PHILOSOPHY

By PAUL WEISS

IN PROCESS

Southern Illinois University Press
Carbondale and Edwardsville

Feffer & Simons, Inc.
London and Amsterdam

COPYRIGHT © 1963, 1964, 1965, 1966, BY SOUTHERN ILLINOIS
UNIVERSITY PRESS
ALL RIGHTS RESERVED
THIS EDITION PRINTED BY OFFSET LITHOGRAPHY
IN THE UNITED STATES OF AMERICA
DESIGNED BY ANDOR BRAUN
STANDARD BOOK NUMBER 8093–0190–3
LIBRARY OF CONGRESS CATALOG CARD NUMBER 63–14293

To Richard Sewall

PREFACE

A WORK of this type demands justification to a degree others do not. Unfortunately, I cannot provide it. But I can offer an excuse for the work in the form of some semi-autobiographical comments.

During the last seven years, almost daily, I have taken out time from the writing of various articles and books, teaching and lecturing, the editing of a periodical and related tasks, to set down my reflections on multiple topics. Some of these reflections are based on what I had previously published and on what I had recently read, but most of them are prompted by questions which arose in class, in conversations, and during the night, re-examined and qualified in the course of a daily morning walk of an hour or so. Some of the observations modify what I had previously written, others represent false starts, discarded projects, or quick responses to questions raised by others as well as by myself; most of them carry out a private dialogue in which I explore, re-assess, develop first one strand and then another of some notion that seemed to be interesting at the time. Most of the thoughts are now being presented exactly as they were jotted down on the typewriter, except for typographical, rhetorical and grammatical changes made on re-reading. I have omitted or changed only what, on getting the manuscript ready for the press, seemed to me to be radically obscure. Since I type almost as fast as I think, these jottings should make it possible for others to observe the nature of one philosopher's thinking before it has been subjected to detailed critical examination, purification, and systematization.

I have heard it said again and again that I am clear when I speak, but that many of my published writings are difficult and obscure. I have no way of knowing how representative these judgments are. In any case, my written works are the product of much, much rewriting. It is conceivable that, in the course of the rewriting, I tended to cut out connective tissue of considerable importance to the reader. The present discussions, which come quite close in form to what I publicly say after having considered an idea in outline at least, make evident that some of the effectiveness of my speech may be due to the fact that I speak with vigor and use many gestures. If listeners are helped over difficult places by the tonalities and emphases of the spoken discourse, it is possible that what I say here may be more readily understood if read aloud—despite the fact that the reader will undoubtedly introduce stresses and nuances of his own.

I am aware that this work betrays many confusions in expression and thought, that it often goes counter to what I had written elsewhere, and that it quite often contradicts what I had said the day before, and sometimes even had written in this work on an earlier page of a given day. But there is value I think in making evident the kind of hesitations and doubts, the alternative suggestions and developments which occur to one given to daily reflection on both old and new matters.

I find it hard to determine whether or not what is here presented is only tangential to, develops and illuminates, or does injustice to the ideas I have systematically presented elsewhere. It is now offered in the hope that it may contribute to that persistent adventure in creative thinking that has been one of the marks of civilized man. It is my hope too that it will further the understanding of the nature of philosophic thought, and that it will offer suggestions which others may find it desirable to develop. For some it may be preferable to read the observations in the order in which they were set down and are now being reproduced; for some it may be more profitable or stimulating to read them in relation to other writings of mine; for some it may be better to approach them in terms of an independent line of thought. A rather detailed index will be provided to make it possible for the first group to make cross-references, for the second to fill in a background, and for the third to locate my discussions of the topics that are of primary concern to the reader.

P. W.

New Haven, Conn.
September 1962

PHILOSOPHY IN PROCESS

ERRATA

June 24

A body can be understood in merely bodily terms, as so much stuff, chemical and physical. But it also can be analyzed in new terms: I would say such terms as mind or God, existence and value or possibility. This means of course that the body is no mere dead thing; it is a thing of unity or meaning, of force and might, and of value. Accepting the body to be this kind of thing, then when we say that body has a mind or soul, we but say that it has a unity of a kind; when we say that it is alive or active we say that it has might; when we say that it is sensitive and good, we say that it has value or is something from the perspective of the ideal. This is the sense I think in which Aristotle looked at the body most of the time in the *De Anima*. He says there that is no more sense to ask if the body and soul are one than to ask if the wax and the impression it receives are one; the soul is the form of the body, the substance itself expressed as form, making the body what it is.

Were it not for the fact that we can significantly ask who makes the analysis of the body in these other terms, that we can judge the body in terms of the value we analyzed it to be, and that we can find it compelled within a universe of might, we would be able to say that mind, possibility and existence were but verbal ways of analyzing the body, and that materialism exhausted the nature of things. But a materialism, even one so flexible as to permit of the analysis of a body in terms which are psychic, valuational and cosmic, is inadequate. Its analyses are of the body defined within the confines of other types of reality. The body in fact, if it be a body functioning at its best, is one which requires that the other perspectives be independent realities, each final; to understand the body as other than these, i.e., as a stuff whose functioning is a palmary instance of all the others, is but to say that those others are realities as fundamental, and thus as inclusive as it. They are independent realities whose fulfillment is to be found in an independently acting stuff, and that is why that stuff can be analyzed in terms of them. The converse is also true: the body must provide a perspective on the others and their independent functioning must involve a fulfillment of that body. That means that body must provide us with a way of analyzing existence, mind and value, and that the full being of these satisfies a need of the body.

Body can be said to analyze existence by providing it with a plurality of present positions; body can be said to analyze mind or God with a plurality of efficacies; body can be said to analyze possibility or value by a plurality of determinations. These ways we accept existence, mind and value and then use body as one of the ways of explaining them. Einstein analyzes existence via bodies; Plotinus analyzes God via bodies; Aristotle analyzes mind via bodies, e.g., by viewing sensation, impulse, etc., as part of, or as exhausting mind. If existence, value and mind each has its full being then body is fully itself, and can be said to find its satisfaction not only in being over against them, but also in the sense that they are the body attenuated into a single might, an eternality of being and a domain of possibility.

When then we come to the question of the union of might and right, we ought not really to say that native rights are alienated for an unalienable right, except analytically. Actually we must say that the body as having its own integrity, as just this body with this native right, can be analyzed as the locus of the other rights and thus as merging its own with them to make the unalienable right to profit from social existence, and that it can also be analyzed as the locus of might and the source of its distribution, and finally that it can be viewed as a social entity. But all the time its very substance is that integral body. Conversely, we must be able to say that the native rights of mind, etc., are carried by the right of integrity of body; that the profiting from social existence is the body treated from the perspective of possibility; that might or existence is analyzed by body as a plurality of efficacies.

Can we apply this type of analysis to the synthesis of judgment? Must we there not say that in judgment the mind accepts the object's diverse perspectived divisions rather than that it divides something (as I say in *Reality*) and then unites them? Error would then be a kind of maladjustment.

July 1

The most complete mastery of any dimension involves the recognition that its meaning is being dispersed, variegated. In itself it is undivided, but in fact it is divided; that which divides it is not alien to it. The divider has to cover the other, there is a variety it does not possess. Its knowledge of anything is one with its grasp of the dispersal of the dimension and thus of the fact that this has a being of its own. Its full knowledge of itself is a knowledge that itself as dispersed has a unitary meaning.

I either have position A by itself, in which case it is indeterminate and excluded, or I have it as encompassing all else and thus as determinate, or I have it as determinate over against itself as indeterminate, or I have it as determinate by virtue of an alien indeterminate, or I have it as determinate by virtue of an indeterminate whose nature we cannot identify (except by abstracting ourselves and thus having A as indeterminate over against a determinate content and its indeterminate unity). The last means that in the dispersal of A we have a unity of A which we cannot isolate without dividing it into two unities, both being substantialized in the dispersed determinate content, A's unity and the unity of its other. The fulfillment of the prescriptive is description; the prescription remains as a unity but one which is self-divided, the determinate content itself being divided into actuality and possibility, or God and existence.

July 2

The meaning of any category in one mode is the being of two other modes, with a third mode in the role of anticategory. The recognition of a being is the same as the identification of the two categories; the accepting of the being is the conversion of it into a pair of categories. Where do I stand when I say this? I stand in one category affirming abstractly what must be in the concrete; that is the meaning of the category. But will the world conform? It must, for the question of conformity is but a question of what the category means. It means nothing other than the content as such and such; this it knows from a distance, if it moves over that distance it becomes the content.

A category has no other being but the reality of the other three modes, with one of them offering the unity governing the connection of the other two. We see from a position in one mode of being and we possess a right to the other three. It is by keeping to our category that we in fact have the content; the having of the others in their concreteness is the use of the category; the having of my category in the concrete is the recognition that these others are ways of analysing it.

July 4

He who pulls himself away from the world in which he is immersed uses logic, in the end, to recover for him the whole and in its proper order. That logic is fulfilled and he achieves his place in the whole when each of the realities achieves its place. At that moment the logic vanishes except as exemplified structure. Right now that we have the logic, we entertain the other perspectives; we are not in them, but then again we are not in our own really; the having of the logic, which is the position of eternity, is the having of one's perspective improperly; it is just as abstract to see the whole through logic as it is to have the other perspectives at a distance. We are immersed in fact while we have the logic; it gives us in an abstract way the distinctions between the concrete modes of being which we are enjoying in a merged way.

There must be analogous formalities from the perspective of ideality, existence and actuality as there is, in logic, from that of (eternity) God. Is it that the ideal sees the world formally from the perspective of some (prescriptive) Ethics; that Existence has the formality of the (dynamic) Laws of Events, and that Actuality has the formality of Rights or Demands (individualization)?

July 5

The difficulty with any individual immersed in the concrete is that he is facing obstacles there which he must endeavor to control, but which, as immersed, he cannot. When we take a more comprehensive view we are actually taking up one of the basic categorial positions; we are once again facing obstacles but this time they are merely the obstacles presented by the beings themselves, and we encompass them within our own system, (though formally and as at a distance from our own unity). Our unity must become dispersed among them to be itself, and this without ceasing to be a unity. The individual immersed in the concrete could gain basic satisfaction if the rest of the domain in which he exists were perfect. The taking of a categorial position is actually the taking of the position of an entire domain, but in the abstract.

The position of logic is eternity or God; ethics is the position of the prescriptive ideal; dynamism and its laws is the position of existence; individualization is the position of the actual, which insists on the subdivision of beings down to a unique substantiality. These all are ways in which one in a position of a category encompasses all. Anybody can move to that position by seeing that he is trying to master other beings inside his own domain. As soon as he sees this he can see the need to deal with the other categories as exemplifications of the one taken as domain. We have a choice then between   A] having opposition by the rest of a domain; and   B] having opposition by the other domains. To be in harmony with the rest of one's domain is to be in opposition to other domains; to be in harmony with other domains is the same as being in opposition to one's own. This is possible only with respect to domains, for each is the analysis of the others.

Each domain analyzes a second by means of a third and fourth; the second provides the fact of the substantiality which is being analyzed. Each says that the second is absorbed in it, and treats the third and fourth as instruments for analysis. How do we know this is true of all four; how do we know that each has a basic position? We are never merely formal, and never merely in our own domain; we are when formal and immersed in our domain also faced with the fact that   A] the second, the third, and fourth each has its own obstinate substantiality,   B] that we have a nature which defies absorption of them, and   C] that we recognize that the being of ourselves, of having this category, is the having of the others as content at the same time.

Usually we oppose without knowing where or what; when we are one with our own domain and thus are over against the very other domains which we in fact analytically absorb, we are aware, so far as we have our own domain and thus our own substantiality, of the substantiality of the others. To lose their substantiality, and thus the awareness of what things are like from their perspective is to lose the completeness of our domain. We absorb all without remainder including the idea of their substantiality, but the substantiality itself must be undergone, and this in opposition to us. We thus know what they are like just so far as we are ourselves substantial. We who know all this are but beings who by a violence have taken a very formal way of being in our own domain—or better perhaps in some other domain. We give up our status as immersed actualities for a formal possession of others [through the adoption of the position of eternity]. We thus through our selves adopt the position of eternity; but then we can say that through our wills we adopt the position of existence, through our bodies that of actuality, and that of ideality through our minds. These we get with violence and without concreteness; to get the concreteness we must actually be bodies with bodies and then find our mind, self and will fulfilled in the more concrete and inclusive domains of ideality, eternity and existence.

July 6

The individual finds himself over against the others in his domain, subordinate and subordinating, recognizes his subordination to other domains, or has the other domains subordinate. He thus finds opposition everywhere. He always has the others in some guise; to be in one category, to enjoy it in any sense is to have the others too.

How, when in one mode do we know the other modes? If we are over against others in our domain, we at once subordinate other domains and are subordinated to them; if we are masters of ourselves we exhaustively analyze the others; as subordinate to them we are exhaustively analyzed by them. We must, when mastering them, recognize their analytic power with respect to us, and so far must be over against others in our own domain.

Does this not require that we, while being where we are, must always be in the other perspectives, while they, though subordinated to us from our perspective, must subject our being to analysis? Our analysis must reveal what analyzes us. If *a* analyzes *b* and *c,* it must do so by recognizing the being of *b* and *c* and thus their power to analyze *a.* The nature of their analysis can be understood by seeing *a*'s unity or substance over against them as that which is to be appreciated by them, as a genuine substance, and thus as that which makes them stand over against it. But by virtue of the enjoyment of *a*'s perspective by *a,* he can know about the fact that *b* and *c* have unities or are substances (since they are there for analysis and are faced with the irreducible core of *a*).

But may not the occupying of the perspective of *b* and *c,* be quite other than what it is thought to be by *a?* No, for the thinking of *b* and *c* as substantial is only the saying that their analysis of *a* is not yet performed; the performing of it by *b* and *c* is but the having of *a* in their perspective. But the having of *a* is what *a* has already. The having of *a* means that *b* and *c* can but restate it, re-present it.

✝ *July* 7

The problem of taking or understanding an alien perspective can be dealt with in the light of the doctrine 1] of the adumbrated, 2] of the nothing, 3] of the bi-focal view of knowledge, 4] of the Golden Rule, 5] of analogy, 6] of sacrifice, 7] of the inevitable opposition which any position encounters, 8] of the acceptance of the other as oneself and oneself as carried in an alien other, 9] of the microcosm. 1] Adumbration: To know is to encompass what is beyond, and to leave over, as the domain of effective reality, an object of ignorance or non-cognitive apprehension, the other. What is encompassed is that other but as now converted into data; to have the other as encompassed content is to recognize it to be effective with respect to us. We subjugate it as that which is subjugating us in another way; our full subjugation of it in our mode requires us to know it as subjugating us in its mode, for otherwise we will not know it fully.

2] 'Nothing' is a terminating and limiting idea. From perspective *x* what lies beyond it is a Nothing: *x* is all-inclusive, yet it terminates. To have something which is all-inclusive, beyond which is nothing else, is but to recognize a Nothing, a being in a counter-move which limits. We can know this because we actively know and thus actively transform the limiting other reality into a Nothing from our perspective.

3] To know something is to take it to have a being and a meaning outside the act of apprehending it then and there; it is to see it from an alien perspective, to recognize it as having its own career and meaning. To grasp anything at all inside one's own perspective is then to understand it in terms not given by that perspective. We hold it to ourselves while seeing it function over against ourselves.

4] When we master others we also have to repulse them; when we retreat from them we must also penetrate them. Retreat is to the subject, repulsion is to privacy and copresence, submission is to objects, penetration is to participation. We require others to act towards us as we do towards them so that we can be passive with respect to them just as they are with respect to us. To be in the world with others is to recognize that they relate to us just as we relate to them.

5] Analogy is the awareness that the principle which we use in our own case is to be used to bring about a comparable or proportionate result in another case. It makes sense only if the same principle is used in both cases and if the mode of application is the same, the only differences being provided by the change in circumstance. When then we grasp what we are, as dominating and dominated, we see this in principle as that which must be illustrated in every object whatsoever, in its own way.

6] Sacrifice is the act of accepting the values of the other. It offers to a disadvantaged equal the opportunity to function as an equal. In knowledge we disadvantage a thing by placing it within our own perspective. We then give up our own enjoyment on behalf of the known, which is so far inferior. We must be aware of its rights if we are to justify the sacrifice we make on its behalf. We must claim that its interests are promoted by our embracing its values and perspective. This sacrifice must satisfy the other; the outcome must bring about more good than was in existence before. This is accomplished by our functioning as beings vis-à-vis that which we merely know. The awareness of our abstractness makes us give up our own enjoyment, in order to be with the others and thus to allow them to do to us what we do to them.

7] To look at the world from one perspective is to view it prescriptively

—unless the content is seen to exhaust the meaning of the prescription, thereby turning it into a description. This turning means that the others have their prescriptive value for the being in the initial perspective, and this in turn must exhaustively satisfy the prescriptions. In a perfect universe each basic approach is satisfied; all prescriptions become descriptions. What is left over in each perspective is its insistence, the fact that the descriptions of it are prescriptively imposed on it.

8] Every being is opposed by and opposes every other. It can oppose it within a common domain, can oppose it as subject to it in another domain, and can oppose it as subjugating it in another domain. It cannot avoid being in one of these stages; to move from one is to move to the others. These others must be present to it as that which enables it to oppose in whatever way it is opposing. The oppositional status it has explicitly enables it to have the others implicitly; its identity consists in its being subject to others and in its subjecting others, in and outside its own domain.

9] We are inside in principle what the facts are outside. We, in knowing ourselves, know that there are other perspectives; when we enjoy one perspective we in fact use the very categories which referred to what ideally supplemented the perspective. As a consequence the perspective is seen to be actually supplemented. That is, the individual has all views or perspectives but only ideally; when he functions as an element in the macrocosm he utilizes his principle of requiring the other perspectives, and thus knows what this element is supplemented by. To the degree that he transforms himself from a being, understanding his own perspective, into a being who utilizes his own perspective, he transforms the other perspectives from something he understands into something utilizing himself. His understanding is then justified, cognitively grasping what, by virtue of the way one perspective is functioning, must be the ways in which the other cognitively grasped perspectives must function.

1] In adumbration we get to the other perspective; 2] with the idea of nothing we have it functioning; 3] in knowing we understand it in alien terms; 4] to be a being among others we must reduce the known to being, by making ourselves passive towards it; 5] analogy tells us that the same principles governing us govern it; 6] in sacrifice we adopt its values, stresses; 7] to have our prescriptions fulfilled, we accept it as having prescriptive power with respect to us and being fulfilled in us; 8] each being is over against in oppositional relation to the rest; in our being we have all the perspectives at the same time; 9] within we are a microcosm; we assume one perspective and have the others outside in the way we had them inside. (Having them all together inside is also a way of having only one perspective. Every microcosm has all four and makes itself a public part of the macrocosm, by expressing the four in the shape of one of them, supplemented by the others.)

To be ourselves we must be passive and active, and that means others must be active and passive. While terminating in an object we encounter its being in knowledge and in fact; that is how we have it as a datum. To have a knowledge of what is we must allow others to take a perspective on us by allowing ourselves to be subordinate to them. We then take the datum to ourselves, allow it to be part of us, and thereupon allow ourselves to be an object for something else. But the datum we take into ourselves is the evidence of that which is taking a perspective on us. By knowing it, I adopt it, and thereby in that activity of possession present myself as a being to be possessed. Might I be possessed by something other than what I know? If I was, the knowing would be distortive. Perhaps it is; perhaps the content I adopt is infected by me and therefore does not answer to a real beyond? I know that I am being acted on, that I am a datum, for the activity requires me to be passive for another, which is A] substantial B] ideal, or C] dynamic. There can be no mistaking its meaning, except of course in the sense that the activity of say the ideal is to be found only in that which is being understood, as that which is being mastered. The tearing away of a datum, the having it for my knowledge is the making of myself passive for it as sheer objective ideality (and/or substantial or dynamic).

The fact that x is a datum, means that when I take it to myself I make myself be with respect to a domain of Existence; the fact that x is held to be true, to be something known means that when I take it to myself I make myself be with respect to a domain of Ideality; the fact that x is then and there, means that when I take it to myself I make myself be with respect to a domain of Actuality or Substantiality. Now x might be nothing other than one of these very categories of Existence, Ideality or Substantiality. In that case what it expressly says is what in fact occurs; in other cases it presupposes these categories. Remaining with the case where we are concerned with the categories as taken from any datum x, as the very being of x purified, as found in x by abstraction, they are all of them data, held to be true, had then and there, and thus make us be with respect to a world outside us in which the categories function.

To have knowledge is to sink into myself with what I master and thus to have myself as passive with respect to whatever in my knowledge expresses ultimacy. But the ultimate for knowledge, is this ultimate in fact? And do I know this truth about knowledge? And where do I stand when I do? The answer to the first must be no; the second yes. When I know about knowledge I use a category of knowledge which makes the original knowledge a datum. I then look at knowledge from the outside, from the perspectives of other categories.

July 11

The knowing of an object involves the holding of the conceptual part of it apart from its being, and the recognition of that being as existing apart; it is a knowledge which at the same time requires some apprehension of the objective of knowledge and of the object over against the knowledge, and of the nature of the actuality which somehow possesses both sides. We who know what knowledge is are aware all the time A] of the way in which the cognized content is substantialized in us as subjects, and B] of the object which is known, the reality beyond. When we know what knowing is we substitute, for the reality beyond, a conceptual version of it which enables us to contrast knowledge (as having an object beyond it) with the original object which lay beyond. At every moment then we are aware of our cognized content as specializing us, and of an object over against it as specializing a reality beyond. We can say that to know datum x is to hold it against object X. To know that x is over against X, we keep X steady, and divide x into "x over against X." We face this with X in fact, and with ourselves. We are over against the "x over against X" too.

July 12

The individual as a knower is, vis-à-vis absolute eternity, a prescriptive absolute, and expresses himself therefore as a desiring being. When he knows, he but delimits his prescriptive attitude in the guise of a mind. The individual who knows himself as a mind must be A] a mind, B] must impose a prescription on the prescription, making it related to external reality. But does this mean that we have an infinite regress of prescriptions on prescriptions, or is there a basic one which expresses the very nature of the eternity as that which has not yet encompassed all else, but stands outside and over against others (rather than as together with the others as fulfilled by them as independent of it), so that its very being is a description of theirs, and these are analytic parts of it? There should be one basic prescription; to know it is but to divide its expression off from it and thus re-apply it; a prescription is thus knowable only when it is used on its own expression.

The logic, ethics, etc., of a man is but the ontological prescriptiveness of his being dramatized, and this he gets by insisting on controlling the others. Why does the eternal (as well as other categories) which is in a way fulfilled by the other dimensions and thus becomes descriptive of them, is exhausted in them and by them, make itself prescriptive in the form of a limited being, such as man? It does this in order to maintain a hold on itself, to be itself in itself, for the prescription, though it is ineffective and thus confesses to be less than it might, is nevertheless by virtue of its being over against the others, possessed of its own integrity.

Man's demands, appetites, desires, search for knowledge and mastery are epitomizations, dramatizations of himself as ontologically prescriptive for the eternal, the instrument by which the eternal recovers the position of being in itself. The sum total of the individuals in the world as having minds is the being of divinity; desire, etc., being the mind as supplemented by other dimensions. From the standpoint of substantial individuality, ideality, and existence the individual is prescriptive in still other ways, again because he is a delimited form of them.

Knowledge by man is himself dramatized, the eternal delimited and prescriptive. We who know this recognize the fact of the prescription to be a dramatization of the world to which it prescribes. The man using the prescription sees himself as something expressed and thus is aware of a world beyond and an eternity behind. As he looks at the prescriptive power he rests in the eternal; as he looks at the mode of expression, he wrests it from the content beyond. The force of the prescriptiveness is beyond itself, and so is its content. How do we know this? Because the expression of the prescription at one point remains the same, and so does the force of the prescription, and the kind of content to which it brings us is the same as before. It is therefore the fact that we arrive at a last point which we can only reiterate that tells us that what we know about knowledge is sound.

The content given to the eternal prescriptiveness of logic as the mind of eternity is denotatively Existence, and is divided into Actuality and Ideality. Each of these dimensions—history, productive activity and ethics, must generate its own prescriptiveness and have the rest as content. But then where do we stand, once again, and how can we know what it is from the other positions? Is it that the finality of the prescription requires an accurate report of the others, so that we know what they are by virtue of the very fact that the pure prescriptiveness, which is the inward mind, is the very substance of these others, one of the analytic factors? We can see what each dimension is by adding to this prescriptiveness of logic two other elements which require reconstruction with it for a conceived meaning of the fourth dimension. Or is it that the very recognition of the prescriptive nature requires a separation over against it of the content as that which demands it and which therefore in turn has the prescriptiveness as a datum?

The fact that the content of a prescription satisfies it is inescapable, for that is where we start, with a prescription with content. The allowance of the content to stand apart is the acceptance of the prescription as a datum for it. It is a presentation of what in the prescriptive is an articulation. The content is prescriptive of the original prescription and in this guise the content is divided and abstracted and categorial by intent. We who say this are faced with prescription and content as needing one another; we find ourselves with a prescription for which this content is a prescription, to which this content makes a demand just like the demand made on it by the prescription.

To prescribe to X I use Y. When I see Y and X in juxtaposition I find Y prescribed to by X. To see this is to take up position Y' making demands on XY similar to that which Y makes on X, and we thus see that the reciprocal demand by XY on Y' is like the demand of X on Y. It is my exhaustion of my prescription as the descriptiveness of the datum, X, which tells me that the way X deals with Y is the reciprocal of the way Y deals with X.

I thus know about the other categories because A] I repeat the use of my own when I deal with them instead of with the content in them, B] I find that the meaning of content is the exhaustion of the form, and that this requires the content to prescribe to the form, as well as conversely, once they are separated one from the other, C] In knowing what I demand when I deal with the other categories I am aware of what they demand of me.

July 18

Whitehead seems to have confounded categories. His eternal objects are possibilities recognized to have some independent status. He neglects their ethical ideality, and their subordination within a single eternal object. He contrasts them with what is obtained on the physical side; but this is not their proper coordinate. The actual entity itself is directed towards the eternal objects, and also directed towards the achievement of a kind of structure or form or eternity, and a kind of epitomization of the world of energy or creativity. These are categorial references. Whitehead ought to recognize actualities, eternal objects, formal structures and creative energies. The actual object prehends other actual objects within the frame provided by the four basic categories, one of which it itself exemplifies. It tries to actualize, tries to turn into itself the categorial features of what is other than itself. It has these as data, and this means it must submit to them in a way; but self-sufficiency and completeness consist in the having of objects transformed into oneself.

July 21

A reality, *a*, has four kinds of connection with any other, *b*. I] It merges with it, (interacts with it, is in a relation of insistence and resistance). II] It stands over against it as an abstract, universal prescription, making a demand on it. III] It is fulfilled in the other; its prescription becomes a description, the other being but the articulation of it. IV] It is alongside the other, a self-sufficient being whose meaning is that the other is there. I is like Existence, II like Ideality, III like God, and IV like Actuality.

It is IV that is most difficult to see and to characterize. We could say that IV is self-enclosed, *en soi,* only because it says inwardly that such and such is outside, and can say this only because there is an outside from which it can be closed off. Or we can say that for it to be itself in itself it must also be for itself, and thus assume the position of *b.* Because no one being alone can exist (see *Reality*), and being in its inwardness must necessarily make reference to what lies outside it, not as that to which it clings (as *Reality* asserts), but as just being there. The reference of *a* to *b,* since it does allow a replacement of *b* by *c,* must be only the establishment by *a* of a place for something other than *a,* with an instancing at that place by *b,* as a particular other of the *a.* To rest in itself it must precipitate an other which can be there on its own; only so far as *b* is that which is independent of *a* and yet coordinate with it can *a* be basic. The basicality of *a* means that *b* is basic too.

July 27

Restricting ourselves to two dimensions, *a* and *b,* the final answer must be that each encompasses the other, but not the fact of the other. Each to be complete, must be descriptive, spread over, be exemplified as the other. The being of *a* is to be found as the rationale of *b;* the meaning of *b* is the structure of *a.* But each is a datum for the other, and each therefore has the other as a brute reality outside itself. So far as it is in itself it cuts itself off from the other; its being in itself is the having of the other in itself.

We seem to have 1] Two points outside totality; these two points are the meaning of *b* for one who is in *a,* not as over against, as self-enclosed, but as all inclusive; it is enabled to spread over the whole of *b* only through the operation of two points of which it does not take account. 2] To bring in the two points is to permeate the whole of *a* with existence; it is to stiffen it, to give it body and therefore disperse it. Before *a* was dispersed over *b* through the aid of something; now it is dispersed as part of its own substance. (In this case it does not know itself in itself nor why it is spread out.) But the two points are antithetical and also over against the rational or Ideal, so that the very being of the rational requires a persistent conflux of alien beings throughout itself. If we separate out those points the rational becomes unextended and applies only through the use of the points; if we cut away from the points altogether to get the rational as such, we frame the rational within the points as unacknowledged, for *we* then offer it to be applied on an alien *b.* That *b* will then assume the role of a point, in that it is outside the rational, and so will we ourselves. It is by allowing the rational to be fulfilled that we get only the two points. 3] We have been looking at the matter from the standpoint of *a; b* in this schema is the analogue of Existence; it is interiorly divisive. At every place *b* is two-directional, confused. To be in it is to have the very stuff of *b* mixed with *a.* From this perspective there are no points, and no way of separating *b* from *a.* 4] To understand *b* we solidify it, gives it a status of its own over against a part of itself, the rational. What remains of *b* has the features of the whole of *b,* and from its perspective the rational which it throws off has the duality in it too. At the limit it allows the *a* to be applicable to it, in which case it assumes the position of a point and *its* entire being will consist in the holding of itself as one point over against the other.

This can be looked at in another way. If we start with *a, b,* and want to say how we can speak of each as encompassing the other as its very stuff or meaning, we must evidently have them together. This having them together can be the having of each as encompassing the other; this is really assuming the position of *b,* and making use of points, *a', b'* to say that there is both one and the other rather than a mere blurred miscellany. These points are the principles of intelligibility; they are the law of contradiction's extremes enabling us to order *b.* Or we could take the opposite stress and recognize the points themselves as the very meaning of *b;* they will then be points in actual dynamic opposition. For such points, *a* will be the law or meaning of the opposition.

When then it is asked where are we when we say that there are two basic dimensions, we are forced to say that we are in one of them as over against the other. The overagainstness will change according to the manner in which we are in one dimension. We are inside one always, as facing alien content; at one extreme we are only a point and what is over against is almost everything, but dispersed and confounded; but at the other extreme we are the content itself, either in the guise of the rational or the existential, and then have over against it two points, ourselves in our inwardness and the content as data for us. But as such points we but offer a frame for the dispersive being of the rational content or for the structuralization of the existential.

Having arrived where prescription is description, we find that the conditions for the conversion, the being of the prescription and the data described, are left out. These can now be made the object of a new prescription, but only if we repeat all over again a prescription which must be made descriptive. When we do this we identify the description with one of the points. We then abstract from the description, do not allow it to be as self-contained as before, but make it refer to the point beyond. Where before we tried to make a prescription rich by filling it up with content, making it descriptive, we now take the description and try to make it more inclusive by making it a demand to be inclusive. But we actually end with it as less than it was. This means then that while we know that the truth is the plurality of descriptions, overlapping one another, we cannot say what they are except　A] confusedly, for the contents blur one another, and reason is mixed with being with opposite tendencies, or　B] clearly, by taking up the standpoint of each from the perspective of one, as purified, a perspective which forces the recognition of the other as over against, as basic, and in root identical with the second standpoint which we adopt within the one, but purified. We recognize as we acknowledge two possible perspectives that the one is ourselves and the other is that which we need in order to be ourselves, i.e. (that the other is *our* other, itself purified).

We are rational beings in activity, and we can make the rational the all-encompassing, or make the activity so, or have each blur into the other, with the being of each over against that blur. As we stress the difference between the rational and the active, hold them apart as points, we allow their merging in fact, and must unite them as different with themselves as merged, and this once again by reason, by activity or merging.

Hegel might be said to start with the view that the final fact is description; but as he looks at each part he sees that to make it rational he must separate out the points of being and rationality. His view that in the end the two are the same is right, but if he makes them one he is bound to restate the problem, and force a need to separate them once more. When he says the rational is real, he must mean that in the end this is so, and then he must say that there is a real outside the rational, and a rational outside the real, for the stiffening of the rational by the real and the structuralization of the real by the rational are not expressed by either. When the scholastics say that God's essence is his existence they make the same point that Hegel does, though of course we could also say if we liked that nature's existence is its essence, which is what Hegel in the end wants. Whitehead's solution (and Hegel's in part) is, to all this, that we first have one state and then the other; merging is followed by diversification, etc. This is Empedoclean, and perhaps also Fichtean. But the problem is internal, dialectical; to throw it into time is but to say that the problem is perpetual, that every solution is a dissolution. It is an answer but only from the side of *b,* Existence; it is no answer from the side of rationality, formality. The dispersiveness of the form as encompassing the content is static, the very law of contradiction itself. This law to be sure requires the dynamic content which is the law ambulando; but conversely, the dynamic process of solution and dissolution is but the exfoliation of the law itself as compulsive even though derivative.

The formal presupposes a content which it would subjugate; the material produces a structure to which it must submit. To say both together is to have a content and thus to allow for a structure which will force a new saying; to say them severally is to use reason, to have them fixed, but to be then faced with their togetherness, which cannot be said.

The essence of the world overflows its existence in the same way that God's existence overflows his essence, i.e., from the standpoint of the world's essence or God's existence, each is the source of the other of itself. God's other is Existence; the world's other is the ideal or logic. But these others have a being of their own. God must fixate Existence, not allow it to be any more in time in order to conquer it; but that it is there is still beyond His conquest. Existence must make logic move, not allow it to hold itself apart and ignore the rules of Existence, but that the logic is prescriptive it cannot handle.

We cannot avoid being in two, or strictly speaking four places at one: *1]* we must either have all the dimensions merged concretely; *2]* we must have them all formally together in an abstract conjunction; *3]* we must have Actuality and Ideality paired in content and sustained by opposite points; *4]* we must have God and Existence paired and sustained by opposite points. *1]* has the points outside and used; *2]* has the content outside and used; 3] and 4] combine 1] and 2] in different ways. Are we in all four of these at once? And so on? Yes. For each encompasses all. We normally bracket, hold some dimension steady in order to master the others better, and when we do this we push aside contents or points as not within our interest or purview. But what we push aside we hold on to as that which allows us to remain ourselves by being excluded.

The contents are all merged and the dimensions are all outside as points. When we try to bring the points together with the content, we but emphasize the fact that the being of the points remains outside. One can continue to peel off content from the points and the points still remain; and conversely one can order the content better and better, distinguish by locating at points the different elements, but the merged togetherness will still remain.

We are primarily actualities and end by being knowers, but in between we do act in time and do yield to the Ideal. The four moments are part of one undivided moment of time and are obtainable by analysis which once again offers us the position of knowers over against the rest. Thus we are all in all four in one undivided moment as existential; in one undivided space as actuality; as one undivided structure as eternal; and as one undivided possibility or ideal, and have all four of these at once, an at-once we can locate in any one of these or in all of them. The one undivided possibility, e.g., has within it the idea of an undivided extension, spatial or temporal, and an eternal structure expressing how it is to be divided.

I allow all to be together by intellectualizing the "and," and expecting it to be concretionalized in three other ways—as a mode of merging, as a mode of possession, and as a mode of acceptance.

Do I in the end have to say that I cannot make sense in thought of the different modes of togetherness, but must content myself with undergoing them in various ways, while I have mere conjunction as my intellectualized mode of grasping the things which are together, and even the different modes of togetherness?

July 28

There is always a kind of gap between any two items. We have them in two ways, an *a.b* way and *a,b* way, *a* and *b* as merged and —separated. And we can go on to say that these two ways are had together in two similar ways, and so on. We are in both ways all the time, and as we try to say what these two ways together are we but multiply the ".";

we thereby cover the entire scheme of things but always with the "." possessed and a content which we want to make one with it. We make the content one with it only by presupposing it as over against the "." The ".", from the position of *a,b,* is but the representation of an endless series of dots; similarly the ",", from the position of *a.b,* is the surface of richer and richer content. To put it this way is to start with what is evidently only a part; more accurately we ought to say that there is a dot which we fractionate and there is a content which we penetrate. Does the entire series of dots exhaust the original dot? When we take dot after dot don't we distort and falsify the original solid one? No, for the fractionization is but the solid dot as active over against content of a special sort. The one thing then that we cannot have is the solid dot and the solid content, both without any divisions in them, except by merely falling back into ourselves and pushing the world away.

What is any being like by itself, without any reference to anything else? It is internally divisive in that it covers the entire field of other beings; it is the pluralization of the dots. Or perhaps the question is what is it like in and of itself? In and of itself each is identical with itself as internally divisive for the others, and divided by the others.

In itself the dot is identical with the plurality of its fractions with respect to the *a,b,* and also is that which the *a,b* needs or points to in order to be just *a,b.*

August 3

Once again: A being may be caught inside the being of others. It may have its activities and being dispersed or governed in ways which are alien to its needs or nature. This will happen in four ways for actualities, since they are not only caught with respect to the other modes of being or dimensions but with respect to one another. In the endeavor to govern themselves they must retreat within themselves; in that act they become prescriptive individuals, beings who would impose their individual natures on all else. I think I was inclined to neglect this stage. It involves the isolation of individual nature as a principle which is unsatisfied so long as it does not encompass, subjugate the beings which lie beyond it. This means that this nature must become diversified as the determinant of all other actualities, that it must individualize the Ideal and make it the object of a concern, that it must individualize Existence and make it into an environment, and that it must individualize God and make Him into its own unity. When the individual has achieved this four-fold individualization he will have encompassed all the others, though they will continue to remain outside him, and will function with respect to him as he does with respect to them. So far as he succeeds in encompassing them he turns his prescriptiveness into a description; his description is then himself as spread over the other dimensions; it is the reversal not of the prescription but of the original state of involvement with others, of being effectively subordinated to them. In the description the others are encompassed but without compromise to their coordinate encompassing of it. The encompassing is but the attainment of body by the prescription, the exhaustion of its meaning in all the content that there is.

Earlier I think I was inclined to move quickly from involvement to a prescription which was attributed only to one being (instead of recognizing that there were four prescriptions), i.e., to the identification of an individual with the eternal meaning of God. If the individual is to look at the universe from the perspective of God he will first have to attain the state where his meaning is descriptive of God, or where he allows himself to make it possible for God to be descriptive of him. Whenever we get a description we get the thing in itself but only as spread over the entire scheme of things; by merely being in itself it is pushed about by all else; it is spread over because the others have their own power of insistence. What I did earlier was in effect to move from the description of God from the perspective of the individual to the acceptance of God in His prescriptive nature, and thus the seeing of the other dimensions from His position. The problem now is the nature and need for this movement of identification; why is not the individual content, once it descriptively encompasses all else? The philosopher might want to ask about the content which makes possible this description and which stood over against the individual as that which defined him to be prescriptive, but why must the individual in its being do this? Before I supposed that part of the being of the individual was divine (and also Ideal and Existential), so that there was no antecedent encompassing of the divine but an identification of oneself with the divine, but this does not face the question in its full complexity.

It is good method to try to dispense with all dimensions, all modes of being, but one; but if *Modes of Being* is right, all four crop up everywhere. There is a togetherness of the actualities which points to the unity that God alone can provide, the connections which Existence alone provides, and the possibility which the Ideal future alone provides, and which cannot be found in any of those actualities. We could say that all four together constitute a kind of space, and that as soon as we ask about that space we impose still another dimension on the space, make more spatiality, and so on. If we did this we would have to say that the to-getherness of actualities is a product from which we can derive God, Existence and Ideality; but we then add to Actualities the reality of space. We in effect will have taken the one to be basic and the others to be derivative, a derivativeness which however does not preclude them from having natures of their own. God, Existence and Ideality moreover are not like space, neutral as it is to the activities of Actualities; God, etc. limit Actualities, dominate them, constrain them, make them be contemporaries in relation to others at a subsequent time, and be governed by a final cause.

A individualizes G, E and $I;$ (I will call the result AG, AE and AI). AG may explicate itself directly on E and $I,$ which is what I dealt with in the previous discussions; it may explicate itself on AE and $AI,$ in which cases we get the environment and the object of concern as a unity of meaning or structure (AG). The final answer might be (restricting ourselves to the standpoint of A) AG, AE and AI as the explication of A's meaning, or it might be $AGE, AGI, AEG, AEI, AIG, AIE$—i.e., the application of AG on $E,$ to take the first example, to give the individualized meaning (AG) of Existence. In this case Existence comes to have a structure as an environment. Or we might get $AGAE, AGAI, AEAI, AEAG, AIAG, AIAE$. $AGAE$ for example is the explication of individualized meaning imposed on Existence as individualized. Since AGE and $AGAE$ are but A's way of representing what G does with respect to E or with respect to $AE,$ they are evidently derivatives. The basic fact must be $AG, AE, AI; GA, GE, GI; EA, EI, EG; IA, IE, IG$. It is when I want to understand how I can have all of these together that I impose AG say on GE. This gives me less than the concrete fact. That fact is the togetherness of AG and GE without further prescriptiveness or descriptiveness. (It is to be noted that since GA is as fundamental as $AG,$ we can get $AGGA,$ which expresses how the individualized or abstracted unity of God is explicated in the divine expression in human souls—i.e., GA tells us what God is as exhausting Himself in the community of the saints, or church or mankind or best of all, nature. As an individual I can submerge myself in the idea of divine $[AG]$ unity. Such a divine unity can then be imposed on GA to give us the eternal meaning, as envisaged by an individual actuality, of God as exhausted in a community, and so on.)

August 4

Every theory is confronted with the fact that if it correctly describes it seems to leave no room for the need to act. If there were four dimensions, and each in its full being encompassed all the others in the sense that its meaning pervaded the being of those others, why should there be any activity at all? The answer is perhaps that in its full being each entity is descriptively applicable to the others, but since those others have their own being and needs, and in fact can never be encompassed as beings within the other dimensions, the descriptions though appropriate, are nevertheless defied. At every moment a description is dissolved by virtue of the activity of the dimension to which it is applied, so that the attempt to apply the description must be renewed again and again. At every moment each dimension is described in a three-fold way by virtue of the spread of the other three dimensions over its being; but when and as this occurs the being backs away and forces a renewed application of these other dimensions. There is then a rhythm in which beings are maladjusted in the sense that they are defied by that to which they apply and must struggle to overcome the defier. There is always a perspective, usually abstract and in this sense prescriptive from that perspective, in which all the dimensions descriptively apply to one another; but this situation is itself immediately dissolved with the transformation of the prescription into a description. A second order prescription, by attempting to be descriptive, dissolves the first order descriptiveness into prescriptions. Because, from the standpoint of what I take to be God, all the dimensions have a unity, I endeavor to make that unity be proper to them; I impose the meaning of God, as I entertain it, on them; when I do this whatever unity they in fact have from God dissolves, and God must then engage in the act of redetermining them. If this be the case we must then face the question as to whether or not there is necessarily a second derivative, and if there need not then be a third derivative etc.

Or is the second derivative only the being of one entity as clinging to the other being and offering that other being to itself? The attempt to offer that other being to oneself would end in a static universe if it dovetailed into the way in which that other being actually was offering itself to oneself. Accordingly the failure of a description to remain fixed is due to the fact that the description itself is A] defied by the described, and B] is held on to the described by the describing being. It is the insistence on x which provokes y, and conversely. The reason why I am not fully adjusted to other beings in this and other dimensions is because I am in conflict with the others as beings imposing themselves on me.

We ought to say that the individual, when it understands the unity of the world, must first A] descriptively encompass God, B] grasp from an individual perspective the unity which God imposes, C] be unable to encompass God's being and thus have its grasp of the unity somewhat distorted. Knowledge will enable us to see, from God's side, the description we impose, and even to know what His being is like, but such knowledge stands over against the being of ourselves and God, and can be known only so far as we confront ourselves as knowers while we confront God.

In connection with politics we ought to see the body as descriptive of the domains of privacy, might and peace. The descriptions are ways of giving them a public meaning. But at the same time we must recognize that the Ideal limits itself to the ideal of peace by making man its agent; that the privacy alienates itself so that it can be the carrier of its rights, and that might uses the body as a location, thereby denying to itself an irresistible status.

No one is satisfied to be merely descriptive; each must also hold on to the being which offers itself as a datum for the description and in this effort it comes in conflict with the being itself, functioning in its own terms. We would achieve perfection if we could accept the being of others just as those others are, not tainted by our insistence. We do this when we know, but only at the price of having the being of the things not yet caught. The individual in grasping what others are from their side cannot get that other side fully without becoming the others.

Description and prescription are only two modes; they are extremes; in between them must be insistence and resistance. The individual resists the grasp of the others, and in that act becomes prescriptive; but it insists on imposing itself and thus becomes insistent, ending with a description. The description of *b* but partially expresses *a*, for *a* is insistent and would encompass the being of *b*. The more *a* succeeds in governing the being of *b*, the more surely will the description it imposes dissolve. That dissolution of the description can be said to be the outcome of the resistance of *b* to *a*, and thus the prescribing of *a* by *b*, with a consequent insistence and description from *b's* side. When *b* is dissolving the description by resisting the intruding *a*, *a* must be doing the same with respect to the description of *a* imposed on *a* by *b*.

The foregoing seems quite confused; also it doesn't deal with the question whether the rhythms of the four dimensions are not different, whether they may not be in different phases, so that when one is insistent, the second is resistant, the third prescriptive and the fourth descriptive. The whole question must be re-examined.

Perhaps each dimension has a way of becoming one with the others: God as Knowledge, the Existent through Action; the Ideal through Ordering its activities, and the Actual through Resistance. That is, just as, when we know, we adopt the position of another dimension so as to have content for ourselves (an act which is preceded by the assumption of an individualized occupation of God's perspective, the I of the *Modes*), so we could also identify ourselves with pure Existence and merge ourselves with the other perspectives but only in the guise of their characteristic activity (which of course would not give us the knowledge form of occupation of those other perspectives); similarly we could, by taking up the position of the Ideal, adopt the way of ordering activities characteristic of the Ideal. Our own way of functioning would be Resistance. (God could be related to description, Existence to insistence, Ideality to prescription and Actuality to resistance.) God himself, to grasp the world from the perspective, say of the actual, would have to allow Himself to adopt the resistance characteristic of the actual; He would first of course express Himself as the actual, divinize it, and then allow that divinized mode of resisting to assume also the position of the being which was being encountered by the actuality.

August 6

Perhaps it would be possible to revert to the idea in *Reality* that reciprocally overlapping vectors constitute a space, but with the addition that this space must be sustained from some other perspective? The theological space of God and the World would be constituted by God and Existence as sustained in opposing ways by Actuality and Ideality, which give us history and art, space somehow temporalized. But if this is so there will be a kind of space relating Actuality and the Ideal (of which the space between actualities would be a kind of limit), and this would be temporalized by God and Existence in the shape of mathematics and science. All four dimensions would be together in a space of their own, but this would have being only so far as one had something, or rather two somethings over against it in terms of which it could be said to be the merging of the two types of space (God-Existence; Actuality-Ideality). But these we get only derivately, by isolating some point in one of the dimensions and having it over against a correlative point. Until we do in fact make such isolation the space of all four, their togetherness, is not as soon as it is; it is a fulgurated product which can be had as having being only as sustained by realities beyond it, realities which otherwise would be the very termini of the space. The nucleus which stands outside space in *Reality* is in a way one of the means by which the vector which it sustains is made one with the vector from an opposing nucleus. The nucleus can achieve that position only by severing off a part of itself as having the function, not of being the source of a vector, but of joining the vector to its reciprocal. This is the case only when we have all four dimensions. Perhaps this is not altogether correct; perhaps it is better to say that we can have all four together in a common space only by virtue of an abstraction, and this requires the breaking up of the nucleus in a new way? In any case not until the nucleus is broken up in this way do we have a genuine space, with a unity of its own, for a nucleus keeps the vectors together when sustained by counteracting nuclei.

If this is the case we ought to have six basic types of "space" — connecting the Ideal and Actual, Ideal and God, Ideal and Existence, Actuality and God, Actuality and Existence, God and Existence. These may be termed, dynamic, providential, purposed, religious, contemporary, and theological. In politics where we start with the public individual directed towards the Ideal, we must evidently start with dynamic space; but we will also have to consider an analogue of religious space, the public and the private individual with their inalienable private rights and public career — morality — ; and a kind of contemporary space where the actuality is connected with its including might. It is the morally determined empowered actuality, in dynamic space, who is concerned with peace, which in turn makes him its instrument of embodiment.

There must be something like art and history within which the dynamic space of the political man is sustained; there must be something like science and mathematics wherein the contemporary and religious spaces of might and morality are sustained. In any case it is not the mere actuality in relation to peace which is the concern of politics but that actuality in relation to private right, as a being constituted by that right, and on the other hand as constituting and being constituted by might. We tend to neglect the way in which the body helps determine the area of privacy, but to balance the relation of the individual to might this must be considered. If it is, though we can continue to think of the actual as mediating privacy with respect to might, we will also think of it the other way, and break the relation up into pairs. In general, political philosophy will be concerned though with privacy as infecting the actual, and that actual in turn as being infected by might.

August 9

The complete account of the cosmos would perhaps show the various elements merged with one another, endeavoring to achieve separation and clarity through the isolation of their substantival nuclei, with a consequent evaluation and exemplification in or on the nuclei of the other realities. But by taking a distant perspective (which is a viewing all of them in terms of the derived position of some one of them), all of the elements will be seen in their separateness. Their togetherness as distinct realities which descriptively encompass all else (i.e., one another), less their nuclei or substantivial points, will be only so far as it (the togetherness) is sustained from the outside by a fraction of itself. The final togetherness in which each is in itself and its meaning is stretched out over the others could be only a severalty, for there is no place in which such togetherness could be. We have all the categories or dimensions together with distinctive natures as in *Modes of Being*, only so far as we take one of those dimensions, isolate a part of its substantivality and view the whole (including itself) from that perspective.

Every actuality (and of course beings in the other dimensions analogously) expresses itself in the area of the others. It can adopt the position of the others and thereby qualify the approach those others make to the rest. This is what the actuality does when it knows, evaluates and acts, for it then assumes the prescriptive position of God, Ideality and Existence respectively. These others express themselves in the Actual; they also then assume the position of the Actual which thereupon individualizes all else, but as tainted by these three—e.g., it is concerned with the Ideal, and God as assuming the position of the Actual thus sees the Ideal as a meaningful individualized object of concern. As a consequence of these considerations, there will be a kind of space or togetherness constituted of any pair of dimensions, and then there will be another where each is infected by some other dimension, and then there will be a third in which each infects its other. Thus

1] Actuality spread out over Ideality; over Eternity; over Existence; thereby individualizing them, making them into an object of concern, a principle of cognition, and an environment. Ideality spread out over Actuality, Eternity and Existence, thereby giving them value, making them into actualizers, agents and loci. God spread out over Actuality, Ideality and Existence, thereby giving them meaning, making them into Immortals, Providence and Power. Existence spread out over God, Actuality and Ideality, thereby giving them energy, making them Effective, Contemporary and Outcome.

2] Actuality as adopting say the position of Ideality will view itself as an individualized mode of actualizing an Ideal, and will view God as an Agent for the Ideal with which the actuality is concerned. And so on through all the above, *AIA, AIG, AIE; AGA, AGI, AGE; AEA, AEI, AEG; EIE, EIA, EIG; EAE, EAI, EAG; EGE, EGA, EGI; IAI, IAE, IAG; IGI, IGA, IGE; IEA, IEG, IEI; GIG, GIA, GIE; GAG,*

GAE, GAI; GEA, GEG, GEI, where the first represents what is spread out, and the second the domain as prescriptive for a third. *AIA* is a concern for a prescriptive evaluation of Actuality.

3] *AIIA, IAAI, AEEA, AGGA, GAAG, IEEI, IGGI, GAAG, GEEG, EAAE, EGGE, EIIE* represent the modes of space where we combine the elements given in 1] above. *AIIA* is the domain of history, *AEEA* is the domain of nature, and *AGGA* is the domain of religion. *IEEI, IAAI, IGGI,* are respectively the domains of teleology, history and providence (*IAAI* is identical with *AIIA*); *GEEG* (or *EGGE*) is the domain of creativity. We thus have spaces of *A* with *I*, with *E* and with *G; I* and *E, I* and *G,* and *E* and *G.*

4] Utilizing the distinctions in 2] above we can have special "spaces" such that we get *A* with *IG,* instead of with *I,* or *AE* with *IG,* etc.

In politics *A* is the Body, *I* is Peace, *E* is Might and *G* is Private Right. The spaces then should be

A with *I*	Social History
A with *E*	Society
A with *G*	Morality
E with *G*	Reasonableness
E with *I*	State
G with *I*	Ethics

But we must also consider the fact that *G* is expressed in *A;* private right is alienated to give a socially significant body. This *GA* makes a "space" with *I, E,* or *G* either in their purity or as themselves prescriptive of the other domains. This would give such spaces as *GA* with *EI,* e.g., Man as meaningful, forming a "space" with Peace as an outcome—note *GA* here is not the space of *G* with *A,* but *A* as infected by *G.* Politics would seem to be primarily concerned with *GA* making a space with *E,* i.e., it is concerned with a society of meaningful, i.e., right-endowed men. Will its problems then be (*a*) to see how men become endowed with rights—*GA,* and then with *E,* the nature of might, and then with their "space"? What do we do about *EA,* the infecting of *A* by *E* to make it a public body, with the diversification of might or *E?* Should we then deal with spaces *EA* with *G,* and *GA* with *E,* i.e., public body in relation to right, and meaningful man in relation to might; the last seems to be the area of conventional political discussion.

August 13

Perhaps one could and should defend the doctrine of proper places and absolute space by remarking that bodies have three dimensions and each of these is diversely oriented. Each dimension has with respect to a mid-point a plus and minus side,—a right-left, back-front, up-down (and if we include time, earlier-later). Each is to be understood in terms of an external point towards which the different sides of the dimension are oriented. This external point might be thought to be the being in its inwardness as over against its own external body. Or if we must take account of all bodies and thus have points exterior to all we can say I think that those points are due to the "secularization" of God, Ideality and Existence, the making of them play a role with respect to Actuality, plus the interplay of the actualities themselves. Thus God is "up"; as taking account of the existence in actualities. He is the point of unification of each. The actualities as swimming in the sea of Existence might be said to be merged by virtue of it; this would be their "down," and as separated off from one another, as pointing away from the common they would be oriented with respect to an up. The actualities as interplaying with one another would constitute a contemporary world of individuals; these individuals would be *right and left* of one another. They would be related to the Ideal in a spatial way if the Ideal could be identified with what was there to be used for the making or achieving of something; and that which we had done would be thrust back as no longer usable except as a kind of form or guide, thus giving us a *front-back.* Existence is where the beings are rooted; this would be Existence as looked at from the standpoint of God. If we start with Existence itself it is a forward thrust which defines the *earlier, later, and present,* and with respect to which God is eternity.

If one takes this latter approach one can perhaps explain the three dimensions of the body as A] the outcome of the integration of Existence with a non-dimensional actuality thereby producing the time diversification, B] this result in relation to God giving the up-down; C] the plurality of the actualities giving right-left, and D] their tendency to act on one another giving their front and back.

August 15

If one were to treat men and women as in nature as differing somewhat as the right hand from the left, one could view them both as actualities directed towards an Ideal, and as related to and in a way incorporating the eternal and the realm of Existence. The male would encompass the whole of the eternal, as meaning, and only a half of the realm of Existence, in the sense that he would have an adumbration only of the rest of it as something enjoyed; the female in contrast would have the same relation with respect to the eternal. They would each as it were twist in opposite directions, but never so far as to be disoriented from the species—where they will be identical in fact—or from what actually defines the other. The way in which the male embodies the principle of meaning (and this will come out in his concern or exemplification with mathematics and abstract formulations) will be in part the way it is also embodied in the female (who similarly illustrates the laws of nature), but there will be a part which the female must surmise—and conversely. Each will directly experience what the other does, but there will be one factor which one will experience fully and the other only partially (but with an adumbration of the something more). There will of course be lower order beings where the difference between the sexes would not be made; there will be cases A] where men exaggerate the male side, or B] where they neglect the male side for the half which the woman has altogether, giving us the A] case of the male who has no understanding of the female and B] the womanly man. There is a counterpart of course with the female. The fact that men and women are so alike and different would mark off the nature of human kind from others.

The twist characteristic of the right and left hand even when expanded into a three-dimensional one—right-left, up-down, back-front—falls short of that of male and female because the right-left, etc., have no consciousness. The twist is due to a difference in direction in space, and thus the deduction of space is presupposed. Why has space three dimensions, each one of which has two end points, two directions away from a middle giving us the incongruous counterparts?

If we take a start with the idea of creation we could say that the first creation of a God would be unextended beings. These would be graded as so many points and thus form a one-dimensional vertical. But the lower the grade the more beings would be needed to express what is the extent or meaning of God. The whole vertical will do this, but the lowest part of the vertical, to be coordinate with the highest, would have to spread out horizontally. This would give a plane which as having God over against it would constitute a three-dimensional reality. God, in short, as understood with the totality of angels to make the heavens, would be an absolute point with respect to which we get a three-dimensional totality.

God's creation of the world would be the attempt to "incarnate" the heavenly reality; he would therefore have to duplicate, i.e., re-articulate the entire scheme. But since this "duplicate" would be lower than the lowest of the angels (otherwise there would be repetition of value), He would have to make it equal with them by providing them with another dimension, to wit time. Through time the cosmos would be equal in value to the lowest of the angelic orders as oriented towards God. Does this mean that the incarnation is the re-establishment in "Christ" of all the rest of the angelic order, and thus of what together with the world in time would come to a duplication of God? The time-span of Christ would reveal his status as a duplicator; its brevity, the superiority of him over the whole cosmic meaning—granting of course that he is in this respect not part of the cosmic whole but the capstone of it. (As part of a cosmic whole he would have a status as mere matter or as a local man who belonged to that part of creation which was in value just below the lowest order of the angels.) But we would in any case have three spatial dimensions and a temporal dimension in which there were lines and volumes, instead of points and planes, connecting what was to belong to God.

Just as the whole hierarchy and choir of angels would be a mode of articulating God, allowing his being to be dispersed (I would say due to the presence of real Existence outside Him, though this is not relevant at this juncture nor to the Christian myth), just so, this cosmos would be a way of articulating that articulation, of allowing the otherwise static expression of God in the heavens to have itself articulated. Or if you take a strong neo-platonic position, the lowest order of the angels would provide the articulation of the highest angel (which together with it would then be the articulation of God), and the articulation of that lowest order would give you the spatio-temporal world. The Incarnation would express an articulation in time of God without the intermediation of the orders of the angels—He would be all the orders in Himself expressed through time. This view is alternative to that above.

August 16

We could say that God created a world in order that there be an articulation of the lowest order of angels. But this creation would both be and not be, in the sense that it actually existed and in the sense that it did not all exist at the same time. The very progressive or successive nature of time means that no being ever fully is. The exteriority of the parts of time means that the being will never fully be unless time is somehow brought together into a unity. The way time is to be given unity is by God tying up the ends of time, by putting a beginning and an end to it. So far as we have such a closure of time the beings in time achieve their full being. The giving an end to time is God's forgiveness, the making the becoming of the non-being of beings cease to be, and give way to full being.

Man's creativity would in a way make him higher than the angels, and yet lower than the angels for he faces part of himself as not-being, not yet, and must make it be. When we have the "fall" in Eden we change from a cyclical time to a historical one; the putting of the angel at the gate is the beginning of history, for there is no returning. This change is in a way a loss and a gain; it is a loss because of the loss of the cycle; it is a gain so far as there is a guarantee of a closure in which a man will be justified so far as he actually makes use of his time to make himself a full being.

When Aristotle speaks of proper places, it is strange that he acknowledges up and down as primary, but not an absolute right and left, or front and back, though he did distinguish these dimensions or diversifications as surely as the up and down. Also if he has all beings inside a place, which is a sphere, how can he get right and left with respect to the centre unless that centre is more than a point? And, similarly, what would be front and back?

August 22

It begins to look as if two central ideas of mine are the result of advances on ideas I falsely attributed to Aristotle and Whitehead. Those ideas which I falsely attributed make Aristotle and Whitehead have better systems than otherwise; had I not made the mistake it is possible that I would not have made the advance I did. But as it now is, the views represented in *Reality* and later, on final causes and on the ground of movement are more novel than I then knew them to be.

I attributed to Aristotle the view that there were real final causes outside the present beings and that these causes effected the present beings and thereby directed and quickened their activities. Richard Rorty has challenged me to show where Aristotle maintained this position, and I cannot find any evidence, except extrapolations based on what Aristotle says about movement to proper places, about the final cause as actual, about the fixity of species, and the movement of things to their proper end. I thought that Aristotle embedded such final causes in actual perfected beings, so that one could say that the kitten grew to be a cat under the pressure or lure of a full-grown cat-nature embodied in the cat. This interpretation would require us to say that were all mature cats to be destroyed the kitten would not grow to be a cat. In *Nature and Man* and in *Man's Freedom,* by generalizing and modifying this misconception, I finally reached the position that there was an all-inclusive but indeterminate possibility towards which all beings were directed and which they first specified as more limited possibilities and then acted to realize in not altogether predictable shapes. I then moved to the position that such a possibility must be sustained by something other than itself, and in "Guilt, God and Perfection" and in *Modes of Being* came to see that it is one of the tasks of God to sustain and to guarantee the satisfaction of that possibility. But the possibility is not a character of God or an idea in Him. It is a reality, independent of Him in being and nature, but sustained by Him as a being concerned with the satisfaction of an Ideal which the actual world might not on its own be able to do justice to.

I attributed to Whitehead the view that "simple location" meant that a body was located in more than one place at the same time. Nathaniel Lawrence has convinced me that by "simple" Whitehead means only "merely," and that what Whitehead is protesting against is the view that a being is only located and not also necessarily describable in other terms as well. Having with almost everyone else made this interpretation of Whitehead, I then generalized and extended the idea to cover time as well. Whitehead did not recognize that an actual entity, to escape the ravages of time, had to be in disequilibrium, had to be not only in the present moment but also in a future moment, and that it continued to be by virtue of the fact that while the present moment passed, it clung to and was sustained by the future moment. Tendency, inclination, desire, aim, etc., are after all present features, and in no way get the being to move, or even to give it a genuine direction.

A being must be related beyond itself to real independently existing possibilities if it is to be enabled to escape the present moment; it must also be subject to a control by Existence if it, though private and independent, is to be contemporary with others; and it must be related to God's unity if it is to have a meaningful relation to all else.

Power or tendency is the beginning of a single process which ends in the realization, at the end of an atomic moment, of the possibility which confronts a being. That possibility strictly speaking is best expressed as an undivided disjunct: *"x-or-non-x,"* and the realization will be the actual carving out and distinguishing of the x or the *non-x*—where the *non-x* is a contrary within a limited range—and the defining of the other as a description of all else that is in the universe or as a prescription more or less exemplified by all else.

A state of readiness is continuous with the state of action, even if it be only a state of re-establishing the kind of hold one just had on the possibility (and God and Existence). Realization of a possibility is the specification of it in such a way that what is left in the general serves not to define an area of possibility beyond all possible realization—which would be a contradiction or a paradox—but to give us a way of dealing with all else, either dispersively in a description, which may be vague, or as a unitary idea which prescriptively orders all else as divergent or opposed to the part that is realized. There must be analogous unused residues in God or Existence which must be given satisfaction. Satisfaction might be given in a different dimension in every case; e.g., "dying" might be viewed as a characterization of God and Existence as over against a fulfilled possibility of non-dying.

Suppose we had before a man the possibility "dying-or-not-dying," and that at the next moment he died. Not-dying at that moment would not be a possibility; firstly it was not a part of the original "dying-or-not-dying" for that is one and undivided; secondly it is not distinct from that whole and over against "dying," for as distinct and over against these it is by the very nature of the case now precluded from ever being realized. Still we can speak of the non-dying of this man as a short way of speaking of whatever else there is in the spatio-temporal world, or we can think of it as a single idea, not to be dispersed over the world, and thus as something which ought or might have been realized, or as characterizing God or Existence. In these shapes it is a prescription, an ideal condition which the others might be said to illustrate in various ways, qualifying and delimiting it; it would stand to them, if one liked, as a kind of possibility which they were diversely realizing. One might say of this non-realized portion of the possibility for this man then that it is in fact the portion which is realized by all else, viewed not from the position of those others but from the position of this man. The non-dying of this man (who is dying) would thus be identical with the birth of that chick, etc.

If we take this last view the whole possibility which confronts a being will be realized at every moment. But this goes counter to the view that there are still possibilities to be realized, that ideals are not necessarily realized, and that God is needed to see that what the world does not realize is realized or exhausted somehow. The answer is that there is a difference in value in "non-dying" as realized in this man, and the "non-dying (of this man)" as realized in the guise of the birth of the chick, or as God now, or as what Existence is now, and thus as standing over against the realized dying of this man. The difference in value must be contained in a possibility comprehending all other possibilities and measuring them; the delimited possibilities then will always be realized at every moment, but the realization will have overarching it a more inclusive possibility which God will utilize to measure all the realizations and thus either exhaust in that totality of realizations or satisfy in His own terms. "Dying-or-not-dying" thus, to use this merely as an example of the all-encompassing possibility, would measure all delimitations of itself, such as dying this way or that, the non-dying of this (rather than that). This evaluation would not be realized so long as the best mode was not achieved; it would stand outside all achievements as defied. It is because we could say that this is not the best of all possible worlds that God (and Existence too) is needed to assure that the evaluation, which the undivided possibility imposes on whatever realizations there are, eventually is satisfied either by the totality of all that occurs, if there be such a totality, or by the addition of a supplementary satisfaction through the action of God (and Existence). In this illustration the "dying-or-not-dying" is used to represent "The Good," and "dying-this-way-or-that" is a delimited possibility, which an actual dying-this-way realizes while other beings realize their own appropriate possibilities. These other realizations are characterized, from the standpoint of actual dying-this-way, as a "dying-that-way."

August 23

A possibility has a range by virtue of its very generality. It should be expressed in the complex form *"x-or-y,"* where *y* is the *non-x* as kept within the range characteristic of that possibility. When *x* is realized what is the status of *y?*

1] Y might be thought of as a shorthand way of speaking of what is common to all the possibilities that are in fact realized by all other things (and/or in other dimensions). But then every possibility would be realized fully every moment, and there would be no unsatisfied ideals, no obligations unfulfilled.

2] Y might be thought to provide a kind of model, ideal, prescription which the possibilities exemplified by all else realize. But then *y,* just so far as these fail to exhibit it, would be unrealized and the question of its status and realization would have to be faced. One could directly say then that *y* was excluded by *x* and had no realization, in which case it would be a possibility which was impossible.

3] God sustains and satisfies the unrealized possibility. But this would make God satisfy all the evil possibilities, happily excluded by the good work that men do.

4] Y could be said not to be a possibility at all, but that the satisfaction of x defines y as that which it excludes. Y would be a logically defined and logically excluded idea. But exclusion is reciprocal and in any case as excluded it must have some status.

5] Y could be shorthand for all else, but there would be the unity of the possibility "x-or-y" which neither the realization of x or of y would contain. That unity would have a valuational aspect; the fact that it was x which was realized in this one thing might be good or might be bad. This goodness or badness moreover would have a relation to the goodness or badness of what comes before and after and perhaps even to a more inclusive good in terms of which all of them would be found wanting. God (and in another way, also Existence) would realize that all inclusive good and whatever possibility, left over, deserved fulfillment. But then what of the evil half of a realization that is good? Whatever "half" there be, good or bad, is realized in the dispersed form of the limited possibilities of all other things, but the evaluation of this, the having of all these realizations in just this way will be related to all subsequent realizations by God (and Existence). God will embrace an all-inclusive possibility which no thing in the world can satisfy—but which all of them together can, just so far as God allows that all-inclusive possibility to be expressed in all these subordinate ones. Individual entities would thus face subordinate ranges of possibility within one which was not fully exhibited in that or any other subordinate possibility.

If what each dimension does to the other is analyze it, and thereby accommodates itself to the being of that other, the realization of possibilities, the suffering of might, the carrying of rights will all be matters of internal adjustment, leaving us with a mosaic of beings, each of which has within it the distinctions expressive of the others while having the others outside it as somehow exemplifying its principles.

August 24

Just what is meant by the realization of a possibility? Does it mean that the possibility actually is transported, embedded in the actual? Or does it mean that the actual reorganizes itself, accommodates itself to the presence of such a possibility and thus exhibits it? The trouble with the first suggestion is that if we carry the idea out with respect to all the four dimensions we evidently destroy what is said to be essential. Possibility, etc., are independent dimensions never to be destroyed and never even to be penetrated. But the second view would seem not to allow for such a thing as the actual realization of a possibility. Moreover it seems to preclude the action of might on a being, of God on Existence, etc. And it seems to stand in the way of the effort to assume the perspective of something other than oneself and the approach to the other dimensions in terms of that new perspective.

August 25

Let us suppose that each dimension accommodates itself to the others. The individual actuality which is at once concerned with the Ideal, immersed in Existence and occupied with eternity retains a hold on all these three; but to be itself it must also stand apart from them. So far as it stands apart from them without inwardly taking account of them it takes a prescriptive approach to them; it is only by virtue of its own adjustment to their natures that this individual has within it the meaning of the others and thus that its own account of them is descriptive. To say all this however is to put the work of conversion of the prescriptive to the descriptive solely on the individual and then as the outcome of an internal adjustment. It seems   A] to jettison the prescription for the sake of being just what the others are and not what is ideally required; it submits the prescription entirely to those others; B] it does not seem to allow for any action of one type of being on another;   C] it does not seem to allow for a thing to take a perspective of another as taking a perspective of a third. The theory of accommodation must take care of these before it can be satisfactory.

A] The prescriptive feature of this being does not preclude the need of what else there is to alter itself as well; a condition remains prescriptive so long as the accommodation must come from the other side, just so far as the other has not exhibited the condition itself. The individual may have to give up that prescription in that form, then or later or eventually or gradually, but what it means now is that   1] the individual has the meaning of the other in an abstract way and inwardly, and   2] that this has a descriptive moment in the way in which the others fall short of this in various ways, objectively exercising a complication of the very structure of the prescription. One might say that the prescription is the accommodation in the abstract to what is ingredient in what is now the case, and that the prescription is satisfied by becoming the very structure of these others, by those others exhibiting it directly. If so, the accommodation is on the one side by the individual but as such remains an unfulfilled prescription, and on the other by the internal adjustment of the others (with their attainment then of an accommodation of the individual) which enables the prescription to be fulfilled and thus be a description.

B] Realization of possibilities, unification of Existence, localization of God, fractionization of the Ideal all seem to involve an action from one dimension to another. If each dimension actually reaches to the others and terminates in them with an adumbrative grasp of their being correlate with its own substantiality, then action would be the way in which it separates and moves towards the other substantially for the sake of the possession of the terminative nature. What is changed then is the outside of the others and this from a perspective outside it. Yet there would seem to be real blows, hurts, cuts in this world. Moreover there does seem to be a difficulty in showing how one kind of entity could conceivably do something to the other kinds. Is it enough to say that the parts of a domain, say the multiple actualities, can act on one another, but that domain cannot act on domain? But we tried to account for persistence in time, deal with obligation, and with politics in terms of such action; must this type of explanation be given up? At the very least we are forced to say that one thing or domain seems able to control others. I must recur to this second point.

C] There is no particular difficulty in x adjusting itself to y, and z adjusting itself to this adjusted x. Nor in the adjusted x adjusting itself to a w. Thus when a body is a bearer of private rights it can as such take account of might, and might can take account not of the body as such but of the body as a bearer of private rights.

Recurring to B] we can say that x adjusts itself to y over where y is, but x will have to take account of y where x itself is, and this will express y's influence. We here speak in a Leibnizian fashion for the active and passive are now characterized not as involving a transference of energy but as exhibiting a difference in power or clarity, dominance or distinctness. Or should we say that x is made to adjust itself to y by virtue of y's view of it so that it is the need of a fractionization of the Ideal in Actuality, e.g., which makes it possible for an actuality to adjust itself to the Ideal? This would lead us from the position just entertained, which is essentially one of a Leibnizian mosaic to the opposite where each thing is intimately involved with every other, and the action of this on that will require a reciprocal conditional act of that on this. Y would then seem able to express itself fully in x and yet x may fail to do much justice to y. We must somehow:

1] take a perspective on y; 2] act on y; 3] affect y in its inwardness; 4] have y independently take a perspective on and act on us, (x); 5] injure, benefit or control y.

August 26

I think perhaps that the problem of action can be solved by recognizing that each being and each dimension makes an analysis of a sort of all else. This is done in itself and where the others are, for no being is merely in one location. But this analyzing is not without effect on the others; this was the point I did not keep in good focus in the earlier examinations of this question. As a rule the thing readjusts itself or offers such normal resistance to the act as to make no difference to its functioning or its appearance; this is what apparently happens when we know. But more forceful efforts involve much more radical readjustments and the outcome of these are known as the effects of those efforts.

The actuality acts on the Ideal not only by making itself embody it, but also by delimiting it, dividing it there and then, imposing specifications on it so that it functions as a limited objective. The Ideal in turn acts on the actuality not only by preparing itself for fractionization, but by actually controlling or luring or directing the actuality to make it a kind of representative of itself. The actuality acts on Existence by possessing a portion of it, and acts on God by its requirement that it be preserved. The Ideal not only lures the actual but acts on Existence by giving it a direction, and on God by its requirement that its demands be acknowledged. Existence not only makes the actual determinate, but enables the Ideal to have a being for this world, and enables God to have a diversification of capacities. God finally gives the actual an eternal context, relates the good to the Actual, and puts limits on Existence.

The above gives us the dimensions as actually making a difference to one another then and there where they are; this is not clearly seen on p. 56 of the mimeographed *Modes of Being.* We ought to distinguish:

1] What the dimensions seek: enrichment, embodiment, diversification, unification for Actuality, Ideality, God and Existence respectively.

2] What they get from one another: Actuality gets completing form, preservation, energy from *IGE* respectively; Ideality gets relevance, satisfaction, being from *AGE;* God gets agent-location, pertinence and effectiveness from *AIE;* Existence gets localization, unity and focus from *AGI.*

3] What they are from the perspective of the others: Actuality is role-bearing, focal point, judged data from *IEG;* Ideality is goal, providence, futurity from *AGE;* Existence is energy, becoming, unpredictable from *AGI;* God is judge, completer and unity for *AIE.*

4] How each responds to the other: Actuality is representative, material (?) and substance from *IGE;* Ideality is good, terminus and expression for *AEG;* Existence is connective, divisive and effective for *AIG;* God is preserver, substance and eternity for *AIE.*

5] How each acts on the other: Actuality delimits *I,* possesses *E,* and demands context of *G;* Ideality lures, directs and requires action by *AEG;* Existence makes determinate, causes and diversifies *AIG;* God insists, imposes and limits *AIE.*

August 29

In one sense we can speak of a single Being which is diversified in four distinct dimensions (no one of which possesses the full meaning of Being). The togetherness of the four dimensions is not concrete, and this fact is expressed in the thrust or reference of each to the others. (The single togetherness of them all is a kind of product, the outcome of the four ways in which the dimensions are together.) Each is together with the others but from its own position; the neutral togetherness of them all is now only an abstraction from them all. It is an abstraction, however, which expresses the outcome that alone would end the striving of the different dimensions with respect to one another. (It cannot be said to be an ideal for the whole, for there is no whole for which it could be the ideal; each has its own appropriate ideality or what ought to be, and each seeks in its own terms to fulfill itself.)

There is nothing amiss in the constant effort of each to seek fulfillment in the face of competition by the rest; the *neutral togetherness* of all four dimensions but expresses the meaning of them all from the perspective of just one of them, the intellectual. As a possibility it offers a problem however, for the realm of the possible is the Ideal which confronts the Actual, whereas the possible neutral togetherness is apparently for all four of them together. But we do so treat it as an Ideal when we view it as an intellectual prospect for the whole.

There is another way of dealing with the Being or the togetherness of all, where each maintains its own integrity, and where we quiet the drive of each towards the others, with the consequent formation of a world of "appearance" due to the interlocking of their perspectives, to constitute common territory. We can speak of the possibility of the togetherness in neutral terms as a projected future thrown off by the very manner in which the beings have perspectives on one another. This raises two questions: 1] the nature of the ongoing, and thus the time of the togetherness and the times of the dimensions other than Actuality, 2] and the nature of possibility as projective over against possibility as directive and as normative.

There is a time which is the juncture of the various times of the different dimensions. Each of the dimensions undergoes change. We are accustomed to speak as though there were only a time for actualities, but there must be a time for the Ideal to realize itself, to make a difference to actualities and the others, there must be another in which God adjusts himself to the data of the others, and there must be a third in which Existence attains stability through the others. This four-fold "time" reflects a disequilibrium in the dimensions. Each is occupied with completing itself through the mastery of the others; each stretches to them and encompasses them "on the outside," thrusting a nuclear phase of those others away from the content which it makes its own.

An actuality is in a process of adjusting itself to Ideality, Existence and God. I have in the past tended to speak as if the first were the essence of what is attained by the actuality and thus was the future towards which the actuality was moving; but Existence and God also have an "ideal" status with respect to the actuality and it reaches further and further into them so far as they are receptive to it and answer it in concordant ways. The Ideal can be said to be the future then not for the Actuality as such only, but for the Actuality as over against it and in interplay with Existence and God. But then we will have to say that Existence and God also have their modes of functioning and that they point to Ideality as their future and thus as expressing the outcome of their attempt to grasp one another and Actuality.

The Future as such is the Ideal as the possibility for Existence; Ideality is the Ideal as possibility for God, and the Good is possibility for Actuality. All three strive for the Ideal in their own appropriate "times" —God attempts to realize Ideality, as Plato saw (though Plato thought it was only an Ideality to be imposed whereas it is also an Ideality which God seeks to embody in himself); Existence attempts to realize Futurity within itself and also in the others.

Similarly there must be an effort to embody the Unity which is God, the Present vitality which is Existence, and the uniqueness which is the Actual. But if we view these seekings temporally we but restate what each is with respect to the Ideal.

The Ideal cannot be brought into the pattern of time unless one supposes it to be occupied with further and further recesses of itself. The recesses are ideality in a non-temporal sense; only the ideal aspect closest to and directed towards the other dimensions is in time. Ideality is occupied then with making its inwardness or implicitness explicit, as the outcome of its temporal involvement with the other dimensions. The other dimensions make themselves analogously explicit. Their becoming is not in public time, but can be defined in terms of that time since it can be defined in terms of their occupation with the Ideal as that which they are attempting to fill out.

But it would be better to say that the making explicit is precisely the function of the Actual as a substantial terminus not only with respect to itself but with respect to the others, just as it is the function of the Ideal, as fixed, to be the future which makes for the being of time. When the Ideal becomes explicit, it fixates itself with reference to Actuality. It is as substantialized in respect to the Actual that it has further recesses which it brings to the fore.

There are analogous characteristic efforts made with respect to God and Existence. Actuality, Existence and the Good all approach God as final. This is neither a way of acting in time or of making something explicit; it expresses a mode of readjustment to God so that the unity which is God can become fully ingredient in them.

God Himself will be faced with the need, as attached to the other dimensions, of embodying a deeper unity than He now has, just as Ideality is always faced with more ideality when it treats Actuality as a terminus, and just as Actuality is always involved in temporal efforts in itself so far as it faces Ideality. God's deeper unity is Himself as *implicit* so far as Actuality is His terminus; it is what He *strives to achieve* when He has the Ideal as terminus, and it is what He *strives to utilize* as a boundary on Existence. But His main task is to be the locus of the togetherness of Himself and the others, and that is what drives Him to subordinate Himself and those others to a deeper unity, and so on endlessly.

Existence finally is dispersive, always dividing itself. When it is fixed by means of attachment to the others, they and it find need for more and more diversification. We have then the following:

Ideality as a *terminus* for all four, which makes them all engage in a becoming in time; Actuality as *substantial* for the others, which makes all *four* (and not only the Ideal!) of them engage in a process of explicitifying; God as a *finality* for all four, which makes them all serve as data for unification; Existence as *content* for all four, which makes them all diversify themselves.

This modifies the foregoing discussion somewhat. What it shows is that there are four modi of time, with all four of them looking to something in the domain of the Ideal for future content; that there are four modi of exteriorization where all four look to the Actual as that which they seek to encompass; that there are four modi of submission with all four of them looking to deeper and deeper unifications; and that there are four modi of diversification with all four of them seeking to be carried further in the process of articulation.

When then we say that the togetherness is not concrete we are primarily thinking of the unification which God provides in His inner depths for the others and for Himself, a process which is unending, but cannot be said to be in time except so far as we orient God with respect to the Ideal. That Ideal is not in any other position with respect to Him than the goals of men are to them.

The situation is analogous to that which we have when the Actual is approached from any of these other positions, for then we have the effort of all to utilize the Actual as a means of making themselves more public. (The Actual makes such an effort too, clinging on to particular actualities and interplaying with them.) If we ask what it is that all seek, we once again treat the Ideal as a possibility, palely stating as an outcome what is, (from the standpoint of Actuality) but the inwardness of each.

We can say in temporal terms what all four of them are attempting to do, but we don't really get a neutral position when we say this, for we then point all dimensions towards Ideality. It is easiest for us to do this, for we always have ourselves pointing towards futurity.

We have four modi of time (instead of the usual one which is defined in terms of the Actuality approaching Ideality), when we deal with God, Existence and Ideality as facing some fixed and further Ideal.

If we take the position of the Actual as substantial, as fixed, the others are seen to be in the process of internally uncovering the very depths of themselves, of engaging in the process of allowing more and more of their beings to become engaged with others.

We can also see that we need to look at ourselves, Ideality and Existence as somehow fixated with respect to Unity. They are then neither in time nor making them explicit, but are being pulled up and transformed by divine unity.

And finally we can see all as present, and so far as we do this we fixate Existence and see it as the agency by which they move through the world, make themselves articulate over a stretch of activity.

God is not only a unity for each but for all; there is also a meaning of the temporal Ideal for all, including itself; there is also a process of explicitness which the Actual provides for all; and there is a diversification which the Existence provides for all. This means that there are four modi of togetherness. Each shears off a part of itself so as to be together with the others, and has itself in that guise as content for itself. We have thus a togetherness in futurity, in uniqueness, in eternal unity and in articulation, but this is only to say that each dimension stands apart with its own finality and that any attempt to understand it in neutral terms but will give us a peculiar and limited mode of togetherness.

To say we have a togetherness as an Ideal in the future is but to say that we have it vis-à-vis the Actual, Existence and God as well (and a specified portion of the Ideal). (We have then moved away from the original suggestion that the togetherness is a projection from the manner in which things have perspectives on one another, to adopt the position that each dimension is thick and that the togetherness is but a way of talking of it and the others from the perspective of the thicker part.) I am not at the end of this problem as yet, but now I must turn to the other point raised above, and also to the question, related to it, of the types of satisfactions there are.

We can always ask of any fulfillment whether it is as it ought to be; no satisfaction in the world, no course of the world, can be taken as finally satisfactory. The good looks to some other being for guidance and perhaps satisfaction. But we must say this also of intellectual ideals such as logic, for though we may be content with the course of the world there is the fact that it may be more complex than it need be. Logic demands a purity which the world can not satisfy. But then we ought to have in addition to ethical and logical norms, one for Actuality and one for Existence—perhaps personal identification is the analogue for the one, and immersion in the present ongoing is the analogue for the other?

Each dimension then will offer a kind of demand which the others will never satisfy, except through the help of other dimensions. God will help the good. Shall we say that Ideality will help out intellectuality, unity, logic, that Actuality will help out immersion, and Existence will help out personal identification? Does Ideality then insist on the unity of the rational and adjust the others to this fact; does the Actual insist on the importance of the present, and make the others submit to this (of course inside and with respect to itself). Similarly does Existence demand that the Actual as now focused, the need to make everything referred to it, be fulfilled, and that others must take account of this, within the being or perspective of Existence? If so Ideality adds something to unity, Actuality adds something to the present, Existence adds something to individuality, just so far as these fail to be satisfied by the others. Ideality adds purity or mere formality to the unity, Actuality adds focal points to Existence, Existence adds vitality and interplay to individuality.

Each dimension could define one of the dimensions as that which is in fact satisfied by the others, or it can, where these dimensions are norms, supplement those others with something from itself to make those others fulfilled with relation to the rest, thereby making them a three-fold togetherness.

There are four norms—the good, translucent intellectuality, uniqueness and activity—answering to the irreducible nature of the Ideal, God, Actuality and Existence. No one of these norms is satisfied by the rest of the dimensions necessarily; each therefore offers either an irrelevant norm, and thus no norm at all; an unattainable norm and thus one which is paradoxical for the others to try to realize; a supplementable norm (which leads us to the recognition of a God,' Ideal, Existence and Individual each with the function of satisfying that norm from within itself while adjusting the values of the other two dimensions to the nature of that norm), or a productive norm which spends itself in the being of the others.

The norms define specifications as more or less good; therefore even if one were to do nothing but the good there would be unrealized possibility characterizing the level not yet attained in the norm. Within the norm, though, as subject to qualifications by the other dimensions, there are subordinate possibilities; the satisfaction of these involves their further specification with a definition of the residue as logically contained in the fulfillable norm or as expressing the very nature of what else there be. None of this excludes the possible case of possibilities being projected and then serving as momentary guides, in a Deweyean fashion; but this case has to face up to unrealized possibilities and unsatisfied norms.

Every norm is prescriptive. It is never entirely cut off from the world; its prescriptive status means that the others are ordered as better or worse with respect to it. They defy it and its evaluations. The norm therefore must attain the state of being descriptive of the objects in the world; all must exemplify it, satisfy it fully. The plurality of realizations one might say is the very substance of the norm, the meaning of the norm fulfilled; the norm as standing apart from all these is but effete, abstract. Still the various cases are of different degrees of elegance; they do not then and there in the same way exemplify the structure expressed in the norm. There must then be a fourth state (after the stage of being unexemplified, being an evaluative prescription, being a dispersed description) in which the things exemplify the norm in such a way that their functioning permits of its re-exemplification throughout.

Every dimension approaches the others in this four-fold way of separation from, evaluation of, dispersion in, and adjustment to these others. (In previous discussions I started with the idea of a being as involved with others, then moved over to separation, evaluation and adjustment. This is the proper order of movement; the just stated order merely gives us the prescription and description status in pairs.) We must say then that the norm starts by being dispersed throughout others, as a kind of description which is accepted by the others in their terms (precisely because the interested being is grappling with those others in a vital way), that it then moves to a position of separation where it achieves its own integrity but only by having a prescriptive nature (which is unsatisfied since it is held off in abstraction from all else), that it then moves to a position of evaluation where the others are as it were acted on, forced within the orbit of the prescription and characterized by it (but without being deprived of their status of independent beings going their own way and thus in a sense defying the prescriber), only to end with a description which allows for the retention of the form of the prescription with a mode of functioning provided by the others so that they continue to re-exhibit that form without undue complexity.

Action is the imposition of one's own prescribing form but it is answered by the others; this is why we have a constant change in the universe; every dimension insists on itself but is answered by the others independently; moreover no one of the dimensions is sufficient by itself; the reality as self-sufficient is all these insufficient dimensions as constantly recovering themselves and insisting on themselves in the face of one another.

Each dimension has certain aspects essential to but not integral to it. We argued to the reality of God in these terms; we have a right to argue to the reality of Existence, Ideality and Actuality in similar ways, though then in each case we must start with the other three as basically real. Actuality is needed so that the other dimensions can be unique, individual, temporal; Ideality is needed so that the other dimensions can achieve clarity, purity, directionality; Existence is needed so that the other dimensions can achieve contemporaneity, vitality, power. There should be arguments in each of these dimensions parallel to the nine basic arguments used in the *Modes* to prove the existence of God.

August 30

We can, I think, say in advance that any philosophic system will be inadequate. But this means that we must then have some overall view which is correct. Scepticism and dogmatism must be warp and woof. We are sceptics perhaps when we adopt the position of a single abstract One and in terms of this evaluate all efforts. Conversely, the dogmatic speculative philosopher, who is articulating a system, criticizes the sceptic for distorting the nature of the Many. The speculative man knows the Many and tries to express the One.

Modes of Being (mimeographed) is in a way biased towards Actuality; otherwise it would not have offered nine proofs of the existence of God and neglected to offer analogous proofs for the other dimensions. Even the neo-platonists with their acceptance only of God as primary, the materialists with their acceptance of Existence, and idealists with their acceptance of the Good seem to see no real necessity for proving the existence of Actuality—they are tempted in fact to deny the reality of the Actual. A strict counterpart of *Modes of Being* would be a neo-platonism, materialism or idealism which did full justice to the other dimensions though starting with one of them.

Spinoza tried to do some justice to actualities while accepting the One; Marx had some appreciation for actualities, and idealists sometimes have room for "finite centres," and God. But there is no system which I know that does have room for all four dimensions. Even with its bias, then, *Modes of Being* is more complete than the others. But I think one can get a richer, more neutral system than *Modes of Being* by genuinely entertaining the status of dimensions other than Actuality, to the very degree that Actuality is entertained. Perhaps this will never be possible for me, for I come to *Modes of Being* out of the position developed in *Reality* (and thus from one which stresses, even overstresses the Actual), and only gradually pushed on to acknowledge the equal reality of the other dimensions, without ever fully enjoying them in their inwardness. It was the argument of the last chapter of the *Modes* that one could never escape one's own perspective, but it was also the argument there that we see everything in terms of another perspective as well.

Each dimension has the others "together" with it. It not only provides these others with supplements which are essential to them (as God does with the others, as is made out in the *Modes*), but possesses the others as dimensions which are over against it. We who know this neutralize the biased togetherness, and we do this by abstracting, getting an abstract mode of togetherness in place of the concrete and biased one. We can do this because the dimension of intellectuality or God can be held apart. It is only when we try to be prescriptive with respect to togetherness or claim that this neutrality is descriptive in any sense other than that of a logical conjunction of the biased togetherness, that togetherness presents a problem. The logical conjunction of biased togetherness is identical in content with the abstract neutral togetherness we abstract from any one of the biased cases. It could be viewed as the description of that logical conjunction, as the prescription of their eventual satisfied togetherness, as the meaning of each, and as the defied case of an applied prescription.

August 31

There is a sense in which there are four normative disciplines—ethics, logic, creativity and representation. These express possibility, divinity, Existence and Actuality respectively from limited perspectives. Ethics is possibility vis-à-vis Actuality; logic is God as pertinent to Existence; creativity is Existence in relation to God, and the representative is the Actual in relation to the possible. Ethics needs completion by divinity and by Existence; logic by Ideality and Actuality; creativity by Ideality and Actuality, and representation by divinity and Existence.

Or more objectively:

Possibility is made into an ethical objective by Actuality
     into finality by divinity
     into futurity by Existence

Divinity is made into logic by Existence
     into the one by Actuality
     into substance by possibility

Existence is made into creativity by God
     into field by Actuality
     into becoming by Ideal possibility

Actuality is made into representation by possibility
     into actor by Existence
     into individual by God

The above table shows that each of the dimensions has a special function for each of the others. But what is not made clear in the above is that if we approach each in terms of its function it needs the other dimensions to supplement it as performing just that function. Thus the status of ethical objectivity is not fulfilled by Actuality; God must supplement it. But as was not stated in the *Modes,* Existence must supplement it too. This means then we must have in addition to the above table the following:

Ethical objectivity completed by God and Existence

Possibility as finality completed by Actuality and Existence

Possibility as Futurity completed by God and Actuality

Logic completed by Actuality and Possibility

The One completed by Possibility and Existence

Substance completed by Actuality and Existence

Creativity completed by Ideality and Actuality
Field completed by God and Ideality
Becoming completed by God and Actuality

Representation completed by God and Existence
Actor completed by Possibility and God
Individual completed by Possibility and Existence

There are then twenty-four completions required. If we add to these the fact that each one of the categories, e.g., ethical objectivity, etc., needs a counterpart in order to achieve that function, there will be a total of thirty-six references which must be made from the base of each dimension, proving the reality of the other dimensions. In *Modes of Being* in the chapter on God nine of these references were isolated. They are the ones above which mention God plus the three cases relating to Logic, the One and Substance. *Modes of Being* (using somewhat different terms) gave a nine-fold argument for the being of God on the basis of the defects of each of the other dimensions as in themselves and as in relation to the other two dimensions. A similar set of nine arguments must pertain to Actuality, to Ideality, and to Existence. We must be able to reach to let us say Ideality by starting with Actuality, God and Existence and showing that these need supplementation by something which gives them what is essential but not integral to them. Each dimension, to look at the matter in another way, must be seen to have nine defects, three of which are satisfied by one dimension.

Actuality needs an Existence for its past, a substantiality for its universals and an other for its inwardness, and this is given by God

needs connections for its present, production for its objective and vitality for its being, and this is given by Existence

needs value for its future, conditioning by a value, and a norm for its being, and this is given by Ideality

Ideality needs substantiality for its exterior status, fulfillment as realizable and a role as a final cause, and this is given by God

needs a ground for its being, renewal for its relevance, a terminus for its reference and this is given by Existence

needs relevance for its meaning, satisfaction for its value and representation for its being, and this is given by Actuality

Existence needs unity to be a realm, intelligibility for its oppositions and expression for its status as present, and this is given by God

needs direction, evaluation and futurity, and this is given by Ideal needs focus, freedom and absorption and this is given by the Actual

God needs specification, utilization and otherness and this is given by Actuality

needs divisiveness, temporality and causal power and this is given by Existence

needs providential interest, expression and relevance and this is given by Ideality

Of the above only the supplementation of God is clearly and systematically stated in *Modes of Being*. The others are touched upon in part. The above characterizations of just what is defective and what supplementations are provided by each have not been thought through and need change of expression, particularly to keep abreast of *Modes of Being,* and also to make sure that the characterizations answer to the different ways in which a dimension is approached.

The basic principle of all this is: Respect the Other, take it seriously, recognize that it deserves every kind of characterization as excellent and as deficient as its original. God becomes not one among actualities but one among final realities, supplementing all else and being supplemented in turn by the rest. But this is only to say that our system is dialectic, or that each dimension needs the others.

September 1

I must have been thinking about the jottings of yesterday throughout the night. It seems evident now that the whole can be simplified. Each dimension should be said to have three defects, not nine, but these are to be satisfied in three ways. Thus,

Actuality's insufficiency of vitality is helped out by Existence. But as past it must have existence made integral to by God, and as future by ideality. Its insufficiency as meaning needs a universal. But this must be made integral by God in the present, and serve to order the past. Its insufficiency as separate needs God as an other. But this does not suffice, and there must be an existential division and a formal unity which provide, respectively, a present and future, for in relation to the Other the actuality should be a kind of past, or finished fact.

Possibility's insufficiency of substance is helped out by God. But as an objective it must have Existence hold it away from Actuality, and as relevant must be made to have some of the reality of the Actual. Its insufficiency as a good is helped out by Actuality which gives it some realization, but it needs further help of Existence to vitalize it and the help of God to make its realizations exhaustive. Possibility's insufficiency as offering a direction is made good in part by Existence which projects it; this addition must be helped out by Actuality which is concerned with it, and by God who keeps it before the cosmos.

Existence's insufficiency of focus is helped out by Actuality. But as cosmic it needs the focused unity of God, and the rational meaning of the Ideal. Its insufficiency of order is helped out by the Ideal. But it needs the law-giving being of God and the stable habits of actualities. Its insufficiency as divisive needs the unity provided by God. But this too needs to be supplemented by the distinct unities of actualities, and the rational unity of possibility.

God too is insufficient. He lacks the simple surface meaning of the possible. But this is not enough; there must further be help from Existence to make Him significant for the world, and from Actuality to make Him effective in a substance. He is also insufficient in worldly creative power and needs Actuality to mediate Him. This must be supplemented by a possibility which conveys His intent, and by an Existence which divides Him throughout the cosmos. He is insufficient finally, as temporal, and needs the help of Existence. But that help is not enough and must be supplemented by the temporal activity of the actual and the temporal expression of the possible.

The above improves somewhat on the categories used yesterday, but is not yet adequate. What is important to note though is that each dimension is insufficient in three ways, and that in each way the other dimensions have different functions, one of them directly answering the defect, and the others adding to this, eking out what the direct answer did not provide. This means that what is said in *Modes of Being* must be supplemented in three ways. Firstly, it must be recognized that the cosmological proofs start with what is not God, but start in three different ways. Thus it is only as needing an other that Actuality refers to God directly; in the other two cases we start with the Actual as existent or as involving a universal. And similarly for the other two sets of cosmological arguments. Secondly, the very fact, that only one of the arguments in each set goes to God directly, means that there is a direct way of going to Existence and/or of going to Actuality and/or of going to Ideality, so that two of the cosmological arguments in each set are really arguments for some other dimension first and only secondarily for God. They point up the fact that we could have taken out of each set two arguments and used them to prove the existence of dimensions other than God. But whether used this way or not, and whether one attends to the direct or indirect proofs of God, the fact remains that God is only one of three supplements which each dimension needs. The job that God does is never sufficient; it is always necessary. What is sufficient is the work of all three for any fourth. Thirdly, it becomes manifest that God needs the support of the others. He asks directly for each dimension, and what this gives is supplemented by the remaining two. He, like the other dimensions, has essential but not integral features which these others must give to Him.

September 3

There ought to be 12 direct arguments of a cosmological sort:

1]	Starting with Actuality	
2]	Ideality	
3]	Existence,	and going to God as providing an essential but not integral element (see *Modes of Being*)
4]	Actuality	
5]	Ideality	
6]	God	and going to Existence in an analogous way and for an analogous reason
7]	Actuality	
8]	Existence	
9]	God	and going to Ideality, etc.
10]	Ideality	
11]	Existence	
12]	God	and going to Actuality, etc.

Or to put it another way, we can start with Actuality and go directly to God, Existence or Ideality (cases 1, 4, 7), or we can start with Ideality and go directly to God, Existence and Actuality (cases 2, 5, 10); or we can start with Existence and go directly to God, Ideality or Actuality (cases 3, 8, 11); or we can start with God and go directly to Actuality, Ideality or Existence (cases 6, 9, 12).

Each can be said to be together with the others but in its own terms; and each can be understood neutrally as together with all the others by abstracting from its bias to get an abstract togetherness, and thus the togetherness which exists only within the limited perspective of God's eternal intellectuality. This tells us what the neutral togetherness is, for the perspective which the abstract intellectuality provides is one which is an abstraction from God Himself. He has in His concreteness a biased mode of having Himself together with the rest; it is only when He denies Himself to assume an abstract position that we have genuine neutrality, but one whose concrete meaning is that it will be distorted in four concrete ways. This neutral position is one which each dimension can in fact attain to by an internal divestment of itself. Each is neutrally together with the rest in one phase of itself. God makes Himself surface, Actuality makes itself private, Ideality makes itself explicit, and Existence makes itself divided. Only God's is intellectual; the Actuality's is an enjoyed togetherness, Ideality's is a formula for it, and Existence is the production of it.

There is a need in 3.08 of the *Modes* to deal with Existence and Actuality in relation to one another.

September 7

The problem of participation seems to arise when one defines the realm of the formal as necessary or pellucid or perfect in some way and the realm of fact as contingent and inadequate. But it would be just as accurate to say that the formal is just what is, a set of facts, though of an inert and formal kind, and that the realm of fact is a realm of constraint, compulsion, necessity. But perhaps it would be best to speak of two types of necessity, the one answering more to the nature of the purely formal, and the other answering to the process of creativity. The one necessity is given in one fell swoop and the other is produced in the course of time. They are not reconciled in a third; rather they are opposing articulations of the Actual. That Actual is in the process of making itself be in time in relation to the Ideal, and as it does this it re-assesses these necessities, qualifying each, delimiting each, giving vitality and body to one, and structure and stability to the other.

It would have been better if in Chapter 3 of (the mimeographed) *Modes of Being* I had started by defining real possibility as that which needed and finally got realization, and distinguished a cosmic and a non-cosmic form of it. The cosmic would pay off in time; the non-cosmic would be a norm, and would not necessarily pay off in time. Even if it were realized in time this would not be enough, for it is such that it need not be realized in time. But as a real possibility it *must* be realized; this is what God does for it, and what Existence does for it, in different ways. God fulfills the real possibility in the shape of a norm by filling it up with His own energies, meaning, value, satisfactions, giving it a completeness and determinateness which the world may fail to provide. He guarantees that it will be satisfied. Existence fulfills the Ideal by making it the very structure of the entire temporal world; it makes the Ideal measure all occurrences. In previous discussions I spoke as if this latter work were God's, and in my "Theses on Possibility" and in *Modes of Being* I neglected to bring out—as I did bring out in the paper on "Guilt, God and Perfection"—the fact that a norm is a real possibility which must be realized, but not necessarily in the actualities in this world.

September 17

History, as having all its evidence in the present, can be said to be exclusively involved in the present. To be sure it ends with a construction, but this, though purporting to be about the past, is also in the present. And the construction though begun in the present and itself existing only in the present is, despite its reference back to the past, actually completed and has bearing on what follows on the present in which the evidence is contained. History then can also be said therefore to be concerned primarily with the future,—a future construction which on the basis of the present evidence purports to report the nature of the past.

The body has a nature of its own; it is also a mode of analyzing right, might and value; and it is also the bearer of right, a unit of might and a representative of value. As any pair of the last triplet, it concerns itself with acting on the third domain. As so acting it unites the pairs to make a whole, and overcomes the division which the other domains made in it. Thus as a bearer of right and as a unit of might it is internally divided and then in two independent ways. By attending to the realm of value the body unifies might and right severally and together. But then there is an analogous unification on the part of might and on the part of right and on the part of value; each of these as divided by the body (and/or some other domain) unites to be able to act on some other domain.

September 20

If there be a difference between the kind of actuality represented by a stone or forest or shoe and that of an organic being, the question remains as to just how the former is in time. Can we say merely that the behavior of the parts of the former is the only behavior which is possible to it? But there is no question but that they age and have a history. If we continue to say, as we ought, that only actual substances— primary actualities I term them in *Modes of Being*—can act, we ought to say that the former have consequences, and that these consequences no less than the outcomes of the activities of their parts, are and take place in time. Therefore we will have to affirm that there is something more than behavior which is temporally oriented. We can combine the two modi of temporal existence by recognizing the activity of primary substances to help constitute the being of time, a time which the secondary actuality qualifies and fills out.

"Being" as applicable to all the four modes must be neutral with respect to all of them. It cannot be dismissed as merely amphibolous, as that which is to be exemplified in diverse ways; it must have some core of meaning of its own; this should be one with the meaning of the "togetherness" which connects them all, each from its own perspective and in abstraction from them all. Accordingly we shall have to say that "being" as such is the mode in which each dimension is together with the others; but as angled in its own peculiar way, and also that it is the most abstract way of referring to all of them as together, as that which they have in common—their being in oppositional and fundamental ways.

September 21

The occurrences in the world can be divided out into three basic groups, without compromising the fact that they are all caught within the same time, are equally substantial, and interact. The first we may term the merely temporal and consists of the inanimate and animate world as sheer happenings, and as in no way expressing themselves as individuals or kinds. The second we may term the historical and consists of all that occurs as expressive of some thing else; the inanimate would then express, perhaps in a monotonous way, the nature of laws and the intent of a God or the meaning of nature. The third is that which may be termed the historically significant, and is the second as caught within the frame imposed by an historian. The historian views the world in terms of some frame which defines the importance of various items; if his frame expresses the nature of man, society, the course of the world, etc., with some accuracy, then his frame, though a means of selecting out only some items, can nevertheless function as a truly objective frame for whatever does occur; it will not distort or relativize what has happened but merely focus on that which is more contributive to the very nature of man, society, etc. There would be nothing in the world that might not come into some historian's frame; history recognizes no limits, just as science recognizes no limits. Each can deal with what the other does, but they have different objectives, different ways of providing a mesh in terms of which different things are selected.

November 10

The concentration on one mode of being to the neglect of others accounts for the various philosophic systems which have dotted the history of thought. Some have insisted on but one mode of being, neglecting, dismissing or treating as subordinate versions of the one they prefer. Others have insisted on two as final and irreducible, doing inadequate or no justice to the remaining two. Others have three modes. Together these make up fourteen philosophies offering delimited versions of a system which acknowledges all four.

A system may of course acknowledge all four modes of being and be quite different from others making a similar acknowledgment. Many more systems are possible, for there is an endless number of stresses and distances and interrelationships which one can exploit. Each man must determine for himself which one of these is most in consonance with what he experiences and otherwise knows.

Nominalism is a philosophy that intends to acknowledge only the Actual. It is now favored by such positivistically oriented logicians as Quine. But these thinkers have no room for the ideals to which they submit in their quest for truth, no place for the unity of their systems and no place for the movement in fact and thought on which their very being and inquiry depends.

Idealism insists on the Ideal as an absolute principle of value or reason, treating everything else as that absolute in a delimited guise. For an idealist such as Blanshard every being, even individuals such as himself, you and I, are the Ideal in some truncated form. Or, as he would prefer to say, it is a complex set of universals, intelligible through and through to the clear mind, and forming part of a single rational, ideal universe. There is no place in his system for the unique, no way in which he can acknowledge the very unity which the whole system has, and no way of dealing with motion, action or time as more than structures or meanings.

Neo-platonism acknowledges only the eternal One, treating everything else in the universe as a derivate or degenerate version of it. For Plotinus actualities have only a shadowy reality, the Ideal is part of God's own mind, whereas Existence, as at the other extreme from the One which alone truly is, is held to be indistinguishable from non-being.

Dynamism takes its stand with Existence, dismissing all else or seeing it as an ex-foliation of Existence. In Schopenhauer it is called by the name of will; in von Hartmann it goes by the name of the unconscious; in Lenin it is given the name of matter. In all these cases, actualities are but momentary knots in a cosmic movement, ideals are faint shadows thrown against the nothingness which environs Existence, and God is but the name of our most cherished superstitions. The systems have no genuine individuals, no true ideals, no authentic eternity, and thus no place for their authors, for the possibilities which Existence realizes, or for the unity which the Existence needs in order to have a nature, and thus in fact be.

Metaphysical naturalism finds room for both actualities and ideals. The position was presented by me in my *Reality:* unfortunately it had no place for the separate domains of God and Existence, and thus could not do justice either to the idea of unity or to the vital movement which keeps all actualities temporally together.

Religious dualism, as in Buber, stresses the reality of actualities, particularly humans, and God, at the expense of Existence and ideals. On this view the central fact is confrontation of selves with selves and selves with the divine. What is neither of these is dismissed as an insignificant though still actual "it." No provision is made for Existence; there is no way in which this view therefore can account for the fact that the selves continue to be together while in time, and no way of dealing with their purposes.

Existentialism has many forms. There are religious existentialists who would be hard to distinguish from religious dualists. But if we take Sartre and Jaspers as representatives, existentialism is the view that there are only actualities and Existence. The view has no room for ideals or for God; as a consequence it views actualities and the sea of Existence in which they swim as irrationalities having no meaning or value. Such a view has no genuine place for an ethics, and no way of accounting for the unity which hovers over all that there may be in this world.

Formalism deals with what existentialism omits, and omits what existentialism concentrates on. It has a religious and a secular form. The religious form speaks of God and ideals as the only realities, viewing all else as the outcome of the interplay of the two; the temporal world of actualities and Existence are the fulgurations of God as trying to realize some purpose as yet beyond himself. The secular form of this view is to be found in a positivistic, even atheistic system such as Carnap's. For him God takes the shape of the unity of all knowledge, and the Ideal takes the shape of the perfect language, and what does not fit into the one or the other is dismissed as nothing at all. As a consequence the individual thinker, on the one hand, and the world of dynamic becoming on the other, is nowhere to be found.

Sceptical naturalism, the philosophy of Santayana, finds a place only for ideals and Existence. Everything, it is said, has a natural or brute origin and an ideal goal or culmination. On this view God is only one other ideal, and actualities are but variant forms of Existence. But once again there is no unity to the whole, and no one to know it, to be sceptical or otherwise.

Anaxagoreanism, like Manichaeism, stresses the reality of the eternal unity and of divisive Existence, pushing away consideration of either ideals or actualities. It is the counterpart of metaphysical naturalism, each making good the limitations of the other. A system, which has no room for the actual philosopher or for the ideals he is endeavoring to realize in the end, has no way of relating its eternal unity to the divisive Existence —as Socrates pointed out long ago.

Personalism, e.g., in Brightman, does justice to three modes of being; it leaves out the realm of Existence and should be supplemented by a dynamism. Kantianism also allows for three modes of being; but since it leaves out the Ideal it needs the supplement of an effective insistence on the Ideal, characteristic of post-Kantianism or idealism. Rationalism, e.g., with Royce, does justice to another set of three; but since it leaves out actualities it must be supplemented by a nominalism. Metaphysical humanism as in Peirce finally includes everything but God and needs neoplatonism to complete it.

These fourteen views criticize one another with justice. They will undoubtedly be used to criticize the position here set forth, but there will be no more justice in such criticism than there would be in any part criticizing a whole for including more than the part can. A fifteenth type of criticism would however be legitimate. This would admit that there were four basic, irreducible modes of being, but would take exception to the manner in which those modes are here presented. I am confident that such criticism will have considerable warrant. In view of the fact that the present formulation of this four-fold system was gradually won over against my earlier accounts, it is quite certain that it will exhibit warpings and distortions, revelatory of my initial and perhaps inescapably persistent stress on the Actual. Unfortunately it is one thing to know that such twists are to be expected and another to know what they are or to have the capacity to correct them; in the nature of the case I am quite sure that there are such twists and quite uncertain where they are or how I might correct them. But fortunately there will be others who can understand a four-fold view without being limited by my present and its particular past. The discovery of their limitations will require still another generation, and so on, without end.

To be and to know is either to exclude or neglect, or it is to stand at a distance from what one knows, and thus be biased in still another, even though less harmful way. It is to be biased towards a neutral knowledge, which tells what things really are, but only by holding itself away from full being. There is no limit that one can antecedently assign to the effort to achieve such neutral knowledge, nor to the subsequent endeavor to make it one with what is there to know. I have tried to reach the first of these goals; an attempt at the second awaits a verdict on how close I have come to the first.

May 31

When we acknowledge something from without, we cannot be said to know it unless what we confront is sustained exteriorly. So far as we know, we know that the datum is exteriorly sustained in one of four ways:

1] Externally, passively received is actively sustained;
2] Existentially, passively received is passively sustained by the world but in a different sense from the way we do;
3] Future self, myself or another, or the community, where we actively produce or control the datum for a future receiving being;
4] Correlative, where we actively take the datum and expect another to take it actively too. This is ourselves as facing the datum as known by another mind.

We have an analogous situation when we assert or affirm from within for this involves us in a claim which is to be tested by

5] An absolute eternal judge;
6] A pragmatic course of experience;
7] A normative determination of its importance;
8] A social world of concurrent actors.

If what we acknowledge or assert is rejected, it is the case that there is a mind other than ours but it is questionable how much mind we have. But it is difficult to determine what is non-acceptance, a just dismissal, and a just rejection, because something else has been accepted as the truth, acknowledged by a mind.

We acknowledge another mind to have the datum as exterior to us but appropriately, in just the shape we have it; this means it cannot be held by God who is superior, Existence which is inferior, or the normative which is attenuated. To avoid being merely adjusted to objects I must view my datum as the object of other minds as well. To know that I know I must know that these other minds are there; this leads me to refer to a mind in the future where what I suppose can be tested; but I must have a closure to that future, and this refers me to an absolute. The active reason is my assurance that I know. But to know that divine or eternal truth I must see the world as God's expression, so that I can also say that the world viewed as His expression is the truth of the datum as an object which I know, or which is known by other minds, or which is certified in the future.

June 4

Lieb asked me if one could make a general proof of the need for four modes of being. I suppose such a proof would begin with any entity x and show that there is a non-essential otherness in it which involves reference to a y, and that the otherness itself is a juncture of two other modes of being, a v and a w. The otherness would have to be more generic than that which relates entities to God, as in *Modes of Being;* it would have to relate to the Ideal or to Existence equally, if one started with Actuality, or to another set of three if one started elsewhere. Or perhaps it would be better to start with the togetherness of all, as a One, and show that this involves the many in the guise of two other modes, and that these two are contingently together, together as a matter of fact only so far as the two are related by a double relation, factually and intelligibly defined, even when it is the case that we are relating Actuality and Ideality. But then our terms are not sufficiently neutral.

The speculative quest might be viewed as an attempt to define the one basic prescriptive category. Beginning with any pair of items, say an actual man and a datum wrested from Existence, we move to the acknowledgment of another actuality, then to Ideality, where this acknowledgment is certified, and then to eternity which gives a closure to the certification. At the end we must come to all four constituting a basic phenomenon or category, which will have in it all the modes; it will be a datum as the juncture of two minds in which the very meaning of meaning or Ideality will be embodied, (and which eternity will guarantee to be so embodied) and in which eternity will be expressed as the very structure and self-completive nature of the datum. The datum in short will be the locus of minds, futurity, eternity and Existence. As a togetherness or prescription it ought to require for its own being the separation of these and their contingent togetherness. The deduction then of four modes of being could begin with the prescriptive nature of their togetherness and show that it has extensive eternality, and also present intelligibility, and then that these are distinct factors.

Or do we get the second pair by recognizing that the initial unity is over against the contingent one, and that each of these is rooted in something other than itself, the one in eternity the other in Existence? If so, our

first derivatives must be Actuality and Ideality as required by the togetherness as constituting the basic many, whose manyness is expressed in the
very being of Existence, and whose oneness is representative of divinity.
But why should there not be a deduction which would give us divinity
and Existence over against one another? There could be, but then their
manyness would be contained in some actuality, and their unity in the
very meaning of Ideality. If so, our general proof then must have the
form of saying that any togetherness we find has a number of items, at
least two, over against it, and that the way in which they, as over against
it, are related is a case of a third item, and that the initial togetherness with which we began is a case of a fourth. Genuine togetherness
is all extrinsic essentiality, perpetual passing away into the four components.

If we say that the one togetherness of all the modes passes away into
all of them we place the modes properly on one level; but then we cannot make a deduction as we did above, and cannot even find in the togetherness one of the categories exemplified. Instead we have to say that
manyness is four-fold. Does this mean that each pair has a relation which
is two-fold, i.e., that the other pair is expressed as a relation between the
remaining pair? It must mean that togetherness is not essential all the
way through, i.e., that everything about it depends on the presence of
what is other than it. If it is the basic category and if speculative
philosophy is the search for the basic category we end with a prescriptive
inescapable four-fold determined togetherness which has no intrinsic, no
independent being. Since each mode is possessed of at least one intrinsic
essential trait, it turns out that there is something more to each of the
many than there is to their togetherness in its ideal form.

August 2

An entity may be said to have four facets: a nature, a
relational role, a meaning and a value. If we start with its nature, the
other three can be viewed as extensions of the nature, as qualified by
Existence, Ideality or God. These are what Actuality becomes as it is
viewed as qualified by these others; or if one likes what the extensions of
its nature outside it are like. If now we start with a relational role, which
is the very being of Existence, then the others are extensions of it, or if
one likes Actuality makes it have a relational significance, the Ideal
makes it have a value, and God makes it have a meaning or essence. If
we start with the meaning, we get four kinds of universals, the Ideal, a
relational provided by God, a meaning given by Actuality, and a value
by Existence. If finally we start with God we get unity, the Ideal giving it

a relational role, Existence giving it a meaning, and Actuality giving it a value.

This is but to say that we can evaluate each of the modes in terms of some other. God offers us a basic evaluation for all actualities; actualities reciprocate, their natures offering a test of the meaning which God enjoys as a value in Himself; Existence offers a basic evaluation of the Ideal, and this reciprocates.

All four functions can be viewed as part of one being, when we distinguish them as distinctive in role and meaning; i.e., as a nature, a meaning, a relation and unity.

In what sense can a being which is here and now be incomplete? It is possessed of whatever nature it has; yet it must be related; it must be comparable and it could be judged as defective together with all others. The comparability of all and the judgment of all point to a power of evaluating. But the relational feature too points to something beyond. Is it that Actuality terminates in the realms of Ideality, Existence and God, and that it acquires a nature progressively as it moves in time and is thereby made determinate in a world with others?

Shall we say that the criminal is outside society? This would define the society in terms of those who were perfectly in consonance with it. But no one is exactly so. A society then is really an Ideal, with individuals being part of it in different degrees. What is opposed to the society is crime as instanced by those criminals and their particular crimes. The society, as including the crime by virtue of its condemnation and the use of its machinery, makes itself into an organic whole, which is to say one in which there is a reciprocity of determination. But if this latter is the case, we must be able to say that the society is qualified by the crime, that it is the extension of the crime in the very way in which the crime is the extension of the society when viewed as a individual social act.

We have then:

1] society as extending to its opposite, the crime
2] the crime as extending to its opposite, the society
3] the society as having the crime over against it
4] the crime as having the society over against it
5] the society as reaching to its opposite and qualifying it so as to make the crime in 3 a case of 1.
6] the crime as reaching to its opposite and qualifying it so as to make the society in 4 into a case of 2.

   1 and 2 are abstractions as extremes
   3 and 4 seem to be abstractions, items idealized

5 and 6 express the reality when taken together.

The crime as qualifying the society (to make it a concurrent crime) at the same time that society qualifies crime (to make it a local social act) defines a real organic social unity.

On this basis one ought to say that a philosophic system is the extension of its denials, and that its denials are extensions of itself, and that they are also in an organic relation one with the other, to constitute what alone is an organic philosophic whole. A philosophic system as extending into its denials ought do this in terms of mere denial, instanced by these items; what the denial should do to the system is to make it a confused or combined set of its instances. But the two as having an organic relation must then be identified with neither side.

The consideration of the nature of crime makes it possible to give another interpretation to Kant's view that a society must not dissolve without having punished the criminal: it means that the very being of the society involves the possession of the crime in the society's terms. What Kant does not see is that the criminal in a way must acknowledge the society as the extension of his own crime, to see that this is justice, that it is himself who is punishing his own individuality. We come close here to Hegel, but Hegel tends to suppose that the punishment of individuality is right and the forgiveness a kind of sadness or regretful incident, rather than valuable and basic. Otherwise he would not have stressed the unity of the outcome. Perhaps in a sense though he is saying the same thing as I am here, for at the end of his Phenomenology he recognizes the principle of negativity as a principle for self-articulation. But still the negativity is adjectival to the whole; he should give it equal status, making the whole a negativity congealed, unified etc. If one takes this view then the progress forward in Hegel might be said to be organically one with the self-diremptive movement, so that the one basic fact would be the two movements occurring at the same time.

When we consider the One and the Many again, is it enough to say that A] they are distinct, B] that each can be interpreted in terms given by the other, and C] that the One is constituted by the Many as I do in my "Togetherness" paper? Must we not add that the Many must be constituted by the One, that there is self-diremption as surely as there is togetherness, and that the Many and the One, precisely because they have their own natures and do make one another adjectives of themselves, must be in an organic unity constituting something which is a kind of One. If so, there must be two senses of One; the first is an item in the Many, which can be thought of as a togetherness of the remainder in that

Many, and the second is a One which is constituted of the organic determination, i.e., reciprocal determination of the initial One and the Many. This final One is a merging just as the original One is, but it is a dynamic merging constituting a kind of time or field.

August 4

There are two ideas of a One involved in any One-Many problem: A] Each one of the items in the Many is a One, and B] all of the items make a One. Remaining with A] for a moment, we must say that each of the items in an aggregate has 1] the other items over against it, 2] is from the perspective of others nothing but the extension of those others; 3] takes a perspective on those others; 4] is organically united with those others in view of the reciprocity of their perspectives one on the other. Each one in the Many is an abstraction as set over against the rest; each in fact is in interplay with the rest; each could be said to be self-diremptive, i.e., be viewed as having the others as mere expressions or articulations of itself, and then be met by what uses it as a component in a different articulation. If this be true the most extreme aggregate will be a kind of organismic whole; space would be perhaps the limit of attenuation of the organic unity.

No entity can be viewed apart from a set of entities which it can be said to negate, express itself as, encompass in its own terms, with them reciprocating. Having accepted this, one can then go on to speak of a One for a Many; this One (B] above) is the Togetherness which they conjointly constitute, the very organism which in fact occurs, so that the togetherness which we acknowledged in 4 is an organic One only in a prescriptive ontological sense which is made concrete in B] as " . ", a unity which is over against the Many, but does not interact with it. Perhaps we ought to say that each item in the Many has two ways of being related to all others; the " , " way is prescriptive and does not tell us just what is there or how they are in fact involved with one another; it says there is a Many: and the " . " way in which the items in fact are together, and which has the definite nature of an organic whole with respect to the items in the Many. Does this mean that there is a Oneness which escapes the Many, since the organic unity is not yet the items in their prescriptive character?

A philosophic system may be said to have a prescriptive togetherness of its various items. Those items must also be together in fact in some way. But what of the negatives of those items? In what sense are they in the system? Is it possible to say that the items as negativing the system

are precisely the items as prescriptive of a togetherness? This would make
" , " a kind of othering relation; or if it be thought not to do so, and in
fact to point out how these negatives are to be together, it would seem to
presuppose an othering relation of the items either with respect to one
another or with respect to the whole which they constitute by the connection " . ". Should we say that that the connection of the items is the
descriptive, contingent variable " . " we would make the philosophic system something adventitious.

Perhaps then we ought to say the opposite: the negatives of the items
in the system are the items related by " . "; the system itself has them
prescriptively, therefore almost aggregationally. But if the system is to
include the items related by " . ", which it must, the total integrated system is the items in a double guise. Then the result is that it is the items
themselves which have a duality of nature. But does the philosophic system include them as having a double nature; is it at once " . " and " , "?
If it is we need a third connective. But this seems to lead to an infinite
regress.

The negative particles are to be disjoined and then they become the
equivalent of the negative of the conjunction of the positive ones, and
this is the same thing as to say that they are equivalent with the negative
of their merging. The negative of $-x \, v -y$ is the equivalent of $x \, , y$ and
of $x \, . \, y$. As the equivalent to $x \, , y$ it is the parts of the system dealt
with as exclusive of one another, or as conjunctive, acceptive of one another. As equivalent to $x \, . \, y$ it is distinguished from the outside, by
the system. By taking the system's items severally we get negative exclusive items; by taking the system's unity as exterior to the items unified we
get the negative exclusive items as disjoined. The philosophic system as a
whole should include the items as prescriptively connected and as merged
into a unity, which is but to say the articulation of the expression
$-(-x \, v -y)$. If we start with that as central perhaps we have to interpret the *"v"* as being two dimensional, one dimension relating the " , "
and the " . ". This would seem to mean that the relation of $x \, , y$ to $x \, . \, y$
is like that between $-x$ and $-y$, or between an $-x$ and an x. A disjunction expresses a generic fact; this means then that it is expressed and
perhaps exhausted as the alternative specifications of $x \, , y$ and $x \, . \, y$, and
also of $-x$ and of $-y$. One might say that a generic case allows for alternative or compatible specifications, and that $x \, , y$ and $x \, . \, y$ are the compatible ones while $-x$ and $-y$ are the incompatible ones. To have $-x$
and $-y$ as incompatible is perhaps but another way of expressing the fact
that $x \, , y$ and $x \, . \, y$ are compatible and also exhaustive; if this be the case

shall we say that they could be represented exhaustively by $-x\,v\,-y$? Shall we say then that a philosophic system is exhaustive in the separate but related specifications $x\,,y$ and $x\,.\,y,$ and that this represents and is represented by the exhaustive disjunction of the proposition $-x\,v\,-y$? The negative of the system's assertions then can be said to contained within a generic unity which is one with the system's unity.

Identity in difference expresses the disjunction of the two modes of togetherness as constituting it (so that it is generic and vague, a kind of contingent togetherness or identity) and the disjunction of the individual items which exhaust it (so that it is generic but prescriptive and thus a kind of demanding difference).

1] Each of the Many

A] is the negative of the rest; it is not these

B] is articulated by the rest; all together express what it is

C] has the others as its attenuation; it views them from its perspective

D] encompasses the rest, vicariously possesses them as that which enables it to be.

2] All of the Many function in similar ways to make

A] an organic unity by virtue of their reciprocity

B] an aggregate by virtue of their independence in being and capacity to move into and out of specific situations

C] are in dialectical relation one with the other, each demanding that there be others.

3] All of the items in the Many are in a specific relation.

A] The resulting unity is descriptive and can vary from that of a sheer aggregate to an effective organism

B] it stands apart from the Many as related by " , "

C] it is constituted by the Many in which the items merge one with the other.

4] Each item in the Many has two relations—

A] a mere demand " , " prescriptive of the fact that there must be others

B] a specific connection with the rest, " . ".

5] The " . " has no primary separate status; if it exhausts and absorbs the " , " then

A] the items connected by " . " are in internal relations and cannot without alteration suffer another

B] the items connected by " . " are as they ought to be, or if one likes there is no ought to be for them c] the "," is a kind of abstraction. But this will not allow us to judge inferences, processes, history, existence as unsatisfactory.

6] The modes as final cannot allow for a distinct "."; their organic togetherness is the way they realize their ",". But the question remains as to whether or not

A] they have a "," which is perpetual and of which "." is a passing instance

B] they are in an Empedoclean love-hate duality, in which case we risk an infinite regress, or

c] they are adventitiously in a "." relation, which seems to make for two entities needing to be related as a One.

7] The unity of each item in the Many requires the separateness of the two ways (x, y and x. y) in which each is related to the others.

8] The x. y and the x, y are basic, coordinate, but not dialectically determinative. They constitute the single generic fact, x. y V x, y, where the V expressed the truth that they are exhaustive and coordinate specifications of it.

9] The unity of the V is distinct from that of x, y and x. y, precisely because it is generic. x, y has a prescribing unity determined from each side, in which the constant fills in what is already prescribed and does not affect the fact. x,— is adventitiously filled in by y. x. y has a descriptive unity which is the merged togetherness of the x and the y. There is a genuine dialectic relation between x and y in x, y, with their unity as x. y immediately correlate but without efficacy.

10] The unity of the V is like that of the x, y since it allows the items to be distinct; it is like x. y since it is a function of the items related. It has another side where it is basic, but in this case it is expressed as an exclusive disjunct, $-x$ V $-y$, where the $-x$ and the $-y$ express what is left after some mode is denied being. The meaning then of V is that it is a function of the two ways in which the modes can be together, at the same time that it is the generic form for the exhaustive set of failures of the different modes—i.e., it is exhausted as $-x$ v $-y$ v $-z$ v $-w$, where x, y, z, w are the four modes. The togetherness of the four modes in two ways gives rise to a generic disjunction of them, mere being which they mutually define. That mere being can be exhaustively expressed of course as the four modes being together in two ways; it can also be exhaustively expressed as the inconsistent alternatives; there are only the three modes, x y and z or only the one mode w, where each mode or combination of them is taken to be the universe.

August 5

Could the negative be the individual, the self-contained?

If so it would be always there; it could not be overcome and include; the whole seems to have positive individuals in it.

Could the negative be the item as prescriptively demanding another, denied this element of prescriptiveness?

The factor of negativing seems to be missing. Also if the items must be together, there can be no genuine negative which opposes.

Could otherness have two sides, one a prescriptive and the other a separative, the latter representing negation?

The negative would then seem to be permanent; the two sides would have to be reconciled; since the prescriptive is also present in the case of the system, with its items in an $x \cdot y$ relation, the change from negative to positive would be the replacing of $-x-y$ by $x \cdot y$, the entire work being accomplished by the ".". But this is excessive. Also in making a transfer to the positive we would lose the individuality of the items, since they would be distinct already as x, y and as $-x-y$. The system would involve the abandonment of one kind of distinctness.

Could we have $-x-y$ *as constituting a domain which gives way to the pair* $x \cdot y$ *and* x, y, *which constitute a disjunction that is instanced by* $-x-y$?

$-x-y$ would really be constitutive items in a disjunct: $-x \lor -y$ which is an abstraction when treated as though it was constituted by the items (instead of the $\lor$), and as if the $\lor$ had being of its own. It would be an abstraction presupposing the system as a whole. Since $-x\lor-y$ is indeterminate, it has something like the structure of $x \cdot y$.

This last seems most promising. It must meet the following conditions:

1] there are negatives such as denials of the system, criminals, etc., which effectively oppose the whole,

2] there is a way in which the opposition can treat the whole as an extension of itself,

3] the whole can be brought about by some operation on the dissident parts,

4] the whole can be recognized to have individual parts which, despite their distinction from the whole, are quite distinct from negative particles.

The specifications of $-x$ from the disjunct $-x \lor -y$ (where they are not really separated out) gives it a determinate status enabling it to stand over against the whole, as required by *1*] As such it can treat the whole as its extension as required by *2*] and can be overcome by being brought into relation with *y* which will prescriptively convert it to *x*, as required by *3*] which are parts, as required by *4*]. What is not clear is the answer to *1*.

What is the relation of —*x* to the disjunct —*x* V —*y?* It must evidently reject this and the —*y* in it. —*x* is a realization of it in such a way as to make —*y* privational. There cannot then be two denials of the system; each denies wholly and everything else; —*x* denies the system *x , y* V *x . y.*

What is to be said about the parts *x* and *y;* and about the other denials? All denials must be equivalent taken severally; they cannot be brought together except by conversion into positives or to make one denial, —*z.*

If it be the case that the negatives are specifications in alternative ways of a basic disjunction, there is no togetherness of them. To have —*x* and also —*y* we must retreat to *V* where we really have neither. They can be had severally because the specification of —*x* V —*y* as —*x* is the determination of the —*y* in the shape of the privational relation of negation to all else, which is to say to *x.* That *x* is separate from a *y,* and this separateness in *x , y* requires that they be together as a one, as *x . y.* The denial of the system is one with the denial of its parts, and the precluding of other denials occurring then.

If a criminal be thought of as a negative, then this must mean A] he is an exclusive item, excluding even another, B] opposes the positive parts and the whole they constitute, C] deals with those others as extensions of itself, while they have him as an extension of themselves, D] be absorbable.

A] will require that there be only criminality, expressed now in this form and then in that. This is the *V.*

B] the opposition of the crime to a part entails, through the part, an opposition to the whole.

C] the basicality and reality of the negative allows it to have the whole system as an extension of itself; *x* is that which it negatively apprehends.

But this leaves over two questions:

1] What is the status of *V* apart from all specifications of it?

2] Must not the negative be capable of absorbing the positive?

1] the *V* apart from all specifications of it is the principle of the negative which the positive system perpetually constitutes and destroys; the being of it is just that *x . y* and *x , y* are distinct but compatible. It is when this

V is fixated by an act or thought that it becomes specifiable and thus has
a distinctive being. But then the four modes will have to have as separate
and nucleal the capacity to make the negativity, which they all constitute
in being together, specified as itself. This would mean that x in itself must
be the negative of what it helps make together with y. This negative will
be derivative though, so that the privacy or irreducible nature of a mode
of being will be derivative from its double positive togetherness.

2] The negative cannot absorb the positive if it is a finality as a product;
but then the treating of the positive system as the extension of it must
either be wrong, or be in a different sense.

The crime would seem then to be a constant product of the societal
whole, but never realized except by the individual crime which rejects all
else to be a world in itself and in this sense to take all else as an extension of itself, as its own generic nature carried to a terminal point.

In the Hegelian system the crime is a genuine other with which the
whole must come in contact, absorb by forgiveness. But perhaps this is
not necessary. We have the whole in the guise of x, y and $x . y$ disjoined;
the disjunction is already the promise of the negative.

The dialectic operates between the x, y and $x . y$, and not between $-x$
and the rest, as Hegel thought. $-x$ is a congealed form of the relation of
the organic unity of the system. The system is organic because x to be
must be in x, y and this requires $x . y$, and reciprocally. The negative
which x must accept is but the reality of the reciprocity. But then the very
being of the whole is negativity, as Hegel held. If V is fundamental and
to be viewed as the negative of the items related in it conjunctively, and
is to be specified by $-x$, then being is a mere negative relation between
modes of togetherness, a negative relation which allows them to be together, and which is itself to be given being only as that which is to be
specified in exclusive terms, as $-x$ or as $-y$.

The negative is a vanishing negative, being constituted by the two
sides. This seems to mean that the society constitutes itself as the very
meaning of crime; it produces this but does not exploit this; but its own
being as over against its members is just this, and it is this which the
criminal will specify. This is an extreme paradox, pointing to something
wrong in the above analysis.

Or should we say that the society as giving the meaning of crime is
still not yet allowing it, since it demands in fact that the meaning be exhausted in the society itself. The definition then should not be of crime,
but of order. This as a principle which is the product of an actual way in
which the items are together, is good order; when it becomes itself the

source of specifications, we get particularization of which the crime is an instance. We say that the criminal takes the law to himself. Could this possibly mean the law and order which is produced by the beings together has no status of its own? Or should we say that law has status as a togetherness which is prescriptive, and that this law as disjunctive, with the people as together, constituting what we have now been terming the principle of the negative? Then what is the case is that the relation of society or law and its members is the principle of negativity which is produced by their interplay and which becomes a negative and the source of crime when given an absolutivity of its own.

If the above is correct then in a philosophic system we ought to say that the relation of the prescriptive and descriptive, of the parts in two roles, is the source of the negativity which its denials specialize. If we want to speak of Hegelian forgiveness we must do this with respect to the types of togetherness, and recognize that their reciprocity is the production of a unity which taken by itself is specified as disjunctive negations of the items in the forgiveness situation.

Is the connection between prescriptive law and togethered men the rights which, when made absolute, become the source of crime? Is the connection between a prescriptive unity of system and togethered items in it the organic system which denials but specify? Is the connection between the various modes as necessarily and contingently together but the nature of being as negation, which each item will specify when taken as in itself? Only the third seems to have some plausibility. But when we see the first as saying that the criminal defines his own case as the locus of all rights and sets this over against all else, crime becomes a matter of right falsely urged: and if we say that what a denial does is to claim to be a whole, it is but the utilization of that whole, in separation from its function as a whole, that constitutes the denial.

Can we define the society as the modes of being as providing the content for the manner in which men will be conjoined in two ways with others, de facto and prescriptively, and that the disjunction of these is what we mean by rights which the criminal identifies himself with and specifies in an exclusive and excluding fashion? But what do we say then of the problem of sacrificing one for many? Is this the conflict between x and y with " , " and " . ", so that, as it were, to give up x or y is to give up some particular part for a whole, such as is constituted by " . "? To make good this decision the whole as a V must continue to carry the meaning of the x which is sacrificed. Conversely if we give up the unity of the " . " for the sake of some individual, x, the V must carry the meaning of that " . ". As carrying either meaning it must make it good by making it sustained by the remainder. But this looks as if the V became effective and this is what we before termed error and crime, etc. The V avoids being crime by retaining the claims of the sacrificed part and thus showing itself to be a function of the part, which a crime refuses to do.

What is meant by forgiveness for the crime? Does it require us to see the $-x$ as outside the system and also to admit the system's inadequacy? Yes; the system as expressed as $x \cdot y \, V \, x, y$ produces but refuses to allow the V to stand apart. It achieves what it ought when it allows the V to function, to be fulgurated without being specified except by it and its correlate, so that the V has only a formal meaning of the emptiest sort. Hegel's dialectic occurs between the V and the $-x$ which tries to be the V. But dialectic occurs between the positive factors to constitute the V; it does not interplay with the negative $-x$, but rather overcomes this by virtue of being the source of the V which that $-x$ specifies. Each negative overspecifies the way in which the parts are related. The negative is without efficacy, having only a formal role, being produced rather than productive.

August 6

The way in which items come together in fact dictates the way in which they will specify the atmosphere in which they exist. Thus the way in which people live together dictates the manner in which they will specify that amalgam of power, ideality and eternity which impinges on them from the outside. It is their determination of this in the form of a single, effective, ideal, prescribing, unitary control which gives the other half of what is needed in order to have society and state.

The sacrifice of one man for many is justified if we view men only as parts of a *de facto* togetherness; when we view the men as also having a prescriptive relation to one another, the problem becomes one of deciding whether to jeopardize that relation or the way men are together. To sacrifice a man, though innocent, for the benefit of mankind, is to insist on the way men are together, despite the fact that one violates the prescriptive nature of that togetherness, since this depends on a separate and equal determination by each one of them. To make the reverse sacrifice, to urge that men submit to another, to be enslaved, is to insist on a prescriptive situation despite the fact that one has denied it the finality and strength which all of men give it. One either infects the system with the values of the sacrificed man as prescriptive or infects it with the substantiality of the totality as it occurs in fact, and demands that the system as a whole make good the energy which was lost.

There would seem to be a becoming which really becomes. This is the outcome of the disjunctive presence of modes of being; modes of being are together in two ways, a " , " and a " . " way, prescriptive and descriptive, *de jure* and *de facto*. As so together in these ways they constitute a relation between themselves which has no other being but the fact that they make it be; the relation passes away when it comes to be. In a sense it is like all four modes: it is indeterminate as is the Ideal; it is existential in that it is in process, but without energy or capacity to be again; it has the finite finality of the Actual; it has a unifying function as does the divine. Process philosophers therefore take it to be the source of all else; they make creativity generate all else. This apparently is what Bergson does; his one *élan* fulgurates in four different (he has only two, actually) directions. But this denies the finality of the modes, makes the *élan* mysterious, goes counter to all knowledge, experience, science. The creativity of Bergson, Whitehead, Schopenhauer, etc., should be viewed as a product. It becomes, and therefore seems to be producing. But Aristotle saw that the very nature of accidents is such as to be in an indeterminate, incomplete state. We tend to fixate the accidents, to suppose that a color is dead. But one can view it as precisely what is in movement, indeterminate in a way. This is a movement to be sure unlike the dynamic movement of an actuality; it is the movement in an effect or as an effect, which is exactly what Zeno was getting at in his discussion of the way in which two bodies moving in opposite directions double the distance. The modern physicists when they view light as an absolute constant in a way confirm this; they recognize that if light is to be a constant it cannot be conditioned by the rest of the things in the world, and this means that its properties are all self-determined, self-possessed. But if light is a process, if it really moves as a result of other more basic realities, then it will have properties which come to be and pass away, which will vary with those basic realities (which alone act), and these properties will be its entire substance. The double distance which Zeno remarked is a transient product sustained by the separate distances, and is in process as an accident.

A part which is put over against a whole must be identical with the specification of the principle of unity of that whole; the abstract unity of the whole, V, is the negative principle specified in exclusive denials, and constituted by compatible disjuncts, $x . y$ and x , y.

There are four types of unity:

$$x . y \quad de \ facto$$
$$x , y \quad de \ jure$$
$$x . y \ V \ x , y \quad \text{organic, final, ontological}$$
$$V \quad \text{produced, transient}$$

the first is something like Actuality, the second like Ideality, the third like God and the fourth like Existence.

The *de facto* is a One; the *de jure* is prescribing and inescapable allowing a many; the $x, y \lor x . y$ is concrete, the source of the others as abstract parts of it; the V is a product, the principle of the negative specified by each x and each $-x$. The x specifies it only as caught in $x . y \lor x, y$, and the *non-x* specifies it as an item taking itself to be a totality. The part when held away without having any bearing on anything else can be viewed as a terminating item, x as at the limit of a situation; taken as effective with respect to the rest it is a *non-x*.

A separated part is that part but only as still presupposing the whole; a negated part is the part as opposing that whole. The whole that is presupposed and opposed is the whole as encompassing the part; it is the whole with the part in a certain relation which the part as separate and as negative opposes, the one opposing it only as pulled away, the other opposing it by standing away, rebuffing. This means that the part has a double role; it is integrated in the whole and yet can oppose itself as there. But how is this possible? If it is possessed of two roles it is possible for it to be outside the whole; yet if it does not possess these two roles how could it be in opposition to itself as integrated? The answer seems to be that the part is entirely in the whole, and when it is taken out it is divided into two, and is then in the whole only partially; what is opposed then is not the whole as it was before but something else. The reintegration will be performed by something in between them, by the tensional unity set up by the separation of the part. The whole $x, y \lor x . y$ could be said to remain but to be divided into two components when we isolate a part x, or a negative $-x$, the other component being x, y and $x . y$ as sheer terms.

The *Parmenides* of Plato is divisible into two sets, the One as a whole and the One in the part. The first hypothesis concerns the V, the second $x . y$, the third $x . y \lor x, y$, the fourth x, y. This is one set. The fifth tells what happens when we take the One as a part, in any of the four guises; the sixth when we deny it is a part at all; the seventh tells what kind of unity is left (an aggregate) and the eighth shows that strictly there is no unity, nothing is left. This is the second set. The truth is the third hypothesis as articulated by the other seven. This outcome is a product of a talk with Bob Brumbaugh.

August 7

An individual man might be viewed as having a juncture of subordinate parts which together define a kind of law or rule which is prescriptive of the way those parts should be together. This rule is the definition of his health and is sustained by the parts as distinct one from the other. The correlative fact of the juncture and the law constitutes life. The individual might be said to attain a self when one of the parts sustains this life, makes it more than an occasional flicker. If this be true then the self has a substantial material base; some material part enables the general principle of unity to have a function in the relatedness of the juncture and rule, at the same time that it assumes a sovereign position and dictates to the juncture and rule which is to be dominant and when, i.e., what sacrifices are to be made to the components as merely together, and what sacrifices are to be made to the way they are in a prescribing relation.

There is a single right constituted by the very fact that there is a rule. The self-denial of individual rights is the enriching of that single right by the deciding self. Where the part subjugates the life to itself we get the tyranny of illness.

In a philosophic system the thinker takes over the role of the disjunct, and can do this by submitting to the system's needs to be properly unified, or it can subordinate the system to itself in which case we get error or perversity.

The strategy of each mode of being is in effect to assume the role of the disjunct between the others as *de jure* and *de facto* together.

In valid inference one submits to the disjunct; in invalid one controls it. This means that inference actually mediates between a *de facto* and a *de jure* relationship between p and q.

The paper on "Being Together" did not take sufficient account of the fact that the " , " connecting separate items had a prescriptive character. Two further questions arise. Can one say that the manner in which or the nature of the objects which are *de facto* together, i.e., in a " . " dictates something about the nature of the prescription? Perhaps it is the nature of the objects which does so, and this enables us to evaluate the *de facto* status that they have? Then we ought to have *de jure* connections depending on different types of objects. But then what happens to the utilization and specification of the other modes by a being which is to be together with another?

August 8

Method: To form a hypothesis in order to explain some phenomenon and then apply it over a wide range of different phenomena, modifying it so as to take care of new issues. This need not compromise the need to have subordinate hypotheses to account for the differences found from one case to the other; but a major hypothesis covering all is needed to make sense of the fact that all the cases are, and are together.

The prescriptive togetherness of items is a function of their number and their natures; the descriptive is a function of their proximity and activity. It is possible to alter the one without altering the other or affecting it even, within limits. It is possible too to require an alteration, which is resisted. Thus a change in the number or nature of items making up the descriptive togetherness affects the prescriptive unity; yet the descriptive togetherness may be kept constant by balancing the nature of the proximity and activities of the items which remain. Conversely a change in the proximity or activity of the items has an affect on the descriptive, making it something different, and yet the prescriptive may be kept unaffected by virtue of the way in which the natures are held together. Or, to say this another way: *1*] the descriptive is a unity whose nature can vary, or which, conversely, can be in consonance with a range of prescriptions. But when the nature of the items in the description is altered, this should have an affect on the prescription, except so far as compensation is provided; and when the nature of the prescription as a whole is altered, this should have an affect on the functioning of the parts making up the description except so far as compensation is provided. In the case of health, we find that the description is of matter of the body, dictating a kind of form which is specified by the items as separate with definite natures; changes in those natures will change the form unless resisted. The form is prescriptive, dictating a kind of togetherness which can vary in intensity, and a change in the form will require a change in the kind of togetherness, unless resisted.

Better—

1] The prescriptive is determined by the number and natures of the items which by their mutality of claim specify in any one of a number of ways a single constant prescriptiveness.

2] The descriptive is determined by the proximity and activity of the items. The descriptive can vary in intensity depending on how the items interplay.

3] A varying of the specifications of the prescriptive or of the intensities in the descriptive can be had independently of the other.

4] A change in the nature and number of the items has an effect on both the prescriptive and descriptive; it demands a change in the prescriptive. This may nevertheless be preserved by anything which can represent itself to be the old nature and number or whatever would make for such an old nature and number.

5] A change in the proximity and function of the items produces a different type of descriptive togetherness when the change is a function of the change in nature and number of items. But the meaning of it can be preserved in the determination to reinstate it.

August 9

A change in the nature of the items will affect the nature of their claims and the manner in which they merge, and thus affect the " , " and the " . ". Still, each of these can vary in independence of the other in specification or intensity within the area of the determination of the natures. The natures in short allow for variant supplementations of claims and of functions.

Despite a change in nature it is possible to hold on to the initial prescription or description; we allow the " , " to adopt some of the energy and activity of the previous " . ", and it must promise to make good what had been lost; one can also hold to a previous " , " by having some item insist on it as a model or ideal for the others to submit to.

Death urges the old pattern despite new mass; morality urges old mass despite new pattern.

The prescription is due to the interlocking of reciprocal penumbra; it is then a kind of space. Aristotle then in his use of the term "form" to refer to shape was not abusing language.

Since items change in nature in politics and elsewhere, and since there is then an automatic correlation of prescription and description, whatever complex occurs is as it should be; but in the case of man with his ethics, and politics with its history, the V between the items holds on to previous imperatives and previous efficacies, thereby subjecting the new organic whole to pressure. It has a unity of tradition and effective sentiment which it urges against what is. No actual state holds on to it all the time, nor urges it properly. The prescription which is steady is constitution; the mass which is steady is associations of various sorts.

Is there an inevitable geometry defined by the very nature of things together; this would seem to be the view of physics, though it is to be noted that the physical geometry here is prescriptive and allows for variation in specification on the one hand and variant aggregations on the other, and thus is not merely a description of the distribution of the matter now.

What should one say of odd geometries? Do they have a real mass answering to them, or should we say that given a geometry there is a real irrational which deviates from the mass of the ordinary geometry? Could they be said to have a modified relation to the real, mediated by the prevailing one and answering to an imagined variation in the mass that actually exists? Must one with Kant go to experience to see which distribution holds in fact to see which prescription holds, supposing that there is always one for the other? Does not every mathematics then entail a special physics?

Can't we know from the a priori what the thing in itself is like, or at least what the non-phenomenal might be like, and therefore know the thing in itself just so far as we know how to get the non-empirical structure? One can ask how we know which non-empirical to choose and thus which answers to the thing in itself; but perhaps it is the whole set of non-empirical concepts which expresses the thing in itself as a series of allowable appearances of which the one we usually face is not better than any others in principle but only in that it has as a matter of fact made this kind of conjunction and this kind of prescriptive set. There is then no problem of synthesis but only the problem of determining, given a given situation or mass, what geometry it in fact entails; and conversely given a geometry no problem in determining what must be done with it to make it be the very structure of the empirical world.

Linguistic analysis is another variant of that kind of Kantianism which takes some form as dictating the very structure of things; but a more orthodox Kantianism and a better one would see the language as having a correlate in fact, but a fact which has variable intensities and which is consistent with variable linguistic forms within limits. Each would have its autonomy and the two sides would be together in one who used language to communicate, as a kind of freshly produced unity of the fact and the grammar.

August 10

The ancient political theorists with their classification of the states and constitutions seemed primarily concerned with the requirements for being a sovereign. They failed to recognize that there are two meanings to their oligarchies and aristocracies, etc. There is firstly the question as to whether the rich or the better born, etc., are alone privileged to take over the sovereignty; and there is second the question as to whether the birth or wealth, etc. can be added to any man to give extra weight to his common rights to vote, to fight or to avoid fighting, etc. One of these may be called political and the other social oligarchy, etc., though this puts the latter outside the political pale; perhaps "governmental" and "qualifying," might be better adjectives.

The classical writers are concerned with man's difference in and out of the state, and thus with what rights he had then and later, what advantages and disadvantages the state confers. They ignore the fact that in a state of nature men constitute some kind of structure and can even assume, if only for themselves, the sovereign role of making a decision on behalf of the structure or themselves, as in the natural environment.

The modern thinkers stay inside the state as the classical writers do, but are concerned with the rights of men in them. They ignore the coming to be of the state and the rights of men as apart from the state, and thus do not understand the state in critical terms. In a sense the Marxists do, but only by turning to a social or historical phenomenon; they do not judge this. The doctrine of the separation of powers is a way of protecting rights.

In a man the emotions, according to Plato, take over the sovereign task; in Aristotle it is apparently the heart which is the locus of the soul and which thus assumes the work of serving it, though this is not altogether clear. Perhaps we get different types of men depending on what organ does take over this work?

The problem of democracy, etc., is a problem of where a man's dimensions stop; the oligarch stops at his possessions; the aristocrat at his past and traditions; the democrat at his capacities (which he takes to be equal with all those of all others); the intellectual with the realm of knowledge; the religious man with his concern; the tyrant with his desires. The doctrine of native rights requires that we first have the men as distinct units and then have them constituting a common right, and a common people. The limits of men in one sense then is just physical and in another is all the other men and perhaps animals and things. In a state of nature, both Hobbes and Locke think, man is a tyrant or a religious being endless in his reach so that his right includes all else.

We ought to start with men as mere units. That they constitute a new unity is a fact; this new unity must make provision for their possessions, virtues, etc., and the rights these entail, and must accredit these rights to the men. But this perhaps is a fluctuating matter to be decided by the sovereign, since it is to apply the structure to a new mass, i.e., a mass other than that which initially defined the structure. This is the cause of trouble; men are aware of their inequalities and want to be equal according to their inward or outward natures.

Aristotle does recognize a democracy in which all have a part in the sovereignty and in which one lives as one likes. But there is also the idea of treating the men as qualified for sovereignty and as living as they like in terms of their capacities, or as we today say, their rights.

August 13

Whatever there be is real; there is then no appearance if this is supposed to be other than the real. Still, there are errors and illusions. These are but realities as caught in a context which is not entirely germane to their implications. Appearance is thus possible only if there are at least two real beings one of which can encompass the other inside its frame. In a way Kant saw this, except that he never did face up to the question of the reality of the ego in terms of which there could be something given. But what he did do that was important was to recognize that one reality might provide a set of inescapable categories in terms of which an alien reality will have to be framed. He had a philosophy of appearances; Hegel had a phenomenology, where the appearances are the real. But Hegel in the end is forced to make a similar distinction, for firstly each stage is somehow to be held apart from the whole, and secondly there is the cunning of reason by means of which it sets itself against itself and thus enables itself to have an appearance.

An appearance ought not to be understood purely psychologically; it ought to be recognized to occur even in relationship to subhumans. The real which is man, if it be a real distinct from other reals, ought to have an appearance for other beings, not merely those that are conscious. Man's appearance to the inanimate is in fact that of a thing, with no other role but that of a quantified object. The positivistic or scientifically oriented philosophers take this appearance more seriously than any other; it is a paradox that Kant did this too and then went back to the individual as though he were providing the condition for the appearance.

A reverse use of this method would consist in "humanizing" objective reality, and then showing how the objective reality imposed humanistic categories on men; e.g., when nature is said to be fateful or a domain of fortune, it is humanized. When we then say that men are the puppets of fortune once they allow themselves to lose hold of God, etc., we make them into appearances for fortune, though in themselves they are supposedly souls and independent of it.

August 14

Plato begins his examination of the state by looking at the parts of man; Locke looks at man as surveying all of nature, and thus at man as alone; Hobbes begins by considering a man in relation to another; Marx views a man as with another and over against nature or with a tool; Aristotle views a man as with two or three others—wife, child and perhaps slave; Rousseau starts with a number of men making a mass.

All of these thinkers are concerned with   A] the kind of mass the men together make;   B] the kind of structure which this type of mass has and the demands it imposes;   C] the locus of the authority to guide and unite *a* and *b;*   D] the best form in which the mass could have (this is really a question of how *b* can be made significant);   E] how to move from these considerations to politics.

A] involves a kind of phenomenological description of the various kinds of aggregates a given number of entities can constitute; the answer should have some dialectical justification. This is achieved by recognizing that the entities contribute individuality, figure, position and number.

B] involves an awareness of how subordinate demands constitute a single demand or prescriptive structure for just that type of entity. Whether subordinate demands overlap and are transformed requires a knowledge of whether some items are superior to others, whether all are on a level, etc., and a knowledge of how these demands can be given unity.

C] since *a* and *b* constitute a single unit, guidance of that whole will come either from without (in which case it will not be a proper exemplar for the state), or from within (which will require the assumption by one of the parts of either the power of the mass or the intent of the prescription).

D] Since *a* and *b* can vary in intensity independently, and since one seeks stability and success in a state, the question arises which combination is best—who is best to rule, how are the parts to be satisfied.

August 16

The modes of being are necessarily four; their plurality is necessary. But Actuality must be carried by some particular Actuality; there is a contingent number of Actualities. Existence inevitably divides into parts; there is a division of Existence which is of the very essence of that Existence. Ideality has subordinate divisions which are inseparable from the Ideal, but occur with it. God has subordinate divisions which He constitutes. Actuality has a contingent plurality, Existence an essential but inseparable plurality of divisions, Ideality an essential but insepara-ble plurality of creases (which cannot be held apart from the Ideal, as the divisions of Existence can be held apart from it); God has an essen-tial but dependent plurality of distinctions and stands over against them.

August 21

One might view the Aristotelian active reason as a kind of minimal form for any human body. As the body becomes more cohesive and complicated the form becomes intensified into the form for just that delimited body. Until then the minimal form, since it is compatible with any degree of cohesiveness and complication of the human body can be said to constitute a unity with the body only in the sense of making it one and human. The subsequent intensifications of the minimal form, because specifications of it, and because at once prescriptive for and a function of delimited intensifications of the human body become more and more integral with the body in its particularity. It is this part of the soul, so intimate with limited impressions and experiences, which Aristotle supposes necessarily perishes with the perishing of the body. It can also be said that the active reason as the source of all forms, indeed as actually all the forms, is correlate strictly speaking with the whole of bodies—which is perhaps the Arabian thesis—and becomes correlate with this or that body only through the process of persistent intensificaiton and unification with limited organizations of the human body.

August 22

Do we have a one and a many to begin with; or is it not rather the case that when we start with a many we define a one which stands over against the many only in that it has a certain nature, and that when we start with a one we get a many inside or below it which is not altogether separable from it? The one and the many then define one another and as defining one another keep one another from being over against altogether. This is really an analytic way of dealing with the one and the many as not altogether free from what constitutes them. If on the other hand we start with a one over against a many we must, as Plato did, explain the individual as the juncture of the two. The classical view of creation makes the world stand with respect to God as a kind of many which does not reach the full length of being separate from him.

Every unity has a form and a matter which are inseparable. Still the matter has potentiality and the form has specifiability, and it is the fact of such potentiality and specifiability which makes it possible to have a form steady and the matter variable, or a matter steady and the form variable.

There are two kinds of dialectic: a static or analytic and a progressive or dynamic; the first shows how given units, we take into account shape, size, compatibility of the parts and the whole they constitute; the second moves along in time passing from one stage to another.

August 25

An entity can be said to have a form and a matter. But if so we must also go on to say that the form is a specification of a larger universal hovering over the form and correlate with a potentiality (itself outside the matter that is correlate with the form). The universal and the potentiality answer to Ideality and Existence. They point up the fact that there must be an "individuality" which hovers over the joint fact of the form-matter (and which is the locus of memory, habits, tradition) and a "divinity" which hovers over all relationality of the form-matter (and makes the individual one of many). We have then A] a unity of form and matter, and B] an encircling unity of universal, potentiality, individuality and divinity. If we realize that the unity of form and matter constitutes a new being and that this has promise for relations of all sorts, we can say that there are two concentric circles of four modes.

1] Do the form and matter, individuality and relationality with which we begin and which are specific and inside the larger whole of universal, potentiality, Actuality and God constitute a unity for the environing four? Yes, if it is outcome of adoption of a role by another.

2] If the inside four make a unity for the outside, is this due to the activity of one of the outside elements assuming a position for the others and thereby specifying itself and those others? Yes.

3] Is it always the case that a set of four is strictly unified so that no change in one can be made without a change in the other, and that all changes are therefore the result of one of the items being specified and thereby involving the others in corresponding specializations? Yes.

4] Does not the inside four require a unity which is to be obtained by getting inside it the very four which are outside it, and does this not involve the assumption by one of the four inside ones of the role of a representative of the other three inside ones? That is, attending to the inner four, must not one of these, taking advantage of its fringe in the guise of one of the outer four and thus as a being capable of change and also of having the ability to represent something which the inner four need, assume the position of the inward unity of the inner four? If so the soul of a man would, e.g. be the outcome of the assumption by a body, or a part of it, of the role of bearer of the universal, individuality and relationability which is correlate with the form.

5] Do the outer four serve as an inner for some still wider one? Or is this the case only when we have some limited field? Yes.

6] Is not the role mentioned in 4 above a combination of four items which itself needs to be unified by some one of those items assuming a role on behalf of an outer four? Or is this possible only when there are realities and not merely roles? In a symbolic activity we need better functioning but no ontological unification.

7] The soul is a kind of microcosm of the environment of a being, and results from the assumption by a part of the body of the meaning of the universal which is outside the form and which prevents it from being entirely one with the body; that meaning of the universal is achieved by taking advantage of the environing potentialities.

8] The outer is accepted to give the inner a better unity. On behalf of its need to be A] individual, B] intelligible, C] active, D] related, the materiate part of a being takes advantage of its own continuity with the source of activity to assume the role of a carrier of the source of individuality, intelligibility and relationality as well. When it does this the being, instead of having merely the nature of something with correlate items, becomes instead a being with an inward "soul" which mirrors what is outside the being.

Staying only with the combination form-matter, it seems as if it is environed by universal-potentiality, the form fading into the universal and the matter into the potentiality. (If we add habit and tension to the form-matter we can add that there is an environing individuality and an environing relationality.) The form-matter is not fully unified. Part of the matter can make use of the potentiality and thereby free itself from the aegis of the form, and specialize the environing universal to make itself into a matter which carries out the role of a representative of the universal-potentiality. (Or is it rather the representative of the form-matter? Does the soul mediate between the body and its form, by representing the body and the form, or by representing the potentiality and the universality? Does the government mediate between law and citizen by representing the law and citizen in one, or by representing the common law and mankind as unified and thus as the very soul of the combination, law and citizen?)

There are at least three different types of family function: 1] there is the family which is a mere correlate of structure with father, mother, child, and which is inside other correlates, just as the correlate beings of its members are inside it. 2] there is the family which follows on some larger grouping such as a state and is the result of a part of that grouping representing the whole. The family here completes the state, and seeks to make the state's traditions, its aims, its energies and power be harmoniously related with others. It is produced by the beings who make up the state, looking beyond it for the elements which they are to unite as the family. 3] there is the family which precedes the state and which the state represents. Here the family members reach to the fringe about them and unite the components of the fringe to constiute a unity for the family, thereby achieving a kind of politicized family, which is perhaps what Engels had in mind when he spoke of the state withering away. Perhaps then there must be a fourth kind of family which is a whole within which there is a correlate making up the state; or better perhaps a family which has within it members as ethical-religious.

August 26

The soul comes to be when every major part of the body assumes in some degree or other the role of a carrier for the form of the entire body. When it does this the soul becomes the body as in fact unified. This unity is something achieved; this means that the living body has the form and the body only as correlates until we get that soul. The unity which is the soul is not yet the unity of the form of the body with the body, for the form is carried by it as a soul only in a representative capacity, and the substantial nature of that soul enables it to be a soul only of some parts of the body. But the unity which is the soul can make a unity of the form and body by reaching beyond them to their environing universal and existence, and trying to possess these. It then possesses them at the same time, but only in the guise of the form and matter, which are thereby made into a unity.

The soul then is a unity serving to make a unity of a form and matter, through the mediation of universals and potentialities. The account needs completion by a consideration of the habits and tendencies of a living being. The soul is a unity also of these two, and serves to unify them by pointing beyond them to a singular past sequence of occurrences and a power of relation, i.e., Actuality and divinity.

The soul is in any case a bodily entity which had incorporated in a representative way the form correlate with the entire body, and is concerned with what fringes the correlates, thereby unifying those correlates. The unity of the soul is achieved when and as it produces a unity of the form and mass of the living body. Let us suppose it is the brain which assumes the role of a representative; then it takes over the task of containing in some way the form and the rest of the mass of the body. It is a unity only when and as it unites the form and the mass of the body. And it unites them only so far as it is concerned with what fringes them. Accordingly A] the brain is a part of the mass of the body; B] a representative of the entire mass;   C] a carrier of the entire form of the body, in a representational way;   D] a unity of *b* and *c*.   E] that which unifies the mass of the body with its correlate structure;   F] that which is concerned with the potentialities of the body and with the universal behind the structure, and which by virtue of this is enabled to be a unity and to make a unity of the body's mass and form.

Must the brain be a unity itself? Yes, because it represents both facets. Must it represent both? Yes, for otherwise it would not be that which works on behalf of both. Must it unite both? Yes, for otherwise they remain only correlatives. Must it point outside them? Yes, otherwise it could not move. The soul then is only the brain uniting the form and matter of a body by attending to what fringes them. This means the brain is A] unity for a being, B] and a control of form and matter, C] needing more than that matter or form.

Or should we not say instead that the brain, when it is able to tap the potentialities of the body at the same time that it taps the universal which fringes the form of that body, thereby makes itself into a power for unifying the body and the form? We must of course bring in the brain as tapping the singular past and the source of relationality, since it must also unify the habits and tendencies of the being as well (which habits and tendencies are not to be found either in the body or the form but are themselves as independent of them as they are of it, and are correlate with them).

It does seem as if I have here given a kind of reification to form, habits and tendencies. But it is a fact that even if we try to locate these in the body there is a difference among them *inter se* and also between them and the body as a mass. In any case we get a soul and a human being only when the living being is unified by a material part that regulates the use of the entire potentiality and common meaning which fringes the living being. Were not the brain to make use of energies not yet manifest and of the meaning of being human which has not yet been particularized, the bodily form and matter would be but correlates, and it would be a thing. The brain, as occupied with these fringes when and as it functions as a part of the body and thus as a part of that which is being unified through its own agency, is what we mean by soul.

Habits as distinct from the body and its form must be thought of as a common source which these two can tap and which in fact is present as a datum. Tendency as distinct from these three must be thought of as encompassing them, as placing them in a setting with others. Tendency then can be said to deal with the body and form from without, but in relation to other bodies and forms, while habits relate to them from without but from a "dead" past. The assumption of the role of uniting these devolves on a part of the body; when and as it taps the potentialities of the body for all, it reaches to the universal, to the singularity of the past and to the context outside. The result is a unity of these four, bearing in them a stability, a dignity, a meaning and an individuality it otherwise would not have.

August 27

Perhaps the soul of a man is the outcome of a number of vital organs acting in concert on behalf of a universal, potentialities, a past and an excellence which fringe the form, matter, habits and tendencies of a body, in which those organs are? Perhaps the psyche of an animal is either the achievement of only some of these functions, or the achievement of them all but without adequate unity? Perhaps immortality is possible if the fringed items as brought together can extract from the organs which bring them together a sufficient substantiality to make it possible for them to continue to be. Perhaps a *thing* lacks the capacity to bring in the fringed items into play with its own four-ply being?

A family is but the members which in various degrees act on behalf of the past, energies, environs and excellence of the group.

Does Plato's state have the philosophers as sovereigns, with the auxiliaries but part of them; or does it have the auxiliaries as sovereigns mediating philosophers and people; or does it have the auxiliaries in an anomalous position, and the decision as to which role they will play determining whether or not we have a good state? The last, I think— and that is best.

August 31

In the symphony we rarely remember what had gone before; we do not always know what is to come after; we are not aware of the dominant structure or theme of the piece, or know what it is saying. This would seem to indicate that we were confined just to the note that was occurring. But in fact this is not the case. The note we now hear is fringed by structure or grammar of music which we discern by virtue of our elementary beats and some knowledge; it is fringed by the actual dynamic world of existence which we grasp even apart from the music, but which the music brings into some focus; it is fringed by what it can subsequently fit with, something we discern in our expectations; and it is fringed by the past which operates in it and us now to delimit the range of what could reasonably be expected. The very notes then that now occur, occur as singularly determined in the past, as caught in a "grammatical" structure, as riding on some phase of existence, and as capable of being followed by only various sorts of rhythms. When we hear it we are also outside it in those fringes, and we bring into the understanding of the note these various fringes, thereby making the note have an entirely new significance than it would have had by itself. We are like an artist but one who stands outside a situation, to make it have a kind of unity and magnitude it otherwise would not have.

September 4

A number of entities together constitute a whole; that whole has, through their conjoint contribution, values which the entities themselves ought to have if they are to be as excellent as possible, fully real, and get back what they gave. A representative of the entities adopts values in the factors of the whole, and thereby gives them a kind of substantiality they otherwise would not have.

The representative first unifies the factors, to make them substantial, then subjugates them to individualize them, then expresses them, and then envisages a new state for them. He thus goes through something like the roles of God, individual, Existence and Ideal.

Different types of groups provide individuals with different values. Thus a gathering of items gives them the new meaning of belonging; an association gives them the new meaning of having needs satisfied; groups, e.g., the family gives them the new meaning of being completed by having their appetites answered; and organizations e.g., the state gives them a new meaning in that it redefines their rights. Each of the accretions from the whole makes a man have a kind of life which is better than that which he could have as alone.

Plato and Aristotle both are individualists in the sense that they do not ask how the family is improved in the village or state but only how man's life is improved. We should see the state as completing both the individuals and the subordinate associations at the same time.

The representative imposes the factors of the whole on the individual members, distributes the values of the whole. Until then the common past, structure, power and function have no limitative value for the parts; they contribute to it and that is the end; the state in this sense is like the wholes discussed in *Reality*.

The representative benefits the factors, himself and perhaps other men. He first makes an attempt to unify the various factors. Apart from such an effort they are simple functions of the individual parts. But unification enables them to be something on their own, and this is good for them; it is also good for the representative since it enables him to be a carrier of a wider meaning than before.

The representative subjugates the factors. This makes them particularized, the past as operative. This is good for the whole since the past is now used, and good for the representative since it makes him more unified, more one with those factors.

The representative expresses those factors in the individuals, breaking them up so that these are benefited. This is good for the whole since it enables it to be sustained in many places, and good for the individuals (of which the representative is one) since it gives them at least what they gave to the whole.

The representative puts the factors in a new form, giving the whole a new role. This is good for the whole since it enables it to have a role elsewhere and thus carry new values; and good for the individual members (and representative) since it enables them to function in new contexts with new benefits.

What is distributed is a belonging, an ordering, a dignity and rights.

September 6

The smallest gathering is a pair. This has one or two representatives occupied with unifying, subjugating, dispersing and relating the factors of the pair. The pair has its factors fringed with more indeterminate versions; the pair also constitutes with others a gathering of pairs and richer combinations. A member of a pair can, because he himself is not wholly bound inside the pair, reach to the fringes; the member of the pair can, because he is also one of a larger gathering, make himself a representative of it and therefore be in a position to use the factors which are constituted by a gathering of pairs. These factors are given to the pairs by the individuals who act as representatives of the gathering of the pairs. The fact that those individuals might also be in a pair but shows that one can first give something to a pair and then take up the role of distrubuting this inside the pair. (The substantiality of the larger group does not seem to be greater than that of smaller ones.)

There must be four types of mass for a pair, four types of structure etc. But the pair itself emphasises tendency, or futurity rather than individuality, structure or power. Major types of pairing seem to be companion, aid, friendship, love; these can accrete by specification in all four dimensions such features as property, tradition, etc., in which case they become institutionalized. In a sense this is a way of intensifying the factors which constitute a pair, and shows that they may have natures which are not the functions simply of the members, but may be the functions A] of larger groups, and B] the specification of fringes by the members. The family is an institution which emphasises past and power; political whole adds an emphasis on structure; both add content to the pair, if it be granted that a pair might be made political without there being any other men brought in.

September 25

The early sections of the *Modes* seem to cosmologize Existence more than they should. Ought it not to be viewed somewhat the way God is—as having a kind of being apart from all else, which is only partly manifest as energy, space, time or any other derivative? This I do indicate; but then Existence by itself could not be a self-dividing reality which must have its divisibility limited. It must have some self-maintenance; this is said in 3.01 but obscurely.

If knowledge adds something to the things known, giving them divisions, focus and eventually, through mind's memory, expectation and inferences, some new connections which jeopardize them in ways they were not before, (since now open to actions they could not engage in before), what happens when we have a system of the whole, and when we know ourselves? Could we say that the system of the whole is but the extension of oneself, a vicarious or abstract possessing of all, which attenuates oneself at the same time and to the same degree it gets to other things, and that the mastery of one's knowledge is the enriching of oneself, so that in the end to possess one's knowledge is but to reinstate oneself concretely in the world, to possess what is outside one by a strategy? In the concrete we do not need the knowledge; in the end it gives us what we were before; but in between we can face all the way what we consciously face now only in part. As to knowledge of oneself this perhaps could be viewed as one's knowledge of others as in turn knowing oneself. But what of our knowledge of the universe as including ourselves?

This would seem to involve an abstraction which achieves concreteness only by being absorbed by all the modes at the same time in their diverse ways. Each gets something of the others by abstracting, and each must make this which it gets into its own being, at which time this, which it had abstractly, loses the value it had. Knowledge should then be the outcome of a need of an actuality to get what it now faces obscurely. Perhaps we have a choice: either be outside and connected with all else concretely, or possess all but have the possessed only in the abstract, and thus as requiring concretionalization before it is one's own.

October 3

The perpetrator of paradoxes has a firm base which for him alone is the locus of true being. He seeks to convert people away from the state of dealing with abstractions. The base can be that of a lover, of an established convention, of ordinary commonsense, of an ethical being, of a realm of religion. Or to refer to the four modes: it is Existence as such, which Brumbaugh says is where Heraclitus remains, and which questions all external divinities, fixities and particularities; it can be the divine which recognizes no genuine becoming, individualities or idealities; it can be the actual which makes paradoxes of the Ideal, Existence and God, by denying them any real being since they lack individuality—which is the approach of the *existenz* philosopher; and it can be the Ideal which rejects all motion, all individuality and all divinity. The lover combines a concern with the Actual with that of the Ideal; the conventionalist takes a dessicated Existence has his base; the common sense man adds to this that of the Actual; the ethical being adds Actuality to the Ideal; the religious man, if not a mystic, adds Ideality to the divine. If we systematically make various combinations we should get other types of paradoxical position, each of which takes some mode or modes for granted and criticizes some evident fact of experience just so far as it exhibits something of some other mode.

Can we not say the same thing of the logical paradoxes—the theory of types, the prediction paradox, the paradox of denotation, etc? If we could, it would mean that what in the realm of the Actual is the paradox of Ideality could be reversed or transformed into the paradox say of the Actual from the standpoint of the Ideal—e.g., a perfect truth or normative truth will equate all assertions as merely others of one another.

One might envisage the origin of the human soul as a series of adoptions, by different parts and functions of the body, of that common form which constitutes the organic whole. The primary adoption would perhaps be by the entire eating-digestive system which approaches the outside world and deals with it under the limitations of the common form; this dealing under those limitations gives the common form a locus in the digestive system. Subsequently the muscular system, treated as a set of habits and thus as the inheritance of a past, deals with the form as that which serves to relate those habits to the other parts of the body, having their own history, but requiring some other mediation and causation than that which they would get from the muscular system if it operated outside the guidance and use of the form of the whole. There can then arise a control by the brain as that which adopts the form of the whole as its own, (and thereby acquires a mind, which is the acceptance of the form of the whole by the brain as that which governs the way it deals with all else). Finally there is the regulative function of the heart which dictates how the form is to be distributed and utilized, or rather how such division guided by the form will be expressed in the rest of the being. When the individual has had these different parts of his body take over these different roles he has one soul which is diffused over the entire body by virtue of being carried by these different parts. When it is carried by each of these parts (before or apart from the others or together with them) the adoption of the form determines something of the way in which past, future, material and meaning are to be utilized or exhibited.

Perhaps the order of occurrence is muscle, mouth, heart and mind?

October 7

The art object has a structure which may attempt to duplicate some object, either as it appears or as viewed in its depths. Or the structure might be a stylized version of something; it may attain a new character by virtue of its achievement of extensionality, temporality and involvement, when ingredient in the world outside the art object. Or the structure may be without any direct application or reference to the world beyond. In all three cases, and ostensibly in the last, the art object provokes an emotion entraining the past of the individual and enabling this to give a ground for the past (in the case of temporal art objects) of a work, or for the tradition and past out of which it springs.

The provoked emotion has a neatness and clarity to it which is not characteristic of the ordinary emotion; also it is a function of the art object, though one which of course must have something to do with the tradition, etc., of the spectator. The emotion becomes purged in all art experiences, by taking up the role of a mediator, of a kind of concern for the world beyond the art object; it thereby becomes ontologized, restricted and eventually swallowed and controlled by the very world to which it directs us.

In addition to the emotion, there is an expectation which is provoked at the same time by the art object to point to an Ideal that ought to be. This expectation also mediates; it relates this Ideal to the world as that to which it may arrive; art appreciation is the tailoring of Ideal expectations to what will ensue.

The art object has its own structure and exhibits an interplay of means and end; it is a significant form, and can be enjoyed just for that reason alone; this is not the enjoyment of the art object as anything other than the outcome of a technique (and then without reference to this technique as a means for eliciting an emotion).

The world outside the art object is at the same time experienced as germane to the area where men work creatively; this is part of the deep abiding sense that we are getting to know the world better, even apart from our reaching to it through emotion; we know as it were where to look right from the start, because as we look at the art object we keep abreast of the world, and sharpen our grasp by use of expectation and emotion.

All art involves a purging because all art involves the transmutation of the emotion from the provoked to the yoked, from what the art object arouses to what is controlled by the world beyond.

Natural beauty is analogous to the beauty in art objects just so far as it is an appearance, and the real world beneath is what is referred to, once again via the emotion aroused. If there be a genuine distinction between the beautiful and the awesome it ought to be between the beauty of the appearance and its counterpart in reality beneath, and not in the magnitude of any appearance. Perhaps one can say that natural beauty makes no reference and the awesome does, but this would involve exaggerating a mere matter of degree into a basic distinction; natural beauty refers, and the real is always manifest to some degree in appearance.

These ideas, as most of the others, worked out with Ellen Haring, are not unrelated to such matters as the origin and nature of the soul, and the nature and parts of the state. Indeed they come from discussions of these originally. The problem of the soul is to understand A] how diverse entities, such as cell and sperm with their own insides can yield a new individual, and B] how this spiritual being can be related to the materiate parts of the universe. A] is something Aristotle could not answer. His doctrine of forms requires that the inclusive form somehow include the subordinate ones, in which case the real individual of these is lost. But if one recognizes that each entity has its own privacy then a number of them can come together to constitute a whole which has a privacy over against and in another dimension from the privacy of the parts. It is the public beings of the cell and sperm which together constitute the larger entity which possesses a privacy.

Instead of holding (as I think I sometimes have held in the past) that the soul is entirely different in origin and nature from the body, one can hold that it gradually comes to be by the various parts of the body taking on various functions expressive of the nature of the whole body. Thus to begin with, the musculature permits of a persistent adjustment of parts of the body to one another; this is not controlled by their common structure, but the individual through his constant efforts and eventually his habits gets more and more to fit into the scheme which he structurally defines. One of the items in such muscle-development is the development of the digestive tract, the mouth and stomach; here we have a part of the body acting as a kind of surrogate for the whole; it acts on the outside world in habituated ways, ways which are mediated to that outside world by an outlook which is a simulacrum of the very structure governing the whole body. The accretion of content from the outside world changes the content available to the parts of the body. When the heart so regulates the body that different parts of the body are there given appropriate powers from the common fund, the heart functions somewhat like an official or officer whose actions are essentially the vivification of the common structure by having it divided in such a way as to make sure that every aspect of it is carried out in the various parts. And finally when the brain deals with the common structure as an object, when it directs itself along the route of that common structure to the future, and thus makes itself concerned with an Ideal, we get the common structure as the structure of a mind, and the brain functions then as an agent for the whole.

When an individual succeeds in having all these four functions carried on in harmony we say that it has acquired a soul. Such a soul thus does not start, as tradition supposes, as a kind of visitor from the outside which must get diffused over the body; nor as a mere inside as I suggest in *Reality* and in *Nature and Man,* but as that which, when as it were diffusion has already occurred, has a single role of carrying out the nature of the structure in these diverse ways and through these diverse agencies. The soul is carried thus by the different parts of the body which then have activities which are as if they were controlled by the structure of the gathering. That soul can conceivably acquire existence of its own, hold on to what is common to these various loci; if so it is capable of immortality, since it can then depart with a characteristic existence, which will not however compromise the existence or the structure of the corpse that is left behind. The corpse has a common structure and a body, but there is nothing there that takes over the representative functions; the body is alive and has a soul when the representative functions are actually being performed by one or more parts.

But if the soul could be immortal, ought there not be an analogous immortal aspect to the state, and ought there not also be an immortal aspect to the work of art which is carried by the emotions and expectations of men in harmony with the grammar and body of the art object and its world? But this would require that the state as a whole, once its various parts have performed their functions, to have the capacity to hold on to the common existence of these; it supposes that the art object, once it has been grounded in these various agencies, which take up representational roles for it, either can itself hold on to the common existence of those agencies, or that those agencies together can carry a soul, which can accrete something of them together. But it is to be noted that the art object's structure is not really the structure of these agencies as together; it is something they adopt from outside them; the proper analogue would be the parts in the painting as a whole. The state gives an even better analogue, for the materiate parts are all in it. The state would then be said to be immortal in the sense that its can hover over the area for a while, after it has passed away.

November 5

All making involves the use of material to be worked over; it ends with a matter encompassed in some form, and has some bearing on a real object outside.

We can view an art object as a physical thing which is carried by a new context, so that the art object has a new role. This is in a way what I said in the paper on the real art object and what Vivas has been arguing for. There is another way of looking at the art object which emphasizes its capacity. Here we view the art object as essentially something significant, as that which encompasses its own peculiar matter in the world of the art object—a matter which is continuous with the matter of the physical thing, but which the form of the art object seals off for the nonce.

The art object could have: a *new* matter freshly made, such as new sounds or colors, which vicariously functions for the art objects as a real matter functioned for that form before; *symbolized* matter, where there is a use of the art object's form and matter to symbolize or represent

analogously what is happening outside; *epitomized* matter, where we find
a new and better medium to carry the form we took from the world;
subjugated matter where we impose a form on any matter we like but in
such a way as to express the true meaning of that form, freed from the
irrelevancies of existence. These various matters, and particularly symbolized matter, must have two relations to real matter and things outside
—be carried by a real object, perhaps even the very matter which is
functioning as a symbol, and which refers to a real object beyond. The
ontological problem of art relates to the physical matter which is continuous with the matter in the art object; the epistemic relates to the
matter which is being portrayed or which performs an analogous function in a thing to that performed by the matter of the art object.

November 11

Why must there be four modes? There must be four answers
to this. Each mode with which we begin demands a different set of
correlatives to answer to different demands. But there is another more
comprehensive answer possible, too. Given a mode of being it cannot be
alone, for unity (as I observed in *Reality,* after Hegel) becomes indistinguishable from Nothing, and Nothing is self-contradictory. Given two
modes of being they must be together. The togetherness has efficacy; it
holds them together. But an effective holding together needs a reciprocal
efficacy to preclude the absorption of the two modes in the unity. Two
modes can provide this opposition but not without making the togetherness be a mode, and then they would have to be united with that togetherness in another togetherness. This last togetherness must have the efficacy
of holding the previous three together, and these must oppose it. The
outcome should be a togetherness without efficacy. But this last point
must be demonstrated, for otherwise we would be driven to five modes
and eventually to *n* modes.

There are then two ways of answering the question of why there are
four modes: A] by showing that any pair requires an effective togetherness, which in turn needs its reciprocal in an effective togetherness in
order to prevent the absorption of the pair; B] by showing that any
pair is in opposition to an effective togetherness, and that this opposition
constitutes another way of being together.

The next questions are: which is preferable, *a* or *b,* and can we stop
with only four modes? *A* and *b* come to the same thing, but in *a* we are
neutral with respect to the pair and the opposition; in *b* we concentrate on
the pair and recognize the other two modes as functional with respect to
it. In *a* we do speak as if the other two were functional only, but since we

recognize that they have their own pairing status we give a more neutral account. But then why can we not say that the two sets of pairs must be together in a paired set of ways and thereby get six modes? The answer must be that the next two modes are the same as one of the preceding pair, or that there is only a self-opposition here without efficacy, a completed togetherness. But why?

If there are only four modes, the togetherness of those four must be complete, ineffective, without power or being, and thus incapable of actually interplaying with the four modes; those modes will have to function in relation to one another and not in relation to their togethernesses. They cannot really make a whole; they cannot stand over against a unity of them all; they cannot be subordinated neutrally, but only with respect to one another; they cannot constitute a common space by the overlapping of reciprocal vectors.

December 21

A temporalized dialectic which produced an antithesis would have to release it in order to have that antithesis in opposition to the thesis. But if it released it we would seem to have two alien elements. The solution would seem to be that there is A] a producing where something still clings to its producer, B] a product, which stands over against, and C] a correlation of the antithesis and thesis which must occur at once when *b* takes place. Or to put it another way, there is a process of negativing which does not go the length of achieving an oppositional term, but merely terminates in it; its other achieves an independent career only by virtue of constituting (with the negativing element) a single whole in which the elements are mutually rejective but also caught inside the process of negativing a synthesis. The synthesis achieves its own independence and must then however oppose the elements, not as contemporaries, but as present over against the past; otherwise the synthesis would not be temporally or logically ongoing.

December 22

Our daily world is a world with which we are familiar. It expresses the area of our mastery. As we look at it we, as it were, are aware that we are sitting on a stone in the cave while we are looking at shadows, i.e., that there is something more. The very need to complete ourselves, to grasp ourselves as other than those shadows is the need to drive on with reason, to make the metaphysical quest, to try to get to the real world beyond. But everyone, though inevitably driven in this direction, as Kant saw, is also repelled by it. There is the desire to complete and the desire to remain as one is with the familiar, for the area where completion is possible is the area of real substantial things which might crush me if I venture into it.

In a sense empiricism is the desire to remain with what one has mastered; it helps me avoid the effort at completing myself by avoiding the risk of challenge and subjugation. Metaphysics is the attempt to find the completing, first abstractly and then also in the concrete, as the inevitable expression of myself; we engage in it only by giving up what we know so well for that which may make us also into nothing. The attraction of Kant is that he points to the metaphysical world beyond as necessary for completion, but then goes on to show how we can remain inside the familiar world and merely attempt to get outside; in this way he preserves the familiar, the drive towards completion and yet allows us to avoid the encounter with real substances, as real as oneself, the knower. The attraction of Plotinus is the reverse; here we are in the world where we have, in a sense, already been overcome, and he points to the way we could avoid taking the realm of appearances seriously. The Indian thinkers have a similar attraction. The limitation in my *Modes* is perhaps my presenting this last type of view for an audience which wants only the first. They are men concerned with maintaining power with the least risk; the others are concerned (and I with them) in completing oneself at the risk of being ruined.

Each discipline makes its own type of demand; each has a characteristic " , ". And each discipline, because it is concerned with a distinct set of things, or facets of these, has a characteristic " . ". Both forms of togetherness can vary within limits without affecting the other. This means that a prescription is compatible with any number of descriptions or factualities of a certain sort, and that a factual juncture of items is compatible with and permits of conformity to any one of a number of distinct prescriptions. No law of logic, for example, is compromised by variations in types of inference—or conversely, no mode of inference is compromised by fluctuations in prescriptive implications. But given an implication or rule of logic and a certain way of drawing inferences which is compatible with that rule, one ought, in order to do justice to the steadiness of the prescription, demand that the way of drawing inferences not be altered—and conversely, given a way of drawing inferences, laws of logic compatible with such inferences should not be varied, if one is to do justice to the persistence of that way of drawing inferences. All that can be demanded of either the structures of logic or the acts of inference is that there be a persistence in whatever co-ordination one has initially accepted as holding between them. Of the various sets of such steadily co-ordinated rules and inferences only that one, however, will in the end be satisfactory whose inferences are otherwise acceptable and whose rules are otherwise significant. Such a set will be a whole, portayable as "$x , y \lor x . y$" where the "$\lor$" expresses the fact that these related satisfactory items are steadily co-ordinate. Similar observations are to be made with respect to science and religion, religion and ethics, theory and practice.

December 31

1] The four modes are on a level ontologically.

2] The four modes can be made to be on a level epistemically, by treating them as norms and prescriptive principles.

3] Any mode can be used as the beginning of a series. An epistemic beginning has an ontological ending; the beginning is an almost inchoate multitude of images, a kind of togetherness; the end is a plurality of parts.

4] An ontological beginning is with one mode by virtue of the presence of others in it functioning as a togetherness; it ends with knowledge as a distillate.

5] Each level is infected by its neighbors to consitute a new intermediate mixed level. We start with Existence as epistemic and thus as an inchoate mass of images and fantasies and move to Actuality or common sense, Ideality or values, and God or eternity or unity.

6] We can go at once from inchoate images to ontological eternity; the mutual infecting will enable us to forge a simulacrum of the realm of Actuality or Ideality.

7] If an epistemic beginning has a sheer ontological ending and conversely, we prove there are only four modes by showing how we end with an epistemic result without being if we start ontologically with some one mode, and how we end with an ontological result without meaning if instead we start epistemically.

8] Ethics has the set: feelings, actions, rules and norms. Other subjects have analogous sets.

9] Plato's cave starts with an epistemic use and ends with an ontological. Why not an ontological beginning?

10] Epistemic beginnings have ontological interiority, and ontological beginnings have in them the source of all categories. The beginnings and endings are thus quite distinct; the ending is clearer but also dependent on the beginning.

11] How are 1, 2, 3, 5, 6, 8 related?

1957

January 1

An entity might be said to have an active role with respect to others, at the same time that it takes a perspective on them. The former is more like an indexical or existential interplay, the latter more like a contemplative but abstract mastery. Each entity in addition is something in itself, when it stands alongside the others, as on a par with them ontologically. And each also adumbratively reaches to the others to make them all epistemically on a level, beings which are equally capable of apprehending the others.

The active role terminates in other beings as more distilled versions of basic realities; it is a way of beginning in ontology and ending with some purged or clarified structure. Similarly the contemplative activity terminates in a world which is the selective distillate of the contemplative structure, and is concrete to the very degree that it is selective. A Bergsonian active turmoil should end with a formal logic; a Freudian domain of uncharted fantasy should end with a reality of discrete items, which clarify the fantasy. Can these be interrelated? Would it be possible to correlate the logic with the discrete items, using the ontological and private turmoils to constitute the principle of their union? And conversely could one correlate two inchoate realms, existence and psychology, say, using the logical and scientific worlds as the principles of union? In either case one would constitute a *tertium quid,* a schematism, a togetherness, whose purpose is to mediate. The mediator would be something produced; it would, in a kind of demiurgotic way, vary in its nature in accordance with the degree of discrepancy that exists between the items to be correlated. But the logic would not be prescriptive, and this is a defect which could perhaps be overcome by having it still subject to the pressures of the inchoate real world of which it is the expression; but then there ought to be a kind of apparent prescriptiveness provided by the scientific world, and a real prescriptiveness which is an expression of a psychological state (whose function it is to endow the scientific world with a descriptive status).

One can approach all this from a different angle. The logical-mathematical structure could be correlate with a scientifically organized world through the double agency of an unorganized totality of possibilities or images and a chaotic dynamic existence. The logical-mathematical would answer to something like God, the scientifically organized world to something like Actuality. The degree to which the first correlation would hold is measured by the degree of consonance of the two rich domains. (These rich domains are ontologically on a level, just as the logical-mathematical and the scientific are epistemically on a level.) But then why need there be the logical-scientific pair; why not just adjust the subjective existence to the objective? The adjustment of these two might be an adjustment which was due to the suppression of one or the other. We test the adjustment by seeing if the logic-science makes a persistent union of the same sort over a period of time; we test the union by seeing if each of the ontological dimensions has an answer in the other.

Because the scientific is the expression of the subjectively rich, while the logical is the expression of the ontologically rich, the mutual adjustments yield an ontological union which has its proper epistemic expression. Apart from the adjustment of the ontological dimensisons we could get a scientific scheme answered by a logic which was inappropriate. We would then find that we could not make the deductions we find the world requires. We could adjust the present structure with the scientifically acceptable world by attributing the aberrations of the latter to the pressure of the subjective, or the aberrations or inadequacy of the former to the pressure of the world. In the first case we would be saying that it is ignorance, wrong analyses, language, etc., which prevent us from seeing how the old-fashioned logic works; in the latter case we would be saying that the rich inchoate dynamic world was inadequately expressed in formal logic and also in the way in which that logic was applied to the scientific world. Once the pressure of the world was relaxed the logic would merely be correlate with the scientific world.

The juncture, logic-science, would express a truth having a subjective and an objective reference, and the consonance of those references would tell whether the juncture gave a truth about the world. Also the subjective ideal and objective existences in their inchoate states would have a mutuality which had a formal structure and an organized world of discrete entities as referents. Their consonance would tell whether or not the structure and world were strict correlates.

Does ethics have the set: commands and intentions as ontological, and rules and actions as epistemic? And politics: sovereign and subjects, government and citizens?

January 2

Hegel's beginning is with what is in fact inchoate and endlessly rich; this ontological base comes to expression only in a dessicated structure. His view is in a way the correlate of Kant, who began with an endlessly fertile ego which came to expression in a scientific world. Neither of these expressions has genuine status; Hegel's lacks substantiality, and Kant's lacks vitality. To make up for their lacks their expressions must be carried by the ego and an ontological base respectively. Without a Kantian ego the Hegelian expression is effete; without an Hegelian origin the Kantian world is fixated. Neither would accept this interpretation. Hegel thought that the substance of thoughts was in the ego, and that the thoughts could have a kind of power of their own, adopt the ego into themselves; Kant spoke as if the ego were a pure id and as if the world that was known was even more real than it. But what their views in substance are is different from what they explicitly affirmed.

Perhaps then the levels in Plato are put badly; ought we not say, as in a way he did too, that there are two items—shadows and perceptions which are on a level and have epistemic significance, and two items, mathematics and the good which have ontological import? But ought we not then go on to say that the shadows are produced by the good, and the perceptions produce the mathematical, and that we must marry the shadows with the mathematicals through the joint agency of the perceptions and the good as in an adjustive relation to one another? He whose perceptions accord with the nature of the good has made a proper union of his shadows with his mathematicals. Apart from such an accord the shadows or the mathematicals might dominate one the other; but it is the accord which gives each its proper place. Similarly to determine whether or not one has properly balanced the good and the perceptions, it is necessary to see if the mathematicals clarify the shadows and the shadows carry the mathematicals.

Do the various modes occupy different types of time and different kinds of space? And if they do what is the nature of the time and the space of the togetherness? Since togetherness is not real, and is indeed just the modes intermixed and neutral, the time and space would be a kind of mere extension of which Whitehead spoke; this togetherness would be specialized in various ways by the different modes, not in the sense that they are derivatives from it, but in the sense that it is an abstract nucleal nature and these are to be understood as concrete realities which exhibit something of the nucleus but in distinctive ways. But why need the to-getherness have any nucleal nature? It could be something having a meaning or nature, though no being—unlike the modes. If so we should have time as four-fold; time is discrete with Actualities, a mere structure for the Ideal, sheer ongoing or duration for Existence, and articulation, mere phenomenological alongsideness for God. The togetherness of all the times is a vivified present of the Actual and the Existent, beyond which stretches the structure of the Ideal and the alongsideness of mean-ing offered by God, the former perhaps marking the structure of the future, and the latter marking the structure of the past. If so the together-ness of the times is a discrete present vital moment, concrete and dynamic, the last term of a set of determinate meanings and the first term of a structure going endlessly into the future.

January 3

The problem of semantics, the relation of the conceptual to the factual, which has been approached by Kant in the most suggestive way in his schematism, needs to be developed further to account for all the cases, to avoid the presuppositions which he makes about their separate-ness, and to avoid his need to use the factual nature of time, rather than a dialectically justifiable *tertium quid,* to solve the problem.

If we start with a false proposition and ask what relation this might have to the truth, we can say that it is a specification of the very universal which the truth specifies. If this were not the case they would not have anything to do with one another; the false would be the irrelevant or the nonsensical. The exclusion which the true and the false have to one an-other is A] contained in their common universality, B] specified by the true, and by virtue of our holding on to the false, is C] specified by the false, to give a mutuality of exclusion which expresses the dissection of what was before an undifferentiated universal. Putting aside for the moment the cases of the irrelevant and the nonsensical, we can say of all propositions, categories, geometries, etc., which are not met by the world, that they are alternative specifications of a common universal, the most common being that of Being.

When we have a truth or a proper formulation of what is objective, we find that the specifications have implications which are in accord. In the case of falsehood we have at the moment an accord provided by the very fact of oppositionality. But the implications of the false assertion lead to a different kind of oppositionality at the next moment; the true is in accord in the sense that the private and the public, though opposed as knowledge and being, are constantly at the same distance; the implications of the one do not involve a variation in its distance from the implications of the other, whereas this is the case of the false and the wrong. If this is so the schematism is as it were being constituted all the time; there cannot be failure of an accord; there can be no semantic problem; there can be nothing like the question of how a mathematics fits a world. There will always be a fitting, but the fitting can be a series of bumps and divergencies in distance, or it can be steady. We either have a schematism which we constitute in such a way that it can persist, or we have one which is reconstituted at every moment to have a different nature. This answer comes close to the demiurgotic answer of Plato if one assigns different moral weights to the nature of the demiurgos, depending on how or on whether or not this or that ideal is being realized through its agency.

When we come to the nonsensical or the meaningless our problem is not really different; what we must find is that common ground which relates the objective being of the expression with another matter of fact in some other domain. What we now have is A] some psychological or linguistic fact, B] its claim to be a truth, C] which must be disowned by virtue of the way in which it is related to an objective fact, or, (as is usually the way), which is disowned by showing it to be only a psychological or linguistic fact. The correlation of the two facts is like the correlation of the private judgment and the objective fact which is mediated by a genuine universal, specified truly or falsely, except that when we have nonsense or meaninglessness, we do not need the universal and can make our correlation one-one, directly. Or better said, truth, falsehood, nonsense all have a factual base and are factually correlate with an exterior fact; as such they are contingently in accord with it by virtue of their mere contemporaneity, and there need be no further correlation. But in the case of truth alone there are implications which ground further factual contemporaneous correlations. The factuality of a subsequent implied outcome of a truth is in accord with the factuality of the consequence which flows from the objective fact. To know something truly is not to be in accord with the object except so far as one continues to draw the implications from the truth. It is those implications as drawn which have the factual correlativity like that had by the initial asserted truth to its correspondent fact.

One consequence of the above is that there is no warrant for the assumption that when there is a discrepancy only one side can be thought to be defective. A "falsehood" is not necessarily a subjective failure; it might be a truth which the world betrayed by virtue of a change in pace or nature. Temporally determined truths have this character. To say it is now one o'clock exactly, is to be betrayed by the world; to say at one o'clock that it is now two o'clock is to assert something false. The first was true for a moment, but while I held on to the assertion the world moved away; the other is false, being in disaccord with what is the fact, though if I hold on to it long enough it will turn out to be true.

The juncture point of two dimensions is a universal; this universal though need not be of a high order; if not, it has a certain thickness and exists close to the plane of the opposing items. One might demand a universal of a very limited and low level kind as the only one which will be allowed to define where one is in accord and disaccord. In such a case we will find items which are not specifications of the same universal; we would then have nothing but mere factual correlation with no truths or nonsense or anything else, but only words and images which are correlate with other entities as a matter of mere fact and for a contingent period. But the claims of truth and knowledge are so broad that it is necessary to find a universal which does justice to the need to have all things brought into significant correlation with what one has in mind or in language, and thus which would allow for false or improper specifications as well as appropriate or true ones.

If we attend only to some such conceptual dimension as a geometry and seek only to determine its truth or falsehood with respect to space in fact, we do not have to ascend to being in its mere being as a universal, and can be content with being as structure, of which space in fact, and the geometry which is true and the geometry which is false of the space can be specifications.

It is hard to see how the time of Kant could mediate geometry and space; nor is it necessary to think of all correlations as temporal in nature, as his solution would require. The problem of falsehood arises even in the correlation of abstract systems one with the other, where what we must match are the implications of both under the common universal which those systems subtend.

There is no need to suppose that the objective fact contains the very essences which are expressed in a truth; the very nature of the truth or conceptualized specification could be such that there was nothing in the world which was its counterpart, identical in nature with it; one need affirm only that it is identical in its rhythm with the rhythm of that truth, in the sense that the pace and consequences of the one were matched by punctuations and implications of the other. I think as a matter of fact though they are in accord, and this because of the existence of that common universal which allows for the specification in the objective domain of what we are providing in the subjective. This does not mean that the object is a mere specification of a universal, but only that there is a facet of it, an abstractable aspect of the object which is such a specification, or rather which can be viewed as such a specification—for there is no need to suppose the priority of the universal. If we say this we can recognize the existence of the object to consist not in its possession of traits and features which are unlike those expressible in thought or language or concept or symbol, but in its possession of a power of generating outcomes which are different in kind from the power by virtue of which implications are grounded and inferences are drawn. We seem then to have the choice of saying A] that the concept and its conceptual outcomes are like those of the world, B] that the concept is like its counterpart but that the processes of the mind and the world are unlike, and c] that the concept and its counterpart are unlike but that the processes are alike. The case where concept and process are both unlike their counterparts is the case of sheer factual correlation or sheer falsehood.

If we have concept and conceptual processes in gear with the world we have the world specified in mind as it is outside; this seems to be the Aristotelian view. If we need have only concepts in gear, and the conceptual processes diverge in nature from the process of the world, we have the view of Hume and other empiricists. If we have the conceptual processes in gear with the objective, but not the concepts, we get the position of pragmatism.

Is there any way of telling which of these views is true? Can we, given a universal, know that the specifications we impose are identical in essence with those which the world provides? The fact that we know truly could be taken care of even if this were denied, for there could be an adjustment of processes, themselves not even similar to one another.

January 4

There is a similar problem and perhaps solution underlying the relating of the unextended formulae of logic or mathematics to their extended counterparts, of concept to an object, of universal to particular, and of a universal to its instances. The *tertium quid* must add something to both sides—this is Kant's solution in the schematism. Time for him allows us to bring together the mere succession of the manifold with the sheer logical necessitation of the abstract logical intellect in the pattern of causality where the succession becomes necessitarian. His time, to put it another way, allows the concepts to be together whereas in logic they might contradict; it also provides an intelligibility and universality to what otherwise would be sheer fact and contingency, to be encountered or felt but not known. Or we could say that the constructions of his schematism dictate the exclusion of some otherwise respectable concepts (such as that of a non-Euclidean geometry) and the exclusion of some otherwise acceptable experiences (such as the sense data and "accidents" of daily experience).

The midpoint is in Kant richer than either side; my account of error in *Reality,* and in yesterday's notes makes the midpoint thinner. Are there not perhaps two-midpoints which are correlative, one thinner and the other thicker? Hegel starts with the thicker and shows the extremes to be effete. Could causality or necessary succession be understood as at once a kind of genus of which necessity and succession are correlate species, and as a kind of basic reality of which these are but abstractions? Do we, when we know an object, have to go through the process of providing the *tertium quid* which is otherwise there in advance? Can we say that a logic and nature are related by the possibility of either, and also by the existence of both? If so we would seem to have the pattern:

$$\text{logic (necessity)} \diagram{\text{(continuity) possibility}}{\text{(dynamics)\quad Existence}} \text{nature (discrete entities)}$$

This would seem to mean that a synthesis of logic and nature occurs in Existence when and as they analyze out the continuity. The analyzing out must be a specifying, such that to the possibility as a continuity is added on the one side the structure of necessity and on the other the fact of discreteness. Such adding is the outcome of the use of the dynamics of Existence by both sides, for the dynamics of Existence is richer than either. Or to say it now in another and perhaps better way, we are able to specify the indeterminate genus, in this case possibility or continuity, by making use of a rich but inchoate power, here called dynamic Existence. The specifications of the indeterminate are thus a way of subdividing the rich correlate of that indeterminate. Does this mean that logical necessity arises through the employment of dynamic Existence on possibility, thus dividing it off into sets of implications (which is a way of breaking up the continuity), and of utilizing the dynamic existence which is after all successively occurring? If this is anywhere near the truth we should say that the two instances of a possibility are in a position to match one another because they make use of the same correlate of the possibility in such a way as to exhaust it. It is because Existence is used up to constitute the correlates, logic and nature, that they can be said to be correlative instances or realizations of the same possibility or genus.

If we turn the matter about we get Existence as a kind of matrix or schema possessing the virtues of both sides, in that it has rational succession or causality as its very meaning, and only by making the logic and the discrete items of nature be mere possibilities, perhaps in a mind, do we succeed in exhausting the continuity of possibility.

January 5

Items to be reconciled can be viewed as abstractions from a single more concrete state of affairs in which their respective virtues are united. Those abstractions are in turn specifications of a single essence, which essence is the essence of the concrete state of affairs. To reconcile the domain of logic (with its necessities), with the mere factual being of things in the world, we must look to a single causal whole in which the necessities of logic are joined to the ongoings of Existence. Logical necessity on this account would be true only of abstractions; sheer factuality would be an abstraction too. These two abstractions would be alternative specifications of a single generic universe of being; this universe is the essence of, the meaning of the very possibility of the concrete state of affairs, the causal whole.

To reconcile a formula of geometry with mere sensuous experience we must recognize that they are abstractions with respect to a pure spatial object, an extended circle for example. Kant would call the latter a schema and would think of it as something constructed. (On this view the Cartesian correlation of algebra and geometry would be rejected for the view that algebra has its correlate in sheer factuality and is reconciled with this by the geometry. This points up the fact that there must be a way of reconciling algebra and geometry; this can be done by recognizing both of them to be abstractions from a mathematics of extensionality.) Kant's answer would perhaps be that they are abstractions from a principle of construction or method employed in time. The difficulty with his or my view is the affirming that this mathematics or method is more concrete than the algebra or geometry.

There ought also to be a reconciling of sensuous experience with the geometry. The source of both would be real shaped objects; the genus of which the sensuous experience and the geometry are instances would be mere extensionality.

If we carry this analysis over to the *Modes of Being,* we perhaps can say that there is a concrete togetherness of the modes in terms of which the various modes are abstractions. That concrete togetherness would be being, and the modes would be derivates of this which specified the unity of the being in diverse ways. If this is correct, then it must be said that the *Modes* was written from the perspective of the genus or meaning of this concrete unity of being, with the various modes as specifications more real than it.

The problem of reconciliation would seem to have two facets: there is the reconciliation of domains—universals and particulars, necessity and factuality, concept and object, and then there is the reconciliation of this concept with this object, this universal with this particular, etc. The first reconciliation requires only the genus to enable them to be together in a world or a mind; the second reconciliation requires the recognition of a more basic reality, for it is a reconciliation of what is true with its object. If we have an algebra which does not answer to the geometry, a physics which does not answer to nature, we can find a place for both by seeing them as different ways of expressing some common genus; they would be correlates just alongside one another. But if there is to be truth and a test of it, we must find that which allows the virtues of both of them to be united and thereby to be supported by one another. We know that our logic answers to the world because we see both logic and world carried in a causal schema; we know that this algebra answers to this geometry because we see both as expressions of the very being of Existence, having a rhythm with the punctuations of both the algebra and geometry, whose essence is given in a mathematics. If we now bring in a new algebra we find we can get a genus for this and the geometry but we can find no concreteness to carry it. How does all this relate to the prescriptive and descriptive distinction? Is the prescriptive the generic, the abstract, the thin which is to be specified, and is the descriptive the concrete, the thick, the determinate which is articulated in the items that specify the generic, perhaps through the aid of the descriptive and concrete?

Kant's view of schematism would seem to consist of a unity of apperception, then a plurality of categories, then a time, and then a world of appearances. The schematism would seem to be the categories as a priori dictating features of time. But if this four-fold scheme were right he ought to have a kind of schematism between the unity of apperception and the categories—synthesis of imagination, etc.—and between a time and a world of appearances—images? His view gives a priority to the conceptual which is unjustified. His statement that the concept must contain something represented in the object would require that no schema be necessary. He supposes that the roundness conceived must be homogeneous with what is intuited in the plate, but gives no warrant for this. Better would be to say that mere circularity lacks extension and the plate's roundness lacks systematic connections with other figures and that the schema is a necessary geometry in pure space. Is the category a subsumed case of the I, and is appearance a subsumed case of time?

A better scheme than his recognizes the correlativity of the I and the appearance or sensuous, and the correlativity of the category and mere time—

Category

I   Sensuous

Time

The schema would be the product of the juncture of the category and time. This enables one to say with Kant that time is not only homogeneous with the category and the appearance (because constituted by universal a priori rules and because it governs every case) but is homogeneous with the I or apperception. Also the way time is homogeneous with the category must be different in type from the way in which it is homogeneous with the I and the realm of sensuous appearance. It is because it is united with the category that it becomes honogeneous with the I and the sensuous, which are correlative ways of expressing both category and time. In the end the schematism, since it conjoins category with time, turns the I and the sensuous from specifications of the category and abstractions from time, into terms of a schema: I—schema—Sensuous. The fundamental fact would seem to be relational, not only temporally but epistemically, with two limits, the I and the sensuous. These can be abstracted by isolating the ongoing of the schema, and can be distinguished by isolating the structure of the schema as their common genus.

Number would seem to combine unity with transitoriness, reality combines being with intensity; substance, (the permanent in time) combines eternity with transitoriness to give us abidingness. Causality combines necessity and succession; community combines coexistence with necessity; possibility combines opposition of beings in the one same time; actuality combines determinateness with temporality; necessity combines temporality with universality. Magnitude is a generation of time, quality an a priori filling of time, relation in connection of perceptions in time, modality is time as a correlate of something belonging to time. Schema are a priori determinations of time according to rules; they are really the categories qualifying time, dealing with it as time-series, time-content, time-order and time-scope. In the end Kant speaks of it as unifying apperception.

To come back to my own formulation, there must, (in addition to a substantial source of the items we seek to relate properly, and a genus of which they are specifications) be a juncture of the source with the genus.

The latter constitutes a relational connection, a vital semantics with the items changed from abstractions or specifications into terms or limits. The relational connection is proper when it involves a unification of the essence of the source with the being of the source, and terminates in what is derived from these two. To relate physics to nature we need a genus of knowledge and a rootage perhaps in experimentation. The combination of knowledge with the experimentation constitutes the proper relation for physics and nature. If these are not able to be the terms of this relation one or the other is unsatisfactory. The physics and the nature which are proper terms are constituted by the generic and rooting components of the relation which unites them.

January 6

In Aristotle we have something analogous to the Kantian Schematism, once the latter has been freed from its hierarchical formulation. Kant sometimes spoke as though there was a primary unity of apperception which the categories specified in their twelve-fold way, and which had under it the pure form of time, and which in turn had under it the gathered manifold of experience. When he spoke this way he spoke as if there was only the problem of imposing those pure categories on the pure form of time, and somehow raising up the gathered manifold into the very being of time. But it would be better to say that the unity of apperception and the manifold are extremes, specifying the categories on the one side, and being abstractions from a vital time on the other. A schematism would then be the juncture of categories and vital time, having the apperception and the manifold as extremes.

In Aristotle the moral virtues have as their extremes two vices each of which, while possessing some good trait, lacks the counterbalancing good trait of the other vice. Prodigality and stinginess are specifications of a relation towards wealth, and a caring about money. The union of the relation with the caring is the virtue of liberality. This has the extremes as its terms. We know this to be the case because liberality has the virtues of both the sides without their limitations. Can we say the same thing about the relation of concepts to fact, physics to nature, etc.? Is it possible for us to find concepts and facts, formulae and extension, theory and practice all to have reciprocal defects which are overcome in something having them as terms? This would mean that the *tertium quid,* though a product, is in some sense richer, more real, more effective, more basic, more desirable than the terms, and to have the status therefore of something like an Aristotelian habit, and to be most germane to doctrines of history which make the historical movement and the outcome of the activities of beings more vital or important than those activities.

If we could say this we would perhaps be able to say the same thing of the pairing of men and women. We would be able to say that there is a kind of relationship holding between them, when they are appropriate one to the other, which combines the partial virtues of each. This relationship could be thought of as the self-sufficient; this could be constituted of the genus "human" on the one side, and of the common drive of any person on the other, a kind of need to be immortal perhaps. The combination of the genus with the drive towards immortality produces the first association, or the pairing of man and woman. The man and the woman are appropriate to one another if a persistence through time (and beyond the two of them through the child) which is at once ordered and capable of outlasting the moment, has one of them as the order and the other as the persistent or reproductive. This Aristotle sees, but he thinks of the order or reason which man possesses as being superior to the reproductive power of the female, when what he should say is that they are correlatives, contraries, equally valuable and equally defective though in opposite ways.

Does this allow us to say that the four *Modes of Being* are so many defective expressions of what is perfect in the togetherness of being which is none of these? If so the modes would be the product of a self-diremption, and the fundamental truth would lie closer to a monism than I have allowed. Or should one say instead that any two modes can be viewed as expressing extremes which the juncture of the other two modes mediate, and that these extremes have reciprocal virtues which the juncture combines? If so the juncture would seem to have more reality or be richer than the extremes, so that a pure mode would be less real than a combination of two of them, and the combined two would seem to lack their virtues or have them subdued inside the virtue which they exhibit as combining the partial virtues of the extremes. If we think of Actuality and Ideality as extremes we would say of them that they lacked permanence on the one side and determinateness on the other. If we think of God as the permanent and universal and of Existence as the determinate and vital, the coming together of these two would give us a permanent (universal) determinate (vital) relation between the Actual and the Ideal. This permanent determinate is what? And does it possess the universal-vital nature which God and Existence have in themselves?

The permanent determinate which could have Actuality and Ideality as extremes lacking permanence and determinateness respectively, and which is sustained by God and Existence as possessing in themselves uni-

'versality (or better, self-sufficient unity), and productive creative vitality—themselves in turn extremes to be united by the juncture of Actuality and Ideality could be said to be the rational order of the universe. If we look at God and Existence as extremes they would have to be said to lack localization and rationality respectively. The juncture of Actuality and Ideality would provide a rational localization, and would allow the Actuality and Ideality to remain outside, with the virtues of individuality and comprehensiveness. A rational localization would be a virtuous effective man, whose God and Existence lack concreteness on the one side and coherence on the other.

There ought to be other combinations: Actuality with Existence; Actuality with God; Ideality with Existence; Ideality with God. Actuality with Existence constitutes a localized activity; Actuality with God constitutes a dedicated man at once localized and purposive; Ideality with Existence constitutes a cosmic time; Ideality with God constitutes a providence. These names are not altogether satisfactory; better ones are to be found in the *Modes*. But they will help us focus on the issue: We now have rational order, virtuous effective man, localized activity, dedicated man, cosmic time, providence as various relations, constituted of two modes, having the other modes as extremes. These extremes fall short of their relation in opposite ways. There ought to be no real difference between the combination: rational order plus virtuous effective man, and localized activity and providence; or between dedicated man and cosmic time, for they are all ways in which a pair of modes is matched with another pair. What is the nature of a four-fold combination, i.e., rational order plus virtuous effective man? This should be a way of describing the nature of togetherness, but this togetherness has no being. The closest we can come to a being apparently as rich or richer than the modes is by having two of them function as a junctured relation, with the other two forced out to be mere isolated extremes. It is only in relation to such extremes that the junctured relation appears to be more real.

Could we now go back and take the Aristotelian vices as items which themselves are to be forced into a juncture, which defines the genus of them and is their primal source in potentiality? Thus stinginess and prodigality would constitute a relation between an impotent relation to wealth and the inchoate activity of giving. Such a relation would be sustained by the virtue of caution obtained from stinginess and the virtue of reference to another obtained from prodigality. Wealth and activity would divide the virtue of the relation whose nature is perhaps best said to be "being economic in fact," the wealth taking one side and the activity the other. And ought we not also say that the transcendental apperception of Kant can be combined with his manifold to constitute a way of relating the categories and the nature of time? Categories and time would then be extremes which are being mediated by this combination of ego and sensed content. Now Kant speaks as if the imagination, or the power of producing a schema, is a mystery he cannot unravel. But is not the combination of the ego and the sensed this very act? The coming together is no more mysterious than is the coming together of the two sides of the schema, its reference to the self and to the world. Kant to be sure argues that the reference is inevitable because he views the matter hierarchically; if we did this we could say that the transcendental unity of apperception subsumes the sensuous, because the unity necessarily includes whatever there be. Indeed there are passages in Kant which seem to suggest this. Perhaps he slipped from one of these interpretations to the other from time to time, now speaking of category plus time as a schema mediating ego and sense, and then speaking of the power of imagination, which is a unity of ego and sense, as mediating category and time.

If all these three interpretations will stand up, then Aristotle, Kant and the *Modes* can be said to shift from one way of relating to another and to deny that there is a single four-ply relating which is more real than the terms. If this is so we ought to get a name for the "power of imagination" of Kant, and a name for the nature of the juncture which two vices produce and which has unsatisfactory extremes. Since vices do have virtues, though only in part, the moral activity will be constituted of those virtues, with the bad portions suppressed, just so far as they serve to mediate properly the activity with the universal. But this begins to sound as if the juncture of the vices was just like the juncture of the universal with the activity, which before we said was a virtue. There is confusion here because one must recognize the components of the relation to possess not their own virtues but the virtues which the extremes severally possess. If this be the case, then the vices must constitute the virtue of having a universal together with activity, the making of a substance, substantiality as such. The vices then in combination make a man, a definite substantial being. Similarly, the combination of man and woman as making a pair should in effect be the concrete being of the union of the form of humans with the power activity of humans. But this would mean that the Platonic view of the state and the association is closer to the truth than the Aristotelian, for the union of the form and activity would be a human. This also gives the truth in the Aristophanic view of men and women being split off a single basic kind of human. However, what is to be noted now is that there is in fact, while there is a man and a woman, a kind of real relation produced by their combination which combines the virtues to be found in a universal and in activity. The species would be constituted by the very togetherness of man and woman, whereas the household would be constituted of the togetherness of the universal and the activity.

What has been said so far is that the relation between the extremes has the virtues to be found at the extremes, though it is not constituted by the togetherness of those extremes. The view of the *Modes* is that all togetherness is a product of a merging, but this precludes the efficacy of the togetherness. What lacks efficacy should be the togetherness of the four; togetherness of two as constituted by the other two has the efficacy provided by those two which constitute it.

We have the following proportions: What species is to household, vital existence of man is to moral virtue, creative imagination is to schema, and rational order is to virtuous effective man, local activity is to providence, dedicated man is to cosmic time.

Let us see what is to be said about the relating of abstract formula to its supposed counterpart in extension. Here we have the analogue of schema, household, moral virtue, virtuous effectiveness, providence and cosmic time. The extremes carry out the virtue of the middle which in this particular case might be termed semantics, or interest, or adjustment.

Is there not something wrong in speaking as if an abstract formula and extension needed a schema? What the schema needs is the structures of mind and body. Or perhaps we ought to transpose the terms and say that the togetherness of the formula and extension constitutes an adjustment or emotion (as Spinoza seems to have held) between the structure of mind and body, and that the togetherness of mind and body treated as structures constitutes an action relating formula and extension, as perhaps Peirce held. Adjustment or emotion would then have its counterpart in species, vital existence, creative imagination, whereas action would be the counterpart of household, moral virtue, schema.

Creative imagination and schema, adjustment and action, species and household, vital existence and moral virtue, are then alternative modes of combining pairs to make a relation which shares the virtues of the terms constituted by another pair. When Aristotle says there is a sense in which vitrue is both an extreme and a mean, is he not saying that it is a term in a vertical dimension? If so does it not have a counterbalancing virtue, and must it not be related by what is not a virtue, as he suggests, the Good, which is divided (as he does not say) into balancing vices? If we take this line we can say that moral virtue is a horizontal schema relating two vices and is itself constituted by the universal of structure and the dynamics of action, but that when the vices come together they constitute the Good, serving to relate the virtue of structure with the virtue of action. The vices can constitute the Good only because each vice is but an unsupported virtue.

Hartmann recognizes the two dimensions and distinguishes them as the ontological dimension of excess and defect, and the axiological good and bad. The ontological he thinks constitutes a continuum of possible habits (potential habits?). He says there is no straight transition from vice to vice. He makes the rectangle into a semi-circle with goodness as an apex. I don't see why this is done. The neglect of the extremes as having virtues and thus as capable of combining to constitute a vertical dimension, defining not moral virtue but vital existence, man as the mediator between the possible good and inchoate activity (the components of the moral virtue), precludes an understanding of the achievement of a status for the good and the activity, before they have and apart from the time when they have the status of components of moral virtue.

Hartmann in effect takes virtue to be the midpoint of a four-fold (and then finally of a three-fold) spread. But if this be the case he ought perhaps provide new terms for the vertical and horizontal components. Let us, to stay with him, then distinguish between character and habit, and treat virtue as their union. Character, however, on this account would be the way in which the extremes of excess and defect came together to constitute a relation between the possible good and the inchoate activity, while habit would be the way in which the possible good and inchoate activity came together to constitute a relation connecting the extremes of excess and defect. Character on this account would be axiological, and habit would be ontological or material.

The Protestant takes God and Man and has them together as Christ who serves to mediate the extremes of faith and practice, supernatural commitment and natural commitment. The Catholic unites faith and practice to constitute a Church which serves to mediate God and Man; the Church is Christ continued, whereas for the Protestant Christ is the mediator primarily.

January 7

If we think of the extremes in a moral situation as Excess and Defect, and Structure and Ongoing, then we have the juncture of the first two to constitute a vertical relation between the Structure and the Ongoing. The Excess and Defect (or adventure and restraint as such), without relevance to what is needed, do not constitute a mean, but rather a Structured Dynamic Relation which is analyzed out as Structure and Ongoing. Similarly Structure and Ongoing together, as merely conjoined, constitute a mean which is characterizable not as Structure and Ongoing together, but as that which synthesizes the virtues of adventure and restraint, of Excess and Defect, along a horizontal direction. The first juncture is Character, the second Moral Virtue.

Another illustration: Man and Woman as companions together constitute an Association whose nature is a mean between Persistent Structure and Vital Interplay; Persistent Structure and Vital Interplay when conjoined constitute a Species whose extremes are Man and Woman.

Question: How is it that the Extremes do not by their conjunction make some combination of themselves but rather a new Relation with a new set of extremes, each of which expresses in an unrestricted way an essential feature of the relation?

Money as interplaying with Giving constitutes Liberality. This new entity has the analytic elements and thus the extremes of Extravagance and Stinginess. Each of these combines Money and Giving but with an excess on one or the other—i.e., Extravagance has too much giving as it were for the money; Stinginess too much money for the giving, or perhaps better, not enough giving for the money. The Stinginess and Extravagance together constitute the character of being practically occupied with economic matters. This has as analytic elements, Money and Giving. Each of these contains both Stinginess and Extravagance in different ways, the Money having to do with the way in which there is a kind of distribution which now prevails and the Giving having to do with the kind of energy and control which must be employed.

The Excess and Defect are thus to be found conjoined in the relation of Character, which connects Structure and Movement; they are also to be found in each of these but in a disproportion. Structure and Movement in turn are to be found in the Moral Virtue whose extremes of Excess and Defect have within them Structure and Movement in disproportion. Men and Women, because they are the extremes for a Species, have within them the Stability and Movement of that Species but in disproportionate ways; because Stability and Movement are the extremes for an association, each has within it the element of Dominance and Passivity which are traditionally associated with men and women. The stability of the association exaggerates the Dominance, and the movement exaggerates the passivity; only the household has them together in a firm "character."

This would mean in connection with the *Modes* that the commingling of any two constitutes a togetherness whose extremes are to be understood as containing the original two in a disproportion. Thus if we use Actuality and Ideality as extremes which commingle to constitute a relation between God and Existence, then God and Existence must have Actuality and Ideality commingled but in disproportionate ways. Conversely, the commingling of God and Existence will constitute a relation between Actuality and Ideality. These extremes make a disproportion between the items making up the relation and thus are capable of being understood as containing God and Existence in disproportionate ways. This means that a pure mode is a disequilibrium of two subordinate modes over against another pure mode with an opposite disequilibrium of those subordinate modes. If we treat the pure modes this way we are in effect looking at them from the perspective of two other modes. From that perspective we get two modes to start with; these are pure. They are then thought to be commingled in various proportions, the mean being the relation between the other two modes. It is only when we begin to look at the original two pure modes from the perspective of the two modes (that are now understood in terms of them) that we see that the pure modes are in fact the outcome of the commingling of the other modes. Each pair thus is taken as pure and in itself, and is commingled to constitute a relation. That relation is treated as stretched in oppositional ways to the extremes, where one of the commingled pair is dominant and the other recessive. These extremes are then treated, as they can and ought to be, as pure modes in themselves to be commingled to constitute another relation which stretches in oppositional ways to the extremes where the original modes are in a dominant and recessive relation.

The Creative Imagination (transcendental) of Kant which combines Ego and the sensuous defines the Category as having an excess of the Ego or Transcendental Unity, and the Time as having an excess of the Sensuous; only the Creative Imagination has them in equilibrium. Similarly the schema which combines Category and Time defines its extremes of Transcendental Unity or Ego, and Manifold or Sensuous, as having an excess of Rationality or Transitoriness, whereas the schema has them in equilibrium.

Given Logic and the Realm of Becoming, their midpoint is defined as Inference. This must be constituted of elements to be found in each in excessive (or correlatively for a correlative, "defective") ways. Now Logic has an excess of formal, internal relations, and Becoming has an excess of material, external relations. The commingling of the Logic and Becoming constitutes Inference and this relates the formal and material in a balanced way. When the formal and material commingle in a stable reasonable habit they relate the Logic and Becoming properly.

But does it make sense to say that formal relations have an excess of

Logic and that Logic an excess of formal relations; that external relations have an excess of Becoming, and that Becoming has an excess of external relations? It would seem then as if Logic had an excess of Logic in it, and Becoming an excess of Becoming, which looks absurd.

But it is to be noted that the items which are commingled are not in the extremes; their properties are. It is not that liberality is money and giving together, but the relation of an attitude or action to a certain kind of item; the items yield up their properties, which properties are exaggerated in the extremes. Those extremes are not the properties, but possess them. When they commingle, the extremes do not unite those properties, but unite themselves as beings to constitute a new set of properties which the new extremes exaggerate.

What is wrong in much of the above is terminology rather than analysis. This becomes evident when we recognize that it is not a commingling of vices that constitutes Character, but that the commingling of the vices permits of the union of the Adventure and Restraint of the vices to constitute a Character, whose extremes exhibit the Restraint in the form of stable Structure, and Adventure in the guise of Movement. When Structure and Movement commingle they sustain a moral Virtue which exhibits Adventure and Restraint combined, and which its extremes unite in a disproportion. If Inference be the commingled result of Logic and Becoming, its extremes are Necessity and Punctuation or Discreteness. These extremes are commingled to produce a controlled Activity, and one part of that is manifest in Logic primarily and the other in Becoming primarily.

Modern logicians distinguish between " '*x*' implies '*y*' " and "if *x* then *y*." In the former case we have two propositions said to have a relation; in the other we have a relating between them. The former is external, the latter internal. When we build a machine to perform logically, we make use of the latter to build in the rules of the former type, and when we engage in detachment, the having of the conclusion, we but take out what was externally there—the "implies." The movement from "if then" to "therefore" involves a risk or leap, the movement from "implies" to "therefore" is but a substitution of externals for externals.

January 8

The previous discussions did not make clear the difference between a being commingling with another, and the nature of the features which the beings thereby constitute and which are carried by other beings, themselves capable of commingling and producing a new feature, which is carried in opposite ways by the original beings.

In connection with the schematism we have Ego, Sensuous, Category and Time. The commingling of Ego and Sensuous we said was the Creative Imagination. This has as its extremes the features of Universality and Ongoing which are primarily carried by the Category and Time respectively, and which it unites in equilibrium. The commingling of Category and Time is the Schematized-Category which has as its extremes A priority and Determinateness, which are in equilibrium inside the schema. We ought now to be able to commingle Ego and Category, Ego and Time, the Sensuous and Category, Sensuous and Time.

Ego and Category should commingle to give the Unity of Judgment; it should have a nature which is divided into opposing features carried by the Sensuous and Time. These in their turn should commingle to constitute The Nature of Experience whose nature is divided into opposing features carried by Ego and Category. Similarly, Ego and Time should commingle to give a feature carried in opposing ways by the Sensuous and the Category. Ego and Time constitute the Form of Intuition, and the Sensuous and the Category constitute the Unified Manifold. The feature of the Unity of Judgment is Identity in Difference emphasized in different ways by Time and the Sensuous, for the one is a universal matrix definitory of all, and the other endlessly fluid. The commingling of Time and the Sensuous in Experience exhibits the features of the Transcendent and the Unifying, which are stressed by the Ego and the Category. The Form of Intuition which is the product of Ego and Time has the feature of Diversity and Unity stressed respectively by Sensuous and Category; the Unified Manifold, which is the outcome of the Senuous and Category commingled, has as its feature Transcendent Unity and Ongoing which are carried primarily by Ego and Time respectively.

Extravagance and Stinginess are Vices which commingle to constitute a Character having the dual-feature of being in equilibrium with respect to a Concern for Money or for the Activity of Giving and Receiving. This Concern for Money is carried by Justice primarily, while the Activity is carried primarily by Man's Self-Interest. The Justice and the Self-Interest commingle to constitute the Mean in which Adventure is combined with Restraint. The Adventure is carried primarily by Extravagance and the Restraint is carried primarily by Stinginess. But now we must go on to combine Extravagance with the Concern for Money; Extravagance with the Activity of Giving-Receiving; Stinginess with the Concern for Money, and Stinginess with the Activity of Giving-Receiving. We always have three sets, inside of which we have a vertical and horizontal dimension. The schematism of Kant and the moral virtues of Aristotle recognized the horizontal dimension of only one set, and hinted at the vertical. In the preceding paragraph it was suggested how we are to recognize the other sets with their appropriate vertical dimension.

Extravagance and the Concern for Money is Gambling; Stinginess with Giving is Short-Sightedness; Extravagance with Giving is Phariseeism, and Concern for money with Stinginess is Economic Conservatism. Logic with Necessity is System; Necessity with Becoming is Causality; Becoming with Punctuation is the Discrete; Punctuation with Logic is Assertions.

January 11

A machine's "thinking" differs from a man's at least in the following respects: *1*] The man follows the rule of "if p then q," where p and q are organically related in an internal relation making a single unity of them, whereas the machine follows the rule " 'p implies q' " where we have an external connection between the two distinct propositions. *2*] The thinking of a man is the risky dissolution of the "if p then q," the making of these have an external relation one to the other; the machine's "thinking" is merely the subtraction of the "implies" from the items to which it had been externally added. *3*] The machine can report when its goal has not been reached or is being missed, but a man can report that it *ought* not to have been missed, that it is a good goal to attain. *4*] The machine can report its breakdowns, its failures, but a man can report that these failures are good or bad to have occur. *5*] A man can lie, deliberately affirm something and have a responsibility for it which he may or may not acknowledge; a machine does not acknowledge any responsibility and has none. We can hold it "accountable," i.e., destroy or modify it if it goes wrong, but we cannot blame it. *6*] A machine can repeat and repeat and thus carry out a universal in instances, whereas a man can know the universal and think it. *7*] A man can acknowledge an outcome and seek antecedent justifications for it, and then proceed to derive not the initial outcome but some prospect which the antecedent justifications open up, and which may be quite different from the outcome. His thought is thus creative. The machine can at best analyze the outcome and get to the established justifications, and then only move forward to where it had started or to some definite, prescribed place. *8*] The machine can operate; its programming, its plans are read into it; man programs himself and the machine.

January 12

Why are we sure that nothing can be red and brown all over, but can be both red and heavy? Is it not that A] each perception terminates in a singular case, excluding all other cases? If the perception involves the use of a single organ, we adumbrate a power which we are then and there acknowledging in a singular case but which must be manifest in other guises—e.g., when the light changes or a different relation exists between perceiver and perceived. But then how is it that the being can be known to be heavy at the same time? Firstly, there is the fact that it is known by means of a different organ. Secondly, there is the fact that the power which is grasped as being manifest as some color or other, is grasped as but a facet of a more fundamental kind of power. We must adumbratively lay hold of the object as having a power which is divided into colorality, shapeness, etc. If we did not have such adumbration of a fundamental power—(is this what Locke meant by substance?) —we could not know that the being was not exhausted as sheer color, and could not know that the being as having this color in this context is the very being as having that color in another context.

If our fundamental set of beings is Ideal and Actual; God and Existence, then the associated features are Structure and Activity; Unity and Divisiveness. When the Actual mingles with the Ideal their structure and activity together constitute a COSMOS, a cosmic unifying energizing, from which one can derive an idea of unity and divisiveness by stressing either the stability or the dynamics of that cosmos. God and Existence can also mingle; the Unity and Divisiveness which they possess combines to constitute a REALM OF IMPORTANCE, a directed normatively determined domain from which one can derive the idea of Structure and Activity by stressing either the rule or the use of a rule.

The Actual can mingle with God to constitute a Realm of Nature having the jointly determined nature of Structure and Activity, which can be separated out to be the features of the Ideal and Existence. The Ideal can mingle with Existence to constitute a DOMAIN OF RELIGION having the features of Intelligibility and Divisiveness which relate Actuality and God as extremes, the one carrying the Divisiveness and the other the Intelligibility.

The Actual can mingle with Existence to constitute a Judgment having the jointly determined nature of Activity and Divisiveness which can be separated out as the features of a related God and the Ideal. The

Ideal can mingle with God to constitute an ENVIRONMENT whose nature is the juncture of Unity and Intelligibility, whose separation gives us the features carried by Existence and Actuality.

Cosmos and Importance, Nature and Religion, Judgment and Environment are midpoints less real than the four modes of being. The pairs, if brought together, would define a togetherness.

Perhaps it would be desirable to distinguish between the midpoint as constituted by the beings, as a mere commingling, and the midpoint functioning as a relation having its components as extremes. Thus the Actual mingling with God is a mystical unity which becomes a domain of nature only as relational. If so we should have

> Excellence or Value as a point and Cosmos as relation
> Creativity   "   Importance   "
>
> Mystical Unity   "   Nature   "
> Historic Present   "   Religion   "
>
> Present Being   "   A Judgment   "
> Perfection   "   Environment   "

If our basic features are Formal Category and Activity, Unity and Divisiveness, we get schematism in place of Importance, and Creative Imagination in place of Cosmos. But if so, there must be a point of Creativity in the schematism, at its centre, and a moment of value at the centre of the Creative Imagination. But also there would have to be something answering to Nature and Religion with their points, and to Judgment and Environment and their points.

January 13

We must distinguish: 1] the forces and beings which are at work in mingling,   2] what is constituted by the mingling as at a point,   3] the relational role of the product,   4] the nature of the extremes which the relation connects and which are separations of it, as carried by the forces,   5] the three sets of minglings, and thus relations and extremes, depending on which forces are mingled with which, 6] the places where this kind of analysis will apply.

1] The forces are Intelligibility (or form, stability); Unity, (or subject, self-centredness, excess); Divisiveness (or field, defect); and Finitude (or object, transience). For the moment I will use Stability, Unity, Divisiveness and Finitude.

2] Stability and Unity make Purpose; Stability and Finitude make Value; Stability and Divisiveness make Power; Unity and Finitude make Mystical Juncture; Unity and Divisiveness make Creative moment; Divisiveness and finitude make Present.

3] The above as relations are: striving, judgment, love, purposiveness, virtue, reason.

4] These relate Divisiveness and finitude; Divisiveness and unity; Finite and unity; Stability and divisiveness; Stability and finitude; Stability and unity.

5] Striving and Purposiveness make one pair, Judgment and Virtue another, and Love and Reason a third.

6] Applied to the Kantian situation we have to interpret Intelligibility as category, Unity as the Transcendental Unity of Apperception, Divisiveness as the Sensuous, and Finitude as Transience. Category and Unity mingle to yield the empirical self; category and transcience give becoming; category and sensuous give the perceptible; unity and transcience give time; unity and sensuous give manifold; sensuous and transience give experience. The relations are Synthesis, Schematism, Nature, Anticipations, Creative Imagination and Cognition. Synthesis and Cognition make one pair; Schematism and Creative Imagination another; Nature and Anticipation a third.

In the case of Aristotle's ethics we get Form, Self-Centredness, Divisiveness and Transience. Midpoints are Self, Becoming, Perceptible; Time?; Being? and Experience. Relations are: (between sensuous and transience, etc.) Actions?, Moral Virtue; Production?; Living Body?; Character; Mind. This means that the pairs would be Action and Mind; Moral Virtue and Character; Production and Living Body.

These terms need redefinition. Also the above discussion must be related to the *Modes of Being.* They can be so related perhaps through a hierarchical idea of the powers.

We have the following hierarchies all beginning with Actuality:

> Actuality, Ideality, God and Existence
> Actuality, Ideality, Existence and God
> Actuality, Existence, God and Ideality
> Actuality, Existence, Ideality and God
> Actuality, God, Ideality and Existence
> Actuality, God, Existence and Ideality

If we go from Actuality to Ideality we transfer finitude; if we go from Actuality to Existence we transfer striving; if we go from Actuality to God we transfer status. Under each transfer there are two possible cases —e.g., the transfer of finitude can now go to God and then to Existence or from Existence and then to God. The difference is that the finitude in the first case is subjectified, made inward to God and thus given a place in his economy, and this is transferred to Existence as a finitude which has been purged, harmonized with others. But when finitude goes first to Existence it is made part of a world of contemporary finitudes and this means that it goes to God as one of a number of items, already inter-related. Given the transfer though we have in effect the mingling of features, treated as the result of the interplay of hierarchies. Thus when Category and Transience, or Form and Transience are treated as powers we have in effect the hierarchy, which begins with Ideality, mixing with the hierarchy which begins with Actuality. The midpoints are perhaps defined by the way in which God and Existence are thereby brought together. It is for that reason that the outcome of the mingling is that which can spread as a relation, whose features are distinguishable and are carried by God and Existence.

The hierarchical idea would require us to say to Kant that we can have a subsumption which begins with the transcendental unity of perception and goes through sensuosity or transience, and can end with any one of them. It means too that one can envisage the subsumption as beginning with a category and ending with transcendental unity (as well as with the others of course); or that we can even begin with mere sensuosity and subsume the others; or that we can begin with transience and subsume the others. Does not the *Critique of Pure Reason* start with the transcendental Unity, the *Critique of Practical Reason* with the Form or Category, and the *Critique of Judgment* with the Sensuous? Ought not an examination of purposiveness begin with transience as is done in the second part of *Critique of Judgment?* (We ought to get combinations of the various Critiques.)

The hierarchical idea will make us say to Aristotle that we can take our start with Form or Self-Centredness or Transience or Divisiveness. Once again the hierarchies ought to prove to be converses of one another. A study beginning with the categories or definitions must be supplemented by one dealing with potentialities; this yields a combination of self-centredness and divisiveness which constitute the moral virtue having each of these elements as unsatisfactory extremes. But definitions should be supplemented also by studies which begin with the Active Reason or self-centredness, and with divisiveness or Perception, etc.

Perhaps now these various historic references should be dropped and a more systematic procedure followed by beginning with hierarchies, getting the mingled outcome, then expressing the relations (vertical and horizontal) with the nature of the extremes. Using 1 for Category or Form, 2 for Unity of Self-Centredness, 3 for Divisiveness or Sensuousness and 4 for Transience, we get the following hierarchies:

3214 1234 1243 1342 1324 1432 1423 2134 2143 2314 2413 3124
4123 4321 3421 2431 4231 2341 3241 4312 3412 4132 3142 4213
The first says, e.g., that a hierarchy starting with Divisiveness and answered by one starting with Transience constitutes a midpoint which can be expressed relationally so as to have Unity and Form as extremes. It is to be noted that each beginning has six cases, so that there are six hierarchies beginning with any one. But each of these six has its own particular match, so that there are only twelve cases to consider. But each of the twelve defines a horizontal or a vertical and must be supplemented by the other;

> Thus 3214 has its match in 1342 or 1432
> "   4123   "   2431 " 2341

Each hierarchy has its proper match to make a midpoint, and this midpoint has its proper correlate in another hierarchy with its match. Thus to start with Actuality and end with God is to be met by one which begins with God and ends with Actuality (or Finitude and Unity, if one likes). This combination occurs together with one which begins with Ideality and ends with Existence, and conversely. Let us then once again (despite our previous remark about not making historical references) look at the Category mingling with Transience which is the combination 1 4; 4 1; this has matching it the pair 2 3; 3 2. This is the combination Kant deals with in the Creative Imagination and Schematism. Instead of having many other cases we have only two more to consider: where you begin with Category and end with Unity or Sensuousness, for this is matched by and belongs together with attempts to take a start with the Sensuous or Unity or Transcendence. In brief, we can, if we like, start with the transcental Unity of Apperception, recognize that this may terminate in a Category, in the Sensuous or in Transience, and that when it does, there is a reciprocal movement going just the opposite way, and that the two ways constitute a genuine midpoint and one type of relation, horizontal or vertical, which must be matched by a vertical or horizontal. If we have Creative Imagination and Schematism, then we have only two more combinations. One of these should have been explored in the Practical Reason and the other in the Judgment.

January 15

We ought to distinguish:
1]   The four modes.
2]   The features they primarily possess: Structure, Transience, Unity, Divisiveness.

3]   The hierarchy of the modes. Each mode can be the first in a series of four. The later terms in the hierarchy are to be viewed as explications of the first, ways in which a selection and articulation is provided for the inchoate totality of the first. Each mode begins three hierarchies, if no regard is paid to the order of the middle terms: 1−2, 1−3, 1−4, etc.

4]   Two hierarchies can overlap to constitute a paired set of modes. Thus 1−2 is overlapped by 2−1, 1−3 by 3−1, etc.

5]   Any pair set of modes has a correlate pair. Thus the pair 1−2; 2−1 has as correlate 3−4; 4−3, and 1−3; 3−1 has as correlate 2−4; 4−2, etc. Let's call them double-pairs.

6]   A midpoint of a pair is constituted of the two modes which are common to a paired set. 1−2; 2−1 have in common 3, 4.

7]   The common modes yield a juncture of features, a new meaning expressive of the overlapping of the common items with one another. This is most readily seen when we treat the midpoints of a pair as in oppositional orders. Thus a paired set of modes should be expressed as 1 3 4 2, and 2 3 4 1 (the second set begins where the first ends). It is because 4 overlaps 3 and 3 overlaps 4 that we get a synthesis of the two modes and a unity of their features.

8]   The separation out of these features yields a relational status between the other items in the double pair. Thus the juncture of 3 and 4 in the above example permits of the isolation of the features associated with 3 and 4 and the attribution of these to 3 and 4 viewed as beginning and end. A midpoint determined by one member of a double-pair is thus the centre of a relation which terminates in the other member of a double pair.

9]   There can be only three sets of double-pairs, for 1−2, 1−3, 1−4 are matched by the reciprocals 2−1, 3−1, 4−1, and the missing elements make up the other members of the respective double pairs.

10]   There is consequently not only the problem of schematism and its correlate creative imagination (both viewed as relations), but also the empirical self and striving, and the perceptual activity and time. There is not only moral virtue and character, but providence and maintenance, and purpose and love.

11]   If the items contributed by the centre of the pair, the sensuous and the ego, are such that they can in fact be carried by the category and transience, then we have the proper schematism of the two and the way in which they can be one. In other cases we find that the relation between category and transience is not composed of items which can be carried by the ego and the sensuous. Similarly we have a proper moral virtue when it carries at its centre the features contributed by stability and transience, but in equilibrium. We test it then by seeing what it, as a centre, is in the light of the contributions of the other member of a double pair, (in this case, character's two components of stability and transience). Similarly character is a relationalization of self and object's commonality.

January 16

The *Critique of Pure Reason* can be said to involve the combined use of the Creative Imagination and the Schematism. The former involves the relating of Category and an Ongoing or *Durée* in such a way as to yield the Schematized Category or Synthetic Unity of Experience. The latter involves a relating of the transcendental unity of apperception with the mere sensuous content in such a way as to yield Experience, Perception or Empirical Content.

The *Practical Reason* may be said to relate ego and category; such relating is a kind of autonomy of the self or Freedom. It also relates Ongoing or *Durée* and the Sensuous to give what Kant sometimes calls pleasure or Happiness.

The *Critique of Judgment* combines Category with the Sensuous in order to attain Beauty, and also the Ego with Ongoing to give Purposiveness.

Kant only occasionally sees these relations as starting at either end; a completed account would have, for example, dealt with the category as encompassing the sensuous directly, as well as having the sensuous somehow lifted up to the category, as it is in the *Judgment*. Kant hints at this in his account of the unity of the manifold, and in his various syntheses. Also Kant should have recognized that any one pair has a correlative pair, as he does recognize when he comes to the schematism and the creative imagination.

We can say two things of the Greeks: they are what they are and that is the end of it, and that they are not as good as they ought to be, as men. In the first sense we cannot say of a Greek that he should not have had slaves; to be a Greek is to do just what Greeks do, and this is what they have historically exhibited themselves to do. But if we remain with this we would have no criticism to make of anyone or any group, for each would be what it is and that would be the end of the matter. We can rightly say that there is an ideal Man which no Greek and no other individual or type has properly exhibited. So far we are with the Platonist and have a ground for an ethics. But the Platonist goes further and says that there is a similar ideal for sharks, another one for beds and so on, and that we can say there never has been an ideal shark, etc. But here I think the idealist is right; a shark is nothing other than what it is; sharks do what sharks do. We can not say of them that as sharks they ought not to eat flesh; we cannot say of them that they ought to be better fish than they are. What the majority of sharks do is what sharks ought to do; what does not do this is a poor specimen of a shark. If female spiders usually eat their mates, the one which does not is a defective spider; it is not better than the others. But if one man refuses to tell a lie when all others do, he is not wrong or defective but is better than they. A man is a being who is defined in terms of an Ideal he only partly exemplifies. Kinsey investigates them as though they were wasps and therefore concludes that what most do is what ought to be sanctioned by the law; but if he had looked at them as though they were not like wasps, whose majority action is normative, he would have been able to say that even though all men do a certain thing it is not necessarily neutral or good.

It could be said of course that the shark does not do as much good as ought to be done in a given situation, but this would be a criticism not of the shark but of the world for having a shark in it. The shark is not criticizable as a shark but only as a being. Therefore one can if one likes put before the shark and everything else the good of being and record that different beings fall short of this in many ways. But even if we do this we must add that man, in addition, has not only the good of Being but the good of man, a Good or Ideal Man before him, which he is to embody. Can one say perhaps that if and so far as he in fact does realize the good of Being he makes himself into the man he ought to be? But the shark in contrast will be one which, when it makes itself into the shark it ought to be, will not realize the good; conversely so far as it realizes the good it does not make itself the shark that ought to be. "Man" then has a normative as well as a descriptive import, whereas the "sharkness" has only a descriptive import from which one can extract or abstract a universal or generalization which can function as a norm.

An existentialist would like to have nothing but the immediate, but this he can acknowledge only mediately. He can have it immediately only by saying nothing. An idealist or rationalist would like nothing but the mediated but then he has lost the immediate fact of having it. We ought to have a mediated grasp of the immediate and an immediate grasp of the mediated. To have the rationalist view alone is to have only concepts, what we say and nothing about that of which we speak, just as the existentialists can have the being but not the speaking.

January 18

There are three associated but distinct problems in the relating of a geometric formula to an object. 1] There is the relation of the two domains, of algebra to extension, of the conceptual to the factual. 2] There is the relation of this particular formula to this particular object as its truth. 3] There is the relation of this erroneous or inapplicable mathematics to a given situation. Perhaps we ought to add a fourth, as relating to the connection between an erroneous or inapplicable particular concept to an object. We can connect them all together perhaps as follows:

When and as we acknowledge a domain of mere structure we acknowledge just so far a counterbalancing domain of mere exterior objectivity, which is inward to itself. When we have a particular formula what we do is imbed it in the domain of mere structures, while we imbed its supposed objective counterpart in the domain of exterior objectivity. Should we have an inapplicable set of concepts we can either imbed them in the realm of structure (when we will have to treat the objects to which they were to apply as not completely objective, as somehow not capable of being fully imbedded exteriorly) or we can imbed the objects we acknowledge in that exterior domain (in which case we will have to treat the concepts as not entirely pure structures). An analogous decision must be made in connection with any particular erroneous or inapplicable concept; either it or its supposed object, acknowledged independently, will prove recalcitrant to a complete imbedding. Normally we think we know what the genuine objective world is, and therefore dismiss this or that concept or system of concepts. But if we go back to the origin of the objectivity, we find it a function of our own effort to keep together our egos with our experience of duration. We then constitute an Imagination, whose meaning involves the thrusting apart of subjectivity and objectivity with the consequent subjugation of concepts and objects. The Imagination has the subjective and objective balanced, and keeps them so even while it distinguishes them, and has them carry the concepts and objects with them. The Imagination, as it were, defines concepts and objects as subjugated to subjectivity and objectivity.

Question: what is the status of the concepts and objects apart from this act of being subjugated? They must intermix to produce an Encounter, which itself thrusts apart the features of fixity and transience which infect and subjugate the ego and duration. We fluctuate, as it were, between the position where we are encountering and where we are creatively imagining. When engaged in the latter we make use of a distinct ego and a distinct duration; when engaged in the former we make use of a distinct set of concepts and a distinct domain of objective reality. Having produced a creative imaginative act in which we succeed in getting a midpoint between concept and object at the same time that we force them into opposition, we are aware of the ponderable nature of the midpoint, and this leads us to attend to the ego and duration. But as soon as we attend to them we make use of concept and object, and constitute an encounter.

Better: We never start with a pure case of imagination or encounter, and as a consequence always have ego and duration, concept and object partly used and partly being referred to. So far as they are used they are concrete in fact but stand out for us in an abstract guise, as not yet embodied; so far as they are referred to they are dealt with as not yet in themselves but as nevertheless forced into the stage where they are completely reified. We are in short constantly epistemologizing the ontological realities of which we make use, and are constantly ontologizing the epistemological data we confront. This is possible because we are men whose minds are not yet functioning in their purity; we exist as it were in the area of the emotions, which not only fluctuate constantly, but which are at once epistemic and ontologic in nature. An emotion, as it were, has a horizontal dimension where it is epistemic with respect to concept and object, and is ontologic in that it is rooted in the juncture of the hierarchies which begin with and require the being of ego and duration. It also has a vertical dimension where it is epistemic with respect to ego and duration, and ontologic in making use of the being of concept and object. As the former it is essentially the stuff of an encounter, as the latter, it is the stuff of creativity.

We can go on to say that the relation of man and woman has its midpoint, and its ontological and epistemological facets. Mankind relates man and woman as "epistemic" data to be imbedded in a nature; the household is the midpoint which man and woman diversely fractionate. It is constituted of a form and a matter which have an ontological role. The species is constituted of man and woman and faces as its data the form and the matter which it must root ontologically, the one in mind, the other in a domain of becoming.

January 19

Apparently the problem of the positivist is not merely the characterizing of various expressions as nonsense and confusion because they do not fit inside his scheme, but the difficulty of providing a means for eliminating only certain expressions, such as the presumably non-sensical or confused expressions of metaphysics, esthetics and religion. Or more generally, since what is being sought is a kind of test, he presupposes some material to be tested; should the material prove recalcitrant he has no way, given just that test, of knowing whether the test or the material is inadequate. This is known as the problem of verifiability or the empirical criterion of meaning. The answer evidently must lie outside both the test and the material; the ascertainment of a proper test of the empirically legitimate must presuppose not only the material or propositions to be tested, but that single reality which is diversely exhibited in the test and the material.

Could we say that the test and the tested diversely fractionate a single Reasonableness, and that this is a product of the overlapping of two hierarchies, one beginning with Necessity and the other with Ongoing? Then only those items would be accepted as meaningful which meet the requirement of being part of the Reasonableness. Here the test might be taken as fixed and the tested items allowed to vary. The Reasonableness would have to be somewhat steady, a matter which could be determined by (*a*) seeing if each of the related items, test and tested, lacked the virtues of the other and (*b*) by in fact making a juncture of Necessity and Ongoing, forcing them together to constitute the very pattern of inquiry. It is then the nature of inquiry as constituted of the double demand, to have necessity and applicability, which defines the Reasonableness that justifies the adoption of some items and not others as appropriate to a test. The test may accept them as they are or translate them; the inquiry defines the Reasonableness, which is that very inquiry as having an epistemic function with respect to test and tested.

Using Hegel's "Master and Slave" as a guide, I once thought that man was in the role of master, but did not see that there was a dialectic which allowed the woman to be master of her master. Later I took another tack and supposed that men and women were analogues, each doing what the other does but in a different guise. But now I am moving to the idea that woman is really in the dominant role, and that the master-slave situation applies, but almost in the opposite way from that in which I once thought when I took the dialectic seriously. The fact that man must go to woman, the medieval idealization and devotion, the very need to use force in order to assert one's mastery, the need for a mother, the fact that man finds himself outside himself in his work, the happy marriages of the mild with the virago, the satisfaction men achieve when a woman goes to them and assumes the role of the devoted wife and "slave," all seem to point to the fact that the woman does occupy a primary dominant role which a man is attempting to overcome. This perhaps accounts for woman's lack of confidence, her lack of need to work or create. How does prostitution fit in here? And the devotion and submission of the girl to the father? Is prostitution some form of revenge, some expression of contempt which the defeated superior might take on the inferior, as a captured king might toady and act abject. Is the devotion of the girl to the father but a recognition that he, by virtue of his strength and outside activity, has already achieved what she is to receive without effort, so that she can profit from him rather than from her mother?

If the above is right the happy marriage is one where a woman is forward, active, without losing the sympathy and gentleness that the man needs; and where the man is receptive, permissive, and willing to express his sympathetic feelings. If she is afraid to love and he ashamed, normally, she must risk her superiority and he must be ready to overcome his inferiority in the encounter.

It is possible to tie up the man-woman situation with the matter of reconciling two facets. Although it be the case that in any problem of test and testing either side can be fixed, it is usual to view only the test as fixed. Aristotle does this when he views man as the dominant factor; if we reverse his stress and take woman to be so, we but use here as a test her self-completeness as an organism and as a source of the future to be; we take this to be the superior of two not yet altogether complete realities. The two together will be fractionations of a species; they will constitute a household or association. In both cases they are correlatives. To say it another way, though one might say man is stronger, has the initiative (and even if one wants with Aristotle, is the more rational) or though one might say that woman was more self-sufficient, the dominant being who ought to give more than receive, these virtues need not be and in fact ought not to be thought of as in order of superior and inferior. We can insist that one is dominant with peculiar and enviable virtues without supposing that the other has not virtues of equal merit. To be a leader or to be the more powerful or the more rational is not necessarily then to be superior or inferior in worth. Still, it is important that the proper virtues be assigned to each; if it be correct that women are really the dominant and the self-sufficient, and that it is a myth fostered by men and allowed to flourish by women, that men are the dominant factors governing all, and that what is thereby governed is inferior, it is desirable to urge women to give more than they do, and men to be in a state of wanting to receive more than they have—not merely in the conventional dimension of being cared for, but in the more basic sense of needing something real without which there is an undesirable dominance of woman by virtue of the fact that she has not met with the man to constitute a new unity which has the two of them excellently matched in the shape of the species itself or an association.

January 21

Let the four basic pivotal points be: Normative, Data, System and Objectivity. They make the following combinations:

1] Normative and Data
2] System and Objectivity
3] Normative and System
4] Data and Objectivity
5] Normative and Objectivity
6] Data and System

1 and 2 make a set; 3 and 4 another; 5 and 6 a third.

The adjustment of the Normative and its data is essentially a problem of a *pragmatic alignment* in time. It is the answer which we can find in root in Kant's schematism, Aristotle's moral virtue, the Regulative Principles and the Hegelian dialectic. The adjustment of the System and Objectivity is one of *Organization.* It is the answer which we can find in the Creative Imagination of Kant, and the Association of Aristotle. The adjustment of the Normative and System, is essentially what is done in all formalization, in model languages. Let us call it *Idealization.* The adjustment of Data and Objectivity is the discrimination of the real from the unreal, the recognition of something other than oneself as constituting what is outside one and yet open to experience. It might be called *Objectification* or Experience. The adjustment of the Normative and Objectivity is the creation of the relevant concepts, the definition of a world, such as is given in the Aristotelian categories. It may be termed *Naturalization,* or Organization of Knowledge or Experience. And finally we have the adjustment of Data and System or *Codification,* the bringing together of the raw material inside a frame of structures to make an intelligible whole out of what is in fact encountered.

There are two "anthropomorphisms"; a humanism which has special valuational categories for man, with lower grades for other beings, thereby ennobling man perhaps unduly, and there is a cosmologizing which applies human categories or categories applicable to man to all other things, recognizing that those other things might exemplify those categories in minor or variant ways. I have been inclined towards the second of these; but the first would be required if a Platonism were demanded of an ethics which might never in fact be fulfilled by man, and yet whatever did occur in the world of subhumans had to be accepted without criticism.

The view that we must accept some things as they are, that there are no residual elements to their possibilities, presupposes that there are hard data. But if we take a Platonism seriously and carry it all the way down to everything—an alternative to "anthropomorphism" just as a radical reductionism is—we would have to say that there is nothing which is to be taken as though it just exhaustively was when and as it occurred, but that it fell short of some norm. We ought not then to say as I have said elsewhere that the Greeks in one sense are just what they are, no more, no less no other, that it is wrong to ask of them that they do not have slaves or that they have had one less or more war, etc. To take such a view is to do as relativists do; it is to carry out the reductionist program all the way so as to encompass man within categories which are recognized to be normally applicable to the subhuman since these usually are thought not to fall short of a norm—(in particular, categories which exhaust themselves in the actual cases). It is to suppose that the nature of the Greeks is self-enclosed, all determinate, a hard datum. If we refuse to say this of the Greeks and of any individual, and on similar grounds *of any* animal *or even of natural things,* we can recover a Platonism which would in effect say that the Greeks who could not be other than they are are the correlates of the norms which they did not fulfill, and which will be fulfilled by God who will make up their defects. In a sense this will permit of an avoidance of a strict Platonism. It requires the realization of all possibilities, though not necessarily in this world, whereas Plato made them self-realized, treated them as perfect already and therefore made a mystery of their need to be realized by anything.

Returning to the supposed matters of fact (which on the humanistic thesis would not have to require any reference to an unfulfilled norm, whereas the ethical man does have such a norm), we will on this modified Platonic view have to treat them as outcomes, as resultants, and not as data given. The Greek who could not have done otherwise than he had done, or the Greeks who had to have slaves, etc., would be seen to be not genuine realities, but instead parts of a larger whole. In short, we can continue to say that such and such happened, but the point is that we would have to add that the happening has a moral weight to it which disqualifies it from being treated as a mere naked matter of fact. We must then not say of a Greek or of anything at all in the universe that it is just this and nothing more or less or other, but only that A] it is just this and B] that its being this is part of a larger frame in which there is an ought-to-be. This ought-to-be makes the "this" be only a part of a whole being. At no point ought one to be able to isolate the "this" and say of it that it is to be treated as final.

We seem here to be on the verge of losing the fixity of past time, but only if we separate out the past time as that which has to have the two factors—the determinate "this" and the qualified feature of value. But the past could be said to be relative to some other time or to eternity, and thus to be able on the one hand to contain within itself the produced "this" and yet to be tied up with something larger and other than itself. In short, though each item in the past might be said to be fixed, to be a genuine "this," the entire past would not be a "this"; it would in fact be related to a value given in the present (if we have temporal relativity) or outside all time (if we have some kind of cosmic value). The fixity of the past would then be a product of the separation of the value from the indeterminate reality which constituted the real present valuational object. The past would of course have a value, but it would have just the value that it in fact incorporates, the "judgment" of its significance being exterior to it; in this respect it would contrast with the present where the valuational element helps constitute it as a single being.

If it be the case that any present actual entity needs Existence in order to be present (which it loses in the course becoming past), and if it be the case, as the above would indicate, that it also needs value (and loses this in becoming past), it would seem to be the case that a somewhat similar state of affairs should hold with respect to God. There ought to be a kind of relation to God in the present which is lost when the item becomes past; this should be the element of interiority, of being capable of being a genuine other, of providing a source for energy and activity, of having a genuine private unity; the past would be the phenomenalizing of this substantial being, and with it the presenting of the actual entity as an extensional spread for God, in contrast with what it was in the present— a dynamic opponent.

Similar things ought also be said about the other three modes; each ought to swim inside the areas provided by the others, and ought to lose something of this exteriorly provided environment (which in fact helps make it a partly indeterminate reality). This loss enables it to come fully self-enclosed but also, though determinate, less real and complete than it otherwise would. There ought to be an analogue of the past with respect to each of the other modes.

Coming to an individual man, it is not entirely correct then to say of Plato that he could not have written another syllable given the fact that he spent his time thus and so when he was not writing what he in fact did write, for that Plato is an abstraction. The Plato that lived, though referred to as that abstraction which is just what it is, was a Plato who always had a reference to something he might have done, and there was in him then a potentiality related to a normative possibility. When we refer to Plato as in the past, we isolate the determinate being which is just what it is, but the isolation occurs within a context where his potentiality is used by the judger or what came later, and in fact relates to a possibility not yet fulfilled. We must say the same thing even of an animal or a plant. We can judge these platonistically by recognizing that each one and each species has a part of itself in a normative state which it does not altogether fulfill. This fulfillment would, as is the case with man the ethical but guilty being, be finally assured by God, who would add to what the animals or plants did, what they ought to have done. The point is that we think we know when men fall short of the good they ought to do, and something of the supplement that God must provide, whereas in the case of the subhuman we think we do not know anything but what they have already exhibited themselves to be, and that if there were an addition which God had to provide we do not know what form this would take. But in fact we do not know just what the Ideal looks like from the perspective of God, and do not know just what He does with the Good which men have not entirely realized. That He fulfills what men do not is true, but whether this fulfillment is nothing other than making good the ethical failures of men, or whether what men call ethical failures are in fact successes in His eyes, we do not know. So in a way we are in relation to man, perhaps in principle, as ignorant as we are in relation to other beings.

January 22

If it be the case that every mode has the others as norms of a sort, which it does not necessarily realize, and which therefore must be realized by the remaining other modes, in what sense does a given mode exist by itself? It would seem as if a mode by itself were an abstraction from a more concrete whole for which the other modes are relevant norms. This would mean that the "non-essential" features of a mode which it obtains by virtue of the presence of the others are features which not merely define the mode as being part of a universe, but actually define it in its most complete guise. It is in short the Actuality as involved with the Ideal which is the more concrete Actuality; the Actuality as by itself, as that which acts or stands apart, or which has a nature to itself and of itself would be a kind of derivative from the Actuality as involved with the Ideal. Now this involvement, if it be a kind of togetherness, would seem to make togetherness more real than the particular modes which are together—contrary to what I tried to show in the *Modes of Being*. But is it not rather a way of "relativizing" the other modes? To be a relevant norm it is necessary for the Ideal, say, to enter into the province of the Actual, to be tainted by the Actual even though it is a norm which the Actual does not fulfill. What would be concrete would be the Actual as inseparable from the Ideal which it has relativized. The full Actuality as it were is that which has succeeded in being in relation to the Ideal; the Actuality in itself then would be possessed of a kind of surplus which answered to the norm and which was evaluated by it, thereby making it possible to say of the Actual that it was not all it ought to be. This surplus might be used in some other way, in which case we have as it were a sin of commission, or it might not be used at all, when we have a sin of omission.

The above seems quite muddled. The issue is one of determining in what sense a mode of being is fully determinate and fixed and in what sense it is not, how it can be more complete and real as the latter, and how this more completeness, since it does involve some reference or use of other modes, can avoid falling into the difficulty of making a "togetherness" more real than the items which are together.

January 23

If every item in the universe has a relevant possibility appropriate to it, and if the possibility has a normative aspect such that it need not ever be realized by that item, then the possibility will either not be realized at all or it will be so realized by something. If not realized at all, this will be because it is already perfect, as Plato seems to hold, or because it makes sense to speak of a possibility which the universe precludes from being realized. But this latter alternative seems absurd. The realization of the possibility by another provides a kind of proof of that other, since the possibility then has features it got from that other.

If we carry this idea out, each mode of being will be seen to be related to a second as its norm, which in turn will be finally realized by the other two, and each of these other two will itself have a normative role with respect to the given mode. In short, each mode will be faced with three norms whose realization will be guaranteed by two others.

What does it mean for an entity to be faced with a norm? Does it not mean that the entity is incomplete if it be cut off from the norm? Does it not mean that the entity as related to the unfulfilled norm is defective, so that the difference between man and the sub-human would be that man is not only natively defective but morally defective also, because he does not add further energy to the realization of the norm? If so, we would not then be able to say that each thing is what it is and not more or less or other in the sense of being fully and exhaustively determinate. Each would have to be recognized to have a potentiality which could have been made determinate in the guise of a realization of the value prescribed by the norm. There would then be a three-ply potentiality in Actualities, Existence, Ideality and God, such that no one of them could be fully determinate except by achieving a status something like that possessed by a past object.

If an Actuality has a three-ply potentiality which requires but never fully achieves a determination in the guise of a realization of Ideality, Existence and God, we have the problem of what happens to the potentiality when the Actuality becomes past or when it ceases to be. In the case of the other modes and of Actuality as such, there is no question of their ceasing to be; they always are, and the potentiality of each always remains. Ceasing to be can occur only with respect to particular actualities and perhaps with subdivisions of the other modes. The subdivisions of the other modes could be said to have potentialities by virtue of the fact that they belong inside the mode; the potentiality and the consequent indeterminateness in the subdivisions is the continuity which the subdivision has with respect to the whole, without which it could not be. In the case of the Actuality we cannot say this without reducing the world of actualities to a monism, when it seems to be the case that each individual acts on its own, and has a potentiality in itself by virtue of its self-substantiality. Could it be that Actuality as such has a being at least sufficient to enable each of the actualities to have a potentiality by virtue of being held apart from it, and that they can make use of that potentiality just so far as they can maintain that holding apart, whereas in the case of other modes of being the potentialities of the parts are essentially relational, between the parts, and not as with Actuality, between whole and part?

But we also have the fact that each of the modes is itself potential, not with respect to its parts, but with respect to the other modes of being. If the analogue of Actuality holds, the potentiality of the parts of the other modes has to do with the realization of the parts of the remaining modes: thus a part of Existence, if it has a potentiality (as it must have on the foregoing account), has this potentiality by virtue of being a subdivision of Existence, but has it with respect to Actuality, etc., thus fragmenting the very norms which face the whole of Existence.

A part of a mode which does not realize its potentiality will have this potentiality made determinate by the evaluation by the norm which testifies to the part's defectiveness. But what is the source of the potentiality of the modes themselves, and what is the evaluative status of each of them at a given moment? Must not the potentiality of the modes be derivative from the common togetherness? If it is, does not this make the common togetherness more real than I have taken it to be? Or is it really the reverse, and the potentiality is the mark of the failure of a togetherness, that it is a togetherness which is paired rather than four-ply? If we could get a single togetherness in which all the potentialities were to overlap and complete one another or at least supplement one another, we would have a new entity which had swallowed up the four.

Each mode we must say has a potentiality related to the other three which, viewed prescriptively, enables one to characterize the given mode as being unfulfilled, as being defective, not as good as it might be, just to the extent that the mode remains outside the other three modes. A fulfillment of a norm is the using up of the potentiality in such a way as to exhibit the norm; the norm will continue to remain outside but will now also be inside the realizing being. So far as a potentiality is unfulfilled one can, from the vantage point of the norm, find it fulfilled in the sense that the moral inport of the norm is filled out as the evaluation of the unrealizing being. In short, a potentiality, whether fulfilled or not, encompasses the norm within it, realizes it then and there in a way which does not do full justice to the being of the norm in itself, but gives it an alien setting in the object either as a whole or in a distorted inadequate form.

Since the normative nature of a mode is one which is not yet fulfilled, it would seem that the mode not only has three potentialities for being realized, but three potentialities, in addition, for functioning as a norm with respect to this or that object. These three potentialities of a norm are always being fulfilled in the sense that their matching potentialities in the objects, to which the norm pertains, are fulfilled by embodying the norm or by being characterized as falling short. In the latter case the potentiality is fulfilled as having a residue serving to relate the partial realization to the norm which it should have embodied. The overlap of the residual part with the norm's own relational reference should constitute the kind of synthetic unity discussed earlier under the headings of Pragmatism, Naturalism, Organization, etc. All this is still quite muddled.

January 24

Each mode of being offers a kind of norm for the others. This means that for each mode there are three norms. These norms can be satisfied with more or less completeness. So far as they are not satisfied the modes are in a state of potentiality, indeterminacy. This state of indeterminacy must exist at the same time as the determinate state does. This is possible just so far as the determinate facet of a being is a part of the whole being and has an added determination reflecting the fact that the norm has not been made integral to the being. Thus Actuality falls short of the other three modes in different degrees. It is in relation to the Ideal more or less *excellent* (or defective), in relation to Existence more or less *adjusted* (or maladjusted), and in relation to God more or less *endorsed* (or abandoned). The Ideal in turn is more or less characterized as *appropriate* from the perspective of the Actual, *available* from that of Existence and *Rational* from that of God. God is evaluatable as more or less *concerned, perfect* and *effective* from the perspective of Actuality, Ideal and Existence. Existence is more or less *congenial* for Actuality, *unified* for God and *organized* for the Ideal.

The characterization of a being as more or less living up to a norm is one with the characterization of it as more or less integral with that norm, as acting in consonance with it. The being will have its own nature and mode of acting but the other will provide it with a context, give it a new import. The perfect realization of the norm will mean that the being's meaning is contained within, governed by the norm; the imperfect realization means that the being's meaning is related to the norm externally. The imperfect realization makes the being be undeveloped within, a locus of conflicts and inchoate activities, unrelated to other subdivisions of the mode as not supplemented by them, and independent of the norm in that it can vary the distance there is between it and the norm, sometimes opposing what the norm may require so as to constitute a kind of conflict with the norm.

A defective being then has a conflict within itself; its own nature does not encompass all its own parts adequately. It is also in conflict with any other being or mode in that its actions might frustrate and be frustrated by those others. It is a being in which there is a lack, a need, a diffusion or failure to have each component self-centred and yet harmonized with the rest. But if this is so, then each mode of being has its parts in some disarray or fails to have itself adequately dissected in parts, and thus is partly inchoate, not articulate, not, as Hegel would say, at once subject and substance, phenomenalized thoroughly. If so we must think of the different modes as not divided into parts properly or as not properly unified as wholes — perhaps the first is the better of the alternatives, except that it does sound as if Actuality preceded actual entities. To avoid this appearance we ought to say that the actualities which in fact make up Actuality are not altogether harmonized, and that until they were we could not speak of Actuality itself as being fulfilled. The harmonization of all particular Actualities will of course involve an adjustment of them to the other modes of being—more precisely, it will involve their achieving excellence, adjustment and divine approval together. The other modes of being too must be then understood as falling short of the stage where they are divided exhaustively into harmonized parts, an outcome which would require that they in fact live up to the norms represented by the other modes.

January 25

1]   Does not the incompleteness of an individual Actuality affect the mode of being, Actuality, defining it to be incomplete? Does not the incapacity of an individual Actuality to have its parts appropriately organized, affect the way the Actuality is related to others?

2]   When two modes of being, or two parts of them, forge a unity, do they function as two norms; as two tested cases; as neither?

3]   There must always be a nucleus of determinate reality in each mode enabling it to be something in itself, and to be fixated in the past or as a datum.

4]   Does not a being at every moment by virtue of its status as defective express the norm and therefore realize its potentiality with respect to that norm? Is it not a "defective realization," but still a realization?

5]   Is the defective being externally determinate and internally not, whereas the excellent being is determinate in both ways?

6]   What bearing does the view that all entities are norms for others have on the matter of hierarchies and the way in which they reciprocally overlap?

7]   Is the realization of a norm a mere internal change, leaving the norm outside, or does it not affect the norm, perfect it?

8]   What is the bearing of all this on the vertical and horizontal combinations, on an ontological juncture and an epistemic fractionization?

It would seem that an entity in realizing a norm reorganizes itself in such a way as to give itself a role governed by the meaning of that norm, and that the norm in turn achieves a role by virtue of the realizing being's new status. The latter point is harder to see than the former; how can a realization by x of the norm y make a difference to the norm y, complete it in any way? Does the realization reach to the norm and in a kind of Whiteheadean prehension make use of it, fill it out in a progressive movement back into itself, the norm all the while holding on to this determining being, or at least to the facet of itself which is being filled out? Or need we say only that each remains in itself while changing its mode of existing? If we say this we nevertheless have to account for the fact that when a norm is realized something other than it is acting, and it seems not to be in fact involved.

If we say the norm is involved in its realization, as I think we must, there would seem to be two involvements—A] that due to the self-organization of a being which makes it have a career partly dictated by another, and   B] that due to the self-organization of another being which involves the first as its form, as that which provides the first with a new meaning or career. It is *b* which is so difficult to grasp, for though on the one hand it would seem to be true that a norm gains by being realized, on the other hand this realization seems to be irrelevant to it. Or should we say that *b* is really the same thing as *a*, but merely viewed as occurring in another? We could then say there are two involvements— C] that due to the self-organization of a being as making itself have a new career, definable by another being, and   D] that due to the encroaching on the territory of the other, reorganizing itself, just as before, but where the other is. Or better still perhaps, when *x* realizes *y*, it does it by reorganizing itself; if this act could be recognized to involve a reorganization of *y* also, both *x* and *y* could be seen to benefit. But we would still have to recognize that *y* must reorganize itself in a new way at its own place, as it were, to accommodate *x's* meaning, and that *x* therefore too would have to be reorganized as being there. We then have two types of reorganization or satisfaction or alteration: E] that which involves an internal alteration in which a new career is established, and F] that which involves the being in the life of a reorganized entity. Perhaps *e* and *f* are no other than *a* and *b* above; I think not.

In what way does an entity achieve satisfaction or completeness by being made into the pattern for another? What is the relation of this satisfaction to the satisfaction achieved by making that other into its pattern? Is there here only a difference between passive and active modes? Is it the case that when *x* realizes *y*, this is the same thing as *y* realizing *x?* Apparently so. But then alternatives *e* and *f* are one; the self-organization of a being is identical with its being used as a pattern defining the career of another.

When matter is reorganized to realize a form this is the same thing as the form being reorganized to give a place for the matter; and this is the same thing as the matter giving the form a new career, and the form giving the matter a new career. When then a being realizes an end through its actions, this must be the same thing as the end reorganizing itself so that it can accommodate the being; efficient and final causality would be one, or to be more inclusive, all the types of causality would be one, if we reckon God and Existence to be formal and material causes. Each would be doing on its side what the others are doing. Does this deny the independence of the different modes and beings? The rhythms could be different in that one mode might be the dominant factor at one time and another mode at another time. Each realization would be a kind of compromise.

A defective object would be one which failed to articulate the norm, to give it a proper filling. The norm from its side would face the object as recalcitrant, but this need not preclude it from assessing it and thereby preventing it from making a union with itself. It would nucleate itself, give itself another border as it were, and by that act define the object as defective. A poor action on the part of an Actuality thus realizes the Ideal, but the Ideal nucleates itself as that which is to have the job done again. A poor realization by the Ideal of itself, the incapacity to encompass all the things that there are in a harmonious way, without distortion, forces the Actuality, which is nevertheless encompassed in just the inharmonious distorted way it is, to nucleate itself, to hold itself away and thus as needing to be dealt with once more. The Actuality thus functions as a norm for the Ideal which the Ideal should realize and whose failure forces the Actuality to withdraw itself.

Suppose we envisage man as facing ideals set by society, an existing environment, and a principle of unity. The actuality tries to live in the context of these, to realize these. This means that at the very same time these others are themselves realizing the actuality, using it as a context for themselves. The actuality's failure forces every one of these into the recesses of itself; their failure to do justice to the actuality forces it to make itself more self-enclosed. According to the *Modes* though it seems to be the case that the failure of one mode is made up by the other two, so that in the end no mode but is complete and excellent—and thus it would seem, since the perfection of Actuality requires the perfection of its parts—that everything is excellent. The answer would seem to be that it is the other modes which enable the nucleated mode to re-establish itself as a full mode, but not with respect to the given norm. If the Ideal is nucleated, unfulfilled by virtue of the failure of Actualities to realize it, it recovers its full being through the compensatory activities of the others. This must mean of course that taken the other way, there is a sense in which Actuality makes good the deficiencies which say God and Existence manifest with respect to the Ideal. Such making good is ontologically necessary and contrasts with the deliberate one of ethical activity. The full recovery of a mode, then, despite its self-nucleation is a kind of reassessing of it. What we find then is that each being, while triply nucleated with respect to the other modes, is nevertheless re-established as a full mode by the very fact that the others are; but this is quite different from the way it could be a full mode through a mastery of the proper being of the other modes.

A defective being faces nucleated modes which *inter se* are realized. It is one which has made use of the other modes, lives in their context but in such a way as to require that those other modes be fulfilled with respect to it, and that it in effect also be fulfilled through the presence of the others.

January 26

The realization of a norm by one being is at the same time the fulfilling of that being; the failure of a norm to be realized is at the same time a failure of the norm to be satisfied. There is a duality in satisfaction; the work of one is sustained either actively or passively by the other or is qualified and hindered by that other. In either case the outcome is a double one in which each permeates the other. The matter is informed, the form is enmattered. This is no pre-established harmony, for where one is passive it perhaps should have been active; its passivity in that case, though allowing for the form, does not actually satisfy it properly, since the form required oppositionality and permeation by the matter.

God and man are correlates just as are matter and form, Actuality and Ideality. That means that God's grace is inseparable from man's acceptance. This has often been said, but what has not been said is that the grace could be viewed as inefficacious precisely because it is effectively blocked by the recalcitrance of man. Or put the other way, man's acceptance of God can be met by God's recalcitrance, his self-enclosed nature, so that the failure lies just as much with God.

When a being realizes its norm inadequately the norm has application to it nevertheless, for the evaluation of the being as defective is the application of the norm, though not as actually permeated by the being or v / v.

The failure to realize a norm is to be attributed both to the being and to the norm, but perhaps for different reasons. Thus the being may be perverse or indolent or overinsistent; no matter what the norm might do, it will find that the being is more recalcitrant than otherwise. Its failure to be realized is to be attributed to itself in that it does not overcome the perversity, etc., but is also to be attributed to the other being which requires additional acts by the norm if the norm is to be properly exhibited.

If the norm does not need to be realized fully there is of course the difficulty that it is not a genuine possibility just so far, and also that it can be potential for what in fact does not allow its realization. But if the norm need not be realized at any given moment, what is the fixed datum, what is the object that is in the past, the being which no longer has potentiality? And what relation has this to the norm? In one sense the norm must pertain to it, so that it can be defective, but this pertaining must be adventitious, exterior, indeed in another locus, the future. What happens to the potentiality of the being? It too perhaps moves to constitute the continuation of being. Is then there a self-nucleating activity on the part of beings which do not realize their norms? Or rather are there not two nuclei created in every failure? Is it rather that the being as permeated by the norm and the norm as permeated by the being are fixated, with the qualification that the remainder of the being is fixated through the exterior imposition of the norm so as to characterize it as defective? So we can say of the past object that only as qualified by the external imposition of the norm is it such that it cannot be other than it in fact is. But if account is taken of a being as having the capacity to realize the norm more, *and this is when the being is in the present,* the characterization of the being as defective is not a fixed one, but one which then and there is being overcome to some extent or is being made worse.

Is this not portrayed in Kant's view that the categories and the manifold are essential to one another and that each completes the other? But carried out this would seem to require the supposition that by themselves they are not so much abstractions as inchoate, and that the outcome is a struggle between both sides. Also if there be four modes then each has a triple struggle; since each mode's lack is eventually made good by combinations of the others, the exteriority of the norm to the defective means that the norm must be realized, made ingredient, serve to complete and be completed by other types of being. Were there such a thing as a perfectly defective entity, without any part of the norm in it, as a Platonic receptacle might be, it would be the case A] that the norm would be realized altogether in other modes, and B] the defective would be the locus of realizations of a different type of norm, such as that provided by other modes. A] Suppose now there were only three modes, and one was like a Platonic receptacle; it would follow then that the norm would be fully realized in the remaining mode, which is perhaps what Augustine thought in connection with the Platonic Ideals. B] What was deficient from the standpoint of the norm, and in this case, the receptable or the nothing, would attain a status with respect not to the ideas in God's mind but with respect to God Himself. The defective being would give a locus for Him. The locus it gives Him would be the reciprocal of the satisfaction which it gets from Him. This should be equal to what the Ideal ought to have given it, and therefore equal to what the ideas in Him require. Also the ideas in Him are satisfied by Him to the very degree that the receptacle fails to satisfy them, and his nonmonistic status with respect to the receptacle requires a satisfaction by the ideas. If we add a fourth mode the matter becomes more complicated in fact, but not in principle.

Potentiality then would not be the result of a being withdrawing from others but would be the result of the surplus which indeterminacy provides; each being in itself would be indeterminate but dynamic, but the indeterminacy would be directed towards the determinate boundary defined by the other; it would be the indeterminacy of latency or immediacy or self-containedness rather than completeness. This would be an acceptable conclusion to all with reference perhaps to the Ideal and even to Actuality or Existence; but tradition has denied it of God; it has claimed that God is all explicit, complete, etc. But this confounds the outcome of God's self-knowledge with his being apart from this, as Hegel saw.

The incomplete mastery of its particular subdivision of the norm on the part of an individual actuality has its repercussions on the domain of Actuality. Realization in that domain is the permeation of the individual actuality by the norm. And if there be three modes, the individual actuality should also have fractionated portions of God and Existence as relevant to it, whose failure to be realized in it requires a failure also of the whole of Actuality to be adequately satisfied by God or Existence.

January 27

Let the four parts of the quadrant be:

Unity or System
Ego   World
Ongoing

The system and ongoing together constitute Inquiry. The ego and the world constitute the Body. The inquiry is fractionated into a subject and object, which divide the unitary virtue of inquiry into a subjective and objective component. The body is fractionated into habit and activity which divide the unitary virtue of the body into a fixed and a changing facet.

The subject imposed on the ego is Mind; the object imposed on the world is Experience; habit on system is Rule or Law, and Activity on the ongoing is Creativity. These impositions are due to the fact that the fractionizations of inquiry and body must be sustained by real beings.

Unity and ongoing are each recalcitrant; they do not satisfy one another completely. Inquiry, which is the permeation of the one by the other, never fully has them; each has a modicum of unsatisfied demand. This satisfaction is provided by the Ego and World. Similarly the recalcitrance of Ego and World prevents the Body from being an ego-permeated world (or what is the same thing, a world-infected ego). What the system fails to get from the Ongoing and thus in Inquiry it gets from the Ego and World together. Ditto for the Ongoing. This means that the Ego and the World must each provide a minimum of that kind of juncture which Inquiry offers; there is an Ego-drive and a World-law guaranteeing the eventual satisfaction of System and Ongoing. *Inquiry, Ego-drive* and *World-law* then together satisfy System and Ongoing.

Similarly, what the Ego and World fail to get from one another in the guise of body is provided for by System and by Ongoing. System and Ongoing provide an inescapable minimum satisfaction of Ego and World, analogous to that which is offered by the Body. System as satisfying Ego and World is a natural language or logic or science; Ongoing as satisfying Ego and World is Productivity. *Body, Science* and *Productivity* then together satisfy Ego and World.

(Combinations of System and World in contrast with Ego and Ongoing, and of System and Ego in contrast with Ongoing and World, must also be recognized as having analogous implications to the above — defining a juncture which does not altogether satisfy and which must be supplemented by two analogues in the items which do not define that juncture.)

The coming together of the drive for unity or System and sheer Ongoing to constitute Inquiry is the producing of what seems to be in one sense more real than the ontological items out of which it is composed, and in another less real. It is more real in that it is the outcome of the mutual permeation of each by each, and thus exhibits them as completed by one another; it is less real in that it is a product not of them but of their properties to constitute a unity having its expression in an opposition of subject and object. Inquiry is not a new entity, but either one of the two — System and Ongoing — now completed. The juncture is no new entity over against them, but each of them enriched, looked at either from this side or that, but in fact not entirely enriched and thus leaving over a fraction to be satisfied by other beings.

When we come to know anything we make a creative unity of an attempt to have System and a process of Ongoing. This is a completing of ourselves—our System being permeated by our Ongoing or v / v. If our knowledge is accurate, what we fractionate from Inquiry is in fact sustained by the Ego and World, when and as these supplement one another to constitute a human body. The body, ontologically viewed, is just Ego as permeated by World or World as permeated by Ego; epistemically it divides into habit and activity sustained by (one hopes), System and Ongoing. If the hope is not realized then the body is not rightly divided and thus does not maintain its balance between counteracting forces, but is instead a distorted version of either habit or activity.

My idea of something and the object to which it is supposed to pertain constitute my experiencing body. They also serve to carry the components of Inquiry. Only so far as they do carry these components as correlatives, as counterparts, can we say that they belong to one Inquiry. Inquiry is superior to those components, but it is not superior to what carries those components, to wit the idea and the object, so far as the judgment is true. My experiencing body is the source of two components less real than it, but the body is not more real than the power of unification or systematization and the Ongoing which must carry those components. Inquiry then is carried in a sense by the pairing of the Ego and the World, and in a sense by the permeating of System with Ongoing; the body is carried by the pairing of System and Ongoing and by the permeating of Ego and World. The first of these senses, the pairing, is not a genuine carrying of Inquiry and Body except indirectly, for it carries their components when these are separated. Inquiry and Body are in fact constituted in the permeating, but need, in order to function, the fractionating of their natures and the carrying of these fractions—without loss to themselves' (i.e., Inquiry and Body) as ontologically real—by Ego and World, and System and Ongoing, respectively.

Logic and Inference seem related as System and Ongoing, whereas Science and Nature are as Ego and World. If so, by permeating logic and inference with one another one constitutes Inquiry whose components are to be carried in correlative ways by Science and Nature; Science and Nature in turn permeate one another to constitute real physical entities whose components are to be carried in correlative ways by logic and inference.

A genuine set of basic realities must then A] permeate one another, B] to constitute a quality which neither had before, C] which is able to function only as fractionated into correlative features, D] which must be sustained by another set of basic realities, E] which in turn constitute another quality, F] which functions when fractionated into correlative features, G] to be sustained by the original set.

If one has an empirical language and wants to know what can belong in it, he must in the end turn to Inquiry as containing the components of subjectivity and objectivity and which are carried in a parallel way by an Ego and a World. What the Inquiry claims is subjective must be what the Ego adopts, and what the Inquiry claims is objective must be carried by the World. If it maintains that to be subjective (say value) which is in fact objective, or if it maintains that to be objective (say an illusion) which is in fact subjective, it will distort the meaning of the Ego and the World, for they in fact will not be carrying these supposed items. Nor will it provide a proper permeation of System and Ongoing either, being as it were a distorted quality produced by the two of them.

January 28

There are two kinds of imperfection, somewhat related: *1*] the imperfection of incompletion, of failing to be permeated by the correlate, and *2*] the imperfection of attribution, the ascription to something of what it does not in fact support. The first can be known by attending to the nature of what it is that needs completion, and discovering that it is inchoate, latent, or that it lacks the virtue of its correlate. The second can be known by a failure of a prediction, the incapacity to draw proper conclusions from the attributed feature. Since attributed features are the outcome of the fractionation (without a dissolution) of the feature which a being possesses, the discovery of the failure of a prediction is tantamount to the discovery of the failure to complete a pair of beings or dimensions—and conversely.

If we start with the view that there is an ego and an object, and that they complete one another, through the activity of interest, to constitute a perceived object (or through the activity of influence to constitute a sensing body,) the two together having the quality of being an Experience, we can go on to observe that this Experience divides into a Structure and an Ongoing. The Structure and the Ongoing are attributed to an Abstract Future and an Activity respectively. These carry the attributed features *just so far* as the Experience, and thus the Perceived Object or the Sensing Body, is complete. (Of course they never fully are.) The Future and the Activity themselves infect one another to constitute an Expectative Item. This Item precipitates out as a Subject and a Phenomenon which are attributed to Ego and Object. The awareness of the discrepancy between Subject and Ego makes one aware of the inadequacy of the expectative Item and thus of the incompleteness of the Future or the Activity, and also of the discrepancy of the Phenomenon with its Object. One's self-awareness is one with the awareness of this discrepancy. The movement of inference is the use of the idea as a principle of inference in the sense that while one fractionates it for oneself one attributes the other fraction to an object beyond.

Suppose we translate this into a body which has a unity of its own (answering to the Ego above), an object of appetite (cf. future), an environmental activity (cf. activity), and an object of interest (cf. exterior object). The body acts to unite its object of appetite with its activity and thereby produces an object of expectation; the body as a unity completes and is completed by the object of appetite to constitute an experience which divides into the object of desire and the act of becoming which are attributed to the object of appetite and environmental activity. These in turn infect one another to constitute an expectative idea which is to be attributed to the unity and the object of interest when divided into a private subject and a phenomenon.

This is not yet right. What is wanted is an explanation of the origin of mind from the being and activity of the body, such that one can see the mind as a power for inferring, without our making unnecessary assumptions to explain it.

Another attempt: When the individual acts to unite the objective of his appetite with himself as acting in an environment, filling out the one with the other, he produces a meaning. This meaning is, as it were, what he means; it does not belong on one side or the other, but expresses him as these two together, as what his action and his presence mean. If there is a stress on the object of appetite we get an expectation, if on the activity we get a perception. This meaning has as its quality an idea or structure or status; it functions only so far as it serves to relate in oppositional ways the two factors which constitute it—unity and content of interest. These are attributed beyond them. Only because the individual can accept the unity of meaning can he have the content of interest directed outside him. His self-awareness of the acceptability of the unity of meaning is one with his acknowledgment of the status of the content of interest with respect to a world beyond it.

This is not satisfactory, for what was wanted was not the recognition that the meaning attributed to the object is unlike that which one has attributed to oneself, but that the meaning attributed to the object has one import for oneself and one for the object. But perhaps this is what is being said? The meaning which I acknowledge as pertaining to myself is the meaning which I recognize to have a different import in the object; I attribute it to myself in order to distinguish the meaning it has for the object. The meaning as reflecting an environmental activity endows the object of interest with an adumbrative component.

January 29

Let a man be viewed as interplaying with some object. If the man also has a common focus with that object in the shape of something which it possesses and he desires, or both desire, or both are converging on, etc., the problem arises of completing the interplaying with the focus by permeating the one with the other. This is done by the two of them wanting to attain a state of self-maintenance. The outcome is that they constitute a Common Datum. Now man has the ability to ascribe this Datum as belonging in whole or part to himself and to ascribe it (in another way) as belonging in whole, or in (a different) part to the object. If and so far as he does this he is self-aware, for he feels the discrepancy between himself and what he has ascribed to himself, at the same time that he is aware that what he ascribes to the other is possessed in some way, affirmatively or negatively by that other. The awareness of this possession by the other is what is meant by having a mind, by knowing the content. (There should be a reverse stress where we start with the man and the object as coming together by virtue of the force exerted by the need to be in some kind of equilibrium.)

In what sense is the completed entity which is the product of the permeation of one item by another identical with a Togetherness? The Togetherness which is a function of both and expresses the fact that they are two is a potentiality which they share; in the completion of each this is what is realized.

When we come to irreducible modes of being which complete one another there must still be a connection between them; the realization of the Togetherness which defines their apartness, as it were, is but the having of them intermeshed, each supplementing the others, and from its own standpoint possessing them. This Togetherness is irreducible and is no potentiality. The togetherness of inadequate entities, of parts which are incomplete and need permeation to constitute what is more real than either has two facets—one which is potentiality for the permeation, and the other of which expresses their inescapable recalcitrance.

We have parts which are irreducible just as surely as we have the modes; there is no perfection attainable, for each part as well as each mode is recalcitrant. So far as it is recalcitrant it is irreducible and it together with other irreducibles make up a Togetherness by a minimum prescriptive intermingling. The modes and the parts can interpenetrate and constitute a commonality. This commonality is their descriptive togetherness carried to its limit. If there could be a perfect completed being the togetherness would vanish; if there cannot we can distinguish a minimal togetherness, the " , " which is prescriptive, and the variable " . " which can approach the state where the items complete one another by permeation or supplement one another by being in rhythm.

Perhaps the pair we must work with is a Future common focus, and a Dynamic Interplay. Teleologically spoken the Future gets filled with the Interplay; efficiently spoken the Interplay gets filled with the Future. In either cases they constitute the common present datum. (Whitehead's Creativity is the supposed power which is outside the Future and the Interplay and serves to unify them; I am supposing here that we do not need it, but can find the capacity to complete in each of the items as related to the other.)

The Future common focus and Dynamic Interplay themselves do not act; the common datum which is shared by individual and object is the product of neither, except so far as they taint the pure causes, as they do in having a common Focus and a common Interplay. The common Focus and Interplay are but the surface of something more dynamic, whose action synthesizes features from Future and Interplay to give a common datum, which is forthwith divided into (in the case of man) a possible self-awareness with an awareness.

When man acts to complete himself with respect to an object and thereby constitutes a Situation, this Situation is tainted by the stresses of the Future and the Interplay so as to constitute A] an item with a career, and B] an item in transition. The Situation carries the Experience made by these two items. The Experience now must be distributed in two ways, structural and progressive. These are dynamic forces of which the Future common focus and Dynamic Interplay are tainted aspects. As a consequence when we have an Experience (by completing ourselves with objects, and conversely), we find this has a forward *thrustiveness* or progression which we use to characterize the *continuation* of our juncture with object, and a *structure* defining the limit of its *variability*. (The analogue of the Common Datum is the schematism and the moral virtue; the analogue of Experience is subsumption in Kant and character in Aristotle. Moral virtue one could say is constituted by the rational and dynamic aspects of man; character could be said to be constituted by the self-centred and outward stresses; the features of moral virtue are vices when attributed to the self-centred and outward; the features of character are instability and habituation when carried by the dynamic and rational aspects respectively.) Experience then must be characterized as at the centre of two phases which it keeps in equilibrium; it has a structure which is essentially future, or rather carried by the future as exterior to it and as dictating the limit of what it is to do, and a progression which characterizes and is carried by a kind of continuation, a dynamic interplay in time.

The Common Datum is a product, a nature which is in fact the quality possessed by a more or less completed Futurity or (what is the same thing) more or less completed dynamic progressiveness, or continuation in time. Similarly Experience is a nature which is in fact the quality possessed by a more or less completed individual (or what is the same thing) a more or less completed object. What is hard to see is how the Future or the Continuation operate.

Man and object constitute a *situation* characterized by *experience* which is divided into features attributed to future and interplay.

Future and interplay constitute an *event* characterized by a *common datum* which is divided into features attributed to man and object.

A] the attribution of features to man and object are due to man; what does this for future and interplay?

B] man and object complete one another through action; what works and how in connection with future and interplay?

C] must one consider the pairs man-future (object-interplay) and man-interplay (object-future) too?

A] Only when man is self-aware does he distribute the features; animals merely share them with their objects. Just so the attribution of features to Future and Interplay is a sharing in diverse ways of the character of Experience. If they really are receptive to those features we have a genuine Experience; otherwise a distorted one. This account presupposes some real being to Future and Interplay.

B] Man and object do not always, and never completely, permeate one another. When they do not penetrate we have a thin experience. Just so the Future and Interplay remain exterior to one another; they apparently do not succeed in completing one another, permeating one another, except in the tainted form of an expectative common Focus and a Dynamic Interplay. These seem to act; their completion is expressed in a Common Datum, which is a kind of feature possessed by either as completed. But the source of the Datum lies outside either in that which in fact can sustain the Datum, to wit, the Future and the Interplay, so far as they are one.

The Event is extensive while the Datum is more or less congealed, just as the Situation is extensive whereas the Experience seems congealed —where Event is constituted of and expresses the completion of Future and Interplay, and Situation is constituted of and expresses the completion of man and object. But if the Datum is superficially more unified through the tainting by man and object, why should we not say that the

Experience is superficially more unified, functions as though it were in the present almost entirely, because tainted by the Future and the Ongoing? But this is not necessary, the man and the object are able to make the union directly, and not in a tainted form, just as it is man and not the object that makes the ascription of the features of the Datum to both parts.

c] Yes, we ought to consider the other pairs. Man and Future would seem to constitute a common purpose, and the balancing pair, Object-Interplay, a physical entity expressive of the wider cosmos, a kind of Cartesian entity. Object-Future would seem to constitute a law-abiding entity, whereas Man-Interplay would seem to define him as a natural being.

In summary: Man and object more or less complete one another to constitute a Situation. This Situation has the character of Experience. That Experience unravels perpetually into a kind of systematic Form and a kind of sheer Ongoing. These two components are in this unravelling attributed to a world that lies ahead and to the Interplay of the man and object. The attribution is not deliberate nor is it accepted; it just precipitates out into these two components; the precipitation would result in its dissolution if the Future were not organically united with the Ongoing (without making an adequate unity with it).

The Future and the Ongoing have no power to constitute a unified reality of them both. But they are somewhat affiliated and affect one another to constitute an Event. The man and the object taint each of them, qualify each of them by their concerns, to make the one into a focused Future and the other into an area of Interplay, and these two, more or less by virtue of the stresses by man and object, constitute a Datum between them. This Datum a man is able to ascribe in whole or in part to himself, at the same time that he attributes something of it to the object. In that act he becomes self-aware, since he knows himself as more or less acceptive of the ascribed Datum, and becomes aware of the object as more than a Datum, since he is aware of what he has left over and thus what must be ascribed and belong to the object. This self-awareness which occurs with an awareness is perception and the use of a mind.

January 30

1] Man and object more or less complete one another to constitute a *Situation* whose fundamental feature is what we normally term *Experience,* when this is viewed as being just as much object as man.

Experience has two limits, a kind of systematic structure and a sheer ongoing, which seem never capable of being held apart. (Earlier I took it for granted that there were real beings which held them apart, but this violates the insight of the *Modes* which tells us in an analysis to remain within the frame of one, two or three modes, and that no one can really hold all four on a level. Also to know how knowledge arises we need not invoke anything more than the activity of man and object.) The hope of man is that Experience can make a unity, that it does complete him and thus the object, and that it will do this without undue change in rhythm.

2] Man and object face a *common future* at which they converge. This I said (in order to give it exteriority), was sustained by something more real—an Ideal. But the fact is that the man and object face no such Ideal, but at best only a qualified version of it, the Ideal as tainted by themselves. Man and object also interplay in a common dynamic *Area*. This too has objectivity apart from them and is to be ascribed to Existence. But they do not face Existence directly; they face it only as qualified by themselves. Now earlier I thought that it took the efforts of the Ideal and Existence, seeking to complete themselves, to bring even these qualified features of themselves together. So far as the Ideal and Existence come together they constitute an Event, but this is not what man and object have between them. They together constitute a common *datum*. Had the Ideal and Existence come together for them, the common Datum would be a feature of the Event; now it just decorates it in part.

The coming together to constitute a decorative common datum is primarily the work of man. It is he, using the object as a pivot, who brings together the qualified common future and the area to constitute a Datum. This Datum, just as the Datum which a unified event would produce, has limits in the guise of a privately enjoyed sensuosity and a publicly located or possessed nature. This distribution is carried, so far as man and object are in consonance, by man and object. But whether properly carried or not, when we have perception man attributes the limits to each side. If he does both at the same time we have a self-awareness accompanying an awareness of the ascribed feature of an object as something germane to that object.

It is possible to take the neglected pair, Ideal and Existence and deal with them as primary, with man and object having only a secondary role. This occurs when we try to deal with nature as law-abiding, in a cosmic physics. What we then have is the Ideal and Existence coming together to perfect one another, thereby constituting *law-abiding occurrences.*

The limits of such occurrences are felt experiences or *qualities* and external experiences or *matters* in an *external relation.* These limits cannot be held apart, really ascribed to something outside them. The Ideal and Existence can be said to converge on an "appearance" of both the man and the object, i.e., on qualified versions of them, versions of them which are the product of the tainting of each by the Ideal and Existence. The Ideal and Existence act to unite these two appearances to yield a *Situational* character. I am not clear whether or not Existence ascribes the situational character in part to itself and in part to the Ideal, analogously to the way man divides the common Datum.

3] Kant's view is to be obtained by substituting Category for Man, and Time for object, with a corresponding "passive" pair to yield transcendental ego and thing-in-itself. The category and time are effective with respect to one another to yield a *Schema.* The extremes of this schema are the *I* and the *sensuous manifold.* These never exist by themselves in their purity; they should be carried by something more real, but in fact are the sheer products of the Schema which fulgurates constantly, with them as limits. Also, the Category and Time face qualified versions of Ego and Thing-in-itself; they work on the *empirical Ego,* and the *x* of experience. The Category and Time unite them (Kant would say the creative imagination works on them) to bring about a realm of Experience. This realm of Experience has two limits, one merely private and the other real. The Category (Kant would say Criticism) forces all into the private side when it is idealistic, into the public side when it is realistic, and holds it between them when it is regulative.

4] There ought to be a similar set of considerations derivable from Kant if we work, as he sometimes does, with Ego and Thing-in-itself as the operative powers. We will then have to say that they are united "by a mysterious power of the soul" so as to complete themselves. So far as they succeed they constitute *Syntheses of the Manifold.* (Kant does not say this is a completion of Ego by the Thing-in-itself.) The extremes of these syntheses are *Thesis* and *Antithesis;* these never exist by themselves but are the products of the synthesis, their limits as it were.

5] Aristotle's moral virtue as the product of a real pair, Reason and Animality, is like 3, his character as a product of Soul and Body is like 4.

February 6

For Plato the norm is excellent. More important it demands excellence on the part of whatever there be. If it fails to be realized the fault lies in the recalcitrance of the world. But then the Hegelian question comes up; the Good must have a power appropriate to its majesty. This would mean that the failure of the Good is in the end not a failure at all, but rather a way of characterizing the Good. Only if one insists that the Good continues to remain with a residuum, and insists upon itself and will do this as it were even after time is done, can one avoid the view that what the Good in the end manifests itself as, is what it in fact is and means. This conclusion is avoided in a way by Kant who thought of God as providing the supplementary needed power to make the Good effective; he admitted as it were the Platonic demand and found a way to have it satisfied. This is the answer in principle which I have in the *Modes,* except that I do not hook it on subsequently and adventitiously as Kant does in his postulates.

The pragmatist takes a somewhat different view. He says that the Good is whatever it manifests itself to be; in short, if over the course of time the Good fails to conquer whatever else there be then this is what the Good is, an ineffective power whose meaning is to be found in a relation between itself and the world, and not solely in itself.

Each mode is insistent and demanding forever; on the other hand no prescription made by any is unsatisfied. The satisfaction is a satisfaction which is derived in places which do not answer to ethics but to ontology; each prescription is ontologically satisfied by all three remaining modes together, but each prescription makes an "ethical" unsatisfied demand on each of the other modes. But can we not reduce the ethical demand to a satisfied one, make it the very structure of time and then in the end say that whatever it has paid itself off as relationally is all there is to its meaning?

A distinction should be made perhaps between the kind of standards which can be satisfied ontologically, those which are insistent on themselves all the way, and those which can be satisfied momentarily. The first is one which allows for the mere relational filling with a consequent criticism of the standard's worth because of its impotence; the second is Platonic, and the third is relativistic. The first makes the demand of the ought equal to its effectiveness; the second detaches the two; the third takes the momentary effectiveness to be enough.

It could be said that the pragmatic and Hegelian and Platonic answers demand a satisfaction only in the area where the norm is imposed; the Kantian and I hold that the satisfaction can be fed into it from other sides when it fails on its initial side. The pragmatist succeeds in getting a satisfaction by belittling the claim in its abstract nature; the Hegelian thinks that the claim has an appropriate power, and the Platonist thinks it has all the power.

If we start with a norm which has being then we must take the answer which says that it must finally get a perfect satisfaction, for in the end nothing can be left over. The answer must be Kantian or Platonic or as in the *Modes*. But if we start with a norm which has no other being but that of requiring exemplification, we can take the other answers.

The problem is one of determining whether every prescription whatsoever has a residuum that no activity or agency, in the realm where it is supposed to be exhibited, could ever overcome. If so, this residuum will provide a burden for the other modes which they will successfully carry off. Each mode of being fails with respect to the other three in three distinct ways, which are the ways it is primarily supposed to act. But since what it fails to do if and so far as it is not performed by a second must be done by a third, each is also faced with three inescapable burdens which it successfully carries.

What man fails to do with respect to his work required of him by God is done by the structured church and the living tradition together — or parcelling out the work, what the structured church does not do to make good man's failure, must be done by the living tradition, and conversely.

That there is a residuum to the Ideal is evidenced by its necessary exteriority. This is shown by its recalcitrance. But might not the exteriority be but that of a time not yet covered? And might it not only so far be recalcitrant? We must find an inescapable exteriority and recalcitrance. This must lie in the fact that it has essential but not intrinsic features — such as its generic being? its very prescriptiveness? its very nature? its degree of determinateness? its determinateness as disqualifying something else? The last, perhaps.

February 7

A genuine prescription should be external to that to which it applies. This means that it has a residuum over and above itself as fulfillable by that to which it applies. But then the One for a Many cannot be prescriptive, at least with respect to the four modes, for then there would have to be a fifth mode which carries the residuum, holds the prescription apart from the world where it is to be exemplified. The One for the Many should be a kind of condition. But then the reconciliations discussed at the end of the chapter on God must be thought of as not involving prescriptions, unless there is also an indication there that there are beings beyond those involved in the antitheses.

Ought implies *can* because there is no obligation to do the impossible; *can* implies *will* because a possibility which the facts exclude is not a real possibility; *will* implies *must* because a genuine anticipatory claim must be fulfilled. *Ought* then implies *must*. But this seems to contradict the idea that what ought to be may not be.

The ought may not be fulfilled with respect to that to which it makes a primary demand; what it leaves over must be fulfilled and this is its secondary demand. Ethically a man may fail to do the good, but he does automatically make good the defects, the failures, which the other modes in their primary relation exhibit.

February 8

If we take account of nature of beings, we seem to be driven to acknowledge something like a Platonic position with respect to norms and ideals; if we take account of the nature of becoming we seem instead to be able to forego such a position for one similar to that given in connection with the One and the Many, i.e., for one where the prescriptive principle is but the other side of a descriptive fact of togetherness, so that the only problem is that of keeping the two sides in a steady relation. This last is the position I take and must take with respect to the reconciliation of inquiries such as ethics and religion, mathematics and physics; it is also the position that must be taken in connection with the modes of being for the prescription regarding the modes does not pertain to their being but only to their "being together," to the manner in which they can come together, become with one another in a common domain.

Standards for each of the modes are in one sense not possible and in another necessary. They are not possible if we recognize the four modes to exhaust reality; each is the mode it is, and there is no alternative. On the other hand each of the other modes may be said to impose prescriptions on a given mode. Viewed this way the modes have natures which fall short of a kind of Platonic standard. It is only when they are placed on a par that the prescription is the structure of a becoming having a *de facto* side. This (no less than the prescription) is a function of the items which, through their action, determine how the distance between the structure and the *de facto* side is to be filled in. By virtue of what is the separation of the two sides produced? This is like asking why there is becoming. Or it is asking about the way the modes connected in these two ways are different. It is because the different modes deal with one another in asymmetrical ways that they can achieve a symmetrical union, be genuinely together.

Remaining only with the pair, *AB,* we have their togetherness in a prescriptive and *de facto* way, and we have a demand imposed on them by *C* and *D,* which they (*A* and *B*) partly fulfill by constituting *E,* the juncture of the demands of *C* and *D.*

February 18

A possibility, which is to be written as "*x*-or-*non-x,*" hasn't the *x* and the *non-x* as distinct. The distinguishing of them depends upon something outside them; there can then be no genuine reference to an *x* or to a *non-x,* except in an anticipatory way, by mentally doing to the possible what the world will do in fact; when this is done there is a contingent production of the *x* or of the *non-x* in advance. But apart from this, i.e., whether this occurs or not, there is the contingent occurrence of *x* when and as it in fact is made to be. *x* strictly speaking is not "possible"; of if one likes it is possible only so far as it is joined with its correlate and merged into a single possibility. The single possibility in turn is always realized, for the realization of the contingent is the realization of the possible. Contingency then entails possibility. We could write "if *p* is contingent then *p* is possible" but this would be misleading since it would lead us to suppose that *p* by itself is the possible; what we should say is "if *p* is contingent then there is a *Q* which is possible and whose realization can be *p.*"

The *Modes of Being* explicates the essential features of the modes, and explains the secondary ones.

Every ideal has a normative residuum, so that while it is true in a sense that every possibility or ideal is realized to become an ingredient possibility, it is also realized in the sense that it provides for the coming to be of its successor, and is also realized over the stretch of time. It has a side which is not realized in this world at all, marking the fact that it is prescriptive and exterior to that world, and thus depends not only for substantialization on something else, but requires that something else to guarantee that it will be realized. If it were not realized, the possible would be that which was excluded by something and to that extent not possible. If it is forever excluded it is forever that which cannot be.

February 22

Mere existence as self-divisive must be made into a single entity; this is a kind of "." status which all its parts achieve. Over against this is a "," functioning as its prescriptive essence and is made of all its parts as together, in an attenuated and neutral way.

It is only when we are able to show that the "," of the essence or of the convergent unity must be exterior to the very beings which constitute it that we are driven to acknowledge some further mode of being. This we do in connection with Existence, finding that its essence needs support and use by God; and we do it too in connection with Actualities, finding that their prospective unity needs to be imposed in an obligating way. But in the *Modes of Being* we find that the prescriptive " , " but points up their disequilibrium as merely *de facto* together and forces them to re-relate themselves again and again, without any better status being achieved in any new re-relating, since the " , " has no ethical worth and no genuine exteriority, since it is their own self-determined lure.

March 27

To assert, "This is a cup" is to assert a truth, not for me, or from this angle or at this time, but for all men and for all time. The claim is extravagant and in the end uncheckable. However there are tests for it. We look to the virtue of man to tell us whether it can be true or not; we suppose that truth is the expression of his virtue and that without this virtue the truth would not be exhibited. The virtue is four-fold, answering to God, Existence, Actuality and Ideality. It is manifest as Sympathy or submission to the facts, as Training or discipline or preparation or habit, as Intelligence or character or self-control, and as Purpose, value, or system.

The common sense truth which I utter is capable of being uttered by me and without a feeling of extravagance, for it merely presupposes that I have virtue to the same degree that others have.

When we come to the abstract disciplines, of philosophy, art, religion and science we must be purer. Philosophy stresses the purity of the virtue of intelligence, art that of training, religion that of sympathy and science that of value or system. To find that one is in error regarding something in one of these disciplines is to find that he has failed to be as perfect there as he ought; to offer the discipline is to tacitly claim to have the virtue. There is then a boldness to the philosopher or creative artist or religious man or scientist about some characteristic of himself as a man.

The philosopher is an Actuality; he approaches the others in a four-fold way. When he comes to know he still takes up the standpoint of Actuality but frees himself from the particularity of his reference to the others; he gets to a neutral position in which there is a four-fold Many, but one in which no one of the Manys and no one of the components (which is the same thing) is stressed over others. But it still is only one of four ways of being neutral.

March 29

The commingling of individuals to constitute a single public domain results in what is inchoate, without genuine being of its own. The single public domain, which can be anything from an association to a state, is most successful if it dissipates itself in the perpetual production of correlative items—a steady structure imitative of the divine, and a constant creativity of energy imitative of Existence. The meaning of the commingled result is to be found in these two items in tension, and so far as it produces these, loses itself as these, it attains a career of its own. (On the other hand, God and Existence also commingle to constitute a cosmic history whose being is chaotic and without boundary.)

When an individual is sacrificed for the rest he is in a way honored, given the privilege of being identified with that which is dissipated as steady structure and creative energy; it is he who constitutes these. To be a hero is to be taken out of the common run and given this peculiar status where one's being is dissipated in the production of something new. It is in this sense one being is equal to the totality. This being can be a unity of a number of individuals, or a source of a plurality of things to do or produce in the structure and creative process. If we, on the other hand, had sacrificed a number for one, that one would have to be worthy of the intensive structure and creativity which the sacrifice produces in eternity and Existence. (I am assuming that the sacrifice of one for many is a production of what that many deserves.)

When a man is murdered he is destroyed, but is given no opportunity to be this for the sake of the rest. Instead the murderer is one who has assumed the role of the state, and thus is one who is to be recognized as real and a full man, only so far as he himself is engaged in the production of a steady public eternity and a dynamic, creative public existence.

Revolution is somewhat similar to the murderer and must be made good by its production of men of dignity and rights; reactionary activity, or better blind insistence on the law, is also somewhat similar. But if we distinguish these two ways of being similar to a murderer, we should also distinguish two types of murder—one in which there is a destruction of the individual actual being who is supposed to commingle, and the other is the destruction of the ideal which the individual is supposed to embody. There is in short the murder of the individual and the shocking of the community's sense of propriety. The more murders the more the murderer approaches the status of a thing, for this is what cannot fractionate itself as eternity and creativity.

The individual as a mere entity or thing should be given up for the many; the individual should be sacrificed for the many if he is most qualified to define the structure and the creativity, i.e., establish a tradition and renew the people through his death. That is why one must honor the heroes and commemorate the holidays. A many then can be sacrificed for the one if the one is thereby enabled to be the very source of eternity and creativity. This is the attitude taken by the soldiers who die for king or country.

In summary: individuals must be viewed as actualities versus an ideal, or as Actuality in relation to some Ideal. In either case they commingle to give the source of a steady structure and a creativity. Conversely, God and Existence commingle to give the source of dignified individuals and a proper goal for them. The two sources must be kept in balance; if they are we have a kind of historically worked out ethical world of men with dignity in which there is a public regard for eternity and for the process of creativity. To remain at the commingled level is to have the inchoate, the thing-like, and what is there produced exists at its best by being the source of a tensional harmonized pair of polarities. To produce the commingling and its tensional extremes, entities must lose something of themselves; they recover it only so far as there is another mode of commingling by other entities. In the ideal case we have men in harmony in relation to an appropriate Ideal under the aegis of a steady structure of law and a genuine dynamism of creativity.

March 30

Men can be said to be directed towards some single objective, or to be directed towards one another as representing some such objective. In either case they interplay to constitute some dynamic field, or association, whose limiting case is a society. This society has its being in an inchoate form, as that which is not yet, just so far as it has no other nature or status or role than that which is then and there being constituted by the interplay. But it is possible for it to constitute a source of two opposed tendencies, of a steady structure and a process of creativity. When some individual usurps the position of the constituted interplay, e.g., when he defies the purposed end through a shocking violation of its ideals, or the reality of some member by murder—he makes himself one who is inchoate, having the guise of a thing or of an absolute standard (since these are the powers which he must represent if he is to destroy with justification the correlative end or men) and can become a being only so far as he divides himself into the extremes of a genuine steady structure and a genuine power of creativity, i.e., only if he revitalizes and makes significant and real the law-abidingness of the community and its source of vital and creative energy. So far as he fails he offers himself as a thing or a standard and thus as that which can be utilized or rejected or confronted but not something to be enjoyed or shared in as a man among men.

Reciprocally there is a coming together of the unity of the world or civilization and the diversification of sheer ongoing. This togetherness constitutes a mere empty locus, a schema of space-time, a mere definition of a type. Restricted to the case of man it defines a mold or frame "man," the species. This gets to have body only so far as it is expressed in a radically diversified form. A man who urges the interests of the unity at the price of creativity is a tyrant; one who urges the interests of creativity at the price of unity is a revolutionary. Both of these stand as types; they have full being only so far as they can in effect re-establish themselves in concrete men and ideals, each with its proper dignity and being.

We have then four inchoate states: thing, standard, tyrant and revolutionary. These set themselves aside, and do not deserve to be treated as men among men. To deserve that treatment they must make good the achievement of the two-sided reality which they, by standing in the inchoate middle, define themselves as qualified to produce. What is true of individuals is also true of organizations. If a state sacrifices any man or purpose it has to make it good by the way in which it re-expresses him in the stable structure of the state and the creative ongoingness of it, in its traditions and laws, and in its ceremonials and activities. On the other hand, if in its career it yields its stable structure or dynamics too much to the other so as in effect to become an inchoate centre, it can recover its proper nature by a more effective focusing on the goal and a better recognition of the rights of men.

April 4

When I make any ordinary assertion, such as "this is a cup" I am implicitly claiming to be a man just like everyone else, with the same degree of honesty, technical competence of observation, intent or purpose to communicate the truth, and to acquire systematic knowledge. This is what I am expected to be, to exhibit and to claim; it is not risky to do these, even though it is an absolute truth that I offer. When I fail to say what is the truth I am to be charged with failure in one of these dimensions. When now I go on to make a philosophic assertion (or one in any other discipline) I go further. These subjects have truths which require for their being the achievement of a more radical kind of honesty and technical competence, a longer ranged purpose and a wider body of relevant information. When I fail to tell the truth I am to be charged as having failed in these various ways.

But why then am I not puffed up in these areas so far as I do tell the truth? Because though there is additional virtue behind the truths I enunciate, these are not to be credited to me. There is a minimal virtue which belongs to me so far as I am commonsensical; virtue additional to this is a function of the truth attained. But how did I attain that truth, how is it that I was able to enunciate it? We can say that there is a reservoir of truth which the common-sense world and the world beyond has collected that I, when I philosophize, represent. The representative truths I, enunciate are carried by superior virtues which are lodged in me. The point is that I do not possess them in the sense that I can pride myself on having them, for I have them only so far as the society allows me to function as its representative, in the sense that it allows me to be a philosopher in that society.

When a man functions as a philosopher he exhibits the extra virtues, carries them out. Were he to attribute them to himself he would by that very act destroy them, for he would misconstrue them as carriers, make them functions of his individuality, and thus taint them with his own desires. But they are objective, transcending desire, showing him to be a man perfected. So far as he knows this, or takes himself to know this, so far as the virtues which he is exhibiting are thought by him to be ex-pressions of himself and his own superiority to others, just so far does he claim that the truth he has is special for him. He has it as a common truth only so far as he recognizes that the additional virtues which he has are the virtues which belong to all, and which he is using representatively.

How do I the philosopher get to the stage of being representative? I surely define myself to be one. This is an arrogance in a way but it is a mark of humility, for should I fail to tell the truth I fail with respect to a precious heritage which belongs to all, and am to be condemned as one who is jeopardizing all the rest. The common-sense man does nothing more than claim to say what all do in fact say, just so far as they are equally men; the philosopher is saying what all the rest should be saying were they to utilize their powers fully. He is doing for them what they should do for themselves. Does this mean that if all were to engage in the use of their powers to the full they would all be philosophers, or that they would together use up the reservoir and thus have no need of a representing philosopher? The latter seems to be the case.

The representing philosopher is no longer needed once every one uses his full powers; all would say in a kind of mosaic but concretely what he is abstractly expressing. He could then if he wished make an abstract statement, but this would then be only a kind of reporting, a kind of abstract record of what was in fact believed by the people together; it would no longer be that kind of venture into the unknown which is characteristic of philosophers and philosophy today. In the end then philosophy as a creative enterprise would be unnecessary if all men were to take advantage of the additional virtue, training, purposiveness and wisdom which is at the root of each.

What is the meaning of this additional virtue or training? It can only be A] an historical accumulation, B] a kind of appetite, C] an innocence, and D] a stability (existential, ideal, actual, and divine elements) which men by just being together constitute, and which the philosopher taps and uses representatively.

At the end a philosopher is an individual in his errors and a *Weltgeist* in his truth. If successful he has presented a myth; if not he has ventured outside the ordinary reaches and ended with something close to a wrong-headed perverse doctrine. This is a truth seen in some way by dogmatic churches and tyrants and the common people. They recognize the deviations of the philosophers to be perverse and dangerous. The trouble is that the churches, etc., mistake the current spirit with the meaning of the reservoir; they misconstrue the history or the appetites of men, the innocent nature of mankind, or the meaning of genuine stable common sense.

The philosopher who fails in any way is one who must be said to have failed to have that minimal virtue which even a common-sense man has. He does not carry out his representative function, for this uses and taps and exhibits higher virtues, but only so far as these are carried by a minimal commonsensical set. If he does not tap this set basically he becomes merely a philosopher of his time.

April 6

Knowledge is a strategy on the part of Actualities enabling them to master what otherwise would be beyond their grasp, due to the limitations of the senses and the restricted locus of the body and its range of movement. This knowledge has within it facets of the enterprises which are in a sense correlative with it—appreciation, sympathy, evaluation, answering to God, Existence and the Ideal. However, it stresses sympathy and evaluation more than appreciation, looking to the totality that lies outside it for a test of itself. Knowledge, in short, has its claims warranted by virtue of the way it is supported by that totality of being which is the province of the divine. Analogous observations are to be made with respect to art, religion and mathematics. Art is a strategy on behalf of Existence; it stresses knowledge, appreciation and sympathy more than it does evaluation. What the evaluative dimension does is to carry the art, justify it; it is by virtue of the way in which art makes possible better evaluations, opens up the world to the Ideal, that it is justified; in process it is instead essentially a productive sympathetic activity guided by knowledge and appreciation. Similarly, religion is a strategy on behalf of the divine; it stresses sympathy, evaluation and of course appreciation more than it does knowledge. It looks to a man as a being of character to sustain and justify it. And finally mathematics or any other formal discipline is a strategy carried out on behalf of the Ideal. In addition to a native stress on evaluation the formal disciplines involve an element of knowledge and appreciation, looking to the practice of an art successfully, to provide a test of its accuracy.

We have then the pairs, Actuality and the divine, the Ideal and Existence each testing the other's claims. Why just these pairs? Why did St. Paul check the prophets by charity and not by a mastery of the formal disciplines or by their productivity—or is it the case that charity is essentially all three, the character of an Actuality, the carrying out of an Ideal and the proper use of Existence? If so, the foregoing must be modified so that it says that knowledge, e.g., while containing within it the elements of the other approaches, is justified and tested by all three. Knowledge as the strategy of an individual is not tested by that individual's character, since it abstracts from this, but by the being of the divine, the Ideal and Existence, since it encompasses these in a biased way and only partially, and they in recompense remain outside it as its test. And so on for the others.

The test for knowledge and for the others, when these are carried to their extreme as in philosophy, fine art, formal disciplines and religion, involve the use of a treasury of merit, as it were, accumulated in the course of time. Each man who engages in these activities to a degree greater than that which is characteristic of his group, in effect holds himself to be their representative, making use of a common store in order to express the strategy most effectively. Should he fail he is one who misrepresented the community, and is to be charged for having stepped out of his commonplace role and messed up what all possess; should he succeed he does not exhibit himself to have any other virtue but that of having acted as a representative, of being willing to allow his own singular virtue of knowledge, sympathy, etc., to carry the common unused goods. What he knows or grasps is for all of mankind, and he can defend his failure to participate fully in daily life by showing that in a way he really is doing this. Did every man for example make use of the common treasury, there would be no need for a philosopher to do so.

We can say then that the philosopher instead of starting with himself as an Actuality, already starts with all the other modes of being as constituting the treasury of virtue accumulated and possessed by all. He is a man then whose knowledge is not only carried by himself as having some steady and decent character, but as one who can and does accrete to that character the techniques of persistent inquiry (or the sympathy characteristic of Existence) the vision of the whole (or the appreciation of the divine) and the evaluation of the Ideal (or formal disciplines). He has them in himself, but they are his only because his being is sustained by the rest in these other ways, i.e., only because he as an individual is helped by the productive, divine and evaluative powers of the community. When he carries out his knowledge he attenuates the ways of apprehending other than that characteristic of the Actual, but in compensation he is tested by them to the very degree that he attenuates, mutes their power. He develops his technical skill for example by himself but as an actual man he must deal with this representatively, and he is judged by seeing just what kind of productive existence he makes possible and perhaps himself exemplifies when and as and because he has this extreme form of knowledge.

The philosopher's claim to truth is not necessarily tested by his own productivity; but it is tested as something which he is presenting, and therefore if we look say to the productivity of the world in which he lives as testing him, it can be only so far as this is recognized either to be a productivity done for him, or conversely that his knowledge is being offered not as his own but as the knowledge for just that objective productive world.

The religious man, on this interpretation, does not have to exhibit charity himself; it is sufficient if he makes it possible in others; his power in any case is due to the borrowing of a kind of charity from the rest, which he partially expresses in his appreciative religious apprehension. He begins in a matrix of charity and is tested by it—and so on for the other virtues, and so on for other types of men.

The test of something then is to be found in its very source. This means that the true prophet will express himself (or be expressed by others) in charity, only because he is one who was able to get beyond ordinary limits by taking advantage of the treasury of charity which the others had prepared. This means that there is no genuine prophesy possible without charity (grace?) and that its test is charity.

What is the difference in the shape which the test and the source give to the same material? Is it that the source is exhausted in being articulated as knowledge, sympathy, etc., and that the test continues to be and function regardless of the articulation as a kind of carrier? Thus the character of man will accrete the sympathy, etc., of mankind, articulate this in the guise of knowledge, and then have the knowledge tested by the type of character, sympathy, etc., which is being expressed in fact. This means that the sympathy, etc., which is accreted is something sheared off from a larger whole—or better that there is a single sympathy which is partly expressed as and through some articulation, and partly in and through a test.

If a man is capable of philosophical knowledge only by engaging in a strategy and tapping the accumulated wisdom of man (the divine component), the techniques of inquiry (existential), the fundamental principles of value (Ideal), and the virtue of good character (Actuality) in the guise of his assertions, he makes a test of these so far as they function apart from him, as a knowing being. In the case of art, a man will go beyond the ordinary by tapping the wisdom, the techniques of production, the purpose and good character in the making of the work of art and look to these sources for a final check.

Staying with only two modes of being this amounts to saying that a given mode can deal effectively with the other only if A] it abstracts from the concreteness of itself, B] expresses the nature of that other in an abstract way, and C] is checked by that other in its concreteness, as functioning in independence of it. And if we suppose the given mode to be a man knowing and that the other mode is represented only in some social form, then the other will be something which he taps when he expresses himself abstractly and as grasping that other, and that other will test him by virtue of the way in which he and it cohere in their functioning.

April 7

When a man engages in knowledge he expresses something of his own being, as organized by a purpose to have truth, a competence in inquiry and a grasp of the unity of what there is to know. The purpose, competence and unity which structures his knowledge are themselves expressions of an accumulated wisdom of the race. The truth which he claims to assert will be found wanting just so far as it fails to be adequate to the accumulated wisdom as it is in fact then being used or recognized.

When St. Paul came to distinguish the true prophets from the false he said that the test was charity. The observation needs qualification. The prophesy itself as a revelation of the divine is possible only in one who is genuinely pious; it must thus express the man as a pious or religious being. But it expresses him only abstractly and then as qualified by the need to speak the truth, the need to convey it and the need to engage in vital activity with the rest. The prophesy in short exhibits in itself an abstract form of charity; it must as it were be a prophesy charged with charity. This prophesy is to be tested by looking to the actual accumulated wisdom of mankind as a form of charity; if we can find in mankind a richer and deeper charity than that which is expressed in the structured prophesy or can find in the prophet a deeper and richer religiosity than the mere prophetic remarks would allow, the prophesy and the prophet are then to be rejected as inadequate. When mankind is better in practice than the structured prophesy permits we know the prophesy is unsatisfactory, not a genuine word of God. And if the religious component of the prophesy as a word of God violates what it is to be a pious man, once again it is known to be unsatisfactory. The prophesy rests then on a base of genuine piety and social charity; it expresses the first in its religious aspect and the second in its structured unity as something communicated and having some claim to truth.

The prophet goes beyond the rest of his community in what he asserts only because he makes use of what is at the root of that community; he articulates this in the shape of the structure of his prophetic utterances, and he tests this articulation by referring back to the root to see if it tolerates it and if it has something further to exhibit. The individual remains one among others just so far as he attributes the prophesy and the structure not to himself but to others; the piety must be his own but the content which the prophesy also expresses must be owing to the rest. So "if he have not charity" must be understood to mean that the prophesy has a charity component and is in fact tested by the charity of the community; what he must have himself is not charity but piety, for the prophesy is the expression of this, understanding by piety a man infused with divinity. If we are to test the prophesy it is not however by looking to him but to the rest.

This account seems to make no provision for a man going beyond the community's wisdom and knowledge, but this is not the case, for the articulation of the community's wisdom is a fresh, free and creative act. What a man cannot do is to have a virtue all his own which marks him off from the rest of mankind in any other sense but that of being a representative of the rest. One who held the doctrine of great men would have to say that the great man has a superior virtue but that he gives it to the rest by using it representatively; perhaps this answer is not much different from the one I have been urging to the effect that the individual has a minimal virtue and that he gets additional virtues from the community. In any case what an individual is admonishing the rest to do is something in their power and thus within the area of their accumulated wisdom.

Ought there not be four ways in which an individual can have his actuality or his piety or purpose or technical habituation exhibited instead of, as above, only two, an abstract and a concrete? Is there not let us say a kind of cognitive prophesy, a kind of dynamic prophesy, a kind of evaluative prophesy and a kind of inspired prophesy, of which perhaps the third is the normative, being structured by the abstractions derived from other modes? Is there not a kind of individual cognition (belief), a kind of structured cognition (logic or mathematics), a kind of dynamic cognition (or inquiry) and a kind of divine cognition (or categorical systematic knowledge)? In each of the four cases there is a structuralization given by the other modes, which in the end also test the nature of the result of such structuralization. But as we have just now put it there seems to be no genuine reference to what is not knowledge. So that in addition to four ways in which one might have cognition, there must be the four ways of dealing with the world, of which only one is cognition. There must be sympathy, appreciation and production, each with its four divisions. This would mean that if we take production as the most concrete, that there are four types of production—individual, rational, effective and organizing, and that each of these, as structured and filled in by content reflecting other modes, offers a test of some one set of four ways of abstractly dealing with what there be. Thus it might well be argued that cognition has four guises of which the philosophic and best is the systematic. This is an abstraction from the individual expressing something of his integrity; it expresses too the accumulated wisdom of men and exhibits this in the shape of an articulation, structuralization and content in the system. This system, as so qualified, is tested by the other cases of the abstract ways of dealing with things. It is tested by the productive mode as primarily organizing, by the evaluative as primarily inclusive, and by the divine as a unity.

April 10

A doctor is a double man; a private being and a representative of a profession, which is to say of a civilized world as channelized through a training, an education, a practice and a tradition. As a private being he is essentially a practitioner and is one who is to be concerned with his patient in the guise of this unique being. As a representative the doctor is essentially a scientist, one who deals with this case as illuminating other cases to come. His patient is a being *qua* patient, a representative of mankind who is receiving the benefit of the institution and of the science of medicine. The problem is to keep these two sides in each in harmony. Each must make himself anew. The doctor does this in the concrete through his living practice, and he does this in the abstract by virtue of his concept of what a man is, thereby enabling him to emphasize this or that side of his double nature. Medicine one might say is the persistent practice of doctors to become men. They are men who are constantly facing crises where they have to decide for themselves just how to balance their "art" and their "science" and correspondingly how they are to define another man as at once private and public, a being to be known and handled through art and science.

What the doctor does and faces is not different from that which is characteristic of every man all the time; we are always beings who are private and public. We are always beings who come into the public world as representative men and thus are to be used for the sake of the rest, but not without recognition of the private side.

If the private side is sacrificed, the public result must contain the private's values; in the very ideals and meaning of scientific medicine the value of the individual must be re-preserved, as the hero's are in the army. Conversely, so far as the public side is sacrificed, the private being must make himself so great that he can represent the others. The doctor who is only a practitioner must justify his ignoring of the needs of his fellow doctors and of future people to learn from him; he must be a genius. And his patient as absorbing all his attention must make himself a noble being. Only this would justify the sacrifice.

Medicine, unlike law, has no one to represent the rights of the individual. The doctor as it were is counsel, prosecutor and judge in one.

April 12

Each mode of being must exhibit four ways of dealing with other beings, of which, one, the most abstract, gets to them neutrally but not absolutely neutrally, since it is the neutral way of one particular mode. All of the modes have four ways of dealing with the others, but the four ways are distinctive in each case. Man, for example, gets neutrality only by *knowledge,* whereas Existence gets it by *relationality* or distinction, Ideality gets it by *appreciation* or *evaluation* and God gets it by *sympathy*. These different types of neutrality touch different dimensions of the other modes. Thus, e.g., knowledge gets the other modes neutrally as having a meaning or form, whereas God gets to them neutrally as beings with interiority. In short we need a neutral way of apprehending beings viewed in their analyzable natures, in their interconnection, in their evaluational significance, and in their individuality.

The neutrality of the Actual is most appropriate evidently to the Ideal; the neutrality of the Existent is most appropriate evidently to the Divine; the neutrality of the Ideal is most appropriate to Existence, and the neutrality of God is most appropriate to Actuality. In short each mode of being has a neutral way of dealing with the rest, but this comes close to doing justice to the nature of only one other mode of being. We thus get the circle of apprehension: *Cognition* of the Ideal, *Evaluation* of the Existent, *Relational spatialization* and *temporalization* of the Divine and *Sympathy* for the Actual.

April 17

Explanation in order to avoid futile tautology requires that one find a predicate outside the given subject, one which is not identical with it. But it would then seem that when we come to being, we would have only an inadequate subordinate predicate by which to characterize or explain it. This is the case if one could have only one predicate. The predicate 'being' is the characteristics of each of the modes of being made disjunctive. To be is to be either "spatio-temporal-or-evaluative-or-self-divisive-or-eternal"; being now is the togetherness of all these, and they are its articulation.

If one asks what is the difference between being and its adequate predicate it can consist only in the fact that the predicate is adequate, i.e., in the fact that the predicate exhausts the being. The parts of the predicate taken severally refer to the being and not to one another; exhausting the being they refer to the respective modes. From the vantage point of the predicate parts, being is defined by the way in which the predicates together refer and leave no residue; if we wish to know what being is from the standpoint of being it will lie in the fact that it puts a bracket as it were around the predicates and says these are its predicates. The Hegelian system with its attempt to convert substance into subject in the end seeks to make the predications of being equal to being, and thus in a way offers a reduction of the One to an interlocked Many.

April 19

If one could ever reduce a substance to a subject, to use Hegel's expressions, one would in effect produce the substance over again. A mere subject, a phenomenalized, articulated substance is one in which each part refers to the others as its necessary counterpart. But once this reference is sustained by the parts themselves the outcome is a single being in which these parts and their references are but isolatable fragments. This is how it is possible for Hegel at the end of his *Phenomenology* to think of the process beginning again. On my view there is never an elimination of the "substance"; it is the One which keeps the items together.

It is conceivable that we have layers upon layers of substance; there is the substance which has had no articulation, and then there is the articulated substance which in turn gives rises to another which must complete itself, etc. What is the difference between the forms of an original substance, and those of an articulated one; can we tell that the dialectic had been gone through before on a previous level? Is it that the knower becomes closer to the object, that the new subject is known not only to articulate but to reproduce somewhat the nature of the substance? There is never an end to such a process; but this is only to say that the Hegelian method throws the residuum of the substance into the knower. On my view there is never a satisfactory articulation in the sense of repetition; the articulated components do not become the substance, but always remain predicational of it. Does this mean that when we come to the Togetherness of the modes that the modes in a sense are predicative of the Togetherness, making it substantial? Or is it not that there is a dialectic here; the modes themselves have being predicated of them, and they in turn have their own characteristics predicated of Being?

May 9

There are two types of defect: 1] internal and 2] external. These divide into two. The internal can relate to A] one's incompleteness, one's failure to have potentialities fulfilled, or B] to one's guilt, one's failure to do what one ought. The external can relate to one's A] security, and B] the need to be more significant. 1a] is satisfied best by rooting one in something more substantial and powerful, making one more of an Actuality; 1b] is satisfied best by the state, where the meaning of the Ideal is altered so that it is appropriate to man and the world in which he lives. 2a] is satisfied best by God, the permanent lover, or by His partial substitute, the church or religion. 2b] is satisfied best by Existence, the domain of time and activity where one is related to more significant and ongoing schemes.

Any one of the two or four ways of remedying the defect can be adopted either as a type of living or as a role. To live a life is to adopt one of the ways as primary and inclusive, but to act on the other ways, so as to subordinate them, give them definite positions within one's life. It is also to offer one's life, without restrictions, to others, for them to reconstitute and to define inside themselves. This answer is the best of possible answers, but it presupposes that one has the willingness and the ability to master all else inside one's frame, and that the other schemes will not distort, abuse, misconstrue oneself and one's meaning. But if the others are living full lives too, analogous to one's own, the solution is the best one. The Yogi and the Commissar or Warrior will have to adopt the other inside—is this what is meant by "detachment from fruits" by the warrior in the Gita? If they do not do this, if they do not have the other mode of being inside themselves, they will just have roles (which is perhaps what the Indian caste system guarantees).

If one adopts a role one allows others to add their stint to one's own, thereby incidentally living a life benefiting from the other roles; one at the same time takes a role in the context of the other, but without alteration or sacrifice. There does not need to be any heroic transformation of others; the others do not have to live perfect lives. This answer is pragmatically the best, but it does not do full justice to a man, for a man must live a life centrally and not incidentally, be himself and not merely be sustained.

June 10

There seem to be at least three distinct types of representative. There is the mere substitute, agent, mouthpiece who exercises in this place the very powers another would have exercised were he there. This is what we have when we make a commonplace assertion about some matter of fact; we represent any man. Then there is the spokesman, the man who makes use of ordinary powers in a special way; he says, does and knows what others would were they only willing to take the lead. And finally there is the creative leader, the man who expresses powers which others allow to remain latent, powers which are resident in them as men but which they fail to bring to the fore. The romantic actor, the philosopher, the scientist, anybody following out some advanced discipline and perhaps even a poet—unless he be one such as Plato thought, a man in a divine frenzy—belong to this class. The realistic drama and actor belong to the first, but the proper mode of acting, the true drama and actor are I think in the second. The Platonic poet like the Hebrew prophet is a mouthpiece not for mankind but for God. He is untouched by his message.

Is there a spokesman for God, who makes use of powers which God uses, but who uses them in a way God does not? This could conceivably be the religious leader who speaks in the name of God but actually expresses the meaning of God in human terms and in a human context. But is there then a kind of "philosopher" for God, a man who actually articulates, uses powers which God allows to be latent, etc. Such a conception, though at first strange, could be made plausible by taking account of the idea of the Incarnation; God one might say allows to remain latent the power to incarnate, and this power can be exhibited by a saint, who incarnates the divine in the human to some extent.

June 12

Natural law has been said to be the product or expression of "natural, primitive, unsophisticated man," of man's instinctual nature, of man's reason, of a divine command and of the common spirit of nations and peoples. These five grounds reduce in a sense to three or four. *1]* man as natural, which takes care of the first two, *2]* man as a mouthpiece, an avenue for the supernatural, i.e., the divine, *3]* man as making himself manifest over a people, and *4]* man as a construction by reason? To these one could add: *5]* man in history, the development of man as more and more social with a consequent production of a natural law, *6]* man as a substitute for God, re-formulating and carrying out in a new context what is religiously right, *7]* man as saintly and thus as utilizing power which God employs only occasionally in such an act as the Incarnation; here the natural law is the product of a divinely inspired man who transmutes this in a radically new way, *8]* man as social with defined ends, as per my paper on natural law, *9]* man as a being of learned reflexes, or tradition, as established by men habitually acting in a society, so that natural law becomes one with the residuum, proven by time and found in common law, *10]* the natural law as a translation of the need of structure of society in an institutional frame, *11]* natural law as a radically new product of a societal structure directed towards the good of mankind, *12]* natural law as an anticipatory formulation of the structure of an ideal civilization. To these "ontological" formulations one should add epistemic ones, such as that of Aquinas to the effect that natural law is man's interpretation of the divine, and analogous ones which would allow it to be an interpretation of common law, possible law, ideal law, etc.

June 13

It is possible perhaps to combine Plato and Aristotle on the question of the state: The state, says Plato, is man writ large, but the man is an Aristotelian not a Platonic man. The Platonic man's soul is a pilot in an alien ship; the Aristotelian is part and parcel with the body. The vegetative soul would be repeated in an *association,* possible to the lowest living forms; the animal soul would be repeated in a *society* possible to animals; the human soul would be repeated in a *state;* the philosophic or transcendent soul, the active reason, would be the structure of *civilization.* The later forms would include the earlier, and there would be the question of "immortality" in the case of the last, the question being whether this is somehow preserved outside all history and whether it does need a "body" or people to sustain it. Also whether or not it precedes the other souls in being, in time as well as in dignity, whether it is one, many, natural or supernatural.

We also have the question of the intellectual and the moral virtues, and in the end the reconciliation of art and prudence, the creative "intellectual" power expressive of the government of the state, and the moral virtue of practical wisdom which is resident in the people. The problem of the unity of the soul and the body becomes here the creation of the political organ. The unity of these two, which is like the unity of the Ideal and the Actual, has as its consequence the proper adjustment to Existence or time and to the Divine or eternal unity, which is to say the test of an organic state in its endurance and its unifying power. (The converse is also true: the juncture of the divine and Existence, the making coherent sense out of history, requires in the end the promotion of the characteristic powers of the soul and body of the state, the juncture of law and people, so that a just state for all men is the test of a divinely ordered history.)

There ought to be political analogues of perception, of the senses, of imaging as well as of knowledge. Obviously knowledge has its counterpart in the formulated laws or the legislature; the problem of the senses and perception and imagining has to do with the relation of states to nature and to other states, and is complicated by the fact that the state is not a substance capable of acting except through the mediation of individuals.

June 14

If we suppose that Aristotle's ensouled body is the proper model for a study of the state, and if we also suppose that the state provides a remedy for what in root is disorder, (so that the soul or structure of the state is in effect a kind of ethical principle controlling and rectifying the lower), ought we not reverse the procedure and look at the Aristotelian soul as a kind of reification of the ethical, some kind of realization of an ideal principle, a sedimentation from some outside domain? How does this precipitation take place? If we are right about the state, it is the product of a utilization of some final cause outside it; a body which is not ensouled, a body ready for living, or an animal body ready to be made human, strives towards something beyond itself. As a consequence it achieves a simulacrum of a lower form of this objective, which gives us a this-worldly meaning for the body. The body would thus be seeking an ideal of a platonic sort and would settle for a soul which would be a this-worldly end to the quest. The need to get a better answer and to satisfy a still further appetite, the appetite to be significant or important, would drive the being on to speculative activity and the acceptance of a plausible philosophy.

June 17

To seek an explanation is to be dissatisfied with things as they then confront themselves either in fact or in thought. If the explanation is in terms of a condition, a locus, a ground for what we have, it is "metaphysical"; otherwise scientific. All philosophers treat something as an "accident" as pointing to some condition outside themselves. If they refuse to do this with matters of fact or some constructive system, they are driven to do this with respect to the metaphysician's. To account for things the metaphysician refers to some other reality. His opponents refer to some reality in him, since what they want to account for or explain is the metaphysical explanation and its error or nonsense. Only one who took things as they present themselves, as Hume seemed to imply by supposing that each thing was or had its own existence (a view which Hume gave up when he tried to account for the idea of causation), could avoid "metaphysics."

Might one not explain by referring back to a cause? One could do this, but the very awareness that there were causes is "metaphysical" *awareness,* since it tells us that there is something in the being as here and now which is testifying to something which is not here and now, and is in fact in the past. To know that there had been a past, that a property had been transferred or produced is to know something about the being of the world; those who content themselves with mere correlations in the doctrine of causation, still have to give a "metaphysical account" of the error which tries to do things another way.

When Russell dissolves descriptions he is metaphysical in temperament since he is not content with the terms as they appear. He is also combating another metaphysics, which claims that there must be a counterpart to the description, by his offering to account for the apparent intelligibility and referential power of the description. This apparent intelligibility and referential significance is, he thinks, due to the mistaken use of language, so that he forces us to something else (and away from what the terms are offered as).

The great problem for all positivists (and for the Enlightenment—as Hegel so brilliantly showed) is to account for the confusion and superstition of their opponents. My arguments for God in the *Modes* start with the conceived natures of beings and try to show that encountered beings have "accidents" because of the action of others. (By "accident" here what is obviously meant is not an Aristotelian accident, since this has no explanation, but something not intrinsic and essential, which is present but does not follow from the nature and yet can be accounted for by referring to some other being as its source, ground, locus.) Because, e.g., an Actuality is an other it points to another which is its counterweight; Existence has an essence which its very nature requires it to escape from but which is nevertheless one with it, and the Ideal, which is prescriptive, is necessarily exhausted by some alien power, for left to itself it would not be so.

These arguments deal not with the items as encountered but as understood. The arguments can be overthrown by one who would be willing to give up all explanation, and would rest content with the beings, accident and essence together, as all on a footing.

June 21

Metaphysics might be defined as the art and science of moving from cosmology to ontology. Cosmology is the characterization of space-time beings in their most universal terms. One then engages in an analysis, whose object is to distinguish the essential from the adventitious. Metaphysics is possible only because there are persistent ubiquitous adventitious features which can be transferred in fact or shown to have a cause in some other domain or type of being. Such domains are the topic of ontology. Once we have arrived at the other domains we can retrace our steps somewhat and consider how these domains affect the original and thereby generate the case where analysis is necessary and possible. This retracing of the steps is part of a wider enterprise of finding out not only what the various domains are, but how they affect one another. Strictly speaking then ontology deals with the basic modes of being and the way they affect one another; cosmology starts with one of the affected domains; metaphysics analyzes and argues to the affecting domains and considers what they are in themselves and in their bearing on one another.

The adventitious features are not hooked on from the outside; the cosmological world really contains them. The domain is actually caught up with another domain to make an integral result; it takes analysis and speculation to get to understand them. Without a feeling of wonder, one would remain with the cosmology indefinitely. The wonder comes from our own grasp of what is essential to ourselves; this enables us to cut behind the common sense of daily life and the speculations of cosmology. We make the discovery usually when we find error or heterogeneity, for we seek to bring order about with truth. The order it might be said is not real, and the result therefore is another error. But the order is an order of explanation or comprehension; indeed it must be granted that it is not the order that exists in fact, for what we have in fact is cosmology and common sense.

The achievement of order is an achievement of something which is not now the case, but which expresses what really is so. We move from an "appearance" to a reality, but do not thereby cancel out the appearance, make it dis-appear, but understand it, make it intelligible, do not leave it opaque; we preserve it by showing what grounds it, makes it be. The adventure presupposes some grasp of what the being is, from which it is to be distinguished, what an essence is. It is one with the adventure of discovering motivations, instincts, drives, arguing to God, etc. We can avoid them by denying that there is something adventitious, that it can be explained, that it need be explained in this way or that. The first is simple positivism, the second scepticism, and the third criticism.

June 27

Unless we are perfect descriptivists, taking every phenomenon (including errors and illusions as they appear) without explanation or qualification, we are driven to divide what we encounter into an essential and an adventitious part. In the west, following Aristotle, we think that the essential part is the Actual, and as a rule believe that the addition of the adventitious does not make a great difference to the appearance. Mystics tend instead to believe that the essential is a simulacrum of God, Physicists tend to believe it is so of Existence, or a limited version of it, and Platonists tend to believe it is so of an instance of the Ideal. These thinkers then trace the adventitious back either to another locus or to its source. Thus the Aristotelian will find a new locus or source, if he be a Thomist, for some cosmic adventitious features. This locus or source is God. The mystic goes to God too, not by tracing back the origin of the adventitious but rather of the essential; he would be inclined to try to explain the adventitious by referring it to some other source or locus. In these various ways, the world is sorted out into a number of domains in one of which there is a residual aspect of the common-sense world and a transferred or transformed aspect of the adventitious aspects of that world.

But having analyzed out the various components we oft times think it unnecessary to explain how those components mixed to give the original data (and some systems seem to be unable to have such a mixture). A test of a philosophy then would be its capacity to take its sorted domains and show that they can mix, and that the mixture will result in something like the data with which the philosophy began.

If it be the case, as I think, that all the modes mix, we ought in our common experience find the residual essentiality of all of them, unless the common-sense experienced world must be sustained by the Actual and not by the others. If all of them are essentially present, what is adventitious would be only a relative thing—given the unity of a being the adventitious would be its individuality, ideality and dynamic qualities as pointing to the modes of Actuality, Ideality and Existence. Accordingly, one could well argue that there are basic ways of proving the existence of the other modes, not from the base of Actuality, but from that of common sense.

It is not altogether clear whether or not the knowledge of the various beings starts from the data of experience. It would, if there be real adventitious phenomena. The proofs of God in the *Modes* speak as though they started with different modes as in the cosmos and dissected out the adventitious features which pointed to the being and action of God. This means that they have already found the modes apart from daily experience; also, that they isolate the adventitious features which direct one to God, when they might (though this is recognized) direct one, from other features, to other modes. Because the proofs start with specific modes they can speak of essential and adventitious traits; and this perhaps is necessary when one is trying to prove one mode, say God. But if one were to start with the cosmological facts then one would be confronted with what is essential to the cosmology, though not essential when one thinks of the ontology where the modes are sorted out. This fact is pointed to in the indirect secondary proofs which begin with infected modes. Thus 4.16 deals with universals, (of if one likes, Actualities as infected by universals in common experience); 4.17 refers to facts; 4.19 does a similar thing for realizability in possibilities, etc. The modes themselves as testifying directly to God, exhibit themselves as "mixed," i.e., as having adventitious traits.

Perhaps another way of saying all this is to remark that an Actuality, e.g., does not only have adventitious traits pointing to the presence and eventual activity of God, but has traits pointing to the presence and eventual activity of the other modes as well. Consequently, it is no simple Actuality but one in which these adventitious traits are combined. To speak of it as an Actuality with these various adventitious traits is to have assumed already that there is a fixed essence and it is that of an Actuality, whereas it is quite possible that these various adventitious traits are themselves essential features of the other modes, having the Actuality as an adventitious feature.

Or, once more, the common content might be one in which all these different modes are in interplay, out of which one can sort any one mode and thereby find the others as adventitious; but it would be the very same fact which gave us Actuality with its adventitious features, say pointing to God, that would also give us God with adventitious features pointing say to Actuality. To take this view is to suppose that the common-sense fact sits in the middle of the modes, rather than being distorted, as I think I ordinarily suppose it is, towards Actuality.

The view that the common-sense object is smack in the middle of all the modes is close to what is said at the end of the *Modes* in connection with the One and the Many. But this means that the common-sense object is also dissolvable into the four modes, since it would have none but adventitious traits.

What is one to say, e.g., to a Platonist who starting with the very phenomena, which I do, immediately finds the residuum to be Ideality rather than Actuality? He sees the Ideal right there and sees it better if we clear away the effects of other modes. Should we say that the adventitious traits I acknowledge to come from the Ideal could be said to be merely transferred from there, and to be manifest here? Because adventitious in this world and in this phenomenon, the Ideal would be adventitious in its career and locus only, and not in its nature. All features are residual and essential in some mode but some behave adventitiously when infected primarily by other modes.

The different modes in their togetherness constitute a new way of acting which is without substantiality of its own. But now we seem pretty close to the characterization of Existence, which seems to be just movement without a nature. The career of the phenomenon as an equal mixture of all is the career not of a being but of a set of fulgurations. The phenomenon would answer to a Humean analysis; it would not have any power or nature, but would be a discontinuity of occurrences which have no ontological import of their own. But what we should say is that analysis reveals that this phenomenon has substantial components, each of which points to a mode of being or exhibits it. The Humean is driven to speak of a human nature which ties the fulgurations together, even if erroneously or without justification. He has as his metaphysical prius a grasp of "human nature," which is the metaphysical real underlying and accounting for, not the phenomenon in the sense just discussed, but a neutral fulgurated stuff, overlaid with a vital force of habitual combining.

Hume might be said to find a phenomenon which has adventitious traits and that he gets rid of this to find the fulgurated stuff. But he does not see any reason to do anything more than accept this analytic result as bedrock; he does not think he has to look at that phenomenon and find in it the stuff of the modes. But granted that we start with phenomena overlaid with human habituational combinations, the fact that this phenomenon is there to be so overlaid precludes us from saying that it is without grounds of its own. If we have sheared off the human contribution we have something over against it as substantial, and contributory to the whole experience. Moreover, Hume is biased towards human nature; the proper approach to the phenomenon with which one begins is to see it to be neutral in nature; the combination of the impressions with the habits of man should be a world (as Kant saw but Hume apparently did not) which is neutral to both, without any dynamic power of its own, and alone expressive of the nature of experience. Hume took his data to be something like what Kant supposed the manifold to be—the residua of an analysis from more complex phenomena. But Hume did know what a phenomenon which was neutral was like. Kant was right in recognizing that this kind of phenomenon must be a product and never an initial fact. So we are back at the root: a series of fulgurations is a product and not a residuum—(as Hume thought) left after we remove the human contribution.

[The above undoubtedly does less than justice to the *Modes* which was not consulted in the course of it. All the observations in this diary are written without consulting previous pages, and usually without looking at any of my previous books. I am trying to think freshly and not trying to make the observations consistent in themselves or with my other writings. My corrections are usually only grammatical. Whoever may be interested in these writings will perhaps be interested in them mainly as an exhibition of an effort at "open thinking."]

July 2

The child meets a resistance to its activities and thereby distinguishes what might be termed an alien realm of Existence over against its own existence. It also finds itself admonished and sometimes hurt; this gives it a realm of value over against its own value. It finds too that whatever insecurity it feels is satisfied by some kind of unifying container, and at one and the same time finds itself to be a unity over against another unity. And finally it finds that its will or intent is defied by beings which are in conflict with one another and thereby discovers a plurality of other beings, some of them humans like itself. The outcome is that it finds itself a kind of locus for a private Existence, unsatisfactory value, endangered unity and defied will. This is its aboriginal set of categories in terms of which it looks out at the world. When it becomes mature and looks at any of the parts which it had set over against itself, it does not contrast these merely with some facet of itself but sees them as loci of a four-fold distinction. It is thus that it approaches Existence or value or God or man. It already is aware of four dimensions of inquiry; it has an a priori category enabling it to understand and divide, come to grips with the nature of what is before it.

The primary fact for the child is a realm of nature, and this is true of man when he begins to philosophize. There is no doubt but that mankind also looms large. This mankind, once it has been separated off from divinity through the awareness that it is divided against itself, is made up of finite beings. It is not yet entirely separated off from nature, or from representing a realm of its own, beyond the individuals and yet less than the divine—e.g., a society or other realm which has something like the same kind of forcefulness and rationale that one might find in nature. This nature is an ongoing affair and the very first distinction that it forces on one is between it as just ongoing, and it as also having some stability or unity or rationale or essence (which is the counterpart of one's own understanding and meaning as embedded in one's discourse regarding it).

The stable and the changing are themselves over against one another in this first elementary state of analysis; their unity would require the recognition of that which helps constitute them severally, for they are not unified in the experience except in the sense that they are had together there, for what the one demands the other defies and opposes. To recover the unity of the two as more than a mere co-presence will require an analysis of their components, and particularly the components of the changing, for this is richer and more immediate.

The basic problem behind all these analyses—into the changing and the stable and into the terminal points of both (if one likes, into the components of the changing which are also the units of the stable)—is just how much of the rich content of experience is to be acknowledged to be in the analytic components and how much of it is to be thought of as a kind of product whose presence cannot be denied but whose reality is supposed to be derivative. We have the choice between A] dissolving the content of experience into encountered components and which, in the end, are to be attributed to other domains as part of the content of other beings, and B] treating the isolated items, the stable, and the terminal points, in terms of which the full complexity of experience is to be understood, as something like props. These, though having a reality of their own (if they did not they would not even be props, and would also not have any apparent locus) would be most alien to what is in fact occurring.

Those who explain the world of experience from within, as it were, by reading its components into it, make the object of speculation familiar in content. But they are to be criticized for being naïve; they abandon experience by giving up its being to the components, leaving over only the thinnest kind of a "togetherness" as alone constituting the "substance" of experience. On the other hand those who explain the world of experience by referring to principles, speculative outcomes, rational laws, etc., offer a modified result, a distant stuff quite alien in nature to the real out of which it issues or which at least sustains it.

An alternative C] is that only some of the content is dissolved into explanatory elements and some of it is retained in the experience. But then the question arises of just where and when to draw the line.

The problem is not whether or not the outcome of analysis is real, for real it must be in some sense. Even if we thought of explanation as just error we would have to separate out that error from the rest of things and give it a locus in a realm which is to some extent not alien to the given realm.

Evidently we cannot suppose that the explanatory realities are altogether alien to what is encountered; if they were, we would have no way of using them, no way of knowing how they operate, no way of knowing what they were. Realities must all be something like what we encounter; the natures they have cannot be altogether alien to the components. To know the components of experience is already to know something of reality, to touch its being. There is no transcendence unless there is some immanence. Nor can we suppose that all the components of experience can be sheered off neatly and then, as untouched natures, be put inside some isolated mode of being. The objects of analysis do not contain all the stuff out of which the analysis was made, for some of this stuff is evidently the product of their interplay.

There is a richness to the world of experience which the juncture of the components produces; to make this vanish altogether or to suppose it belongs to one of the components is to misconstrue the reality of appearance; it is to deny the world we are trying to understand, or it is to distort it by making it the function of only one of a number of factors as operating together. The only alternative therefore is c]. When we ask about the being of togetherness, when we ask for the explanation of experience, when we engage in analysis, what we must do is to dissolve the experience in part into components which are to be attributed to other realms or modes of being and into a residuum in the form of a togetherness of those components where they are perhaps transformed.

Does the *Modes of Being* tend to tear out of their joint togetherness all content and read it into the modes themselves; does it, in connection with experience, go the other way, and account for that experience in terms of categories, etc., which are at maximum distance from the given experience? Does it not then seem that while I am commonsensical in connection with experience, I am excessively rationalistic in connection with the modes of being? Or to say it another way, though I give maximum being to the togetherness of the items in experience, since this is the area I seem to refuse to abandon, I also give only a miminum being to the togetherness of the beings, since I reject the idea of a fifth mode. If there be a One which is self-diremptive we could have the four modes in somewhat the position I put the components of experience; if there be a mere appearance to experience we would have the components of experience somewhat in the position I put the modes.

Is the nature of experience such that the four components of it can possess only part of its content? Is it a reality biased towards Actuality, or produced by the four modes (in contrast with the togetherness of the modes) so as to have nature and dignity of its own? Or is it not perhaps the case that the four modes intermingle not in one but in four distinct ways? Staying now with just two of the ways, must we not say that the modes constitute the world of experience by virtue of their minimal natures, that they help bring about a richer experience in which they themselves cannot be found, and that at the same time that they constitute the world of prescriptiveness for this experience (or rather that they provide the components of sheer togetherness for the very content that is experienced)? If this is the case, the content of experience will be a togetherness whose components are as alien as possible to the explanatory principles of it, but the meaning or prescription or togetherness itself as an idea or meaning will have components which are the very being of the unitary realities, which in turn are the terminal points for both the content of experience and its unitary meaning.

Could we envisage experience as a kind of circle, thinning out as it moves from a base point to apex, with terminal points in between? The base point would provide the original stuff of all knowledge, and the terminal points would be halfway posts (no less real for that) in the determination of a sheer togetherness. If one were to take this view it would seem that experience is basic and everything else is real only by some process of self-diremption, that all explanations would be props, and that the prescription for the experience would in the end be a fake, being sustained and constituted by, but without power over experience.

It is the halfway points themselves which must be taken to be real; they also provide the stuff of a togetherness which is rich experience, and the rationale of a togetherness in the form of a prescription. They themselves, in turn, are constituted of both elements, a stuff and a rationale. The child's initial four-fold category immediately puts us in touch with all four elements; we do not first have the experience in its richness and then dissolve it, but rather as we attend to the rich experience we already dissolve it in these ways, leaving a residual qualitative stuff of experience as an analytic component.

But we still have to face the fact that there is something through which the four-fold division moves. Is this not the very "being" which exists only by being dissolved, which has no being as it were of its own except as this neutral centre, and which is no more contentless than it is irrational, or just as contentless as it is irrational—which is to say, which is strictly speaking not at all, since to have it is to dissolve it? Is not the very being of being a non-being? Is not the unity of being just the unity of this which cannot be? Would this not mean that before we ever begin, or at the very beginning, we have already begun to analyze, and that the togetherness of all the forms of togetherness, the mere rich experience with its prescriptive element and with its component realities involved with one another, is a construction which cannot be made intelligible?

On this last hypothesis we take as unintelligible, as the last irrationality, as that which is not real, whatever offers to be the togetherness of all, which offers itself as a primary source of all being. The very nature of being requires that each be by itself to some degree—a position maintained in *Reality*. There never is then an altogether unsorted reality; the very fact that the child approaches the world which is over against it, and that it comes out with a set of categories in terms of which that world is to be understood, points up to the fact that we start with some things over against others. But still the fact remains that what is over against, is connected with, and that there is a way in which the connection must be understood as having some kind of being. Though reality is not altogether unsorted, there is a togetherness of all the items, and thus of all the different types of togetherness. This seems to give us a fifth mode of being, and a repetition of the question as to whether or not the togetherness dissolves utterly into components leaving nothing at all over, or just the mere fact of a togetherness without content of any sort. And in any case we would have the paradox that the outcome of all the elements in the world would be the emptiest. The answer is perhaps that the elements are connected one with the other but not all in the same way, so that to go from one to another one must move through a third to have that other in a certain way. There would then be no single way of being together; though the items are never entirely sorted out, they are never entirely just together. They are together in diverse ways, themselves incapable of being together except in the shape of the elements which sustain such separate togethernesses.

Or once again, since the knower stands over against the known, in facing the togetherness of experience it is necessarily the case that the knower has the whole of experience in one guise with the experience itself standing over against him in another guise. To be sure, the knower is one with the world, but this one-ness is also one of the topics for the knower and is not to be confused with the knowing itself. The knowing of course is together with the known in another sense, for there is a knowing going on in the world. But this togetherness is the very thing which a substantial being constitutes in its own inward being. Accordingly, so far as there is a cognizing act there is a sorted-outness to the world; this is sustained by the being as in the world and thus as not yet sorted out. The knower as sorted out and the knower as not yet sorted out, and thus the knower as a mind and as a being, are themselves sorted out so far as they are distinct from the single individual which is both. They are not sorted out as constituting that being. Once again if we ask about that being, whether its possessions and its inwardness are sorted out from one another, the answer must be that they are sorted out in the form of the knower as being, and the knower as cognizer, and not sorted out as constituting one inwardness.

We always have then a kind of togetherness and a kind of separateness, and if we ask about the way in which they are together, we get a "togetherness" answer and a "separateness" answer, and never one without the other as its inseparable counterpart. From the standpoint of the "togetherness" the counterpart is not altogether separated off; from the standpoint of the separateness the counterpart is not altogether together with it. And if we try to stand in between we find once again that we have the two modes of separateness and togetherness in opposition and as merged, and that we are undetermined as to just which one we are to specify.

The modes of being then must be separate modes which are at the same time together not only in four ways (since each of these is consistent with the separateness of the modes), but also together in one unity of four ways. That unity of four ways stands over against and is also merged with the four distinct ways. But if there be any real unity of the four which can stand over against them it would seem to destroy the ultimacy of the four ways; but this is only to say that from the standpoint of the four ways the unity of the four is really separate, whereas from the standpoint of the unity the four are not separate. But this would seem to mean that there is a unity over against them and thus a fifth mode, and also that there is nothing besides the unity. Should we not say then that from the standpoint of the four ways the unity of the four is not separate, but from the standpoint of unity the four ways are separate? If this is the case then the togetherness of all the modes is defined by the modes to be something which they constitute. It would have no prescriptive component and no nature. Also, from the standpoint of such a togetherness, there must be over against it four ways which defy it and deny it. The four modes would then not allow themselves to be absolutely neutrally together; their unity, by the very nature of its being, would require that there be that which denies and defies it.

Since there always is a separateness there never can be a full concrete togetherness or merging. If one wants to speak of the separateness and the mergng together, one will once again have them as apart at the same time. The being of a number of items together, whether in experience or as the four modes, is always abstract and requires an antithesis in the form of a separateness, and any attempt to deal with these two will but give us the antithesis once again, showing that the merging is abstract in the sense that it requires as its counterpart the separateness. Is the argument then that if we have, say four modes, they require a non-separated One, which is themselves as in fact together, and that this in turn requires a separated One facing a separated four?

Or is it not better to say that if we start with either the One or the four we find the other in a double relation to it; the four together will have the four as separate from one another and it; and the four as separate will have the One, in which they are together, not separate from themselves. A pre-analytic datum could be had only by a man who, to start with, had all his items apart; but he who has them all apart must have had them somehow together. It is a matter then of which is concrete and which is abstract in relation to the other component. Is it then that the meaning of each mode is to have itself with the others in four ways (or to keep to two modes: in two ways), of togetherness and separateness in relation to the others? Does the separateness require itself to be sundered from the items it relates, whereas the togetherness requires itself and them to be merged?

My being as one who knows requires that the world be divided into two parts, a part where I and the world merge, and another part (which is most airy) which stands over against me and the world. But then it seems as if the contingent rich togetherness in experience requires an oppositional other, a sheer togetherness over against it. But this One for the Many no less than the one in the many is not a new being, a new mode, for firstly it is but half of a One since the one in the many is inseparable from it, and secondly it is constituted by the very many which it has over against it.

Must we say that our separateness requires a One which is not separate and another which is, must we not then also say that the more our togetherness includes the One which is not separate the more it forces apart the One which is separate? If we could ever have the four all separated out then they would require a fifth; but if they are kept together in a One, they do not allow the separated One to be separated in being from them but only in intent, as that which is separate just so far as the modes are, and which is not separate just so far as the modes are together. It is, in short, not yet One enough to be either; it depends for its being on the decisiveness of the modes to be really separate from one another. Because the modes cannot be entirely separate they cannot allow for the being of the fifth mode, or what is the same thing, just so far as the modes are together in the richness of the cosmos they preclude any being to the togetherness.

So far then as the child looks out at the world in a four-pronged way, a way which is one in the very being of the child, it does not allow the four modes to be separate. The child has the modes all together by virtue of the fact that its diversity is nothing but its own unity exhibited, and never allows its terminal points to stand apart from it. But since it does know them as having a being apart from it, it must at the same time allow itself to stand apart from them as an alienated being who (though identical with a part of one mode) has all the modes, in their inwardness, altogether foreign to it. It can know them just so far as it gives up its inwardness as wholly private, and exhibits this as the diverse categorial apprehension of the four modes.

If I were to be a unity in myself I would have to solidify in me the togetherness which is a separateness, and the togetherness which is a merging. But as soon as I did that I would find myself merged in being with another being and at the same time over against it. The four-pronged approach of knowledge was not then rightly said before; the child as making such an approach deals with others in various ways.

Each mode of being might be said to be the unity of another two while it stands over against the fourth. One of the two which it unifies will be separated, the other will be merged with its being; one of them will be had as a kind of cognized object, the other as an assimilated one. As having these other two in a unity it will stand over against the fourth in a double way, separate from and merged with it, and thus have that fourth as at once cognized and assimilated. Accordingly we cannot get the four modes all separate at the same time, nor can we get them merged. To speak of a mode as related to another in two ways is also to speak of it as having these two ways both exterior to it and interior to it, which is to say as separate and merged. We cannot call this a dualism for the two ways are not altogether distinct; nor a monism for they are not altogether merged.

At the beginning of our experience, or of our investigations, and also at the end, we have a state of affairs in which there are not only separated and merged items, but their separation and merging is itself separated and merged. It is the case then that the rich experience has props which are its explanations, and also that there are more basic somewhat alienated realities which stand apart from this merged reality and have it as something over against them in their privacy. The experience is not over against them as a being, or rather, so far as they are over against it, it is one of the modes of being itself over against the other three. So we can say that rich experience with its props stands opposed to three other modes of being; these define it to be not experience in its richness but rather another mode of being claiming to be something more. The merging of the four modes then is a mode of being, but it is not a fifth but one of the four as opposed to the other three—or it is all of them together in such a way that they lose their identities, or it is both of these states at once.

(In a sense in which I did not realize originally these notes are somewhat random in the sense in which statisticians use the term. The foregoing is perhaps a good sample; it is written straight away without any
looking back or to a side and contains a mess of inconsistencies as I try
first this tack and then that.)

Let us distinguish between Experience and an experience. The former
is neutral to all the modes, but does not exist at all. An experience can be
either in this mode or that. It is Experience displaced. When we encounter
something in experience we find all the modes merged but as biased towards, as sustained by some one particular mode. If we wanted to get the
neutral point of all these various experiences we would get only the
mere ideal of a togetherness of Experience as such. Accordingly we can
rightly say that there is a kind of appropriateness of experience to
Actuality, and that consequently all the other modes are somewhat alien
and have to be derived by speculation, with Actuality as a residuum.
Actuality will then have some of the quality which the experience exhibits (since it is its expression), though exhibiting some of the nature of
the other modes. This is the position rightly taken in the *Modes*. But what
was not there seen, and what is not seen above is the fact that there are
other experiences, and that one can move into them, taking up *as it were*
a position for example as one of the merged components in an experience
oriented towards or in God. In this case the experience is suffered, since it
is God who is having the experience; it is God's experience which one is
helping constitute. We can call it a mystical experience of God because
we, as one of the merged components, actually qualify and merge with
the being which is God, at the same time that we merge with the other
modes to constitute God's content of experience. And so on for the other
modes.

We can find ourselves now experiencing and then experienced by
these other modes, and from these different positions get to know the
various modes. When we are being experienced we can learn about the
experiencer by subtracting ourselves as it were and leaving the experiencer as a residuum in the same way that we get to ourselves as a
residuum. We speculate in short to ourselves, deducing ourselves as it
were by virtue of the fact that we have qualified say (as in this case),
God. Such deduction is not effete, for it does tell us something of ourselves as having the capacity to qualify; it tells us how we can add to the
experience of God. This phase of ourselves as merged with others to
constitute the experience of other modes of being is not exploited in the
Modes.

There is no midpoint of all the experiences, any more than there is a
midpoint of my experience and the experience of another man. All ex-

perience is displaced Experience. We can to be sure refer to all the experiences but this requires a reference to what is not an experience, to wit Experience, the juncture point, the mere idea of the togetherness of all of them in a neutral way. Such a neutrality is presupposed; it is something we need to refer to as the normative togetherness of them all, and is analogous to the object which we focus on in diverse ways in our diverse experiences. There is, however, an object for us to focus on.

Is there an Experience, a Being, a Togetherness which the diverse experiences, that are oriented in the various modes, all specify or focus on? It would seem not. There is a difference then between the intersubjective experiences of a public object and the experiences of the various modes. This lies perhaps in the fact that intersubjective experiences take place inside one mode, the mode of Actuality, whereas the other experiences do not. We have then two types of experience:

1] As Actualities we confront other Actualities and possess them as substantialized and displaced in us.

2] As representatives of Actuality we have the realm of Experience which is constituted of the other modes together, and which is our initial data of the world, not yet broken up into Actualities, or Existence, or God, or Spirit, or Value. Our Experience in the second sense has no object in common with the other experiences by other modes. There is no object on which all of the modes of being focus; the togetherness of the modes of being is not one which is being acknowledged in biased ways in the various experiences.

The various experiences of the different modes do displace or have in a biased way the Experience which is their neutral point. The experiences do not do anything but contain the modes, and we dissolve them to find the modes in their severalty. But when we come to daily experience (1) and attempt to know objects other than each of us, we find that though we now have the object as a qualification of ourselves and can dissolve the experience in order to get ourselves and the object, the object is a residuum for us and for others too. The Experience (2) characteristic of the various modes is ontological, whereas ours (1) is epistemological; theirs is without an object over against it whereas ours has one. Or should we say instead that the Experience (2) of the modes has all four modes as its real objects? But then must we not say that our daily experiences (1) have our different selves and their object distorted in the experience (1)? There is a wrong comparison being made here, for what would be analogous in our daily experience (1) would be our experience of one another (1) and not (2) of some object apart from both of us.

We have an experience (1) of other selves in the same way in which each mode has an Experience (2) of the other modes; we have here a genuine entity over against us to know but it is not the convergent object of our diverse experience (1) but rather something which we can get in one way in our experience (1) and which is obtained in another way in the other's experience (1). The experience (1) here can be said to be ontological, though perhaps, since we are cognizing the other in some way, it is not altogether wise to say this. It would be better than to say that the Experience (2) of the modes, of one another, is interlocked, is reciprocal, whereas the experience of an object is not.

But we still must ask about the neutral point of the Experiences (2), of the nature of Experience. But this is like asking about the neutral point of our experience (1) of one another, as if there were a place where these experiences were neutralized.

Our initial datum is an Experience (2) which is oriented towards us and out of which we can extract a knowledge of the other modes of being, a knowledge which is equal to what they would extract from their Experiences (2). The fact that they in their diverse ways could analyze to the same outcome we can is the meaning of the one Experience, of the sheer Togetherness, or the meaning of Neutrality. Accordingly we have on the one hand allowed that there is nothing like a single all-inclusive Experience which is neutral to all the modes, but we have at the same time allowed A] that there is no exclusive orientation towards Actualities but that in fact the Experience (2) of Actualities moves into what is an Experience (2) by other beings, and B] that the dissection of any one of these Experiences (2) will yield the same set of components the other Experiences (2) do, though the process of dissection will have to be different, and C] that the neutrality which we sought originally of all Experience (2) is Neutral Experience, which is experienced by nothing and which is nothing other than the meaning of the four modes as separate, not yet constituting different Experiences (2) of one another by virtue of the infection of the others in each.

The concrete, transitory rich togetherness of the modes has layers; it has four levels in each of which some one mode is the possessor. There is no way of standing in between them all; to find an in-between, one would have to break up the Experience (2) on all levels and see how they are together. But it must not be forgotten that we then and there will then have them together in a concrete way. Thus to revert to the case of two to focus the point: the Experience (2) of each distorts the component coming from the other. To get the in-between place it is necessary to isolate each of them out of the Experience (2). But as soon as we do this we find that they equally contribute to constitute that midpoint, and at the same time overlap one another on two levels so as to constitute their diverse Experiences (2), with which we began.

We can say then that our initial data dissolves primarily towards one mode and derivatively but finally and irreducibly toward the others; it does reveal to us something of one mode and is somewhat alien to the rest. God is not had in *propria persona* in our Experience (2), though he has presence and makes a difference there. But at the same time we cannot separate ourselves off from Him; we can feel Him adumbratively, recognize that he is Experiencing (2) us. We have then no necessary bias in principle towards one mode. On the other hand so far as we really separate out all four modes and keep them apart we do make the midpoint of all the Experiences (2) into a fifth mode. It is only because the modes, while apart, immediately take account of one another that the presumptive fifth mode of the Experience or sheer Togetherness loses its vitality to become but a point, an indication of the fact that the diverse Experiences (2) will dissolve in the end in the same way.

July 3

When we experience something, particularly the other modes as qualifying us, we move inevitably over to those qualifying items and thus grasp something of what the being which Experiences (2) us is like. We do not, except, e.g., as mystics, know how we are being experienced as, for this requires us to be experienced while we are in fact being active. Perhaps though there is a faint awareness of this, a tiny element of mysticism even in ordinary experience.

The overlay of modes makes Experience (2) in four dimensions, and the modes themselves are contentless as outside it; the modes as contentful act towards one another to constitute a midpoint which is contentless. The union of the two togethers, the contentful of Experience (2) and the contentless of the midpoint are unified in each mode. But there is no central point for such unification; the different modes are restless, now stressing the midpoint and now the content, or if one likes their own public and their own private natures, and never having them in equilibrium.

July 31

What is it that requires explanation—is it experience (1) or is it human judgment? Most philosophers think it is the former, and therefore infer back to some prior principle or reality to account for the way in which experience occurs. Even the classical empiricists took this approach. Locke referred back to substance, Berkeley to God and Hume to human nature. The modern empiricists however would like to reverse the trend. They would like, with the pragmatists and with reductionists of all sorts, to explain (and often to explain away) human judgments by referring them to experience for a test. When experience is used in this way it is given a normative status which it does not have intrinsically, and just so far it is taken out of itself and made into an hypothesis or explanation. To say that one wants to determine whether or not an expression is meaningful or true by referring us to experience is in effect to have made the hypothesis that experience has a testifying worth and thus is, even for a modest empiricism, to be bold metaphysically. The only escape possible from any kind of speculative theory is the view of a simple phenomenalism which merely describes every phenomenon as it appears; but this no one has ever the time or the interest to do. We seek to explain and this requires us to retreat from the data as given, to something in terms of which it can be organized, reduced, integrated and/or understood.

August 1

Strictly speaking it is "exists" rather than "existence" which is the predicate, except in some special or strained cases such as "this book has existence." "Exists" is like "smiles," except that it characterizes the object as a unit whereas "smiles" isolates some facet. "Smiles" is contained inside "exists" but not comprehended by it. "Existence" on the other hand is a term with existential import; it is a logically proper name, a true denotative. It is analogous to Kant's possible experience. All denotative terms, "this" "John" "he," are delimitations of "Existence."

We can significantly say then that "Existence exists"; our assertion is not a tautology unless it be a tautology to say that "this exists." It is not tautology, for "Existence" points out a domain which contrasts with other domains such as Actuality, Ideality or God, and which contrasts with its delimitative parts; "exists" on the other hand tells something about the career of that which it characterizes; it tells us that it has implications which logical rules do not encompass, that it is involved in becoming, that it is a terminus of relations.

Plausible but improbable: Each race of people has animals of the same color: all swans, cows, dogs, horses, etc., are black in negro communities, white in ours, etc.

Probable but implausible: The distribution of the colors of animals in the different tribes and continents is roughly equal.

The doctrine of detachment is to be found in the Pythagoreans and Plato. What it in effect says is that an action, which must in any case be started from within, is not to involve the individual in its course and in its outcome, but is to be allowed to be carried by the body and the environment. Man initiates and must initiate action, but he ought, on this doctrine, keep his soul unaffected by the course of the world. One can defend this position by arguing that the consequences which are appropriate to the soul are always other than those characteristic of the body, and that while the body is ennobled by virtue of having actions started by the soul, the soul would be injured if it allowed its activities to be redefined by those of the body. What remains over is the question as to why there should be action at all; the soul would have to gain something from the fact that it did ennoble the body, and it would have to gain its maximum in this way, thereby precluding its need to involve itself further in that body. Accordingly, it would be the fact that the body was made to act, the fact that action was begun, which alone was valuable to the soul. This would mean I suppose that the soul benefits from the opportunity to be an actor, to initiate, to start something off, and in a sense then to create, and that this which is created must for the soul's good and for its own good go its own way. This doctrine says that there is nothing to be gained by continued control, except so far as this control was but another manifestation of the detached soul as initiating activities in an alien medium.

We today seem to take the view that the soul ought to be made more integral with the body, that continual control or involvement with the body is good for both the soul and the body. There is no doubt but that this view does give us a more completely unified man, and answers to experience, medicine, psychiatry, and common sense; but it does involve a loss of the soul's integrity and (what is often overlooked) of the body's. Rationalists see the latter point but not the former; pragmatists see the former, that the soul's values and meanings are modified or qualified or lost when they are involved in the world, but do not see the latter, that the body is itself affected by those transferred meanings and is then no test of them. (Dewey at times saw this point and took the mind and body each to test the other rather than, as James and Peirce were inclined to do, to take the body to test all that goes on in the soul or mind. In this sense Dewey was a good Aristotelian.)

August 2

Whatever term or concept one uses, it serves as a kind of focus, and may be employed again and again. Faced with content which does not respond as one has been accustomed to have the objects of the term or concept respond, one has the alternative of qualifying the concept or replacing it by another. These two procedures are opposed, and the attempt to follow one is in effect a criticism of the other. If the being addressed as "ma" does not answer, it may be, we can suppose, because she does not want to or because she is in fact not "ma." The second is the more radical answer for it in effect makes one have recourse to a more inclusive frame, either in the guise of oneself as the centre of the judgments or in the guise of the world as the source of change and novelty and disappointment. Sooner or later one takes this position, and then has nothing but qualifications of it to insist upon until he comes to the point where he orders the qualifications and therefore uses subordinate organizing concepts. These in effect make some of the qualifications, say of the I or the world, into qualifications of one another.

There is no principle for organization given by the ego or world; they are just referential points whose uncharted activities provide an answer to the source of the plurality of occurrences. The subordinate concepts which order the concepts used on experience are initially among the latter concepts; they are the ones for which the others are made to serve as qualifications. Just why these are chosen is perhaps a matter of tradition, language habits and accident. In any case, they are soon found to be inadequate. The drive of the individual to make his content ordered drives him to use his reason and thus to recognize the recalcitrance of some concepts and facts to the organizing concept. Alternative organizing concepts are then used and an effort is made to reconcile these. Until this is done we either have the "paradox" of making one of these concepts do the work that really requires two, or the "incoherence" of having the two concepts unreconciled. The attempt to avoid both paradox and incoherence is what drives the philosopher and the scientist to speculate, to reconstruct, to offer a new concept not necessarily answering to any used before.

The idea of "God" might be an extension of "father" originally. As used by a theologian or a philosopher it is intended to organize subordinate concepts in such a way that justice is done to the phenomena of experience at the same time that there is a single totality of knowledge, with explanatory unity and without paradox.

August 5

One might envisage experience as a kind of togetherness. This experience is subject to four different types of pressure. There will be a kind of "irrationality," a kind of odd activity which one will eventually credit to Existence. There will be a kind of value, insistent and demanding, which one will eventually credit to Ideality. There will be a kind of drive, effort, appetite, an insistence which one will eventually credit to Actuality, particularly oneself. And finally there will be a kind of unity, or order, which makes it possible to bring all one encounters into one purview; this unity we sooner or later credit to God.

If we explore these final foci of the irregularities in our experience we get to metaphysics. Another thing we might do is to see how one in fact gets to recognize these final foci—this is the study of the growth of consciousness and self-consciousness which Freudians and phenomenologists have made. (Thus Ideality is first found in the demands of the powerful parent, and the individual is found in the guilt which comes from the awareness of the departure of the parent, when one does not live up to the parental ideal.) Such a study allows one to move gradually from experience to what might be termed bearers or representatives of the modes. It could precede the *Modes;* the *Modes* would then be begun at the point where one discovered that these bearers, taken to be final by Freud, etc., are in fact only bearers and representatives and that there is a reality greater than these. It would be possible then to go on and consider how it is that the various modes come together and thereby constitute experience. This procedure would be the reverse of the above. One would first try to see how and why the modes took on bearers of various sorts: in order to fulfill themselves they become incorporated in beings which are instances of other modes, since these instances give a purchase and are available in a way that the pure modes are not.

Since, in order to act in any way one must make use of the modes, it is possible to write a number of "phenomenologies" in which one made use of two or three modes in order to see what can be done to read two or one other mode into the very meaning of experience. It is not possible to make use of only one mode and to bring in three modes at once, for it is necessary to use one mode, and to have another as a guide or principle. This is what Hegel did. He started with "experience" and later took account of individual Actualities by using the Ideal rationality as an operative principle, one which told how to transform indices of Existence (and eventually of Actuality), within the frame of an Absolute totality or unity.

If this is a correct account of what Hegel was doing there should be a number of comparable works which are occupied with other modes. Thus one could start with the counterparts of the "this" of Existence—pleasure for value, desire for the individual, or a unity of a pair for God, and then attempt to use, A] Actuality and Existence, God and Existence, Actuality and God as agencies for moving from pleasure on and on until we had individualized or naturalized or divinized value and thereby made it part of a richer experience; or B] used God and Existence, Ideal and Existence, God and the Ideal as agencies for moving from desire on and on until we had divinized, naturalized or rationalized desire and thereby made it part of a richer experience; or C] used Actuality and Existence, Ideal and Existence, Actuality and Ideal as agencies for moving from a simple unity on and on until we had individualized, naturalized or rationalized unity and thereby made it part of a richer experience. It is to be noted that Hegel could have, in his attempt to bring in Existence and Actuality into the very substance of experience, made use of the divine idea of unity or totality, while keeping as his principle or guide the meaning of the Idea. If he did this he would have said, not that the rational is the real and the real the rational, but that the real is unity and unity is the rational. (Evidently there are other slogans related to the other modes: the use of Actuality as an agent allows for the slogan: the individual is the real, the real is the individual; and the use of Existence as an agent allows for the slogan: flux is the real, the real is flux (or energy, or events, or activity, or process).

Hegel tried to make experience rational, keeping in mind the fact that the divine totality involved a real unification of whatever was known. Accordingly he fastened on any item of experience which pretended to be something substantial, showed that this referred to another, and tried to give an intellectual reinterpretation of this item and the way in which it was related to its other so as to make a whole. He saw in life and death, I suppose, testimonies to powers beyond mere experience and then tried to bring these powers into the phenomena by making them provide the dynamics of experience with its coming to be and vanishing—and its persistence. He got deeper and deeper into Existence, probing new depths of evidence of its power, and coming to the end of his quest when he found that experience had over against it no longer a depth but just itself, or a depth which was itself, and that this enabled him to complete his phenomenology. Later in his work he tried to do a similar thing for Actuality, acting as if this were just a continuation of what he had done before; but he did not affirm that his studies in conceit and consciousness, etc., are probings into the being of Actuality and not of Existence. He could have started at these places and worked along quite different lines from then on. He could have tried to rationalize desire, or to divinize it, or to naturalize it; instead he used it as though it were a phase of Existence itself. There is then a need to write a phenomenology of the individual.

This would begin with desire as indicative of the reality of an individual outside experience or knowledge of the body, and show how this could be understood as in experience or knowledge, or as being bodily. To do this the Ideal or Existence or God could be used as agencies with corresponding frames given by some other mode.

Hegel thought of Existence as involving or as essentially an other; but this it is only because he has taken his stand in experience and looked for existential indicators. If one took this approach with respect to other modes one could view them as others as well; or, taking a stand with the divine as an agency one would be able to see that Existence was not merely an other in a rational relation to the experience, but that it was a rational prop in a relation of oppositional unity to experience. But one could also start not with experience, but with knowledge or language or action. And one could also start not with any of these forms of togetherness, but with some one mode either in itself or as a locus for the other modes and thus itself as a kind of togetherness. Thus one might start by taking the individual as a basic fact and attempt to bring into the phenomenology of his being all the items which indicated other realms. This would require three distinct treatises. They would see this individual in relation to Existence, or the Ideal, or God. These three treatises would have each two parts; what was agent in one would become frame in the other. Thus the individual in relation to the Ideal (which is the study of ethics) would have a part where the Ideal was vitally identified with the individual, making ethics personal, under the aegis of the idea of unity; or the individual in relation to the Ideal would be unified in itself and with respect to the Ideal in the attempt to achieve practice. The individual in relation to Existence (which is the problem of man in nature) would be rationally dealt with under the aegis of God, somewhat as Hegel in fact does in dealing with the community of animals, or it could be dealt with as a problem of unification with the idea of achieving intelligibility. And finally the individual in relation to God could be rationally dealt with under the pressure of a doctrine of flux or vital movement or it could be vitally handled with the desire to attain an intelligible account.

In all these schemes there is an implicit supposition to the effect that the agency which is being used exhausts its power by the end of the system, and that the agency which is the frame at the same time achieves its full realization. The incorporation of a mode inside some other then is completed with the exhaustion of the power of a third and the realization of the import of the fourth.

If Hegel's phenomenology is

1] God made concrete, the Ideal realized and Existence made explicit (and the Actual transcended), we can have the following alternatives:

2] Existence made explicit and the Actual transcended with God realized and Ideal made concrete.

3] Actual explicit, Existence transcended, God realized, Ideal concrete.

4] Actual explicit, Existence transcended, God concrete, Ideal realized.

5] and   6] Existence explicit, God transcended, Actuality or Ideal realized.

7] and   8] God explicit, Existence transcended, Actuality or Ideal realized.

9] and   10] Existence explicit, Ideal transcended, God or Actuality realized.

11] and   12] Ideal explicit, Existence transcended, etc.

There are, in other words, three main cases each where a mode is made explicit, e.g., Existence is made explicit with   1] Actuality or   2] Ideality or   3] God transcended.

In each of these cases there are two subordinate cases: in one of these subordinate cases a third mode is realized, and in the other of these subordinate cases a fourth mode is realized, the remaining mode being made concrete. Thus

1a] Existence explicit, Actuality transcended, God realized, Ideal made concrete.

1b] Existence explicit, Actuality transcended, Ideal realized, God concrete.

2a] Existence explicit, Ideal transcended, God realized, Actuality made concrete.

2b] Existence explicit, Ideal transcended, Actuality realized, God concrete.

3a] Existence explicit, God transcended, Actuality realized, Ideal made concrete.

3b] Existence explicit, God transcended, Ideal realized, Actuality made concrete.

The above six cases concern Existence, the world at large, mere process and activity or its representative experience. To seek to make this explicit, to convert its "substance" into "subject" is one of four basic enterprises.

A] Which way of making explicit should one choose?   B] Which of the four modes should one seek to make explicit?

A] There is much to be said for transcending God, i.e., ignoring Him, overlooking Him, trying to deal with the world as apart from Him, since

He seems to be so obscure and outside the purview of a "science." If this
be so we reduce the ways to trying to make only three modes explicit
(this answers question 2) and in these three modes to consider only two
cases. We would then have:

1] Existence made explicit, God transcended, Actuality realized, Ideal
made concrete

2] Existence made explicit, God transcended, Ideal realized, Actuality
concrete

3] Actuality made explicit, God transcended, Ideal realized, Existence
concrete

4] Actuality made explicit, God transcended, Existence realized, Ideal
concrete

5] Ideal made explicit, God transcended, Existence realized, Actuality
concrete

6] Ideal made explicit, God transcended, Actuality realized, Existence
concrete

The first two might be thought to deal with the nature of things, the
second two with self-knowledge or the realization of the self, and the
third with the achievement of values in the world. Since the last seems
like a myth, and even where recognized (as in the case of effective or
demanding Ideals, and even personalized in the guise of society or parent), there is interest in the way in which it can come to full expression in
the course of knowledge or being. If so this leaves us with the first four
cases, of which the second and third are closer to the Hegelian idea than
the first and fourth. What interests mankind are perhaps the third and
fourth, where man comes to be manifest in its richest, the fact and being
of God is ignored, and the whole is seen to be making the Existence or
the Ideal concrete, finding the whole as an embodied Existence or Ideal.
The embodiment of Existence is a way of naturalizing, the embodiment
of the Ideal a way of cognizing; they could be thought of as supplementary, with naturalizing involving the temporal realization of the Ideal,
and completed cognition as involving the exhaustion of the powers of
Existence. Since the latter seems not to suppose that cognition is equal in
reach or power to the whole of Existence, the former answers more
readily to our antecedent suppositions. A new phenomenology could
therefore profitably start with the case where the Actual would be made
explicit while the Ideal was realized and Existence as a frame became
more and to be concrete, to have its full being in the domain where the
Actual was made explicit.

But then, in this case, what is the dialectic? It would seem to be
Hegelian in that the real is to be made rational, but not Hegelian in that

it is Actuality and not Existence that is made explicit, made into a phenomenon, understood as manifest. Existence is a domain of otherness, of the opposed, but the self is the domain of the possessor, of the master, of the judged, and evaluated.

Should we say that each individual is to be made explicit, phenome-nalized, by seeing how it dissolves into a confrontation with what ought to be interrelated by possession and judgment? Is it not this that the existentialists saw in Hegel's discussion of master and slave? Hegel supposed that these expressed the subterranean forces of Existence; the other thinkers saw that they expressed the subterranean forces of Actuality and that the so-called negativity principle was not in operation. Instead there was a power of genuine self-and other-mastery, i.e., of self-possession and the possession of others.

August 6

Speculative philosophy is the art of providing the most cautious hypotheses to cover all the facts.

There are four disciplines which represent all the dimensions neu-trally:

I] Actuality through knowledge yields philosophy
II] Ideality through evaluation yields mathematics
III] Existence through co-ordination yields art
IV] God through appreciation yields religion

Each of these neutral positions has been won by a strategy. These strategies are achieved in one of four ways by each discipline, depending on which tonality of the whole is desired. Thus philosophy can have a naturalistic, a personalistic, a moral or a religious tone, depending on whether it is Existence, Actuality, Ideality or God which it uses to counterbalance the native bias of a given mode. (When one makes use of the same mode to counterbalance a given bias, what one in effect does is to re-assess that mode, give it a new centre of gravity; it is in this way that a personalism or existentialism can avoid a bad subjectivism.)

We have then four kinds of strategies, occupied with overcoming a characteristic bias and ending with a tonality which reflects the nature of the mode used in order to overcome that bias. Let us designate these as:

1] cognition through the use of a counteracting Actuality
2] qualification through the use of a counteracting Ideality
3] vitalization through the use of a counteracting Existence
4] re-organization through the use of a counteracting God

Each mode of being has then four strategies, and thus four different neutral guises. Naturalism in philosophy is the outcome of a vitalization imposed and counteracting the natural bias of Actuality; personalism is the outcome of the recognition of the individual, and involves an over-coming of the bias of Actuality by emphasizing the interiority, the individualized side of Actuality; morally toned philosophy is the outcome of the qualifications imposed by the Ideal as it subordinates the Actuality and other modes; the religiously toned philosophy is the outcome of a reorganization of the data which the Actuality confronts in a biased way, a reorganization which is appreciative of the various values and stresses of the different modes. Similar observations must be made with respect to each of the disciplines.

Each achievement of neutrality through strategy must be embodied in three subsequent grades, thereby enabling the abstractiveness of the neutral position to be overcome without falling back into a reaffirmation of the original bias. We have—

A] the position of abstract neutrality to be exploited by the discipline,

B] the position of interpretation carried out by some one of four enter-prises which itself has four possible phases,

C] the position of the enjoyment adopted by some one type of being,

D] the position where the import is determined in one of four ways.

A, B, C, and D have four guises each, for each discipline. Thus philosophy (I) in the guise A, has the four guises of 1, 2, 3, 4 of neutrality. There will be an analogous set for it in the position of interpretation, enjoyment and import. Thus a naturalistic philosophy will find its primary interpre-tation in some principle of permanence, its primary enjoyment in some idea of value and its primary import in the individual. Each of these has less important variations; it is possible, for example, for a naturalistic philosophy to have its primary import in its effect on society and thus in a form of Existence. These variations can be designated as *i, ii, iii, iv*— individual, valuational, dynamic and unitary.

Each of the modes then, say Actuality, yields a neutral discipline (1) by any one of four strategies, e.g., vitalization (3) to give a natural-ism, which can receive an interpretation (B) through the use of an individual (*i*).

If we apply the above to the arts we get:

III. 1. drama, the position of neutrality through the use of counteracting
                                                                   Actuality

     2. poetry, the position of neutrality through the use of counteracting
                                                                   Ideality

     3. music, the position of neutrality through the use of counteracting
                                                                   Existence

4. sculpture (architecture, painting), the position of neutrality
through the use of counteracting God

The playwright's work is III,1, A. He is interpreted (B) by the actors primarily (*ii*) as alert to the value of the Ideal, who look to the written play as an Ideal and attempt to make it vivid by virtue of the way in which they embody this Ideal in themselves in an existential or dramatic context under a guidance of a permanent order. If they do not treat the play as an Ideal they can take a minor variation, and view it say as an individual expression by an author, as an historic document or as a divine vehicle. (*i, iii, iv*) Having interpreted the play it is open to enjoyment (C) in the primary form of an existent occurrence, an ongoing in which the audience can participate. This is a primary form for III,1, A, and (*ii*); there are three others. And there is finally the position (D) where the import of the play III,1 can be determined by viewing it as a permanent fact in the world, the meaning of some such eternal truth as the tragic meaning of life, etc.

We have an analogous set of steps for poetry (III,2). It is to be interpreted B primarily as an actual occurrence, as a matter of fact with an individual nature (*i*); is to be primarily enjoyed C *iv* as a kind of permanent fact in the world, as the locus of eternal verity; and is to be primarily evaluated, have its import determined D *iii,* by its role in the vital course of history.

Music (III,3) is to be primarily interpreted B *i* as something eternal and perfect; is to be enjoyed C *ii,* as so interpreted as a kind of ideal we want to embody, and D *i* is to be primarily determined for its import by the effect it has for the individual, by its facing the individual as an individual item of enjoyment.

The manipulative arts finally are to be interpreted as a kind of domain of Existence, as the very world caught within a limited confines, are to be enjoyed as individual objects, and are to have their import determined by the way in which they serve as ideals.

The four: music, drama, poetry, sculpture form a circle in the sense that if we begin with one of them, its import is in the same domain of being as is the neutral formulation of the next kind of art. If we knew with which one to begin we could then make a circle which embraced the others. I think it most plausible to suppose that manipulative arts offer the most immediate and available and the historically first of all the arts. If so our sequence must be: after the manipulative, poetry, music, drama, . . .

Can we make a similar sequence of the naturalistic, personalistic, moral and religious philosophies, each of which has its proper interpreta-

tions, enjoyments and import? If the above is to be a guide we have
religious, moral, naturalistic and personalistic.
This seems to answer to the historic situation quite well. But which one is
the *Modes?* It would seem to be primarily moral, in which case there
ought to be revisions of the *Modes* made with stresses on the naturalistic
and the personalistic. Also what are the primary interpretations, enjoyments and import determinants of philosophy? Shall we say the reader
interprets, mankind enjoys and civilization provides the import—these
differing of course in their primary stresses, depending on whether or not
the philosophy is naturalistic?

When we turn to the arts again, and particularly drama, we see that
the position of a neutrality is achieved, as in all the arts, by a kind of
epitomization. The playwright makes a unity of the four modes in his
play, by making a use of the individuality of Actuality in order to overcome the bias of men which they exhibit unconsciously and more or less
conventionally. He makes the Actual function as a kind of norm and
realizes this in an idealized medium in a dramatic (or existential) effort
guided by the principle of unity. It is his outcome which the actors make
vivid, by viewing it as an Ideal which they embody in an existent medium,
in an effort at perfection and under the guidance of the nature of man.
The acted play is enjoyed by the audience when it views it as an existential occurrence which is being embodied in something permanent in an
individual experience, under the guidance of what one takes to be man in
the ideal frame. This drama as enjoyed is evaluated by civilization as the
locus of all values; this evaluation is embodied in individuals, where an
Ideal effort is made under the guidance of the existential purpose of
history.

August 7

There would seem to be four usages of the term "subject." There
is the naturalistic or realistic use, which takes a subject to be something
to be rooted in an existential realm, in effect an "object," thereby making
meaningless or useless any term such as "exists" when made to have the
role of predicate. There is the idealistic use, which thinks of the subject as
a grammatical subject, as something to be correlated with the predicate, or
explicated by it. Such a view makes useless or meaningless the characterization "true" or "false" of the entire assertion. There is the actual
use, which identifies the "subject-term" with a real "subject," the individual or I; here the subject-term marks out a sphere of interest of the
individual which the predicate then delimits, qualifies and reorders. Such

a use finds useless or meaningless the characterizations, "I assert" or "I believe" or "I suppose." Finally there is the theological, and in which the subject is in effect a reject, an item contrasted with God, in which the predicate serves as a kind of rectification or ,qualification, serving to bring back that reject into God. Such a use finds useless or meaningless the characterization "is real," "is excellent" and perhaps even "is finite," "is imperfect."

The kind of reduction which Russell imposed on the use of terms like "existence" and his reduction of descriptions to characterizations of existent entities, has a counterpart in reductions which could be made on behalf of idealistic or judgmental logics, such as Bradley's; personalistic or individualistic or existentialistic logics such as Kierkegaard's and theo-centric or monistic logics such as we have in India.

Each one of these logics has its own peculiar "existential import." In each there is a term which states the domain and therefore can be said to be a genuinely proper name. The term is the name of a mode of thought. In the naturalistic or realistic logic, "Existence" is a proper name, and every subdivision of this, designated by "this" or some other denotative term, is consequently a proper name too. When it is said of "Existence" or any portion of it that it "exists," the second term is redundant, firstly if one is making use of the naturalistic logic, and secondly if the predicate but repeats the meaning of the subject. In the other logics, "Existence" is not a proper name. And in a naturalistic logic there is no need to suppose that "exists" but repeats in predicate form what the subject embraces. One may treat "Existence" as a proper name without making it improper to use "exists" as a predicate. As such a predicate, "exists" would characterize the subject as being involved in the realm of Existence; it would in effect say to us that the subject term was a genuine one, a true proper name. The Russell analysis supposes that the true proper name is self-evident, self-revelatory. If this were the case then one could say that "exists" was effete; but only if one supposed that a proper name was the name of something which in effect existed. Russell's analysis presupposes that we are already in nature, that "Existence" and the referents to its subdivisions are truly proper names, that the nature of proper names is self-evident, and that the predicates which are used with these but redescribe what these proper names implicitly express.

In idealistic logic, "truth" is the outcome of an adequate or appropriate articulation of content, which is exhausted in that articulation. The subject and predicate strictly speaking have no being; they are abstractions which only in their synthetic unity have meaning and function. On such a view the characterization "true" but summarizes the fact that we have an articulation. If we sought to speak of "The Truth" or the Ideal in this logic we would find that it was only the proper name for the entire set of articulated expressions. Whereas in the case of Existence the subject-term was supposed to be a qualification of the term "Existence" and have a referent which was rooted in the whole of Existence, here we have the entire assertion making a subdivision, and its referent part of the domain of Truth.

"Truth" could be said to be the proper name for the Ideal. To say of it then that it was "true" would seem to be redundant or meaningless. But once again it is being supposed that the subject term is repeated in some way by the object term. But in the assertion "Truth is true" or in more conventional language "The whole of scientific or articulate knowledge alone is true" we have a subject and a predicate which are correlatives. Each by itself says something other than it does in relationship with its correlate. "True" is a universal and could conceivably be applied elsewhere; applying it to the "The Truth" is in effect cutting it down to this specific case, the universe which in fact exists.

In existentialistic or personalistic logic it becomes redundant to assert "I assert"; and when proper account is taken of the nature of the assertion and the way it issues from the subject, it becomes redundant also to say "I believe." These are in effect proper names for the Subject itself; every assertion is but the expression of that Subject and in a way but explicates this, rounds it out and resolves it or adjusts it or improves it, by means of the predicate as completing some limited version of that Subject. When it is said for example that "this table is brown" what in effect is being done is to provide a way in which the Subject comes to expression in some such form as "I believe this to be a brown table." The "I believe" here is a reflection of the Subject, and the rest of the assertion is a kind of predicate of this, which can be analyzed into a subsidiary subject term "this-table" and "brown." The "brown" completes the "this-table" to make the whole into a kind of expression or counterpart or continuant of and therefore completive element for the Subject. It is effete then to say in this logic anything like "I believe"—as Spinoza, who had I think a different logic than that of Actuality in effect said. Spinoza thought the "I believe" unnecessary not because the proposition qualified a Subject inescapably but because he thought it exhibited interiorly the kind of rationale this modal term expressed. Spinoza got rid of "I believe" by finding the assertion itself to be self-sufficient; but it is on this logic removable only because the very presence of the assertion—and perhaps the kind of assertion it is—requires that it have a certain relationship to, be sustained by the Subject in a particular modal way.

Strictly speaking though, the assertion is no simple removable tautological predicate of the Subject; it tells us something of the Subject's state, condition or knowledge.

Finally, in monistic logic where the subject of an expression is in effect a reject to be modified and corrected by the predicate, all claims on behalf of the reality or excellence or finitude, any claim about the status of the Subject term would appear to be redundant, since the function of a predicate here is not to tell us about the subject but to reduce this to a position inside the absolute. Here the proper name is given by the predicate; it pulls up the subject term as it were into the domain of the divine. The best proper name is the predicate "God"; this predicate, a unique description, which is not reducible, is a proper name of God only so far as it does lift up the Subject. "God," when used as though it characterized the divine rather than whatever did occur in this world, would be like an ordinary predicate. Every ordinary predicate lifts up only this or that Subject. It achieves the status of a true proper name by virtue of its function and not of its denotation. It is as it were by absorbing the subjects which we use into itself that "God," which is pertinent to all of them, attains the status of a genuine proper name for that mode of being we have called by that name. The rejected terms here are not simply redundant; they tell us what is to be rectified by God.

To say that something exists is surely significant from the standpoint of the Ideal, from the standpoint of individuals, and from the standpoint of God. And unless one adheres to the assumptions made by Russell it is even significant in naturalistic logic. In each logic what the others take to be proper names are denied this status. Any sense in which "Existence" could be a proper name, the other terms are not, and conversely, where those terms are used as proper names "Existence" turns out to be a subject correlate with some predicate articulating something richer and bigger than "Existence," an expression of the individual in relation to a world beyond, or a term which must be qualified and modified until it is indistinguishable from the name "God."

What logic do we have who view the whole? Is it not a logic whose proper name is Togetherness or Being and which divides into one of the above four as soon as we characterize it? The mode of characterization forces the Being to have the shape of this or that type of Subject, and therefore to be in such and such a relation to the predicate. Being or Togetherness is the proper name to which no predicate is proper; as soon as we try to make it into a single Subject we find that we have ambiguously related the predicate to it, and thus have not made a true proposition. To say that "Being is four-fold" or to say that "Togetherness is not a mode of being" would be tantamount to saying four things at once, either because the Subject is broken up into four terms, or because the way in which the predicate is related to the single "being" or "togetherness" is four-ply. What we in effect do is to adopt one of the four logics and thereby speak of "Being" or "Togetherness" not as it in fact is but as it is from the perspective of that language.

Strictly speaking then we ought to say that there is one proper name and this is not characterizable, or alternatively, that this proper name either denotes, acts as a pivot, serves as the beginning of an act of expression, or is something to be absorbed and transformed. Another way of saying this perhaps is to say that when we begin with a proper name in one of these roles we are dialectically driven to consider proper names having other roles, or alternatively, what in a judgment is taken to be a proper name with correlative predicate, adumbrated, and subjective unity is found to be itself a predicate, adumbrated, or unity for some one of these others in the role of Subject. Thus if we begin with a supposed existential term, such as "This" or "this table" and have it correlate with "brown" as predicate, adumbratively connected with an actual perceived table, and united by a knowing subject, we can also look at "brown" as a name in an idealistic logic with the "this table" as a kind of predicate or localization of it, which functions as a kind of correlative in an assertion but in effect has only a subordinate status; we can treat the previously adumbrated "this-brown-table" as the proper name in a monistic logic and the "this table" as an incomplete adumbrated fragment from it; and finally we can treat the unity of the assertion, the meaning of it, as a proper name for the Subject, with the "this-table" serving in an existential logic as a unified way of focussing on a facet of the unity.

The four-fold analysis of a category or judgment in effect then is undetermined as to just what is to serve as subject or predicate or adumbrated or unity. The decision to use one item say as subject and another as predicate, etc., is the decision to adopt one mode of being rather than another as one's pivot. The category as not yet used in one of these ways is once again the category of being or togetherness; it cannot be used on being or togetherness without first making a division in beings. The category in its undetermined, multiply determinable guise is being; it is the proper name which is one with its object, the proper name which has no predicate; the proper name which no one can use; the proper name which is a kind of blur of different types of proper names; the proper name which is so general and vague that it is neither a name nor proper.

The Subject, we might say, begins by expressing itself, and what it produces must be localized. The localized product must be correlated with its other so that it can be co-equal, and then must be re-absorbed in a higher unity, must become the Subject in order that it be completed. This constitutes one epoch or stage, and is to be followed by three others which begin respectively with localized production, correlation, and absorption. When we have gone through all four epochs we have arrived at the present. In this activity, which can be said to be a voyage of self-development, of enrichment, of articulation, and of the achievement of the absolute, we but find the meaning of the present in all that has gone before. The next epoch gives us a new and more inclusive standpoint, requiring us to engage in the entire activity again with this new standpoint as our new beginning, as the very substance of the Subject. At the end then we find out what the Subject was with which we began and which we knew only through its expression; the end is the Subject itself making itself manifest.

We start with an expression of the Subject, the Subject as past, and end with the Subject in the present. The next cycle is the repetition of the first except that now we have the old present Subject possessing its past expressions, whereas before we merely had the expressions outside that Subject. If we take the two of them together we can define a new present and a new epoch. The Subject as manifest in such and such expressions is a repetition of the expressions and the stages which follow on it, but in a self-consciousness; when we make both the Subject and its expressions into a new Subject which is merely expressed, we get a new standpoint, in which the Subject and its expressions are absorbed in an unknown Subject. This Subject expresses itself with new meanings in the old places. Thus if we start say with the Greeks, we express what they are from the standpoint of the Subject in the present whose nature we do not know until we get through the four cycles, and end with a Subject which is to express itself.

August 8

There are four *cycles* to an *epoch*. If we begin with say Actuality and its kind of Subject, we must go through the stages where this is supplemented by the domains of Existence, Ideality and God, in order to get a full expression. If we start with "I believe this is a cat," the "this is a cat" is in effect the Subject so far as it is oriented in the real Subject through the "I believe."

We must posit this Subject, relate this, root this content, as dislocated from the "I believe," in the domain of Existence, in order to give it objectivity, to make it something that has been expressed, to give it a role apart from the fact that it is being expressed. This in effect reduces "I believe this is a cat" to "this-cat," a denotative term or proper name embedded in a real situation. The Subject now is without any role in discourse; it is a subject only in the sense that it is part of an object; it gives us an objective point of view but no genuine term. We have not, to be sure, changed the initial Subject into a new type of Subject, the kind used in naturalistic contexts; we are merely referring our old Subject (to which we still cling) to a domain exterior to it. If we had wanted to get a Subject as something existing we would have had to add an act of denotation, would have had to move to the Existential domain and submit ourselves to it; but what we now do is to use our expression to characterize that existential domain.

Since that domain is outside our Subject we cannot make any significant use of it until we translate it into the correlate of our initial Subject, to give us something like "this-cat is brown" or "this-cat is moving" or even "this-cat exists." Here our original Subject, collapsed in the guise of a grammatical Subject, is supplemented by a term which the exteriorization of our expression allows us to surmise. (There is no such grammatical subject as "this" unless one starts either with an existing Subject or a grammatical Subject; if our cycle begins with an expressing Subject we always have a unit of discourse, expanded or collapsed.)

The "this-cat is brown" remains in part an expression of the Subject and in part an articulation of the existing object. The new predicate now takes over the position of dominance to become in effect the new Subject defining what is excellent or real. It is an evaluative predicate in this sense, and though it still allows the Subject to express itself, still allows for orientation in Existence, and for the having of a correlate, it now has the additional function of making what before was an expressed Subject, with a subtended base or correlative predicate, into a Subject for a higher Subject. The predicate "brown" lifts up the "this-cat" to make it into a Subject which is sustained by a higher Subject. This is a "this-cat" because it is subjugated in a certain way by brown; because it is brown, or more obviously because (say) it meows we can acknowledge "this-cat" to be a genuine cat.

In this cycle what we have is an expression of a Subject which is supplemented by other domains, without losing its status as an expression. We complete, inside the area of the Subject, the expression it offers by taking account of the fact that there are points of reference for that expression before it can achieve the status of a real Subject on its own. The expressed Subject, through the three subsequent activities, is transformed in the end (through the predicate as oriented in the divine) into something which is thereby substantialized. One may say then that the cycle is completed with the substantialization of the expressed Subject—what Hegel would perhaps call the conversion of substance into subject. Of course there is no genuine substantialization; there is only a reference to the power by virtue of which such substantialization could occur. The original Subject still remains what it was, but we end with the recognition of a unity which could operate through the predicate and thereby give us a genuine Subject made from the original expressed Subject and its correlative predicate as rooted in Existence. But we end before there is the operation of the unity; we merely recognize it as a factor in the entire complex of which the expressed Subject is just the initial item.

We begin a second cycle with the effective operation of the unity, with the change of the Subject, "this-cat" through the agency of the transformative predicate "brown" (or because it is brown and meows, etc.) into a proper name of the excellent or real or eternal. It is this reality, "this-brown-cat" which is now to be seen to require expression, to come out into the open, to have a being apart from the divine in which it attained its substantiality. It is something which can be articulated, adopted, affirmed, treated as something which could be believed or asserted. The divine, in which the "this-brown-cat" is but a fragmentary part, knows this part only so far as the divine sees that it could express itself as such a part. The expression is but a fulguration, a mere exposure, unless it can be oriented in something outside it, in Existence. It could not be used in discourse, known to be what it is, unless it is given that Existence as a correlate in the form of an item in discourse, such as "is moving." We end this cycle with the assertion "this-brown-cat is moving" or better we end it with the awareness that this subject "this-brown-cat" could be expressed, does have an existential counterpart and does have a correlate, all of which are given a role inside and yet over against the unity with which we began this second cycle.

A third cycle begins with the entire expression "this-brown-cat is moving" as a unit, as a kind of subject in which "this-brown-cat" is the grammatical subject. This judgmental subject, as one might term it, needs to be sustained by a power which it does not have of itself; its predicate must serve to lift its subject up into a unity of the two of them. But in this cycle it merely points to the fact that there is a unity which makes it one, a single judgment in which these elements are in fact held together. For it to be one the grammatical subject in the judgmental whole must be distinguished as something around which the discourse can pivot. When the grammatical subject is oriented in Existence, "this-brown-cat is moving" at once achieves a unitary meaning, a genuine expressive subject, and an objective orientation. But the "moving" still stands outside the subject as it were. If, instead one used the entire expression, "this-brown-cat is moving" as the initial subject in this cycle, one would have to provide a locus for it. It there could be enriched by some transformative power, such as "because it is alive," and then allowed the opportunity to come to expression either as a single term or as a unit in an inferential whole, and then oriented in the existing world beyond.

A fourth cycle begins with the actual rooting of the outcome of the third cycle. Here "This-brown-cat is moving because it is alive" is given substance, allowed to have implications which it formally does not possess. As so embedded in an external world, as functioning as a proper name for a real being, with its rationale, "because it is alive" built into it, there is need to make manifest what these implications are. Reference must be made to some further characterization, such as "in our kind of world" to make evident the nature of the subject as it in fact can act. And this addition must, under the power of a unity, be able to transform the entire subject "this-brown-cat is moving because it is alive" into a single reality, a genuine solidified subject, which can now come to expression. At this point we end the fourth cycle and the entire process of using four logics, each in four dimensions.

We began with the logic of Actuality and found that there was need to take account of the roles of other modes, though without allowing them to change the function of the Subject, but only to add to it, to complete it. We then moved to the logic of the divine or eternal and found a similar need for completion; similarly for the Ideal and finally for Existence. We end with a new Subject, the solidification of "this-brown-cat-is-moving-because-it-is-alive" as the very substance of a self or mind or individual, and which must now come to expression in a new round of four cycles.

In each cycle the beginning is with a Subject of a special sort, and the dialectic but shows how this might be completed by giving it a role with respect to other dimensions, which themselves are not used but pointed out. A new cycle begins when what is pointed out is in fact made use of. The provision of the domain which was pointed out is the achievement of a new type, an enriched Subject, since what had been gone through before in principle is now in fact added. When we come to the end of the four cycles we have in fact given to the Subject, with which we began, three counterparts, all of which could be viewed as equally good Subjects. We in effect are, if we hold on to all the cycles, providing ourselves with some such complexity as: "this-cat"; "this-cat-is-brown"; "this-moving-cat-is-brown"; "this-living-moving-cat-is-brown" (to express all these in the language of a Subject). A new four-fold cycle begins with the adoption of the richest of these subjects (the last).

The movement *inside* a cycle, the movement *from* cycle to cycle, and the movement to a *new set* of four cycles must be due to the fact that there is something in the first expression which requires something beyond it. The "this-cat" requires that there be other roles or ways of being a Subject; the Subject which expresses itself in this way is still not fully expressed; its attempt to be fully expressed makes it subjugate itself to, correlate itself with and submit itself to other powers; when it has spent itself in these ways, we are left with it in its purity as a mere expression, and as qualified by the other three modes. If one were to turn away from a consideration of Subjects, one could have the four-fold cycle followed by one in which there was a consideration of the dynamics of orientation, by predicates, and by evaluations. But we are in no position to move out of a consideration of Subjects unless once more we invoke a power which needs these other cycles in order to complete whatever it has begun.

Whether then we have a four-fold cycle of Subjects to be followed by another, with a richer Subject and so on, or whether we have such a cycle followed by a four-fold cycle of existential connections, another of predicates, and another of rectifications, the end of our set of cycles must be shown to give way to another—or we would have to say that we had come to the end of time and system. It is only because there is some prospect which still needs to be realized, only because wherever we are we are faced with something which needs to be actualized, that there is a necessary movement beyond the point where we are.

In the course of history, the point which is the present is that which is fulfilled by all that has gone before. We can say then that we start with the present, with the final complex subject, "this-moving-living-cat" as the partial proper name of an eternal being, and that we provide the other stages in order to articulate this; the earlier stages then are earlier only in that they are partial formulations of what we have in the present in an unanalyzed way. We look back at the past, as it were, as a way of analyzing what we start with in the present. When we pass to the next moment we are then confronted with the alternative of looking at all that has gone before as a way of analyzing this next moment, or of looking at all that has gone before the previous present as a way of analyzing that previous present, and of having the previous present as an additional item analyzing the present. Or to say it another way, though for the present every past item is part of its analysis, inside the past the successors offer themselves as that which is analyzed by their predecessors. Every past occurrence then has the role of being an analytic component of the present that is now, and of the presents that had been and which had succeeded that occurrence. The present therefore can have as its analytic datum just the previous present, since this already epitomizes all that had gone before, or it can have that previous present as one item alongside the other items, or it can have it as that which is in fact analyzed by what had been, and yet allow this, which had been, to be analyzed from the perspective of a further present.

Given the second world war as a present, and the first world war as a previous present, the first world war could be said to be that which must give rise to the second. But since it is itself that which had to come about because of the war of 1870, let us say, the war of 1870 has the role of being A] that which is to be understood in terms of the inclusive meaning of the first world war, and B] as that which is to be understood from the vantage point of the second world war. The first world war will be found to be a kind of explication of the war of 1870, and also to be that which can be dealt with as an occurrence without any role with respect to the war of 1870. The present is exhausted by all that had gone before, and when we get a new present, we do not merely add to it another past moment, but subject this new present to a new analysis over the new totality of past items. The war of 1870 is one thing from the perspective of the first and another thing from the perspective of the second world war. This does not result in a relativity of history, for firstly the analysis of the first world war is correct, and can itself be absorbed and made into an analytic component of the second world war—i.e., 1870 as involving 1914 can be a datum for 1940, and secondly the datum, 1870, is in no way denied, but merely re-assessed, given a new role.

The present makes the past items take the position of analytic elements of itself, so that when these are seen to move beyond themselves it is because the present is the leaven, the actual power that was used to give them the status they have as items. Though the past preceded the present the status of the past is determined by the use of the present to make it a set of items, to make it move into the present, and to explain and be explained by that present.

But when we come to the four types of four-fold cycles of subjects, predicates, referents and unities, we would have to say that what guides the whole is the meaning of being. Being seeks to be and in this process dissipates itself over the entire 4 x 16 shapes in which the components of knowledge will appear. At the end of such a venture Being is, not as *a* Being, but as beings; from the beginning then it is the undetermined residuum of being that is trying to be which makes one go through the various cycles. But then what happens at the end of the 4 x 16? I think we must say that in one sense being is exhausted, for we are at the present, and in another sense not, for now we must consider not only the Actual in the guise of subject, or as predicate, etc., but must have it as active or as unified or as desirous, etc. But what is the case when we have gone through all these stages? Is this the very coming to be of Being, and there the making of a new Being which must start all over again, but with a richness we have not had? But since we can go through this process in thought can we not anticipate the new shape Being will assume? No, we cannot. We cannot bring together all the expressions of being to make one unexpressed Being; this occurs at the end of the four cycles of subject, predicate, etc., and what shape it will take we cannot know until we in fact get there. When we complete the system and collapse what we have done into the unexpressed reality of Being, we really have an unending process to go through, for the collapse is something which, though theoretically expressible in a word, must be in fact undergone in order to have it be.

At the end of the theoretical completion of the cycles we go through the process of making a new present. The present of this epoch is here now, and the analysis of it is a reformulation of it. While we were exhausting Being in this vast articulation, we were building it up on the other side with just this wealth of articulate material being made to be together, and when we come to the end of our cycles we find that what before were expressions of Being are now a Being expressed, and that Being must conquer these expressions. We will then either see what we have before us sullied again and again by the expression of Being through it (which will force us to make use of ourselves to start a new round of thought), or we will ourselves adopt the position of that Being which is on the further side, which has somehow collected itself while we were articulating and thus dispersing it. This collected Being is in fact three distinct Beings, a substantial, a unifying and an ideal. To adopt any one of them is in effect to be carried by new forces.

We must move to a higher level where the fact that there had been these carryings and the previous elaboration of being suffices as data for a new dimension of unexhausted Being. In effect we never get rid of some kind of togetherness no matter how we disperse it in a plurality.

If we take our stand in experience we find it a diffuse unity in its horizontal and vertical dimensions. To find ourselves in it we break it up by emphasizing different parts and thereby getting an abstract unity of the modes as related by abstract relations of togetherness, making them a genuine many. In order to be able to make a unity of our own being, since it too is diffuse, we are forced to distinguish the various forms of togetherness as abstract, and to recognize that they are united concretely in the different modes. We always have diffuse unities and clarified neutral but abstract sets of items. The diffusion is genuine Being which must be expressed in real articulated items, but only by then and there solidifying on the far side. It is like an Empedoclean rhythm. We never get to an extreme; as we disperse Being we collect it, and just before it is wholly dispersed we find ourselves confronted with a denser version of the counterpart than we had before.

More exactly, the dispersed Being occurs together with a triple intensification of Being. This means that at the end of the four-fold cycle of cycles where we have the subject in four cycles, the predicate in four cycles, etc., we find a unity held over against us, which is at once dynamic, transcendent and ideal, and that we, through our need to hold on to the dispersed totality which we produced, yield ourselves to the unities. When those unities are completed in a four-fold cycle of cycles for each of them, we come back to the point where we have solidified a new Being on our side; this is the Subject that needs expression. This new Being is different from the old because it is newly forged; it is a new precipitate.

The movement which we go through in speculative philosophy is a schema for an endless movement at the same time that it does report one actual movement of speculation. Speculation is an actual movement which offers the schema for all movements, each one of which is novel in the sense that it had a specific content produced in the course of activity in thought and fact.

To return to the simplest case of a single cycle of a subject as being supplemented by references to other components of a judgment, we come to the end by exhausting Being in the guise of an expressed Subject, but in that exhausting we in effect make Being collect as the domain of, e.g., Existence in which the given subject is forced to adhere, etc. And when we come to the end of the four-fold use of Subjects we get three more cycles.

August 9

We can distinguish   *1*] a *completive moment,* where starting with, say the idea of a subject, we follow out a dialectical course in order to complete its categorial structure by taking account of the possibility of other items which could be added to that subject.
2] a *thematic cycle,* made up of four completive moments. In connection with the subject we have the subject as an expression or ejaculation of a

Subject, as a referent or objectification, as an articulation in discourse, and as a datum for a transformation.

3] a *dialectical cycle,* made up of four thematic cycles. There is the thematic cycle of the subject, another of the object, and a third of the predicate and a fourth of unity.

4] an *epoch,* made up of four dialectical cycles. There is the cycle of the individual, of power, of essence and of unity. The dialectical cycle which is mentioned in 3 is that of essence. Thus the treatment of the subject occurs in our *epoch,* inside the *dialectic* cycle of essence. The treatment of this subject from the standpoint of an Individual Subject is one moment in a *thematic* cycle of the Subject, and the subject is but a fourth part of the *moment.*

At the end of a completive moment we are ready to move into another part of the thematic cycle. This movement is the outcome of the solidification of the very being which is made articulate in the provision of the elements in the completive moment. The being that is made articulate is the togetherness of the subject, (in this case) with other modes; the separation out of those modes is negatively performed by concentrating on the subject, and positively performed by referring to the roles these other modes might play alongside of and correlate with the subject. Each moment in a thematic cycle then is the articulation of a form of togetherness, and gives way to another form of togetherness which, relative to it, has become more concentrated than it had been before, allowing for its articulation.

It has been the view of the *Modes* that the various togethernesses are co-ordinate; it is the tendency of the recent discussions here to view them as having special affiliations with one another, and that we properly move from a togetherness appropriate to Actuality to one appropriate Existence to one appropriate to Ideality, and finally to one appropriate to God.

That the completive moment seems capable of a serial development without distortion seems clear, but it is not yet clear that this is true of the various types of togetherness; that it is necessary, with the completion of the category of the subject as an expression or ejaculation of the Subject, to move to the category of the subject as a referent or objectified item, rather than say to the subject as an item in discourse. We can conceive of six distinct orders for thematic cycles.

Whether there be only one order for a thematic cycle or six, each one of the cycles must be supplemented by three other cycles with their own characteristic themes, to constitute with those others a *dialectical* cycle. Whether or not there is only one proper neighbor for a given thematic cycle is to be determined by knowing whether the completion of the thematic cycle of the subject (whether in one or six possible orders) requires a thematic cycle of say an object rather than of the predicate or unity.

It would seem that one could complete a dialectical cycle of four thematic cycles in any one of six ways. Each one of these orders would be the result of the exploration of a togetherness as it makes itself manifest in discourse, language or knowledge, and thus in the realm of essence.

The dialectical cycle of essence can be followed by any of the other three, and thus gives rise to six possible ways of producing an epoch, depending on which solidification of being is selected as deserving clarification on completion of a given dialectical cycle.

Perhaps it is more correct to say that the completive moments too are without any necessary order, and thus that any one starting point in a completive moment gives rise to six orders. If this is the case we evidently have: 6 x 4 completive moments. But there are not twenty-four thematic cycles. Also there are only internal differences in most of these completive moments; though ordered differently internally the completion is the same for each topic. Consequently there are only four completed moments for items in a thematic cycle. But these can be related in six ways to give twenty-four thematic movements. These when completed make up only four items to be united in a dialectical cycle. But this cycle can be completed in six ways, for the different thematic cycles can be related to one another in six ways.

The relating of the thematic cycles to one another, once again gives four dialectical cycles. These can be interrelated in six ways to give six different types of epoch in which individual, power, essence and unity are the products as interrelated with and sustained by one another. In a sense then we have many, many choices in the type of serial order which we are to follow.

We have six orders of completive moments, and four of these moments; six orders of thematic cycles and four such cycles; six orders of dialectic cycles and four such cycles; six orders of epochs—24^3 x 6. But no matter how large or small our number, it is still finite, and one must face the fact that at the end of an epoch or of any one of six orders of epochs we seem either to have come to the end of the universe, or are faced with an endless repetition of what we had before. Hegel seems not to have faced this problem. The most plausible answer is that the solidification which we arrive at when we come to the very end of the epoch is not necessarily like anything that had been before; it is something new, produced by the very articulations through which we went. As we try to articulate that solidification, we can follow the schematic lines laid down in the philosophic discourse, but we cannot cover the same route. It will have the same structure, and in this sense we will have a repetition, but it will be in effect an entirely new universe. Hegel emphasizes the ideal, has only three stages, stresses the power of the negative, and tends to ignore the individual; he also has a lack of sympathy for the other modes. But I, like him, also start with "universals," find them solidified in Existence, then made into articulate essences, and finally substantialized by what he would call the Absolute. How well does this answer to history as reported by the *Phenomenology?* Does it enable us to do what that could not, to restate our epoch in our terms and for today?

Hegel's larger logic makes a basic division of Being, Essence and Notion. Since Being comprises quality, quantity and measure within which are to be found something, finitude, etc., it is evidently close to what I have been terming the Subject. His essence, which deals with appearance, and contains Actuality as a subordinate case, and does include the thing and its properties is, as essence, (and as involving causality, the idea of the dissolution of the thing) closer to what I have termed Existence, the domain of the object. Finally the notion, with its syllogisms and elements of the idea, etc., and its idea of the true and the good, is close to what I have termed the Ideal.

Hegel moves on (though not in the logic) to an absolute idea in which logic, nature and spirit are the three terms. I have included inside the realm of logic what he is terming the absolute idea; and inside the domain which he has forged out of logic, nature and spirit, I have added the Absolute itself. So far then the main difference is, apart from his idealistic bias, due to my addition of another step, my change in the type of dialectic, and of course, my lack of subtlety and my failure to make all the dialectical turns. There is also the fact that Hegel never really takes the various positions as really basic; he sees that they are real stadia, but he also transcends them, makes them give way to other modes as it were, instead of seeing that the other modes are supplementary, and that when the whole is laid out in dialectically articulate form we have once more to engage in the process, because this articulation is but one half of an Empedoclean rhythm. In a way then I reverse the entire Hegelian process, for the last stage is one in which, what before was only an expression becomes substantialized; the phenomenon, the subject, becomes substance rather than the reverse. Or better, when and as a subject becomes substance, the initial togetherness which was a kind of diffuse substance, becomes subject to a counterpoint in the coming to be of another togetherness.

There are at least three processes going on: 1] the phases through which say a theme of subject goes through. 2] the last phase where the subject becomes substantialized. 3] the coming to be of a new togetherness, the reciprocal of that which is being dissolved in *1*. Hegel knows *1*, and seems to speak sometimes as though the very inverse of 2 was required, though in fact his system progresses to the more and more concrete. What he does not see is the third step, the congealing of a new togetherness which itself must now be dissolved. This new togetherness is one of three in fact. Only because it does take place does it make sense to speak of a new epoch with a novel outcome arrived at while following the same kind of route as before.

Most important, the Hegelian system has no way of requiring the continuance of the world or the system; having attained the end it has no other place to go, whereas what I am saying is that the end is but one outcome inside the whole, and that the true end, as he himself saw, is the articulation of the whole with that end as one part, and that, (and this is the most important consideration) the articulation of the whole involves a correlative precipitation or concentration on another togetherness which must then be articulated.

One must distinguish A] the substantialization which occurs inside any cycle, and in ordering this as the last term if one begins with the subject, B] the substantialization which is a phenomenalization by means of the articulation of an aboriginal togetherness, C] the substantialization by precipitation of another togetherness which must now go through an ordered articulation ending with the substantialization A. Hegel, and I think I too, confuse A with C again and again. Once they are distinguished we can see that to be a substantialized subject is to be but one kind of subject needing the others as supplementation, and that if there is to be a movement to a new cycle it is not because we arrived at a substantialized subject but because all the phases of the cycle had been gone through, making the original substantial togetherness dissolve into a phenomenological whole at the same time that a new togetherness is substantialized.

As we have been viewing it the present is the substantialization in the last phase, and not the substantialization of a new togetherness or the dissolution of an old togetherness. It seems then that once again a number of things were confused earlier. When we speak of the past as an analysis of the present we are really viewing the past as having the present as its togetherness and as articulating this. We are not thereby provided with a reciprocal togetherness because in effect the new togetherness, the present, is not actually dissolved. A new present would then give us another togetherness to be dissolved in a new way. But we should say instead that the entire sequence, including the present, is the dissolution of a to-getherness of an entire history and that this is in effect the making of a new togetherness which begins with the original datum but extends to the new present. As we change epochs, the togetherness which is to be dis-solved is changed. This I presume is what is meant by the rise and fall of civilizations, etc. But now the question arises as to just what is a new present which is the terminus of a dissolution of a togetherness? The last present must involve a terminus to a genuine dissolution of a togetherness of all of a history, or we can analyze all the past as a kind of necessitating of the present.

If now were the last present it would not be by the accident of history but because in fact the togetherness of a certain type was exhausted then and there. This supposes that we can call a halt to history at any time and define a togetherness for the whole of what has occurred up to that time. (This is a significant idea, but not in ontology). It does perhaps tell us what to do in history: so define a togetherness that it dissolved over the course of time, culminating in the present. The very next significant event need not on this view have another type of togetherness, but only the old, stretched and with a new meaning. That is, if we start with the kind of togetherness characteristic of Actuality, it does not follow that the new one, which we must have in order to cover the next period of time as well, must be a different kind of togetherness; it could be one of Actuality with a meaning that it did not have before.

The acknowledgment of a temporally stretched togetherness from the past to whatever we take to be the present involves a reciprocal coming to be of a new togetherness. This means that though from the standpoint of a new present, one might employ the old type of together-ness, the interpretation of the world from a previous present requires one to use a new togetherness.

The past necessitates the present because the togetherness is defined as coming to an end just then; it is the last present for just that way of defining togetherness. Accordingly, as we look at history we see that the world hereafter must have an entirely different perspective. When the world that comes later does appear it can adopt the very kind of together-ness or perspective we had. But as having a longer stretch it will have a different meaning and content, showing that we had previously construed history too narrowly.

When do we have a new present, requiring either a new form of an old togetherness or a new togetherness? Is it not that we start with one type of togetherness and subtly alter its meaning as we go on in time so that at every moment we have a completely articulated form of that togetherness, while retaining an attitude which fills it out with more content or meaning so that it can include the very next moment? But this does not tell us A] when we have another epoch, and B] when we have a significant new moment in history, a present inside an epoch which requires a change in our original togetherness.

Must not the second question be answered by saying that every moment is significant, though it may not make an appreciable difference, not change the meaning of the togetherness in any ascertainable sense? If so, different occurrences have different weights, and we must allow them to come into the entire situation before we can see if the togetherness in which the whole set of occurrences is comprised is altered. Or, since the togetherness which one uses is a kind of constructed one, designed to come out where it does, perhaps it ought to be supplemented by three others, and the whole together offered as the meaning of what has happened until then.

But we still would have to decide about the nature of the new epoch. This could be done by trying to do the same type of job again and finding that the correlativity of the togetherness did not work as before; the very attempt to use the same type to begin with and then adding on or also doing it from the other sides would be found wanting in the sense that the necessitation of the last stage, the explanation of the parts would come easier for one approach than another. Accordingly, the historian would have to begin with four approaches to history, all terminating in the present, settle for that one which illuminated the most, while recognizing the other togetherness as precipitates ready to be used in a new treatment starting at a later point. It is only when he tries to stretch his particular accepted approach on and on in the course of time that he finds the other approaches which he had tentatively formulated become easier to use.

Can we say that a new moment in history, any history, is one which A] makes a significant palpable alteration in the togetherness with which we began, or B] makes it possible to have a better, clearer, easier, more complete explanation by trying one of the other approaches. Is it, shall we say, that the war requires, e.g., the approach which emphasizes Existence, and that as soon as it is over we begin to see the value of men or ideals or something like that? A whole history might then be said to allow us to go through all these phases, and that an epoch will come to an end when we have to start all over again.

But we must also attend to the fact that for Hegel whatever we start with is in the process of becoming other to itself; this would in the above terms be the coming to be of a precipitated mode of togetherness, to be articulated over a course of time. Each togetherness, each diffuse whole of history before articulation would be in the process of producing the other of itself and then come to be out of the articulation of that other. Hegel thinks that the point from which one began, the togetherness, never lets itself vanish but offers a kind of fake sacrifice to itself and then recovers itself more fully. In a sense he is a more radical substantialist than I with respect to the togetherness (as I have called it). He sees only that the totality, before it has been articulated, makes something other than itself be and then takes this into itself; but the totality is dissolved while its other is then and there produced.

There is of course no complete dissolution, and no complete precipitation; if the former occurred, there would be a loss of a needed togetherness; if the latter there would be a genuine being made out of togetherness. As it is, togetherness is real being (of which we always have something in the present) merged and not yet itself. When we begin history from the present we in effect see it as not yet distinguished from its past; the making the past analyze a togetherness and culminate in the present is a way of separating out the past from the present and allowing each to be itself in itself and by itself, and yet with the other.

Once again my refusal to start off with four modes in understanding anything meant that I had to go through a circuitous route. I should have seen that past and present are two correlates, the one representing a kind of Actuality the other a kind of Ideal, and that they involve the dissolution of one form in which they are together while they constitute another—the latter having three components.

August 10

The climax of a play is something like the present in history; it is the culmination of what went before, but it would be a mistake to think of it as the meaning or interpretation of the whole, for this is given by what I have termed the togetherness of the whole, which is being articulated over the acts and scenes each with its own integrity and value.

The togetherness could be said to be the position of one who interprets. It is easy to slip into the mistake of supposing that an interpretation looks to an Actuality, an Ideal, Existence or eternal unity and exhibits this, or that it makes some combination of these. Now it is often said that a play, for example, gives us a report, is a realistic portrayal of what perhaps had even been lived previously by the actor, as some of the discussion in Wm. Archer's book would seem to indicate. Others speak of the interpretative artist looking to some Ideal, a great man or spirit, which he is trying to exemplify, and which lies beyond anything the author might have said. And there are those who think of the actor as one who allows himself to be caught in the situation, to improvise, to constitute the situation then and there. Finally there are those who speak of him as though he had within him the principle of unity guiding the whole and which he is allowing to be made manifest in his acting. Acting makes the matter most acute, but the situation is common to all forms of art and interpretation. The basic mistake of these approaches is that they forget that there is something to interpret; they use the art work as a stimulus rather than as material to utilize.

There are four basic types of interpreters: 1] the artistic—the dancer, the actor, the musician and perhaps builder, occupied with making themselves into Ideals through an interpretation of the initial work as an Ideal; 2] the practical man, the soldier, the craftsman, the technician, occupied with making themselves into loci of action, of living out an existence as an interpretation of the initial work as an Ideal; 3] the teacher, the administrator, the priest and parent, when interpreting what is given to them in law, history, books, etc., making themselves into the loci of some comprehensive vision, some principle of unification as they look on the initial work as an Ideal; 4] the terminal interpreter or spectator in the arts or in sports who starts with the very works which concern the first three, or with the products of these three, and integrates them with himself in the primary role of an individual actuality, thereby refining or purging himself, reconstituting himself by making himself the bearer of a richer totality.

Each one of these interpretations has a primary stress as here indicated, and secondary stresses in the other dimensions. The primary approach to a work is as something Ideal, as indeterminate, a possibility with some excellence which needs vivification and determination. If one refuses to deal with the work of art as an Ideal, one approaches it as a mere Object or thing, as is done by factual historians; or as a sequence of events, as a kind of occurrence, as is done by biographical and constructionistic historians; or as a locus of some myth or truth or value of civilization, as is done by literary historians. Now these could be called interpreters too, and if one wished each type could be subdivided into four. Thus starting with the work of art as a sequence of events, one could conceivably give this an artistic interpretation in written history or even in some art; or give it a practical significance by incorporating it in some ritual or ceremony; or give it a meaning inside one's own comprehensive vision; or finally allow it to be integrated with oneself as an individual. It is perhaps only a verbal matter to decide whether to call these different usages of a given entity interpretations or something else. If we call them interpretations, then we will have interpretations of the kind first discussed, which might be called *Creative,* since they start with the work to be interpreted as an Ideal and thus as something needing determination, the work of a free being.

There would then be four Creative types of interpretation, one of which is that of the spectator. These would all be occupied with giving a new body, a new unity and a new dynamics to some work which, though perhaps, as in the case of a painting and in some respects a written play, is already determinate, is treated as an Ideal for the interpreter. He knows his job is to give it a new meaning. He deals with it as the playwright or composer or architect might have dealt with some genuine Ideal outside himself. (The playwright, etc., need not attend to any Ideal, but may in fact look to the world or to an individual or to the eternal. But wherever he looks, his product is an Ideal for the interpreter.)

The second main type of interpretation is one which begins with the work to be interpreted as a brute matter of fact, as an item in the world, an object, an Actuality. One can deal with that Actuality in all kinds of ways, from a dating (which is itself a kind of re-actualizing of the Actual in a context of time), all the way to the interpretation of it as having some role to play in the affairs of men. It is this unit item, this object which is sold at auction, which is owned by so and so, etc., and which may make a difference to the rest of the world by virtue of its factual import. To be sure it is not a mere physical entity; it is a work of art, but not looked at in terms of its meaning as requiring a creative interpretation but as something occupying a place and having some role. We can call this type of interpretation, *Acknowledgment.* When we make acknowledgments in the arts, we tend to submit to the brutal fact of the art object, to allow ourselves comment and commentary, as is sometimes done even in acting, when the author has been over-insistent on his directions and the actors over-submissive to the script, merely using themselves as mouthpieces. However, this mode of interpretation is, like the others, distinguished not because of what the interpreter does but by the category in which the object is taken to be. It is possible for one to view a painting or a script as an acknowledged object and then subject it to a fresh and vitalizing acknowledgment in which this fact is brought into a new and important context. Thus to take a simple illustration, it is possible to put a play inside a play, or better even to use some picture or some book as an item in a play, transforming its meaning radically by virtue of the associations in which it has been put.

A third mode of interpretation looks at a script or musical score, or set of drawings not as an object and not as something to be filled out, but as a history in miniature, a kind of ordered sequence of occurrences, a dynamic activity, an ongoing. Here the work is entered into, but not for the purpose of finding outlines which are to be filled out, but in order to analyze it and determine how it fits together. This is the sort of thing which interests literary historians. It could be made the object of a genuine artistic effort, made to serve as the carrier of an Ideal (or Actuality, Existence or God) or conversely, brought inside a scheme where an Ideal, etc., is the dominant fact and thereby given a new role. This third kind of interpretation may be said to be *Historical.*

Finally we can take the object to be interpreted as the locus of an eternal truth or meaning or unity. This which may be said to be the interpretation of a myth or viewpoint can itself be used in an artistic work, as illustrated just now, or could be dealt with, as could the others, in practice, in teaching, etc. What is done with it is to start with it as a kind of meaning, already determinate in a way, and not (as in the first case) as already accepted as indeterminate and requiring filling. There is no need here to suppose anything added; when interpretation is imposed it is to give it new significance in new contexts, allowing it (as in the case of the last two), to be untouched as a work, and only to be decorated, or reassigned a position. This *Mythological* interpretation is most often used in interpreting paintings and poetry rather than other types of art, though it is perhaps the dominant outlook of most historians of art.

I have used the guise, in which an object to be interpreted appears, to determine the different types of interpretation. One might instead take interpretation to be divided not according to the type of entity to be interpreted, but by the manner in which it is interpreted. If one were to take this approach, instead of saying (as we did in connection with creative interpretation by an artist) that the artist is occupied with a making of himself into an Ideal by using the initial work as an Ideal, one could say that an artistic interpretation makes itself into an Ideal, and can do this by approaching a work of art as itself an Ideal, an Actuality, a dynamic occurrence or a unitary meaning; that a practical interpretation makes itself into a locus of action of that which is itself approached as an Ideal, etc.; that an evaluative interpretation makes itself into a locus of a vision with respect to a work of art treated as an Ideal, etc.; and finally that a spectator makes himself into an individual embodiment of the work of art viewed as Ideal, etc. This division of the term "interpretation" is perhaps better than the former.

Acting is so vivid a case of making a work of art real in a new way that it can serve perhaps as the model for all the others, though each of the others has its own rationale and ought to be dealt with in its own terms. Acting shows up the difference between the object to be interpreted and the interpretation in a radical way, allowing one to see what interpretation as such does. Other forms of artistic interpretation will be clarified by considering acting. Though these others start with other types of art (music or drawings) and make use of different media, they approach their objects in the same ways as actors do, i.e., as Ideals, etc., and come out with products through the utilization of similar dimensions.

Daudet's paradox of acting contends that the artist must stand at a psychic distance from his work; the work is dramatic and ought not to repeat the world of every day. It ought not, but then it in fact does not. We would take it amiss if one were to say to us after we had done a kind deed in life that "that was a fine gesture or fine way of acting"; just so we would, were we actors, have to take it amiss if it is said that we act the part of a villain because we are in fact diabolic. We need not re-live, as some followers of Stanislavski seem to think, the very part as it is in real life. What is the case is that one does bring oneself into the acting; one must vivify through oneself what in fact is offered as a text. Not to do this is to deny the dimension of Actuality to the material which is given. Even where we have something offered as an Actuality to the artist, it is necessary for the artist to add his own Actuality; otherwise he will not be acting but merely allowing himself to be used as an instrument, as a mere translucency for the expression of something other than himself.

The actor must have some grasp of an Ideal, some perfect way of acting; or better, some good or result, some artistic end, which is to be achieved, and which therefore he must look to even though he may use a script which, in relation to his acting, is an Ideal. When one looks to an Ideal outside the script while using the script as an Ideal, one remains inside the artistic activity just so far as the outcome is an Ideal, and leaves it so far as the outcome is something else, as it is with the practical men or teachers, etc. The two Ideals should be merged, as should, in the previous case, the two actualities, the object and the actor.

The actor must be involved in the situation; he must act here and now with respect to this actor and that, this scene and that audience. To ignore these is to allow him to act by himself, not to change his rhythms, not to respond in fact to his fellow artists. He must offer a situation then to the work he is to interpret, even if this be itself taken as a kind of situation, or dynamic historic sequence.

Finally the actor must have some awareness of the whole which is being played; he must have the whole within him as a unity, somewhat as a baseball player—and here the word player is significant—has from his position an apprehension of the entire field and his role in relation to the others, not merely as in the game and over against the others, but as one who is in a particular position as a kind of precipitate or localization of what is the unity of them all.

The actor then must bring together four dimensions, one of which is provided by the work to be interpreted. He is like the practical man, the teacher and the spectator in this regard, but differs from them in his production of an Ideal object through the amalgamation of the four dimensions. The practical man also has four dimensions, and may in fact face the very same object which the actor starts with but, since he is occupied with the production of an ongoing, his mode of "interpretation" is different from that of the actor. The teacher is concerned with producing a vision, an outlook, and the spectator with producing himself in the shape of an enriched man.

A work of art taken in the very shape in which an actor takes it can be the material used by practical man, teacher or spectator. The reader of a play is then evidently distinct from the spectator, for the reader of a play starts with the very play the actor does, but makes it part of an individual being, whereas the spectator starts with the *actor's* play and makes this part of his being—and the two results might be quite different.

A reader of a poem is like a man reading a play. Though a terminal interpreter, a reader of course can himself in turn be made the object of an historical study, of a work of art, etc., etc. The reader is terminal only with respect to the work of art which he is interpreting, and in this respect contrasts with the actor; but he may not be terminal for some further work of art or other activity, in which case one starts with him as a man, either in the guise of an Actuality, or an Ideal, or an Existent or a Meaning, and then treats him as something to be creatively understood or handled, dealt with as an object in practice or in an historic or biographical account, used by a teacher or guide, or brought within the aegis of some new vision or outlook.

There is something analogous to this situation in the theories about mathematics. Three are dominant today—intuitionistic, formalistic and logistic—Brouwer, Hilbert and Russell-Whitehead. It is usually overlooked that there is a fourth of long-standing, the Pythagorean-Platonic, in which mathematical entities dwell within a domain of their own without real distinctiveness and yet with sufficient tonality to enable them to be carved out. The intuitionistic program of constructiveness, which had its modern origin in Kant and its first good expression in Kroneker, actually presupposes the Platonic-Pythagorean. Kronecker said, "God made the natural numbers," i.e., Kronecker took them for granted. Having accepted them, the mathematician proceeds somewhat as an activist and carves out of the eternal, divine-like realm the particular determinate entities in which he is interested. His work is presupposed by the postulating, formal mathematician who abstracts from all content and objectivity to give us the purely structural assertions of mathematics. But such formalism depends upon the achievements of creative mathematicians; it is in effect a form of idealism without any genuine orientation beyond the syntax of mathematical discourse. This idealism is presupposed by the logicians of today, who start with an orientation towards actualities, and attempt thereby to give concreteness and pertinence to the achievements of the postulating and formalistic mathematicians. The logicians are presupposed in a sense by the Platonist, for the Platonist builds on the visible entities of the Pythagoreans; it is the mathematics as laid out empirically which the divine mathematics of Plato (see the *Republic* with its dialectic and the *Phaedo* with its awareness of number as possessing such features as oddness forever) perhaps rests upon, not ontologically but cognitively as a base in terms of which the dialectical movement can be expressed,—unless it be the case that logistic needs a theory of types for this must be rooted in an "intensional" ontological base. If this be a correct statement then no theory of mathematics will be adequate which does not take account of all four. A number must then at once be an eternal essence, a power of synthesizing (as Kant suggested), the outcome of a postulating and a derivation in a purely formal way from postulated entities, and the characterization of some isolated phenomenon in the world. It is impossible though to have all four of these approaches at the same time; we must solidify two of them by means of the others serving as perspectives or agents. Thus we can combine the intuitionistic and the logistic view of numbers (to take the supposedly established persistent rivals) in a view which makes each logistic formulation to be a product of an intuitionistic carving out of numbers from their eternal Platonistic domain, and a placing of these formulations inside the frame provided by the formalistic mathematicians.

The problem of interpreting mathematics in physics will in principle not be unlike the interpreting of a script by an actor or a reader. It will be taken as an indeterminate schema, as a kind of Ideal, which must then be enriched by the world itself, the physicist himself and the Ideal of science which he seeks to realize. The mathematics may be intuitionistic, etc., but it will be treated by the physicist as an Ideal. Physics is like an interpretation which is not final, for it is itself something to be interpreted by technologists and engineers. It is therefore not the agency by virtue of which mathematics gets actualization, but rather the agency for giving it another guise in Existence. It "existences" the mathematics, and the result is in turn looked at as an Ideal for the engineer, who in his turn gives it a being in some actual matter of fact.

When dealing with a work of art we recognized that there could be four ways of turning it into an Ideal in an activity of artistic creation, and this whether one started with the work of art as an Ideal or in some other guise. Is there something similar to be said in connection with mathematics? Can we take it, not as a schematic whole, but as a fact or event or vision, and so interpret it that it has a kind of physical import in all cases? Would not this be the way in which historians of science, historians of culture and historians of civilization see mathematics? And if this is so will there not be practical interpretations (say in numerology or astrology), interpretations in terms of import (say by teachers of mathematics), and spectator interpretations (say by those engaged in working puzzles and examples)? In any case what we will have in connection with physics is a mathematics transformed, with a primary need to make it integral to the existential part of another four-fold scheme. The mathematics which would be used would be some kind of unified whole of the four types of mathematics; this whole would have its four dimensions, but still would have a kind of diffused unity, particularly as in the guise of a datum for the physicist. He would take this four-dimensional reality, without discriminating the dimensions, as a single block and give it the role of an element in a four-dimensional scheme where it in effect became part of Existence.

Physics, though having only one role with respect to mathematics, has three other roles of its own—it does look to nature, it does look to an Ideal at which all inquirers (as Peirce argued) might come to a rest, and it does look to the individual. As looking to these different places, it must, to make use of them, bring in other dimensions as filling and backdrop.

We can start with something to interpret and have four disciplines which will engage in this (e.g., acting, teaching, etc.). And we can take any one of these disciplines and have it deal with a different type of entity to start with. The teacher or the actor can look to nature, or to some vision, or to the individual. And in the same way we can have a physics which looks to mathematics, or nature, or men, or eternity. And just as the work of art can be approached in four ways so mathematics can be approachd in four ways, of which physics is only one.

Although I have not been consistent in the way I used terminology and have switched now to this perspective then to that, I think it is now clear that a given item can be viewed in one of four guises, and that this can be interpreted, given a new role in some new guise (which could be of the same mode of being as the old), and that the field or discipline which engages in the interpretation could not only take the object in each of the four guises to bring it to the new guise characteristic of the field or discipline, but could also turn to other types of objects and do the same kind of thing for them. Thus we can view a written play in four guises— fact, schematic ideal, existential occurrence, unitary meaning. We can interpret it in an interpretive art by making it have the role in that art as an Ideal. But an interpretive art can also look to some other things besides works of art—it could look at nature, or men, or myth. When it does any of these it looks directly at what it was making the play do representatively, when it began with the play in the guise of occurrence, object or vision.

If now we start with nature and think of interpreting her, we can do it first by seeing nature in one of four guises, then by engaging in four ways of handling each of these guises, to end with four translations in each case. If we approached nature as a brute datum, e.g., we could engage in an artistic or an intellectual use of it so as to make it be an ideal, etc., for some engineer or in a play, or could make it, by some formal activity, into an Ideal or other type of entity.

When physicists look to nature, they take account of the mathematics that is available as representing the unity, the ideal of a settled truth, themselves as trained honest men, and of the actual course of nature through which they in fact live. As a rule they take nature to be an existential domain which they will translate into an Ideal by means of mathematics, truth, honesty, and experience.

August 11

The work to be interpreted and the outcome of the interpretation can be in the same mode. But as a rule they are in different ones and are brought into being in different ways. A script which functions as an ideal for an actor who in turn represents a kind of ideal for the spectator is produced as a rule by looking primarily to nature or man. It is embodied of course in words. The actor takes this ideal content, this indeterminate schema and gives it body. He becomes an ideal for the spectator not in the sense that the spectator looks to him as a model but that what he portrays is an outcome which the spectator can now use as an indeterminate schema giving meaning to himself. The actor might make himself the primary locus of the play, as some emotional actors do; granted that he was successful the fact is that the outcome of acting is essentially a dynamic whole, which can be used as an ideal by the spectator.

The spectator could embody the acted play in himself by making himself into a kind of situational being, analogous to an actor, as some excited spectators do, but the primary task and the outcome, even in such a case, is a man transformed. The Stanislavski method is one which is aware of the need of the actor to bring himself into the total situation. It is misconstrued when it is thought that this method requires the actor to repeat life, rather than to use his body as a vehicle and a locus for the situational activities, but in such a way that he becomes involved as one component in a whole. There should be analogous Stanislavski methods for musicians, dancers—for any interpretative art.

Tragedy might be defined as the realization of a value in such a way that the resultant four-dimensional whole has less value than it otherwise would. The more acute the discrepancy, by virtue of the magnitude of the realized value and the failure of the total value, the more poignant the tragedy. There is tragedy therefore in the area of some success, which is what Aristotle insisted on; but this is not inconsistent with workingman's tragedies. The value which a man might exhibit in himself might involve a loss of value for civilization; this is the tragedy of the futile sacrifice, the wasted life on behalf of a lost cause. But the reverse is also possible, for one can succeed for civilization and have an empty life of one's own. The kind of tragedies are evidently then to be determined by A] the primary values which men seek to achieve, and B] the primary values which they in fact ought to be exhibiting. The second is the outcome of the way in which they make themselves be when realizing the first. It is as if one had focused on a climax and lost the togetherness.

The fatal flaw theory takes account of the fact that the rhythm of becoming a value is not identical with the actualization of a value; the theory of the conflict of loyalties or values is aware that the value, which is embodied four-fold, sometimes opposes the realization of some other value, and conversely. It is not the doing of two opposed things in the same dimension which sets the tragic situation of Antigone, but the aim to realize one value with the need to reject the embodiment of another occurring at the same time, that there is an embodiment of one value with the rejection of some realization of a value. The latter would not be tragic by itself. To be loyal to one's relative while giving up the realization of this or that narrow value of success in work or in the good opinion of others is unpleasant, sad but not tragic. Nor is there tragedy in the fact that in becoming one type of being one is not also some other. It is not because loyalty to brother precludes being loyal to country that makes the tragedy, but the need to act on behalf of the brother while rejecting the state of being loyal to country, together with the converse need to be loyal to country, and the related necessity to reject an action on behalf of the brother, that makes Antigone a tragedy.

All interpretation is involved in a situation which is analogous to the tragic. The production of the interpretation (and initially also of the work of art) is the result of an aim at one dimension through the use of other dimensions. The achievement of the aim may produce a failure to get to the desired outcome. All techniques are faced with this problem, for they tell us how to attain the end aimed at, and too often risk destroying the outcome, of which the realization of that aim is but one factor, since it ought to be accompanied by supplementary efforts to bring in other factors. The artist and interpreter—and this would apply to practical man, teacher and spectator as well—is caught in a tragic failure just so far as he succeeds in his aim and fails thereby to make something embody a value that it might.

The purpose before one is but a factor in a larger purpose, a kind of outcome, a togetherness if one likes, which is not aimed at. To aim at something is to put it before one, to put it on the same plane and is therefore not to allow it to permeate, to fill out what one is, but in effect is to make provision for the filling out of some other value. The art of living wisely is like the art of interpreting correctly; it involves the aiming and realizing of a value in such a way that the outcome is something excellent, and not necessarily the same as the value aimed at. By trying to be helpful a man might make himself into a courageous being; by trying to make himself courageous a man might become honest. By trying to be a "professional" philosopher a man might become wise; often he becomes foolish or remains unchanged in important ways where he should have changed.

Any one of the four modes could be an object for a philosopher, and any one of those modes could be taken in one of four guises. But whatever he does the philosopher must use the strategy of the Actual and deal with these items in terms of knowledge. The approach of the *Modes* has been to take each one of the four modes as an object, and to approach each in its own proper guise. It looked at Actuality in its actuality, the Ideal in its ideal role, etc. There could then be a four-fold philosophy taking account of all four modes, which however saw all these various modes as in the same guise—say, as brute facts, or something to be made determinate in another realm, or something vital and ongoing, or something fixed and basic, or some combination of these.

The very same four modes which philosophy translates into a neutral language from the perspective of Actuality, can be approached by art, religion and mathematics. These too can look at the modes in any one of four guises, but all of them reconstruct what they take as data until it has the form of a neutrality approached through their characteristic strategy.

The tragedy of life and drama has a counterpart in the intellectual world. The philosopher who aims at clarity, organization or systematization may miss the truth both in himself and for all the modes. The philosopher who aims at truth or flexibility or freedom may obscure the whole, or end with a kind of disorganized pattern. It is the characteristic mark of the piece-meal philosophers of today to aim at and to some degree realize some limited aim, such as clarity of expression. They are not as successful in this realm as their concentration of effort would lead one to anticipate; but successful or not they fail in their efforts to make any progress in the achievement of vision, wisdom, insight into the universe and knowledge, into man and other beings.

An interpretation brings the interpreted into a new realm, A] with a minimal distortion of the data—and then we say that the interpretation is true or accurate, and B] with a genuine embodiment of the four-dimensional value which is characteristic of the interpreter. There is no question here of truth or falsehood, but only of effectiveness, of efficiency, of achievement. The more the data are distorted, the more the initial work serves only as a stimulus or occasion; the greater the failure to attain the value of the interpreter, the more is he to be understood to be over-submissive, a mere type, and this even when he in fact succeeds in transposing the initial data into the new medium. One can give a good translation of a poem in the form of a dance, and yet fail to have a genuine dance; one would have the appropriate gestures but the dance would lack body.

If of course one thought of the initial work of art as seeking to embody say an Ideal, one could then use the interpretation as a way of seeking to embody this too, but in a new way or place. If one takes this approach an interpretation would be accurate to the degree that it parallelled the success of the initial embodiment. If it goes beyond this it is in effect the production of a new work of art. This sometimes happens. The actors transcend the script; the musicians improvise and modify and thereby go beyond the score; and one can say that the painter or poet who looks at nature for his data may give what he finds there an embodiment it did not and could not have there. If the philosopher or scientist were to do this we would charge them with mythologizing, for we think that their primary task is to keep to the data. But this attitude fails to recognize that the very act of knowing is a kind of dramatization, a kind of dislocation of data, a kind of allowing for a new re-organization of the four modes in a new medium where they may in fact be together in a way they cannot empirically be.

Ontologically there are only the modes and representatives of them.

But any part of such an ontological scheme, any empirical expression of it could be improved upon in knowledge. The improvement we do make by virtue of our dramatization is taken away, is balanced by the loss which abstraction provides. Since the empirical expressions are themselves in a way abstractions, the act of knowledge in connection with them may prove to be an improvement on the whole. We cannot through knowledge improve on the cosmos, but through knowledge we may be able to improve on some portion or expression of it.

To the question then as to whether we ought to interpret the law, or the world or a work of art by transposing what it says or intends, we must give a third answer to the effect that the value, which it in fact does exhibit, must be re-established as a result of an attempt to attain some end such as peace or prosperity or justice. The judge or the policeman, and even the legislature (if we think of this taking its start from the will or customs of the people), ought not then attend merely to what the law expressly says; nor ought they go beyond the law and see that what the law intended to realize is actually realized in the new medium; but they ought to re-establish in a new guise the result of the achievement of an aim. One might conceivably argue for the establishment in the new medium not of the embodied outcome of the formulation or realization of the law but of what ought to have been embodied when the law was forged. Thus if the presence of the law is in effect the being of peace (and this can occur even where the law is a threat or the expression of violence by a dictator), the carrying out of that law will involve   A] the use of the law as data,   B] the aiming at something characteristic of the work in the new medium, and   C] the realization in the new medium of the old value, e.g., in this case peace.

The judge need not attend to what the lawmaker had as aim; he need not be content with re-establishing the values which the lawmaker, by virtue of his work excellently done, in fact embodies. He can embody that value or a higher form of that value by aiming elsewhere. To be sure his embodiment of the value in the new medium will make it have a weight it did not have before. The judge could of course embody another set of values, but then he could not, strictly speaking, be said to be giving an accurate interpretation of the law. If he accepted the law or its aim and embodied some other value than that which in fact was embodied in the realization of the aim of lawmaking, he would be a new lawmaker.

The problem of the division of powers is in part the problem as to whether the different powers in a state are in effect new lawmakers, each through the acceptance of similar aims or the adoption of data from one another trying to and perhaps succeeding in embodying new values, or whether those different powers are all designed to embody the same value.

The latter view seems preferable. It requires one to look at the living law, the positive law, the judicial decisions, the work of police officers, etc., as different ways of expressing or exhibiting in different media one or the other dimension of the embodied value of stability in government. The quest for justice then, which might be said to be characteristic of the courts, would be a quest for a value which, if properly embodied by a proper judiciary, ought to result in stability in another medium than that provided by say, legislation. The people would look to these pronouncements, or their agents would follow these pronouncements, in such a way as to enable the government to continue or prosper. This is not inconsistent with the formulation of laws and the carving out of decisions which are upsetting to established ways. It in fact could even be geared to the idea of trying to make new laws; it is not the aim but what is embodied in the realizing of that aim, embodied by supplementing the dimension of the aim with three others, that dictates what the meaning of the legislature or judiciary, etc., is. The outcome of the well-ordered state would then be a plurality of embodiments of some cherished value in different media, all of which together would add to the fulfillment of that value, because in the different embodiments now this and now that dimension would be the carrier.

It is the truth, the vision, the insight, the ideal, the import of the play then that the acting and the spectator ought to embody, each in his own medium, and through his own way of aiming and of using the play as a datum. If the play is treated as an ideal schema, it will be filled out by the actors who might aim at what the playwright aimed at, or at the filling out of the play, itself treated as an ideal. In either case the actors will embody worth, import, value. If they are successful interpreters they will embody the value or worth or import which the play embodied. We will see the play then as having "truth" in two dimensions, and if we bring in ourselves as spectators, and also the civilization which will evaluate us, we will see it in the two dimensions while enjoying a third and projecting a fourth.

We fall short again and again, and this is the tragedy of interpretation, or the loss of value embodied in the course of attaining some aim, such as the acting of that play. Since we are concerned with the play as an ideal, which we could conceivably act in a way that the play itself does not require and which is better in its import than that which the play itself provides, we can embody what the play does not and yet avoid something tragic. We can make something new and fresh, be artists going beyond the play. But in life where we are aware of the values which ought to be embodied, where there is no better embodiment than that of a four-dimensional plenitude, there cannot be a failure to embody these. We can improve on plays but cannot on the ought-to-be. This does not mean that there are not new horizons to tragedy all the time, that there is no renewed vision, as Sewall remarks, which points to values critical of what we have achieved. It means only that embodiments have limits; that they are to be tested and judged by values as yet unembodied. In the case of art we start with some kind of embodiment, and this embodiment, if it falls short of the perfect embodiment, can be improved upon in some other art. That other art will be doing a needed thing, but it will not be interpreting the initial work.

The analogue of much of this in epistemology is that our interpretations of the world as expressed in judgments and assertions need not have a point for point identity with the world, but ought to embody in the realm of mind the value which the object embodies in fact. And in a way we have said this by remarking on the fact that in mind we have a category which is to be unified, and that the object has a unity in itself. In knowledge we try to construct the item and impose a unity on it, whereas the object has the unity to begin with and may express itself in a plurality of ways.

To know that we have interpreted properly we must have the capacity to recognize that we on our cognitive side do have the embodied value which the object has. We would not have to aim at what the object aims at, we need not have the same structure that the object has. We might conceivably embody a value which the object embodies only partially, and thus in our interpretation of the world go beyond what the world in fact exhibits to reach in our knowledge (which in contrast with Plato we can say is produced by us and involves a genuine construction and realization of an aim) what the world did not in fact reach. Whether we duplicate the embodied value of the object in our knowledge, or whether we go beyond this and embody what the object should have but failed to embody, we ought, if we are to know what the truth is and when we have it, be able to recognize the value in us as answering to the value in the object or the value which ought to be in the object. This we would know by virtue of the commonality of our rhythms. If we have the same embodied value we would be productive in the same way, though in a different medium and with different objects: we would be in harmony with the object throughout its career.

It is, as the pragmatists have observed, our capacity to continue to act without hindrance, our capacity to fit in with the world of the object which determines our truth. In the case where knowledge goes beyond what the object was capable of attaining and is thus in effect a genuine artistic production with the object as a stimulus or occasion, it would in effect be not what is called knowledge, but myth or an imaginative, idealized construction. Though desirable as showing what the better state of affairs is like it is not what is wanted in knowledge. To know something is to embody the value in another medium, and is thus to keep apace with it. We ought to say the same thing of a good interpretation of the will of the people, of laws, of musical compositions, of plays, of acting, of science and thus of anything whatsoever which starts with something outside it as data, aims to realize something, and embodies a value as a consequence of the realization as supported by other dimensions. But whereas the object in fact goes through a career and we ourselves live in time and thus can test the similarity of our rhythms, this is not the case with a composition or a law. Here there is just an item given. How then are we to test ourselves as answering to the value it embodies? One answer is to say that we as spectators and readers find ourselves in the same degree of alignment; we are equally at home or familiar; we find our way in it with the same degree of facility in both cases.

Where, as in the usual case, we do not know the composition or the script, and find ourselves watching the play or listening to the music, we cannot know whether the music or the play is in fact a new creation. But we sometimes on the other hand, as a consequence of the music or the play can come back to look at the composition or script, and when we do this we can find ourselves in consonance with the composition or script in part because we have read into it the meaning which the play or music gave it. We make the play true, we true it, because it has the value we want it to have, and therefore we go back and give this to the original.

The reverse process is a romanticizing. If we (because of the values which a composition or script might have and which answers to us, the readers, through the consonance of our rhythms, so that we read it correctly), were to go to the play and impose our rhythm on it, we would find that it was resistant in the first place and in the second, so far as the play was malleable, that we in effect re-created it, when what we sought to have was something which answered to the script. We could of course re-create the play according to this established rhythm, as we do in criticism, particularly that tempered in such a way as to get out of the play what we ourselves cherish or embody, but then we cannot speak of the play as being true to the script, even when it turns out that our recreating is a way of giving the play the value which the script had embodied and which we ourselves as readers made our own in our own way, enabling us to be affiliated with that script.

While every inference involves a risk, there is a kind of immediate knowledge, a consonance which the philosopher has with what occurs in fact. He holds together in his being the various modes, and the togetherness which he then constitutes answers to the togetherness which the

world exhibits. Now the world in fact exhibits four distinct modes of togetherness which never in fact get together except at best in the vaguest
kind of blur. But this is exactly the case with man; he has a single
togetherness which is dominant in him and which is not altogether sundered from the kinds of togetherness that are beyond him. As not altogether sundered he makes with them a kind of blurred realm of experience. It is when he isolates himself and finds this isolation answering to
the activities of the modes as together in one way that he can come to
truly apprehend what is outside himself. As he dissolves the togetherness
into its components as they are in him, he can also have items whose
activities as in him will answer to the activities of those components in the
guise of modes outside him. We "know" with certainty then, but not of
that which we infer or hold before our consciousness as the aim of
knowledge, but through the agency of these. Because I have a good
though inchoate and non-duplicating concept of say Existence I can be a
full man in whom Existence can have a role analogous to that which it
has in itself and in relation to other modes. The virtue which I have,
enabling me to be true to the world, is one which I have representatively,
as acting on behalf of men who are already true to it. Truth then is but
the adjective of an ontological truing of men with what lies beyond them.

This outlook makes it possible to provide an alternative to the usual
ways in which referents to the subatomic in physics are understood. In
contrast with the realistic theory which supposes that all such referents
have real objects, even though they are not directly known and though
their behavior seems to conflict with the behavior of some commonsense
macroscopic things and thus with the domain where there are predictions and evidence is to be had, and in contrast with the conventionalist
theory which holds that the subatomic referents have no object at all but
express ways of manipulating and interrelating gross phenomena, and in
contrast with the constitutive theory which supposes that the categories of
knowledge help constitute what is in fact real so that the subatomic entities are real because of physics and are kept real by the very fact that
there is physical knowing, we have the alternative that   A] they are
creations of man and in this sense conventional,   B] that they are real
inside physics and thus far are constitutive of it, and   C] do make
reference to something real outside them and thus are realistic, but
D] primarily are ways in which we with our instruments and aims in
physics are able to embody the very rhythms and make predictive anticipations of what is going to occur.

Terms in physics do not portray real entities as existing in just that
guise outside physical discourse; but they are not idle or conventional or

arbitrary. We have an analogous situation when we look in a mirror. To see the object we must look at a certain place in the mirror; the object which exists apart from the mirror and the mirror-image are true of one another. If one takes the former as the standard the latter is a truth of it, but under the conditions of a mirror. To speak truly as it were of the real object by means of a mirror we must speak of the object as located in the depth of the mirror. We can live in consonance with the object by attending to the mirror-image as sustained by the mirror. We ought not to ask whether the object in fact is just like the mirror image; in some ways it is, and in some ways, by virtue of the reversal in the mirror, it is not. There could be distorting mirrors, mirrors with tints to them, and the object can be just as truly known via the mirror-image once the condition of the mirror be considered.

The language of science has its own grammar and makes a difference to what it embodies; but it is not arbitrary and what it says is not disconnected from what occurs. It is what occurs, but subject to a conditioning, which conditioning may allow us to know truly, just so far as it is a conditioning which enables us to keep apace with the object. Of course we can always keep apace if we take account of just how much distortion our new medium is providing, but such a way of speaking presupposes that we already know the object apart from the new medium, whereas what is now being argued for is that we have all the truth we need and ought to have (without supposing we have an antecedent acquaintance with pure and naked data), when in following the course of what we formulate we in fact live adjustedly to what lies beyond, as is evidenced by our continually being able to derive from the world outcomes in consonance with what we are deducing inside the new medium. The subterranean nature of the physical world can be said then to be portrayed by subatomic physics in the sense that the deductions of that physics are in consonance with the careers of things, as is evidenced from the fact that the very content we have deduced can be derived from the world when the worldly content is subjected to conditions imposed by the physics. Deducibility answers to external dynamics somewhat as the feeling of enjoyment of a play answers to the unitary value embodied in the play.

August 12

To realize their aims men must sacrifice something of the value which the integrated life of woman embodies; to have such an embodied value women must sacrifice something of the kind of aim men have.

Men in their realization of intellectual virtues slight the moral, and women in maintaining themselves in the moral neglect the intellectual virtues. But more, one can envisage men and women each aiming at what the other embodies. Thus a man could aim at a full life and achieve a kind of stability, while woman could be said to aim at security and achieve some kind of mature and integrated life.

A man might be sacrificed in order to assure the preservation of a number of men. This decision by a commander is directed towards victory and embodies peace; the victory is to be defined as the retention of one's men while the objective of the battle is reached. The loss of the man is in effect a partial failure to attain the victory. On the other hand in ethics no man can be sacrificed for another or a multitude. The aim here is the attainment of some usable good and the preservation of a unique value. The preservation of the value may involve a refusal to realize the good which the state or the commander can bring about in public. To choose between the two is impossible. There is something to be gained by giving up one man for the sake of saving many, and something to be gained by giving up public order or public goods for the sake of preserving a man. What each side ought to do is to incorporate the lost value at which it aims into the value it embodies; the state should be stained with the value of the men sacrificed to maintain it; the ethical man, the kingdom of ends, should be stained with the value of the goods which were ignored in order to maintain that kingdom of ends. This is possible because they are both ongoing, and can try in their next adventures to make good the need to remove the stain; they ought to so aim and act that the value they lost will in fact be recovered. Until then the value lost becomes a kind of condition in them of the price they paid to have values embodied.

When we look from an art to an interpreter, we can then distinguish: *1*] the embodied value of that art, *2*] the guise which that embodied value has for an interpreter; *3*] the degree and kind of realization which the interpreter gives to that embodied value by putting it inside the interpreter's medium; *4*] the embodied value which the interpreter achieves in the course of the realization of the interpretation. *1* and *4* can be the same in degree and kind; but *1* may be achieved through the aiming at values which *4* neglects, and conversely.

The embodied value of the art, i.e., the art object as it is in itself, a four-dimensional reality which supplements an aimed-at value with energies and powers, etc., from other dimensions, is in a way a completed fact. But since the interpretation does make use of the embodied value in the guise of something aimed at, that value does gain something by being interpreted. The script is itself a work of art; but the script as used by the actors gains another dimension. This is good; each work ought to have roles in all dimensions and the multiplication of the script in the play and then perhaps even in a reading, while it does not add to the value of the script itself, does add to value in the world, making possible in fact that play and the reading. Just so the use of a man's aim by a woman, the acceptance of a woman's embodied value by a man, the acknowledgment of the preciousness of an individual life by a commander, and the acknowledgment of the need to engage in public service at sacrifice and risk, all involve increase in value, by virtue of the assignment of the value of one domain to a role in some other without affecting the first. To be sure when the commander sacrifices he affects the first, but if he makes it good in a civilized career of the state there is a way in which the first is retained. In the arts, what is sacrificed to achieve the embodied result is not guaranteed or promised satisfaction somehow, for the art is no larger than the embodied value. In compensation the art does not use up the art which it interprets; it allows it to be.

The case of men and women is partly like that of the public/private problem of war and ethics, and partly like that of reciprocally interpreting arts, where each allows the other to be, while putting it in another context. So far as each tears the other out of his normal rhythm—the man aiming at objectives, and steadily and gradually attaining an embodied moral virtue, the women incidentally aiming at this or that, and only as subserving the attainment or retention of a moral virtue—each owes the other something; each must carry out the need of the other and satisfy it, the one through and in the aim, the other through and in the embodied life. What the man wanted in the achievement of his aim, self-confidence, virtue, satisfaction, etc., the woman must also provide him with when, in sacrificing the pursuit, he partakes of the family; what the woman wanted by allowing herself aims, refocusing, sense of achievement, etc., the man must also provide her with, when in giving up her undirected existence (the household's well-being is what she wants, but this is not aimed at) she shares with him the organization of life in order that his aim be achieved. He must see to it that the realization of his aim involves the attainment of a civilized life for both. He ought to change his aim, make it richer when she shares it with him; she ought to change her embodied value, make it capable of sustaining a steady aim, when he shares his life with her. Should he try to act as she normally does, he will be in effect a shiftless or lazy man; should she try to act as he normally does, she will in effect be a fanatical or dislocated woman. This is not inconsistent with great achievements by women and a civilized life by men. But the achievements by women cannot be dissociated so quickly from their integrated value; this is their steady core, and the achievement is significant only so far as it is allowed and carried by the value. The civilized existence, the having of the moral virtues in their fulness by men, cannot be attained as it can by woman by merely growing and including more within an aboriginal fulness; the civilized existence always requires some external focus for him, and not necessarily in the guise of something to be successfully achieved in a public world of praise and honor, but always something in the guise of a work done, of something made. He is primarily the maker, she the doer, and each uses the dimension characteristic of the other as an agency for attaining what is wanted, with the eventual possession of the other dimension in its full being. But men and women are also like reciprocal arts, in that the value which each insists on is given a new interpretation by the other. The aim of man, both when realized in him and when not, is evaluated by woman as having a role in a larger context; the embodied value of woman, aimed at or not, is adopted by man as an element in his aim. Man does not take much account of the aims of women, holding them to be incidental and transitory; women do not take much account of the embodied value of man, holding this to be trivial and childlike.

The Stanislavski method, particularly as expressing in *Building a Character,* is essentially the method of teaching the individual actor how to bring himself into the situation in such a way as to in fact embody the value in the situation of the play as it ought to be, and presumably as presented in the script. There could be similar manuals prepared for other interpreters, particularly those who like musicians and dancers put so much of themselves into the activity of embodiment. Stanislavski does not make the mistake of wanting the actor to be emotionally involved in the play; he is alert to the need to make the embodied ideal value have a dimension of ideality and vitality, as well as be unified and individual. A manual for teachers would be something different, for the teacher is trying to embody the eternal value of a vision. But the teacher does need to learn analogous things, subordinating himself to the problem of the eternal rather than (as is the case of the actor) to the presentation of the ideal as script and the play as ideal for spectator. A manual for practical men, say soldiers and particularly officers (since the privates are essentially tools), would carry out the same method but with a stress on the need to embody the value of Existence when and as they made themselves effective. And finally a manual for spectators, e.g., Adler's *"How to Read a Book"* would take account of the individual's value as that which ought to be embodied, which ought to be something achieved in the course of the entertainment and use of the play or poem. Stanislavaki aimed at doing something with the actors precisely because he was concerned with the embodiment of the value of an acted play, which as a datum had an ideal status and will have that status for the spectators. The analogues, because concerned with the embodiment of something eternal, existential or individual, would aim at other things.

The aim for a manual for spectators would presumably emphasize the content of what is being read, as Adler tried to do. But it must not be forgotten that the individual's fulfillment is the final aim of being a spectator, and the manual would aim in one direction, at the spectacle, only because in this way the spectator's full being would be achieved. The aiming at the spectacle must of course be distinguished from the realization of the value of that spectacle in the individual; woman-like that value must be the primary fact and the realization of the spectacle be made to give way to it.

Whatever aims women do have and which they do pursue with some success do affect and distort what they want to be; and since they do share the aims of men and make these aims be at the price of their own established unity, there is always the tragedy for woman in the fact that she, in being successful with man, is a failure with respect to what she ought to be in herself. And this perhaps is the story of Medea. As to Antigone, if we say that her aim is to be politically obedient and her need is to be sisterly loyal, the tragedy either is to be found in the fact that there is a decision to be made one way or the other, or that the tragedy arises only so far as one sees that the former achievement endangers the latter. But this is a difficult case; I must reread the play.

If we turn to politics, the same problems arise. But there is the antecedent question as to whether a state in the effort to achieve an aim embodies some value, or whether it is not itself the product of an effort on the part of individuals to achieve some result, so that it in substance is the togetherness of them all made to have a reality as an embodied value with four-dimensions, but which itself lacks being in the very same way in which any togetherness does. A togetherness could be said to have some kind of being, and even to have a history and an epoch; it could be thought of as diffused over a people and to come to concentrated form as the people divides itself into essential classes and these occupy different positions over against one another. If we take some such view as this we can think of starting with a kind of inchoate unity of the people, as a kind of cultural whole, where though there are individuals, definite roles and some character to the totality, there is nothing but the beings as interlocked with which the state is to be identified.

The situation with which we begin would then be analogous to a kind of Existence, or a togetherness as existing. This would attain its first degree of clarification by becoming articulate, by having the different individuals assume roles in relation to one another. There would be a translation of the togetherness into the guise of an Ideality, but one in which there would be components in which there were stresses and meanings at different points, in contrast with the previous togetherness which was essentially a domain of activity in which there were no genuinely definite parts. Some one or more of these components would precipitate out and subordinate and qualify the rest to make them into slaves or citizens or workers for what might be termed a sovereign, the combination constituting the entire situation. And finally there would be an expression on the part of the sovereign, there would be a dictation and a manifestation of him so that the whole became nothing more than a moment of him. And finally, to stay within one cycle, there would be a rooting in the existing world, by virtue of work and command, a control of what was in fact.

In all these stages the individuals would, as real beings, stand outside the cycle; they would be the beings for whom and out of whom the togetherness came to be. If this were the nature of a single cycle there would be some one togetherness which was characteristic of the group with which we began and which would have to give way, not to that togetherness in another guise (which would keep it in the same cycle), but a new togetherness which had an emphasis on Ideality and thus was a kind of law; a togetherness which had an emphasis on unity and finality and thus was a kind of divinity; and a togetherness which was a kind of commander or individual. The completing of a cycle would be the allowing of a new togetherness to take over. There is no need to suppose that there was an internal power in the state which forced it through these stages; it could be compelled to move through them by virtue of the way in which individuals actually aimed and realized that at which they aimed.

If one were to take this point of view men would be occupied with definitive objectives and the state would be a product of their achievements though, as a rule, the achievements would fall short of the aim just so far as the state itself was what it ought to be, since the proper being of a state is one where the achievements of men with respect to some one aim are supplemented and modified, and therefore something other than a mere achievement or realization of an aim could be. As they made one type of togetherness move toward the vanishing point the men would by their activities make another come to the fore. The various forms of the togetheress could not be together without forcing the men to be sheer individuals. They are able to be individuals with some kind of interlocking, some way of being in a form of togetherness just so far as there are other forms of togetherness which stand out over against them (though constituted by them) and are ready to be made manifest by virtue of the appropriate activities of those individuals. These will progress by making themselves more and more into parts of this isolated togetherness in the sense that this last will be diffused over them. Or, looking at the matter from the other side, there could be a beginning with a diffused togetherness which precipitated out or allowed for the precipitation out of individuals who, at the moment that they were at the limit of such precipitation for that given togetherness, would become caught inside another togetherness and so on through a major cycle.

We have then a togetherness of four kinds of togetherness, which stands out over against the others in a condition of diffusion or solidification, and which as moving away from the state but allows for the coming to be of a new idea of togetherness in a condition of solidification or diffusion. Unless we are to give power to a togetherness we ought to say that the togetherness is in diffusion, bringing about what for it is a solidified togetherness of a different sort. That solidified togetherness is in fact fused over the entities which were precipitated out of the original diffused togetherness.

Men are caught in four distinct forms of togetherness, each of which was diffused over them to constitute a particular way of being together — an existing society, a mythologized group, a religious community and a contractual whole of individuals. As the men in one of these begin to act they form a contrast with themselves as in the other ways of being together. They in effect attenuate the mode in which they had begun and intensify the other modes. The men would still be subject to the diffuse togethernesses, each distinct from one another, on pain of making the men blur with one another, but they would be in them in different ways and with different degrees of concentration or immersion at different times. But then it would have to be true that men were always together in one of these and perhaps all four of these ways. But if the latter the state has always been with us, unless we are to say A] that the different types of togetherness are not yet altogether distinguished one from the other, and B] that until in fact the togethernesses begin to precipitate out their elements, they are in a less than maximal state and thus cannot be known as functional entities but only as prospects. We would have to say that if the state is that type of togetherness which is of an ideal sort, that this exists forever, once we have men of reason, for in the reason is the pattern of their mutual understanding and ideal togetherness.

If the state is a kind of togetherness and therefore is inescapably present always in an explicit or latent form, must not the state's organs, its laws, etc., also have this kind of being? Or should we not say instead that the laws are the genuine products of the activities of men under the aegis of an inescapable togetherness? But then once again one can look at the state as one such product and attribute (as is done in the *Modes*) the togetherness to the modes in their basicality, and not as expressed in such momentary and non-cosmic beings as men. On this account the state is a togetherness but not a permanent or basic one; and the same thing would be said of society, a mythologicalized group or a religious community. They would be something like microcosmic forms of the four types of togetherness.

Or perhaps better still, the state in particular and perhaps these others too can be viewed as the joint product of a produced togetherness of subordinate beings such as men and of an antecedent inescapable togetherness of the modes either in their purity or as delimited and thus as particularly pertinent to men. This result would make it possible to take account both of the fact that the state is produced in the course of time and that it has a power and a meaning and a history which is no mere function of the activities of men. But by virtue of what is the agglutinating of the aboriginal togetherness with the one produced by men possible? And will there be similar combinations produced by society, etc.? Do we not here complicate the issue and make combinations needed where perhaps one component can serve? But we have indicated the need for the combination. What must be shown is how we can unite the two kinds of togetherness, the aboriginal constituted by the modes, and that which is produced by men. But in a sense they do not need to be united; the mere concurrence is enough. We would have a state when the kind of togetherness produced by men is in consonance with the delimited version which is inescapable and sustained by the modes.

One can see an analogue in a religious community since this can be thought to bear the marks of something transcending men's practices and in fact governing them and directing them. And one can see a similar analogue, though not as good a one, in the idea of mythologized group for here once more there seems to be a kind of ideology beyond the power of men to control, and which seems to justify such views as Toynbee or Spengler about the dominance over men by something other and outside them. What is hard to see is an existing community under a larger dominance, unless we adopt the view of some such thinker as Jung. On all these views the state and other forms of groupings would be the outcome of some ways in which the modes were together and of a produced togetherness through the actions of men.

The vibrations in the cosmos would cause changes, as astrologers and similar folk have urged; and the activities of mankind would also cause changes, as most others say. The state would alter by virtue of both of them. And it would, if there is a need for cycles to continue, or if there is an end to our epoch, give way to another way in which men are grouped. There would always be a kind of latency of grouping of all types, but the actual one would require the precipitation out of a special one through the activities of men.

August 13

It is reasonable to begin the consideration of politics with men interlocked not in a state of nature or by contract but as facing nature, as having an environment over against them. This environment can be faced as datum, occurrence, ideal or as definitory of them. If datum, nature is taken to be something outside, to be struggled with, and the history of the people would be the chronicle of its conquests of nature. But to get something in the guise of a datum means that one is able to focus on it, to hold it over against one, and this is undoubtedly a late development. The environment can also be faced as an occurrence, an ongoing, a domain of energy and power to which one ought to be adjusted. It is this which is the primary fact we all face as individuals and as a group; we must constantly keep apace of a nature outside us in order to maintain ourselves. It is only after we have managed to go through the four stages of such adjustment that we will be in a position to look at nature as an ideal, a model, a locus of rules to which we must submit. Though we incline to think of this as the highest and latest development, there is no doubt but that man would not have been able to survive without some elementary apprehension of the idealized aspects of nature in the patterns of recurrence of the seasons, birth and death, growth and decay. And once this has been attained, nature can be viewed as all-comprehensive, as the sea in which the people itself swims, and under whose benign or malign dominance it lives; here we have nature as the source of powers and mysteries and eventually of gods and finally of forces to be used. It is after we have mastered this mode of having nature that nature can be faced as a brute datum over against the enclosed world of civilized living.

In all these stages there is something like a work of art that is being produced. There is a hard matter utilized and a power outside which makes use of it in order to attain something, and incidentally to embody something. The product is contingent and unnecessary in the sense that there is no compulsion in the world that makes it be; people can die out and the opportunities may not be available for the movement to any particular cycle. There is no need to suppose latency of any of the outcomes, but only the desirability of the realization and embodiment of something, to which the people will address itself if it has successfully passed through a previous cycle and does in fact function at its best.

A people is an interlocked group of individuals, not yet a society and not yet a mob. It is the outcome of the natural union of the sexes and the need of men to remain together in order to function and prosper. How much of this is accident and how much is of the very nature of man, is not important for our present purpose, though it seems evident from the rhythms of men, their appetites and dependence when young that they could not continue unless they had some way of mutually supporting one another in tribes or families. If they discovered these unions by accident then it was an accident which had to occur if man were to continue; it is thus better described as something dialectically desirable and contingently produced—as the state also is. A people is not yet a society, for it need have no stability or structuralizing customs, though these will belong to it after a period, since they are the products of the inevitable repetitions of activity, due to the lack of imagination, daring and flexibility on the part of men.

The people face an ongoing nature, an occurrence to be made one with themselves. This requires that they supplement it with some awareness of what it is to be an individual, what it is one seeks to obtain and a *Weltanschauung,* an attitude expressive of native fears and hopes. It is only when the occurrence is supplemented by these that the people makes itself into the locus of that occurrence and of these supplementary dimensions, and thereby becomes not merely a people but a people in nature, a people at home in a territory, a people which, even when nomadic, owns and makes use of the environment as part of itself. They make a people in nature in which in fact there is an ongoingness with a rhythm other than that which nature itself presented. The outcome is a matter of practice, of activity, and not of artistic design or production. It is the way in which the people respond to the environment which dictates how it will embody it.

Nature could function as an ideal for the people, but this is a late development on the one hand, and on the other has to do not with the coming to be of a state but with the coming to be of civilization. The ideal which a people faces is its own standards, established through custom and in this sense conditioning and limiting the fresh activities in which the people engages every day. Every people in the very course of adapting itself to nature, forces out over against itself the habitual patterns which it has acquired unknowingly over the years. It is in possession of its own past and uses this as a determinant of its present. It is able to do this because there are young and old inside the people, and the old, by making reference to the stabilized activities in which they themselves engaged, criticize and evaluate the people. The ideal must be supplemented by considerations of what in fact is happening, with a grasp of the nature of the whole, and with some appreciation of what the individual men are and need. But these are supplementary dimensions, enabling the ideal to be assimilated and thereby permit the embodiment of a vitality which it is the purpose of sheer activity to make possible and to exhibit.

The confrontation of an ideal by a people gives way to the confrontation of its own outlook, its own unitary meaning. (Nature, and also customs, could themselves occupy this position; but these are late developments and have to do in any case with the achievement of religion.) The people come to solicit the help and to try to manipulate the powers which govern them as a whole, and so far as they do this they turn their own unitary meaning into something which they stand over against and which they seek to utilize and reintegrate. The parts thereby make use of their own whole, bring it down into themselves, giving it body and themselves a representational meaning. This is possible because the *Weltanschauung* has been congealed in ceremonial and ritual and has inevitably accreted various members whose task it is to represent it and to urge it as having an overriding import. But this outlook does not become integral to the people except so far as there is some consideration of the nature of individuals, some sense of direction, some grasp of what is happening.

Finally, the people confront themselves as individuals, recognize the rights and worth of men as something which they ought to make part of themselves in the very course of practice. There must be a respect for the individual, and this no matter how brute and savage the community be, for there is always at least the need to elicit their co-operation and respect. (Nature, the idealized customs, and the divinely characterized outlook could all be dealt with as individuals; but once more these are the developments and in any case have to do with the evolution of an ethics for a people.) Each individual being remains, no matter how firmly nailed to his group, how immersed in public affairs, how intimidated by the rest, an individual with a privacy, of which regard must be had if the people is to be sustained from below, as well as alongside through blind custom and habit. The awareness of the individual is in part a function of the achievement of the practical presence of the unified outlook through ceremonial and ritual. Each man makes it possible for such an acknowledgement to take place, but the people do not actually embody the values of the individual until there is some supplementation of the acknowledged being of privacy by a sense of direction, of outlook, and of what is happening.

If there be a movement through all four processes of practical identification of nature, customs, outlook and private rights, a people through its practices will have covered all phases. These occur in sequence and what was gained by one would be lost if some part of the people did not in fact adopt the achievement as its characteristic possession and used it representatively so that the rest of the people could continue to have it. It is when we have these representative subdivisions that we get a state. The state is the people subdivided into representative groups which through their practices exhibit the import of nature, customs, outlook and individuals in the new medium of the people. Since a people with customs is a society, a people with an outlook is a nation, and a people with consideration of individuals is a community, the state is a set of representative groups of people occupied with the distinctive features of an exterior environment, a society, a nation and a community. One can stress, inside a state, one or more of these subdivisions and representative groups. One will then get states which are primarily natural or technological, primarily cultural or civilized, primarily religious, or primarily ethical. If this be the case, then strictly speaking the religious state does require a nation to have been developed conspicuously. Now this seems to go counter to the view that religion is primitive and might even find its origins in nature. But there is no inconsistency between the views. Religion can have many origins and can terminate in a religious state from many different angles. But if one does envisage the state as issuing from a people, as having in fact a genuine representative part engaged in the promotion of religion, religion in the state will require that the features of a nation, its outlook, its unifying meaning, be practically embodied and be sustained by some limited group.

And although it is the case that law has its roots in nature, does reflect custom, has a religious sanction and does have some regard for the rights of men, as relevant to the state, the law takes account of the structure or features of society and makes these into representative structures for the whole. The law, the outlook, the rights, and the force of nature will, as carried by representative groups in the state, be subject to their own internal development, requiring cycles in which they are completed through other dimensions and the assumptions of other roles. The law is not merely embodied in and expressed by some representative group on behalf of all the people in the attempt to preserve the essential practical acceptance of the import of the customs; it is also a mediator between the law of nature, a natural law, a divine law, and an ethical law; or better said, the positive law, though it begins as a kind of adopted structure of the prescriptive customs, is through supplementation made to take account of other dimensions, and issues in the course of its own cyclical advance as a single law enriched in all these ways. So far as it emphasizes one dimension over another it is the reflex or instance of these other types of law—natural law, laws of nature, divine, or ethical laws.

In the *Modes* it was said that there were three representative classes over against the might of the people. But the above would indicate that there are four classes, and that the what might be called the pedagogical class—priests, teachers, etc.—is representative of a divine outlook. Might will then have the role of a kind of togetherness in the state? But if this is the case can one speak of organs as the joint product of divisions of might and the representative classes? This is possible so long as one recognizes that the dispersion of a togetherness allows for its solidification in various areas. The divisions of might would then not occur just simply and in the abstract but in the very course of the movement of a cycle from subordinate class to subordinate class. The account in the *Modes* did not make a progressive study of the representative classes and therefore missed the fact that this involved the dissolution of a togetherness. But then the problem which earlier was thought of as a problem of adjusting the divisions of might to those of the classes would be automatically solved, and organs would come to be just to the very extent that classes came to be. This is the case so far as one views the classes dialectically; it is not the case when account is taken of the fact that the classes are themselves the double product of men working together and of the dissolution of the common might. In a sense then there has been only a shift in emphasis: where before it was thought that political organs were joint products of divisions of might and classes, here it is said that the classes are themselves joint products of the divisions of the might and of the co-ordinate workings of men, leaving over no people in fact, except in the sense that there is always a rooting of all the classes in nature. The state would not have a synthetic function of uniting classes and institutions but would instead be the product of a dissolution, with a consequent congealing of other types of togetherness to make possible the movement to a stadium beyond and other than that of the state, such as religion, ethics, rationality (which are not functions of the state but instead actually prescribe to it).

The state will have over against it not only individuals in their privacy, but also the Ideal in its prescriptive character, the divine in its unifying nature, and nature as an ongoing process. What is not readily seen is that the Ideal as over against the state is involved in the very being of the state, for it not only functions as a moment in every type of state but is the primary feature of a law-abiding, prestigiously determined state. The realization of the Ideal in the state has somewhat the same difficulties for the Ideal in itself, as the state has for the private individuals. And the divine as embodied in the outlook of the people, and the practices of what I have termed the pedagogical class, is inseparable from the divine in itself, and the realization of the one will involve some kind of affect on the other. And finally, the powers which are in nature are not discontinuous from those exercised by the people and by the empowered class, though the latter is geared towards the other classes and members, and therefore must conflict occasionally with the temper of the free movements of nature.

The sacrifice of the public for the private or conversely, and analogously in the other cases, must be compensated for by the incorporation, in the remainder, of the values lost in the former. And in the end then there is no preference, apart from efficacy and opportunity, between the denial of privacy in a preserving public world and a denial of the public dimension in favor of a privacy. In both cases there is an irreparable loss in fact; the loss can now be compensated only in the form of a promise to realize the lost value in a new way in another setting.

A corporation is a juristic entity, a quasi-person, constituted by law. If one with Kelsen were to treat the state as a corporation one would have to subordinate it to some law, and yet law seems to be the creature of the state. One could overcome this impasse by recognizing that the law transcends the state so far as it is a common or a natural law. But what Kelsen supposes is that the state has rights and duties by virtue of the positive law and that it is identical with this; but it would seem to be the case that the rights and duties are those of the government and this is inside the state and therefore can be under the state-produced law. If the state is one with its law in what sense is the state a person with rights and duties? However, the state does have a history and a place in history and therefore must be recognized to have some kind of being. Its being is not that of a real man, nor of an ideal order, but rather of a set of classes together, indeed with a minimal togetherness of one sort, which these classes explicate while productive of a maximal destiny of a new togetherness which the coming to be of those classes inevitably produces. The minimal togetherness gives the state its name and characteristic note, for this minimal togetherness is due to the separation out of the classes as sustained by the divisions of the people. It is the people as divided while attending to this or that mode which makes the state be in the form of the interlocked classes and as having over against it the pure modes. The precipitated dense togethernesses which are thereupon produced become the ground for the treatment of men in other ways.

Men could be conceived to be together not in the dynamic way characteristic of a people, but in an ideal way, as a kind of spiritual unity (as Hegel seems to view it, as well as those who speak of the common or community mind); or they could be together as constituting an invisible church as the very substance of divinity; or they could be together as a single actual individual, as a kind of organism as facists say. The unity men have by virtue of their common heritage and belief—their spiritual import—is outside and apart from the state, and sometimes opposes it; they could be together as part of a church, once again in opposition to the way they are in a state; and finally they could be together to constitute an organism by virtue of blood ties or nationalistic feelings of solidarity.

The state's final achievement is the opening up of the opportunity for the Ideal, divine or organic unity of men to make itself manifest in the same way that the people did. The outcome will be not a state but a kingdom of ends, an invisible church or an harmonized mosaic of men. In each of these outcomes the initial togetherness is dispersed through the coming to be of subdivisions or groupings of men, which are different in kind from those characteristic of the state.

In this account there seems to be shifting back and forth in a confused way from the perspective of a togetherness like the people, to that of the Ideal or nature which it utilizes, to that of the state which it constitutes with the Ideal, nature, Actuality, etc. And this is evident in the last paragraph.

August 14

Some questions to be faced: 1] Is there something in the field of art, analogous to politics, where the achievements in and between cycles is preserved in representative parts?   2] Does not the problem of politics involve the re-definition and exhaustion of the multitude in the shape of   A] a populace,   B] a people,   C] a public,   D] citizenship?   3] Is not there an analogue here in which one ought to see an interpretive art not only approaching some other in the guise of some one mode, but also finding itself to require a four-fold exhaustion?   4] Is not the state the equilibrium of the four specifications of a multitude, in the form of distinctive divisions, each at maximal intensity with the populace, etc., at minimal intensity?   5] Is it not necessary to go through the cycles of cycles just to get the multitude to use up nature, so that if there were a recourse to the ideal, etc., it would involve still another movement?

A] Do we not have a start with a populace and the coming to be of a people through the production of four classes, each class requiring a four-fold movement in which the class is focused on and the others made possible, with the result that the four classes all bear something of the nature of one another and each thus contains something of the possibility of the entire whole, and can therefore act representatively?   B] Do we not have the coming to be of a public, citizenship and finally a populace (an educated, living community working in harmony, a "classless" society) through the forging of other divisions which are but new dimensions of the ones which were forged in the dissolution of the intensive populace?   C] Does the achievement of the state lead to the production of something new with the same multitude or does it force us into another domain, with attention paid not to nature but to the Ideal (say international law), and then to the divine (say mankind or peace), and finally to the Actual (say to the fully adjusted, free and fulfilled individual)?

6] What contrasts with the state when we speak of individuals over against the state: is it the members of the populace, people, etc., is it the individuals as the bearers of the classes but viewed as apart from them, or is it the individuals as expressed through these classes?   7] How can the state act on the individuals or constrain them?   8] What is the source of sovereignty?   9] Is it not the case that the state itself is occupied with a four-fold purpose: A] the expression of its parts and the compromise of conflicting interests;   B] the control by a superior power and the reconciliation of the opposition;   C] the preservation of the past and the adjustment to the present;   D] the prescription of laws and demands, and the flexibility of accommodation of the individual case?   1] In the sense that arts are accumulative either through memory or through their own retention of their productive paths, e.g., in architecture, the achievement of a four-dimensional phase (say of the interpreted art in the guise of an Ideal as supplemented by the possibility of other dimensions) and the achievement of a sequence of these phases (say of the Ideal as faced by the interpreting art in the guise of an individual, a process, an Ideal or a unified meaning—a side neglected earlier), to constitute a single interpretation of a given work of art in the guise of an Ideal, there does seem to be an analogue with politics. We do not then go through a sequence of four phases of a given art in a given guise, but hold on to these and solidify previous positions in representative portions of the product, so that at the end there is in each something of the whole, something like a Leibnizian world in which there is a plurality of independents each of which contains the others in its own characteristic way. 2] If by a multitude we understand a sheer plurality of humans, then we would have to term this in the area of politics the analogue of the four types of togetherness as being blurred together; though this plurality is made up of distinct individuals, as a plurality, and thus as in a sense one, it is the most confused or indeterminate one possible, and the progress of the state consists in its dissolution, with the consequence that the individuals cease to be as independent as they were before. Their individuality is achieved on a different plane, a plane which allows them to be distinct while involved, whereas the plurality insists on their distinctness to such a degree that the involvement is maximized and their individualities are lost just so far as one looks at them from the standpoint of the whole. The whole absorbs them and points to them as individuals only as outside it and away from it; the dissolution of the populace is the having of the individuals together in such a way that they are significant terminal points and have significant natures; whereas in the populace they are distinct only as units, in the other cases they are distinct as having some kind of natures, precisely because those natures have been freed from the blurred involvement they have in the making of the plurality. In a sense multitude is the most dense form of being together but also the least determinate.

It is doubtful if there ever is a stage where we have nothing but a sheer plurality of men. The dissolution has already occurred no matter where we start; men have natures to begin with and these are possessed in themselves while they make reference to one another to constitute a populace. It is this populace which is dissolved in the production of four classes. These classes are themselves the product of a four-fold reorganization, in which first the class is stressed and then provision is made for the presence of the other types of classes. It is only after each class has been supplemented by formal penumbra which allow for the other classes that we are able to have four classes, each of which fills out the penumbra of the others. This four-fold set of filling out classes provides a maximal exhaustion of the idea of the populace; it makes the togetherness of the populace reduce to a minimal, at the same time producing a maximum in the multitude of what may be termed a people.

A people is an intensification of the multitude brought about by the expression of a populace in the shape of four classes. As occupied with the adjustment to nature in the same way that the populace was, it too must go through the process of producing divisions through the use of nature.

(It was not clearly seen in connection with art and the treatment of subjects earlier that the being which is dissolved has four dimensions and requires four-dissolutions.) It is not only that an interpretative art must deal with a given art in a four-fold way, making it as an Ideal have supplementations from the other modes, and that it must allow for other types of interpreting agents, such as practical men, teachers, etc., which allow that Ideal initial art to have another role, but the interpreting art itself must be understood to have its being in a four-fold dissolution, as something personal, as purposive, as productive, and as an achieved meaning.

The divisions of the people are independent of those of the populace. But unless they are made commensurate with the populace, the exhibition of the populace will not cohere with that of the people. Comparable to the four classes produced by the dissolution of the intensity of the populace are four functions produced in an analogous way by the dissolution of the intensity of the people. The functions could follow one on the other, to give us complexities of various sorts, all incomplete and making a significant whole only from some outside perspective which included them all. But the classes can accrete to themselves the various functions which the people permits, and the functions can promote the solidification of the classes. Apart from the dissolution of the people the classes would have roles but no definite tasks to perform; they would have positions and would act but would not be for the sake of functioning in certain ways. Moreover the functions may not be properly assigned, so that the prestigious class, e.g., might conceivably be engaged in exerting power.

The production of a functionalized people is followed by the institutionalizing of a public. The public was initially produced by the solidification of a togetherness occurring with the dissolution of that of the people. It is a coming to be which could succeed that of the people, to give us an historic sequence; or it could be retained inside the multitude and be divided in that multitude. In the ideal case the institutions are but another dimension of what we had in the classes and the functions. The institution formalizes, lays down conditions for membership in the classes and for the exercise of the functions; these in turn sustain the institution, give it body and energy.

The public gives way, in the same way as the others, to the citizenship. This divides into four rights in which the citizenship is to be divided — the right of the life of the individual, the right of speech for the mind, the right of movement, occupation, property and thus of dynamic existence of the temporal being, and the right of worship and belief. These rights ought to be institutionalized and supported by appropriate functions and classes. The same individual of course can exercise the four basic rights, but as exercising any one of them he acts within the area of an institution, is engaged in a specific type of function and belongs to a particular class, just so far as there is a harmony in the four-fold dissolution of the multitude. The outcome of that four-fold dissolution is four classes each with four dimensions, each reflecting in its being the possibility of the others. It is this mosaic of intertwined classes which constitutes the state.

3] The third question was answered above in the affirmative.

4] The state is the populace, people, public and citizenship at a minimal intensity; that is, as capable of being and acting as a unit at its minimum and yet at its clearest, most focused. It is because the multitude is at once and equally populace, people, public and citizenship that a state can be; but this condition is inseparable from the condition of having an intensification of four classes, functions, institutions and rights. There is no power which holds these divisions in being nor assures the persistence of their equality or the concurrence of their activities. The state is in a constant flux, sometimes tending towards the condition of a populace, a people, a public or citizenship, and thus becoming manifest as a class-ruled state; a state of struggle for functional dominance; a state dominated by some institution; or a state in which some right is preferred over others.

5] The state results from the use of nature by the multitude. After it has come to be there is still a need for the multitude to take account of the Ideal which lies beyond it. And then of the divine and of individuals. Shall we term these new kinds of complexities, or are they only completions of the state, providing it with purpose, meaning and individuals? Or do they instead define the world of myth, religion and ethics as embodied in mankind? If the latter, they must with the state constitute something larger than any of them—perhaps civilization. If the former, we seem to lose realities such as the religious community and the epicurean garden. The latter then is the preferable alternative: after the completion of the state there is the supplementation of it by other treatments of other modes of being by the multitude. If we can hold on to the state as we go through these others, we make a civilized domain be; if not, we have the state as an item in a process, which alone can be termed civilization. In the latter case civilization becomes one with the course of history so far as the history goes through these various cycles. The former is surely possible; the being of the state and its meaning can be preserved in the shape of laws, traditions, etc., while one goes through other cycles, and supplements the state by these other dimensions. If we do this, the state will be but one dimension of a four-dimensional whole of civilization which will presuppose a "class-less" society, or a state of equalized beings. The state will be followed on this view by the multitude dealing with the ideal of law, with divinity in the guise of peace, and with individuals in the guise of free beings, and the whole will be a mosaic of mosaics, ending an epoch.

It would be appropriate to call the outcome of the dissolution of the intensity of the populace, "a gathering," that of the people, "a community," that of the public, "a society," and that of the citizenship, "a commonwealth". These are all mosaics of four divisions, and together constitute that mosaic which I have termed the state. On this interpretation the state contains within it the community and the society as well. What is usually termed a society in which the state is a part is a civilization or some part of this. This does not deny that the society with its institutions, traditions, customs, etc., might precede the state in time and sustain it, in the sense that a state could stress the public more than the other sides and thus would be a social state, a state-like society. But to this it can be objected that there is a kind of sophistication to the idea of the state; that it necessarily comes late on the scene and that mankind can live in society for a long time. This is tantamount to saying that mankind can live in gatherings, communities, societies, commonwealths without coming to the stage where all of them are retained and kept in equilibrium. It still could be the case that the society would be the outcropping of the dialectical achievement of the state, but one which had not yet attained completion and which therefore could properly be characterized not as a state but as a society.

6] The state contrasts with A] each of the ways in which men are together, B] all of the ways in which men are together, which is to say both with the multitude and with the four-fold residuum of the disolution of populace, etc., C] with each class, function, institution and right, D] with combinations of classes, functions, institutions and rights among themselves and with each other, E] men as one group but as belonging to this or that class, exercising this or that function, belonging to this or that institution, having this or that right, i.e., men as class-beings, functional-beings, institutional beings, beings with citizenship rights, and any combination of these, F] different modes of being— nature, the Ideal, Actuality and eternity, either in their purity or as pertinent to the multitude, G] combinations, H] dissolved populace, etc. These can be summarized:

A. 1. state in contrast with populace
A. 2. state in contrast with people
A. 3. state in contrast with public

A. 4. state in contrast with citizenship
B. 5. state in contrast with multitude
B. 6. state in contrast with minimal populace plus people, etc.
C. 7. state in contrast with class
C. 8. state in contrast with function
C. 9. state in contrast with institution
C. 10. state in contrast with right
D. 11. state in contrast with class with function or institution, etc.
D. 12. state in contrast with class with class, or function with function
E. 13. state in contrast with class-men
E. 14. state in contrast with functioning-men
E. 15. state in contrast with institutional men
E. 16. state in contrast with men with rights
F. 17. state in contrast with nature
F. 18. state in contrast with Ideal
F. 19. state in contrast with Actuality
F. 20. state in contrast with God
G. 21. state in contrast with nature and Ideal, etc.
H. 22. (see 12) state in contrast with gathering
H. 23. state in contrast with community
H. 24. state in contrast with society
H. 25. state in contrast with commonwealth
H. 26. state in contrast with gathering plus community, etc.

These contrasts raise various problems for the state. They may be designated as *1*] obstacles to its might; *2*] diversity in rhythms; *3*] plurality of estates; *4*] need to respect; *5*] organization against inchoateness; *6*] correlates; *7*] partial and representative activities and the problem of confinement; *8*] adjustment; *9*] definition and limitation; *10*] acknowledgement and opposing privilege; *11*] combination of 7, 8, 9, 10; *12*] (see 22); *13*] individuals as bearers of publicly significant roles in contrast with the area in which they can be carried out; *14, 15, 16*] ditto; *17*] the state in contrast with fundamental modes of being (also *18, 19, 20, 21*) and thus as the artificial over against the ontological; *22, 23, 24, 25*] the partial over against the whole, the incompleted organization against the completed; *26*] the almost completed with the fully completed.

7] On this view the state has no powers, but any part of it might act representatively on behalf of it, and as so acting may restrain the rest. This is particularly evident when we take account of classes, functions, institutions and rights. Though these stand in contrast with the state and have narrower objectives, even when four-dimensional and supplemented by the rest, they can nevertheless carry out these objectives in such a way as to encourage and delimit the operations of the others. There would be no overall objective of the state which would work on the various parts or contrasting items, unless we can speak of the dialectic which makes use of the state as one moment in a larger civilization. From such a position, the state would be able to act, but as an instrument and agent, as a congealing of a power which was going through other stages and which, because going through other stages, could stop at the state as having some kind of being and meaning, and which the state could have because it exhibited the power or nature of some mode. If we think of civilization as essentially a manifestation of some such mode as Existence, then the state as a stadium in the development of Existence would have a power which it exerted over against the above contrasting items, with the possible exception of 17 (though even here there would be a contrast in view of the fact that the state would be Existence as involving men, and would have it in a restricted way). It is in terms of these exterior modes that the state can be characterized as having a history, a purpose, etc. The state then has no unitary meaning; it is not even a whole or aggregate; its being consists in the movement of its concordant parts, and it has a unitary characterization only by virtue of the presence in and governance by exterior modes. Cut it away from those modes and it is a mosaic; subordinate it to those modes and it ceases to have being in the classes, function, etc. In the end then some combination of divisions of a mode, as infected by men, make up a set which contrasts with some mode in its purity.

Restricting ourselves for simplicity's sake to just a limited portion of the state, we can characterize a class as one of the outcomes of the use of nature by men. That class stands over against nature as a whole, and even more sharply, with Existence as a whole. And if one takes account of a second class, then the state as a complex of the two classes will be intermediate between the classes in their severalty and the pure mode, and can be said to constrain the former and qualify the latter, though the activity is entirely outside it, in both cases.

8] The state itself would be sovereign with respect to any of its subdivisions precisely because it included them all; it would be sovereign too so far as one subdivision acted on behalf of it as a whole; it would be sovereign too so far as any pure mode or delimited version of it acted through it to govern and limit the function of any one of its parts or the men with which it contrasted. This means that the state is sovereign as an expression of the nature and rights of individual man, as an expression and congealing of the Ideal, as an expression and localization of Existence, and as an expression and imitation of the divine. A stress on one of these makes the state sovereign ethically, juristically, through power and by designation. Its sovereignty is thus distributed, though when it is exercised it is singular and dominant. The state has rights and duties and privileges only as the complete over against the incomplete, and then as a complete which has no substantiality of its own, but only the being of a concordant mosaic. In the end the sovereignty both in principle and in fact would be the outcome of the modes of being beyond it that express themselves through it by virtue of the persistence of a dialectical progress which insists on holding on to that through which it has gone.

9] The state takes a number of forms, such as democracy, constitutional, dictatorship and authoritarian. (Democracy is here used in the sense of the state as a vital process of efforts, constraints, movements without regard for the whole, and dictatorial is here used in the sense of the state as a kind of superior power. The terms are perhaps ill-chosen, for there is no question but that we can have constitutional democracies and constitutional dictatorships, and that we can have both authoritarian democracies and dictatorships.) In each of these forms there is a kind of stress which is balanced by an opposite one. The democracy encourages the expression of diverse interests and tempers and expects these to work themselves out, but in the end it blurs the opportunity for expression through forced compromises and majority rule. The constitutional state prescribes through the agency of laws, but in the end it blurs the functioning of law by accommodating itself to the needs, resistances and appetites of men as individually manifest. A dictatorship is occupied with controls, but in the face of resistance and even opposition it must mute its efforts in order to conciliate antagonistic groups. Finally the authoritarian system is occupied with not losing any of the goods, of making a unity of all that had been achieved with what is now available, but it is forced to adjust itself to the new demands in the present and to sacrifice some of the things it had gained.

These forms of the state have sometimes been spoken of as forms of government. So far as this is the case they are evidently ways in which parts of the state operate on behalf of the whole and with respect to the parts, and particularly of men both as together and as broken up into subdivisions of classes, functions, etc.

August 15

There would seem to be four types of sovereignty: *de facto* the exercise of the role of making decisions; *de jure,* legalistic, assigning some one to the role of making decisions; coercive, the expression of some individual or group will by virtue of superior power; persuasive, an acceptance by habit and tradition of a dominant outlook so that the tonality of the activities is altered. These answer respectively to the dimensions of Actuality, Ideality, Existence and God.

In the movement from populace to citizenship, or better subject, there is at once an expansion and a contraction. The expansion consists in the extending of an acknowledged status to more and more members, and the contraction consists in the imposition of conditions which in fact will be met by fewer and fewer members. Thus though every man, woman and child is part of the populace, the people and the public, and is also a subject, individuals in these different groups might have different weights. Slaves in the census determining slave states were counted in fractions; there can be proportional voting; children, women, etc., can be represented by men; the unit might be a family, etc. On the other hand, a member of a populace must as a rule meet a new condition to be a member of a people; he must not only be a unit but must be capable of functioning in some way and be qualified to function. A member of a public must be qualified to engage in various roles, must achieve a kind of status, say that of a man of property or of one who has passed various initiation rites, etc., in order to be acknowledged as one of the public. And finally, not every one is given the rights which characterize a subject; aliens might be thought to be part of a populace; the young might be included among the people; the women might make up the public, but all of them might be denied the rights of a subject. What is hoped is that as the requirements for admission to one of these groups is raised there is also a raising in the opportunities and the removal of obstacles in the way of men being acknowledged to belong to them. Thus one might put up a reading qualification and this would eliminate those who could not read; but one might be able to extend education and also would not exclude any one for any other reason but the failure to meet this requirement. There would be no arbitrary caste or classification of men which, regardless of achievement and ability, was excluded.

The four types of sovereignty could be sustained by any one of the four types of groupings. A mob-rule is *de facto,* an inclusive democracy by law is legalistic, the force of custom as defined by all the populace is coercive, and the common will expresses the persuasiveness of the sovereign populace. A people would be *de facto* as offering class pressures, *de jure* as expressing the demands of various trades, coercive as manifesting a common energy, and persuasive as having a social cohesiveness. The public would be *de facto* by virtue of its institutional pressures, *de jure* by virtue of the attainment of a status, coercive by virtue of the weight of its dignity, and persuasive so far as it expressed a national spirit. Subjects would be *de facto* sovereign as expressing interests of groups of various sorts, *de jure* as having such civil rights as that of voting, coercive by virtue of the accumulated force of individual resistances and insistencies, and persuasive through its loyalty. The state as comprising all four groupings would be *de facto* as expressing a general will, *de jure* as being defined and limited by law, coercive as authoritarian, and persuasive by the respect one accords it.

The various terms such as "democracy," "monarchy" seem to refer sometimes to the number and nature of the beings who make the decisions which will have the support of the force of the whole, and sometimes to the number of people who are assigned or allowed rights to express themselves by some such device as voting, or the use of force. Strictly speaking, the second is but a special case of the first: we have to decide where it is best to lodge the final decision which will be carried out. There is no doubt but that whatever system one does pursue, there will be expressions by the men, and some limited number of beings to whom one can look for responsibility or at least to pivot the decision, as an executive or officer of some other sort. Accordingly, there can be no clear and oppositional distinction amongst these various forms of political organization. But if we want to make a distinction in the light of the primary source of decision then we can define a democracy as A] involving all the subjects, and B] having its decisions carried out, rather than merely expressed or taken account of or even yielded to by all. Whatever operates in the state would operate as the instrument of the democracy.

But then there could be only a numerical difference between types of government. There could be the rule of the few, the rule of the one, the rule of many and the rule of all. The rule of one would be the rule approximating the mode of divinity; the rule of the few that of the Ideal, since it would require taking account of a principle of selection of that few; the rule of the many or majority would approximate that of Actuality, since those who constitute the majority would at that moment be the actual subjects, and the minority would be part of the world of subjects only so far as it also made the view of the majority its own; and the rule of all would approximate the mode of Existence, since this is the domain embracing all actualities.

We have then 1] *de facto* democracy as consisting of all the men; a democracy consisting of the majority, the few who are qualified to vote or who are free; and a democracy consisting of only one whose decisions are made on behalf of the many as its representative, as is the case when the president takes over in an emergency. We also have 2] democracy as constitutional, as *de jure,* where the difference between one type and another is in the kinds of things the law encompasses: there could be a *de jure* consideration of men as mere units, as involved in activities, as having various positions in institutions, and as loci of rights. 3] We also have democracy as coercive, where the difference between one type and another is due to the exercise of force, or to the functioning of a legal system with its punishments and rewards defined in principle, or to the outcome of a conflict of wills on the part of men in a dynamic interplay, expressive of their diverse individualities, or to the coercion by a locus of command, where the whole is unified to express a single common will, or a general will. 4] And finally we have democracy as persuasive by the sheer massiveness of its expression, by the ideal it portrays, by the moral natures it allows to be exhibited, and by the unity it stabilizes.

This kind of four-fold division with four parts, modifies and improves on what had been said just a while before. It also makes it necessary to find new ways of differentiating democracy from other forms of government or state. But before this it is desirable to recognize that there can evidently be 4 x 4 x 4 x 4 or 256 different forms of democracy depending on how the various subdivisions of one of the four forms is combined with the rest. Thus we could have a combination of 1 with its first subdivision, 2 with its second, etc. This would be a democracy in which we have a *de facto* coverage of every man, a *de jure* treatment of them as engaged in various activities, a coerciveness expressed in the conflict of the wills of individuals, and a persuasive one which appeals by virtue of its stable unity. This combination would give us a democracy which at once embraced the men, the legal system, the power, and the locus of command. The *de facto,* and then in only some of its cases, alone seems to have been considered by most theoreticians, although occasionally attention is paid to some forms of constitutionality.

When we speak of an aristocracy or oligarchy we are not actually opposing a democracy, for as we saw before a democracy can in fact have a single member, providing he is occupied with doing good for all, as their representative, though he need not necessarily be elected by the rest. Or if this be refused the title of democracy, then one can acknowledge a single executive, who is subject to recall by the people. We would distinguish him from a tyrant or dictator only in the sense that there is machinery made available for restraining him. Machinery is of course always available, for this is what rebellion makes use of; but what is here intended is that the executive is subject to conditioning, not necessarily by laws but by force or persuasion or allowable opposition in the shape of wills, if there is to be a democracy. So our first distinction must be between states in which the multitude of men in some representative way express themselves and control the agents of decision. If they are instead controlled either by what they themselves instituted—for one can elect a tyrant or dictator, as in effect happened with Hitler—we have the rule by some or one.

We have then states which are controlled by the multitude in some form or other—populace, people, public or subjects, through majority action and acceptance, through a common will, or through the mediation of some chosen instrument. And we have states where the control lies elsewhere but there is consideration for the multitude. Both of these have been called democracy; we have the latter in the guise of our elected representatives. But this last case is to be distinguished from those where the control lies elsewhere, and there is no established, non-violent way of controlling the control, limiting or qualifying it. Once we take account of custom, violations by omission, neglect of dictator's edicts, etc., without harm in fact, the distinction between the democracy where there is representative decision controlled by the whole people, and a dictatorship where there is a consideration for the whole but no machinery for the express purpose of limiting the dictatorship, is a matter of degree in theory and may vanish in fact. But we cannot define a state in terms of the consideration it shows to the multitude; a state can allow the privilege of voting or of freedom to worship to all, and yet this all may in fact produce a result which shows no genuine consideration for its own needs. A *de facto* democracy can be one which is effectively in opposition to the needs of men. Accordingly, if we are to distinguish democracy from other forms it must be by contrasting it with those other forms in the sixteen shapes listed.

A *de facto* state can call for some or one to constitute the state, whether or not consideration is given by the some or one to the rest. This some or one would be of the populace, people, public or subjects. In this sense we never have anything but a non-democracy, for no democracy has ever included everyone, since children, the insane, the criminals, the aged, the aliens have been excluded, though not necessarily denied all rights and all representation. A *de jure* state can have class-legislation, or can in fact allow the laws to apply to only some. But if there is a discrimination it is so far not democratic. Yet every democracy has some discrimination; it denies to those who do not live up to some condition—say proper sight—the right to engage in certain activities, say flying a plane or driving a car. A coercive state can distinguish between ruler and ruled, impose conditions on groups and to this degree enslave them in contrast with other groups. Once again a similar thing seems to be true in democracy, for income tax differentials, the denial of freedom of movement and voting to criminals, pure food acts and the control of manufactures involve some differentiating among the membership of the state. Finally, a persuasive state might be one which has its focus of persuasion in an individual or a limited group. This is also true of a democracy. Not all the different elected or controlled representatives of a democracy have equal persuasive power.

If we say all the above things, we seem to have lost any way of differentiating democracy from other types of state. There is of course the question of the determination of succession of sovereignty; there is the question of the final locus of decision in the usual course of events; there is the question of the legal determination of the powers of the executive; there is the question of the right, *de jure* or *de facto,* of expressing dissent and allowing for diversity of opinion to be made manifest. If one takes account of these, one moves towards real democracy. The difference then between democracy and other forms lies in the fact that the democracy has within the state—and not as opposed to it as it would be by rebellion—the machinery and the right to determine who the sovereign is to be, in the sense of a representative executive or locus of decision, and of its succession, its allowed powers, and its status as that which could be opposed within the state. The opposition is between the state or some representative of it, as a kind of unit, and the different forms of togetherness and their subdivisions, and finally the individual members taken severally and as having this or that role, this or that function, etc.

If the state is not the subdivisions and not the mere unity of them all, but the subdivisions as making a single set, then the proper and even inescapable form of the state is evidently a mixture (as Aristotle saw) of democracy and other forms. This mixture can be given (as Aristotle wanted to do) a constitutional, *de jure* definition and control. But there is no need to do this; the mixture could be maintained as a matter of habit and tradition; it could be maintained as a kind of ideal or principle which is being realized constantly through the activities of the parts; it could have a kind of meaning which the parts exhibit by the manner in which they harmoniously work together; and it could be maintained as a matter of ethical decision and will. These are often as effective and sometimes more effective than the judicial. But the judicial does allow for clear expression and the knowledge of limits, and through its use of language can come closer to expressing the neutral position where all the parts and the mosaic of them all have a rule and a right.

If it is the case that there are four types of sovereignty—*de facto, de jure,* coercive and persuasive—it would also seem to be the case that these could be found in any of the forms of democracy already distinguished. It is possible for a *de facto* democracy, a state where all men make their decisions manifest, to have a *de jure* sovereignty, i.e., to assign to the men the right to make their decisions manifest in this way. Or one can have a persuasive democracy, to take another example arbitrarily, and have this exercise a coercive sovereignty; a democracy which is effective by virtue of its appeal may nevertheless function in the guise of a series of compulsions which exist even while they are being submitted to in such a way as to make unnecessary an untoward expression of the force involved. If we then multiply the 256 cases by the different types of sovereignty which they could express we would get 1024 kinds of democracy. Or is it the case that the four ways in which we divided a *de facto* democracy for example are but four ways of expressing the kinds of sovereignty which a *de facto* democracy could have? No, because the divisions of the democracy were not determined by a consideration of how it arrived at the stage where it was *de facto* or *de jure,* whereas this was what we did in connection with sovereignty.

To make the democracy sovereign by law is still not to decide whether the law demands that the democracy function as a force or a conflict of wills or as something persuasive, etc., and is not to determine just what kind of *de facto* being the democracy is to have, i.e., if in the form of a force or conflict of wills it is to express itself in a legal or a persuasive guise, etc.

What is now evident is that the having of laws is no guarantee of a democracy or of justice, for the laws may serve to sanction the sovereignty of one or a few without regard for the needs or rights of all. Nor is any other device a guarantee of this. The members of the state alone have the power and alone have the decision as to just how they are to function in relation to limited groups which exercise the power and the will to decide what the whole and its parts are to do. The members of the state, when they go counter to the express will, are of course in rebellion and the price may be death. They can in fact yield to the laws without real consent, and yet be thought to have made them, just as men can yield to a tyrant without real consent, though thought to be in opposition to him.

What perhaps is at the centre of what most people think is democracy is not the exercise of rights or the acknowledgment of them, since these have in times of crises been severely limited, but the having of genuine alternatives A] in elections, B] in the expression of wills, C] in the facing of charges in the courts, D] in the hierarchy of appeal, E] in the exercise of speech and worship. It is then a pluralism over against what is thought to be monolithic. The democratic way (and one can have this even sanctioned by a single individual despotically exercising force) exists only when there is a real set of alternatives, and the decision as to which is to be accepted is determined in the open market place of discussion and by the expression of a majority view.

August 16

One can distinguish   *1*] the causes of sovereignty,   *2*] the manner in which it is instituted,   *3*] the manner of men who exercise it,   *4*] the numbers of men involved in the exercise,   *5*] the manner in which it is exercised, and   *6*] the outcome of the exercise. *1*] The causes of sovereignty are   A] decisions on the part of some individuals;   B] historic accident,   C] direct or incidental realization of some aim;   D] a precipitation of established folkways. The first supposes a rather extreme form of rationalism and wise calculation; it can be one of the means once men have seen what states are like and have decided to set one up deliberately. But in the beginning this surely was not the method, particularly since men could not come together to agree unless somehow they had agreed beforehand to unite, to do the wise thing, etc. The second,   B] seems to be the correct view in the light of what we know of history and the various ways in which men experimented with ways of coming together, the gradual unfolding of the outlines of the state, the non-existence of it in places where it could have been, and the existence of it where it need not have been. This point of view should not obscure the fact that there is something in the nature of men and their needs which makes it possible for them to act, under certain circumstances, in ways to make the state come to be. There is a disposition to produce the state, but no necessity.   C] It is possible to aim at the production of a state, to envisage it as a possibility and then to proceed to bring it about. Or it is possible to aim at something else, such as peace, prosperity, justice and in the course of attempting to attain this bring about the state. This alternative shares something of the features of the other two. It expresses something like a decision, and it shows the marks of accident. But unlike a decision which may be arbitrary and non-purposive, just an expression of a private act to make something be, without consideration of it as an objective, the aim at the production of a state sees it as something desirable, and acts in various ways (and not merely through decisions) in order to make it real. As a rule we make an effort to reach something other than the state, and have the state as one of the incidental products, not of history but of our efforts to attain something, and which remains an objective which we will thereafter try to preserve and realize with the help of the state. We thus make some state be in the course of attaining some direct objective for ourselves as men, and the state thereafter can be used to help us do that job better; though of course it can be the case that the state can be effete, an unnecessary outcome of such an effort to realize some aim.   D] Finally, the state can come about as the consequence of the rigidification of customs, the articulation of rules, the formulation of what had already been established over the course of time. In this way the state becomes, as sociologists have long insisted, but an attenuated, formalized expression of an established society or community. But it surely is the case that the state has other virtues as well and that such precipitation is on the whole but an occasion for the achievement of the sovereignty through the other agencies as well.

The causes of sovereignty can evidently operate severally; but they can also, as was just suggested, operate together. The cause of sovereignty would seem to be an amalgamation of all these causes. Men decide to do something definite about their organization; if they do not, it is hard to see how they could come to the stage of setting up special agencies and expressing themselves in deliberate laws. But the time when they will make such decisions, and the success of their endeavors to express their decisions is in good part a matter of accident, of good fortune and opportunities. And for the most part, though the state could be the very object in mind when they are deciding to do something about the organization of themselves, men as a rule aim at just harmony or peaceful working together (and incidentally attend to the state as one of the instruments for this), and come in fact to produce the state in the very effort to bring about the peaceful working together in some way or other. And finally this effort at realizing some aim, such as peace, is precisely that which may force the germane folkways to come to expression. The accounts of the causes of the state as a rule over-emphasize one of these factors, ignoring the role the others play.

2] Sovereignty can be instituted: A] deliberately through agreement, B] by deliberation and interplay of different forces, or the conflict and compromise of wills,   C] by constitution or other legal agencies, and D] by the command of some superior power. The first is the theory of social contract. Here individual men are supposed to act as individuals to make themselves into a single body. But of course they are such a body to begin with, and would have to be a rather tight knit one to be able to forge a compact or contract with one another.   B] There is a struggle amongst men for control, and in this struggle there are victors and victims. The outcome of the struggle may be complete mastery or some compromise in which one gives up the right to challenge others for the sake of the security which is produced, as Plato observed. c] A state can be a juridical entity, constituted by means of legal devices, started through the formulation of a constitution. Here one can lay down its privileges and the rights of its subjects, and regulate in impersonal ways the activities of the various component parts. Such a constitution is the product of a rational understanding of the state and the formulation of its necessary structure. D] Finally a state, as some theologians have urged, may be commanded by a superior power such as God, or by some superior leader or other powerful man who redefines the whole system in which men otherwise live together.

All of these modes of instituting a state can operate independently, and can and usually do have an effect on one another. One deliberates and makes a compact which in part expresses the different tempers and tensions of the people, formulates it in a constitution and insists that the constitution is demanded by one's ancestors or God. The interplay of forces can lead to the making of contracts, the expression in a constitution, and the acknowledgement of a superior's desire to have it so. The formulation of a constitution can have the shape of a contract, can reflect the nature of conflicts and the dictates of some superior being. Finally, a superior being may demand that one should make a contract, compromise among the conflicting forces and formulate the result in a constitution. But it is possible to have a contract and no constitution or compromise or command; conflict and compromise without contracts, constitutions or commands; constitutions without contracts, compromise or command; and commands which have nothing to do with contracts, compromise or constitutions.

The four cases in   1] can be combined in all ways with the four cases in   2] Thus we have:

1A. and 2A. decisions expressed in contracts

  2B. decisions which result in conflict and compromise

  2C. decisions which produce a constitution

  2D. decisions to yield to a superior command to act together

1B. and 2A. accidental production of a contract

  2B. accidental compromise of conflicts

  2C. accidental production of a constitution (say, by making one available at a propitious time)

  2D. accidental adoption of some supposed superior command

1C. and 2A. realization of an aim with a consequent deliberation to have a contract

2B. realization of aim with a consequent adjustment of conflicts

2C. realization of aim with a consequent formulation or establishment of constitution

2D. realization of aim with a consequent submission to some superior command.

1D. and 2A. abstraction from folkways and the expression in contract

2B. abstraction from folkways and the overcoming of conflict

2C. abstraction from folkways and expression in constitution

2D. abstraction from folkways and a readier submission to command.

3] There are different manners of men which exercise sovereignty; earlier these were distinguished as A] populace, B] people, C] public, D] citizens, each with a distinct quality and way of being. Any one of the above sixteen ways of producing a sovereign (a production here being understood to combine causes with a manner of instituting) can be exercised by any one of these combinations of men, or all of them together.

4] Not every member of the groups in 3 necessarily functions in the state or engages in a sovereign act. The numbers of men who are involved in the exercise of sovereignty may be A] one, B] few, C] the majority, and D] all. Though this quantification is an exclusive one, it is possible for some functions of the sovereign to be exercised by one of these quanta and other functions by others.

Numbers 3 and 4 are independent. It is possible for only one, a few, the majority or all of the populace, people, or the public, or the citizens to be involved, and this would yield sixteen more cases. What is usually meant by democracy is the case 4C, (4D is close to what Rousseau seems to have in mind, but though this in a way is presupposed by 4C, for all the people must agree in advance in a sense to abide by the majority, it is not what one has in mind when speaking of a functioning or political democracy). The populace is too large and undefined, the people too conventionally bound and socially immersed, and the citizens too late a product and one of the outcomes and not one of the conditions for a democracy, to enable any of these to serve as the area where a democracy is to be located. Accordingly we have 3C, the acknowledgement of a public as the proper group to consider in a democracy. That public is to act as a majority (4C) to decide on its own limits, conditions, laws and rulers.

5] The sovereignty can be exercised in a *de facto* way, in a *de jure* way, through compulsion, and through persuasion, as has been suggested earlier. Each one of these ways of exercising sovereignty, of just being a sovereign regardless of whether or not one has been elected or has a legal right to the position, has, as has been indicated, itself four dimensions, depending on which groups will exercise it. Though there can be a democracy of the populace, and this brought about or acting *de facto,* or by law, or through pressure or by persuasion, and another set of four centered around the people, a political democracy concerns itself with a public. That public may just as a matter of fact exercise sovereignty; the laws may require it; it may have the power to do so; it may have the persuasiveness to do so. All of these in fact seem to be necessary at once. But what we think of as a political democracy is one where the public exercises sovereignty under the sanction of laws. Accordingly, tying this up with the foregoing, a political democracy would be one in which the majority of a public is legally authorized to determine what is to be done.

Such a political democracy can come about in the sixteen ways discussed before, though the 2C cases are the ones which, since they involve a constitution, must be considered as primary. There is then only the question as to which of the cases under *1* is to be thought of as primary. *1*A and C require too much in the way of deliberation and focusing; *1*D, and even C, can be viewed as special cases of B, the historic accident. Whether then there was some decision on the part of individuals, whether or not they had some particular aim in mind or many such which had as a side effect the production of a state, and whether or not the state is an attenuation of the established folkways in whole or part, the state would seem to be the result of an historical accident in the sense that it came about only because certain contingencies happened to take place. The ground had to be laid in the appetites of men, the kind of satisfaction which the state produced, the kind of folkways that had been established, the kinds of decisions and aims men had, but it is essentially a dynamic rather than an individual, ideal or unifying principle which governs its origin. Accordingly, we can then say that a political democracy is a contingent organization of a people legally authorized to determine what is to be done.

Given a political democracy there are a number of effects it might produce. According to some critics the effect is to injure mankind; it is in outcome undemocratic either because of the ways A] it deprives some individuals of rights and opportunities, B] the kind of instability it allows or promotes, C] the kind of irrationality or perverse ideals it sustains, and D] the kind of conflict in the whole which it brings about. A genuine democracy would be one where these effects were at a minimum. Since every state should promote stability and seeks to, since all of them should pursue a rational ideal, and since all of them should make possible the embodiment of the richest meaning, it is only the first,

A], which would seem to be characteristic of democracy, since this pledges a consideration for a majority or all men. Accordingly the political democracy must be said to act in order to preserve and promote the rights and opportunities of individuals. We thus get the following definition:

> A democratic state is a contingent organization of a people legally authorized to determine what is to be done, and effectively preserving and promoting the rights and opportunities of all its members.

In all this no attention has been paid as to just which political organization is preferable. (Nor have I asked if there are advantages which a monarchy or a mixed government or an aristocracy or an oligarchy has over a democracy.)

Is it better to have an inherited source of power; is it desirable to balance powers; is it desirable to determine the selection of the individuals who are to be sovereigns (even when perchance there is a universal privilege of voting, it may be only for those of a certain privileged class, in which case we would not have a genuine democracy but only a democratic mode of selection of members of a non-democratic state, except in those cases where the privileged class is open to all to enter, regardless of antecedent condition or irrelevant factors of appearance) out of a limited class or out of all the people? The inclination of those in a democracy is to answer that it is not good to have an inheritance of power, that it is desirable to balance powers, that it is desirable to select the individuals who are to be representative or to be sovereigns in their activities from out of all the people so far as specialized knowledge, as in the case perhaps of justices or technical experts on civil service, is not required. But these, though large questions for practical politics are incidental and minor for political theory.

September 15

If it be the case that the denials of a philosophic system are specializations of the unity of the system as such, what relation shall we say holds between the actual items of the system and the unity of the system as such? Can we say that those items do not illustrate the unity of the system? If so, it would seem as if they are outside the unity and what it embraces, in which case they would seem to be a heterogeneity, exactly what the denials are. Or is it not the case that there is no such entity as a unity of a system, and that the isolation of it is in fact the specification of dislocated items? The unity of the system as in the system is precisely the exhaustion of the unity in the relations which the items in the system bear to one another. But if the unity is a kind of relation, then all denials will be relational, since they are all forms or cases of that unity. Is it then that the relations which in fact connect the items in the system become forms of negation when they are taken away from their terms? Is it then, e.g., that "non-causality" becomes a relation for such items in the system as causation and ideality only when held apart from those terms, and that when these terms of the system are brought into account the relation changes to become the unity of the system? But what is this unity as it functions in the system? Is it a relation? If it were, the negative relation would seem to change to a positive relation of unity when in the system. Or is it not a kind of togetherness? If so, we must say that when togetherness is held apart from the items which are together (and thus made to seem as if it were a genuine mode of being) it takes the form of specific negations of the items that are in fact together. To make togetherness oppose the items that are together is to forge the negations of those items, and have these negations as a mere aggregation. When we take any one of these negations and try to put it in the system we find that we must either generalize it until it becomes a functioning togetherness, or that we must negate it so that it becomes a substantial item in a togetherness. In the *Modes* I assumed only the second way; and this is strange for I there said that the items were specifications of the unity of the system, and should therefore have said the reverse as well; the unity of the system is a generalization of the individual negations.

There are then two ways of negating the negatives of a system: we can convert them into one togetherness of all the items in the system by generalizing them, making them relate the items in the system in such a way that all their being is exhausted in the activity, or we can convert them into their opposites and thereby retain in them their being while changing their values. In the latter case there will be a functioning togetherness which does not owe its presence to any act of negation of the negations of the system. However, if a system be viewed as a kind of distillate of experience there must be a way in which its unity is a kind of conversion of the items of experience, for there is a sense in which the items of experience are negatives of the very items in the system which are supposed to report them; they oppose them and are at the very least their correlatives.

Since there is nothing like a negation of the totality of things, the togetherness of the four modes must be incapable of specification, of isolation, and since it functions to connect in such a way that its very being is exhausted in that act, it must be incapable of generalization as well. The togetherness of the modes must be unique, and all systematization must, even when attempting to express this, be but one of the items which the togetherness relates. Such a related item, Actuality as manifest in the guise of mind, will have its own concrete unique togetherness. But since there are things outside the system this togetherness will be capable of specification; it will be capable of generalization too but only by going outside the system in another direction, towards the world as encompassing the system and other things.

If it be the case that God is unity, and this is somewhat analogous to togetherness, might one then not say that all that lies outside God is a specialization of the abstract version of his unity, and that the items are preserved in Him only by being transmuted from negations, in the sense that they are outside Him, into positivities (or the unity for these positivities) when made part of Him and preserved? But then preservation would seem to be an inversion of what things are.

What is other is a negative, but it is not a negative which can be expressed by a simple negative sign; or better perhaps, negation has various thicknesses, and the thickness of the negation by God of the world and by the world of God allows for the preservation of things in their excellencies. It is only thin negation, the negation of logicians, which requires one to invert the very items which are outside one's system. There should then be a thick negation relating the philosophic system and the world, and the latter should be convertible into the former in somewhat the way in which it is converted in fact into the unity and components of a preserving God. Since God is together with all else we can say that the thick negation of God and the world and other modes is just togetherness, so that once again a negation will be a specialization of togetherness. But what is not clear is that this specialization should have the guise of one of the items in God when subject to a negation.

September 16

There are four ways of dealing with an art object. One can follow the lead of idealists and take a coherence-theory approach. This is what the New Criticism does. It stays with the poem and tries to find its internal self-sufficing rationale. This is an approach which is most germane to poetry and painting, particularly when these move to the stage of being purely syntactical, verbal, musical, paradoxical, a tissue of meanings. A second approach is perhaps the classical which wants the art object to report, represent, tell the truth about an objective world. This is the art object as a message or restatement; we find it best expressed in realistic drama, portraiture, prose, historical narratives, etc. A third approach is that which interests the amateur; it is the point of view of those who see the art as defining a new dimension of value and being, as a kind of divinity in terms of which everything thereafter is to be measured. We take this approach when we deal with the major works of art — Homer and Shakespear, Raphael and Rodin — in every variety. A fourth and somewhat neglected view takes the approach of Existence — in contrast with the above which dealt with the work as a kind of miniature Ideal, Actuality or God — and says that the art work first says "stop," keeping us within its confines, and then tells us how to subject ourselves to reorganization so as to make ourselves in harmony with the punctuation which this contains. We look at the art object in order to "purge ourselves," to re-define ourselves, to get a new rhythm, one which accords with what this art object exhibits. This is the point of view we usually take in drama and music.

All four approaches are legitimate and with respect to all objects. All four can be accepted by those who deny that there is anything more to the art object than a kind of stimulative power, or by those who suppose that it deals with a special facet of reality, or who think it has its own object.

Even in the first case, the view of Actuality, to the effect that the art object is a report, can be applied in a four-fold way, though it then should be a report of the subject experiencing rather than of something real outside.

September 29

Whatever the universe be thought to contain, in the end there must be no principles for it but those which are descriptive of it. The theory that there are only descriptive laws or principles is in the end the theory that they are always fulfilled. There can be no normative principles which are unrealized in it, without setting those principles over against the universe and thereby holding in effect that what by hypothesis was the universe is only a part of the universe. If one expanded the universe in this fashion one would be driven over an infinite regress (unless the now expanded universe would have no normative principle unrealized, which was questioned to begin with). But if this is the case, why then is not the program of naturalism to the effect that there is no realm of possibility, no antecedent set of prescriptive principles in logic or mathematics necessary, a tenable one? The answer must be though all natural possibilities are rooted in the world, revealing that the so-called merely logical possibility is just a word, there are norms which may never be realized. We can say of the entire *natural world* that it is not altogether all it might have been. But we cannot say this of the *entire universe,* for whatever is said of it is said within it and not over against it. The normative principles of nature are over against nature, but inside the universe. Might one not then go on and say that normative principles are possible in nature if one sets one part of it over against another? This surely is the answer that naturalism must give. It can offer man a set of norms by looking to the rest of nature as a model, or as the locus of principles—or conversely, man can be a norm for the rest of nature. But what still remains over is the fact that one cannot then say anything about the defectiveness of the whole of nature, as together with man. Yet these would seem to be less than they ought to be. There is no locus for this "ought to be" and indeed no way in which naturalism can affirm such an ought to be.

But might it not be said this is exactly the position in which one gets when one looks at the entire universe? Indeed one might say that naturalism or any other position, by taking up the view that this or that set of items make up a universe must suppose that there are no prescriptives for it. How can a naturalism then be dislodged, except by showing that there are more items? Can it be dislodged, as *Modes* supposes, merely by showing that nature and man together might be defective? After all the universe is not identical with perfection; or if it is, why may not nature and man together be identical with perfection? The answer must lie in the fact that nature and man together are the concrete and can be judged as defective, whereas nature, man and a standard for them, even though the standard be real and ultimate, has no concreteness of the sort which will enable a principle to stand over against them; there is no principle in short appropriate to both standards and world, though there can be principles appropriate to the world, as including nature and man.

If we suppose nature is the universe we will have no way of showing that the next stages of nature must conform to the rules dominant today, even if we were to go on to say that those rules are of the very substance of natural objects and are known to be prescriptive because they are definitory of anything that might occur.

In connection with nature it is to be noted, that A] there is in the universe something which is prescriptive for the rest; indeed, each mode is a norm for all the others, and B] the norms are irreducible. We know what the universe always must be like because it contains substantial realities (incapable of passing away by the very nature of their being), which by their interlocking yield the very structures in terms of which one might try to deal with them.

But once again, why may not something in nature be used as prescriptive for the rest, and conversely, and why may not nature itself be irreducible? To the first point, we must again say that all of nature (with man) can be judged, and that we have no proof that a mere nature (with man) is irreducible, whereas one can prove that a universe is. Consequently, the argument boils down to the fact that we can prove the irreducibility of nature (with man) only so far as there are other irreducibles which it needs to have be in order that it might be, and in terms of which it can be evaluated, and this can be only so far as there is a universe larger than nature. The whole universe has necessary components, components which never can be cancelled out, but the universe itself is not concretely (but would be formally) necessary, since it is not possessed of any definitive being in the concrete. There would be, strictly speaking, no being which was the universe, but only a universe of beings, the universe as a togetherness stating the formal necessity which the modes constitute. (The universe as a togetherness could be viewed as prescriptive with respect to some other phase of itself, and these phases could together be viewed as prescriptive of the modes, and conversely, but then what is really meant is that the universe is not merely the modes, but the modes together.)

It is the modes together which has no substance and for which there are no prescriptions; anything less than this has substance, and has prescriptions in the shape of realities it does not include. Nature and man therefore cannot be treated as final, out of whose being one might analyze some basic principles to which nature and man might or must conform, and which therefore will allow for the use of something like prescriptions for what is to be later. Any principles to which nature and man ought to conform, might also be violated, and are in fact not yet embodied anywhere, and might never be so.

But if the modes are concretely together, and have a formal togetherness which with them makes up the entire, exhausted universe, do we then not have something more than the modes, and therefore are we not on our way on an infinite progress? Is the formal and material necessity a single whole? Is this whole necessary? The answer must be that so far as the modes are well-interlocked and possess the components they contribute to the common togetherness, there is only one necessity and this is concrete; so far as the modes are viewed as pure and over against one another, they are less than all there is. So in one sense it is the modes together which exhaust the universe without residue, and in another sense the modes as over against and thus "together" with a togetherness do this.

The necessity which is the universe is in the end the only necessity there is or can be. Here Kant and Hegel are right. But what they did not see was that if the universe be too narrowly confined, we will face necessities outside it in terms of which it is to be judged. And the way to know if it is too narrowly confined is to recognize that it is temporal (and therefore has not yet succeeded in being all it should be, and may never succeed); that it is substantial and thus demands something over against it; that it does not contain certain required items. What is temporal might always be defective; what is substantial allows formal principles to be applied and does have a boundary requiring other substances; what is ineffective has no necessary control over what it contains. The universe is atemporal, non-substantial and non-effective and therefore is as excellent as possible, has no principles over against it, no beings to contrast with, and is dependent for whatever meaning it may have on the fact that it comprises necessary modes which are necessarily together.

The total universe of the four modes is not temporal; as including the modes and the togetherness of them, it is not substantial; as dependent for its meaning on the being of the "togethered" modes, it is a product of and not something dictating to them, and thus cannot offer them prescriptions. Nature is "prior" to the things it contains; the universe is in contrast "posterior"—though no temporal meaning is here involved. For the naturalists to make out a case for the finality of naturalism, then, they must show that nature (including man) is not temporal, is not substantial, and is not prior to its content.

No "game" or arbitrary limited language can have ultimacy; if the rules for a game are prescriptive, they must have some being over against the game, and this means there is more to the universe than the game or the language—which is to import into one's account an ontology. But most people who hold this view at the same time seem to say that the rules define the game; but then the rules are grounded in the game. Consequently this account turns out to be a most ontological one, with the rules constitutive of a reality, here narrowly supposed to be a game, inquiry, language or something like that.

September 30

Is the art object like nature or like the universe, i.e., is it temporal, substantial and effective, or is it atemporal, abstract and without control over its parts? It would seem to be the former. It was made in time and goes through a process of decay; it is over against other objects and its creator, and it does control its parts, since the art object is an organic whole dominating and modifying the very parts out of which it might even be said to be constructed. There is difficulty with this interpretation only where it is thought that effectiveness must be physical, that substances are necessarily alive, and that the temporal status of a being requires it to be devoid of any steady meaning or value. If, however, we attend to the value or meaning, then we can say that it is atemporal, for though it may come to be and pass away, it does so as a single unit which has been given or deprived of a carrier; that it is abstract in the sense that the value is adjectival to the art object itself; and that it is ineffective in the sense that it is a product. But the temptation of many contemporaries is to identify the value of an art object with the art object itself, and to suppose that the art object is therefore outside the world of substantial, effective, temporal beings, and is instead an idle adjective of some idle knower.

October 3

If it be true, as I think it is, that Descartes reached an impossible impasse in his treatment of mind and body, having no way in which he could bring together an unextended with an extended to make a single unitary being, it should be true that we get a similar problem in Kant, particularly with respect to the Aesthetic. If the things in themselves are without extension, and if, as must also be the case, the sensuous manifold is without extension, how can they become extended even when dealt with through the forms of intuition? What kind of juncture could be made here? The manifold or the transcendent objects (whether or not different from things in themselves) and any other material which Kant requires for his categories and forms must have within them that which is congenial to those categories and forms. The world to be dealt with by the categories and the forms must be already in some sense categorized and extended. But one need not go the length of the absolute idealists and suppose that the world contains categories and forms of extension. All that is needed is to recognize that the objects are not somehow transmogrified by what is entirely alien to their nature. All we need say is that something latent and submerged and thus infected by content is so treated by the categories and forms of intuition that the infected category and the temporality and spatiality of the object is brought into focus.

This same problem must arise in reverse when we start with the forms of intuition or categories, and ask how they are to be realized. The filling they are to receive must be appropriate; it cannot be just stuff. This is possible if the forms and categories are already stretched out, are attenuated versions of the very filling that is to be given to them. And such an account is most consistent with Kant's own treatment of the modalities, which treats the possible (and thus I should think the categories and the forms of intuition) as the necessary, lacking some conditions. The mistakes indicated above come about because the difference between mind and body, form and content, and perhaps even essence and existence is taken as radical, requiring a juncture of alien beings having no feature in common and no capacity to make a unity. If the mind is but the body attenuated, and the body is the mind quiescent, subjugated, not yet functioning as mind—a kind of concrete in which a meaning, which is mind or which allows for mind or which belongs to mind's domain, can be isolated—there is no problem of their juncture.

If now we turn to the modes, the question will then arise as to just how they can be brought together. Essence and existence, the nature of proof, the capacity to be religious or to have knowledge, the problem of testimony, etc., bring this question into sharp focus. The *Modes* says that from the perspective of each mode the others are attenuated versions, and that there is no true way of expressing what a juncture of them would be like, either in a being or as neutral to them all except by speaking a] of the other modes as subjugated by the being, and b] of a neutral togetherness. But the other modes as in a being must then be capable of being there. This means in effect that each being has within it all the other modes, and therefore when it in fact meets the other modes as over against it, it brings to the fore the components in it which answer to what is over against it. The togetherness of all the modes in contrast does not constitute a being; so far as it has any nature at all, and it does, it allows for the meeting of each with each, because each has in it what answers to the others, thereby enabling them as it were to contribute components to one another which would suffice to make a new mode, were it possible (which it is not) to isolate what they contribute and hold it apart from the contributors without thereby annihilating those contributors.

October 4

When one tries to reconcile different entities and looks to a *tertium quid* one is doing in effect what is done when one looks for a substance to serve as the locus of a number of distinct characters. The unreconciled are in the end shown to be abstractions and to oppose one another only as abstractions; the *tertium quid* owns both of them, and expresses itself as them. They are its dimensions. When we turn to things we find that any characterization is categorial; i.e., it is an exhaustive instance of one category, and stands opposed to other categories and of course to other instantiations of its own. Thus to say that something is yellow is in effect to say that 1] yellow is *the* color of it, and 2] it is not a shape, etc. Just what are the categories governing things is hard to see. Certainly the categories of Aristotle and Kant are much too general. Color and taste and smell are qualities but each is categorial in the sense that each is exclusively exhibited in some instance and these instances are compatible since they can be in the same object. Color is instanced as yellow, and taste as sweet, and there can be something which is both yellow and sweet. A thing cannot be yellow and green, because the characterization of the thing is in terms of the categories or dimensions of a thing. How many categories and dimensions are there?

A preliminary listing of non-relative qualities of things, giving only one of a pair:

1] Existence: insistence, resistance, motion, rest, change, continuity, relation, uniformity, variation
2] Quantity: size, figure, number, length, breadth, depth, mass, growth, coherence, order, sequence, unity, duration, repetitiveness, location
3] Power: causality, strength, productiveness, agency, vitality, tendency
4] Form: symmetry, circularity, convexity, sharpness
5] Motion: impulse, rapidity, direction
6] Matter: density, hardness, elasticity, tenacity, texture
7] Organic: vitality, pleasure, touch, taste, odor, sound, color

These are part of a list from Roget. Is there any way to get an ordered classification and proper subdivisions? What principles must be invoked? If the *Modes* is right there ought to be a three-fold basic classification of qualities with at least four basic subdivisions in each.

October 5

The view that one dialectically considers the reality of an inferred entity whose being would make it possible to explain entities otherwise in conflict or unintelligible or abstract, might be termed a reconstructive view, since it engages in a construction for the purpose of reporting what there is in fact. The "thing" as the locus of qualities is such a reconstruction. If use is made of the four modes, the first division of qualities is three-fold. These would be compatible qualities having loci in the same thing; each one of these would be instanced in a way which precludes another instancing of that quality there; the localization in the thing is the exclusive instancing of a given dimension or quality of the thing:

Actuality has three sets of qualities:

1] In its existential dimension it has dynamic qualities,

2] In its ideal dimension it has valuational qualities,

3] In its divine dimension it has organic or unifying qualities.

1] Existential or dynamic qualities: insistence, resistance, motion, rest, change, stability, growth, decay, duration, repetitiveness, place, causality, strength, productiveness, agency, vitality, tendency, impulse,

2] Ideal or valuational qualities: beauty, ugliness, the pleasureable, the painful, attractive, repulsive, symmetry,

3] Divine or organic qualities: continuity, discontinuity, uniformity, variation, size, figure, number, coherence, order, unity,

This triple division mixes many different types of qualities. Can these be sorted out by dealing with qualities in one mode as referring to the others? Thus dynamic qualities in themselves might be one class, another in relation to the Ideal, and another in relation to the dynamic. And a fourth might be the qualities in relation to one another.

1A. Dynamic in themselves: conatus, change, disposition, duration

B. in relation to one another: insistence, resistance, motion and rest, position, productivity, agency, vitality, impulse

C. in relation to the valuational: growth and decay, tendency

D. in relation to unifying: part, self-maintenance

2A. Ideal in itself: beauty, ugliness

B. in relation to one another: better and worse

C. in relation to unifying: harmony, disharmony

D. in relation to Existence: satisfaction, pleasure, pain

3A. divine in itself: unity, uniformity, variation, figure, number

B. in relation to one another: concurrence, size, coherence, order

C. in relation to the Ideal: attractive, repulsive

D. in relation to Existence: purposiveness, randomness

October 7

If the mere One is indeterminate and is in this respect indistinguishable from Nothing, and if Nothing is self-contradictory because it is indeterminate and yet determinately what it is, there must always be at least two beings. Since each is only because the other is too, each must be related to the other, hold on to it in order to be at all. Each to be something fully in itself must endeavor to possess the other. Accordingly the first feature we must insist upon as characteristic of a being is that it has a conatus, that it makes an endeavor to master something other than itself. As a consequence it can, depending on the success it has in reaching to and subjugating the other, have the features of rest and motion, growth and decay, change and stability. As standing over against the other it has a definite boundary, and therefore has the additional features of size, shape and number. Since its insistence is met by a counteracting resistance, and since the insistence of the other is met by its counteracting resistance, it manifests any one of a spectrum of qualities from that of texture and color, continuity and discontinuity on its surface, to that of sound in between, and to taste and pleasure and pain at the place where the other is being suffered to intrude. Each of these considerations gives us a new category or dimension of the being, each one of which is instanced in an exclusive way. And so it is possible for there to be a being which, though not capable of being red and green at the same time and in the same respect, can nevertheless be round and growing and pleasurable.

Red and the pleasurable are in the same dimension, with different stresses on the degree and locus of the resistance and insistence; one might therefore argue that a object cannot be both, that it cannot even be sounding and colored. This is not the case because we have different organs by means of which we can exercise and receive different degrees of insistence and resistance. Sound and color are not in the same relation as are red and green, for the latter are instances of the same universal, whereas sound and color occur in different areas and exhibit different degrees in which insistance and resistance can be exercised.

October 8

An individual organism is in a circumambient environment. It's status as over against that environment is that of a kind of vague feeling which can be indifferently termed a sensitivity or a consciousness. The readiness to discriminate something in the environment, due perhaps to the articulate structure of the organism, involves a forcing of something to the forefront of the environment vis-à-vis the organism, with a correlative precipitation out, of a correlated consciousness. The original sensitivity thereby becomes a kind of whole over against the precipitated part which is the consciousness of the object.

Self-consciousness is the vague ontological-epistemological total sensitivity facing a subdivision of itself in correlation with a focused part of the environment. Having once achieved the correlations, due to an "alertness" as Rotenstreich calls it, there is A] the task of systematization, elucidation, clarification, organization, and the task of endeavoring to understand what the world is from the side of the world. This requires use of the original consciousness as an adumbrative, and of speculation and dialectic to make sense of what is encountered.

October 9

In 1.01 of the *Modes* it says that non-extended things cannot become extended by the imposition of an extended frame; or more narrowly that non-spatial things cannot become extended by the imposition of a spatial frame. In 1.09 it says that possibilities may not be in space though spatializable. It says there too that possibilities do not have extensionality but can acquire it. My students feel the two are in contradiction. But are they if we can say that there is a kind of extensionality in possibility and in God and in the Actual, and that this comes out to be a genuine extension through the process of interaction, cognition and the like?

Also, 1.08 says that primary Actualities are persistent. May not they last for just a moment? The moment to be sure may be extended, but why must they last more than one? Even though it resists, even though it does not pass away in a Cartesian or Humean way, the Actuality might, though capable of lasting more than a moment, last only for one moment. It is as it were persistentable, rather than persistent.

Also, it is said that compound Actualities are resistant and insistent but exert no power; what must be made clear is that their resistance and insistence is derivative from their parts; also that resistance and insistence are not dynamic activities but structural or analytic components. Insistence for example is really a vector or directionality, and resistance is but another way of talking about irreducibility as reactive to that which threatens it in fact.

October 12

Though it is remarked in the *Modes* that the various modes are analogues of one another, having different but correlative logics, times, divisions, etc., the accounts of them are not parallel. One can, however, forge a kind of urphilosophy in which the analogical features are expressed in a neutral language, or with variables, which the different modes might be expected to specify in divergent ways. Thus a proof of a mode might be stated as "given w, route x and process y, z can be inferred," where w, x, y and z are the different modes.

To find the urphilosophy in the *Modes* one might begin by classifying the propositions thus:

7]   1.03 (1.02)   Necessary truths for each mode; this relates particularly to parts of the modes, and should therefore follow on the characterization of the whole.

1]   1.01, 1.04–1.08   Necessary and residual features. (include 1.10?)

2]   1.09–1.13   Acknowledgment of other realities.

4]   1.14   Imperfection

3]   1.15–17   Ingredience

5]   1.18–24   Action with respect to others

6]   1.25–29   Mutual effect of all

7]   1.30; 1.33–44   (1.31–32 belong under nature of Actualities); relation of parts of Actuality to one another

8]   1.45–1.55   (a special type of a subdivision of Actuality, man and his features)

9]   1.56–1.69   Supreme function of Actualities

11]   1.70–1.85   Other modes from perspective of knowledge

10]   1.86–1.89   Inference and knowledge as activities of Actuality

       1.90–1.104   the category in knowledge

12]   1.105–1.117   Actualities and the Ideal

       1.118   Actualities and all the modes

1]   2.01–3   Ideal

12]   2.04–5   Ideal and other modes

7]   2.06–11   parts of the Ideal

13]   2.12   comparison of modes

14]   2.13–14   satisfaction of Ideal

4]   2.16   incompleteness of Ideal

12]   2.17–19   and other modes

6]   2.20–22   mutual affect of modes

12]   2.23–31   action of Ideal on Actual

15]   2.32–37   enhancement of men by Ideal

15]   2.37–56   rights and duties of men because of ingredience of Ideal

15]   2.57–63   right of might

12]   2.64–83   Ideal in relation to Existence

16]   2.84–88   men as escaping the Ideal

15]   2.89–94   men enhanced by Ideal (see 2.32–37)

2]   2.95–97   testimony

14]	2.98–104	satisfaction of other modes
1]	3.01–2	Existence's nature
12]	3.03–5	Existence affected by other modes
12]	3.06–12	Existence from perspective of others
12]	3.13–14	function of other modes for Existence
11]	3.15–31	Existence and knowledge, concrete and abstract logic; history; 3.67–75
11]	3.32–36	inference and process
12]	3.37–48	Existence and Actuality. Also 3.59–65
17]	3.49–58	purging of the modes
7]	3.76–91	achievements of Existence
12]	3.92–99	Existence and other modes
2]	3.100–102	testimony
14]	3.103–6	satisfaction of other modes
18]	3.107–9	modes as relations
20]	3.110	proof
3]	4.01	ingredience
3]	4.02	needs
3]	4.03	adjustment
14]	4.04	satisfaction
12]	4.05	burdens
2]	4.06–7; 4.14–24	testimony
18]	4.08–9	relation; 4.25–4.35
19]	4.10–11	detachment; 4.38–4.49
20]	4.12–13	proof; 4.52–57
1]	4.58–59	God's nature 4.65
11]	4.60	idea of God
12]	4.61–64	and other modes 4.67–75; 4.84–4.98 (also ingredience)
7]	4.66	divisions of
18]	4.76–79	modes as relations
19]	4.80–83	detachment
2]	4.96–99	search for God
20]	4.100–104	a kind of proof
21]	4.105–9	the disciplines.

The above twenty-one numbers are tentative subdivisions; the duplications show the analogues. We can thus say:

1] Necessary and residual features 1.01; 1.04–1.08; 2.01–3; 3.01–2; 3.76–91; 4.58–59

2] Testimony, 1.09–13; 2.95–97; 3.100–102; 4.06–7; 4.14–24; 4.96–99

3] Ingredience, 1.15–17; 4.01, 4.02
4] Imperfection, 1.14, 2.16
5] 1.18–24, Action with respect to others, 4.03
6] 1.25–29, Mutual effect, 2.20, 22
7] Parts of 1.30; 1.33–44; 2.06–11, 4.66
8] Necessary truths regarding parts of, 1.02, 1.03
9] Special subdivision of and its features, 1.45–55
10] Supreme function of a mode, 1.56–69; 1.86–89
11] Category in its uses 1.90–105
12] Other modes from perspective of the characteristic function, 1.70–85; 3.15–31; 3.32–36; 4.60
13] The modes in relation and affecting one another; 1.105–17; 1.118; 2.04–5; 2.17–19; 2.23–31; 2.64–83; 3.03–5; 3.13–14; 3.59–65; 3.37–48; 3.92–99; 4.61–4; 4.67–75; 4.84–95
14] Comparison of the modes, 2.12
15] From the perspective of others, 3.06–12; 2.84–88
16] Burdens of the modes 4.05
17] Satisfaction of a mode, 2.13–14, 2.98–104; 3.103–6; 4.04
18] Enhancement by another mode 2.32–63; 2.89–94
19] Purging of the modes, 3.49–58
20] Modes as relations, 3.107–9; 4.08–9; 4.25–35; 4.76–79
21] as activities, 4.10–11, 4.38–49; 4.80–83
22] proof, 3.110; 4.12–13; 4.52–57; 4.100–104
23] disciplines, 4.105–9
  Can we not restate these then in the urphilosophy as:
1] A four-fold account of necessary and residual features
2] Each gives testimony to all the others
3] Each is located in all the others
4] Each is imperfect in a distinctive way
5] Each has a characteristic action on the others
6] The action of each on a second is qualified by the others
7] The nature of the parts of each, and their relation to one another
8] Necessary truths regarding the parts
9] A primary subdivision and its features
10] The four-fold primary functions
11] The four-fold use of the category
12] Other modes with respect to some given function, such as knowledge or sympathy
13] The modes in relation and as affecting one another
14] Differentiation of the modes
15] The modes from one another's perspectives
16] The burdens of the modes

October 13

Is the neutral account given in the twenty-three propositions of yesterday an explication of the One? It is, in the sense that it too is radically indeterminate, being essentially a paradigm properly expressed in variables. This means they must be reformulated in a better way:

A   1] There are four types of features, and four ways of being resident — necessary, associated, accidental and residual.

E   2] There are three degrees and kinds of testimonies which each offers of the others.

D   3] Each is in the others in three distinctive ways.

A   4] There are four distinct types of imperfection.

B   5] There are four ways of acting.

B   6] All actions of one mode on another are qualified by the remaining two.

A   7] There are four distinct types of parts, and these differ in the ways they interplay.

A   8] There are four necessary truths regarding the nature of parts, the relation of parts to whole, the nature of the whole and the relation of the whole to the parts. The Ideal has a necessary truth regarding the whole to the parts — necessary realization; Existence has it regarding the nature of the whole as self-divisive; God has it in the relation of parts to Him as a unity. These match 1.02, 1.03.

C   9] Each mode has a distinctive primary case.

B   10] Each mode has a characteristic way of functioning.

A   11] There is one category having four roles.

C   12] All the modes can be approached by means of a strategy practiced properly by only one; there are four strategies then to be employed on all four. The *Modes* overstresses the strategy of knowledge.

E   13] Each mode grounds a different type of relation to and interacts in a different way with each of the others.

A   *14*] Each mode is to be distinguished in a special way from the remaining three; the having of the four defines a final way of being distinguished.

C   *15*] Each mode can be dealt with from three perspectives.

F   *16*] Each mode assumes burdens left behind by the failure of two to deal with a third.

F   *17*] Each mode is satisfied in a distinctive way.

D   *18*] Each mode is ingredient in the others in a characteristic way, and must be freed from them in special ways.

E   *19*] There are four types of relations.

B   *20*] There are four types of activities and therefore times.

G   *21*] All the modes can be proved through the use of the same paradigmatic form.

C   *22*] The characteristic enterprises grounded by the different modes have parallel tasks, relations, activities and reconciliations.

These can be reduced further:

A   *1*] There is one category with four roles.

2] The roles allow for four ways of being distinguished one from the other.

3] Each role is exercised by a mode with its own type of features.

4] The features are resident in four ways, necessary, associated, accidental and residual.

5] There are four types of imperfection.

6] There are four types of parts, differing also in the way they interplay.

B   *1*] There are four ways of acting and four types of time.

2] There are qualifications of acts by the various modes.

3] There are characteristic ways of functioning, with characteristic tasks.

C   *1*] There is a distinctive primary case.

2] There are distinctive strategies to be employed on any and all.

3] Each mode can be dealt with from the perspectives of three others.

4] There are characteristic enterprises grounded in the modes and these have analogous tasks, relations, activities and reconciliations.

D   *1*] Each mode is in the others in a distinctive way.

2] Each mode must be freed from others in special way.

E   *1*] Each grounds a different type of relation.

2] Each acts on the others in a different way.

3] Each offers the others a special kind of satisfaction.

  4] Each fails in its own way.

  5] Each leaves a burden for the others.

F 1] Each mode can be proved and can have a role in a proof (Ideal).

  2] Each mode can produce in one of four ways (Existence).

  3] Each mode is normative for the others in four ways (God).

  4] Each mode stands over against the others in a different way (Actuality).

A. says there are four ways of being, B. that there are four modes of activity; C. says that there is a most excellent way of representing each mode; D. says that the modes are to be found in each; E. says that the modes have corresponding functions and tasks, and F. makes use of B, showing how the activities lead to one another.

These can now be collapsed to:

I] There are four ways of being.

II] There are four forms of activity, functions, tasks and therefore ways of "proving" and going to one another, satisfying and burdening one another.

III] Each has a distinctive type of excellent representative, and a characteristic strategy and discipline.

IV] They are ingredient in one another.

I seems to speak of all four as from the perspective of God, II from that of Existence, III from that of the Ideal, and IV from that of the Actual; they are in fact the ways in which the One of the four modes is articulated, the ways in which it is dissolved into four modes—as Beings, as Agencies, as Values, and as Components. A four-fold procedure would break up each of these into four sub-divisions and explore these in four ways, by assuming first the position of one mode and then of the others. The result would be that the account of the four modes would be broken up into sets of propositions and into individual propositions which were the analogues of one another.

Also, the beings would all seem to have types of extensionality as well as unities, meaning and substantiality—though this perhaps is a matter to be dealt with in IV. They would also seem to ground four times, four logics, four "makings" and four unifying principles. They would have different clusters of values, and they would have their own ways of being components in one another.

October 16

All action for Descartes is either cosmic or enclosed inside the self. The former alternative drives us towards cosmologies and their associated phenomenologies where every item is on the surface, without interiority and therefore without potentiality; the latter alternative drives us towards monads, the noumenal self and the private life of the existentialist. In all these cases we lose action, and therefore history, ethics and poetry. There is no place for either doing or making. These require A] something which is, and B] something potential. If we had only being there would be no need to act; if we had only the potential there would be nothing able to act. The modern's world, since it is from the philosophical standpoint a world without substances, a world of phenomena without interiority and promise, cannot contain beings who make beings who act for good or ill, beings who do creative work.

October 17

English empiricism is a theory which starts with the construction of sense data out of commonsense objects, and then makes a vain attempt to recover the initial objects from the constructed elements. They and their opponents are also phenomenalists, denying any real potentialities and possibilities and therefore unable to deal with acting, making and doing, and consequently to have a place for history, art and ethics.

There is however something odd about the references to "insides" of inanimate things. Perhaps even we have no right to talk about out own "insides," privacies, our status, en soi. But if we do not, we have no ground for all the phases, characters, facets in terms of which we know anything. There would be no real beings. But if we acknowledge an inside for men, how can we avoid saying that there is one in animals, in vegetables and also, (unless we tear the world in two) in the inanimate as well? The domain of the active requires that the beings in the world which can act (and I would assume that even the inanimate can) are already stretched towards the future, and thus are already outside their present, here and now boundaries. The being outside, the stretching is already "metaphysical"; the inside is a terminus on one side, as the prospective future is on the other side, with the body in fact and the here and now as loci of their expression.

October 19

If it be correct that the philosopher representatively uses the powers of all men, it is also correct that the ordinary man uses philosophical truths representatively. He takes into himself the meaning of an entire philosophic system in the shape of an implicit or inner power sustaining the limited specialized truth which he representatively expresses on behalf of all men.

Every one of the items in a philosophic system can be said to have its independence, not merely as that which defies the entire system but as that which has the entire system as its substance, congealed in the shape of the individual who offers that isolated part. The part defies the whole only so far as it denies itself, i.e., defies its own background, and thus is existentially absurd, explicitly going into conflict with what it requires in order to be.

The philosophic system, as the idealists saw, if it absorbed its parts, would have no individuals to sustain them; the parts of a system, if held to as such, with the entire import of the system behind it in the shape of a man, are what the analysts and the existentialists exploit. The analysts recognize that the way to exhibit the system behind the "ought" or prescriptive power of the system (which is in fact the being of the man urging the truth of a part of the system) is to see the part in all kinds of contexts, to explore all possible cases of it, to allow as it were the "ought" behind it to be exhibited as the totality of the contexts or variants which the given part might enjoy in this world. The existentialist instead puts himself (as having just this or that posture with respect to the selected part) in relation to other parts; the "ought" of the entire system, which is his very inwardness, he allows to be expressed and in a sense exhausted by the totality of contexts in which he finds himself manifesting a given attitude.

The philosophic system with its parts is developed in an existential manner, since part is presented after part by a single thinker. Unlike the existentialist though, the systematic thinker maintains a hold on the system itself as a totality answering in an articulate way to the being of the individual as dealing with part after part; the outcome of the existentialistic adventure is thus in principle had in advance, and is in fact exhibited as the totality of the parts when those parts are themselves of an abstract sort. There could be more concrete assertions made involving or requiring as a background the individual in a more radically concrete and decisive manner; but if we go to the extreme of having such concrete assertions, without generality (in which the individual either is present or is the essential locus) we will speak as individuals and not representatively, and thus will be unable to really communicate. The philosophic system uses the existential being representatively when it moves from part to part.

Analytic philosophers can use the expressions of the parts either representatively or existentially. If they do the latter they run the risk of nominalism, taking the particular part to be final and to have a radically new meaning in a new context; if they take the former way they see how the meaning of the assertion changes in different usages. When in a philosophic system there is a reference to other parts, the analytic method is in a way being pursued, for the given part is given new contexts. If one were to put each part in a special relation to every other to see how it changes from case to case, one would have analytically explored the entire philosophic system.

A philosophic system thus is outside the living individuals in the sense that it is a whole which abstractly formulates any one of them, states what any is representatively, and thus not what he is in the concrete. But as the system is actually written down the individual must move from part to part; though he is a representative he has made his very being function as the representative, rather than allowing the representativeness to usurp (as a *mere* metaphysician might) the role of the individual. The total system is congealed in the shape of the individual acting representatively in writing part after part; when the system's parts are referred to one another, they carry that congealed system into open in the guise of the totality of variants which a given part has in its diverse junctures with every other part.

If one were to make a study of the habits of smoking in college students the analyst would see what such habits mean in social contexts, in legal contexts, in health, in relation to other habits, etc., etc.; the existentialist would see what such habits meant with respect to other outlooks and behaviors of the students themselves; the systematic thinker would isolate the fact that there were students, and see the habit of smoking as one way of expressing this nature in relation to the others, and would, in referring the habit of smoking, say to the habit of studying, see what this meant in a new context, i.e., how much one habit affected the other.

We can urge the pursuit of particular disciplines either in an existential or analytic manner. We can try to adopt some one outlook or procedure or attitude, and exhibit this in different cases in the hope that the totality of cases will give us the full meaning of the concrete reality which was left implicit in the given initial case. Or we can take the initial case and put this in all possible contexts in the hope that the totality of those contexts will reveal the nature of the being which was unmentioned and unrecognized (in contrast with the existentialist) but which was in fact acknowledged in the admission that it is the same man who is putting the case into the different contexts.

There are then three senses in which an "ought" or prescription of a system is made explicit: it can be articulated as the total system, it can be exhibited as the meaning of the parts of a system as exhausting it, and it can be exhibited as the parts in their mutuality of reference to one another. The first gives us the structure with obligatory power; the meaning of it as a prospect or possibility for the parts. The second gives us an exhausted reality, which has no other role but to keep the parts phenomenologically together or similar. The third gives us an exhausted reality which the items themselves carry. The relationships in the third case are the outcome of the use of the ought, but the being of the ought is in the items being referred to and referring. The ought is exhausted in the changes in the meaning of the given item. The first answers to the possible, the second to the existential, and the third to the actualized meaning of the ought. A fourth meaning is the three together as constituting a unity, in which the three of them are equal to one another. Such a fourth sense must allow for the being of each of the others; it provides the measure which the three exhibit in their diverse ways, prescribing to them that they must be equal. One can also use any one of the other three as offering a prescription to the remaining ones. Thus the existentialist might offer a prescription to the divine measure, to the total unified system, and to the referential parts, saying that they must all be equal, i.e., that the unity of the parts of that whole must be one with the meaning of the whole and to the parts as referring to one another.

It is not clear from the above just what the meaning of the "divine" ought is in the philosophic system. Is it the relating of the whole and its parts, as just suggested? Is it then the demand that the totality of an existentialistic and/or analytic inquiry should be understood to give the entire meaning of the totality, that the totality must accept them as exhaustive? Without the divine there would be no way of making this equation.

In what sense can one prescribe to the divine? Would it be that one would demand its use at such and such a time, so that, e.g., one who had the entire system would demand, when he had arrived at it, that the other facets be now made equivalent with it or be shown to be wanting? An existentialist would say on such a view that the meaning of a system must be understood to extend no further than the existentialistic use of it as the production of just these parts, the assumption of human attitudes just this far.

The above account would make the divine ought as it were the secret behind the modes, for it is that which requires the exhaustion of the meaning of the entire system in the plurality of referential parts. But there should be a more neutral position achieved in which the divine no less than the others is seen to demand the realization of something that ought to be. We ought to see each as demanding something of the other three. But the position which sees this cannot be, as it seems to be above, a position which straddles the unity and the referential and explicit parts. It must also encompass the demand that the unity and the parts be in harmony; it must be able to say to that demand as well, that there is a demand imposed on it. There must be a position entirely outside the system, occupied by a being in its full substantiality. The existentialist apparently has this in mind.

This being is not a philosophical being but being in its being, a being which is correlative with the philosophic system and which is that entire system with its four oughts made one, substantial and final, having no additional adventures, a man concrete and fulfilled (by the system). To be sure a system, since it can be complete, does not do full justice to the existentialistic and analytic requirements; each of these concerns itself only with the parts of a system. A full existentialistic and a full analytic activity would get us down to the most particularistic of acts and expressions, and have over against them a purely rational unified articulate whole. If we could ever complete the two former activities we would, together with what it equated, presuppose a more substantial actor whose being would be spent in the activity of equating. This would seem to mean that a full system with full particularity involved in exhaustive references, and in which the parts were in full consonance with the whole, would always have outside it something which decides. This outside decider would have to exhaust itself in the act of deciding if the system were to be all there is.

There is much ambiguity in what is here being said, and particularly there is difficulty in seeing whether I am taking up the position of the divine or am really neutral with respect to it and the others. But what is important is that the right position for the philosopher to take is to urge that the parts of his system (and then by extension, all studies of particularity), be pursued existentially and analytically and with a submissiveness of himself and them to a divine equating—which itself must in some sense be subject to an equating (by each of the other three) — with respect to the others.

Since the most abstracted metaphysician is a man, and since the most extreme nominalist or existentialist deals with repetitive situations and articulates in a kind of universal language, it would seem to be the case that these are extremes on a spectrum and not altogether alien approaches. The substantial inwardness of the existentialist infects his particularities; the metaphysician, like the analyst, allows himself to be expressed over the entire material with which he deals. The existentialist's inwardness is a congealed system; the metaphysician's inwardness might be said to be the congealing of the existentialist's particularities, or of the references of the analysts. The existentialist has an inside which is the congealed expression of the metaphysical system, but he does not keep this to himself. He expresses it in the connections between the particularities. To convert him into a mere metaphysician (in the sense of having a mere whole system; not I hope, the type exhibited in the *Modes*) one would have to explicate the nature of the mutuality of reference of which he makes use, the nature of the change in context to which he subjects his particularities. The metaphysician is prior if one takes exceptional powers exercised by few to be the generic forms of powers exercised by all; the others (existentialist and analyst) are prior if one takes the powers exercised by all to be specialized powers which are, in the case of the metaphysicians, epitomized in the form of exceptional powers exercised by some.

Answering to metaphysicians, analysts and existentialists there ought to be a fourth class. Are these theologians? Or are they substantial beings exercising their wills? It is the first so far as this be understood as requiring the reassertion of the V, or unity of the system in every part and reference. Such a theologian would also congeal the V of the system. He would be like the metaphysician in that his activity leaves no inwardness over. But like the existentialist he would allow his inwardness to infect his referential acts. So we have A] metaphysical unity as exterior to or exhaustive of the being of man; B] theological reconciliation as exhausive in acts which are infected by his nature; C] analytic systems as exhausted in acts where the individual is expressed in mutual references; and D] existential commitment as an inwardness which is to be exhausted in attitudes as encompassing a totality of acts. The last two are sequential, time-consuming, never coming to an end, whereas the first two, since they make use of abstractions, can have a completion. In the case of B] the completion is also an incompletion since the individual as infecting what he does in reconciliations is not altogether exhausted in the act until the whole existential and analytic activity is finished. The existential and analytic activity in a system is only partial, since it never gets down to ultimate particularity. The activity, in so far as it is partial, can be completed in a system; so far as it is concrete it is too particular for inclusion in the system. It is only by tearing the parts away from the whole and giving them full being as involved in a plurality of real contexts, or as expressions of a substantial inwardness, that we get genuine analytic and existential treatments.

Perhaps better: The unity of the system is the divine analogue; at the opposite extreme is the individual immersed in an absolute particularity from which he is not distinguishable; he and the particularity congeal the unity in the shape of an inward man. In between is an existentialism and an analytic approach. This can be on the side of the individual, in which case we get something like Kierkegaard or Nietzsche on the one side, and something like robust common sense on the other. Or they can be activities inside the system, the system as dealt with as having parts. So far as they have this function the material dealt with will have a kind of universality and thus have parts over against it, and the individual who is working with them will be in part exhibited in them, and never be the wholly concrete individual that is outside the system.

The philosophic system rests on the radical individual outside it; he combines and expresses himself in and through the unity, and the existential and the analytic use of parts. The individual thus makes himself manifest as the system while holding himself unmanifest over against it. And in the system he makes himself manifest in one moment as the mere unity, then sequentially by virtue of the insistence of the various parts, and then referentially as the parts presented in new contexts. The outcome of the system is then the individual in the guise of unity, in the plurality of parts, and in the plurality of the meanings of each of the parts. The entire system is a strategic way for the individual to become complete through an abstract mastery of all else, a completion which requires him to be exhibited in and through the content that is mastered. He, as it were, becomes the divine unity, the existing diversity, and the ideal multiplicity of meaning, at the same time that he stands outside these in himself.

October 20

The actual individual gives up part of himself in order to engage in any activity. In the intellectual realm he engages in the strategy of making unity take the form of the unity of a philosophic system. This unity expresses in the most abstracted form what he is on the inside, at his very centre, but freed from all that is peculiar to him. It is as it were his super-ego, himself turned inside out and made to face himself as individual in the guise of an obligating unity. It would be a self-imposition of an obligation were it not that such a unity is in a sense the divine subjugated, made subject to the intellectual unfolding of an individual.

The unity of a system is static, and by itself is just a part and inarticulate. If held apart it would in fact deny the individual which sustains it and the philosophic system which it helps constitute. But the strategy of the individual also involves a subjugation of something ideal. Any particular act or idea is in isolation an oppositional element to the entire system; but if given new contexts it achieves an enrichment of meaning. One way is to put it in different contexts; another is to redefine it in terms of all other entities in accordance with the generalized pragmatic principle of transformation as given in the *Modes*. The individual also gives himself to the particular act as being related to all others or in various contexts. He becomes the totality of imposed changes on a given pivotal particularity; he is now outside himself and the particular. If he has done his job correctly he will be the very unity of the philosophic system, but one multiply perspectivized in the sense that it has a plurality of applications or strains within it connecting the given parti-cular with other items.

The individual can multiply its acts while keeping to a steady attitude with respect to them; the plurality of acts and the particularities which result exhaust the meaning of the fragment of the individual which was allocated to the production of the acts. If the acts produce particular parts of a philosophic system, they are expressions of an intent whose full meaning is exhibited in the totality of parts, for these are its exhaustive expressions. The individual here is an existentialized being engaged in some inquiry or activity, and not lost inside his own recesses. The existentialists fail to distinguish the self (which is the centre of the actual individual, outside and grounding all activities, and engaged in the strategy of lending part of itself to subjugate aspects of other modes of being) from the id, which is one of the fragmentary expressions of that self.

Super-ego, ego and id (to use the Freudian expressions without any supposition that these answer to Freud's items, in nature, function, origin or meaning) are expressions of the self, having the role of unity, mutal reference and the production of particularities inside the philosophic system. All of them state the nature of the self (though as engaged in subjugating some other mode of being, and as abstract and expressed). The self in itself is over against other modes of being; it is concrete and unarticulate.

The id is properly expressed through the body, in action; the ego is properly expressed through the understanding; the super-ego is properly expressed emotionally. (Judgment, Understanding, Reason are the Kant-ian counterparts). If we eliminate all three we are left with their products in the form of a collection of related parts sustained by a self which remains outside them all and just owns them; if we recognize the three we recognize the sense in which an inquiry or philosophy or any other stragetic expression has a triple unity of its own and does justice to the meaning to the self as involved with other modes.

At every moment the individual is engaged in acts of various kinds; that means that at every moment he has isolated a facet of his self and is engaged in the activity of making that facet manifest, either as an obligating unity, as the attitude sustaining the production of a number of parts or acts, or as the activity of referring parts to one another, thereby endowing them with meaning. When the individual changes the nature of its obligating unity, its attitude or the items which it wishes to understand, it changes the nature of its strategy.

A philosophic system does not differ from other enterprises except in the sense that it makes use of all three expressions of the self, and does this in such a way as to exhaust them. Other enterprises uses thicker fractionations of the self, do not continue long enough enough to exhaust their natures, and do not fractionate them systematically in such a way that they answer fully to one another.

We can make an analogous use of these ideas by distinguishing the idea of Perfection, History and Comparative Civilizations as strategic expressions of an Individuality which could be adequately expressed only by being faced with modes of being which are as substantial as the Individuality.

October 21

The unity of a being would seem to be a *diffused* unity having over against it a plurality of dissected parts as sustained by a *simple* unity. This latter is the unity of a subject as at once encountering at a distance and being in some comparative relation with it. When we come to know, we must at once be diffused and simple. But this is true of all other beings as well. Consequently, we must differ from them only in the way in which we deal with entities which the other beings never isolate the way we do. We are beings with a dominant unifying power and a radical inwardness, which are in both a simple and diffuse relationship to one another.

(Positive law has a simple unity, natural law a diffused. These two are united in one way by living law, and in another way by normative law, the former answering to men in their inwardness and the latter to a divine prescription. These two latter types of law are united in one way by natural law, and in another way by positive law.)

When we come to the modes of being in their severalty they all have the problem of the one and the many with respect to their parts. Since the parts of all except Actualities are not fully distinguished, they evidently are diffused unities which have over against them whatever dissected members of themselves are sustained by a simple unity beyond; in the case of individual actualities there must be a simple unity characteristic of Actuality, since this presupposes its parts. Accordingly we have the simple unity of Actuality over against the diffuse unities of the other three modes. These other three should be diffuse in different ways, since they have different ways of being related to their parts. All of them need the simple unity of Actuality to serve as a focus for those parts, and all of them have parts in some sense precisely because they have over against them the unity of Actuality. It is a neat question whether or not the simple unity of Actuality can be dealt with even abstractly, for it does not have being except so far as there are many actualities, each one of which is at once simply and diffusely unified, and each one of which, as over against the simple unity of Actuality, ought to be diffusely unified and have its component parts somehow focused by the Actuality. This would mean that Actuality itself not only makes divisions in other modes of being, but also in the actualities which are within it; the possibility as it were of indication and predication are already determined by the fact that all actualities are within Actuality and thus have over against them a simple unity.

October 22

One could identify the diffused unity, which is what a being is with respect to others, (and which can be identified with the root of existential being and with positive law) also with Kant's form of Intuition. The simple unity can be identified with the root of analytic knowing and natural law, and also with Kant's Understanding. Then normative law would be Kant's Reason, and the living law would be the Kantian thing-in-itself, the manifold, or the transcendent object; the first, the Reason, would be like the divine unity, the second, the thing-in-itself, would be like the unity of an actuality. The concurrence of these two would dictate the manner in which and the extent to which the Intuition was made coherent with the Understanding. The doctrine of the Schematism in Kant would then be resolved not by referring to the double form of time (which in a way supposes that the problem is one of reconciling not Understanding and Intuition, but cognition and being), but by the joint use of two unities.

Analytic understanding and diffuse apperceptive existential being are to be found in all beings, in the form of a private unity over against other objects as at once having a nature and a locus with respect to it, and in the form of a substantiality which encompasses in a continuum what it is in itself and what it is on the surface. What the former does by putting an item in multiple contexts the latter does by putting itself in multiple contexts; the former exhibits itself as the plurality of contextual connections, the latter as that which is the steady unity in a plurality. All empirical inquiries attempt to achieve the neutrality of the analytic understanding; they put the ego outside all content as a mere simple unity, as what Kant would call an "I think" accompanying all that is known. All insistence on methodology, on procedure, on techniques make the diffused unity basic and merely fill out this unity by making it encompass all data.

The normative divine unity is the condition which is explicated in a principle of value ordering content in a hierarchy; the substantial actual unity is a condition which is explicated in an activity making the understanding and intuition active at the same time.

October 28

In a society men's actions are met with habituated types of response; the substance and structure of the society consists in the stabilized and therefore secure and reliable outcomes that the activities of others guarantee on the basis of something done by some one. From the standpoint of that one the others constitute the society, since the activities of that one are themselves habituated—or interpretable in the light of the habituated responses of the rest. A society by virtue of these habituated responses imposes on actions and things a set of conditions, forcing them to have implications and consequences that apart from those responses they would not have. A language in a society can be understood to be sounds which elicit certain habituated actions on the part of others; a given word may entrain a whole series of responses of a certain sort, such as the preparation of a fire, the readying of a net, making other noises, etc. The grammar of the language would consist in the requirement that these responses be produced; that grammar then is the tissue of expectations which is grounded in the habitual responses of men.

In a society the activities of men, their private natures and private objects achieve new implications and consequences. The society is needed just so far as these added implications enhance the individual, satisfy some needs of his. It is not then that the society is required in order that man's daily or recurrent needs may be given satisfaction through mutual supportive activities, but rather that needs in a subtler sense (which even

when answered by quieting responses should be more fully exploited)
require to be enriched, made to have a new import. When they do have
this new import they make a man have more dignity, fulfill him in a new
way. This means that men have a need to be more than they are. They
must not merely have their natural needs satisfied, but must have these
needs altered. A satisfaction of these altered needs will amount to a
satisfaction of a being who, as possessing those needs and as satisfied, is
quite different in nature from a merely natural being.

What does a man need to achieve, and why is it that it is not enough
to satisfy the needs he has as a natural being? Is it not that men are, even
when their needs are satisfied, A] still potential, B] insecure, C] defective, and D] insignificant? Does not then a man desire to become explicit, to be sustained by others, to have limitations overcome, and to get
a new status? Is it not for the sake of attaining these outcomes that men
allow their needs to be transformed through the kind of responses others
provide, and which are then (and then only) satisfied?

A man might conceivably have enough organic material to nourish
his body. But he wants to eat together with others, and wants to eat what
the others eat because only in this way does his eating serve not only to
satisfy his body but to make him a being whose eating satisfied his deeper
need to be part of that community. He wants to be part of that
community because otherwise he would be without the support of
others and thus insecure; he also would lack singificance, and would have
potencies and defects which no mere eating could overcome. To eat
accepted food in accepted ways is to satisfy a potentiality and overcome a
defect with respect, not only to nourishment, but to meaning as well.

Do we, when we add these meanings, absorb within ourselves what
is other? Do we identify ourselves with what is first an other to ourselves?
Must we have this other in order to be ourselves? Must we recognize that
something means something to another in order that it should have
meaning for ourselves? Do we want to make the meaning it has for the
others also part of our own meaning and thereby become fulfilled? If so
do we not also move on to more complex societies only because we find
that they make possible greater fulfillments?

The mores give us stability but no impartiality or equality; the positive
law of the state gives us equality and impartiality but not necessarily
justice; the natural law gives us the justice and proper aim but does not
evaluate us in basic terms as men who ought to be evaluated not merely
as items in a community but in themselves, and whose communities are
not final but are to be judged in terms of what they do to satisfy man's
need to be full beings. I am social, as Mead saw, when I see myself as that
to which another can respond and can myself respond to myself in a

similar, analogous or in an alternate way. I want, for example, my eating to be something for me as it is for others; to eat as a social being is to deal with my eating as a kind of terminal final cause for both of us. When I do this, do I then possess something of him? Or is it that I then make vivid my true final cause? Or is it that I then in fact have an object which is richer than what a mere bit of organic matter would be? Is it then that I am a being who has an appetite for more meaning? Is it that I am keyed to a universal? Do I delimit this in the form of items in the world serving as terminal final causes by virtue of the fact that they are the pivots for me and others, and that, as a consequence, in adopting them I in effect am realizing my end? This would mean that the eating of something is in effect the realization of the good but in a concrete form; it is the good as carried by something concrete.

The very items which otherwise would function in the concrete or as answering a specific need of the body are made into carriers of the good with which a man is also occupied. If this is the case can we say that they might be made into carriers of the divine and the existential as well? Is the focused item, as sustained by fellow man, an item in society which functions as a carrier of the domain of existence? Is it a way of quieting the external world by making it sustained by some object which we in fact can use? Is an item in the state also a way of utilizing something Ideal? Is civilization also a way of utilizing something divine? Should we say that men need to be in society, etc., because they then in this way, while satisfying particular needs, also make provision for the adoption of dimensions of being they also need? On this view men go into society in order to satisfy a need which is four-fold in nature—a specific need of themselves as actual beings, and a need to master the Ideal, God and Existence, and that they move away from one form of association to another in order to be able to take in more and more of what they in fact need in order to be full beings.

In root men are driven by a need to be masters of Ideality, eternity and vital Existence. These are to be mastered only in a certain order, i.e., first, Existence in society, and then Ideality in politics, and then eternity in civilization. Such a view must accommodate the fact that men are aware of the divine and the Ideal sometimes even before or at least at the same time as they are aware of the existential aspect. Right from the start objects are seen to be carriers of them.

The very nature of life forces into the fore those carriers which enable us to master the world about; the very activities of life, of living and breeding require that we isolate those items which elicit the cooperative activities of others as relating to the forcing away and subjugation of nature. Only when this has been accomplished to some degree can attention be directed to those items which are in some sense loci of the Ideal, i.e., meaningful termini, and which therefore enable us to have a meaning beyond that of beings in nature.

Existential control enables us to be better adjusted in the universe. Ideal control enables us to have an excellence or a value. We turn to the divine element when we become aware that there are higher goods or standards than those which are germane to us as members of the society. But why should we not then instead turn to deeper meanings of the Ideal rather than to an entirely different dimension such as God? Is it not that what is now wanted is sanction or justification, some awareness of meaning, some grasp of our own individuality as worthwhile, not only in the community or even with respect to some Ideal of excellence, but with respect to some fixed principle, so that we can be matched with any being, or better can be found to be sustained regardless of our excellence? Do we not need the divine in order to be assured that, even if we fall short of the excellent, and thus live in independence of it, we have a status which is fixed? We turn to the divine in order to have a kind of assurance or stability which, though sustained and encouraged by the Ideal and the Existential, in the end operates in independence of them. We turn to the divine then not to complete the Ideal but to find a principle which is inclusive of it and which may overrule or govern it.

October 29

Men are imperfect because they lack the reality others embody. This reality is four-ply, as expressed by the various modes of being. To become perfect in some way is the strategy of man; knowledge enables one to grasp all else and thereby be perfected though only abstractly. To be perfected concretely a man must have beings in the concrete. He engages in activities of mastery, of realization of the Ideal, of activity and creativity, and of worship and mystical identification in order to apprehend these other realities directly. But in order to have them here and now, in the concrete form of himself as an individual actuality, he needs to get them as embodied in the items with which he daily deals. The objects which answer to his bodily needs (and perhaps some intellectual needs as well) through the agency of his habitual associations of them with items with which they are not normally in association, give those objects the roles of carriers of the meaning of fellowmen, of the Ideals he shares with those men, of the nature of the vital Existence which links him to those men, and of the significance of himself and them in a permanent setting.

Aristotle has too material a view of man, even though he is aware of the fact that he needs knowledge and perhaps even religion, for he does not grasp the various objects (as a kind of generalized Franciscanism would) as their carriers. He does not see that there are realities which would not be possible in this world except as facets of, dimensions in actual entities.

Will the progress from habit, to positive law, to purposiveness, to final significance be a dialectical one? What makes one give up the living law of habit for the positive law, or at least supplement the former by the latter? Is it that only the positive law would allow one to bring out into clear focus the fact that there is a kind of relation of each man to every other and that this has a prescriptive component? Do we go to the next stage by taking account of the fact that man stands outside his society if only to see a justice which it ought to exhibit, and that finally he does stand outside?

Are the foregoing needs related to the need to realize potentialities, to achieve security, to be better ordered, and to attain a new significance? Objects as carriers actualize potentialities in richer than brute ways. There is a kind of belongingness, of fitting inside a stable whole which gives us security; the act of dealing with a purposed end is also a way of obtaining a special order for one's powers; new significance is attained when one, as habituated, is dealt with as a single being having a permanent value. In other words, the needs to realize potentialities, etc., are not to be thought of as mere needs of the body which are given opportunities by society, or even as needs of the natural man, but as needs of an ontological man, as it were, to become completed in new ways.

Are the heroes of history equivalent with the saints in religion, the noblemen of ethics and the wise men of history? Do they differ in that the heroes are too individual, the saints do not get present satisfaction, the ethical noblemen are too few and too dependent, and the wise men have not yet appeared?

The state deals with public man, and in a utilitarian spirit; it cannot distinguish good and bad intent, between loyalty and submission; it protects the intrenched, denies privacy, cannot see that other societies and states are as basic as itself.

November 4

The real object can be said to be a scientific object subject to local qualifications, such as those of interest in the humanistic disciplines. In contrast with those who take a scientific view of the world these qualifications will be said to have their own integrity; and in contrast with those who deal with the humanistic side as primary, the universal aspect which is dealt with in the sciences will be said to have an area of genuine functioning. It is the individual man who is married; his man-ness is operative there as surely as is his individuality. He is a single being, but his singularity requires a reference to him as having a universal side, where he is interchangeable with others, and an unduplicatable side, where he is contextualized either interiorly or exteriorly. The context is reducible to the scientific neutral universal aspect only so far as it is public; so far as it is sustained from within it adds something to the meaning of the science and in fact has the science itself as a limiting version.

It is organic matter that is food; the food is the organic matter subject to new conditions which localize the functioning of that organic matter without destroying it; it is a way of adding special conditions to the situation, locating the scientific object. We make use of the law of gravitation only by looking beyond it to the location of the object and the nature of the *t,* in the formula. These the science cannot get to. Conversely the humanistic approach to a falling body does not give us the generalized form of it, where it is like every other; to get this we must smoothe out the local conditions, see the object in its potency and promise, rather than as that which has now made itself manifest in this singular way. So in a way our problem reduces to the old one of the relation of form and matter, of the universal and the singular, and the answer to this is that they are both abstractions, that each makes a contribution, and that each has some kind of status within the more inclusive individual being.

With this as a guide one can reduce the ontological four modes to a cosmology in which there is only the Actual. Unity, its most generic feature, will represent God; its governing nature will give the meaning of the Ideal; its effectiveness will express the meaning of Existence, all three having a universal import greater than the individual itself. One would then answer the question of concurrent action in time, of the unity of Existence, the reality of the past, and the meaning of guilt by supposing that the cosmos adjusts itself in order to take care of them. Yet other modes than Actuality could also be taken as prior. This means that the cosmology which starts with Actuality is arbitrarily chosen.

November 5

The realm of science is the realm of what is analyzed out of encountered unities. What is analyzed out is dealt with in cosmic terms.

The encountered unities are understood in science to be the product of different laws and constants confronting and qualifying one another in such a way as to leave some residual features, and permitting of a mutually qualifying continued action. Thus water is analyzed out as oxygen and hydrogen. These are to be spoken of in cosmic terms, as subject to the laws of chemistry. The water is to be thought of as the juncture of these two, a juncture which precludes their functioning as gases, of manifesting the same boiling point they had before, etc., but retaining their atomic weights and other powers. The activity of the water, say its flow in relation to other items, is to be understood in terms of the energies given by the constituents as qualified by still other reduced items or conjunctions of them. A complete scientific account of the world would then give us an interlocked set of laws whose juncture points would have consequences because the juncture happens to persist and to interplay with other laws and junctures. The *Geisteswissenschaftliche* approach on the other hand starts with the juncture as having a definite nature, and accounts for the extreme analytic cosmic items of the sciences as the outcome of activities in thought or act by social men in which they turn the unitary items into abstractions.

To suppose there is hydrogen and oxygen in water is to subject water to the new conditions of human interest in quantitative activities; to obtain hydrogen and oxygen from water is to express an interest in freeing them from mutual qualification. It is to lose the water as surely as the gases were lost when they were combined to produce water.

There is no need to suppose that the scientific and humanistic positions exclude one another. The water (to use this as a case of a socialized object, even though it is also a good topic for the science of hydrodynamics) has a nature, and this has consequences. Both sides agree on this. Also water has a certain weight, and can be produced from and can yield items which account for that weight and other related properties. On this too both sides are agreed. Where they differ is that the scientist thinks that the juncture is adventitious, and the consequences merely follow on it (so that in the end we must say that water is not real), whereas the humanist thinks that the analytic components have no real status in the unitary item (apparently the unitary item for them functions in human contexts independently of any contribution that could be made by such components). But we can say at one and the same time that there are analytic components in the unity, though these are not what the components are when apart from the unity—since they mutually qualify one another—and that there is a significant unity with implications and outcomes. What the scientist takes to be a mere juncture followed by other junctures, the humanist takes to be a unity requiring certain consequences. The former has certain consequences *required* by the analyzed elements; the latter merely acknowledges consequences for the unity. But there is no reason why we cannot have both, though to be sure if we start with the one we seem to have no need for the other. But there is need for the other since from the scientific side we are forced to speak of continued adventitious junctures, and from the other side we are forced to speak of the submerged character of the analytic components and the contextual nature of them.

The items in the world are complex with unitary natures having implications of their own, inside of which are muted elements that yield combined features or juncture natures. Taken at any one moment the juncture natures and the unitary natures are identical, and the entire entity can then be treated as a scientific item; taken dynamically, as part of a situation, each is forced to have consequences as a unity, consequences which can be reduced to the scientific only by making the situation past and thus static. The forward thrust of unitary items if not to be found in the forward thrust of components, for these components are already muted. But the object is at once present and thrusting towards the future, so that we have a scientific present and a humanistic incipiency towards the future. But this would seem to be saying too that in the past we have only scientific objects; history would then be impossible. Scientific objects have an historical import when viewed serially, as carrying out a necessity to yield what in fact comes after. We save history in the past by recognizing a necessity in the past, though the dynamics of that necessity, its actual reproductivity is no longer. We have then 1] a necessity of the component parts as operative by themselves, 2] a necessity of the unity which can be treated as a juncture only by making it followed adventitiously by other junctures; and 3] a dessicated necessity of the past which is the necessity of the unity freed from its dynamic thrust.

November 7

Having learned that physicists think that every single property of such gases as hydrogen and helium can be derived from a knowledge of the subordinate elements, and aware that I overstated the matter of unity the last time I wrote on this topic, I think perhaps what one ought to say is that there is after all something that is being explained (to wit the unity's nature) by what is different from it. This nature is adventitious only in the sense that it is other than its constituent items; it is the meaning of their unity. From the standpoint of the subordinate items there is a unity. We can say that it persists and can know how it will interplay with other unities; but we cannot then know its meaning as a pervasive unity which provides a standpoint from which the analysis and public treatment of the object are to be conducted.

The error of the humanistic and the scientific approaches is that each supposes its item to be fully determinate. Each is determinate in fact only so far as the other is allowed to be radically indeterminate and yet essential to it. The real object is at once the social and the scientific, a one and a many, but these as in the object are neither fully determinate nor fully indeterminate. What is wholly determinate is the fact that these two are related and are partially indeterminate. Though we are inclined to speak of water in two senses, as embracing the components, and as over against them on a different level, we can nevertheless effectively distinguish it from its components both as a social or public or observable object, and as the topic for hydrodynamics etc. As such it is not yet fully determinate; it lacks full intelligibility and sufficiency. The atoms of hydrogen and oxygen in water are not yet determinate; they lack the kind of power they would have were they freed from their molecular careers.

The case is analogous to that of the Aristotelian matter and form. His matter is wholly indeterminate; but this is necessary only because the form is defined to be wholly determinate. In Thomas the form becomes that of God over against a wholly indeterminate matter, with subordinate cases of forms of species over against the indeterminate Aristotelian matter. Ditto for Plato with his forms and receptacle. But the converse stress is also possible. One can take matter to be wholly determinate, a matrix of distinct items, as in the atomism; but then one will make the One a vague diffuse order of nature. But what we have in fact is not altogether indeterminate form and matter together, constituting a determinate being. The indeterminate form and matter become determinate only by being abstracted from the determinate being. Such abstraction requires that we the knowers become their locus.

The determinate being which is the locus of the indeterminate form and matter, of the social meaning and the physical elements, of the one and a many, is itself determinate only with respect to something other than it; i.e., only with respect to its indeterminate components, or with respect to some indeterminate that succeeds it. In the first respect determinateness means that which is to be expressed in a plurality of correlative indeterminates; in the second respect it means that an item is determinate in the present only because there is an indeterminate future for it. The four modes of being seem to make a determinate cosmos in the first sense; we individuals seem to make it in the second. The first says that there is a determinateness having analytic indeterminate components; the second says that there is a determinateness which in achieved by virtue of a correlative futurity.

What is the relation of the determinate being to its components or to the future? Must it not be said to be the relation of unifying, i.e., not yet unity and not yet diversity, an activity rather than a state? Does it require us to suppose that the future is the determinate being itself made indeterminate and thus one in which the components cannot be found? The components in the determinate could be found only by taking the future and using this as a way of analyzing the determinate being in the present. Similarly if the knowing individual is a kind of indeterminate before he has synthesized the data, he is the indeterminate form of the determinate object. The object has real components only from the perspective of that unity.

The components of an object, its matter and form, are to be found in a three-fold way. They are the divisions into which the determinate object falls when defined in terms of the possibility which that object faces; it is the components into which it falls when we approach it as cognizing beings; it is the very items which are being subordinated, kept indeterminate by the object as a unifying whole.

The object as in the present is only relatively determinate, for one of the components of the entire real object is the indeterminate possibility which is now future to it. The real object is a present indeterminate which has a relatively determinate pluralized set of tendencies focusing on a single prospect. Can we say that the object too is abstract? Yes, it is abstract precisely because it is not wholly in or outside of time. Does this mean that in the end we must say that whatever is determinate is derivative, i.e., not as real as the indeterminate elements? I think we must say neither the former not the latter. If we say the latter then all composites will be relatively unreal; if we say the former it would suppose that the elements must precede the determinate object in being or time.

The determinate is the abstract only where it is in fact initially part of something larger or more real. In the case of a real item which is diffuse in the sense that it is partly in the present and partly in the future, the present state of it is to be thought of as determinate just so far as it is held apart from the future. But the real item, though determinate, is not itself abstract (unless there be some larger context for it), because it is pure. Determinateness is one with purity or perfection, and this is achieved by abstracting from other concrete beings. But then why not say that determinate being is present being? Present being has potentialities and faces real possibilities; it has the status as a mere present only by becoming past, no longer on the edge of the future.

November 8

Let us distinguish form and matter in an Aristotelian way, but take the form to be individually referential and not a mere species feature, and the matter to be quantified, a plurality of items, a many. The form and the matter can then be said to have a double convergence, two limits, one defining them as having issued from the past, the other defining them as issuing into the future. The form as converging on the future limit is the object as essentially historical and requiring something still to come, though that something is indeterminate. But though indeterminate it is a something to come which will encompass both a form and a matter; it is the indeterminateness which results from the fact that A] it is not identical with that form and matter as constituting a being now, and B] can encompass more than the form. But the future limit as the convergence of the form and matter is determinate; its determinateness is thus a boundary between the indeterminateness of the form and matter themselves and the future which lies beyond them. The limit from the past is also a convergence of form and matter and is also determinate as a boundary between the form and matter and the past that lies behind. When we speak in this way we are close to an Aristotelian position in which form and matter are primary, and efficient cause and final cause are not altogether separate from the beings and may be said in effect to be even less efficacious than the form and matter.

One can take another approach and see the past and future as realities having effectiveness now. This is what Whitehead does with his data from the past and his eternal objects. What happens then is that the two converge to constitute a unitary meaning and a locus of energy as limits of the nature of a now. These limits will be abstract determinate boundaries, and the future as directed back towards the energy will be the meaning of the luring future, and the past as directed towards the unitary meaning will be the conditioning of the object in an habituated sense.

The entities studied in history will be A] limited unitary meanings in the present, B] prospective unities which are indeterminate because they have not yet been quantified by the material side, C] the past as effectively conditioning the meaning of things in the present, and D] the combination of A, B and C. A similar statement must be made for the objects of science. When we isolate the boundaries or isolate the limits of the now we isolate the objects which are studied in history and science.

These objects are concrete only so far as they are related to the indeterminate future and past. These are indeterminate in the sense that they need quantitative or qualitative components which they do not then possess. The future is not yet quantified, the past is no longer qualitied but is in fact dessicated and in this sense divided.

November 9

If we start with an object here and now we find that it is at once qualitative and quantitative, a kind of form and matter, meaning and energy, but in such a way that neither can be had without the other. But as embracing the other neither is distinctive enough. Thus water as actually embracing the atoms of oxygen and hydrogen is more than water as mere fluidity, the mere item as caught within social contexts. Conversely, the molecules of H_2O would also embrace the unity of themselves as having a kind of stability, so that it would be in a sense more than their mere conjunction. In order that each of these sides should have its own distinctiveness it would have to become attached to something distinctive. The two sides together in fact constitute their own boundaries, the one boundary marking off the way it issues out of the past, cuts itself off from that past, the other the way in which it requires the future. These two sides, these two boundaries are abstract, dependent, but nevertheless determinate. If we start from the side of the boundary we find the form and matter to make a single volume over against the boundary.

The form and matter also have the status of boundaries with respect to a real past and a real future, each having a kind of diffused presence, by virtue of their overlapping, to constitute a real ongoing future. It is only when it is seen that the past and the future together constitute a Now, one side of which is the determinate meaning of time and the other side of which is the determinate meaning of energy or the quantity that now exists, that the past and the future achieve distinctiveness and determinate natures.

The being which confronts us as having had a past and capable of a future is both qualitative and quantitative, a unity of the two. If we insist on understanding what that unity is we must look at it from the perspective of the determinate boundaries which its components determine. Each of these components deals with one of the boundaries as constituetd by an alien other. Thus the qualitative defines the past as having been sustained by the quantitative; the quantitative defines the future as that which will be governed by the qualitative. But if we seek to be neutral and to see both the qualitative and quantitative together as distinctive we must approach them both from the boundary defining their distinctiveness.

Conversely, starting with a real past and future they together are diffusely in the present. To have them as distinct they must be recognized A] to determine together a single Now in which we have the structure of time and the energy of an aggregate of items, and B] to be dealt with from the perspective of these as defining them to have distinctive functions. Past and future stand out over against one another only because of the way they refer to the different sides of the now and are approached in terms of that now. The past defines the time side, since it is an indeterminately defined past, lacking a qualitative component; this component refers to the time side to provide it with its meaning. The future on the other hand defines the energy-side of the now, making it have a determinate hold on existence then and there. The future, apart from an approach from that energy side, is indeterminate.

The historical object here and now comprises the scientific side by virtue of the fact that it defines a border which intrenches on a real future. This dictates what kind of quantitative being as present the scientific side is to have; the scientific object here and now comprises the historical side by virtue of the fact that it defines a border which intrenches on a real past, which in turn dictates what kind of a qualitative nature the present is to enjoy.

November 11

Some of the characterizations of the last few days must be modified and perhaps even reversed. If we start with a real future and a real past interfusing with one another, we must acknowledge them to converge in two ways to define the meaning of a quality and a quantity in their existential, that is their present and effective being. Starting the other way, with an acknowledgment of an interfused form and matter, a meaning and energy, we must acknowledge them to converge in two ways to define the meaning of a now, the one a form or meaning stressing the fact that it is cut off from the past, and the other a matter or energy that is to be followed by a distinct future.

The real past is the domain of fact; it is concrete and internally indeterminate with respect to its quality; a present quality contributes its definiteness to the real past at the same time that it achieves something of the concreteness of the past. Conversely the real future is the domain of possibility, concrete and internally indeterminate (with respect to the parts and specifications); it is attached to the quantitative present. The future achieves something like the definiteness of that quantified world, and the quantified achieves something of the ultimacy and promise of the future.

The real object, taken as now in the present, is a matter and form interfused; they get their distinctive parts, say fluid water and hydrogen and oxygen molecules—only so far as the water can be closed off in a present moment. On the other hand when we see the world as a coming together of past and future, we see that the definition of a being as at once qualitative and quantitative is but the restatement of this fact, with a separation of the two components. The past and future achieve separation by the production of quality and quantity, now. The one entity that exists, if by existing we mean here and now, is the matter-form combination closed off from past and future; is we mean the dynamic, it is the past-future combination constituting a quality and a quantity here and now.

Ought one to say therefore that the present object quantifies the future, or conversely that the future is the possibility for the quantified object; that it qualifies the past discrete reality; that the object as at once intelligible and existential is limited by being cut off from the past and the future? Should we say then that the (quantified) hydrogen-oxygen grounds the possibility of a fluid with atoms in it, and that the quality of water sums up the meaning of atoms which could have been organized as water? And should we also say that the state of being closed off from past and future grounds the intelligibility and existential facets of the object before us?

What is important to see is that we cannot acknowledge a real world of existence containing only the scientific objects (which Northrop identifies with the ontological) except by recognizing that this must be understood to be closed off from the past, and to help constitute a closure from the future; and that we cannot acknowledge a real world of qualitied objects of an Aristotelian sort except by recognizing that this is closed off from the future and helps constitute a closure from the past. If we want to speak of the epistemic side of this fact we must speak in terms of quality and quantity. In that case we must see the present object as the determinate juncture in two ways of an otherwise merged past and future. If the light ray is a reality now, then it not only (with color) defines the way the past is cut off, but exists as that which is cut off; if the color is a reality, then it not only defines the way (with the light ray) the future is cut off but it exists as that which is cut off. The light ray denies or negates the past; the color denies or negates the future. That is why we can encounter the light ray; that is why we can enjoy the color. The light ray is of course also cut off from the future but it allows implications to it; the color is also cut off the past but it allows implications to it. Thus the light ray grounds predictions but not a knowledge of what had been; the color warrants reference to what had been but does not ground predictions. We feel that the color is impotent, that the consequences which follow on it are not its doing; we feel that the light ray is dynamic, present right here and now, defining the past as not existent, but grounding justified expectations as to what will be. To know what a man will do we must refer to his body, but a body which implies a future which is more than bodily in content; to know what could have been we must refer to human nature now, but one which is the outcome not only of human nature but of the working of the human body in the past.

The humanistic side is impotent but at once cuts off the future and implies a past outside; the scientific side is dynamic and at once cuts off the past and implies a future outside. The implied past and future are determinate in the sense that they are focal points for both sides, but they are indeterminate in that they are implied. The implied future is a future which is a possibility for specific scientific content; the implied past is a past factuality sustaining an unspecified universal. There is no science of human nature, but there is a history for the human nature which science grounds; there is no history of scientific realities but there is a future which they implicate.

Because Whitehead starts with a real future and a real past he can get nothing in the present but a momentary Actual Occasion—actually an abstract entity with two distinguishable sides, a mere quality and a mere quantity. The Aristotelian approach is to start instead with a form and a matter, the intelligible and the dynamic, and to treat the past and the future as themselves only boundary conditions of the object as in the present. The Aristotelian is the more congenial view for man, because of its stress on the reality of a substantial being in the present; but it ought to be supplemented by the other since it does make sense to speak of the present object as having these two distinctive abstract limiting aspects of quality and quantity, nature and spread-outness. The actual course of a being would be a shift from the one position to the other, for as moving into the future it must be a kind of abstract involved in a real future, and as having moved into it, as having achieved a position, it must be a present being which has cut itself off from its past and from a future to be.

November 12

The quantity of a present object involves a preliminary demarcation in the realm of the future. By virtue of the nature of the quantity in the present we know something of the magnitude, the areas of activity in which further quantities will be exhibited. The quantity now, which is in fact a product of the togetherness of past and future, is distinct from the quality that now exists just so far as it is implicated in the possible future. That future can be said to be oriented in the present by virtue of its terminus in the quantity.

The quality of an object now offers a principle of unification governing the otherwise discrete items in the past. By virtue of the quality now we know something of the way in which the past in fact is divided. The past on its side is summed in the quality in the present; this is its meaning, what it amounts to, the unity it now has.

The energy of a present being is interfused with its intelligibility; quantity and quality are but limits of these, abstract and distinct. The energy involves a closing off of the past. It defines the kind of past that could be, one in which this energy is to be found. The principle of the conservation of energy is but the cosmic formulation of the theory that the energy in the present requires that there be this amount of energy in the past.

The intelligibility of a present being involves a closing off of the future. It defines the type of meaning that can occur in the future. That meaning is a product of the intelligibility and the energy, just as the defined past, or conservation principle, is a product of both the intelligibility and the energy. But the future is primarily referred to by the intelligibility, and the past by the energy, so that the future and the past are indeterminate in the sense that there is a reference to the contribution which comes from another source. The intelligibility offers a meaning in the future to be filled out by energy, and which can now be specified quantitatively as a magnitude, etc.; the energy offers a type of past which is to be unified by the kind of quality which we now have.

The quantity of the present has a contingency to it; it involves certain distributions of items, a realization of one of many possible formulae for the activity of physical entities. The contingency is what the future contributes to it. The contingency of the quantity is to be found in the fact that there is a type of future which alone is possible and which limits the kind of things that the quantity can become; it roots the quantity in our world at the same time that this future is demarcated by the quantity so that certain types of qualities will occur. That the hydrogen and oxygen molecules, viewed as quantities of a certain sort, should be in a world of water is guaranteed by the fact that it requires the future (which is in a way qualitative) to be broken up in certain ways and not others. It makes the future be a future for water and its implicates. It also imposes a condition on any characterization of the past.

The energy in the present is the physical activity of the hydrogen and oxygen in the present. It has a certain range, putting a limit to the past and the future to give the magnitude of the present moment. Primarily stressing its limitation of the past, it tells that the past could be, is one in which such energy was. Did we not know what the energy of the present was we could not know what energy was distributed over the past moments; if we did not know what the future was like we could not know to what conditions the quantity would be subject in the future.

The quality of the present might be a Platonic form were it not that it depends on a real past for its being; it is rooted in this world by virtue of the fact that there is a past which has isolated it in the present object and particularly from its total form or intelligibility. The situation then is similar to that of quantity, which is found to be just this quantity and not some other type or amount by virtue of the fact that there is a future governing it.

The intelligibility in the present (if this be viewed as the counterpart of energy, to be identified more or less with the form in a thing) which interfuses with the energy to constitute a real present object, exists now. As now it stops at two limits, one at the past and the other at the future. Primarily stressing the future limit it tells us in what areas, under what kind of contingent qualitative unity the quantities and energies are to be in the oncoming future. It tells, as it were, that the future will be a domain of a certain energy-quantity activity.

An object as a qualitative-intelligibility offers a measure of unity for the past and a prescription for the energy-quantity in the future; in turn it is rooted in the world by the past, and thus is no Platonic form. At the same time it emphasizes its presentness by allowing the determination, in fact insisting that the determination of the future is to be provided by the activities of the quantity-energy. As a quantity-energy the object offers a principle for demarcating the future, and a measure for the conservation of the energy of the past; in turn it is rooted in the world by the future, and thus is no mere mathematical formula, at the same time that it emphasizes its presentness by insisting that the meaning of the past, the way its occurrences are to be divided and combined, is to be given by the qualitative-intelligible.

The beautiful or fluid or criminal or ominous is to be treated as a qualitative-intelligibility, and thus is to be said to tell us A] how to look at the past, since this has its items unified by this type of quality-intelligibility, B] what kind of activities in the physical realm are to be possible; C] what in fact is the case and not something outside the sphere of this world.

This which we say is just a physical thing, a matter of atoms and quantities is to be said to tell us   A] how to look at the future as demarcated, divided in a way that it does not itself control,   B] how to measure the energy-quantity of the past since this is conserved and thus identical with what is present,   C] what quantity is real in contrast with what might have been.

Attending only to the future, the qualitative-intelligible side tells us the contingent limits within which the activities of the physical world are to take place and the principles for the distribution of the energies in that future; the quantitative-energy side tells us how the real future is divided into magnitudes which are to be filled out by qualities, and that those quantities are to be controlled in the sense that they will be confined within those magnitudes. In brief, the one tells us the limits and the control which the physical will impose, and the other tells us the limits and the control which the non-physical will impose. To say then that this is a beautiful thing is to say at once that an understanding of its beauty requires an awareness of how in the next moment that beauty will be confined and conditioned, and also how the physical components of the thing will be limited and controlled.

The reconciliation of free-will and a divine pre-ordination of the future can be found in the above account of the quantity-energy and the intelligibility-quality with respect to the future. God will, on this account, provide the limits and a control of the exercise of free will, and free-will on man's part will involve a secularization of God's intent with a sub-mission of man's achievement to the limits which that intent then has.

Once again: intelligibility defines a principle governing the action of physical elements, and quantity the kind of control this will exert on the elements; energy defines the distributions in the past, and quality the way this was organized.

Once again: quantity tells what kind of principles will control the energies in the future, and intelligibility tells what the qualitative nature of those principles must be. Quality tells us what kind of formal, intelligible unities control the facts of the past, and energy tells us what the quantitative expression of those unities was. A grasp of the being will involve a union of intelligibility with abstract quantity to determine what the concrete future is like, and a union of energy with abstract quality to determine what the past was. The Form, because non-Platonic, entails a kind of future physical course, and the Abstracted Quantity, by affecting a real future possibility, provides a control for the expression of the energies then. If this is beautiful or ominous then if it is something merely suffered, a mere sensuosity, it will but say how the undifferentiated future is to be made into areas of activity; if it is something intelligible it tells what kind of qualities can be in the future, qualities which are the filling out of the differentiated future areas of activity.

Once again: The future has a certain type of quality prescribed to it by the form that the object now has, and a principle of the distribution of energy dictated by quantity which fills out the quality. The future quality is the shape in which the law governing the future energy is exhibited; the past quantity, defined by present energy, is the ground governing the kind of past intelligible units which quality prescribes.

Is it the case then that the meaning of a form today, beauty, etc., is that it tells us how a similar form is now prescriptive of the way in which energy must behave? The realm of the humanistic then entails the future qualitative form of the laws of the scientific, and the realm of the scientific entails the past quantitative meaning of the facts of the humanistic. To say this is beautiful is to say that, e.g., the blood will be controlled by a resultant emotional enjoyment; to say that I weigh 145 now is to say that in the past I was a skinny boy of 90 lbs., or that I was 90 lbs. skinny. The emotion entailed by beauty will dictate how the heart will beat; the weight I now have, prescribes a weight for one who was skinny or undernourished, etc.

Once again: The physically conditioned possibility which confronts us because of the energy in the present has the qualitative character of an entailed feature of an intelligible form. The unifications of the past, which a present intelligible form demands should hold of the past, has the quantified form which a conservation of energy demands. What must be is that the hydrogen and oxygen in the water will act in such and such a way inside water or steam, etc. What had to be is that the water that had been had the weight and properties which are demanded by a conservation of present energy. The present item on its humanistic side guarantees the kind of qualitative nature that the possible quantity will appear in: the qualitative nature of the future is abstract, lacking real quantitative content; it is like the quality now, but it exercises a control that the present quality lacks. The quality colors as it were a possibility which was made relevant by the quantity of today; just so the quantity fractionates the past relevant to the quality today.

November 13

The diffused object in the present can be understood as having its two sides, first distinguished as abstract limits in the guise of quality and quantity, and then in fact united in a real possibility which stands outside them and the object. That possibility is qualified by both; it is the quality as charged with quantity, the quantity as charged with quality, or better, intelligibility affected with the kind of energy which the present has. That modified possibility is abstract and related to a diffused object in the present which realizes it. The diffused object in the guise of the possible enables us to understand the object now as at once the terminus of science and history, intellect and sense, matter and form. The snub-nose now entails as it were a possible concavity in the flesh and it is this which enables us to understand the snub nose as a unity. There is no problem of having the concavity in flesh, for the flesh is a materiate universal, a universal of a material, and can be one with the possibility, whereas the snub nose seems to have added something; the concavity in it is intermixed with the material flesh in fact, and the flesh has been mixed with snubness rather than concavity. The schematism of Kant is as it were outside the categories and the manifold; because it unites them, there must be a possibility for the union in which they are modifications of the possible. This seems to put the stress on possibility and thus to be biased on one side. But the same thing with the opposite stress can be said of the past, and in any case the possible, as infected by the quantification of the present object and specified by the quality there, is not identifiable with either one or the other. The form of the present object is strictly speaking not intelligible, since it is interfused with the matter.

We must distinguish the present diffuse object; its abstract form and abstract matter; the future possibility quantified in an abstract way; the past facts conceivably formalized from a distance; the diffused state of becoming; and a past and future abstraction representing being in the present.

The diffused object by itself entails a distinctive form of the possible qualitative future and a distinctive settled quantified past. If one wanted to have these two together, to understand how there can be a past and future, one would have to recognize the present as a kind of possibility of them both—a future qualified by what had been; what had been, generalized by what is to be.

The union of positive and living law is that possible state of affairs in which the future tonality is given by the living law and its articulation by the positive law. The present living law with the present positive law defines a single possibility, which may fall short of the combination that should in effect be, and which is to be judged by natural law.

The possibility defined by the diffused object is realized through the action of the parts and restrained by the form. It can be grasped as that which is to be made determinate. The diffused object by itself is faced only with an intelligible future form and a brute factuality in the past; these modify one another to constitute a present which is knowable because the form is specified, the brute matter clarified. But these knowables are specializations of a prior given possibility and a prior given past.

The present object could be re-analyzed into two components and then be understood as having them qualify one another. What will be the difference between this view and the above? The mutual qualification is that of abstractions. But why instead of projecting it into the future don't we say that there is an abstract aspect in which the limits of the object are unified? Were this the case we would still have the question of the relation of the original object to the abstract unity. We would then either make the object into a kind of surd which sustains what alone is intelligible, the abstract combination, or treat it as an appearance hiding the intelligible.

But does not the previous view say that the object in the present is a surd with respect to the future? No, because that future really operates on it and thereby infects it. It is as if the parts of the diffuse object were to have a life of their own, making new combinations and affecting the original diffuse object. But perhaps there is no diffuse object? The future would then not be a different from the present or past. We would then have only a world of qualified possibilities succeeding one another, which is perhaps what the phenomenalists suppose. Why not? Because there is the effectiveness of the qualifications, the real movement of the scientific objects. I am saying that the diffused object is real and that it is intelligible because it has a real future, so that neither the diffused object nor the intelligible unity, is an appearance. One could try to avoid this by supposing that the unity is in my mind, but then the object seems to be a plurality, and unity only an appearance or imposition.

November 14

The converging rails are not qualities of the real scientific rails; they are the outcome of the imposition of qualities on the quantifications imposed by the scientific rails. The saying that the convergent rails are parallel is ambiguous: it means primarily that they would be seen to be parallel if seen from right above. Now the scientific rails measure over a set of places equally apart; the parallelism of vision is coincident with the parallelism of the scientifically known object. The parallelism held in vision does not become the convergent item; but the convergent, since it is a way of dealing with the parallelism from a special place, is the scientific parallelism as qualified by a transformation of the visual parallelism that holds here and now.

The future is that which is constantly quantified in a constant way with variable qualities. The past is a constant from the position of the qualities open to vision, as imposed on as yet undetermined distributions of energy. The past star is a construction from a present star as now at once seen and subject to astronomical characterizations. When we refer back to the past we refer back to that which could have been seen if in fact there is a quantification present there, a quantification which we know now by reading back into the past a transformation of the quantification that is now characteristic of the seen star. The local qualities modify the implied distribution of quantities.

When we construct the past star in this way, we are not able of course to know about it as that which is not visible in the sense in which the present star is visible; we do not have the instruments for referring to the star as just over the chimney; the past which lies outside the range of human perception would have to be reached not through perceptual features of the present star but through some other agency. Also the star (as reconstructed in the past and having different quantified properties or distributions of energy than that which is characteristic of the present seen star) has some connection with the present star. Does it determine the time and position for the appearance of the star now, so that we in effect impose, on the possibility which the past star quantifies, a quality which is the implicate of the quality we now see, just as we do in connection with the convergent rails? Is the object seen then today, because there was the old visible star, because it affected a possibility, and this possibility was realized qualitatively by me? And would there be a realization of the possibility (which vision seems to produce) only through the use of the quantified items? We seem to realize the possibility that there will be an explosion only by virtue of the activity of the scientific side; yet there seems to be a visible star because of some activity on the qualitative side. Is it that we must first reduce the visible star to the normative case and then get the quantity? Do we not then deny that we really see the external world; do we not also have the problem, in connection with the star, of dislocations in space and time?

November 15

The rails now are equidistant. This equidistance defines a pos-sibility which is quantified and which, when a perceiver is present, becomes actualized as a quality, "parallel" or "convergent"—and the latter in any degree. So far as the equidistant rails are concerned they specify the possibility to be expressed over a whole series or family of perceivable qualities. One member of that family, e.g., seen parallels, is not only presently perceived but is sustained by an energy in the rails, i.e., is coincident with the rails. However, it is also true that the convergent rails are coincident with real rails. What we have in fact in connection with the rails is not only then the quantification of the possibility with a realization of one member of the family of qualities from a certain perspective, but the realization of the rails as genuinely qualitative and energized. The real energized rails sustain an entire family of qualities, all of which in their interrelationship express the meaning of one of the members, usually that one selected to represent the meaning of equidistance, i.e., the parallel ones. But the seen parallel rails from above are but one of the family.

The seen star is not seen only from here; it can be seen from many positions. It embraces a family of lights at different positions with respect to me now. If there is a star now, then the family of positions of the star is in exactly the same situation as is the family of appearances of the rails. If there is no star now the quality seen is dislocated, and must be said to be either in my mind, or to be located now with reference to some earlier location. Since the seen star is a star which is the beginning of a scientific inquiry, it must be a quantified star. Unless we are really cut off from our contemporaries it is an energized star. (The present star presumably can be seen at later times. But this adds a complication.)

If the present star could be seen later, then what we see now might conceivably be an earlier star. But if there is a real star now that is being seen, the time-toned quality of the star belongs to two families—one of the energizing star now, and one of the star that had been, which has many temporal locations. Now the star that had been is a star of the past. It does not possess energy. It possesses only quantity. The visible star now offers qualitative closures on the energy that had been, to constitute it as a set of loci of quantities, so that we who see the star now can speak of an entire set of such quantities as constituting the past. The past star then is only one of a member of quantified stars, stars which are given a kind of quantified being.

But what then of the energized star that had been? We said above that the star now with its energy could be seen later. But it will be seen later only as that which has been a quantified star. This means that no later position enables us to get to the real star that had been. It means that the real star that had been can be known only through a scientific extrapolation which ends with a merely quantified, abstracted kind of star. The supposition that this quantified abstracted kind of star is the locus of an energy that had been is but a way of congealing the entire series of quantities from today until then into one time, just as we can congeal the entire series of appearances of the rails into their being parallel.

November 19

In the present we have an intelligible empowered being whose present existential energy permeates it, having its limits in a quality and quantity. The being in its existential nature, but via its status as empowered, quantifies the future possibility before it. That quantified possibility can be made real in the present in two ways: the energy can be made to quicken it (thereby turning the possibility into a quantified nature), or the intelligible side of the being can be imposed on the quantified possibility to make it a perceptual object. The first of these ways gives us a being which is not perceived; the latter, one which is without efficacy. Both objects contrast with what is in the present for us now, since this is at once quantified, energized and qualitied. Consequently, it is sometimes the case that an energized present object can be perceived.

The object as in the present defines a relevant past by virtue of the way in which its intelligible nature makes unities out of the endless divisions in the past. When these unified divisions are endowed with quantities related to the quantity of the energy in the present we get a reference to a real past object.

The problem of the perception of the stars is whether the perceived is a kind of possibility which is realized in the form of perception, but which lacks the real energy to make it a present real being, or whether it is a real being and the past object is only a construction from it. Perhaps the best thing to say is that the present perceived object has a quality which epitomizes present energy not located where the quality is. The world which the energized quantified possibility presents for perception is not necessarily one which will be perceived as possessing a characterizing quality; what is perceived is an epitomized quality which may or may not be located where the energized quantity is. When we start with that present object, we must say that the future will be determined by the quantified energized object, but not necessarily as possessing the epitomized quality; it may possess some other of which we may know nothing. When we refer back to the past, it is however via the perceived quality. This dictates what the relevant past will be. What we hope for in the sciences is that the references to the past in this way will yield characterizing qualities, and thus qualities inside of which there could have been the energy which is now distributed outside the range of the perceived quality.

November 27

Any idea can be transformed into any other by some operation or other. The transformation must not be supposed to eliminate the original idea, and is not supposed to answer anything in fact, since it is something conceived and has to do with meaning. But one might with justice demand that one keep to only some types of transformation, either for the sake of keeping abreast of what things in fact are, or for the sake of keeping inside the areas of a given discipline. More important, one must ask if the outcome is contained in the original. It seems that this must be said to be the case in connection with A] such ultimates as the modes, and B] such excellencies as the good and the purged qualities of art. We cannot extend the idea to every item without supposing that each and every object of knowledge contains within it the totality of ideas or meanings. 1] Why can we not say that no entity into which we transform a given one is contained in that given one? 2] Why not say that the Good or God is something entirely alien to the given items of experience and are only the outcome of arbitrarily imposed operators? 3] Or why can we not say that God or the Good are ingredient in actual things, but that when we subject them to the operation of dislocation in the attempt to get them in their purity we but suppose them to have a status which they in fact do not have. The answer to the third question is that the given item cannot be understood except as subject to a prescription stemming from an exterior reality. The answer to the second question requires a reference to direct testimony, to the acknowledgment of facets in a given item which are values, unities, qualities, etc., and thus exhibit the transformed reality as subject to qualifications by the being in which it is ingredient. But we cannot suppose this is true of every entity; there are radical transformations which give us something quite alien to what we start from, as it is most evident from the fact that we can use the operator "othering." The first question asks why should not all transformations be thought to be modes of othering. This they can be thought to be, provided that othering be not conceived as doing more than changing something about a being, and not necessarily changing everything.

In some cases we can change everything, and in some we do not or cannot. But it would then seem as if, to answer the second question

again, that it is the simple which can be completely changed by a transformation. This supposes that the simplicity of an idea means that it is
open to alteration; its very simplicity means that it is to be altered from
the state where it is ingredient to enable it to have the status where it is
apart.

Why should it not be possible to explain God, e.g., as a transformation of some kind of Actuality or Ideal or Existence? Ought we not in
the end say this is possible only so far as He is in fact contained in the
other modes? In short, no free ultimate mode can be explained by
transformations except so far as it is already present elsewhere in some
other way. If we did not say this we would not be able to put the modes
over against one another. It is not then that the Actual, e.g., can be
transformed into God, but rather that the Actual has a facet or aspect
which can be so transformed because it is God in a modified way. But if
Actuality cannot be transformed into God and *v/v,* there are limits to
what can be transformed, and thus areas where no unity of meanings is
possible. I think we must say that the Actual can be transformed through
the strategy of an abstraction, when it becomes intelligible and thereby
relatable to God. It is the kind of transformation which is not possible in
reality, as is the transformation of desk to ashes; it is a transformation of
meaning which can be obtained when we recognize that Actuality is a
being with such and such powers and activities that can be abstractly
transformed into the meaning of God, but which cannot be made into the
being of God without God's aid.

December 1

Phenomena are just what they then and there are. They have
no potentialities, no power, no energy, no substantiality, no privacy,
no promise, no resistance. Whenever we confront phenomena we are
inescapably driven to acknowledge a domain beyond them. That domain
is the numinous, the fearsome, the uncharted. We find quite soon that it is
compulsive in four ways: it has a dynamic life of its own, it has localized
foci, it has a valuationally prescriptive or judgmental facet, and it is the
locus of ourselves and what we do and encounter. In short we begin to
distinguish in it an existing, actualized, idealized and divine side. The
compulsiveness of each one of these, drives one to acknowledge four
modes of being.

In order to focus on this numinous side below phenomena we
engage in private ways of accepting it. That is why we are creative in
the arts, are adjustive with respect to our fellows, make ethical decisions

and act in terms of them, and worship and pray. These are private answers, and are to be supplemented by ourselves in the guise of parts of larger corporate wholes. Our creativity in art is supplemented by us as part of one total history; our adjustive acts with respect to our fellows is supplemented by us as engaged in collective knowing; our ethical decisions are supplemented by political and civilized social living, and our submission to the divine is supplemented by institutional religion.

December 2

A better set than those given yesterday would be: Decision-ethical activity in consonance with others; Selfevaluation-Civilization; Art-History; Worship-Church. The first of each set tells us how we master the domain which lies beyond the ostensible phenomena—Actuality, Ideality, Existence and God. The second of each set tells us how we as corporate beings give an interpretation to the different modes. Ethical Activity is the meaning of Actuality for man; Civilization is what man takes the Ideal to be; History is man's interpretation of Existence. The Churches as institutions are what men understand God to be. Of course the different modes lie outside these interpretations, for these interpretations are evaluatable as A] incomplete expressions, B] manifestations of man, and C] inadequate expressions, that fall short of the prescriptive powers of the different modes.

1958

January 14

There seems to be some justification in the following historic summations:

1] We have a tendency to push back the achievement of a synthesis into the past, and finally into a rudimentary form of one of the elements. This is what we do, e.g., in understanding the coming to be of Christianity. The historians push it back into Greek thought or Jewish thought, and eventually find it to be already contained in an embryonic form in one or the other.

2] We have a tendency to skip steps of a doctrine or plan in order to move on in fact. A clear case of this is the Russian Revolution under Lenin which jumped the steps prescribed by Marx.

3] We have a tendency to get to higher and higher positions in order to deal with all beings equally. The most conspicuous case of this is Augustine's saying that from the position of divinity there is almost (?) an equality of desert in the good and bad men in this world.

4] We have a tendency to get below the phenomena to a final destining power. This is most evidently done by metaphysicians, and particularly by Schopenhauer who went below all ostensible phenomena to the will in terms of which the powers and activities of all are to be understood.

These various activities involve supplementation by *1]* a principle of persistence or identity of the initial case through to the present. *2]* a principle of regularity or drive enabling one to maintain the common position despite the jumps; *3]* a secularization of the divine allowing for the acceptance of the lower and its diversity in spite of the divine equalization; and *4]* the translation into experience of whatever is metaphysical so as to enable one to have evidence and meaning for the speculations.

Are individual beings substances? The fact that they pass away and are dependent on one another would seem to indicate that they are not. The true substances would seem to be the modes of being. Yet Actuality as such is not substantial. Actuality can qualify as a substance only so far as it is represented by individual men or is constituted by the plurality of interplaying beings, by "nature" as it were. Should we then say in an Aristotelian fashion that a species of animal is substantial in that it can represent the whole of Actuality? The whole species would represent the whole of Actuality in somewhat the way men as individuals do—they would act on other Actualities and other modes of being, becoming an other with respect to them. But does this mean that a species must be permanent or that it is immortal? Or is it that the laws of the species, the species nature as such would be integral to the universe, having been localized and fleshed by individual beings?

January 15

No individual actuality is a substance in and of itself. It is one by virtue of its representing the whole of Actuality, which alone is over against the other modes of being, themselves substances. The primary simple actualities, e.g., an electron or something like that, is substantial just so far as it is the instantiation of the laws characteristic of any Actuality whatsoever; it is a substance in that it is "any" thing. Living beings are substances just so far as they instance these laws and at the same time localize, specialize, vivify them; they provide the laws with a being in themselves; each of the living beings is an instance of a grounded form of the laws, qualified and restricted. Whereas the in-animate's being is, qua substance, nothing but an extraneous carrier of the laws governing all, the being of the living is permeated by and permeates the laws. In the case of man, the individual goes one step further and inwardly represents the whole of Actuality; he goes beyond law and beyond grounding, to be in himself the very meaning of inwardness.

In the case of the complex derivative beings, such as a stone, etc., we have instances of common laws but restricted and qualified. They are not genuine substances. The living beings are genuine substances because in the grounding of the restricted qualified laws they compensate for the restrictions and qualifications and thus can act as genuine representa-tives of all Actuality. What is here said modifies somewhat the view in the *Modes,* and yesterday's observations, for it was not understood in these places that inanimate beings were representative of Actuality as such in the same way that man is, though not by virute of an inwardness of status but by an instancing of the laws governing Actuality as such. The inanimate instances the laws of Actuality, the living grounds it (and so far gives Actuality body and career) and the human provides Actuality with the inwardness which opposes all other realities. The law of Actuality is over against and in this sense other than the rationale of other modes; the living has a body which is over against and in this sense other than the divisions of the other modes; the human stands opposed not to divisions of the other modes or to their structure but to their very being, but does so only as representative of the nature of Actuality as such, which has no inwardness of its own.

To the paradox then that "Being altogether is not," we must join the paradox that nothing in this world of Actuality is a substance is and of itself, but only representatively, and that Ideality (with Plato) must be said to be a substance, that God (with classical theology and Aristotle) must be said to be a substance, and that Existence (with Descartes) must be said to be a substance (he calls it body). The three of them have rationalities, divisions and inwardness answering to the inanimate, living and human which are, through representativeness, their absolute others. (There must be a kind of immortality which Ideality and Existence provide which is distinct from that provided by God, e.g., Ideality will give it by subordination and Existence by providing consequences. This point is made in the *Modes.*)

January 16

If one were to take a Kantian approach to the idea of possibility, and treat it as the consequence of a relaxation of some condition defining the actual (which in a way is what is done when it is defined as a qualification of a categorical assertion), we get something like abstracted ingredient possibilities in all the modes, even that of Ideality. This meaning of possibility relates not to any ontological realm but to one's attitude or status with respect to that which is in fact; it could be viewed as what a mode of being is when viewed from a distance. Thus we can say that Actuality when looked at from the perspective of Ideality is a relaxed Kantian possibility. But we ought also to say the same thing of God and Existence. In the case of the Ideal we can contrast the Ideal in itself with some division of itself. And in a similar way we can look at three modes say from the perspective of God, in which case they would be abstracted unities; if we look at them from the perspective of Existence they would be abstracted fields; if we look at them from the perspective of Actuality they would be abstracted individuals.

If we say "it will rain" and it does in fact rain what is the nature of the assertion before it has rained? Is it not that it is a relational statement connecting the present with the possibility of rain and does not attain full being as a relation until it in fact rains? In that case it is a relation of truths. Until then it is only the relation of intent or promise, perhaps to be understood as saying that "rain is a genuine possibility" which is relevant to what is now the case, the assertion serving to relate the present with the possible rain. If so, we have then a kind of variable meaning to "it will rain"; until it in fact rains it must be a structure which has one steady meaning, and which it maintains even when it rains; and it also has a meaning which varies in content, becoming a meaning of truth of fact only when the fact arrives. The matter is not changed if we say "it rains on January the 16th at 10 o'clock" and say this before the date specified. The assertion will still refer to a possibility; it can refer to an actuality only when the rain occurs. It will not have the status of relating the past to the present in all the cases. But it is also true that it is an assertion which claims to be true of something and must have a terminal rather than a relational status.

The proposition, "it rains on January the 16th at 10 o'clock" must be said to have a variable relation or a variable terminus. If the former it moves from the status of being possibly true to being true; if the latter, the truth it has moves from the status of being possibly applicable to being in fact applicable. In the one case we deny that it is true in or by itself; in the other we allow for this. In the light of the meaning of logically true, we can perhaps say that as not yet realized or instanced, it is formally true, or syntactically true, and acquires semantic truth later. But since "it is raining" cannot in itself be said to be true at all apart from all actual raining, we are forced to say that the semantic approach to truth is prior, and that if "it is raining" can be characterized as true in itself it is a derivative from the semantic one. Accordingly we must say that the proposition "it is raining" as having pertinence to tomorrow is now only possibly true in itself and possibly true in relation to the world, and that when it becomes true of the world by a change in the world it accretes the property of being true in or by itself.

The question of instancing of a proposition, universal, etc., is similar to the problem involved in the Incarnation. Just as there are those who think of Christ as merely man perfected, so there are those who think that an instancing of a universal is but the fulfilling of a potency, having no reference to any possibility beyond. And just as there are these who think of Christ as God and not at all man, with a kind of apparent body, so there are those who view instancing as nothing but the presence of a universal, with "presence" being only an apparent other. And just as there are those who maintain the doctrine of two distinct natures in a single being, so there are those who think of instancing as a kind of reciprocal duplication in the realm of the actual of that which is merely possible. Better answers involve the mutual determination of particularity and universality, or the recognition of the nature of creativity.

The doctrine of the mutual determination of particularity and universality in effect holds that instancing or participation is a joint affair. The two come together and each is enhanced by the other. The trouble with this view is that it supposes a *tertium quid* to do the uniting, and that it also denies the independence of the two items; it speaks in the Aristotelian-Thomistic vein of a soul and body, neither one of which is able to fully be itself without the other; a similar view was presented by me in *Reality* in connection with the doctrine of synthesis. But these are only analogues; if there are real Actualities and real possibilities they have beings of their own and do not need completion one from the other in order to be, but only in order to be perfected. The possibility gains something in being realized, as does the Actuality, but it is not (as the body-soul or synthesis doctrines hold) something which they need in order to be at all, as if they were fragments torn off some richer whole. If we view the modes as independent, their coming together will be the production of something richer, and will take place not in between them but in both of them.

An Actuality realizes the Good A] by becoming better organized in itself—this is like the doctrine of the realization of potentialities, and B] by implicating the Good in new situations, a matter which has its reciprocal in the Actuality being implicated according to the nature of the Good—and this is like the doctrine of synthesis. And since there is no transportation of possibilities from one realm to the other it is also like the dualistic view. And since it is the possible which is realized, it is like the gnostic view. The Actuality by organizing itself implicates the Good and is implicated in new ways. And what is true of the Actuality is true of all other modes.

January 29

Why should one not say that a possibility, which should be realized and is in fact not realized, does achieve some kind of realization by virtue of the fact that the actuality where it should have been realized is thereby characterized as defective? Is it necessary that the possibility must be fulfilled, enriched, realized in the most excellent way possible, that things in fact exemplify them? This last is surely not the case, for things are defective. Is it necessary then that the possible be fulfilled, enriched, realized somewhere else? Must the Good become fully good; may not there be a constant tension between it and the Actual? Or is it the case that every mode is fully satisfied by all the others, that its needs are answered, that each becomes relevant to the others through the medium of a second, that each functions as a norm which no one alone but all the others must realize together? Why must a norm be perfectly fulfilled; is this the same thing as a realization of a possibility? Or should we say with a kind of Hegelian backhandedness that the possibilities, normative and non-normative, are always related to the Actual and thus fulfilled but at various degrees and positions, and that this is enough? But were it enough why should it ever be realized more? Because this would give it a greater satisfaction? Before the final satisfaction, it would always be realized to some degree. Such a view is tantamount to one which says that the Good, the Ideal, the possibles by virtue of their relevance to Actuality are already realized to some degree, and that this degree is sufficient to show that they are not impossibilities. Taking this interpretation, all possibilities and the Good are realized at least by virtue of being relevant and therefore as now characterizing the actualities (to which they are relevant) as incomplete or defective and striving perhaps. There is need for fuller realization on the part of both the Ideal and the Actual. But this does not affect the ontological question as to whether or not the Ideal has not been sufficiently realized to avoid the paradox of supposing that it is a possibility which may never be realized.

Relevance is realization enough to make unnecessary a reference to God. This view would be Platonic, with the difference that there would always be some relationship to the world beyond the forms; it would be Hegelian in that the possible always gets its realization, for the relevance is a mode of realizing it by giving it locus in the world outside it; it would be Kantian in the sense that it would still allow for further filling; and it would be Aristotelian in that the filling would benefit both the Ideal and the Actual.

The assumption made in the *Modes* is that the possibility must be perfectly fulfilled, if not at this moment then later or over the whole of moments, and if not here then there, or over all possible beings. But what does it mean for it to be completely fulfilled? Is not a judgment or evaluation or characterization of what is other than it, as being something negative, a fulfillment?

Do I not here assume in root the view of *Reality* that all beings strive to complete themselves, and that this is possible in the sense that they are attracted to what they have not yet mastered, that the defectiveness of them is but the other side of a genuine striving to overcome and master, and possess the perfect, and that until this is achieved neither the possible nor the Actual is satisfied? But would there though be anything wrong in the universe if the modes remained outside one another, evaluating each other as defective? Indeed, do I not say this in the *Modes,* and merely add that the rest of the modes add up to the satisfaction of the demands of a given mode? But do they satisfy it in fact, do they actually go any further than merely serve as its counterpart? Why must there be a completing in the mode itself; why should not the fact that it has a perspective on them in terms of which they are limited or defective be enough to satisfy it? Is not judgment that x is defective from standpoint y a satisfaction of $y;$ why must it want x to be perfect, and thus for itself to be in x or realized there? And if it so wants it what is wrong with its not attaining this end? If there is nothing wrong in its not attaining this end we must modify the position taken regarding the Ideal in the *Modes,* and give up the providential view we have of God, and also the view of the completeness of the incursion of Existence in the other modes.

This alternative is not satisfactory, as can be seen if we start from Actuality and ask why it should strive to complete itself; the above alternative says in effect that it is already satisfied by virtue of the fact that as distant from the Ideal it already is satisfied by that Ideal if only in the sense that the Ideal is thereby characterized as defective from the vantage point of the Actual—as perhaps by not being articulated, pluralized enough into independent components. Since actualities do strive, the striving would have to be thought of as a mistake, as some Hindus think, or it could be the product of some other kind of need—perhaps to master other actualities and not other modes of being. But there is something perverse about the Hindu upside-down denial of what is omnipresent and effective and which is also acknowledged by them when they eat and sleep. The need of actualities for one another does not cover the fact that men, at least, not only strive with respect to one another but with respect to the Good which is common to them, and by virtue of which they can, through their concern for it, be members of one class and move into the future together. The striving of beings for the Good, beyond that which it realizes through relevance or desire, is due to the fact that what they now are makes them to want to make the Good encompass all else and thereby be realized in them. But if we say this we reverse the original remark to the effect that beings strive to realize the Good, for now we are saying that they act to encompass all else, including the Good. But these perhaps are two sides of the same effort; to try to encompass all else is to move to where the others are; to strive to realize is to bring them to where one is. Both are necessary for fulfillment, for the beings are located both here and there.

January 30

Those who try to reduce the various modes of being to extensions of the Actual in effect make the Actual realized by denigrating the other modes. The objection to the view that any being is final is that it fails to see that a being is incomplete, that its incompleteness requires that it hold on to what would complete it, that this will make it be in tension, and that this tension is relaxed only so far as the being in effect lays hold of and possesses, makes interior to itself the beings which are outside it. The minimization of the other modes of being in effect allows Actuality to remain as it is and to be satisfied by virtue of that denigration. It is as if one were to say that "sour grapes" is the way to achieve satisfaction. And it would, were it not that one is in fact hungry, that one indeed needs the other modes not merely as what is other than oneself but as possessed by oneself, translated into oneself somehow.

January 31

There are two stages in knowledge. The first is one where we focus on, attend to the object, take it to be at the border of ourselves (at a distance from where we normally locate our bodies, at least with respect to the perceptions involving sound, smell and sight). If we accept this as the object we in a sense, without judging it, pass a judgment on it. It is analogous to the judgment of something at a distance as being desirable, or of something being judged as defective. The knower in this stage offers the basis in terms of which the object of knowledge is to be evaluated; he is the real, and the object at which he terminates is, as terminus, just something for him. We move to the second stage where there is a concern for the object itself, when we acknowledge that our relation to the object is abstract, that it transcends the reference to ourselves and gives us the object as it is, though under the limitation of abstraction. The first stage is analogous to the stage where the individual being in fact reaches to and masters others from its own angle and for its own use; the second stage is analogous to a situational one (which on the ontological level might be said to precede the mastering one), where both the being with which one starts and the being at which it terminates are on a footing. In the ontological situation the footing is provided by the fact that they are both in space; in the epistemological situation it is something achieved by overcoming the initial bias of attention through an abstraction. In this overcoming of the bias which is achieved in neutrality.

We thus have ontologically: first the case where beings are in situations, and then the perspectives each takes of the others, mastering them from its own perspective. This second stage can have many subordinate stages from that of apprehension at a distance, to touching, to assimilation. The second stage is in effect the first stage of knowledge; to attend is to focus on, to reduce the being of something to the status of an adjective of another. This stage is necessary because the togetherness one has with others in the first stage allows them all to be so on a footing that they have no definite direction in which to go. (If one takes the position of *Reality,* of course, the first stage is a product of something like an interlocking on what is here termed the second stage.) But what is important now to note is that given an interlocking there is the fact that each entity takes a perspective on another and reduces it, from that perspective, to the stage where it is adjectival to itself; it can do this while it is in the situation. When it does this it evaluates the other; if it remains in that position it in effect qualifies the other as nothing more than a limit of itself. The fact that a being makes this which is now merely a terminus for itself into something which it ought to struggle with, leads it to engage in an abstraction in the case of knowledge, and to act in the case of the ontological situation. Faced then with the terminus of attention, a man can either act on that which lies beyond the terminus, or abstract from the act of attention to get the acknowledgment of that which lies beyond the terminus. Epistemological approaches to reality find it difficult to see how either of these is possible. The pragmatists do recognize that action is required, but do not see that the speculative entertainment of the being in the realm of thought is an analogue of action.

The neutrality of looking at the object of attention as on a footing with oneself is analogous to the action of handling the object in its own terms. The major difference is that action starts with the taint of the individual and ends by achieving neutrality in the struggle with the object, whereas abstraction (though to be sure it also begins with a bias) expresses the status of the terminus of the effort to deal with the things in their own terms. It would be desirable therefore if one could find an epistemological term which, like action, expressed something of the fact that it A] goes beyond the bias of mere focusing, and B] while it goes beyond that bias, begins as a biased act itself and ends in an objective interplay.

Perhaps abstracting is the analogue of action. If so we can say that having focused on something, the next stage is either the progressive moment to an objectivity in knowledge or in action. The end of the knowledge movement is neutrality, and the end of the action movement is interplay. After this we get a third stage where the content as neutrally known is adopted as one's own, which is the perfecting of oneself through the agency of knowledge, or the assimilation of the object taken in its full-bodied being, which is the perfecting of oneself through the agency of concrete use.

In order to make use of the real objects outside us we therefore first denigrate them into termini, then re-establish them as coordinate, and finally, adopt them for ourselves. The last stage looks like the first, but differs in that it does take account of the objects as they are, whereas the first deals with them under the perspective of an abstraction (the second deals with them under the perspective of a vital struggle).

We must first give up the status of being superior to the others by evaluating them in our own terms, in order to attain the status where we are superior to them by virtue of a conquest. There are in short two kinds of conquest, the conquest which results by denigration through the conversion of entities into termini of attention, and the conquest which results from the re-achievement of objectivity through abstraction and action, in order to make the others into components of ourselves.

Those who criticize the *Modes,* on the ground that it reifies what is in fact nothing more than an expression of Actualities,   A] engage in an act of dislocating the modes from their setting as alongside one another,   B] attend to them as mere termini of attention,   C] allow a judgment to be passed, without making a judgment to the effect that these are nothing more than termini. The result would make Actuality complete; there would be nothing for it to become. But the fact of prescription involves an imposition on us, pointing to the reality of the Ideal; the fact of dynamic concordance points to the reality of Existence; the fact of permanence, of satisfaction of the Ideal and of otherness points to the reality of God.

Actuality is an other   A] as prescribed to,   B] as effectively concordant, and   C] as sheer inward. Also, Actuality is intruded on, the intrusions having the form of demands by a becoming in a field, by that which is absolute alien, and by that which is bodily effective.

The *Modes* says that The Ought-to-be Can Be, but it denies that What *I* ought to do I can do. But in a sense the way it deals with the first involves a rejection of the denial. Thus it maintains that to do all that I ought to do I must make use of whatever powers there be, either directly by accepting them as instruments or by adopting their results as my own. Now this is evidently what I can do. Accordingly though I cannot by myself do all that I ought to do, I can do all that I ought to do by taking advantage of whatever there be. But this is of the same order of answer as that which says that I am required to do only that which in the circumstances I can do. This latter answer allows me to make use of various powers and agencies available. For example, I ought to see my dying friend within the next five hours. It is no avoidance of this obligation to say I can't walk there in that time; if it be the case that I can get there by car or train, I am under obligation to use these. Accordingly what I am asked to do is what I can do, when the "can" is understood to include the using of whatever agencies and instruments there be. The cosmic problem of the Good then is solved with the recognition that I can make use of the various modes (and in the end even the Ideal) in order to satisfy that Good.

I know that I am ignorant (and therefore that my knowledge is abstract); that I am defective (and that therefore there are prescriptions); that I am involved in an environment (and that therefore there is an Existence); that I have an inwardness which retreats before all (and that therefore there is a God); that I am injurable (and that therefore there are other actualities). These results are not proofs; they are testimonies, pointing to the kind of things which must be proved, which are there to be proved, which have a being equal with our own, and which must be recovered in order for us to see ourselves as equal to them. We must then get to the stage where we acknowledge our ignorance, etc., as the outcome of an approach from without us. We might be said to start in unknown ignorance, etc., and to go to the point where we know, where we make others into termini, etc., and still find ourselves not perfected.

The attempt to view all the modes as forms of the Actual but says we are perfect already, with the other modes delimited into boundaries of ourselves. But no matter how much of the world we reduce in this way we are left with our own awareness of our ignorance, etc., and thus of our awareness of ourselves from a perspective outside ourselves, and which we evidently occupy by virtue of the fact that the termini of our knowledge, etc., are achieved, derived from a more basic ontological situation in which we are together on a footing with others.

February 25

We can think of the space between two actualities as a kind of "lebensraum" or empty place of a togetherness. This can be filled in three ways—by works of art, by social realities, and by sacramental things. The first of these involves the use of Existence, the second of Ideality, and the third of divinity. From this perspective we start with the area of togetherness and fill it up; the object of art for example is to fill up the empty space and time. The social reality is brought about in the same way. To use John Wild's illustration, when I say "I promise" there is no separation of self from the expression. I would go further and say we must expand the expression to "I promise you." The promise is here the substantial reality, and the I and the you are to be thought of as limits of it. We know that there is a you so far as we know there is an I, and we know there is an I, since we see it making itself in the course of the promising. The promise is lived through in time and its career reveals the contours of myself and you; if I, faced with an obstacle, give up or alter the promise, I also do something with respect to you; and you too, in response or apart from it, may alter the shape of the promise and thereby redefine what I can do. The I and the you as limits of the promise have no separate being; but if the promise be but one of many substantial realities with the I and you as limits, we can define the substantial I and you as the product of the overlapping of the many "shadows" which the different substantial processes cast in both directions. The substantial I is then the limit of a set of social processes.

The relation I have to God is similar, and is expressed in the sacramental object; and this relation once again is like that which I have with respect to the natural world beyond, and which I attempt to see in the art object. From this point of view the art object does not represent; it is the universe, and though perhaps it may have its source in a prior knowledge, from the standpoint of a phenomelological account it is the basic reality. The material which I use for art, like the material I use for a promise is in the art itself; it must be viewed as the work of art in inchoate form. Nature then for the theory of art in this account is not something over against the artist; it is something which is found out in the course of the art activity; it gets substantiality only from the totality of art objects.

I, you, nature and God have a being of our own. This means that the above is but a correlate of an ontology which begins, not with the realm of the togetherness, but with the togethered items. In the end the two parts must be brought together, in which case we would have society, art and sacraments as various strategies which seek to achieve neutrality between the various parts of the ontology but in a way that a man can perform. In the *Modes* it was seen that there is a togetherness which is sustained by God and exhibited as a special form of His apprehension. It is that apprehension, but sustained in part by us, and largely or at least in part produced by us, which is exhibited in the sacramental object. This like the art object and the social object is in a process (of which the I and the other are limits), achieving substantiality only through the multiplication of their work as limits. So far as we suppose them to be substantial apart from these ways of being substantial we take the opposite position of an ontology.

A possibility is made concrete by an actuality. The ingredient possibility that we then can abstract can be viewed as an attribute or predicate. But it also can be seen to be a specialization of the realm of indeterminate possibility. When we see it in this way we are forced to take a position in the past, for it is from that position that it became a particular possibility. We don't look back into the past, we don't create it, we just recover in ourselves a position which enables us to see in a temporal stretch the process of making the indeterminate totality of possibility into a particular one. When I see snow on the ground I can make a judgment, through the use of the ingredient possibility, that there is snow. Or I can assume the attitude that the snow is not irrational, that it is open to my experience, that it can be adumbrated, that I can make the generic possibility specific. When I do this I move back into my own past. That is, I remember. Remembering then is a direct contact with the past, not the dead past but a layer of pastness which I uncover in the very effort to see the specific possibility as that which has been made specific, and by me. To know that the possibility is determinable by me is to know that I must go back into my past to find the position from which it was made determinable. I roll back time by attenuating the possibility until I am faced with the indeterminate possibility, and I proceed forwards by tracing the way I went from the past until the present. (This is only the germ of an idea, but it is a big idea!)

February 27

Formal and material implication, as mentioned in the *Modes,* also inferences and processes, the formal and thicker ways of inferring to God, the two types of logical constants, etc., can be dealt with in three ways. *1*] They can be treated as distinct, and in such a way that there is a discrepancy between them in the requirements they involve. *2*] One of them can be thought of as prescriptive for the other, with the other as a kind of degree of the first. Thus if we start with formal logic, or formal proofs of God, or inference, or one set of formal constants, the material forms could be thought of as thickenings of these, as adding additional content which slows their rhythms and even may alter their original structure—so that the movement to the concrete necessarily involves a risk. But also, conversely, the formal can be viewed as a kind of attenuation of the thicker, as involving a reference to an endless time and an endless community. The latter approach enables one to do justice to the pragmatic idea of habits and the necessity of having a genuine logic which is not confined to this or that situation. The former procedure though allows one to have a prescriptive logic and to measure the concrete in terms of purity; this makes possible the use of logic and mathematics and the evaluation of matters of fact as not altogether "rational."

We complicate this situation of course when we recognize four logics in the four modes, and think of a fifth type of logic as being constructed within the "space between" all of them. This new logic would be but the vitalization of the togetherness, the enriching of it in a way analogous to society, art, history, etc. It would be the logic of science were it but the logic in between the Ideal and the Actual, making use of Existence; it would be the logic of God if it made use of Him; etc. But as the logic in between all of them it is the logic of being, and achieves being only when constructed as the togetherness of all — in which case of course it lacks prescriptive power for the modes and their characteristic logics, taken substantivally. *3*] The third alternative is to view any logic in between the modes, in pairs, triplets or even all four together, as prior to the pairs, etc., so that a logic of science or being for example would provide the neutral, nuclear meaning which the other logics would diversely illustrate.

The second alternative is the preferable one and should be treated as having three stages: *1*] beginning with a formal or material side and viewing the other as a limiting case, *2*] the converse activity of the first, and *3*] the constructing of a medium over time, analogous to the way one constructs an art object, which will enable one to see these first two starting points (the limits of them being viewed as continuations of them and not genuinely over against them) as correlatives not of something prior but of something they help constitute.

March 8

The affiliation of words with ideas is a fluctuating one. As one increases one's vocabulary the value of the words one already has is modified; the words get new weights and powers, and each therefore has a bearing on the ideas already possessed that it did not have before. But also as the ideas or understanding increases, the given words take on different nuances and thereby alter. Since a language is not merely the possession of an individual man, the words also must alter in terms of the weight they have in one's entire life, not only as an individual but as interplaying with others inside a common society or state.

If one's normal vocabulary and speech is prose, in writing poetry one inevitably distorts one's own meaning, as carried out by such a vocabulary. The poetry tells a "lie" in the sense that the rationale of the poem requires certain words, to provide which is to falsify what one intended to say. Conversely, if one tried to say exactly what one meant (and this is for the mature man adequately expressed at least for most purposes in his prose), one will write poor poetry. If there be one who "lisps in numbers" then he will have the reverse experience in dealing with prose; what he says in prose will distort what he sees and says in poetry. A similar situation prevails in connection with the language of mathematics over against that of every day. And of course a similar situation prevails with respect to the languages of different countries. One cannot translate French into English, for example, with complete accuracy, for the words in French have overtones revelatory of the way in which the French use their mouths in speaking, eating and kissing and all the rest. It is only when we identify a limited pragmatic realm for convenient action that the translations are satisfactory. We then abstract, prescind from the overtones of the words, to use them as hard counters for specific items. When the items are made rigid and the words are used as isolated pieces in external relations to one another, it is possible to translate from one language to another without distortion. But such translations do not give us living languages; at the very best they give us the habitual usuages suitable for pragmatic action.

It is foolish then to look at poems to find out what poets are thinking; or conversely, to look at the obiter dicta of poets. To be sure they may be exposing themselves, revealing unconscious drives and interests. But this would be hard to substantiate, for the unused language instead of answering to the deepest parts of oneself may answer to the one's more superficial ideas.

March 12

A pluralism, and therefore the view presented in the *Modes,* if it has a dialectical grounding, offers an ontology which immediately expresses itself as a cosmology. It is an ontology in the sense that each of the plural entities is a genuine reality in and of itself. But since each is the other of the rest, and needs the rest in order to be itself, each exists only in a cosmic whole. Atomists such as Democritus and Leibniz have ontologies which are rather arbitrarily made into cosmologies, for there is no justification in them that there should be more than one of the atoms. On the other hand, phenomenologists have a cosmos which has no ontology behind it and thus have a single interlocked set of realities which never get to the stage of being entities on their own.

If an actuality can be said to be an Absolute Other only with respect to God, it would seem that only as such is it self-identical through time. As the other of other actualities it will change. Accordingly a being may be said to be self-identical and immortal only so far as it achieves the status, through God's aid, of being a representative of all Actuality and as such over against God. Different actualities will assume the representative function from different starting points; their individuality will be preserved only as adjectival to their representative function.

March 15

The self ought to have four roles as it stands over against other selves, Ideality, Existence and God. As over against other selves it is unique; over against Ideality it is active; over against Existence it is substantial; over against God it is private or inward, His absolute other. It is the last three so far as it has a representative role. In these four ways it is also immortal, though in different senses. As over against other selves it is immortal in its perpetual orientation to the situation in which it dwelt; over against Ideality it is immortal as forever linked in time to the Good; over against Existence it is immortal in the sense that it maintains an existence of its own when it is sundered from the body; over against God it is immortal in the sense that nothing can get into it to destroy it.

Which immortality is pertinent to identity and responsibility? Is it not with respect to other selves that it is persistently responsible? And is it not identical over against Ideality? If so what is it with respect to Existence and to God? Is it as a root reality for Existence, powerful enough to be over against a world; and is it as having the dignity of being a man, as being a genuine representative of privacy as such, that it is over against God?

Conversion involves the adoption of a new language. Is this necessary because in the very attempt to use it we see better what lies behind it? If so it is good to learn a foreign language because in speaking it badly one sees what ought to be said even in one's own language, which has become dead and flat with time and familiarity. Or should we say that one is converted because one sees a new truth and then finds the new pattern? If so, we would want to learn a language because we see something which our own frozen language does not let us say. Or does the convert merely enjoy the new music, the new rhythms and retains his old beliefs? If so, in languages we would be really be thinking as we had before but would find some extra quality of aesthetic value in the adoption of the new language. All three ways of being converted and of using languages seem to be in operation.

Leibniz said that the ontological argument presupposed that God was possible. He thought that he could show He was possible by showing God was the locus of all possibilities. But all possibilities whatsoever are together incompossible, thereby showing that God is impossible. Indeed, starting with God as possible will lead to just the opposite of what the ontological argument was supposed to do. If that possibility really is had apart from existence it is the wrong possibility for the proof; the only possibility that the proof can use is one which is indistinguishable from the actual. If one must begin with possibility one must begin with a possibility which is not that of God. Thus one might begin say with the possibility of man and show that there is a distance between that possibility and the actuality which is man. By an argument of convergence one can then proceed to think of the limit where the distance between the possible and actual is non-existent. There is no argument in fact when one gets to the possibility which is God; there is a kind of argument before one gets to that possibility. That argument would be something like a cosmological argument. And if I am right in *Reality* the argument would show that it was the entire cosmos, or (according to the *Modes*) the four modes which alone were proven to be real and identical with their very possibility. The argument in the *Modes* perhaps could start with mere possibility, the mode of being which is Ideal, and then show that its own completion would require that there be the other modes. Its own meaning would thereby be changed to be the possibility not of this or that but of the other three modes; it, as their possibility, would be indistinguishable from their unity, just as they would be indistinguishable from the articulation of it.

The traditional idea of God can be obtained in the *Modes* by making the Togetherness the concrete or basic reality, and viewing the God in the *Modes* as a principle of unity, something like Northrop's macroscopic atom. But better would be the view that men working together with the rest of the world forge a living togetherness which can have the role of a traditional God (or a history or a society or an art or a way of being in communion or communication with one another). One can then go on to treat it as the reconciliation of the various modes with one another, particularly as represented in some discipline. Thus, e.g., if one were to suppose that there is a philosophy and a theology, the one representing the natural world and the other God, one could forge the idea of a "living" God in the shape of a community or perhaps better in the shape of a virtuous man, (i.e., a man who combines in Existence the meaning of the Ideal) in which the two disciplines were reconciled. The disciplines could be said to be on a level, and each could be said to have similar vices and virtues. Thus we could say that philosophy was foolhardy because it tried to view the universe as God does, but also that it was timid in the sense that it did not commit itself to a basic belief; and we could say that theology was foolhardy in talking about that which transcended this world, and timid in that it refused to allow itself to follow the guidance of the logos. Courage would be their reconciliation, a courage manifested in a living existence in which one showed oneself to be an intelligent man of sensitivity. A church would be the place where such men were trained. On this view Aristotle's *Ethics* would offer a splendid way of dealing with basic antitheses. However, in Aristotle the contraries are of different values; in the above they are taken to be of the same value. Consequently for him the contraries have different virtues and vices, but in the above they have similar virtues and vices.

March 20

We can be said to be trying in multiple ways to fill out the emptiness which separates us from the rest of the world. These activities are: dreaming, thinking, speaking, behaving, acting, making. Dreaming fills out the space between our privacies and all else to constitute a world; imagination is its daytime correspondent and constitutes an environment. Thinking connects substantialities to constitute a manipulatable universe. Speech connects the individual with all else to constitute a language. Behaving connects a body with bodies to constitute a realm of becoming. Acting is transitional to other beings and with them constitutes an event. Making is productive and constitutes a work of art or manufacture. The earlier activities are to be found filling out the later. For each of them there is a corresponding other: reality, learning, hearing, resistance, reaction and data.

March 30

Four distinct types of excellence can be distinguished. There is the excellence of integrity, of being what one is. Each entity in the universe has a value peculiar to it, and the allowing this to be, freed from extraneous and mutilating and obscuring conditions, is a way of allowing it to be excellent. Secondly, there is the excellence of completion, where the entity is raised in status through the imposition and incorporation of some other reality. The introduction of formal rules into the fluent activities, the institutionalizing of prophetic utterances, the conversion of natural objects into the objects of a civilization are similar ways of being excellent. The first mode of excellence is not necessarily lost, and may in fact be exercised alongside of the new way. The enhancement of a completing unity takes advantage of that original excellence; it makes use of the object as at its best.

The alternative between a repetitive use of some principle in every context and the analogical use in different contexts, which characterize the Franciscans and the Dominicans respectively, is to be faced with a third or Lutheran alternative to the effect that the principle or Divinity is self-identical (with the Franciscans) but answers to the particular excellences of the different objects to yield what (with the Thomists) one can call analogical results. (This makes analogy not a method but a product, and this perhaps is the only useful form it has.)

The third way of being excellent is the reciprocal of the second. Here an entity functions as a completor. It gives itself, as it were, sacrifices itself and thereby while giving some other entity a higher dignity through completion, gives itself an excellence which comes from service. The Incarnation, the trying of criminals by the court, the imposing of reason on the world, the use of speech and categories, are different ways in which something becomes excellent by helping to enhance something else.

The fourth way is that of supplementation. This is a modification of something like the juncture of the second and third ways of being excellent. But it is a genuine and separate way. The being now has a place in a system, it has role and position, and by virtue of its being in that position it achieves the excellence of doing its job. My station and its duties, the *Monadology,* the view of the *Bhagavad Gita,* the cooperation and usefulness, the meaning of the parts of a harmonious object involve this type of excellence. As in the case of the others, this is compatible with all the others.

One can perhaps associate these different excellencies with the different modes. God is essentially the being whose excellence lies in being Himself; traditionally Actuality is that which needs only supplementation in order to at its best; the Ideal, as is evident in Aristotle, is that whose primary function is to complete, to add dignity and meaning to what is otherwise a mere potentiality; and finally each part in Existence supplements every other to make Existence excellent in every part but not as a whole.

This kind of associating of the excellences with the different modes must not be allowed to obscure the fact that all the modes are supplementary, completing and completed by others. This means not only that there are two types of togetherness (at least) answering to the supplementary roles of the modes and to their roles as completing and completed, but that the outcome of these roles is not an excellence except in an abstract sense.

The supplementary role of the modes is "at a distance," and allows for a prescriptive togetherness, whereas the completing-completed roles provides a descriptive togetherness. Each of these is perhaps subdivided into two types to give four kinds of togetherness. On this view the supplementary role will be primarily exercised by two modes, and the completing (descriptive) by two others. God and Existence would give the prescriptive, and Actuality-Ideal the descriptive.

April 2

Against Leibniz:

If God entertains all the "possible" sets of compossible worlds, He must entertain them in a disjunctive relation. Conjunctively they would make a self-contradictory set. The possible worlds He says have a degree of perfection and make a proportionate claim to exist. The existence is not integral to them; otherwise they would exist. God gives an existence to one of the compossible worlds. Why can He not give an existence to all of them, retaining the disjunctive relation which holds between them as in the mind? Is it that there can be no disjunction in fact? But disjunctions do occur in time and over species (that is why the Thomists invoke the principle of analogy). Is it that to make one universe it is necessary to exclude the being of the others? But why? Is it that God has only a certain quantum of energy and that if He endows one compossible set with existence He exhausts His capacity to create? Or is it that if He did make all the different sets exist, there would be no way of adding them up to make something more excellent than the best possible world, so that the making of the others to exist would be a superfluous act? The more He held them apart as disjoined existent worlds the more He would be unable to make them add up to anything, and thus He would not, on the basis of sufficient reason, have a reason for making others be. But then in what sense were they possible? Did not God's goodness exclude the state of possibility from anything that was less than the best possible set? Or must we say for Leibniz that a possible set of compossibles can be entertained in His mind in abstraction from His goodness and yet without making it a merely logical set, but allowing it to be one which makes, as he says, a claim to exist?

Also, Leibniz defines action as decreasing in effectiveness with distance; but this reverses the way in which he should proceed. Instead of supposing that there was a distance between monads or between composite substances, a view to which he is not entitled, he should have said that where we have vividness or clarity there we have not only action but nearness. Distance is then to be defined in terms of obscurity or lack of intensity, and not the reverse.

April 15

Using art in the broadest possible sense we can say it involves the imposition of man on Existence in such a way as to create a simulacrum of Existence, ennobled. When man acts on Existence primarily through his body we get the art of production, economics (?); if through his mind the art of communication and inquiry, the sciences; if through his will we get the art of conquest, e.g., turning things into property (to be distinguished from the study of politics which relates to public man and the Ideal); if through his emotions the fine arts. These different ways of acting are infected with the values and meaning of one another; there is for example no pure emotional expression, one unaffected by body, mind, etc.

Correlatively, social science can be said to be the imposition of Existence on man so as to create a simulacrum of Man, ennobled. When it acts on man primarily in the order of space we get anthropological and comparative studies; when in the order of energy we get vitality; when in time we get all three, history. History will divide into political, ideational, biographical and aesthetic, depending on whether it makes evident the will, mind, body or emotions of man.

Returning to art, since Existence has three strands, space, time and energy, we evidently have the following basic fine arts: emotional reconstruction of space, of time, of energy. We must now account for architecture, dancing, poetry. These combine the first and third, the first and second, and the second and third. All three are combined in opera, drama.

Each of these arts is dominated by conditions offered by one of the modes. Taking the standard given by the Ideal we get comedy and tragedy in all these arts; if God, we get destiny and fortune; if man we

get slavery and mastery; if Existence we get order and novelty.
We then have: painting
music
sculpture

architecture
dancing
poetry

drama

We must take account of prose, (novels), gardening as a type of sculpture, pantomime as a type of acting, etc., and show what is the meaning of comedy and tragedy, destiny and fortune, slavery and mastery, order and novelty in all the arts. Shall we say that comedy comes out as a special case of criticism, and tragedy of appreciation; that destiny comes out as a special case of completion, and fortune of accident; that slavery comes out as a special case of the authenticity of the medium, and freedom of man's conquest of it; that order comes out as a special case of rules, and novelty comes out as a special case of spontaneity? If so we get the following approaches to all the arts:

1] Criticism and Appreciation

2] Aim and Accident

3] Authenticity and Conquest

4] Rules and Spontaneity

The Ideal *1]* provides a test of excellence; *2]* of worth; *3]* of creativity *4]* of degree of individuality. They need one another.

April 16

Susanne Langer in *Feeling and Form* deals with the arts as constructing new domains. She thinks these are "illusions." Avoiding this supposition (which would also make the world of society and state, of history and religion all illusory), we can say with her that each art produces a simulacrum of something real in Existence. It transforms Existence so that Existence has a new role analogous to that which it had before. Taken in this sense there are three basic arts: architecture which gives us a new space in which we are to live; discourse which gives us a new time, and music which gives us a new energy with its own rhythms. All these intrench on one another.

Inside the basic space of architecture is sculpture which fills space, and orders it; inside discourse is story which fills and redefines the nature of time; inside music is acting. We can recognize painting to be a more radical way of dealing with space than architecture, one which does not allow any additional filling; we can take poetry to be a similar final use of time, in which there is no reading or acting or gesturing which can add to it (except in the way framing a picture helps it); and we can recognize a more radical way of using the energy of Existence in dancing as a finality. There is still the film, opera, photography, gardening, cooking, etc., to be explained. These are all non-basic, and belong inside the basic ones—film goes with painting, gardening with architecture, opera with music and dance; cooking goes under architecture. What of photography, and what of the sensuous enjoyment of the various arts? Is not photography a subdivision of the architectural realm, so that it is quite distinct from film? Is not the enjoyment of a smell or taste, and thus the outcome of the cooking, etc., a form of the art of music?

April 17

Just as painting does in a more radical way what architecture does, and thereby precludes a subordinate art such as sculpture, just as poetry radicalizes the activity of discourse and has no such subordinate art as the novel; just as pantomine radicalizes music and has no such subordinate art as drama, so property radicalizes conquest, invention radicalizes science, and work radicalizes economics.

We approach the world primarily through the agency of our bodies to make an economic domain; we thereby reveal that the arts which make use of economic materials (and in the end all do) have an aspect which can be brought under economics. Similarly the use of will in the arts means that they can also be brought under conquest; and the use of the mind in the arts means they can be brought under philosophy.

We can approach nature as open to mind, body, will and emotions. When we do this we say that it is to be grasped in the abstract, by control, by dominance and by interplay. How does this approach differ from that which yielded science, economics, conquest and art? In no way. What we have in addition is a division in terms of A] whether men are concerned with some other mode of being than Existence, and B] how they deal with the different strands in Existence. The forms will give us enterprises concerned with the Good, God and Nature. These should be approachable in terms of mind, body, will and emotions too, and if they have subordinate parts, there should be subdivisions. Each subdivision presumably will subsume some activities and have final ones too.

April 18

Since it is possible to convert a cave into a home, there is a way of having something approaching architecture through intent. Perhaps we ought to distinguish an artifactual area as provided by intent in architecture, an art which is merely building something, and fine art which is architecture proper. Analogous to the artifactual area of space is the artifactual area of time which is provided by expectation and which dictates the length of discourse, the rhythms of speech, etc. Similarly there is an artifactual area of energy taking the shape of a pulsation and which is produced by an attitude of identification or adoption inside of which the music can occur. Architecture, discourse and music, as it were, provide firm boundaries to what was achieved through intent, expectation and adoption. In the production of the boundaries something is added.

We live in the world of artifacts from the very beginning; there is still however a mode of life outside this area; we do fall like stones. The artifactual world is real with its own logos; the alternative theory is that the natural world is real and art is an illusion, an exteriorization, etc. If the second theory were correct, we would have to say for similar reasons that society, law, history, politics, as well as the distinction between property and possession, tort and injury were illusory.

The expression of the will on Existence gives us conquest; on the Ideal, Ethics; on God, worship; on Actuality leadership. Mind on Existence is science, on Ideal is mathematics, on God is theology, on Actuality is cosmology. Emotions on Existence is art, on Ideal is mythology, on God is faith, on Actuality is love. Body on existence is economics (?), on Ideal is ethical behavior, on God good works, on Actuality is making.

April 19

If fine art, economics, science and social living together constitute art, and if this makes a separate domain, each of these divisions and the whole should be able to function on man once again, and should be able to act on the four modes again. If we suppose that the the reciprocal of art is history, then all the arts together will, as imposed on man, constitute an artifactual history, the history of man as already in civilization. Such a history should divide according to the divisions of the arts. It should show:

Existence dominating mind   to yield industrial history: the market
                        will   moral history: sports
                        body   geographic history: environment
                        emotions   myth: stories, lore

Existence, since it breaks up into energy, space and time, should divide once more; to stay with the last case, the reciprocal of art, we ought to have space dominating the emotions, which is the ethos, time dominating the emotions which is the temper, and energy dominating emotions which is the vitality of a people. And so on with the other parts of man.

Since the product of Existence on mind, and conversely, is a separate domain, we ought to have a kind of history in which Art affects Existence, and we ought to have a kind of history in which, say, industrial history affects Existence; and we ought to have a kind of art in which history is affected by man, and a kind of art in which music, say, is affected by man.

April 25

It is the task of the actor to behave in the light of an assumed motivation. This motivation characterizes his "character." It has the form of a conditional contrary to fact—"If I were Romeo I would kiss Juliet vigorously, on first seeing her." The actor has here lost himself in the part of Romeo in a given situation. A man in ordinary life perhaps would say "If I were Romeo I would not die for Juliet." He, this unique individual, would then exhibit his own character, and not that which the situation is thought to demand as a dramatic and effective enterprise. The critic stands in between these two. He would say to the actor, "You are too old and fat to play Romeo, and the situation calls for kindness and timidity any way"; and he would say to the individual, "If you would not die for Juliet you wouldn't be Romeo." The true teacher has the same attitude.

The actor purges himself as it were of pity and terror as surely as the audience does; the simulation of the motivation is analogous to the adoption of the actor's position. The emotion of the actor is dynamic, that of the spectator is produced; the one thrusts forward, the other builds up within; the former is the implicative power for obtaining the consequences; the latter the sustaining substance of the watching of the play.

April 26

The tragic hero has a kind of pity for other men and is aware of the vastness of, and thus has some terror in the face of the universe. The actor is like him, though his feeling is simulated; he takes a role because his focus is the universe and men; in the course of a response to them, as the loci of the grounds for the pity and terror, he purges himself, makes himself one who acts regardless of the fruits, with detachment from the realities of the world; he does justice to the situation but does not involve himself. This does not mean that he does not act with his full being, but only that his emotions are not those which he would have as an individual.

The individual responds as himself and makes the situation conform to him, and in this way is like the hero too. The hero is an individual in a role, and the ordinary man and the actor each stress one part of this; the ordinary man learns to become detached, the actor learns what it is to be involved in himself. Perhaps then the actor acquires pity and terror? No, for then he would not feel relieved when it was over; he learns though what it is like to be worthy of pity and terror.

The critic is like the tragic hero; so is the teacher except that the beginning for critic and teacher is simulated and referred to another; they are heroes vicariously. The spectator is like that too but he focusses instead on the situation and is thus like the actor.

April 29

Through the agency of mind, body, will and emotions man tackles the external realities. If his object is to master Existence he engages in science, work, dominance and art. Such mastery enables him to make as his own what is external to him. The Existence remains external in fact, but he does achieve it in art in somewhat the way he achieves it in judgment—we deal with abstract or symbolic features and subject them to new relations which are maintained by us, and thereby have the entire reality in controllable terms, though in an abstract form. We have the world within us or for us as subject to a limitation. But that world is real in the sense that the implications, to which it subjects the initial data and thus the actual items as apart from our new implications, do affect the careers of the initial items.

For me to know that something is an oak is to bring it into relations with other trees not there present; I also implicate it in the world of tables and chairs, with Oak street and with people living in Oklahoma. All art has this status. The space in a painting is not an illusion. The colors in the painting with their shapes are made (via our emotional apprehension) to have new relations and thereby define and give us possession of real space, though of course in our context. The brute reality remains outside.

Kant's first *Critique* might be said to give us a set of conditions for knowing which could be carried over for art as well, since the categories re-organize the manifold and give it a meaning it otherwise would not have. One need not go with Kant and suppose the manifold is without any meaning or being, unless one assumes it to be brute matter which remains outside whatever context we deal with. But if knowledge be one context, the manifold for it could be well-organized by some other context, for example art. Is there then a manifold neutral to all possible contexts and approaches by man? I think we do not need to affirm that there is.

We also have the fact that pity and terror are purged in drama because they are modes of living through the drama in the idealized situation; they are expressed in that context rather than in the rough. Is there not a similar purging of other emotions for the other types of art—spatial and temporal ones? There should be. There must then be various kinds of emotion.

Spinoza's list: fortitude: strength of mind or desire to preserve oneself and generosity or desire to help another. Then we have joy and sorrow, astonishment, contempt, love, hate, inclination, aversion, devotion, derision, hope, fear, confidence, despair, gladness, remorse, commiseration, favor, indignation, over-estimation, contempt, envy, compassion, self-satisfaction, humility, repentance, pride, despondency, self-exaltation, shame, regret, emulation, gratitude, benevolence, anger, vengeance, cruelty, fear, audacity, consternation, moderation, ambition, luxuriousness, drunkenness, avarice, lust. There is no terror on this list (commiseration is pity).

If we have pity and terror in connection with "energy," in connection with time we ought to have the feelings of concern and fear, and in connection with space we ought to have the feelings of compassion and alienation. How different are these characterizations? The names do not seem well chosen; we must show the common nature characteristic of Existence as affecting the individual and as affecting all of us men.

May 2

Answering to the pity and terror of tragedy is the diffidence and despair of comedy. In both cases there is a dramatic presentation with a "psychic distance" enabling one to engage in the emotions which would be spent awkwardly and with human involvement in ordinary life. In comedy the diffidence one has of oneself is overcome in the defeat of the pretensions of another; and the despair one has that mankind will ever overcome the world is overcome in the recognition that there is a prevailing value and truth despite what men do. And in each of the arts there must be an answer to these four emotions—pity and terror, diffidence and despair. In fact there are three ways of answering them:
A] With the *Gita* one can act in the world with detachment. The emotions are themselves involved but are purged in fact because the situation

is given an artistic boundary. This is roughly what one does when one anticipates that a cave is a dwelling, that prescriptive grammar is a world of discourse, and that adoption yields a world for a conquering energy. B] Classical art starts with man-as-involved-in-the-world who makes a new world detached from it in which the emotions are purged. The representationalism of classical art need go only so far as to elicit the simulacrum of the emotions which are to be purged. The distance between A and B is not very great. This is easy to see in tragedy and in comedy. But we can also see it in architecture and music, etc., for we there note the reorganization of what we already in a way encounter, and live through it with a vitality which expresses either our terror or despair, or our pity or diffidence.

c] Modern art does not begin with a world in which we are emotionally involved but rather attempts to give us a world which has its own rationale and in which the emotions are elicited for the first time in the way we want them to be. Thus while classical art shows us how to become detached, the modern starts with a detached world.

If one takes A to be a first stage of B, i.e., if one takes us to already engage in artistic activity by the very fact that we respond to something as tragic or comic and thus give it some detachment from the totality of natural occurrences, we can say that A and C do somewhat similar things, for in the case of C we convert raw material into a new world, and in A do so but preliminary to the reusing of the product to make still another world. We could therefore envisage a stage D, following C, where the modern art was thought to give us a material which we could use to give a more dramatic form. E.g., if modern architecture is the frame for modern painting, we can see the former as a kind of eliciting of emotions which are purged but in too large a context, and the concentrating of those emotions in a more controlled situation. Painting would then stand to architecture somewhat the way in which a dramatic tragedy stands to an actual occurrence which has either been evaluated as a real tragedy or which has been even more deliberately sundered from the context of the actual world.

When in art we make a new space, time, energy, and thus Existence, we are in effect conquering the exterior Existence in somewhat the way in which we conquer it when we know, for though we do not destroy it and in fact though we subjugate it to new conditions, we have it in a fresh and manipulatable way. A painting is neither two nor three dimensional; it is colored shapes which behave as volumes in three dimensional ways; we, through their means, have control over a space which otherwise would confront us with arbitrary neighbors and activities and therefore would make us sooner or later bring about real pity and terror, diffidence and despair.

May 3

Since in our acknowledgement of ordinary experience we subject what we confront to some kind of encapsulation, and thus in some way follow out a Kantian treatment of a "raw" manifold, there are two directions in which we can then go: we can continue the process of encapsulation or categorization, or we can continue to focus on the content. If we do the latter, we keep to the emotions which we initially elicited, but now elicit them in a new way, as having a psychic distance and thus as being capable of being purged. If we do the former, the new categories will produce a new content and thus will involve a new eliciting, and thus presumably a new set of emotions other than those which we had when we initially encapsulated or categorized. This is the procedure of modern art.

We engage in art in order to conquer Existence via the use of the emotions. That Existence had conquered individuals and man, and that is why we see it as the ground of pity and terror. But this is only to say that we approach the world as already caught within the patterns of history; it is the awareness of historical man as subject to forces of Existence that sets the problem. We must first neutralize the historic stress by virtue of our initial encapsulation and emotional response, and then we must continue to satisfy those emotions in a controlled setting, or produce new content and thus new emotions under control. Presumably there should be a reverse stress coming from history which confronts the arts of man.

The mind faced with Actuality finds it absurd in its individual guises and disordered in its cosmic form. The Existentialists see this. But what they do not see is that the mind can now proceed to re-present the occasion for the absurdity and disorders, and thereby get rid of it through purging; or that it can proceed to reorganize the content of Actuality so that we can see the whole without any absurdity or disorder. The systematic existentialist concerned with therapy does the first. The philosopher does the second; the mind which faces Actuality in this guise is one which is somehow captured by Actuality. We conquer Actuality by freeing it from this capture and then going on to have it more dramatically or in an entirely new guise. We therefore move on to such an approach as that of *Nature and Man* where we see man conquering the forces of nature through an eventual understanding of himself. (Or should it be said instead that this is the function of epistemology?)

From the perspective of the body, individual man is alone and mankind is without meaning. The practices of the individual are found to be repugnant and those of mankind to be futile. The body is therefore driven to engage in work of a sacramental sort. In this way God is brought in to fill up the emptiness of the individual. We assume to begin with that God has already caught the body within His orbit; the repugnance we find in the individual acts and the futility of men are then reflections of the fact that they are being judged by God. The effort of the body should be to recover man from this control. The first act is to neutralize the judgment of God by virtue of an act of control by men. This control can be increased, thereby altering the significance of man, or its initial product can be re-presented so as to enable one to exhibit the control in a new way. If we do the first we have the work of service and charity; if we do the second we have the use of symbols.

Finally the will is faced with Ideality. Ideality, as overwhelming man, reveals him to be individually perverse and collectively undeveloped. The will endeavors to free man from this dominance, by continuing the process by which the recognition of the perversity and undeveloped form was begun or by engaging in new activities (ethical) which would elicit new usages of the will. In the former way there is a rectification of the will, the submission to the dictates of obligation, whereas in the latter way there is a creativity of the will which controls the obligation.

In summary we have:

Our answer

emotions elicited by a conquering Existence; art
mind   elicited by a conquering Actuality; existence
body   elicited by a conquering God; service
will   elicited by a conquering Ideality; ethics

The reciprocal of the above answers tells us what the nature of the domain is defined to be by a conquering mode of being. When Existence conquers we have history; when Actuality, cosmology; when God, divine judgment, and when Ideality, politics. If this is correct we have the following pairs: art and history; existenz and cosmology; service and divine judgment; and ethics and politics. If this is so *Nature and Man* must be a form of existenz in which an attempt is made to show mind freeing itself from Actuality and allowing us thereby to overcome the attitude that man is individually absurd and collectively disordered. By Existence then is meant the conquest of limitations; Existenz philosophy says that this conquest is to be achieved by re-presentation; in *Nature and Man* it is done by reconstruction and thus by creative work changing the content.

May 4

The case of God and of the Ideal were not properly worked out yesterday. What should have been said is that we confront man in the stage where he is overwhelmed by God both as an individual and collectively. This evokes in us an awareness or an attitude which reveals that man is insignificant, and that mankind is engaged in a futile struggle. Through the agency of our bodies we sacrifice ourselves on behalf of the individual and engage in service on the part of the whole, thereby overcoming in a controlled way this failure to have encompassed God properly. It is by a proper control of God through sacrifice and service that we possess Him and thereby complete ourselves, though to be sure only in the shape of ourselves as having worked.

The Ideal overwhelms the individual and the collective, making the one a failure and the other incompetent, without genuine integrity. This evokes in us a need to will. Through the agency of our wills we obligate ourselves to act on behalf of the individual and to partake of community work so as to act on behalf of the whole. We thereby master the Ideal which otherwise remains outside, overwhelming man.

There is a sense in which comedy offers a rectification of tragedy. If tragedy is the awareness of the regrettable mastery of one of the modes on man, individually or collectively, comedy is the rectification of this in that it sees the side where the mastery is good. The individual is seen with detachment and the whole with objectivity as properly assessed by the mode. When in the course of any artistic creation we tend to become too involved in pity and terror, the comedy enters to show the value of the overcoming. The comedy of course has its own value. The individual and the people are seen in ordinary experience as properly suffering from a dominance by a mode; this we can see just so far as we are impersonal and detached. But such impersonality and detachment could make us cold; the idea of dramatic comedy is to control these attitudes so that we can spend them without "fruits." This means in connection with tragedy, that we can view ourselves as beginning with raw experience and as providing a kind of impersonal and detached way of handling it (as Kant does with the categories) which give us confidence and judgment that the right prevails. We can then go on to a representative form of this in drama where the content is refined, or to a more modern form of comedy where there is an imposition of a new set of dominant terms, e.g., Existence in a new way.

There ought to be four types of comedy—answering to an appreciation of Actuality, Existence, God and Ideal; and these four types should break up into the case where we face the individual and where we deal with mankind. Comedy in connection with Existence is dramatic comedy; in connection with Actuality is the recognition of man as one being among many; in connection with God it is the comedy of salvation of individuals and mankind; in connection with Ideal it is the comedy of the final worth of man achieved through his finding a place in a rational evaluative order.

Remaining wholly within the area of art, and thus considering only the problem of Existence as confronted through the emotions, we must conclude that comedy is a recovery in the direction of history, but history seen as redressing the stress which makes for tragedy, i.e., the stress where Existence overwhelms man and thereby elicits our pity and terror, Comedy, in contrast, by virtue of our detachment and objectivity, is seen to re-assert the rights of Existence and the recovery thereby of man's rightful plane.

The transition to history from art requires the gift of comedy, just as the transition to art from history requires the awareness of tragedy. And just as in the latter case the art enables us as it were to intensify this recovery from the objectivity and impersonality of history, so comedy enables us to intensify the activity of freedom which history will provide for the excesses of art or the involvement in pity and terror.

We laugh in comedy because, identifying ourselves at once with man and Existence, but holding to an objective position, we recover man as properly placed, and thereby in fact enhanced, for it is only by virtue of his being placed in the context of Existence that he is fully himself. We cry in tragedy because, identifying ourselves once again with both factors, we recognize that man has a dignity and value which is being crowded out by Existence. The real objective of both comedy and tragedy is the recovery of a midpoint, where man is in a proper relation to Existence. If we insist on the tragic element we are bound to awaken the comic and conversely. To be sure the tragedy and comedy are inside a drama; but the position can be generalized, so that when we have the tragic element dominant what we find coming to the fore is not the comic dramatic element but the comic element as recognizing the neglected right of Existence with the consequent recovery of man. If we had a re-assertion of a comic dramatic element then within the frame of the drama where Existence is in fact being redefined, we would merely emphasize its meaning more than we had; our ordinary response to drama, and this whether it be tragic or comic, is to re-assert the comic side. The natural role of Existence, Existence as not yet redefined by us in drama, is made manifest in history and it is to this history we inevitably turn in order to overcome the bias of art.

"History" here is perhaps a misused term; for what is intended is not history as merely temporal but as spatio-temporal-energetic and thus as Existence involving the mastery of men. In a tragic drama the recovery of the proper position is not of course the assertion of Existence as dominant over men (for this is what the tragedy shows) but a simulated form of this. So that we can say the comic spirit forces us from the dramatic tragedy to historic tragedy, so far as the latter is understood to express justice, the proper role of real Existence as dominant over real men. The revolt is in fact not against the dramatic tragedy but against art itself as involving the use of Existence, the subjugation of it, even when it is given the role of being a dominant factor. Just so the revolt against history as expressed in the tragic spirit which makes art possible and relates it to play is not a revolt against history as such but against any excess dominance, and the incapacity of man to manipulate Existence. What we want is not to repeat the history but to overcome its dominating Existence, which we discern is tragic; the achievement of art is therefore a relief, since it overcomes what we saw before was tragic. Just so the return to history which is prompted by the comic spirit ends with a kind of deflation since we then find ourselves and mankind and others caught within the control of a dominating Existence.

Men seek relief from objective Existence in art, from God in service, from the Ideal in ethics, and from Actuality in a kind of phenomenalism of appreciation. Such relief is achieved through the provocation of the tragic spirit and ends with this spirit being spent (either with respect to refined content or a new kind of content) in a harmless though dramatic way. Men on the other hand seek a resolute objective truth by moving under the stress of the comic spirit from art to history, service to worship, ethics to politics, and appreciation to knowledge. Once they attain that position they are deflated, lose their vitality, and merely live shorn of "fruits."

The comic spirit in the various arts—architecture, sculpture, painting; discourse, poetry, drama; music, acting, dance—is thus to be understood either as allowing inside the dramatic work something of the import of history, or it is to be understood as in fact forcing us to attend to an external history so as to redress the art itself. It functions as the former when we get dramatic comedy; this tells us, within the context of our control of Existence, that Existence ought to be in control.

May 5

There are two kinds of rectification which a tragedy requires. There is the one within which involves the recognition of the dignity of the human spirit that shines through the crushing of an alien mode of being. And there is the rectification which results from the recognition that there is a pretension to human beings which deservedly is crushed. This latter is what is made evident by the comic spirit. The rectification of tragedy in these senses comes inside the area of the art. There is also the rectification which is provided by the recognition that there is a world outside the art and that there the forces of alien modes of being dictate what in fact will occur. This rectification is supplemented by one which takes men sympathetically in the concrete, recognizing that they are worthy of love.

This four-fold rectification of tragedy is met by a four-fold rectification of comedy. A comedy awakens our awareness of the pretensions of man. It is rectified by an awareness that man has some dignity of his own; and is rectified also by seeing the rights of the mode of being to define what a man should be. The former is the alertness of the sombre and tragic possibilities in man. There is also the external rectification which consists in seeing that exterior man has his rights, and that if men identify a mode with themselves it is in the end vain.

There are then two recitifications within and two without; the rectifications within involve either the acknowledgment of the rights of one component of a combination of man and a mode of being, or the use of the correlative efforts of comedy or tragedy. The rectification without is the acknowledgment of some reality outside art, either the mode or man, or it involves the recognition that men deserve love or criticism. The comedy needs rectification in the shape of tragedy, or in the giving us a proper perspective on the nature of a mode and man in relation to it; it needs rectification on the outside of itself, as an art form, through the giving of a genuine status to the mode as that which does not allow a man to identify himself with it, or as cutting away from all reference to a mode and recognizing that man has rights which he is to maintain on an objective basis.

May 6

The rectification of comedy would seem to be the stress on the value of a mode of being in itself, apart from men, and the turning away from man in the drama to a consideration of the real mode of being as dictating the proper position which man should occupy. If drama be as basic to reality as the so-called natural world, perhaps one beginning is in puns and play, from which we move not to art but rather to nature or history, where the comedy can be rectified by giving the mode of being a proper role, so that in the end we come to say that man is properly evaluated. The movement then to an understanding of the different modes, particularly when one begins with the testimony in which the modes are involved with man, is essentially a movement in the spirit of comedy.

May 11

If, as Robert Thom suggested to me, the feeling of terror is expressive of a self-exposure of oneself, might it not be proper then to say that what tragedy awakens is a feeling of pity, terror and despair for the other man, for oneself, and for mankind respectively? I think we ought to go on too and say that there are three kinds of conditions for the coming to be of comedy. There is the taking the stance of art. Here there is an acceptance of the artistic condition, a condition attained through the tragic acknowledgment of a crushing reality. There is also the acknowledgment of the right of the artistic form to dominate and transform the items with which it deals. Finally there is the return to the real world with the admission that its powers, particularly over against the pretensions of man, deserve to be dominant.

The primary stresses of comedy also ought to be three—oneself, another and the world beyond. The world beyond, or the power or right of some mode of being to assert that itself is objective; this is natural or divine comedy. There is also the right of another to maintain himself as over against the world and myself; this is the comedy of dignity of the unquenchable power of mankind. And finally there is the insistence on oneself, on one's own values, and thereby an insistence on one's superiority to others. In the case of oneself and the other, perhaps it is necessary to enter into a sphere where the exterior powers are first tragically acknowledged, so that we can have a norm in terms of which our pretensions can be evaluated.

May 13

We find Existence over against ourselves, other men, mankind and other types of reality. This awakens in us feelings of terror, pity, dismay and awe. It is the attempt to master these feelings and thereby to be in possession or control of Existence which drives us to art. The arts are divided into those which stress space, time and energy, and subdivide in each case into those which provide the frame, those which fill it out, and those which are final.

June 10

The world exhibits a constant re-aligning of values; new units appear and old ones disintegrate. The appreciation of the old ones, of the total situation which once prevailed, and the attribution of the elements of that situation to some residual item, as essential to it and its value, is what provokes despair; the appreciation of the new value, by virtue of the separation out of an item from a larger context as irrelevant and obscuring, is the occasion for the provocation of a feeling of hope. To control these emotions, and thus to purge them, we continue the process of re-alignment begun in nature, either by emphasizing the act of separating out of a situation, or the nature of this which is being separated out, so as to give modern and classical approaches to the item. Art is produced as a controlled epitomization of the process which originally provoked the feelings of despair and hope, expressed as pity and terror on the one side, and of impartiality and confident detachment on the other. The movement to the realm of art can be viewed as itself a kind of abstracting of the individual, and thus as justifying despair, or as a kind of finding of the entity's proper meaning or career, and thus as justifying hope. In either case the resulting art can itself be treated as an object which deserves to be criticized for tearing men away from their proper place, or as deserving praise because it at last enables things to be in their perfect epitomized status.

December 31

Some of the various occurrences which I face daily are unified by me to constitute concrete correlates of my experiences. I possess them, take them to be mine. What I do not possess I attribute to others, if the same in quality with what I do possess. The more surely I infect the ones I possess with myself the more surely must I do a similar thing for their similar correlates. I take this to be my act of pained experience only so far as I also take a similar act to be owned by others, and conversely. In some cases I start with my fragment and in other cases with theirs. We can be mistaken as to just what is possessed. It may be that what I take to be like my material is not; in that case I am wrong to say that it belongs to another. In some cases I am glad that he or I is not aware of a certain type of experience that is thought to accompany a public activity; we don't want pain. It is possessed but the absence of pain means that some parts of the possessing experience will not occur. In some cases we regret that we do not have the accompanying experience—e.g., certain types of moral action. This means that we think the experience would make some items occur in the future which we do not want to occur. But though not experienced the items are thought to be possessed by the "character" of the individual.

If no one possessed the residue which we do not, we would view the whole of what we do not possess as owned by some supernatural being and focalized into apparently possessed items, deceptive counterparts of our own. To get over the acknowledgment of other minds then, we must suppose a God who deceives. Not because God is not a deceiver but because we do not see why we should suppose there is, we take the counterparts of our possession to be real counterparts, possessed by focalized substantial beings in fact.

When and as we undergo our own private inward experience we adumbrate the other's. Physical occurrences have a unity only so far as they are united with an adumbrated intensive unity. If we start by acknowledging such an intensive unity we can affirm that the plurality of dispersed occurrences which we encounter belong together in fact. We have a world of laws and publicly separated occurrences only because of the possessive note we acknowledge in them, referring to another's intensive unity. If we start with the public set we recognize an intensive unity for them which remains the meaning to which they are contributing. They tell us what the possesser is. We want possession to define the order, the character. If he has no consciousness it is still his, but without sufficient control.

January 27

In the realm constituted by art, i.e., apart from the perceptual object, the art work is the Actuality, i.e., takes the role of the Actual; Existence is the space, time and energy in the work of art; the Ideal is the prospect which the artist tries to achieve, and the artist as the unity for the art is in the role analogous to the God of the *Modes.*

If we look at different types of workers they have different positions towards their work. Thus the artist is like God, but the scientist is like the Ideal, the politician is like Existence, and the existentialist is like Actuality in role and position.

Is it correct to say that the art work is the artist endlessly multiplied under new conditions? Is creativity externalized in a plurality of external identities? Is the prospect of the artist his way of encompassing all that he does? Is the space, time and energy of the art, the artist externalized? None of these seem very plausible; if they do not apply, the analogue of the artist and God falls to the ground, at least if God be understood as in the *Modes.*

Creation is the articulation of a sense of beauty, the finding that, beginning here in the making we are forced to do thus and thus there. Each step is an adventure. We can know that the result is right only by virtue of our recognition that the indeterminate beauty is being made concrete; we must sense its embodiment, recognize that it is being formed without distortion. The problem then is like the problem of recognizing a Platonic form, or better an Aristotelian essence as it alters its specific nature from case to case. To suppose the form or essence does not do this is to suppose that it rides on the surface of the matter or locus. If the form becomes integral in different places it alters. In what sense do we then have the same form; when can we tell if it has been distorted? Is it that the form has implications, a career, consequences of its own, and we can tell if the form is distorted by seeing if it can do these things? Thus if a man's soul has been distorted by his body, or blocked by it in some way, it must be manifest in the shape of perverse actions, and perhaps in the discrepancy between the soul and the body. We have a distorted form when it does not fit properly, when there is an unused surplus of matter.

But this would be tantamount to saying that excellence is in the fitting of form and matter, in the complete articulation of the matter, the permeation of it by that form so that its career is governed by the form. If that were the case in what sense is the beautiful different from say the form of cat as in a cat?

Would "beauty" be but the name for any form as fully articulated? No: the sense of beauty, the form of beauty allows for all forms; it is a transcendental, a sense of the fittingness of any form with its matter, and in the realm of art it is the articulation of a form in the matter of the art. But instead of there being a preconceived idea or form of some object which is then made articulate in the work of art, we have instead a process of articulation living up to the basic demand of beauty, and in the course of this articulation with these means in this place there emerges the nature of the form that is being articulated. The form is then made when and as the articulation or use of the matter takes place, under the guidance of the sense of beauty. This is something like the way the scientist works; under the guidance of the sense of truth he experiments here and there making some idea or meaning evident inside the frame of an existent world.

The artist humanizes the realm of nature, and in this process makes himself (as representative of man) manifest, so that in the end his work is an analysis of what it means to be a man in the universe. If we attend to the totality of art, Croce—as is almost inevitable in the light of his idealism—is right; art is expression. The intent of man in art is one with its achievement. Wimsatt and Beardsley are right that intent is in the object, but only where the object is all art objects and the intent is that of mankind as artist. The intent of mankind in art is one with its achievement.

January 29

Every being thinks it is doing something of importance. The fly sitting on the lion's tail thinks it is keeping the lion warm. And it is too, you know. But not as much as it supposes.

It is commonly accepted that the art object is self-enclosed. But the admission is almost immediately negated by two insistencies. The one which is most common is that the art object appeals to a man's feelings, or means those feelings or is to be understood in terms of those feelings. The other is that it has some bearing on society or men's attitudes. There is no question but that these may be outcomes and most desirable; what is in question is whether they are essential to the being of the work of art as a work of art. As something artifactual it is of course involved in the implications of human interest; as enjoyed it does have repercussions on man; as made by men and placed in a public setting for them, and even as something judged and thus faced by representative beings, it does have references beyond itself. To be it must mean in these ways. But it has been made to be, and it is a work only so far. If this be the case the meaning which it has is self-constitutive no matter where it originates. It is like an Aristotelian substance or the world as created by a God. The meaning in it is the articulation of the sense of beauty, the making of this concrete. There are as it were many possible worlds and the artist makes the best possible one be; it is the best possible because he is the creator who sees the defects in the others. We cannot measure his work by any other agency; we can only re-articulate it, analyze it, show how it does this and that, and how this helps that to make the whole.

From where do we get the sense of beauty? It is a generalization from experiences in nature, say of a non-useful but pleasurable kind; is it a derivate from some Platonic heaven, some highly general Ideal; is it some combination of these? We seem to be bound by our history in what we want to say in art, and yet we also seem to be able to criticize the past and go forward into new places. Is the category of beauty something a priori? But what warrant have we for saying this; what kind of meaning could we give it beyond identifying it with the transcendental ego or the absolute? It would seem rather to be possibility, the Ideal, the very same thing as the Good but now viewed not as subjugating the Actual, but as constituting it, as permeating it and reorganizing it. It is possibility in a new way of acting, the possibility as at home in the sensuous; it is less than the Good in the sense that it sees the Actual or Existence as being more than idea; it is more than the Good in that it infects the Actual.

If this be the correct meaning of beauty, there ought to be an analogous way in which the other modes function. Thus we ought to say that the Actual does not merely stand over against other things and somehow takes them to be extensions of itself; that the realm of Existence does not merely drag things along with it, and that God does not merely see all things as kinds of identity, but that there is a way in which the Actual adjusts itself to the others, that Existence takes account of their insistencies and that God preserves them in their root nature. These were seen to be true in the *Modes,* but what was not there seen was the fact that they define new usages of the four basic modes. The Good becomes Beauty; the realm of Actuality becomes the Human or Cognized when it accepts all else, merely permeating it with its own category; the realm of Existence becomes the realm of nature when it accommodates itself to all else; and God becomes the eternal judge and preserver when He allows all things to remain within the ambit of His being. In all these cases though the category functions as the generic concept "Being" does. In these cases the categorical meaning of a mode is that which makes itself be by diversifying itself in the body of the other modes, thereby providing testimony to itself as a unity and unifying element, but not necessarily as having a being outside those modes.

The Actual as having being in itself for example manifests itself in the other modes; it affects them but from its own standpoint it also subjugates them to its meaning or perspective. It is when it gives itself up to them, allows them to be its multiplicity with their own obstinate substantiality that it in fact is enabled to be itself over against the plurality, and in fact allows itself to provide testimony to itself. Testimony is provided when the reality accommodates itself to some other mode, but the testimony is not to itself as accommodating but to itself as capable of subordinating, as being something in terms of which the others are to be understood. In the domain of the activity the mode imposes a testimony to itself as outside the activity, as superior to all else.

Beauty then is Goodness as not subordinating, not obligating, not defining another mode, but as sacrificing itself to be integral to the other, thereby testifying to the reality of a Goodness which could subordinate what is in fact being organized. To understand making and art then we must see the obligating Ideal step down and do work, thereby losing its own self-sufficiency and unity but gaining body and accommodation. In art, in contrast with nature, the artist deliberately infects Actuality with Goodness or beauty, forcing a simulacrum of the Actual to be thoroughly infected with the Goodness, which is thereby multiplied, articulated, diversified and in that process deprived of its Goodness. The artist in effect takes his stand with Existence and not with the Good; the Good is instrumental, but in the course of his effort he turns it into an integral Beauty. When he looks to the realm of Existence, and instead of merely giving meaning to this from the perspective of the Ideal accommodates the Ideal to it, he makes the Ideal have the shape of an Architecture, Mythos and Music. (Does this mean that the accommodating to Existence as in the Actual has the shape of Sculpture, Story and Acting, and that the accommodating to Existence as in God has the shape of Painting, Poetry and Dancing? The Ideal for the artist accommodates not Actuality or God, but Existence as qualified by these. Were it to accommodate pure Actuality or God, it would be a Universal Form in Aristotle's sense—for the one, and a Measure for the other's being—in Plato's sense of the Good as a measure of the Demiurgos and of all else.)

We are driven to create because we are in one mode, take another seriously, and make use of the other two. It is the fact that we are here in the Actual looking at the Ideal which we would like to have here and now, not by submitting and acting for it, but by making it accommodate itself to us, that we force it to take the shape of a human political plan or an historic terminus or a destiny (so far as we make it consider the drives of Actuality, Existence and God as pertinent to man) or offer it fresh and more accommodatable material (Actual stuff) to which we add our action (Existence) and our own being as unities. Did we do the same thing with respect to the accommodation of Existence, we would offer Existence material, ourselves as unities and, instead of providing action, would provide it with some kind of meaning; this would give us the enterprise of science. Did we do the same with respect to the accommodation of God we would offer God material, ourselves acting and the Ideal as a meaning; this would yield a value-drenched, sacramental universe.

Is the accommodation of the full bodied Actuality to the Ideal a matter of craft, and the accommodation of representatives (or better of manipulatable portions of the Actual in the guise of mere matter) a way of engaging in an art? The craft could be engaged in a real making, but this is related to an end beyond; the art begins by taking boundaries, volumes, colors, language, sentences, rhythm, sounds, gestures and movements as its material, thought of as needing the Ideal in order to be self-contained; the craft starts with what is already a being and enhances this. Play makes something but does not enhance it with the Ideal; it opens up the material, whereas art in fact closes it by means of the Ideal. The material for art, though part of an Actuality, is offered as functioning for Existence, as a guise in which Existence appears. In craft it still is Actuality, and in play it is God as ignoring the need of the Actual to be governed rather than manipulated by God. Art takes an Actuality and makes it be manipulatable in the light of the Ideal—it goes towards the freedom of play. Religious participation takes an actuality and makes it feel the weight of God—it goes towards the craft of participation of observance away from the acceptance of destiny.

In art then the actual man offers his unity and action to make material of the actual world (functioning on behalf of Existence) accommodate the Ideal possibility, which as being so accommodated has the meaning of Beauty. Beauty has a different concrete form in each case; we know we have it when we have made the work into the norm for all others, in which each of the parts is expressive of its own sensuous base, the kind of dimension of experience it is to represent and the power to maintain itself as self-enclosed and thus as perfect. It is the self-enclosedness of the otherwise accidental which shows the presence of beauty. If we do not know what the beauty is, or that it is self-enclosed we must retreat back to the Ideal in the form of the Good and recognize what it demands in the way of unity, inclusiveness, enhancement on the part of what contains it. Accordingly we can approach art in terms of ethics in the sense of saying that were Actuality perfect in the sense of living up to the Ideal, the Ideal would be concretely Good, though it would have given up, so far, its own insistence on subjugating the Actual. But this perfected Actuality can provide a guide to us as to just what perfection is.

The work of art keeps insisting on the rights of the material to be what it had been, as ethics does not, and it diversifies the Ideal as the ethical does not. On the other hand, ethics perfects the thing as it is, allows a man to be more fully a man, whereas art manipulates the material. However, given the perfect man ideally conceived, the classical artist took this to be what he wanted to present in his work. This need not be done; the perfected man can stand merely as the concrete measure for the concrete work, to tell us what perfection in the concrete is like. The artist in short can look to the ideal perfect man to tell it of the kind of result that is to be reached, though by a different route than is followed to get that perfect man.

This is not to fall into the error of using a model for art which is alien to it. It is not to use man as the model for art. It is only to use man as perfected to give a concrete illustration of the lineaments of a perfect work – purity, fulfillment, composition and scope. (cf. Aquinas who has clarity, integrity and proportion, leaving out scope). So we get the perfection that ethics tells us to get but by an integration of the Ideal with a materiated Existence, in which the latter is allowed to show its quality and the former is forced to become articulated.

Like the idea of being, beauty has no meaning as in itself but only as diversified, but like the idea of the Good it has the power to control, though not by virtue of itself but by virtue of the fact that it is nothing other than the Ideal, forced by us to take up an accommodating residence in this insistent sensuosity.

When an artist has a specific idea in mind he makes use of a relatively concrete surrogate for the general idea of beauty which pervades every one of his works. As a rule he does not have such a surrogate; or if he has it he is not aware of it.

The perfect man has been made to be, partly through his own efforts. How can we use him as a model for the arts, particularly since in his case his being and nature is accepted, and the Good, which could be known apart from him, retains its integrity? The answer lies in the fact that once we accept the work of art as having a being in which the beautiful must be an ingredient the only thing needed is to complete the work, give it a completion through scope, purity, fulfillment and composition. In short we must start in art and once we are in it we have the same kind of problem we have in perfecting man. In both cases we know what we have—an Ideal which is to be embodied more fully than it has been. To be sure the completion in art does involve the making of the Ideal concrete and thus the further diversification of it, in contrast with the completion of man which requires only the embodiment of the Good. But on the one hand the Good in the concrete is distinct from itself in the abstract, and on the other hand the beautiful in the incomplete is continuous with itself in the abstract. The answer then is that the art object already defines the kind of thing which would complete it, and the artist in the process, knowing where he was and what its excellence was, should know whether he is or is not completing it. We who stand on the outside and do not know where or how he began can get into the picture through analysis and see that the whole continues what was in a part, it being understood that the nature of the part is changed when account is taken of the rest.

It is revelatory that Kant speaks of the Aesthetic Judgment primarily, rather than of the object on the one side or the process of creation on the other. Moreover his antitheses of idea and feeling throw the issue into a subjective frame. If there is to be reconciliation of idea and its other, it should be between idea and the sensuous content taken as that which is other than feeling—and here we come close to the use of the term Aesthetic in the first *Critique,* leaving the third to make a subjective reconciliation by virtue of a lifting up of the content into the domain where the idea is entertained.

Aesthetic distance can be understood to be nothing more than the isolation of the work of art, the holding it away from its environment and the observer, or it can mean the avoidance of intimacy, the allowing of the sensuous to become outstanding rather than the idea. But the latter way of speaking puts too much emphasis on the idea. Though it is beauty that is being embodied it is for the sake of possessing Existence that one creates. We are ethical to do justice to the Good, but we are makers of the beautiful for the sake of Existence in the guise of actual boundaries, volumes and spaces; languages, stories and meaningful wholes; energy, vitality, and creative fulfillment in action.

Were there nothing to works of art but the sensuous, they could be completed equally well in any number of ways; were there no standard at all possible, and thus no Ideal, we would be driven to rest with incomparable tastes. But we need not. It is right to criticize men for being superficial, insensitive, unperceptive, ignorant. We can see something in what the connoiseur shows us. Part of the problem about tastes is the fact that we do not know if those who disagree with us are in fact more (or less) sensitive than we, or whether they (or we) have allowed some extraneous factor to intrude. There is a disputing of tastes in the latter cases, not of the tastes themselves given these conditions, but of the tastes as allowed to be corrupted. And of course if we deny the legitimacy of the approach via the Ideal we have nothing but our several tastes—or we must use some external criterion such as the needs of society, etc., to guide us.

A statement that a photograph is "exactly like its original" really intends as Charles Morgan has pointed out, to say that the photograph represents "in an accepted convention of black and white." But is there then no value in the theory of art as imitation? Could we say that it imitates the way in which beauty is in fact exhibited in nature, though of course with respect to the new medium and thus in a new way? Must we then suppose a beauty in nature is first seen? Yes, but only as it has been approached aesthetically; it is this which is imitated, and that from which it originates is to be cued in the work of art itself.

Gisele Brelet has remarked that music "like sound, projects its form upon a background of silence which it always presupposes. Music is born, develops, and realizes itself within silence . . ." Does this mean that the energetic dimension which music masters is held over against the other dimensions of Existence, or over against everything else, or that silence is part of the very same dimension as the sound? The answer must lie in a distinction. There is the silence out of which music issues and into which it passes; this is outside the work and can be said to be the other dimensions. And then there is the silence which is inside the musical piece and it is this which is part of the very same dimension; it is only through silence-with-sound that we have music. The first form of silence is nothing but the background against which the music exists in the very way in which a picture exists over against nature. We could say if we want that the picture exists over against color, for it is a fact that there is noise in the world outside, which we call silence only over against the kind of sound we accept in music; just so we have color in the world but this is not the color in the painting.

The fact that there is a sensuous component in the beautiful would seem to require that the beautiful be experienced in order that it be, and in this respect once again it would differ from what is good. But the perfecting of the sensuous is an objective fact; music as unheard belongs with story; but of course the performed music must be heard, the performance involving a joint participation of maker and audience.

January 30

We have on the one hand the insistence of a mode in another; the other is viewed in terms of this. We have the embodiment of one mode in another; the other carries it. We have the transformation of one mode in another; the other alters it. Thus the Ideal makes Actuality, Existence and God intelligible, obligates and measures them. And a man realizes the Ideal in the shape of the Good, carrying it. And he makes himself and the Ideal over, adjusting one to the other, to make himself at the next moment, realizing a possibility there, giving it a determinateness it did not have. Accordingly we can make the following classification:

Insistent mode:	Receptive Mode:	Result: Receptive Mode is
Ideal	Actuality	Intelligible
	Existence	Futurity
	God	Measure
Embodied Mode:	Carrying Mode:	Result: Carrying mode is
Ideal	Actuality	Realized Good
	Existence	Purpose
	God	Excellence
Transformed Mode:	Altering Mode:	Result: Altering Mode is
Ideal	Actuality	Realization in time
	Existence	Ordered (change)
	God	Providential Intent

The ordered change in the last triad is what is "imitated" in art, through the use of entities serving to present the dimensions of Existence.

Each of the other modes—Actuality, Existence, God—can be treated as Insistent, Embodied and Transformed with analogous results. And each of them, as well as the above, has a private experiential meaning (e.g., art) and an objective one (e.g., history) which deal with the transformed Ideal and Existence.

Ruskin said that Bach had an incorrigible faculty for going on and on. This raises the question as to just when a work of art is completed. This is the counterpart of the question how long one must continue to work in a given medium with a given work in order that the beauty be exemplified. Having arrived at the exemplification one finds that it is possible to destroy it by continuing. The very meaning of beauty, in other words, requires that there be a definite ending or boundary to the work. And yet it would seem that the totality of sensuous content should be organized by the ideal beauty. This is true—but there is no ideal beauty except as mediated by a particular concrete idea and thus by a specialized and distinctive case of beauty. Because the universal beauty is not a single idea but the most abstract formulation of all actual beauties (which of course it makes possible in the sense that it functions as an Ideal transformed in organizing the material), one cannot bring all content together to make one beautiful object. Each limited expression of the general idea has its own scope. But this too is perhaps a misleading way of expressing the matter. It is the organizing of the sensuous content under the driving lead of the ideal of beauty that enables us to forge the kind of idea or form which is ingredient in that content in a beautiful way. The form itself must show its own limits, pointing to the fact that some other form, perhaps also beautiful, is now beginning to operate on the content, showing that we are reaching the limit of the previous form.

De Selincourt remarks: "The piece that seems long is the piece that has failed to suspend our consciousness of real time." This is but to say it is that which stops having the status of a work of art; the question is why does it stop? I have tried to indicate that it is when the content, which is being organized, ceases to embody the same unity it had. Now such a failure can be overcome by getting a wider idea than the one which prevailed just before and the one which is now beginning to be embodied; in short the work which is running on too long can be made part of a work which is longer than itself, thereby making the work which was running on too long find its own limit inside the larger. But this opens up another question: there comes a time when we have had enough of art and want to get back to life and the concrete. Why is this? Why does beauty pall? In part it is the fact that it is held over against the vital world, that we are fatigued, and that the kind of idea that beauty sustains in the concrete lacks the power that the real objects have. We after all must sustain the work of art by providing it with determinateness and implications, and to do this we must belong to the world and give up art, just as we give up thinking so that we can eat and sleep. The lower demands are insistent and presupposed by the higher.

It is also the case that when one has engaged in an art for a while one is caught within its orbit, and while possessing a critical power in one sense, a power of internally working on it with effectiveness, one at the same time lacks the power to see it from a distance, as something which another might note. It is not only that everyone needs the eye of another, and can provide that for himself only by starting off where another might be; it is the case that an art object has a double status. It is part of the world of art objects and the creative domain, and it is something which must be made to stand away from the rest of the world. After a while when we come to look at what we have done we see it in the context of other interests and discover not only the flaws which are discovered by other artists but see at last what its value is, its deadness say in comparison with the work of a master. This deadness is the objective component of that complex feature of the work of art, its being composed of an objective self-sustaining nature and a subjective engagement in it.

The foregoing is related to the fact that to be immersed in an art is to be incapable of significant thinking, and conversely. The problem of the art is the concretionalization of beauty via the bearers of Existence on the one hand, and some subordinate idea on the other; the problem of thought is the entertainment of a meaning, usually by an abstraction from an object, and the consequent immersion of that idea or meaning in the systematic context of meanings, or the Ideal. The processes are thus the reverse of one another. Even when we consider creative thinking as another variant on creativity we get a contrast. The creative thinker does entertain possibilities and does try to reach them through an effort which begins with some premiss or idea that can be thought of as a kind of matter for the prospective conclusion. But it is the case that the premiss is left behind on the one hand and on the other is *aufgehoben,* transformed, made to appear in the context of that which was before a general possibility. In thought we move to a pre-destined or at least preliminarily accepted possible end by coming under its aegis, whereas in the practical dimension we bring the possibility into the present and make that present accommodate it. If we followed out this procedure in thinking we would take a possible conclusion or outcome and make it alter the beginning. E.g., if we entertained as a final idea "cats are happy" because we took it to be true that "cats smile," the procedure in an art-wise way would be to make the latter into "cats happily smile"; in a creatively thinking way the conclusion or outcome would be "cats are manifestly happy."

Raymond Bayer: "What each and every aesthetic object imposes upon us, in appropriate rhythms, is a unique and singular formula for the flow of our energy." This is surely sound; what it says in effect is that the spectator's pace is set by the object's internal rationale, and that this pace is a matter of another rationale, which in some sense must match the other. We have here the analogue of knowledge; the ideas we obtain from reality need not duplicate those guises they have in the world, but they produce consequences at their own rate which at a given terminal moment should coincide with what is derivable from the world. Just so the spectator need not keep abreast of the object; the rhythms in him are his own, but they are rhythms which must coincide all along with the object's pivotal points. It is the spectator who is emotionally charged and the object which has a structure; the two are in accord but only in the sense that what was done to get a beginning for the spectator will, when done again at another point, find the spectator once again—or starting with the spectator, what was done to fasten on one part of an object, (while the spectator has an aesthetic satisfaction) will, when engaged in at another part, continue that satisfaction.

January 31

The most obvious truth for any one working in a given art is the self-containedness of the work, the fact that it is non-representational. But it is very hard to accept this with respect to the arts with which one has no acquaintance. A second difficulty is that every practitioner of an art recognizes that the art work is but a residue, and at the very best but part of the entire work of art; the process of creation is for some even the whole of the art, the art work being in fact irrelevant. But obviously from the standpoint of the spectator, since he begins with the art object, it is the art object which is either the whole of art or the major or central part of it. A reconciliation is possible here by recognizing both the process and the product to be in the domain of art, the creator stressing the one, the spectator the other.

Leo Steinberg offers three explanations to account for the rejection of representationalism in modern times and the apparent acceptance of it in previous ages: *1*] representationalism was adventitious and has now been avoided in what is today pure art (Fry, Barnes); *2*] previous art was one form, and we today have another (Ortega y Gasset and Malraux); *3*] modern art is representational (Steinberg). He ignores a fourth alternative; *4*] there never was real representationalism, even in the period where it is said to occur.

Is technique but the mastery of the conventions which have prevailed? This seems to be the case when we think of perspective, problems of color and depth. And yet to have no technique at all, to be a mere primitive or untrained worker in a given field would seem to be a disadvantage. There are in fact two meanings to technique: one is the mastery of the conventional usages, and the other is the disciplined use of one's tools. The latter is usually the product of one who has first immersed himself in the former and then freed himself. We become trained in a technique in the second sense by virtue of our participation in the first, and our ability to free ourselves from its restraints. We have then two kinds of failures in art: the remaining inside the conventional technique with the consequent reduction of art to craft and schools, and the being free of any technique and thereby avoiding the first failure by thereby not getting the success technique could have made possible.

We are left with two problems: the possibility that one who was not trained might train himself in a technique which is new. This surely is possible but rare, particularly since we cannot entirely free ourselves from some acquaintance with previous art forms, including perspective, rhythm, etc. The second problem is that it would seem to be true that Oriental art has remained within conventional techniques with profit, and (what is the other side of this question) merely to produce new techniques is to put a premium on novelty. Here perhaps we can say that the Oriental technique might be like the sonnet form—a deliberately accepted restriction inside which the new technique is in fact being developed. The innovator is not being taken as a model so long as we emphasize the fact that there is something gained in the training. Consequently the proper thing to say is that the technique in the sense of the conventional is good if A] it disciplines, and B] is used as a condition or restriction, a definition of an area rather than as constitutive, or as something which must be rejected and replaced by another technique (which of course would have its own conventional warrant and nothing more).

To return now to the first question of the self-enclosure of art and the ordinary man's response to it, it would seem a reconciliation is possible with the recognition that it is the work of art is a totality that represents, that it has its own mode of articulation of that which is faced in another way in perception, etc. What is being represented though, is not this or that object but something of the very being of Existence; we now learn what it is to be space and time and energy, by allowing it to function in ways in which it cannot in the common-sense world, due to the common-sense attitudes on the one side and the heterogeneity of random objects which hem them in on the other side.

Paul Klee: "The modern artist places more value on the powers that do the forming, than on the final forms themselves." Is it the case then, as Steinberg suggests, that the modern artist, recognizing the aboriginal power which he wants to depict, instead of following the classical lead and giving this an ideal expression, seeks to find or express its multiple forms? He sees the hand as force, grasp, rake, pestle, etc., and portrays these. Does this offer an alternative to the view that all art is contrary to fact conditional? I think not; it merely tells us what particular form of a contrary to fact we want to use. We must read the hand as in this or that position, whether it be idealized or not, as expressive of the meaning of hand or the power of hand or the power of Existence. The modern artist, though, may take the appearances as more immediately revelatory, whereas the classicist takes the ideal form to be so. For the one, the ideal form or classical approach hides the power; the reverse is the attitude of the classicist, for he supposes that the contingent forms which the power assumes in nature are masks, deceptive, hiding rather than revelatory.

Helmut Reinold says: "Music is sounding motion in temporal space." Here is an independent confirmation of the view of music developed from the consideration of Existence. He goes on to say: "The tension between the equipollent and complementary elements of time, motion and space is of the greatest importance for the understanding of music."

February 1

It is the peculiarity of play that it has no "closure" in the sense used by Gestalt. This is not true of games, work, craft or art. It can be said to be true of toil, but not because there is no closure but because this has been abstracted from. If this be the case, there is something odd about play, for unlike anything else it faces an open universe and does nothing about it. It is not concerned with realizing possibilities; but this is true one might say of toil as well. It is occupied with manifesting energy, of making oneself externalized, of expressing, not necessarily oneself but what one is or has, without intent or purpose. Toil is more limited, monotonous, whose justification would lie in having a proper terminus; it has no merit in itself, being deprived of the only thing which would give it merit. Play on the other hand has some merit or value in itself, not merely in the sense that it involves an improvement of tonality in the player, and gives him a needed release and adjustment in himself (for then it would have to be thought of as essentially therapeutic), but in its exploitation, its being a mode in which Existence in man is allowed to be Existence. Play is Existence coming into its own rights, joining the Existence which lies beyond, to make one cosmic in his rhythm and meaning. Taken in this way it is evident that there is a component of play in everything we do, even toil and drudgery, for we cannot help, when we act, meeting the rhythms of the external world and sharing in this release.

Craft is closer to work than it is to art, in the sense that it is occupied with means, though it makes and uses them beyond the strict needs of being merely means. It enhances the means, makes them means in the best possible way. Decoration would seem to be a craft which goes beyond this point. But to this one might reply that in the first place it is an art, though of a subordinate kind, and in the second place so far as it is a craft it is one which has been allowed to get in the way of its own necessities, except where it makes the means memorable, available, attractive in the sense of making one want to use them or own them for a proper end. We find play and art closer than craft and art. Like play, art has its elements of spontaneity and openness; it brings us back into the universe of Existence, allows us to join with the larger world. But unlike play, art has a value and a closure of its own; it makes something excellent, something primary whose carrier is subordinate to itself. In craft the decoration or aesthetic values help the means; in art it is just the opposite.

In sports and games play is subject to rules, conditions, arbitrarily defined closures; in art the closure is defined by the art itself, and the rules are generated and sustained in the production. Play leaves no residuum except a possible feeling of health. Games and sports have a residuum in the score and the memory of the process. It is in art that one has the product as an essential element, and treats this as a kind of residuum and summary of what had been done.

Another similarity between play and art (which is shared by the other forms of expending energy) is that they, despite their involvement in Existence, form a domain apart from the every day world and the world of nature. They produce items which involve new implications among themselves; they forge new links inside themselves to constitute new types of wholes. Game and sport do this too; theirs also is an encapsulated world. But work does not make a whole except so far as the end is brought about; toil fails altogether, it having implications only by virtue of its place in human interest and economy. But play is the exercise of forging new connections; this is also true of art. In work and craft and sport we get new connections but this is not the purpose.

Play and art then are human existence articulating itself in the arena of a larger Existence with which it joins at the same time that it holds itself off. Play and art reach out into a larger world but only to get to a limit within which they operate or use as an initial starting point for a further forage into the larger world. Each movement outward is however held to and added to by the player to constitute an open set of relations or, by the artist, a closed set having value in itself.

Art then is like play in being an opening into Existence with a forging of connections inside the captured domain. Like sport and games it has rules or techniques and can be pursued in terms of an outcome desired. Like work it is arduous and occupied with means, for the outcome is also the terminus and puts an end to the art as it does to work. Like toil it involves much preliminary and isolated activities of preparation — training, which is an important part of art learning, is in good part toil. Like craftsmanship, it is occupied with having and using means excellently.

Should there be two definitions: One for art and another for fine art? Shall we say that art is making something excellent come about; the pursuit of that which has great value, engaged in with sincerity and devotion, and that fine art is the production through the use of sensuous content of that which is beautiful or excellent? The attempt to relate the artist to the common man, which surely ought to be done (contrary to the romanticists with their insistence on a special breed of man or being as alone artistic), has led some thinkers such as Dewey to view art as a kind of craft, craft apparently being but an embellishment and continuation of work and play. But one can maintain the commonality of the artistic endeavor and artistic power in the same way one does the philosophical; all men express it but in different degrees. The artist carries out more persistently and representatively the very activities characteristic of others; this does not mean that it carries out the craftsmanship which all men might exhibit, but the very artistic effort which is distinct from craftsman-ship—but which like craftsmanship answers to a more basic need, that of self-completion through mastery, submission and adjustment.

All art uses pre-existent materials within which are fixed patterns. The text of the musician and the actor are more closely grained than the language usages with which the poet begins; the poet is freer in his use, he has a wider "text," but it is not mere words but grammatical words with the meanings of daily life with which he must begin. This does not show that he is engaged in a craft, but on the contrary that though he uses the materials of every day he goes beyond them to make something which adds to the patterns of every day determinations. Thus, it is necessary to go beyond my paper on the reality of the art object and recognize that the artist not only adds implications to natural objects but also to certain human artifacts. This recognition of course is already made in distinguish-ing the kind of field which architecture provides from the filling which painting gives that architectural space. We have accordingly the determi-nation which comes about through involvement in human artifactual situations, the determination which comes through the aesthetic use of this in an encompassing manner, the determination which results from the filling of that encompassing art, the determination which results from the creation of secondary arts, and the determination provided by putting it in a wider context of education, therapy, etc. This would seem to indicate that the art object is never fully determinate, particularly when account is taken of the fact that there are many more usages for it than we have already discovered. The physical object would seem—in consonance with the physical theories—to be a universal.

We need not suppose that all universals are abstract; there can be concrete universals, not in the Idealist sense of something which persists through time taking on new forms or shapes, but in the sense of being substantial, even individual in some respect, and yet lacking specification with respect to this or that set of universals. If this be the case it would seem that we cannot speak of actualities as being fully determinate. This truth is in a way affirmed in the *Modes,* for it is there said that fact is determinate. But even fact, and particularly past fact, would seem in one way capable of being lifted up and brought into a new context, as it is in the mind of God. This does not destroy the full determinateness of fact as in the past, but only its full determinateness as substantial or as part of a substantial whole. The most determinate aspect of the real in short can be thought of as indeterminate with respect to the kind of role it plays in the world. The very fact that a determinate reality can be made to function in mind or in theory, that it can be remembered, etc., means that without loss of its full determinateness as fact, it can be indeterminate with reference to its role in something more.

We have then the determinateness of a thing in itself, and the determinateness of its being. They are independent. The existence of art would seem to indicate, particularly when attention is paid to social contexts and subsidiary arts, that there is no end to the determinability of a being, until we have encompassed all the modes in all their specificity. We are moving more and more to full individual concreteness but never arrive there until we have in fact found the being in every context whatsoever. To be fully an individual then one must first find oneself in every possible context. Is it the case that we men are now in one sense in all possible contexts and are individual so far, and yet that we can be taken out of the contexts in which we are, or better that in some partial context, such as being in the space-time world, we still are indeterminate and can have determinations added? But were this the case in what sense are we capable of this additional determination? After all as involved in all the other modes we are presumably fully determinate; how then can something be added, without thereby making us be something other than the individual reality that we were, an individuality made determinate through participation in all the modes? Or must we not say in view of the fact that there is time in this space-time world, that no one of us is ever fully determinate, and if individuality means determinateness no one of us ever is fully individual? Would it not be better not to equate individuality and determinateness? But must not we go on and say that concreteness is partly indeterminate, and that it is only the wholly factual, as kept within the province of past time, that alone is determinate?

The more dimensions we add to a being the more categorial determinateness we provide, but the more open we allow it for relational determinations. Or should we say that the individual in his inwardness somehow comprehends and possesses all the categorial determinations and makes them specifically determinate—while allowing that he may be extrinsically determined in various contexts? This denies that the determinations affect the being. If this were the case we would have to say that the being of an art object is a kind of adventitious being added on and not really affecting the being of the physical thing. But the physical thing's career is involved. Perhaps we can say that it is involved in the categorial determination provided by being also a work of art, and that the specifications of the categorial determination do not impinge on the physical? This would be tantamount to making the specific determinations outside the realm of the physical, and yet is it not these which have their influence? Or is it? Is the determination of this picture as a Picasso effective with respect to the picture as physical, or is it only its status as a picture which is so?

As a being the object is complete so far as it falls into all the modes, and the picture is complete as already in the Ideal realm, even without appreciation. Appreciation gives it determinations inside that realm, which is but to say that the work of art becomes a work of art only through a recognition and not through a new involvement, except in the sense that new details are added. The object is complete categorially and is incomplete in time, in aesthetic status, in divine value, and in its own expression of powers. The paper on the objective status of art then needs to be qualified so that it is said that the work of art adds not to the physical object but rather to the real object as already idealized, as already involved in the dimension of the Ideal, and even in the dimension of the Ideal as involved with Existence. Human involvement is merely the making the possible dimension specific via the use of human effort and being.

February 3

If beauty is a controlling pervasive idea which becomes articulated in the course of a production, it would seem to be analogous to the transcendentals of being, unity, goodness, something which the scholastics recognized to pervade all the categories and not be subordinate to them. But there would seem to be some content to the term, and it is not altogether clear that this is what the scholastics affirm; for them it would seem to have no other meaning than that of a kind of blurred amalgam of distinct though analogously proportioned realities. It is as if God had entertained the idea of being before he made any beings, and manifested this being in the guise of a plurality of beings which exhausted its meaning. Or it is something like the idea of a totality of which Kant spoke? But perhaps best: it might be viewed as having its root in some actual entity and reach beyond this; if one could abstract it from all affiliation then it would be vague and blurred; but by virtue of the fact that there are beings and some beauty we can see these as comprehensive terms which, though oriented in some one, have application to all. Of course in a way this is the scholastic answer, for they already have God as the primary case of being, unity, goodness, etc. But it is not necessary to affirm that the entity with which one begins is a primary case of the transcendental, but only that it is one case of the transcendental, having been specified in just that way, and leaving over a range which requires different specifications. If we abstract from that one case, the transcendental becomes indistinguishable from the entire realm of possibility; it is only because there are other modes that possibility cannot be dealt with in this way; or better, since we already have other modes, the realm of possibility is sundered.

The treatment of transcendentals as though they had a kind of surplus beyond the specification they in fact have raises the question as to whether or not individuals in a species are to be treated in a similar manner, despite the Aristotelian outlook—and it would seem this is the case. Individual differs from individual in the way in which each specifies the humanity which is common to them all. But putting this matter aside, the question of importance is that starting with the idea of beauty or any other so-called transcendent, one gives it meaning and definiteness only by virtue of its differential use. It is because in entering into the aesthetic domain, we already have made use of the idea of beauty that we can go on and create. But how did we get that idea in the first place? This is one with the question as to why we move away from simple noting or observing in perception to aesthetic enjoyment. Is this a result of involving it in our affairs, and thus is it that we always are ready to bring such an idea into play; that we already, right from the start as we begin to perceive, are involved in other activities and have only the problem of integrating ourselves, i.e., of either abandoning the peculiar human involvement to lose ourselves in the object and its affairs or to bring that object into relation with us? The fact that we are faced with this alternative shows that we already have the idea of beauty, i.e., the readiness to deal with Existence from a position which involves the Ideal. Beauty is the existent as made to embody the Ideal, an existence which of course is being manipulated in the guise of limited bits of Actuality.

In a sense we have three alternatives: There is a primary beauty and everything is an analogue of it; there is a rooted beauty and everything is another form of the abstracted version of that rooted beauty; there is an abstract form which is diversely or commonly exhibited. The first requires us to affirm a primary being; the second supposes we are in the realm of aesthetics to begin with, and the third identifies it with possibility. We could combine the second and third. Beauty can be said to be identical with mere possibility when taken in and of itself, but when faced as a purposively entertained object, or as necessarily utilized when one adopts an aesthetic attitude, it becomes inseparable from some rooted outcome, and only then does it have the guise of beauty, rather than mere possibility.

When we perceive, have we already settled our accounts, forced ourselves away from a vague entertainment of beauty and the aesthetic attitude; is perceiving a deliberate rather than an antecedent step? If it be a deliberate outcome of some differentiation in an attitude, we could say it is a mere accident, a matter of a leisure, a matter of interest caught, or something conspicuous which makes us make the undifferentiated attitude take the shape of perception or the shape of an appreciation. I must initially be undetermined whether to master, submit or adjust, to accept things as they go, or to bring them within my set of needs and activities.

If the problem is to make a unity of the Ideal and a localized sensuous Existence, there ought to be a kind of diversity which is also required. If there be two types of being brought into a unified togetherness, there must also, according to the *Modes,* be a togetherness of mere external relation. The very being then of beauty which involves the merging without seam of the Ideal and Existence also involves their separation. As merging without seam they are pulverized in themselves, pluralized endlessly; as separated one from the other they are themselves without internal specific differentiation. It is only by infecting Existence with the Ideal in such a way that each is pulverized at the same time that each is allowed to function in itself as over against the other, that we have a realization of beauty. The beauty would be exhibited in both together as correlatives. When and as we have the work of art in which the beauty is the unified product we must have beauty as the spread between the mere Ideal and Existence, the one functioning as that which forever lies beyond our activities, as the final purpose of all and the locus of all possible further determinations of the work, the other functioning as its materiate base and allowing it to be part of nature.

Can we suppose that beauty deals only with the merging of the Ideal and Existence, and that the other half, the case where Ideal and Existence stand as sheer plural elements at a distance from one another, is a kind of being? Were this so, we would then have to say that beauty is a kind of being matched by a correlative kind of being, which perhaps could be properly termed Unsatisfying being. Beauty and the Unsatisfying would be correlative ways of having two modes of being together, the one intimately, the other at a distance.

February 4

Along the line of Aristotle's practical syllogism one could say that we first move to a terminus in thought and then, retreating back to an actual starting point, move on through the concrete to get to the actual terminus. If we hold the conceived end before us, we and it are related by an abstract relation. This one can view as a kind of model for the production of beauty. The beautiful would then be a kind of formal stretch between what we now have and the Ideal which lies beyond, and the making of something beautiful would involve the actual concretionalization of this formal pattern, by moving to that designated end. Put this way the beautiful is not the Ideal, but the relation of this to what is here and now; it would be an obligatory relation satisfied with the transformation of the actual existents here and now into idealized forms. This would also require one to suppose that the perfecting of something according to its own nature would be a making of it beautiful. This will cause no difficulty if what is recognized is that the entity which is being idealized is Existence as manifested in these sensuous objects. Also one ought to say that the reaching of the Ideal is the reaching of it as beautified—the pattern is realized not only in the process but as an accumulative terminus. But none of this is really clear to me.

The problem might be put as that of quantifying the quality, of knowing when a quantity suffices to exhaust a quality. How many cats exhaust catness? If there is no possible exhaustion how can one say that "catness" has been realized? And would one not have unrealized possibilities? A Platonist can say "yes," but can an Aristotelian or a Hegelian?

We ought to say that the Hegelian thesis and antithesis are equally abstract (and so is the relation between them), and that progress consists in shortening the distance, making the relation more concrete by making the terms more concrete through mutual infection. At the lowest level the infection is minimal; at the upper level there is no way of distinguishing the two sides; they are one another.

In art we would have to say that the meaning of beauty is the juncture of the Ideal and Existence in such a way that the one cross-grains the other, articulates it, gives it locus and function. But we still have the case that there comes a point where additional quantity makes a difference in quality, and a subtraction in quantity makes a difference in quality. The idea of beauty is not a conceptual idea because it is achieved only in the cross-graining of other elements, Ideality and Existence. When form and matter are one we say we have beauty. But the problem is when are they one? Why this form should have just this amount of matter and not more or less? Is it a purely empirical discovery that we find we have beauty at such and such a point of interpenetration?

How does Hegel know (or Being know) when Being has had enough of Nothing, has come close enough to it to turn into Becoming? Is there some point which is found by mere trial and error, or is there something in the nature of the terms? Do different media and different ideas or forms have different ways of being one? And do we learn what these are only by trial and error? McTaggart observes that as the dialectic of Hegel progresses the items lose their stability. Does this mean that the substantiality moves from the terms to the relation of otherness, so that we can say that there is a progression in the substantialization of otherness? But this progression has moments, and the question is when and how we find a moment? But putting that question aside for the time, we can say that different forms and matters are more or less impervious to one another, and that they sustain one another only by being made permeable either by virtue of their own meaning or (on a lower level) through the imposition of another meaning. Or perhaps even better, though it is not Hegel's view, different forms and matters are permeable by virtue of their own meanings but in different ways.

Being stands outside Nothing because Nothing does nothing to divide being in itself. Quantity stands closer to Quality than Being to Nothing, but does not cross-grain it except as an idea to make Measure. It allows Quality to become many qualities without making it into just Quantity made concrete, whereas the final absolute being is all the categories which must be traversed. The fulfillment of the Hegelian dialectic requires that there be a radical plurality as expressing the full meaning of a unity. Nothing, or endless division, does not serve to divide Being properly; yet there is no proper other for Being but this.

Hegel surely thought that forms, or better an idea, could be embodied only in different degrees in different media; his classification of the arts assumes that stones are more resistant than canvas to ideas. He supposes that there is no more to an idea than its spiritual basis; architecture could then be said to have its own appropriate idea, and tragedy another. But would we not be left with the spiritual component which architecture could not assimilate? If so, we would be viewing the medium of art as appropriate not to a certain type of idea but to the being of the idea, the kind of thing it is. In the language of the *Modes* we would be saying that the problem of beauty would be that of finding the kind of existent which would be most appropriate to the Ideal. But strictly speaking, the existent would have a core which could not be brought into perfect unity with the core of the idea. The sensuosity of speech would offer a core beyond the reach of the spirituality of the idea and this could be said to be even more resistant than stones, precisely because it was so self-assertive.

According to Aristotle there is a proper size to man. What is this? That which enables him to do all the things a man should do? What are these? Whatever the soul permits? But how do we know that the body of an Aristotelian man is appropriate to the human soul? Only by piecing together and idealizing the different parts of man and seeing that these various sides are satisfied in a body of such and such a kind? Or by saying with Aristotle that soul and body are two sides of the same thing? But this does not seem to allow for the defeat and failure of the body to provide for all the aspects of the soul. We are no further along than before I think. What will satisfy an idea? How big must a many be for a given one? When does an Hegelian synthesis occur, at what point in the process of synthesizing does the synthesis take place?

February 5

The suggestion of Kant and the post-Kantians is that there is a purpose to be considered in connection with the understanding and regulation of the realized Ideal. Not only then do we have the idea (say something spatial, temporal or energetic as encompassment, use and filling), the sensuous material which is being used as a medium (stones, marble, paints, etc.) and the beauty which is the result of their juncture in such a way that each is the cross-grain of the other, but we have the purpose of the work, the relating to the enjoyment or use of the work, which enables one to determine whether or not the work is too large or small, too minutely divided or too grossly expressed. It is because the picture is to be seen that the colors should have their "clarity" and "vividness"; because of the nature of colors there must be contrastive effects; because the building is to be lived in it must be of such and such a size with such and such windows, etc. The problem then of the realization of beauty (and art or fine art can be defined as the making imaginatively and freshly something excellent or beautiful) is possible only because it has a correlate in the shape of some external evaluator. The beauty here has the status of the divine and the evaluator or external referent that of the Actual. Consequently what we have in art is the juncture of Ideality and Existence in an intimate way in shape of beauty, and in an external way in the shape of man, these two ways being themselves capable of being treated as at once merged (in appreciation) and as outside one another (as the prescriptive and the descriptive) with the consequence that Ideality and Existence will serve as mere relations between them, the one serving as a prescriptive and the other as a descriptive condition. Appreciation would be the merging through the use of Existence under the correlative guidance of the Ideal; Objective Judgment or valuing would be the merging through the Ideal under the correlative guidance of the Existential relation which in fact holds between the object and the individual. There is evidently also a way in which the individual rather than beauty can give the very essence of the merging of the idea and the medium; this lies in the act of creativity, with beauty serving as the external conjunctive guiding this activity. We have then:

idea and sensuous existential medium intimately joined as beauty and externally connected by man, the correlate of beauty

and   intimately joined in creativity and externally connected by the ideal of beauty, the correlate of creativity.

and

beauty and man intimately joined in appreciation with a correlative union under the guidance of the ideal or idea.

and   in judgment with a correlative union under the guidance of the nature of Existence with its divisive demands and expansive powers.

We know then where to begin and end in creativity and appreciation, in judgment and in the objective acknowledgment of beauty by virtue of the correlative acknowledgment of beauty, judgment, appreciation and creativity.

A better definition of craft than that given some days ago is: the skilled making of something desired, skill being the excellent use of means. Art then would be craft which has been vitalized by imagination and freshness to produce that which is excellent, the excellent here being the beautiful. Fine art is to be distinguished from art as such, as involving a sensuous medium.

Beauty is perfection in the domain of the arts. To know it is to know what is the Ideal for art, and what art is and can be. There must be something in the confronted world or art object which indicates its incompleteness. This is either inchoateness or monotony; beauty is the Ideal made articulate, the sensuous given meaning by virtue of the interrelation of its parts, each of which must have some value while serving the whole. There must be integrity or freedom from irrelevance, proportion or articulateness according to the content's powers, and clarity or vividness (the content's nature allowed expression). In a sense then I go back to Aquinas' definition, except that I add scope and ignore the problem of pleasing or giving pleasure. The beautiful could conceivably disturb.

February 6

The link between the aesthetic domain, (or simple unfilled unity) and the sensitive individual is given on the one side by possible space (or time or energy), a space which has fluidity in dimensions and geometry, and on the other side by an existential vital connection between the sensitive individual and the aesthetic domain. The sensitive individual's category of observation is the possible space which will be specialized in the aesthetic domain in the shape of beautified space, or in the shape of private pleasure. The material for the art work is the existential connection which will be specialized in the sensitive individual in the shape of a satisfaction, or in the art work in the guise of sensuous content. Possible space and existential connection are correlative ways of relating the aesthetic domain and the sensitive individual; the latter are in turn correlative ways of relating possible space to the vital existential connection. The satisfied individual is the sensitive individual made concrete, just as the beautified space is the unity of the aesthetic domain made concrete. Both are the products of the merging of the possible space and the existential connection. The latter two can themselves be made concrete, made to relate the aesthetic domain and the sensitive individual, to produce an aesthetic space on the one side and an appreciation on the other.

Creativity produces the union of possible space and existential connection; satisfaction is the outcome of such a union on the side of the individual. The latter is not produced by the former, but is correlative with it and can be stressed in independence of it, and *v.v.* The activity of adjustment bridging the vital connection between the realm of aesthetics and the sensitive individual produces appreciation; aesthetic space is the outcome of such a union in the aesthetic domain.

Aesthetic space is the union of the aesthetic domain and the sensitive individual inside possible space, but it is biased toward the former, whereas release, which is a similar but passive union, is biased toward the latter. Beauty is a product biased toward possible space; it is the aesthetic domain made concrete through the union of possible space and vital existential connection. One of its components is a sensuous medium, which is the vital connection passively made concrete, with a bias toward the beauty. The release of the individual and the sensuous medium are both outcomes, incidental to the achievement of an adjustment on the one hand, and an aesthetic space on the other. It is because beauty is biased toward aesthetic space that the sensuous medium is a passive product; it is because the satisfied individual is essentially one who is adjusted that release is a passive product.

The creative act uses a possible space in such a way as to make the aesthetic domain concrete, with the help of the vital connection between the artist and the aesthetic domain. The creative act too converts possible space into an aesthetic space with a correlative conversion of the vital connection into a sensuous medium; it is accompanied by the achievement of a release in a satisfied individual which is a correlative to his adjustment to the realm of the aesthetic. The creative act in short produces beauty from the aesthetic domain because it makes aesthetic space from possible space at the same time that it makes a sensuous medium out of the vital connection interweaving these two. An incidental product of its achievement is the satisfying of the artist, by virtue of a juncture of possible space in the form of a feeling of release, and a vital connection in the form of an active adjustment to what lies outside.

There are a number of guides in the production of beauty: *1*] the satisfaction of the individual gives a subjective note; *2*] the achievement of an aesthetic space in a sensuous medium gives one the components; *3*] the aesthetic space in relation to an adjusted individual; *4*] release in relation to a sensuous medium. In the latter two cases the beauty is defined in part in terms of the object and in part in terms of the individual. The last two cases can be combined.

It is possible to think of the production of aesthetic space and adjustment as primary objectives. When this is done beauty becomes one of the products and guides to the achievement of the aesthetic space, while the satisfied individual becomes one of the guides and products of the achievement of adjustment. If beauty be said to be the outcome of creativity, the satisfied individual can be said to be the outcome of a re-organization, and where we are concerned with the production of aesthetic space this can be said to be the product of an aesthetic insight.

Correlatively we could then say that the achievement of an adjustment is due to the acceptance of oneself as aesthetically concerned.

When we concentrate on the production of an aesthetic space we make use of the individual's release on the one side and the aesthetic domain on the other. Analogously when we concentrate on the production of the adjusted individual we make use of the sensuous medium on the one side and sensitivity on the other.

February 7

Perception has a double orientation. As rooted in the object it has the note of Observation; as oriented toward man it has the note of Feeling. When the feeling component is treated not as having its terminus in the individual but as forming a link in a chain of feelings and other occurrences in the individual and other men, when it is allowed to have its own implications and thereby involve the perceptum, giving it a contextual meaning in human affairs, we get the Aesthetic Domain. If we make primary reference to the perceptum in the Aesthetic Domain our attitude is to be termed an Appreciation; if we make primary reference to the context of meaning we have Detachment (from nature), or Distance.

Since it is the case that the perceptum has its place in a life, it would seem that all percepta are possessed of some aesthetic significance. The origin of aesthetics lies in data which we confront at any moment. But it is also the case that on the one hand we do lose ourselves in a world and follow out its contours; there is not only a realm of Observation, but an implicative set which is Nature, and an attitude of Submission and Acknowledgment which goes with one's acceptance of this Nature. On the other hand there is the fact that the data which we appreciate is often caught in conventional contexts. In between the realm of the pure aesthetic and Nature we place a kind of second Nature, a conventional world which we observe in the way in which we observe Nature, and which is nevertheless constituted of data that have meaning only because of the context which we have provided.

Aesthetics initially means something as broad as in Kant; the specific delimitation of it to that which is appreciated apart from any use or conventional import comes later. Perhaps it would be better then to speak of the domain where feelings are given implications through the involvement with other things in the individual and other men as the Human Orbit, *Lebensraum,* Social Context, Domain of Meaning, or Import.

If we start with the Human Orbit we distinguish within it a Pragmatic or Conventional Dimension and a newly forged one in which, exercising our freedom and our initiative in Appreciation, we produce new connections and involve the perceptum in new relations in the Human Orbit. The newly forged relation can readily fall back into the pragmatic and does this sooner or later. But until it does, it constitutes a genuine Aesthetic Dimension or a domain of objects which are being enjoyed. It is this domain which confronts the photographer; it is this which one acknowledges when one recognizes the passing show, the shapes and colors to be attractive, pleasant, joyous, beautiful.

Every entity in experience can have a place in the Aesthetic Domain. Even those which are ugly, painful or merely useful can be arrested by the eye or intent of an individual and swung out of the context of nature or usual relations. By holding it apart from the connections which are available for it in nature or in man, it is first sundered, made to stand apart, given a separateness of status, and then, by virtue of the nature of man and in fact the contribution it makes to his own nature, it achieves new implications. New implications can be insisted on; one can forge them deliberately or throw oneself into a position where they are achieved. When we do this the isolated datum, (which is merely enjoyed) is given an Importance; when the new relations are allowed to appear, either because we keep up the attitude and thus have more and more isolated, encapsulated data of an aesthetic import, or because we approach the world with some novelty or creative stress, we forge the beginning of a world of Art.

The Art world has its origin then in the isolation of perceptual data with a consequent use of them in a context which is not Nature's (since the data were isolated from it in the first place) and is not conventional (since the attitude toward subsequent terms is not that of the conventional). When the artist begins to act, to make something through the manipulation of some sensuous medium, he makes use of portions of Existence to institute, (through the help of the ideal possibility before him) more objective conditions on the kind of result he had obtained aesthetically.

It is not necessary, however, for the artist to begin with an aesthetic appreciation. He may look at the world of nature or accept conventional usages for whatever he happens to perceive, and begin to be an artist and have aesthetic appreciations only when he has begun to be active. The converse is also true; one may stop with mere appreciation and never be actively productive of art. One can look at a cave and take it to be a dwelling, a place where one is going to live. Here one isolates the cave, separates it off from the rest of nature on the one side, and on the other ignores certain other usages it might have in human affairs, such as a storage place or a hiding place, etc.—whatever it be which a hole in a natural surrounding might ordinarily imply. Had one instead burrowed out a hole in the hill to make a dwelling, one would have made use of the portion of Existence which that hill was presenting and would impose the meaning or aesthetic setting on the hill when and as one was making it into a hole. In the one case we would confront a natural object and view it in a special way; in the other case we would start with a special way of dealing with a natural object and operate on the object to make it have another weight or meaning.

Because a man started with an aesthetic attitude toward the hill he made the cave dwelling. Had he merely worked on the hill without this objective he would be a man who worked, exercised some skill, or more sharply, who had labored on the hill. When he finally makes the hole and signalizes it as a dwelling he is like the man who came upon the cave as a natural formation and took this to be a dwelling. In short, the fact that a hole in a hill was made by nature or by man does not affect the fact that it is a dwelling for one with a certain attitude. (The artist has an attitude toward material which is to eventuate in the cave dwelling. He is an artist because the cave dwelling is the outcome of work performed in an aesthetic context.)

When a man approaches the hill as a possible place to make a cave dwelling, he has brought the idea of a cave dwelling, which is defined inside an aesthetic context, to bear on the hill and has thereby defined the hill aesthetically. He does not appreciate the hill aesthetically directly but only indirectly through the operation of the idea; the idea serves to isolate the hill from its normal implications to give it the implications of the aesthetic, without any intervening enjoyment of it as separated off from nature or human conventional usages.

The aesthetic object is held apart from three connections; it is held apart from its involvement in natural events; from its involvement in human conventional contexts; and from the feeling or inward tonality of the individual. But while it is held apart from these to constitute an item in a new domain it also is of course inseparable from other sides of itself where it is as a matter of fact caught in these other ways. The cave as a dwelling can and does crumble; the cave as a dwelling does look like a hiding place and tempts the use of it this way; the cave as a dwelling has an affect on man and helps constitute his inward state.

If there were difficulty, as there is for some, with the idea that there could be a separate aesthetic dimension over against nature, one would also for the same reasons have to give up the idea of a human contextual one for society as well. And if one gave up only the idea that the aesthetic dimension was held over against nature one would be tacitly supposing that the social context gave us nature as it in fact was. And finally if one gave up the idea that there was an aesthetic dimension over against the purely subjective enjoyment, one would have difficulty in understanding the meaning, importance, the criticism and the beauty in a work of art, for these are over against the individual and in part test the kind of inward feeling that he has.

February 9

The parts of a work of art have a primary function when they serve merely to make a composition involving combinations, contrasts, relations and tensions, without reference to anything beyond. They have a secondary function when they, by conventional associations and usages, serve to arouse consideration or reference to entities outside the work. Colors in interplay offer a case of a primary function. If the color and shape "portray" say a moon and a sea, the colors can be said to have a secondary function. They have a tertiary function when the referents are associated or symbolized elements of the secondaries. Thus when a moon and a sea are taken to represent eternity and change we have the colors exercising a tertiary function.

To have only primary functioning parts is to have mere "decoration," or composition, and one is forced to look for cues and clues to read the work. To have only secondary functioning is to have a didactic art. To have only a tertiary functioning is to have a sentimental art. The purely didactic art of course has its compositional aspect, but this is ignored, obscured or bad; the sentimental art has its compositional and its didactic side, but these are ignored, obscured or bad.

Ought an art have all three functions integrated? Classical and religious art is based on the use of all three; modern abstractionists take only the first. But if I am right about cues and clues, then even here we have all three but in a new way. The clues might be said to be primarily ways of giving us a referent via suggestions rather than conventional usages; the cues might be said to be metaphors going beyond the suggestions to what the suggested might refer to or be connected with.

It is a problem in the literary arts to attend to the primary functions. Poetry is too often involved in the consideration of the secondary and tertiary; even the New Criticism, with its concentration on paradox, deals with the paradoxes involving the secondary usages, somewhat as Surrealism does. Drama has too often a story to tell through the use of quite definite conventional referents. When we put a stress on the music, rhythm, assonances, etc., in a poem we bring back the primary stress; when drama becomes an interrelationship of gestures, positions, re-alignments as it does in Japanese plays or in the "play within a play" in Hamlet, we also return to the primary stress.

To define the motion picture we must know what its primary stress is—is it the relation of frames to frames? Then it is a set of photographs. Of scenes to scenes? Then it is a kind of drama. Or is it not rather sound, color, shape, movement in free association which is its primary meaning? Has not the movies overlooked its primary function to concentrate on the didactic side, the side of conveying a "story"? This side need not be eliminated; but it ought to occur with the others. Experimental movies tend to have only the first side—and sometimes only the third.

Perhaps it is correct to say that we do not have art except where the primary status of the parts is of major, though not necessarily of exclusive interest. Significant form is a major part of any art, but its occurrences need not prevent the use of secondary and tertiary functions.

The Japanese Haiku poetry stresses the primary usages without ignoring the secondary and tertiary, usually going directly to the tertiary as the proper object of emotion. It is perhaps a good thing to use secondary referents only as cues and clues to the tertiary. A new movement in current abstractionistic or non-objective art could be achieved, which allows for the conveying of some idea with a consequent emotional involvement on the part of the spectator, by slighting the secondary functions but not eliminating them entirely. The work would be a composition which, through the cues and clues in it, makes a transitional referent to conventional objects but only as themselves cues or clues to something which they can be said to symbolize, not necessarily in any specific way but through the invocation of a mood or sentiment pointing one toward the great values of nature and of life.

February 13

There are at least three levels in a work of art—that of significant form, the interrelationship of the parts; that of the conventional referential meanings, which would by itself make it didactic; and that of the symbolic referent to something outside the conventional context. The picture of a lamb has to be made to have its own interior power and value; the significant form is the most important side to a work. The lamb in the picture is a picture of a lamb by virtue of conventional interpretations; it looks as a lamb might look were it transferred from there to here and made "two-dimensional." But the lamb also symbolizes purity or Christ.

Were one to have this dimension stressed or alone one would have sentimentality; the first dimension alone would give you mere decoration. The work of art, though emphasizing the first dimension, does include the others. The second is inevitable, and the third perhaps also, for we make associations no matter what the artist intends, and we do adumbrate beyond the immediate data of daily life, particularly when we put ourselves in the mood to look at a work aesthetically.

The aesthetic attitude is a component within a larger perceptual one. That perceptual attitude has two poles, an objective and a subjective. On the objective side there is the given content, the appearance, the meaning in public, the phenomenon, and also the adumbrative, substantial, inward side of the being. The latter is the object of metaphysical speculation and of love; the former is the object of perception, strictly speaking; it, in its interrelations, makes up the content of science.

On the subjective side we can distinguish, 1] the attitude of recording or noting the phenomena; 2] the attitude of observing and interrelating the phenomena; 3] the attitude of aesthetic appreciation of the phenomena. These three attitudes have in common the isolation of the phenomena, the encapsulating of it. The first however allows it to be merely related to other similar isolated items, perhaps under the aegis of some system or law. Science as a domain of knowledge arises in this way. The second dimension is one which brings the isolated item into the context of human interests. It relates the item to other things via the perceiver, adding implications which the science does not affirm. The third dimension not only brings it into the context of human interests, which in a way already has its structure, but institutes new relations, forces the item, in part through the mediation of emotions, to take up new implications, to be involved in new ways.

There is a problem as to whether there are not multiple strands in the last dimension. Thus one might say that in religion or in politics, etc., one deliberately involves perceived items in new relations. And on the other hand, it makes sense to say that the aesthetic dimension is in fact nothing else but the items as related to one another to constitute a significant form. And perhaps this is what ought to be said. It enables one to go back to the dimensions of the work of art itself, and recognizes that when one identifies its significant form one is treating the work as a perceptual object and stressing the subjective pole of the perception. This subjective pole of course, because it does relate to the object, does not yield a mere private impression, but gives us the real object as subject to new connections. The dimensions of conventional reference and of symbolization would be ways in which one attempted, through limitative means, to add implications to the aesthetic in order to get back to the objective pole as the correlate of a mere recording or noting. In short, the use of references and symbols in a work of art, though they add to what is aesthetically enjoyed are employed in order to free us from the aesthetic dimension and bring us into the state where we merely record what is a mere objective phenomenon or its adumbrative substantial base.

The English empiricists with their attempt to get to the world of common sense by means of a reconstruction of "sense data" held this view in essence. But if the artist is correct and these are in fact additions which, though not without warrant, are restrictive and distortive except as subordinate notes, the adding of implications beyond those aesthetically enjoyed would be a way not of recovering what the object is in fact but a way of producing something which is satisfactory for some common-sense purpose. But this is also a way of inverting the common-sense position; it supposes that the aesthetic dimension is in some sense primary and that the additions are made to it, even granted that they go beyond it and tell us something of the adumbrative side of things. Does not the answer lie in the recognition that a perceiver is at once a being in interrelation to other beings, and the relations of the data are in part commonsensically defined by that interrelation, and that he is also an appreciator who is in a more privately sustained but also a more abstractly intended relationship to what is beyond him? This problem needs further clarification.

The problem can be put in a paradox: To get significant form or the merely aesthetic dimension in perception one must add to the implications which the object has in nature, not only those which are brought about by virtue of the human conventional involvement, but also those which relate to the individual, and those which have to do with some purpose being creatively achieved. The physical or natural object lacks determinations, and the determinations of the aesthetic are the final ones it attains. From the perspective of that attained outcome the other implications are of course only background; but they do involve the thing which is being aesthetically approached. But on the other hand, the work of art, when dealt with as the locus of significant form, can be related to the world only by adding to the attitude or meaning that the work of art possesses; it would seem as if the work of art lacked some implications, that it was indeterminate in the very way in which the object in nature was, and this not merely because it was taken to be a mere object (which of course is possible) but because it was taken to be an aesthetic object.

Is the answer perhaps that the aesthetic dimension does not make the natural more determinate, but that the natural and the aesthetic as well as all the rest are correlative, supplementary ways of making determinate that which is not determinate, with the proviso that there never is a state of affairs where the object is entirely indeterminate? A cat, e.g., could not be fully determinate in nature, without making impossible aesthetic and human implications as actually involving the cat. But one ought not to go on, as I have done earlier, and suppose that these implications are ways of making the natural object be more and more determinate. They are instead co-ordinate ways of determining the cat. We speak of an object as in nature when the initial way of being determinate is provided by nature; we speak of it as an artifact when we treat the human involvement as the first mode of determination.

When we approach the work of art as an object we deal with it as we deal with the objects in nature; we then isolate not the significant form which the artist has produced but a significant form of that object—e.g., the significant form of the picture as an object on the wall, rather than of the colors inside the picture. But we can also deal with that picture on the wall as the locus of a significant form. When we do this we are in effect analyzing the picture. It is to start with some part and reinstitute the kind of implication which in fact helps make the whole a whole of significant form.

The above discussion supposes that the significant form is not an ingredient of the things as in nature. And there is surely this meaning, for we do add implications to the things, giving them new relations, new import, jeopardizing and enriching them by virtue of the kind of connections we by our interests produce. But there is also the fact that inside the simplest connection in nature there is a phase or aspect which tells us only of the kind of structure it has, the kind of interconnection that holds among its parts, and which conforms therefore to one of the original meanings of "aesthetic," as that which is immediately apprehended. This can be dealt with, though, as a limited or variant version of the other sense of aesthetic.

A given entity in nature can be related via human interest (which abstracts from the concrete involvement to stress only the appearances), to the very objects it is ordinarily related to in nature, or it can be related to other entities or in new ways by virtue of human interest. Human interest thus provides us with a new primary or stressed set of implications for a given entity; those implications may merely abstract from a natural set or may bring about new types of connection which supplement the natural set. The abstractive act yields a structure which may have aesthetic immediacy but it has no aesthetic value except so far as the attitude itself involves some kind of emotion and thus represents a significant human

effort; the involvement characteristic of the aesthetic approach of appreciation includes the abstractive act as a part of a wider enterprise in which the
object becomes involved with other things in ways consonant not only
with the natural relation but with the abstracted aspect of this.

February 14

The mere structure of the perceived object as the terminus of
perception is a form which has been isolated; it exists only for an aesthetic
attitude. It is not appreciated. To appreciate it is to take it as a whole and
give it new implications via human concern. It may however be a
component in an appreciation which starts with one of its termini and
subjects that terminus to new implications, so that as a consequence the
terminus has the implication of being structurally related to some natural
object in a natural situation and of being vitally related to that object or
some other in an appreciation. When the photographer gets ready, or
when one in the course of an enjoyment of nature attends to what is about,
one is alert to the structural connections in the objective situation, and
perhaps appreciative of it in a wider context.

Let us take the case of a green next to a blue.   1] One can recognize
the structure and appreciate it as a case of the oddness or contingency of
the world.   2] One can absorb the structure in a more intensive appreciation of green having a contrasting relation to the blue next to it.   3] One
can go on to take the green as having a supplementary value for another
green nearby. When we deal with nature we have to move to the last
position from the first; when we do this we try to ignore the first as a
kind of factuality. When we deal as spectators with a painting we start in
the same way with the green next to the blue and then try to ignore it
except so far as it can be read as an element in an intensive involvement of
the green with the blue (case 2).

When we appreciatively have the green in relation to the blue or to
another green we are taking the work of art as an aesthetic object. But
there is a reference made, either through conventional associations or by
cues of various sorts, to a world beyond, and there is also some vague
apprehension of the substantival character of the data encountered in the
world beyond, or its import in the cosmos or for mankind. And there are
perhaps also recognitions of the role the green plays with respect to blue in
a scientific or psychological scheme, in a religious one, etc. To deal with
these it is necessary to adopt one of two alternatives: the aesthetic
appreciation and the other modes are purely subjective, humanistic elements having no reality beyond the human domain, or they supplement

what is structurally real and objective, either in the sense of being also integral to an exterior reality or in the sense of being added to it in fact, by virtue of man's presence in a real world.

In the "Reality of the Art Object" I took the last alternative but concentrated only on the art dimension. The danger with it is that it makes one suppose that apart from man the world is very thin in fact, being nothing but structure; it denies that what is discerned in science or religion or art is actually an integral part of the world apart from the human system of science, religion or art. The view, on the other hand, that the dimensions of science, religion or art, though discovered by our involvement, are in fact objective, integral parts of the real world apart from us, makes the values of these subjects integral to objects, and defines man to be one who discovers rather than creates these values (or better perhaps, who creates values which in fact are there apart from his activity). If we try, as is the usual procedure, to take the world of scientific discovery to be the world that is there in fact, but the world of religion and art to be additions which merely add to, from the outside and via man, what is objectively real, we wrongly split off these dimensions from the real, for in principle they are on a footing with the scientific. We make a prejudicial judgment if we say that green being next to blue is an objective truth, but that green contrasting with blue nearby is not. And we cannot take the first of the alternatives, to the effect that these various dimensions are merely subjective, without denying not only the objective status of what is discerned, but even its phenomenological status, its role as objective for us—and thus the evidence we have every day.

Whatever theory we do entertain, eventually must find room for the fact that in the aesthetic dimension we do have references to the matter of fact and the symbolic (and thus to the common-sense, scientific and religious systems) as real and outside the aesthetic. But this allows one to say that these dimensions are merely supplementary and are no more real than the aesthetic; it could be that they were all (including the aesthetic) supplementary to some nuclear reality, though the usual supposition is that we have here a case of the second type, with the non-aesthetic or at least the common-sense and scientific aspects alone being objective.

Perhaps all of the dimensions are presenting the same object under different conditions, so that it is one and the same thing to learn of it in one dimension as in another? The object as dealt with via scientific instruments has such and such implications, and as dealt with via human involvement has these other implications. We have a kind of parallelism then, but one which takes the different conditions seriously as making a genuine difference, so that the real cannot be said to be divided into mere aspects. But what happens then to supplementation? What kind of being has a condition? It would seem to be constitutive of a realm and yet be that which is in some sense outside it in order to make the realm possible. Also there would seem to be no error, and no better or worse; there would be no truth in the view that something is lost or gained in one dimension or another. And why should one make a reference outside one dimension? How could he? The conditions evidently add something real to the world, in this view, and the references and supplementations are needed in order to take account of what in fact is effective, objective and real.

The best answer would seem to be that there is a real object with power having (to take a simple case) two types of relation to another real object—a direct and an indirect. The indirect is mediated by another object, which serves as a condition for the determination of new consequences in the second for the first. We can say of the first object in relation to the second that the direct relation alone is real; we can read into the situation the relation which is needed to bring about the new consequences in the second, and in that case we take the contribution man makes to be in fact a discovery of what is there already; and we can suppose that the indirect relation is supplementary or subjective, distorting the pristine awareness of the mere direct relation. The direct relation, it could be argued, is itself a kind of indirect, since it is known only by a perceiver; it is used merely as standard or limit, and any objectification of it, any characterization of it as reporting what is the case would have to be extended to the other implications which man provides. We have here a case where we can speak of A and B in a relation which is taken to be objective and dyadic when in fact it arises only because of an externalization of a triadic factor, the contribution made by man. Have we any warrant for taking any one of these as objective in preference to any others; any warrant for taking any as objective; any warrant then for a supplementary view or a subjective one?

We reject the subjective, for this takes only termini to be real, and unwarrantedly denies reality to relations; moreover it cannot explain the addition which man makes without supposing that he is a reality outside the interpretation which he imposes. We have then only the supplementary view which says that man, in diverse relations to the two objects, involves them in new relations and implications. Depending on what his attitude is, the implications vary and make different systems. No one of the dimensions is altogether adequate; all are needed in order to give the full contribution of man and therefore the full meaning of the object in the world. Since the object is in fact related to man, the discovery of the new implications but explicates, realizes, makes actual the potential power in the object. When we read into the dyadic relation the additions which the triadic situation provided, we suppose the additional elements are part of a structure which would be there apart from the triadic; but there is no warrant for this. And yet we can say that there are genuine dyadic relations, which are in no way dependent on the presence of man. To find these one would have to perceive and thus have the objects in a triadic relation. Like "primary qualities" they would belong to the largest possible system; they would be the common components of all triadic situations, the elements which could be found in all of them, and thus were in some sense constants.

Reference from a work of art to the objective common-sense reality would be a reference to either the common dyadic elements in all relations or to a supplementary set of triadically determined relations. On the other hand, reference to the symbolic objects would always be to that which was triadically determined. But if we can legitimately claim that common sense does yield the common elements we can with justice claim this to be true in the aesthetic or religious dimensions too. What we would then have in the case of common sense is a conspicuous use of the dyadic relations. In short, there would always be triadic relations, but in different cases the common dyadic elements which hold in every system would be conspicuous in different degrees. In art we ignore them, and bring them back again when we make reference to the common-sense object of daily life. When we become didactic or prosaic we incline to suppose that the emphasized portion of the common-sense referent is basic and real and objective, whereas it is a partial element in the common sense and also present in the aesthetic dimension, but now shorn of the common sense additions. It is this blue here on the painting which is contrasting with the green that is thereby defined to be *next to it,* though it may not be "next" according to a ruler.

February 16

A scale holds up objects and also makes it possible for them to exhibit a relation say of balance, or equality of weight. A poor balance would hold them up also, but it would make them exhibit a relation of inequality. The equality and inequality are equivalent when consideration is given to the scale, the good scale serving merely as a norm for the use of the terms to describe the features in the things, the kind of relationship they have to one another apart from the scale. There seem to be some features of which it is not true that they become manifest via some mediator—thus the smaller size of an object can be defined as equal to a part of a larger; perhaps this can be said of weight as well, but it is not perhaps the same thing to say that things differ in weight as it is to say that they will balance or not, for the balancing does require the use of the scale and the weight does not.

Man the knower, the scientist, the common-sense man, etc., act somewhat as the scale does. The objects (or the parts of the objects in interrelation) which the one type discerns in one type of relation, the other discerns in another type of relation. The discerned relation, the relation which is seen to to to be exhibited between the entities, is there in fact, though its presence is made possible only by virtue of the activity of the mediator. His mediation is not read into the relationship; it constitutes a new fact. But as a consequence of the mediation there is made manifest a kind of relation between the entities which would not be made manifest in any other way. The manifested relation is not something latent in the entities or the world; there are the entities, and the relation they have is made manifest in this way or that depending on the mediator. If one wants to speak of the nature of the relation as apart from all mediation, one must provide a transformational formula for moving from one mediator to another, and then naming this in terms of some basic relation. Normally we suppose that the proper name for the relation is that which we encounter either in common sense or in science, and forget that this should name not the particular relation which is manifested but the principle of transformation by means of which one can move from one type of relation to another through the introduction of different kinds of mediators.

When we perceive we normally have a cluster of manifest relations: there is the conventional common sense, habitual relation; the adumbrated, substantival, intimate ontological relation; the aesthetic or purely surface connection; and perhaps some hint of the social import in science, religion or industry. Each of these connects in different ways. What is a direct connection of two objects is for another a mediated one; in both cases the connection is mediated by individual men. It would be a mistake to suppose that one of these manifested relations is superior to or more objective than any other; if it were, the others would be relegated to some minor position, and perhaps even designated as subjective or unreal. The only difference is that we take one of them as normative for the use of our terms, and ought to use it to name not the manifest relation but that relation which is being manifest now this way and now that, depending on what the mediating individual brings into the situation an attitude of noting, surmise, enjoyment, cognition, interest, etc.

When we turn to the artist we find that he substitutes for the aesthetic forms, which he encounters as he enjoys the world, a new, freshly created set. It is not that he need attend to the aesthetic forms in nature; it is sometimes easier for him to ignore these altogether. But whether ignored or not, what he does is create a new aesthetic content, keeping all the while a reference to the other dimensions. That is why one readily interprets his result as having a common-sense, scientific, religious, etc., import at the same time. It is to be noted that the aesthetic work that he in fact produces has these dimensions itself. There is in short the scientific object which is taken to be the referent of the form of the art object, and there is the art object as having a scientific side itself. The picture of a house refers to a house that will eventually fall down; the colors of the picture are physically related and the picture itself hangs on the wall. These two scientific objects have nothing to do with one another so far as the artist is concerned—or the spectator. But a scientist would relate the falling house (if there be one in fact and not merely referred to) to the physically colored picture, or to the picture as hanging on the wall. The fact of the reference indicates that though the aesthetic dimension of the picture is a locus of forms in interconnection, which say exactly the same thing as the colors (as physical things) but in terms of different modes of mediation—the one in an aesthetic spirit, the other in a scientific or common-sensical—the cluster of other relations (because man is more than a recorder, conventional being or religious one) is manifest at the same time.

The normative use of the aesthetic dimension is what makes one use the others as referents. Just as the common sense normative use of the term "blue" would refer to a blue seen under certain fairly well known circumstances (daylight, arm's distance, normal eye sight, etc.), but intends to tell us what the color is in fact (with the name "blue" being a way of referring to the whole array of colors which will appear under different circumstances—blue having a different look at twilight than at mid-day, as next to red over against next to yellow, etc.) so the aesthetic dimension takes itself to be normative and refers to the correlative and equal dimensions of science, etc., which are discerned when and as it is. It is as if we saw a blue in normal circumstances at the same time that we saw it looking reddish in others, and understood the blue not only to be the name of the color in itself (in which case it would be the neutral meaning of all the "appearances" under all the different circumstances) but to refer to or be used as the beginning of a reference to the other appearances.

The difficulty with this account is that it puts all appearances on a level, so that there is never anything in error or wrong, except in the sense that it violates typical usage or normative acceptances. The advantage is that it does enable one to use any of the dimensions as a norm, so that one can look at the world from a scientific perspective or a commonsensical one or an aesthetic one, etc. It is this advantage which weakens the difficulty of having only typical usages.

The usual view of typical usage takes one of the dimensions as primary and forces one to deal with all others in these terms alone; but there are typical usages in all dimensions as it were, and only for certain purposes does one dimension stand out as primary. In this respect the approach through a theory of perception, which stresses one kind of norm, a commonsensical one, and is not faced with alternative manifestations and thus has no immediate pressure to consider them and thus to refer to them, differs from a theory of perception which recognizes that all the dimensions appear at the same time. Such recognition forces a reference to the others by any one dimension which is taken as a norm and thus which A] is manifest in a primary or stressed way, B] names the nature of the relation which exists in fact, C] can be portrayed only by a transformational formula which equates the different manifestations, and D] precisely because it is a norm, is used as the accepted datum and ground for a reference to the others.

The aesthetic dimension, given the fact that it is being enjoyed by the perceiver or appreciator in such and such a way, strictly speaking, needs no support in any other dimension. But the support does enable one to see that what is revealed in it, when it is taken to be a norm, is more than it as then and there; it needs supplementation by other dimensions in order to have the role of naming, not a mere appearance, but the very substance of things. As involved in such a reference it functions as the substance which is being manifest in them rather than as their correlate. A correlate places the mediator not alongside or on a level with the objects which are having relations made manifest, but underneath them as a kind of support, making the other manifestations and their media to be mere qualifications of the dimension and the mediator.

It still remains true that any spectator will have some relation to a work and will, on the above account, be on a level with any other, unless inside the aesthetic dimension there are normative or normal usages. Just as it is true that horses are flies for a madman, and that it is the very horses and flies which he identifies that are also distinguished by one who is sane, and that his identification is (given him) identical with the diversity of the other (given the other), so one spectator is related to another spectator. Our usage says that the spectator who can discern more forms, whose set of implications is richer, is properly to be taken as a normative spectator, for in this way we make better sense of the supposition that the manifested relations that he makes possible could be used as a norm. From that position we can get a good name for the substantival nature of the dimension as having all the other manifestations as instances or expressions.

We are inclined to suppose that the spectator who sees more forms or has more implications is the normative type—and this is also true of the scientist and common-sense man. But when we come to the dimensions themselves we are inclined to suppose that the scientist has a dimension which itself has more implications than the others and therefore is the proper dimension which should give the name of the reality that is being manifest in all these different dimensions. We are inclined to suppose that science will in the end explain common sense, religion, art, etc. But these dimensions seem equally basic; one can take any one as normative.

If this is the case is it not also the case that we can do a similar thing with the mad man and the sane? A mad man can in fact be said to see connections the other does not, even when seeing what the other does; for him the horse both is and is not a fly, and in this sense could on the above supposition, be said to be more basic than the sane. If we insist on restrictive conditions of communication, etc., then we can still say that the madman and the sane are on a level in the sense that what is discerned by the one is theoretically as available as the other, and that we in fact do suppose this when we are trying to deal with the mad and trying to understand what it is he discerns and fears and knows. The madman's contradictions can even be included; no restriction need be imposed on him. This means that we cannot say the proper norm is given by that which has the most implications; it can only be that which can explain the other dimensions by making use of the principles of transformation that we in fact possess.

But if it is the case that we can explain the mad by transformations from the sane, can we not do the same thing in the reverse way? We are left evidently with the question as to the warrant for taking some perspective as primary, when we are inside some one dimension. Perspectives which are normative in the various dimensions can be equated, and all of them can be said to be equally basic; and in each dimension we can have normative usages for the names we employ.

The answer to the question of the madman and the sane, is that we take the man who, in a given dimension, through the use of accepted means and extensions of these, is able to discern more elements. The madman gets his additional elements by abandoning the usages which are accepted. The expert is a man who sees more but not because he is using new devices. We take the man who sees less to be insensitive so far as he is inexperienced or inattentive; with education, training and attention, he should be able to discern what the others do. Consequently we can say that in the aesthetic dimension we can have standard spectators, and that in the scientific we also can have our standards, but that there is nothing in the one which makes it superior as a test of the other. To be sure there are things that happen in the one that do not in the other, but it is not a question of more or less, but of the following out of distinctive methods. The analogue in connection with the mad and the sane would be that of allowing each to be basic, each with its characteristic normative cases. The mad would then not be compared with the sane, but would be made correlate with it—provided that we have a typical or standard madman in terms of which others are to be judged as atypical.

It is not correct then to hold as I did in the paper on the reality of the art object that there is a natural world in which there are partly undetermined objects made more determinate in art. The object as in nature is determinate fully; the problem of the work of art is not getting it into nature but into reality, of which nature is but one facet. The illusory nature of art follows only when nature is taken as normative and thus is made more substantival than the art. The art would then not be a determination of it, but one of its manifestations as subject to some external condition. But strictly speaking the art is equally basic and can function as a norm for nature.

Our usage of terms does not make evident which is to be taken as normative in the sense of giving the name for the substantival reality; sometimes we speak in common-sense terms, sometimes in religious, sometimes in natural and sometimes in aesthetic. The philosopher as one who seeks to avoid the partiality of these various views might perhaps be permitted to name the substantival mode, in which case the various dimensions would all be expressions of his substantival mode which, however, unlike the dimensions, would not be perceivable or encountered, but like mathematics would nevertheless be neutral and all-encompassing.

February 17

De Witt H. Parker listed six principles in the logic of aesthetic form: organic unity, theme, thematic variation, balance, hierarchy and evolution. By the first, organic unity, he means unity in variety, self-containedness, completeness of the work, in which each part needs the others. Perhaps this is better described as an internal tension and resolution. He recognizes that all the other principles serve it; the hard question then is whether they are really needed.

Theme is the dominant character, such as melodic pattern, dominant shape, etc. This cannot be separated from his other principle, thematic variation. Indeed what ought to be said is that the work must connect all the various parts through a plurality of themes, each of which is instanced with variation, so that there is a persistent identity with novelty. The plurality of themes or patterns constitutes a plurality of unifications, and the unity of the entire work is the way in which these patterns support one another.

The principle of balance seems to be included in the idea of unity and resolution; sometimes Parker speaks as if there is central axis needed, but this surely is not the case; there are as many axes as there are themes. Sometimes Parker seems to think balance means symmetry, but he also goes on to think of it as primarily rhythmical, where rhythm is defined as thematic repetition and balance. A rhythm is a combination of accented and unaccented beats; it is a way of making a unit out of sub-units and repeating this with variations. It indicates that the thematic variation is not haphazard but involves stresses and submergencies.

The principle of evolution, in which the earlier parts determine the latter, but tells us that the thematic variation is not mere replacement but involves reference back and forth, and this of course is involved in the very idea of tension and resolution. Parker wants the work to move toward a goal to show development, but development is but one form of thematic variation with regard to what had been before. He thinks of evolution as dynamic and balance as static, but of course with thematic variation we have the two dimensions at once.

Hierarchy involves the idea of primary stress on some element, but it is highly questionable whether this is a significant item, since we can have many different stresses in the work. Starting with one of these stresses though, it can be said to define the pinnacle of one hierarchy. In that case we would have to say that the work of art is the locus of a plurality of hierarchies. But this is only really to say that one thematic set can be stressed over against others, in such a way as to allow the others to be dimly ascertained in its background.

Can we not bring all these elements together in a single characterization? A work of art has a number of patterns in which there are tensions and resolutions; any one of these patterns can be stressed, and all of them ought to be varied as they proceed, the variation having a retroactive as well as a progressive effect.

The perceiver or spectator or connoisseur is superior to others who, using the same mode of observation and powers, is able to discern more themes and variations (or their absence) than any other. He is the ideal observer or appreciator. If he uses other agencies not within the power of the rest he is aberrant, so far as what he discerns cannot be discerned by others; he is thought to be endowed with miraculous powers if these results are eventually discovered by the rest through the use of ordinary devices.

In each dimension of the noted object—scientific, rational, common-sensical, ethical, aesthetic, etc., there is an ideal perfect observer, who because more persistent than the rest, and freer than they of conventional limitations, sees all they do and much else besides. Whatever he sees may be seen by all the others together, but each of the others sees only a part. Instead of staying in one domain they slip readily into some other; he remains in it.

The ideal spectator lives through the thematic patterns in their internality, their relation to one another, and does this under the guidance of an overriding sense of beauty, in which the diversity of the themes is harmonized. The different domains in which there are ideal spectators all have the characteristic of relating the totality of confronted items. It is to be noted that in each domain there are often subdivisions, such as the several sciences, the several arts, the branches of practice and so on. These divisions should each have their own ideal spectators and should, like the domains themselves, encompass all the items confronted in a certain way. We call that branch of a subject subordinate if it does not attend to all the items within a domain which have been approached through some particular agencies or methods. We call that dimension not basic which does not deal with all confrontable items. And we call that spectator defective or insensitive whose treatment of a division or domain is such as to preclude a recognition of the theme in its internal variation, contrast and resolution, and its relationship within the total unity of themes. Oil painting is a subordinate branch of painting, in that there are effects it cannot render. This is the analogue of looking at nature through colored glasses which do not permit the grasp of all the colors. Needlework is not a basic dimension, since it lacks the full encompassment of space—which is characteristic of sculpture. This is the analogue of an approach to nature, e.g., in terms of what could be used only by a wood-working machine, for this leaves to a side, without discrimination, a host of distinguishable objects.

When common sense is thought of as defined within the area of familiar names or usages it turns out to be a subordinate branch or a non-basic dimension. But everything we confront, in another sense, has a rough-hewn nature and a place within our unreflecting totality of experi-ence. In this sense, it is basic. Strictly speaking no human enterprise discriminates perfectly in every area of experience; we can distinguish basic areas only if they are in principle ready to or capable of being extended to places where they are not extended now. A science has universal principles capable of indefinite extension throughout the confrontable world; it is the supposition of aesthetics that the creative powers of man are coextensive with such cognizable principles. This is also the basic supposition of religion and of common-sense mankind. It is not the point of view of mere practice (for it is thought that some things are worthless and as such are not to be distinguished from others) or politics or history.

Are these the basic dimensions: science through its transformational laws; mathematics through its universally extendable principles; aesthetics through the omnivorous appetite of the creator; common sense through its human discriminations and social combinations? Philosophy's categories, since they do not allow for full discrimination in the realm of the encountered world do not offer a basic dimension in the realm of perception. Philosophy's basicality would be the result of the fact that it defines the unity in each of the dimensions, and the unity for all of them. It would subtend the rest. The dimension of religion would be on a par with science, etc., just so far as it had an idea of mercy or apprehension or conservation which embraced all the items in the universe in the light of their differences in being and relation. History could be basic if it were made cosmic and embraced all the eddies and cross-currents of all existents, just as science, through the complication of its laws and conditions, attempts to encompass every experienceable item at least in principle. Psychology, and sociology would be subdivisions, the one of science, the other of common sense, and could not be thought to be basic if not encompassing all items, but which can be so treated that every confronted item would be included by them as items having discriminatory natures and thematic interrelations.

The thematic variations in the basic disciplines—science, aesthetics, common sense, mathematics, religion (perhaps as including history)—differ. Science proceeds by complications; aesthetics by inversion, nuance, discriminatory stresses; common sense by language, practice and attitude which involve sudden shifts and breaks held together by the habitual rhythms of society; religion by evaluations which involve gradations in a hierarchy of classes inside of which there can be discriminations. The scientific approach tends toward the monotonous; the religious, despite the hierarchy and gradations, toward the atomic; the common sense toward the episodic. It is only in aesthetics that we have a full insistence on the thematic variation. The price we pay for this is the lack of constantly applicable laws, as in science and mathematics. Mathematics though could be said to have the same kind of variations as aesthetics, and in this sense, as traditional views have so long stressed, mathematics and aesthetics might be thought to be more basic even than science and religion. Because art allows for jumpings across intermediaries, for intensifications, inversions and the rest, it is richer than science. The rationality of science, like the consideration for the individual case in religion, provide results that the mathematics and art do not.

Mathematics for most is submerged in science, and science in fact is practiced only by few. The basic approaches, and perhaps these alone, make a supplementary set in terms of which one can have normative usages. They are aesthetics, common sense, as concerned both with nature and the schemes of mankind, and religion. The aesthetic approach is one which, though adequate to give us the encountered world as mediated by a sensitive man, offers itself as normative, and thus as having the others as manifestations of itself (and itself too as a manifestation when it is taken to be a dimension alongside the others). As normative there is a necessary referent of the aesthetic content to the world of common sense and the world of religion.

The opposite stresses are also possible. One can look at the world from a religious point of view, and taking this as normative see both the aesthetic and the world of common sense as co-manifestations of the reality which is being accurately portrayed in the religious dimension. A proper religious approach would then require that what is discerned is to be understood to have manifestations in common-sense experience, nature, society, and the aesthetic. Similarly, a proper common-sense approach which took common sense as normative would see the religious and the aesthetic as supplementary manifestations to which a reference must be made in order that the common-sense dimension should serve not merely as a dimension alongside the others but as a normative index of reality. This last is something like Plato's view, for he took society as normative, a society which, though as set up by him was not the society that in fact is sustained by common sense, is supposed to engender such a common sense. From that point of view the role of art and religion are secondary, each serving, when properly treated, to report the very truths of the society in their own way, and needing to be referred to in order to allow the society to be a root reality, with these as expressions.

We have then A] basic dimensions which deal with encountered data having its roots in perception, B] ideal explorers of these dimensions who master all the thematic developments in themselves and in relation to one another under the aegis of a guiding unity, C] the normative use of one of the dimensions and the necessary reference of that one to the others, when the dimension is recognized to be something which is also being explored,   D] the subdivisions of the dimension as comprehensible by some limited method or approach,   E] the derivatives to be achieved through combinations and modifications of the dimension.

In producing a work of art a more intensive aesthetic dimension is substituted for the one that is usually discerned (except by photographers who proceed in just the reverse way, or rather who start with an intensively appreciated aesthetic dimension and partially reproduce this), but with the usual common sense and religious dimensions continued as a rule. Is there a similar substitution in common sense and religion? Is there a way in which common sense redefines itself, and provides something better than what it otherwise gets from a direct encounter? Is it not the case that this is the function of the use of language and of societal solidification through manners and established beliefs? And is it not the case that religious practice, the following out of religious customs and participation in religious institutions, is a substituting for the religious dimension of ordinary perception, when this religious dimension is taken as primary? The religious man, as a member of a religion, offers a more subtle and comprehensive set of interconnections than the data is seen to exhibit.

May not the situation be reversed? Is it possible to substitute direct aesthetic perception for the art dimension, rough-hewn common sense for societal good sense, and religious awe or acceptance for religious practice? To do these things one would abandon something which man has more or less deliberately made, for an immediate contact with something more primitive and perceptual. We do hear again and again of a revolt against such deliberate makings in favor of a more primitive acceptance. We are asked again and again to turn to nature's beauties, to nature's realities, and to nature's awesome majesty and values, to trust our senses and experience rather than the artifacts we have created. We would then seem to deny the value of man's mediation in the guise of a creator, to suppose that his creation is a distortion or dislocation, an abstracting or a confusing. Since this is the case at times, there is point in urging the return at those times. And in fact we do turn back to nature occasionally, without knowing that we do. We turn from art to nature with our perceptions heightened, relieved to be away from the merely humanly created; we turn from religious practice to practice in fact, with some acceptance of the cosmic realities as primary and immediate evidences of the divine; we turn from the conventional usages of language and society to a more pristine acceptance of the currents of nature as being more basic and objective.

When we return to the realm of naïve apprehension or when we stick

with it we are in effect placing ourselves as naïve and innocent in a
position superior to ourselves as creative. And we can justify this only so
far as we somehow find in nature itself the very dynamics and increase
which we find in the artifactual world which man brings about. Otherwise
we unnecessarily dismiss the values we do in fact find in the substitutions
of art, religions and society.

Could we make up a new combination in which two or all three of the
dimensions of ordinary experience are made to give way to the artifactual?
Could we in short have a world of art which is supplemented by common
sense as societally determined, and by the realm of religion? Not only can
we in fact engage in just this kind of substitution quite readily; it is indeed
the position of the iconographers that this is exactly what is done. Yet the
origin of art lies elsewhere; it involves not the use of sophisticated
common sense and religion as supplements and objects of reference but
the naïve common sense which looks at nature in partial freedom from
society, and the naïve religious acceptance of things as having an import
for man, the being who lives, loves, fears and dies in lonesomeness.

For the dimensions of aesthetics, common sense and religion in
perception, let us write $A, C,$ and R. For these dimensions, as the product
of human creativity beyond that involved in mere perception, let us write
$Ac, Cc,$ and Rc. Then we have the following possible cases:

1	A	C	R	where the first item in each row represents the normative case
2	C	A	R	
3	R	A	C	
4	A	Cc	R	
5	A	C	Rc	
6	A	Cc	Rc	
7	Ac	Cc	R	
8	Ac	Cc	Rc	
9	Ac	C	Rc	
10	Ac	C	R	
11	C	Ac	R	
12	C	A	Rc	
13	C	Ac	Rc	
14	Cc	Ac	R	
15	Cc	Ac	Rc	
16	Cc	A	R	
17	Cc	A	Rc	

18	R	A	Cc
19	R	Ac	C
20	R	Ac	Cc
21	Ac	A	Cc
22	Rc	A	C
23	Rc	Ac	C
24	Rc	Ac	Cc

There are thus 24 cases. In four of them the aesthetic dimension of perception is conjoined to supplementary common sense and religious dimensions of both the perceptual and artifactual variety. (There is no need to distinguish the order of these supplements. *ACR* and *ARC* are the same in light of the fact that one need not go through the common-sense dimension to get to the religious or *v/v*, though the former is the usual practice. If these distinctions are insisted on the list doubles.) In *1* we have no substitutions, but simple perception; in case *8* we have all artifactual. In *4, 5, 6* we have perceptual aesthetics combined with sophisticated versions of the others. In cases *2, 3, 12, 16, 17, 18, 21, 22,* the aesthetic dimension of perception has the role of a background. In cases *15* and *24* we have full substitution but with common sense and religion as normative.

If we stress the fact that the aesthetic dimension in perception and art is concerned primarily with patterns, rhythms, significant form, then the supplementary use of common sense and religion can be accounted for as providing objects as involved with human interests on the one hand and as providing terminal entities of value on the other. In short, without these supplements there would be patterns not necessarily having any pertinence to human interests, needs and focal acts, and not necessarily having any pertinence to what has dignity and value and bearing on human welfare and value. We seem to need patterning, interest and value, and the more we stress the one the more surely must we refer to the others as manifestations of a single reality, properly named in the light of the one we stress, but underlying and manifesting itself as all three. Were it not that one was taken as normative, all three could be said to be doing the same thing in collateral ways.

February 18

We perceive with a triple vision. For most of the men in our orbit of culture, the primary stress is on the commonsensical dimension. This is a shifting combination of naïve common-sense distinctions and relations with those stressed by society, with a tincture of those which have been adopted, modified, qualified and rationalized by science. Because this dimension is normative the other two are had as referents. Despite the quip of Wilde that we see a nature which imitates art, the aesthetic dimension in perception is naïve. Photographers might be said to sophisticate this to some degree, though perhaps it might be more accurate to say that they merely attend more carefully to the naïve content of the aesthetic dimension in perception. In addition there is the religious dimension which perhaps (except at crises) is quite overlaid by the sophisticated versions of the data which we obtain in the course of our religious training by religious organizations. The formula then which expresses what we perceive is:

$$C\text{–}Cc; \quad A\text{————}Ac; \quad Rc\text{—}R$$

where the size of the dash measures the degree of incursion of the creative or non-creative component into the other component.

According to the above formula we are creative to some degree in perception, more creative in religion and most conspicuously in the aesthetic dimension. The creative component thus is not one which we are then and there instituting, but nevertheless is constitutive of what we discern by virtue of the kind of approach we are making to the referent of the common-sense dimension.

The creative component can be said to be read into the religious dimension when and as we refer to this. The creative component of the aesthetic is also read in when we make a reference to the correlate dimensions of common sense, but this component is largely a background, a qualification, a mere addition to what is naïvely apprehended. The creative component of the common-sense dimension is had when and as we have the non-creative component, because our perceptions are qualified and guided by judgments and outlooks which already bear the marks of creative work in the past.

Confronted by a datum of this perceptual type we have no need to go elsewhere. Indeed, did we not take the common sense to be normative, did we not occasionally distinguish (because we note a diversity of custom and an ambiguity in some of our perceptions) the creative from the non-creative components, and did we not discern the other dimensions when we had the commonsensical, we would never move away from the perceptual. The normative use of common sense forces us to take account of the other dimensions as coordinate with the dimension of common sense; the distinction between the creative and non-creative components in a dimension leads us to the reflective study of epistemology; the discernment of the other dimensions leads us to focus on them when our need for common-sense objects, our interest in them, our awareness of their incapacity to satisfy us fully, make themselves manifest, due perhaps to our leisure, our weariness and our vital concern with a world beyond.

Men become creatively religious and aesthetic when they shift the stress from common sense to the other dimensions and attend not to the content as had in perception but to it as within the power of man. The shift to the other dimensions could have been a shift in perceptual stress; it is possible just to enjoy the passing forms of nature. We do this sometimes when we idly glance at the patterns made by shadow and sun, or the waves in the sea; we do this at times when we are fearful and alert to our possible destiny. Such a shift could be accompanied by normative usage and thus give us a world which has common-sense objects which are instances of, or occasions for, or termini of the aesthetic surface and the religious meaning.

The problem of the origin of art is not the problem of the shift to another dimension of perception, but that of the abandonment of perception altogether in the dimension of the aesthetic. This abandonment could occur without in any way disturbing the dominance of the commonsensical dimension in experience. When this occurs it is not altogether correct to speak of art as merely substituting the creative component of the aesthetic for the non-creative as it occurs in perception. However when the artist engages in the creating of an aesthetic dimension he looks at the world with this dimension uppermost. If he does not disturb the perceptual order of the common-sense, aesthetic and religious components, what he refers to can be portrayed as:

$$Ac; \ (C–Cc; \ A———Ac; \ Rc—R)$$

What we have here is not a substitution of the aesthetic dimension of perception but the replacement of the primary dimension (the commonsensical) by the newly forged aesthetic one. It becomes normative and the total complex (in brackets above) becomes the referential dimension within which three dimensions can be discerned. If we take that referent as a single block, it would seen necessary to make reference also to another block expressing, not the object which is over against the aesthetic, but the religious import which is correlative with that aesthetic dimension and which functions as a block within which three dimensions can be discerned. Thus:

$$Ac; \ (C–Cc; \ A———Ac; \ Rc—R); \ (R—Rc; \ Ac———A; \ Cc–C).$$

The religious dimension correlate with the newly forged artistic aesthetic dimension has three dimensions in which the creative and non-creative components are given the reverse stress from what they had in the perceptual object in its common-sense role. When and as we make reference to a commonsensical object in which an aesthetic and a religious factor can be discerned, we also refer to a religious dimension. Here to the fore is the religious component in which the primary contribution is given by something naïvely discerned, as qualified by what we have learned. The aesthetic dimension is a simulacrum of the original aesthetic dimension which we create, except that it is partly qualified by the aesthetic dimension of the world as we in fact perceive it. There is also in this block a reference to the common-sense dimension, but it is one in which there is just a slight predominance of the meanings which society and science have imposed on common-sense data.

Starting with perception we find three dimensions. When we move away to artistic production we not only create an aesthetic dimension richer and more controlled than what we had confronted, but we discern faintly and make reference to a kind of reverse image of the three-dimensional perceptual block with which we began. The movement to the newly forged aesthetic dimension is the outcome of a desire to have the aesthetic dimension be more valuable and mastered than it is in perception. But the reason we do want this is because we see something of its independence and of course are aware of its possible normative use.

What we did with the aesthetic we could have done with the common-sense and religious dimension. It could be possible, as is evident in sociology and the growth of forms, for one to isolate the common-sense dimension as an objective of creative control, and to hold this over against the common-sense object of perception and an aesthetic block of dimensions. Similarly one could, as is done in the forging of a religion, make a new religious dimension and hold this over against the common-sensical object and an aesthetic block of dimensions.

Where we isolate and create a common-sense dimension we engage in a substitution; we replace the perceptually dominant common-sense dimension by a superior one, retaining the former however as the dominant dimension in the perceptual object. The aesthetic and religious creative acts could occur in a similar way, but this would require that there first be an inversion of the ordinary perceptual approach to things. Some teachers seek to have this inversion occur first; they force one to turn to nature and look at it in a non-common-sense way. But it is perhaps the case that the inversion occurs only afterwards, so that the perceptual object is seen (and this is the truth of Wilde's quip) to have a dominant aesthetic rather than a dominant commonsensical component.

The artist when he turns from his creation of a new aesthetic dimension tends to see as the perceptual object not Cc–$C;$ A————$Ac;$ Rc—$R,$ but either A————$Ac;$ Cc–$C;$ Rc—$R;$ or Ac————$A;$ Cc–$C;$ Rc—$R;$ or Cc–$C;$ Ac————$A;$ Rc—$R.$ That is, he either places the perceptually discerned aesthetic dimension to the fore, or places a reverse image of this, in the light of what he had created, or has that reverse image replace the original aesthetic dimension as it occurred in the perceptual object, which is to say put in place of the aesthetic dimension, as an object of reference by the common-sense dimension, an aesthetic dimension which reflects the additions which the artist has produced through his creative work.

Is it the case that when we engage in creative work we not only forge a dimension which has a normative value and thus a referential object in the shape of the original perceptual entity, but that we also force into being or make evident another object, and that this object is a kind of inverse image of the perceptual? Is there anything more than a need to reproduce the perceptual situation that forces one to maintain this hypothesis, and is there any need but symmetry which makes one say that it is an inverse image sort of thing? We do need the second object of reference, but this could be treated as a kind of discriminated element in the original perception, forced out of place by the very creation of a new aesthetic dimension. In fact it might be because we are interested in the isolation of just that factor that we engage in the creation of a new aesthetic dimension. Were this the case we would have to say that it is because we are occupied with the religious side of reality beyond what it is discerned as in perception that we engage in the creative artistic act. We would then also have to say that it is because we are interested in discerning the aesthetic side of nature that we engage in the creative act of forging a religion or a socially acceptable common sense—and this does not seem to be the case.

The creation of the artist does enable us to grasp something of the religious dimension that we could not grasp in the perceptual object. Would it also be true that the creation of a religion enables us to grasp something of the aesthetic side of things? This would seem to be true. Is it also the case that the society's creation of the common-sense object enables us to grasp something of the religious and aesthetic as coordinate? This seems possible. But it is not yet clear that there should be an inversion in the new referent, whether or not this referent is first isolated, or is isolated because and through the operation of the normatively employed creatively produced dimension. Perhaps it would be best to say that the inversion can occur, but that as a matter of fact the new referent can be the very perceptual object we had before, but now with a change in stress. In this case the religious or aesthetic dimension of the perceptual object would be forced to the fore when we supplement that perceptual object by another referent, and in being so forced would constitute the new structure of the new object. That object would seem though to be a kind of shadow of the original and this unnecessarily multiplies entities. Better then is the contention that when we engage in a creative artistic act we are confronted by the original perceptual object, but that behind this is a continuation of a modification of either its aesthetic or religious dimensions.

More sharply put: In perception we are confronted with objects which are primarily commonsensical in import and secondarily aesthetic and religious. Each of these in different ways has imported into it something of the creatively produced elements from man's past. For the sake of better mastering an Existence which is forever escaping him, or under the stimulus of an attraction for the aesthetic dimension in the perceptual object, or to focus on some other dimension better, a man engages in the activity of producing a work of art. The art object is the aesthetic dimension mastered and enriched, and has over against it the original perceptual object and a somewhat distinguished and modified vaguely apprehended domain of natural aesthetic forms or something of religious import. The art object itself of course can be dealt with as a perceptual object from which we must take a departure in order to master its aesthetic dimension better in a new fresh creation. The spectator of course, does this, the artist does it too when he uses the art object as one of the occasions for the production of another type of art object, perhaps one having art as a perceptual object.

The perceptual object, as having three dimensions—commonsensical, aesthetic and religious—is an illustration of the three modes of being—the Actual, the existential and the divine. The aesthetic production which the artist provides is essentially the achievement of an Ideal, the beautiful as a category having evaluative import for the other three as integral in the perceptual object. When a man, instead of creating the aesthetic object, produces instead a social or a religious one, he still provides a kind of Ideal—social or a divinely sanctioned one. In the course of reproducing and mastering Existence by making an art work, he on the one hand produces an Ideal, and on the other hand, gives independence to the dimension of Existence by allowing it to serve as the heart of the referential act.

When, instead of producing an object of art, we produce a socially satisfactory common-sense entity or a divinely sanctioned religious one, we dislocate the existential factor of the aesthetic in the perceptual object. Some of it is still used in the act of reference, but since in these cases what is not really distinguished is the actual common-sense dimension in the perceptual entity or the religious component of it, these must have primary use in the referential act. This means that in their cases the reference to the perceptual object is different from that of the artist. The social man refers not existentially but via actualities, which means through the mediation of human beings; the religions refer not existentially but via sacramental objects. What this amounts to is that when we create a dimension we also use that mode of being in a referential way. The creation gives us a mode of being in the shape of an Ideal, in the shape of a kind of reference, and as a part of a perceptual object. If we took reference to be primarily existential and the perceptual object to be an actuality which taints the dimensions in it with Actuality, we have three types of qualification: the Ideal, the existential and the Actual. This would seem to indicate that when we dislocate an item, no matter what it is, it assumes the status of a divinely qualified one.

Starting say with the art object, we have then the aesthetic dimension as Ideal, the aesthetic functioning as relation in a dynamic way (the very being of Existence), the aesthetic as a component in a perceptual object, and the aesthetic as divinely sustained. According to the foregoing analyses the last must be such as to be almost entirely submerged in the divine, for what is dislocated is the religious element in the perceptual. Starting with the socially determined common-sense object, we have common sense as an Ideal, functioning normatively; we have it carried by men assuming the role of representatives for vital Existence; we have it as a dimension in the perceptual object; and we have it as a submerged element in a religiously separated dimension. And finally, starting with a religiously determined reality, we have religion as an Ideal; we have it as a sacramental relation; we have it as a component in perception; and we have it as the meaning of a dislocated aesthetic part of the perceptual object.

The created object then is part of a four-fold situation which has its ideality expressed in the created object; its existential side expressed in the way reference is made beyond that created object; its actuality expressed in the way in which the perceptual object contains it; and its divine side expressed in the way it stands outside the perceptual object from which it was dislocated in part.

The aesthetically produced dimension is pure as reference; the idea of beauty is pure only as an ideal created dimension in the role of a norm; the perceptual object is a pure case of Actuality only where the common-sense side of it is dominant; the dislocated dimension is a pure case of the religious only where the ominous side of the perceptual object is dislocated. If we could have an ideal of beauty existentially mediating a common-sensical object with a religious background we would have, in the realm of perception and creation, the best possible case of an illustration of the four modes of being.

February 19

If $C–A–R$ is an accurate formula for a perceptual object, with C representing commonsensical, A aesthetic, and R religious dimensions, all with mixtures of naïve and sophisticated acceptances, then it is evident that empiricism has made a number of blunders. Firstly, it supposes that the aesthetic, i.e., the immediate or surface is on the surface; the aesthetic aspect is in fact recessive and is to be found in a stressed position only occasionally. Secondly, it supposes that the aesthetic is atomic when it is essentially a pattern, a matter of structure, form and interplay. Thirdly, it supposes that it is entirely divorced from the other dimensions, forcing one to postulate or construct these, whereas it occurs only together with them. Fourthly, it supposes that one could construct one of these dimensions out of the others, whereas each is self-contained. Fifthly, it supposes that the isolation of a dimension involves no alteration, when as a matter of fact it is essentially constructed, a new creation replacing the other. Sixthly, it ignores the referential nature of the new creation, and the distorted component of the perceptual object which its isolation involves.

The aesthetic dimension need not be to the fore in order that one should be interested in creating. It is enough that one should note that as in nature it is shot through with irrelevant contingency and is not an excellent as it might be, and that it is in fact a form of a mode of being—Existence—which deserves and needs to be mastered by us.

The three-dimensionality of the perceptual object means that we take three attitudes toward it at the same time; appropriate to the commonsensical object are our interest, needs, habits, usages; appropriate to the aesthetic are empathy, pleasure, enjoyment; appropriate to the religious are feeling, emotion, sympathy, and perhaps even sexual involvement. And when we treat the art object as a perceptual entity we have the three of them again. The act of creating any dimension in a nobler form is an act which need not involve the same kind of evaluation or attitude as was characteristic of the perception. The creativity of a dimension overwhelms the acceptance of it.

The appropriate attitude in creating the aesthetic dimension is appropriation or mastery; that of the common sense is adjustment or concurrence; that of the religious is submission or acceptance.

The created dimension has a referential connection with the perceptual object and with a dislocated component of it. This referential connection rides on the surface of a vital existential relating. And as all existential situations do, it is at once divisive and connective. As divisive it keeps us at a distance, the very distance which interested Bullough; as connective it gives us the conventional and emotive meaning which didactic and sentimental art tend to exaggerate and hold apart from the very dimension which refers to them and gives them value and locus. Bullough overpsychologizes the relation of distance, and mixes up a basic view with references to attitudes and similarities on the part of spectator and object. Also it is the entire object, even as possessed of an aesthetic dimension that is kept at a distance. Bullough is inclined to hold that it is merely a putting the object "out of gear with practical needs and ends." It is this, but it is more; it is a putting aside of the perceptual object entirely, for the sake of concentrating on the creative side. But staying with the perceptual object and ignoring the creative, we face another difficulty with his view: He supposes that it is only the aesthetic dimension which we keep at a distance, but in fact, when we want to have a simple perceptual relation to the perceptual object, and thus enjoy a psychical distance from it, we push the naïvely apprehended aspect of all three dimensions to a side.

To know what a perceptual thing is in itself we must free it from extraneous additions. Since every one of the dimensions is tainted by our contribution, we have no recourse in ordinary experience but to distinguish the more from the less. Consequently we try to separate off and attribute to ourselves the sophisticated, inherited and obviously imposed components of all three dimensions, leaving at a distance, as characteristic of the object, the naïvely apprehended common-sense, aesthetic and religious aspects. The object as substantial, pertinent to ourselves, and as having a bearing on human destiny, is as "distant" as it is as having a significant aesthetic form.

Distancing is the other side of empathy, the one separating, the other uniting. There is a kind of empathy for the sensuous or aesthetic side, another for the commonsensical and a third for the religious. The criticism often made of the last two is precisely that they read into things what is characteristic of man. Those who would like to stay with the surface of things, as Russell sometimes did, are inclined to say that we read into common-sense objects the elements of volition and resistance characteristic of ourselves, and that we objectify our fears and hopes in the content of our perceptions. These are thought to be critical remarks; but the very same temper of criticism can be expressed with respect to the empathy we express with respect to the aesthetic dimension. One who took common sense as basic, as Moore was inclined to do, would object to accounts of the good and beauty which read into them anything to do with our needs and appetites and satisfactions. And naturalistic approaches to religion (such as that which was characteristic of Dewey), say the same thing of religion, objecting to the fact that it reads into the common-sense objects the purely subjective fears and hopes of men. But one could take the religious position with all its values as normative. From that perspective, one wrongly reads into the aesthetic dimension values it does not have. This is the puritan objection to art. And one can take common sense not to be important, as mystics and other-worldly men have done through the ages.

We have an empathy in all dimensions; it does not arise from us but, as Koffka observed, has its roots in the object; the structure or "rising" or whatever is a phenomenal characteristic. We ought not then to speak of ourselves as reading ourselves into the object, but only of having a connection with it at the same time that we remain at a distance from it.

Since the perceiver and the artist both are in the position of an Ideal with respect to the perceptual object, the normative use they make of their categories and products is different from that which is characteristic of the dimensions in the object. The categories and art object are taken to be normative in the sense that the object beyond is subordinated to it, explained by it, absorbed into it, subject to it. The white shape is the very essence of lamb and purity. To be sure the perceptual object and its dislocated dimension continues to transcend the referent; there is always a distance. But this means only that there is a tension from the side of the perceiver, one which in fact is being partly resolved by making the act of reference function existentially. The perceiver starts as an Ideal which would subjugate, but the subjugation, because it must be carried out over a vital existential distance and be exercised with respect to what is in fact independent, is one which makes the perceiver fall back into himself and have over against himself a world which is not subjugated except in an intent. That intent never gets the length even of reaching the object but remains always as a kind of hope or attitude which cannot escape the confines of the category or product which guides the perception.

El Greco said of Michaelangelo that he was a good man but not a painter. By this he could have meant only that he did not paint as El Greco did or that he did not measure up to the standards set by El Greco for an El Greco kind of painting. It was evidently not a judgment about Michelangelo in his own context. And this brings us back again to the criterion of a painting or any work of art. This can be nothing more than the endless proliferation of nuances in themes themselves encompassing the entire object and together constituting a unity which can be properly termed beautiful. That beautiful unity is not the product of a deliberate effort to bring beauty about; the objective is some ideal meaning or goal defined by the nature of the medium and the dimension which one seeks to create. It is in the creation of that medium as having endless patterns that beauty is achieved. But the patterns cannot be merely multiplied; they must have tensions amongst themselves. And in the course of producing the unity one at the same time makes a subjugative, distancing, empathic connection with the world of perception suggested by, and sometimes conventionally related to the aesthetic production.

By what warrant can one claim that the philosophic account of objects is free from the humanistic intrusions characteristic of perception, both naïve and sophisticated? Must it not be that the very activity of speculation tears one away from the context of bias and puts one in the area of neutrality? But this would be a fictitious domain were it not that some hold is kept on the object. The speculative approach actually continues to maintain the perceptual categories; it acts as a kind of Ideal (despite the fact that it is rooted in an actual man and takes in fact the approach of Actuality to all the other modes), but it does this in such a generalized way that it can subjugate perception with a minimum of distortion. More important it isolates in the perceptual object the very distinctions which characterize it as a category. To this it might be objected that instead of indicating just what is the case in fact, it but reveals how one, taking the position of the Ideal as sustained or expressing an Actuality, distorts the real in the light of that position.

Malraux is surely right in emphasizing the fact that artists learn primarily from artists and not from nature. This is but to say that the aesthetic dimension in the perceptual object is not the primary condition for artistic creation. There is a dim awareness of it and of its inadequacy, but the way to master it is to attend to previous ways of mastering it and to learn from these how to engage in a mastery in a new way. And that art is most suitable to one which has for him endless possibilities of creation. The true painter is one who having just finished one painting is aware that it has limitations and that he ought in fact to engage in the production of another which avoids those limitations, thereby permitting of a better (i.e., relative to the limitations characteristic of the previous painting) mastery of Existence.

If emotion is pertinent primarily to the religious dimension, then the purging of emotions is and can be but one of the elements in any work. It is the involvement with plot and character that leads to a consideration of purging of emotions. If, on the contrary, were one to attend to the aesthetic dimension alone, with its element of pleasure and enjoyment one would take as the main objective of art the production, intensification and preservation of pleasures. And if one were to take the common-sense dimension as primary one would, in the light of its involvement with human interest, consider the satisfaction of human interests primary. Tolstoy's moralism is due to his emphasis, despite his religious remarks, on the common-sense dimension. This is of course also true of Marx. Freud's primary interest would seem to be in the aesthetic dimension, since he emphasizes the element of pleasure. His view is one with Santayana's. Aristotle's primary interest is in the religious dimension, since he emphasizes the element of purgation and is concerned with virtue and vice, and human destiny. His view is one with Maritain's.

We have then a purging of emotions which are unordered with respect to the religious dimension as discerned in experience; an intensification and focalization of pleasure and enjoyment affected by irrelevancies and our subjection to the contingencies of Existence, in the aesthetic dimension of experience; and finally a satisfaction and completion that is provided by the proper creation of common-sense objects, which perfect and control the dimension that would in experience be mixed with dissatisfactions and constant transitions and involvements.

Is it the case that the purging is the proper object of a temporal art, that the intensification of pleasure is the proper object of an energetic art, and that the satisfaction and completion, the relaxing of the tension of need, is the proper object of a spatial art? Or should we not say that all of these occur together, though the different types of art emphasize one of these achievements rather than the others?

Whatever the answer to the foregoing question, it would seem to be the case that in experience the emotions are excessive, the pleasures impure and the satisfactions blurred and incomplete. But is it because of these facts that one engages in the arts? Is the drive behind the artistic activity the need to take care of this subjective side, rather than to consider how to master and control? Also, if it be emotions we wish to express properly ought we not to have recourse to a religious reconstruction rather than to an artistic? If it is satisfaction we wish to achieve must we not make new common-sense objects? If this be the case then a partial answer to the foregoing question must be that if the temporal arts specialize in purging and the spatial in satisfaction, they can do these things only by functioning as surrogates for the creations of religion and common sense respectively. Should we then say that story telling for example is a kind of secular religion, and that painting for example is a kind of fictive social order?

February 20

The problem of the response to art is a problem which needs an antecedent solution of the problem of the response to the perceptual object. This response is that of using, enjoying, and being involved with it in one's substantiality. All these occur together, one being emphasized at one time and another at a different time. In addition there is the activity of subjugating it to ourselves by means of categories having a referential role. We deal with the perceptual object as the terminus of a judgment which brings into play the associations of society and experience, as the terminus of the aesthetic object produced by the artist, and as the terminus of the meanings and values introduced by the organized religions.

The art object has the three-fold nature characteristic of a perceptual object; it also can be dealt with in the six ways in which the perceptual object is dealt with—use, enjoyment, involvement; judgment, art and institutional religion. When one speaks of a response to an art object, presumably what is meant is the enjoyment and judgment of it. But such enjoyment and judgment is, according to the above analysis, directed at the entire art object having the being of an object rather than of the purely aesthetically produced component which is given residence in some physical object. The above analysis dealt with the enjoyment and judgment of the work of art as having a weight and a frame, etc. What is wanted then is not enjoyment and judgment of the work of art, but something quite different—the isolation of the aesthetic dimension and the proper apprehension of this. This requires a dislocation, an inversion of the art object. Instead of being faced as *C A R,* it must be dealt with as *A C R.* In such isolating one makes use of concepts and attitudes, but with the act there is a change from concepts and attitudes pertinent to a common-sense object to one of readiness to feel and enjoy. This readiness to feel and enjoy is directed not at the art object as a mere object of perception, but at it as predominantly aesthetic. This aesthetic component must now be participated in; one must find the basic themes and follow them through. The most sensitive appreciation of the work will involve the discovery of a plurality of diverse themes each of which is developed, and all of which together harmonize, constitute an excellence which is beauty. Without a plurality of themes we have thinness; without development of theme we have monotony; without a unification of themes we have chaos; without a tension amongst the themes which are being united we have uninteresting solutions, mere elaboration.

The isolation of the aesthetic side and the dissection of it into a plurality of themes all held together by the concept or fact of beauty occurs without regard for what the artist intends. It is not the case, as Wimsatt and Beardsley claimed, that no knowledge of the artist's intentions is possible; we can read evidences of such intentions in the work of art as surely as we do in psychiatry and law. But it is the case that, except to provide us with guides, there is no need to refer to the intentions.

The pursuit of thematic developments in the art object distinguishes the approach we make to the aesthetic dimension which man creates and that which we confront in the perceptual object. We enjoy the play of forms in nature, but we do not try to unravel them, partly because they are so shot through with contingency, so complicated by irrelevancies and impurities, and because they, except for someone like Berkeley who thought of the play of phenomena to be the language of discourse of God, are not thought to have such a development. The recognition of the plurality of thematic developments also helps resolve the question as to whether or not the artist works without thought or control. The thematic developments are for the most part deliberately instituted; the main one is so instituted, but not necessarily through any mediation of concepts or well-formed ideas. On the other hand there are many subordinate themes and relationships which the artist produces incidentally and without clear knowledge; it is these he often corrects, works over or at later times perhaps surprisingly discovers. Each builds bigger than he knows.

The isolating of the aesthetic dimension in the work of art does not exclude, but in fact must involve the dividing of a medium into an aestheticized and a physical side. The medium is something worked over, and as worked over is evidently something which is not yet part and, as material, never can be part of the aesthetic side. But we work over the medium to make it the embodiment, the carrier, the indispensable component in the artistic work. A theme without such embodiment would be merely in the mind of the artist; a theme which was merely carried by material and was not integral to it, would be one which had no being in a medium but only localization there. This is how Hegel seemed to treat architecture, forgetting that the lights and shadows, the use of the module, the organization of the building was more than having stones exteriorly glued through the use of ideas that could not find proper lodgment in such unthinking entities. The thought of the architect is one with the art object he creates, though not one with it as having a material body. But even the highest art, poetry or drama for Hegel, has a material backdrop in the form of physical bodies and voices and larnyxes, etc.

There is, because the medium is integral to the art object, a texture to all art objects. The theme must explore the texture, the quality of the material. It elaborates this, makes it integral to a pattern; the pattern is an interconnection of textured foci, the texture always making us aware that there is a background behind the art object but which is being held apart, put aside. The use of the texture helps constitute the art object in its aesthetic dimension as a distinct entity. The fact that it is a locus of interlocked or relevant developed themes makes its appreciation a matter not of simple enjoyment but rather of work, effort, initiative, imagination and even struggle.

Something similar can be said of the sociological common-sense object and the religious institution or its objects. These are not, when viewed as the termini of genuine appreciations, to be approached as are their naïve counterparts in the perceptual object. In each there is a new medium provided, a new texture is given, and themes are elaborated which are not to be found in the perceptual domain. We must learn how to participate in them, and must look to masters to show us how they are to be further elaborated. It is not the awareness of the nature of the dimensions in the perceptual object which teach us how to deal with them in the created world. We may have to turn to the perceptual object for guidance, for an occasional hint, for basic patterns even, but not for a training in the art of appreciation of the created work.

An institutional religion is not merely the religion of the numinous forced inside some organizational pattern or subject to new implications and involvements in human affairs; it includes the making of something new. There is something wrong then in the views of men such as Dewey who think of institutional religions as the enemies of a true religious apprehension of nature. We can view the institutional religions as laboratories and instruments for the renewal of a genuine apprehension of the divine. But there is a sense in which the institutional religion has nothing to do with this; it has its own life and value, helping define a culture. Such a religion is no more to be made subservient to the religious dimension of the perceptual object than a work of art is to be made subservient to the aesthetic dimension of the perceptual object.

Similarly the elaborated objects of socialized common sense have their own integrity; their texture is given by the language and values of the society. Their function is not primarily to make one organize the common-sense objects of daily life; their function is to constitute an entirely new domain which can have referential relations to the common-sense objects of daily life, and are which is to be judged and enjoyed, i.e., appreciated, in its own terms.

When men create in art, society and religion, they are enabled to complete themselves through a mastery of Existence, Actuality and the divine in ways they could not in mere perception. Perception is limited in its range, without thematic variation, shot full of contingent and irrelevant details, terminating in objects which are also impure in these ways. But this mastery is not merely the perceptual dimension newly confined and controlled; it is the dimension newly forged in the body of the medium. We can use the perceptual object as an instrument for getting to this result, and we can use the created object as an instrument for making us concentrate better on the perceptual. But they have their own values and integrities and need no justification through a demonstration of instrumental use.

Having achieved an independence of being, the created object has a categorial value; its meaning can be read into and is read into the body of the perceptual object, via habits, expectations, associations and altered usages of the organs. But these additions then suffer a sea-change; as in the perceptual object they are to be dealt with, used, enjoyed and undergone in the same way as the rest of it. And so when we approach the perceptual object in the course of experience we find there the transformed residue of previous creative efforts. So far as this is true there is a need on the part of the creative man to get away from the perceptual world, not merely because he is engaged in mastering the dimensions in a way that the perceptual world will not permit, but because there is a likelihood that he will unknowingly be dragged down to see in nature what in fact was not there in the first place. Though Wilde is wrong in thinking that after Turner we saw Turner sunsets in nature, it is the case that after Turner we saw Turner-affected sunsets, sunsets which are qualified by the achievements of a Turner. To see the pure sunset one would have to isolate the mere object of apprehension, break away from the contribution which we have made to the aesthetic dimension in the perceptual object.

Were the contributed element (which is read into the perceptual object, from the vantage point of the created domain) there without any alteration, the isolation of the pure component in perception would leave over this contributed element; a study of it would then tell us what men had done in the past. But we cannot learn what men had done in the past, what they had creatively brought about, by examining what is left over in the perceptual object after one had isolated (if one could), the pure component, for as was just observed, the created element, when brought into the perceptual object is changed, submerged in some cases even, and in all cases altered by the other components and by the new medium.

The medium can be said to affect the meter as well as the tonality of the work or the object, for media are resistant and compliant, tensed and easy, etc. But one need not attend to the medium in appreciating a work of art, for as in the work of art it is part of the pattern. The medium gives the substantiality, the locality, the "visible" power to the pattern. It offers a kind of key signature to the pattern, telling us what kind of pattern should or can be carried out. It is the medium which defines the range of patterns. Because words have alliterative powers, consonance values, as well as the capacity to convey meanings, we can look at a poem as the locus of elaborated paradoxes, rhymes, alliterations, etc., etc.

The critic need not stay with the art object as a mere aesthetic totality.

He can attend to its commonsensical referential powers—what is some-times called its capacity to communicate—and to its religious referential powers—what is sometimes called its mythopoesis. He can and ought to bring in some consideration of its social affects, its import for traditional religion, its place in its own genre, its success in living up to its own professed intention and so on. Such considerations need not involve him in a rejection of the work as aesthetically satisfactory, or even in considering it on the whole as such. It is possible for one to see a work as having a deleterious effect in society or on certain people and still praise it as a work of art, and even comment it on the whole, recognizing that the limitations it may have or even the errors it might promote or incorporate are overwhelmed by the artistic merits. The important thing for the critic is not to confuse the different positions of evaluation, and not to condemn the work as a whole because of its failure to live up to a standard characterizing excellence in some non-aesthetic dimension.

In what position must the critic stand that he can look at the work in all these different roles; what position must he take in order to evaluate the merit of the work in one of the roles over against all the rest? Evidently he must have a position which involves the apprehension of the Ideal which is expressed as the Good, the Beautiful, the True, and be able to judge how well the art object as a totality of *C A R* embodies this and helps promote it elsewhere. The judgment in the end is in the light of an all-encompassing excellence of which the excellence in art, beauty, is but one illustration, and which has no rights that take precedence over all others. It has its own rights, but these, like the rights of other specializa-tions of the Ideal, must in the end be modified and varied to make them consonant with one another, so that they end by becoming an elaborated articulation which exhausts the meaning of the Ideal.

February 21

When I went to New York and began to paint a good deal, I found that I began to write less and less in my philosophy book and that by the time I was at the end of my stay I gave up writing altogether. When I returned to New Haven I found it almost impossible to write anything. I concentrated on writing but found that the thoughts would not come. But the painting, which I relegated to the weekends, continued to improve. And then suddenly I began to write again, and though I continued to improve for a little while in my painting I soon found that I began to lose vitality and freshness and focus in the painting. This long range effect of the one on the other has a counterpart of course in the short span. He who takes an intellectual approach to the arts will tend to make his art a mere vehicle for an abstract idea and will tend to lose the interior development of the medium—which is what Hegel apparently never understood. And he who takes an aesthetic attitude toward his ideas will watch how they flow and interplay; he will be a punster rather than a thinker.

In thinking, one's body is but in the background, kept from intruding, and a trance-like focus on it is achieved in the mind. Keeping the body in the background does not mean it cannot act, sometimes violently. A thinker might gesture, grimace, write, but the direction of his energy is dictated by the idea and he assumes the attitude which makes such dictation possible. In art, though much of the body is not used and though there can be a good deal of fatiguing use of the mind, the approach is essentially existential; one expresses oneself through the hands primarily but as vehicles for the entire being.

The entire being must be involved in thinking, but it functions primarily as support and vehicle for the exercise of the mind; in art the hands serve as the vehicle for the use of being who is then said to "express" himself. The thinker betrays, exposes himself; the artist makes himself manifest through this restricted channel. The spectator engaged in the gruelling work of tracing out the themes stands somewhere in between these two. His approach is initially and perhaps at the end from a distance, and is thus somewhat like the intellectual's; but since he is concerned with the work of art, he looks in terms of his being. The seeing or hearing is not on a par with the actual making.

Can it be said that the poet, the choreographer and the composer, and perhaps the conductor and director, are mediating their entire beings through their hands? This does not seem to be the case. They do express themselves and may do nothing more than exercise their imaginations. It is not then the effort which one expends through the hands, or the use of them in fact to make something which is the central fact, but the immersion in a medium and the pursuit of the theme through it, mediated or channelized by some part of the body. Even the botanist or naturalist or other empirically oriented intellectual, who may be wanting to just record patterns encountered, transmutes the items in such a way that they become integral to the pattern of his own thought.

Thinking is the most successful of the arts; it effectively controls its medium, i.e., the objects in the world as transmuted into concepts. The different concepts have no tonality; they do not resist in different degrees. Some may be clearer or vaguer than others; their affiliations may not be known. But they are themselves translucent, through and through what they are then and there. Their capacity to be analyzed or completed is not due to a potentiality in them, but to the thinker who in effect replaces or modifies them to give quite new ideas. The objective relations, even the substantial being of the objects and their relations are brought into the realm of mind on condition that they continue to be beyond it, as is the case in all art. And though when we think we may conform to the pattern that holds in fact, it still is true that the thinker absorbs without residue the pattern that he in fact is thinking through. The thinker, though guided by the facts and in the end subservient to them, nevertheless in his attitude has already conquered the medium. There is no texture to this thought which he owes to the world, even though his thinking is geared to it and his problems and pace are set by it.

The contrast between the two attitudes would seem to be then the allowing oneself to be involved in a foreign medium, the having one's being involved in a new texture, or the insistence on one's own pattern to control and absorb the medium and the corresponding texture. There is something realistic about the creator which is not true of the intellectual: he allows the objective world to have its own intrinsic quality, whereas the intellectual does not. On the other hand the intellectual, where successful, is able to "appreciate" the object and its relations, get an "imitation" of their essences into himself and thus do more justice in another way to the object.

The artist does justice to the world beyond by taking account of its texture—though the texture may be only that of a canvas and paints, or sounds and instruments (with perhaps an attempt to make a semblance of the texture of actual things beyond)—whereas the intellectual though concentrating on the nature of things does justice to them only by insisting on the use of his logic, inferences, constructions and speculations.

The problem raised by Lessing as to whether or not there are distinct and appropriate media for different arts has, on one level, a rather easy and obvious answer. There are temporal, spatial and energetic arts and there are arts which use paints and others which use stone. But if the question is whether there are some things which can be said in some arts and not in others, the issue becomes more difficult to resolve. Surely one cannot say with Lessing that sculpture cannot express anguish, that there are some ugly expressions which therefore cannot be artistically presented. His view overlooks the transformative power of the work of art, and the capacity of one art to express in ways other arts do not. A piece of sculpture need not express anguish by showing an anguished man; that is a simple-minded representationalistic view of sculpture. An anguished man can be shown in an endless number of ways—indeed his entire body can exhibit the anguish, with the expression in the eyes and hands and face offering but one thematic variation on the whole, or serving to provide subordinate themes to a dominant one of anguish. Lessing thinks that there are some things which the artist must conceal in order to achieve beauty; but this is not really a concealment but a minimization of one theme in order that the whole should be beautiful. It is not, in short, because there are some things an artist may not do that he for example is said to veil the face of one who is undergoing terrible suffering, but because, in order to convey such suffering, he must not exaggerate one avenue through which the suffering is expressed, that he does not allow the face to reveal it. In short, Lessing seems to be right: it is because the artist wanted to successfully produce something beautiful that he minimized the presentation of the anguished face. But Lessing is wrong in thinking that there were some things that could not be shown or should not be shown. The anguish of the face could have been shown and could have been beautiful, but then some other theme would have to be used to support it. The picture of Christ on the cross, and the statues of him would seem to indicate that Lessing's case can be made only by ignoring what is evident on all sides.

Modern paintings show how mistaken Lessing was in thinking that the painter must confine himself to one single view at one moment. The cubists give one illustration of a plurality of views; so does Picasso at many stages of his career. But even classical painting gives the lie to him, for there can often be many perspectives presented on many different levels in a painting; and oriental painting of course often shows scenes in which a series of events take place. To this it might be objected that we then have just a collage of momentary single views. But this once again forgets the dominance of the theme which interlocks these various views, prohibiting the approach to them as isolated views. Even the piece of sculpture which is thought to be all present in one frozen moment, portraying a frozen moment, is a locus for a plurality of themes. If the themes all add up to anguish on the whole, they themselves need not express this. It would involve a fallacy of composition to assert that the nature of the whole is a repetition of that which occurs in the thematic development of the parts.

Lessing takes essentially the view of the spectator and then with respect to the topic presented rather than the aesthetic values. He wants the artist to promote the free play of the imagination; he wants him to show us a man sighing, for then we can imagine him crying; but if, thinks Lessing, he shows him crying we cannot imagine him in any other condition but one which is less interesting, such as groaning or being dead. But the imagination can soar in any direction; and groaning or being dead are not necessarily less interesting than crying. Lessing thinks that signs existing side by side can represent only objects side by side. This overlooks the way in which the space, time and energy eddy, curve around items, that the theme grows, ties up earlier and later, the near and the far in ways which are other than that which they exhibit as mere physical entities.

Bosanquet says we cannot make the same things in clay that we can in iron. But this is an error; what must be said is that clay imposes conditions which iron does not; but the patterning of them in one way need not preclude the patterning in another in order to say the very same things.

February 23

In the act of perception we find not only a commonsensical component, an aesthetic, and a religious, but have these caught in a judgment which allows them on the one hand to be internally divided into contemplated and indicated, and to merge into an adumbrated version. The "it" which is indicated has all three components; so has the contemplated and adumbrated. Since we approach the percept by means of a category which is qualified and directed by a concern for some possibility, and is expressive of some interest in what is to be, there is an idealization which affects the perceived. The judged aspect of the perceived moreover is dislocated from the rest and made part of mind; in this act it is subject to new transformations, characteristic of logic, etc. The perceived, since it is not entirely freed from our past understandings and habits must be said too to contain in its common-sense component primarily something of the past as well as of the future, made evident to the sensitive expectant perceiver.

The possibility which primarily concerns common sense is that which has been realized; common sense is primarily conservative and sees in the perceptual object primarily what had been seen before. The aesthetic dimension is primarily fresh and open to new prospects; it is the locus of the play of unfulfilled possibilities. In the religious dimension we find further possibility sustained on the opposite side from that which sustains the habits of common-sense perception. What we have then are possibilities established in the past read into the common-sense object; possibilities now being brought into play on the present aesthetic content, somewhat in the way in which Santayana spoke of essences illuminating the realm of matter; possibilities still future, being sustained by a power outside them which makes them germane to human destiny. In addition to these possibilities there are those which are germane to the perceptual object and the reality beyond it, and this apart from man and his knowledge. The individual who is the locus of the category and through which the past habitual ways of perceiving are manifest makes something of his individual nature and stresses manifest in the object, just as the religious background of the possibility is manifest in the religious dimension. These various possibilities ought to be sorted out and some systematic presentation of them provided.

There are also the relations which the perceived has to others both because of man and by itself. When in the course of judgment one isolates the perceptual content and subjects it to the patterning of logic or aesthetics one has the problem of truth, and the problem which Peirce raised—why and how we hit on hypotheses which in fact answer to the facts. The answer is perhaps that we do not need to look for any accordance of nature with the hypotheses, art objects and other things we create. We are constantly separating out content in perception as we live through experience. Consequently we are inevitably forging and manifesting relations between the content with which we start and the content with which we end some span of judging. The habit of coming to a certain content, after we have had another and in a certain way, grounds an habitual way of inferring. It is because we have perceived this book here as having such and such a shape, and then, by moving our eyes and position, have perceived it as having another shape at the same place, that we are able to relate these two contents (not merely as having come to us at different times) as being related through shifts in perspective. A shift in perspective is lived through and need have no direct correspondence with the way in which the shapes are related in principle or in fact. But if we can always get them in that order through that change in perspective then we have a living rule. What we call the formal principle of the connection is that abstractable residue in the living rule which can be ascribed to the shapes. In short, if we know the way in which the shapes are in fact related, through a consideration of shapes and perspectives and not through a consideration of our thinking or perceiving them, then we can use this as the normative component in our perceiving, attributing the rest to ourselves as merely psychological or dynamic or inferential activities, in which the formal component is made manifest.

An alternative account: The common-sense, aesthetic and religious dimensions of the perceived all exhibit something of the past, under the pressure of habituation, experience, art history and religious training. All of them exhibit something of the individual's contribution, and all of them bear the marks of the substantial object of which the perceptual is but the surface. But in addition, the common-sense object is related to a discerned possibility through the expectative attitude of the individual, who brings that possibility to bear via the expression of his interest. The aesthetic dimension has its possibility brought to bear on the aesthetic content through the agency of an attitude towards beauty. The religious dimension has its possibility brought to bear by means of a power which we can only vaguely discern. The individual's interest and the religious power are active both in the sense that they in fact bring the possibility into the present and in the sense that they impose themselves on their respective dimensions. But in the case of the aesthetic dimension, the ideal of beauty is more neutral. It is the individual's concern with the possibility that makes it come into the category of beauty; it is the individual's vital occupation with the realization of beauty which makes the possibility via beauty have a locus in the aesthetic object.

February 24

We can distinguish the following components in perception: 1] The naïve common-sense element;   2] the sophisticated common-sense element, reflecting the residuum of learned truths from science and accepted versions and demands of society;   3] the naïve aesthetic element;   4] the sophisticated aesthetic element reflecting artistic production and inherited values;   5] the naïve religious component;   6] the sophisticated religious component reflecting human interest and cosmic control;   7] the realm of possibility which is being mediated by the categories of judgment, the sense of beauty, expectation, and religious attitude;   8] the analytic components distinguished in a judgment, having the form of the common-sense object serving as the terminus of a denotation, the aesthetic dimension as the item contemplated, and the religious as the copula;   9] the adumbrated substantial reality of the object as outside the judgment, and functioning as substantiality for the common-sense object, as that which is ponderous, tangible and active, linking spaces and times for the aesthetic component, and functioning as an adumbrated background for the religious component.

When we turn to the art object we find all these components too. To isolate the aesthetic side of the art object we delimit the aesthetic element in the physical frame, the canvas, pedestal, paper, bodies, instruments, etc. This aesthetic object like the naïve and sophisticated aesthetic components is to be seen as the locus of patterns. The common sense part of this set of patterns gives it its texture, and the religious part (for the common sense and religious components can never be entirely freed from the aesthetic) gives it its bearing on other aesthetic elements. The human judge or appreciator enables one to avoid the mere geometrical and chronological connections of the elements in the aesthetic situation and to determine relations of another sort. These latter relations are present in the aesthetic dimension, but they come into focus only by virtue of a being who can in fact directly relate what is spatially and temporally distant.

The observer or appreciator in a sense then provides a kind of space and time which is distortive from tht standpoint of the physical object. This distortive space and time is to be found in the object but only so far as there is one who can as it were move through it. The ability to see distant connections is the same thing as the ability to synthesize the termini of these connections to constitute a way of being together which is not mediated by flat space and time.

Neil Welliver's paintings of the round-faced people shows an interweaving of the convex and concave. As one concentrates on the convex side the faces become very close; on the concave they are at a distance. The two-sidedness conveys a numinous terror; the fact that they are faces makes them answer to the commonsensical side of things; and their aesthetic quality is determined by the way in which the shapes and features interplay. What is not clear is why the features and shapes have the colors they do.

Perhaps "grain" would be a better term than "fabric" or "texture" to express the qualitative difference which the components of a pattern make. Thomists speak of the clarity of a color, musicians of the tone of a sound or its purity, the dancer's body is a source of the grain of the gestures he undergoes, and so on. The problem as to whether or not some things can be said in one art and not in another is the problem in part of the role which the grain plays in any portrayal, as well as of the kind of patterning which the medium permits. The medium in short has two roles: it is that which is patterned and it is that which infects the pattern with the quality of the material. Putty can be stretched, and sounds can be made to intensify one another; but these show only how they can sustain patterns. In addition each has its own texture, and thereby once again limits what can be expressed. But it is not precluded that in its own way anything which has a common-sense meaning or a religious one, and even any encountered aesthetic pattern, can have its translation in every art. To suppose that it cannot is to suppose that there is a radical division among the arts, precluding a common convergence on the same realities; it is to refuse to see that the kind of difference which one kind of material makes for one art is answered by the kind of difference another kind of material makes for another art. To say "anguish" is to verbalize what might be painted, or sung, or sculpted and so on. (Can we bring it into architecture? Perhaps through the play of light and dark.)

February 26

Is sport a craft, a kind of technique having winning as its objective? Or is it not rather an art of educating, of making men, a part of a larger *paideia?* If the latter, is it still not a kind of craftsmanship, with the winning or the contest as a form of stimulus, lacking the concern for the production of beauty or the achievement of a plurality of themes, each developed for its own sake? Could there be too much stress on training and discipline and rules, and not enough on the fresh innovations that could be achieved after one has mastered the training? Is it then that a sport could be an art but is in fact dealt with as a kind of craft?

A sport as an art is perhaps approximated in the field events and in gymnastics, though one can well argue that the actual carrying out of some game does reveal an immersion in the production of what is beautiful or at least graceful. After all it can be reasonably maintained that any art might have as its goal the achievement of some result and that the beauty that ensues is just an incidental result. Or should it be said that the training one receives in an art school is either to make one an academic artist or to prepare him for the production of genuine works of art, but that in sports we have only the former as an objective, with the goals well-set, the rules well-known, and the measure of success accurately defined?

A sport provides us with evidence, as a contest or criticism in the arts do, regarding the efficacy of training. It is as if one were training one's students to win the *prix de rome* or to get a scholarship. If this is the case, would not an athlete or a school of athletics seek to move beyond this point and introduce new activities for the sake of the promotion of grace and virtue? These are now being promoted, but only incidentally in the attempt to conform. Is it not then that there is too much being done in the way of competition, in the marketplace, so that one is never allowed in sports to make a fresh start which could end in failure, but is constantly forced to see if one can do a little better than before, along the lines followed in the past? Is it not then as if one were a part of a vast school of artists, insisting on keeping within it? Is it not that every new type of sport opens up for a while a new avenue of inventiveness and reorganization? But is it not also true that there is no genuine concern, as there is in the case of the so-called fine arts, for the production of a plurality of themes, the pure production of significant form? If so, what is it that we are looking at in a sport? Is it the dimension of common sense, or religion, or something quite different?

In sport there is a stress on the common-sense aspect of the activity; it is a race, or a jump, or a game. But there is also an adumbrative aspect contained in its festival side; mankind is revealed in a religious dimension at the same time. Perhaps here we must include the spectators with the performers. A sport minimizes the element of form, to put it paradoxically, where form means the aesthetic dimension. It is primarily didactic and sentimental, held in line by virtue of the contest in which it is exhibited. It is when one stresses the sentimental, religious side that the art value of sport comes out best, for then the spectators and the performers (as we see in a tribal dance, which is a kind of sport) make up a new unity having its own aesthetic quality. But once again this is not really sought after, so long as the audience is not a genuine participant, acting on and reacting to the performance.

The professional sportsman, who like the modern artist makes a living from the activity, is in a position to introduce freshness and beauty; but he too is beset with the need to demonstrate his excellence in a result. Would anyone else be interested, if he were not interested in the result? In graceful sports such as diving, casting, skiing it seems that there is such an interest. But once again diving, etc., seem to demand of the individual a conformity to some initial set of principles, and do not encourage the breaking away of the individual from established ways.

It would seem then that sport is the most academic of arts, the art which becomes free only when it becomes dance, ballet, or drama. To become these there must be a greater stress on spontaneity, creativity (and a neglect of the testing of excellence) than is usually the case. But does it then remain sport? Is sport a kind of academic dance or drama, or is it the preliminary to this, the craft of it, something like the training that ballet dancers get, but without any desire on the part of the coaches to have their pupils ever exercise this training in a fresh, creative merely artistic way? In the light of the strong "religious" dimension of sport it is best perhaps to assimilate it to the drama than to the dance, and then to one which is constituted by occasional improvisations by men who are primarily overwhelmed by or live too much in consonance with established rules.

A sport is an improvised dramatic event, with a conquering "hero." It is governed by strongly controlling rules, and reveals the nature of men. Could one encourage improvisations for their own sake and not under the dominance of the idea of victory it would be more manifestly an art. But does not the dramatic hero struggle for victory? Yes, but the contest has a plurality of dimensions; the theme of the struggle is pluralized and given an opportunity to develop. The sport is to be compared to a melodic kind of drama, a drama with a single theme carried out in different circumstances, which under the drive to win, defines the kind of improvisation which is appropriate. There is no script, no story for the sport; it is a drama which has over-regulated actors and an under-prepared plot.

If we took a drama and threw away the script we would lose the encapsulated nature of the drama, the element which makes it remain inside a limited border and express itself there. Also, the script makes one behave in terms defined outside the present situation. Since a sport is without a script it is driven to take on the shape of a real contest, limited though by multiple conditions. The individuals performing in a drama or dance are performing with respect to a script which interrelates them; without the script they lose this "fictive" relation and would be brought into real and vital contact. Even in the improvisations of jazz musicians there is a script from which they depart.

A sport is a dramatic event without a script in which there are disciplined players improvising solutions to reach an excellence defined antecedently in the form of some result. The coaches prepare the individuals to reach this excellence; they discourage improvisation and a consideration for the merely aesthetic values, preferring to stress the common-sense import, and to bring about the religiously significant result. The contest is the making evident of the excellence in the light of some fixed standard. Even in sports where there is only a single individual, say a runner or a diver, there is a contest against the result that others provided at other times.

In the case of those sports where there is a stress on grace, it can be said that there is a kind of script, to which one is asked to conform too closely. Just as the art of sport is more academic than academic work, just as the professional is more of an artist than an amateur, so the sport which stresses grace and seems interested in beauty is further away from art activity than the others.

We seem to have two kinds of sports: the improvisation, without script, in which the contest provides the context, and the skilled attainment of grace, in which there is a set measure of excellence one seeks to exhibit. In both types the definition of excellence is set by something outside the activity; we have as it were an a priori definition of what excellence and success are, whereas the other performing arts, precisely because they at once use a script and allow for the fresh and vital expression of various themes, exhibit excellence in a new and fresh way, beyond the reach of any antecedent definition.

A real struggle, a war, differs from a sport in its absence of rules defining excellence, its absence of a predetermined time or space. Like the sport it has no script; like the sport it may be engaged in by over-disciplined men. It allows for more improvisation, however, and even for genuine creative thinking. In short, it is less of an art than sport on the side of its lack of "distance"; it is more of an art than sport on the side of its spontaneity and creative activities. But like sport it must be thought of as a degenerate case of drama or a preliminary exercise in the craftsmanship of drama, which is how it is practiced in the war colleges and their war games.

It is perhaps arbitrary whether we call a drama without the script a real art or not. It would seem that we should call it an art, though it is the case that the absence of the script makes difficult where not impossible the development of themes. Where situations merely call forth disciplined and habituated responses capable of being charged with spontaneity and even creativity, they do not necessarily elicit vitalizations of structures already known. It is as if antecedently known structures in a recognized art pertain to the entire work, whereas in the case of sports they pertain either to the individual or are used as standards defining an excellence which must be approached or reached but never freshly interpreted. (A sport of course is not pre-regulated; there are, as in every complex occurrence, details which are novel and even innovations occasionally. But the stress is not on these.)

A sport in contrast with a game necessarily involves the use of the body; it also requires the use of the mind, usually though only of the intelligence, which is to say the ability to make connections between what is now perceived and what is about to be. There is no exercise of the imagination, the source of the innovations, novelties and creatively new items of the artist.

February 28

The two great opposing views on the origin or need for art are perhaps that art is a form of expression, and that it is a form of mastery or self-completion. The former starts with the artist and takes the work of art to be the outcome of some surplus in him, of vision, power, need, truth, emotion. The difficulty with it is that it makes the spectator's role difficult and leads to the problem of the artist's intent. Why should any-one be interested in another's expression; how does he get anything out of it himself? Should we say that the spectator expresses himself along the lines provided by the artist? Even this would make the matter too personal.

The view of Aquinas, Maritain, Croce all go back perhaps to Plotinus and his doctrine of the overflowing goodness of the self which must make itself external in order to be itself more, or just because there is an excess. Once we say this the consequence which Croce draws and which Plotinus emphasized becomes evident: the produced work is somehow inferior to the source; it contains but a part of the goodness; the very production is itself a diminution or at best no addition at all. But this is surely incorrect.

The second view takes seriously the making of the work. It starts with the real world beyond and tries to show that the artist must provide a new way of dealing with it in order to master it. Art is that new way. This view makes it possible to see art as constituting a domain of its own, with an excellence which others might appreciate. It brings in a moment of expression, since the material which is being molded and given an aesthetic import must be mediated by the individual, who gives it new implications. It also provides one with a way of classifying the arts: Croce rightly draws, from his theory, the conclusion that there is no proper classification of the arts. This is inevitable for him, since the only proper classification depends on the material or medium or topic, all of which require an orientation outside the "intuition" that is for him the essence of art.

In the classification made on the basis of the three dimensions of Existence (the area which one attempts to master through art, by taking one portion of that Existence and subjugating it to the implications provided by man), I place music with the performing or energetic arts. The temporal form of music should be the composition, and this is perhaps to be included under myth. Myth is the articulation of time, stressing the religious dimension of it more than the commonsensical (which is stressed by story) and the aesthetic (which is stressed by poetry).

In Aristotle's theory of the birth of a human, the mother contributes the matter and the father the form. This view has the advantage of dealing with human birth in naturalistic terms. Its disadvantage is that the Aristotelian human form, as Thomas Aquinas stressed, transcends bodily need and condition, showing that it could not have that natural origin; also, it is faced with the fact that there can be parthenogenesis on lower levels and in principle on the human, which would seem to indicate that the female has within her all that is needed for the generation of a man. The Thomist answer, which requires one to have resort to God for each and every human birth, makes birth a miracle and makes God responsible for the fact that the embryo of the crippled and the insane are alive.

The most hopeless congenital idiot would be one which had a body into which God deliberately inserted a soul, knowing full well that the life would be brief, painful, ugly. We need a naturalistic account which avoids the embarrassments of Aristotle's original view. One way is to reverse his stress on matter and form, while taking into consideration the reference of a form beyond itself, as that which is already tensed towards and terminates in the future.

We can say that the inside of a human being, the unique and permanent part of him, is that which was in germ in the egg. The contribution of the male (where it is more than a stimulus to the growth of the egg), as biologists have persistently indicated, would be to the constitution of the body. The sperm of course has its own inside, but this inside can be said either to be dispersed, fragmented, allowed to become the insides of the cells of the body, or to persist in the shape of some one cell. The first of these ideas seems preferable since it does not make the sperm really exist forever and ever over the generations. Accordingly, it is the inside of the egg which is the unique inside of a human, and this has as its dominated body the biological interplay of the outside of the cell and the outside of the sperm.

This view does not make the individual a female on its inside; it says that the very egg which was fertilized provides the inside of whatever being there does eventuate. The inside of the fertilized cell of course has an inadequate body; and it becomes a hard question to decide whether it could be called human. The human inside is a continuation of this, enabled to grow by virtue of the body it dominates, and not until the self has a body capable of certain types of acts can we say that it is a true self. Until then it is a constant, and the locus of rights, but almost on a par with the self of a genuine idiot. It exists but does not function except to enable the individual to be over against all else.

But why should we not say the same thing of animals? Would not this view really require one to say that all insides are in root the same, but that there are different bodies which they may possess and therefore have different roles to play? If so, our view is close to Plato's rather than to Aristotle's, and in principle ought to allow for something like metempsychosis. But it could be the case that the psyche of the animal is a kind of mixture or a function of an interplay of the insides of cells. Or better we could say I think that the psyche of the animal, though an inside originating with the egg, never achieves a status of independence and definite concern transcending the activities of the body, and thus cannot be like a self. But the idiot, though it cannot do more than the animal (and perhaps less) would have a true self. He would have powers he could not use, while the animal would be using all the powers it has. The resulting actions could be the same but their reasons would be different. And this is the answer I think one must take, even though there is no verification possible apart from the recognition that there is something wrong in the slaughter of idiots and the denial of rights to them, as over against the slaughter of animals and the denial of rights to them. This could be prejudice, but on the other hand it may but articulate something discerned. In any case the supposition of the eggish inside of the human individual does allow one to accommodate the facts of parthenogenesis, of human self-identity through time, the biological and psychological inheritance from both parents, and the assimilation of the idiot to the human race.

March 2

One art accompanies another when each retains its nature, but one plays a subordinate role. One art supplements another when each retains its nature but they are coordinate at least part of the time. One art unites with another to constitute a new art when each involves a modification of the other. The problem of the nature of painted buildings and sculpture, of poetic and prose discourse mixed, of opera, and of motion pictures is that of deciding which of the three alternatives holds.

The Statue of Liberty seems to be an art object in which sculpture and architecture are supplements. A merely painted sculpture or building is one in which painting is subordinate; but a genuine painting of a sculpture which changes the kind of painting (and involves a reconsideration of what is sculpted) would give us a new art. In a sense tapestry tries this. If musical composition is included in the realm of the myth, then this can be combined with a kind of painting as in the musical calligraphy of John Cage. An epic would seem to combine myth and poetry and some story-telling. As such it is a distinctive art and not to be reduced to poetry or story-telling as such. Opera is a genuinely new art if the acting and the music are radically modified, as they seem to be, in the light of the needs of one another. They should no longer then be thought of as primarily music or acting, or criticized in these terms primarily, but in new and fresh ones.

In the dance we can make music subordinate, supplementary or united with it. Stories and a kind of drama are also to be found in the dance every once in a while, but these are usually supplements rather than correlates. In the movies we have a new art form in which acting and dancing (and occasionally music) are combined. The dance has to be understood as the exhaustive occupying of the medium, in contrast with acting in which there are pivotal points occupied. The judgment of a work of art such as the movies must be in terms which are not reducible to those that apply to either acting or dancing.

Though each art is an art because of the dominance of the aesthetic dimension, each can also be said to stress, in a way the others do not, the religious or the commonsensical or the aesthetic role. Thus architecture, myth and music all put great emphasis on the numinous element even while they are being pursued as purely aesthetic activities. (Architecture of course has had a long tradition of usefulness which has prevented the practitioners from recognizing their need to be concerned with pure enclosure and the geometrizing of space regardless of use; it encompasses car-designing, landscaping, city planning, arabesques in space, pavillions, etc.) Sculpture, story-telling and acting all put an emphasis on the common-sense role. Painting, poetry and dance are arts in which one's attention is riveted on the aesthetic role.

March 4

The phenomena acknowledged in science (which is an extension of common sense) subject to the clarifications and extensions of mathematics and thus of Ideality, and the phenomena acknowledged in art, subject to the clarifications and extensions of an encountered Existence, are reconcilable in two ways. One can see them reconciled in the religious, numinous dimension as the counterpart of an idealizing judgment on the part of an Actuality, or one can see them reconciled as the unity of the object viewed from the perspective of eternity. The object is both of these items making one integral unity. That object, with its unity, can in turn be described as that which, with the divine, lives through a concordant time and diversely realizes a common Ideal.

When we turn to ordinary perception, we can deal with such things as the broken oar or the seen star in an analogous way. The actual oar is in one piece for touch, and is broken for sight. What is it as neutral to these? It is that which functions as a substance, that which through time realizes a possibility and which does this while in the relation of concordant otherness with the divine. Or it can equally be said to be the numinous adumbrated unity of the two aspects over against which the perceiver stands, and which he also encounters by expectantly converging on its possibility.

The star that is now seen over the tree top and the star a billion light-years ago can be said to be the very same star treated in different ways. It is that one star which, if dealt with abstractly in mathematical terms, is to be located in an astronomical, abstract time some billion years ago; it is that very star, which, if dealt with abstractly in a phenomenological vision, is to be located over the tree top. Where is the star in fact? It cannot be said to be in either the time or the space of astronomy or phenomenology. In previous writings I supposed that the latter was somehow primary. But it is no more primary than any denotative object would be. The actual star is now enduring a time and filling out a space, and this is not the case either in astronomy or phenomenology.

Suppose I want to go to the star? I can traverse over a mathematically defined space in a continuous way for some mathematically, accurately defined time. I can also travel over a phenomenological space in a discontinuous way for some predictable time. When I arrive at a star it will be at the point where these two types of space and time converge. In perception I keep myself attuned to the numinous adumbrated aspect of a reality at which the two types converge; in judgment, apart from perception, I attend to the real star as that which makes itself continue to be in the world as the unity of two types of aspects. It is the latter position which Whitehead takes; his actual occasions synthesize the two aspects as seen from the position of eternity. But it is consonant even with his own view to look at eternity from the position of the actualities; when this is done the star is seen to be the divine in an accentuated position, the divine functioning as the synthesis of the two aspects to constitute the real nature of the star.

The two aspects of the star are reconciled either as and in an ongoing, or as and in a nature. Whitehead and the process philosophers take the former alone; but the other, which is perhaps the line an Aristotelian should take, take the latter tack. These answers will not satisfy either phenomenological common sense or astronomy, since they force the answer to be elsewhere, and don't even show us how to move from one of the aspects to the other. But on the one hand no reconciliation of the two is possible in the territory of either; and on the other hand it is possible to define one of the aspects in terms of the other by taking account of the juncture of both and using this as a transformational principle. When we interpret common sense as a kind of complicated and blurred use of the astronomical truths, as the classical rationalists did, we use the real star as a principle of translation. When we interpret astronomy as a kind of rectification and extension of common sense, as we do when we view science as common sense extended, we in fact take the real star, which undercuts the astronomical and the phenomenological or commonsensical objects, to translate these latter into the former. This translation involves the use of the adumbrated aspect of the star.

We can reconcile astronomy with phenomenalism by A] seeing

them converge in the adumbrated, B] seeing them converge in the perceiver, C] making one of the aspects into a transformation of the other by use of the adumbrated as a rational principle, and D] by taking the perceiver as a source of confusion. The latter two ways (c and D) are biased towards one aspect or the other; the former two ways (A and B) recognize that there is a reality beyond either and which is in fact supposed in the latter two ways (c and D) of reconciliation.

What is here said about astronomy and phenomenalism holds of course with respect to aspects of a phenomenal situation—the felt and seen oar in the water, the parallel and convergent lines of track, etc. And it holds of the worlds of science and of art. These are to be seen either as extensions of one another under the transformational operation of an adumbrated real or an actual perceiver, or are to be seen as aspects of a religiously sensed reality or of a substance in a lived-through time and space. In the last two cases they are correlative means of articulating what otherwise could not be said.

The foregoing treats 1] art and science, 2] two phenomena for the same organ (straight and convergent rails), and 3] two phenomena for different organs, all in the same way, as types of subject-predicate-adumbrated situations. Part of the difficulty men have felt in reconciling the two types is due to the fact that they suppose that predicates characterize their grammatical subjects. But if predicates and subjects be seen as correlative components of an articulation of what is neither of these, it becomes evident that the two "stars" are distinct abstractions having their locus in the real beyond the judgment, where they are intertwined, and in fact mutually infect one another to give us a being with a nature, a real star which is not merely the one or the other. The real star is an astronomical star qualified phenomenalistically; it is a phenomenal star which is inseparable from an astronomical star, which qualifies it and is qualified by it; it is an astronomical star made phenomenal by perception; it is a phenomenal star made astronomical by reflection. The real star, as neutral to both astronomy and phenomenalism, is neutral to both perception and reflection, or is, if one likes, the object of the two together. The real star is to be reached through an emotional acknowledgment of it as a substance.

Since in perception we have three dimensions answering to the Ideal, Actual and divine aspects of an object, a concentration on the first two will lead to the acceptance of the real as essentially religious in nature, i.e., as essentially loaded with implications for human welfare and cosmic destiny, or as essentially that which articulates the nature of man as expressing itself in diverse channels.

March 5

Architecture is the art of bounding space. This art need not be restricted to buildings. It encompasses landscaping, gardening, the making of automobiles and in fact anything at all that can enclose a space or give a limit to it, as that within which certain things are to be done. The bounding is not a mere putting of limits, a mere framing, but an interrelating of the space by virtue of its limits. The architect makes a new entity, a work of art; the relations which the spaces have to one another are hereafter of a new type.

There are in root four problems which he confronts: the outside, the inside, the cosmos and the finite. The outside is that which is at once held over against nature and is one with it—as well as over against the environment which is man-made and one with it. The inside has to do with the nature of the delimitation to which he is subjecting the larger space, the kind of finitization he is using to express the numinous nature of the entire space.

The three elements which Wotton offers as the marks of "Well-building," commodity, firmness and delight, are translatable into the numinous import and ethnic significance, into common sense and utility, and into aesthetic significance. The primary stress of architecture is on the first, on commodity, though the current theory is that it is on the second. The second alone would make the architect a craftsman, the first alone would make him a reflection of society, and the third alone would make him a mere designer. But if he has all three he must have them in a proper relation. The very fact that he seeks to enclose a space and hold it away from tht rest of space shows that he has as a dominant problem the dealing with the numinous, the larger regions of space as that to which he must refer and which in some sense he must capture. The common-sense side is the way the thing is to be built; it must have firmness, which involves stability and proportion. Here there is a great emphasis on symmetry, to save the balance. The delight side is that which, once it has been decided to encompass the space and with firmness, comes into play with respect to light and usage.

The quarrel as to whether architecture should build in sympathy with or in defiance of nature is readily resolved with the recognition that the two are actually parts of the same effort. To hold off the space is to be in defiance of nature, and to make the architecture part of the wider world of space is to make it in consonance with nature. But it is not only nature but the man-made environment of which this is true. This is due to the fact that the negative space between architectural works also constitutes an architecture of the community.

Functionalism claims either that function follows form, or that function and form are identical. In either case it stresses the aesthetic and commonsensical dimensions. The more complete definition would say form, function and fulguration. The last refers to the brightening, the illuminating of the meaning of the whole of space in a limited context. The form of course is the aesthetic, and the function is the commonsensical dimension. But though all three belong together and make an integral whole, the dominant fact is the fulgurating one, so that we have a world in which we can live.

It is hard to separate architecture and sculpture; a chair seems to be describable as either the one or the other. And sometimes it is hard to know whether the sculpture is merely accompanying, supplementing or is a co-constituent with the architecture in some larger still unnamed form of art.

March 7

A philosophic work should be written as though it were the last possible work, though it can never be more than the latest comprehensive work claiming to be true. When presented as final it makes evident what its borders and claims are, and thereby elicits out of the world and men the type of evidence and problem that can reveal its inadequacy. To deal with the work in a tentative way, to offer it as mere hypothesis is to allow all data to make a mere miscellany and therefore not to have anything stand out as a challenge to it. (It is the case, of course, that works in the past, though not presented by their authors as being the truth, have been found wanting. This is due to the fact that they were so treated as last works by others; even a critical philosophy is offered in a dogmatic spirit or is so accepted.) The value of offering the work as the truth is to make evident what is actually being maintained; a false sense of modesty makes some men attempt to hide what is in fact outside them, the system which they themselves once made and which is now part of the public domain.

A philosophic system thus is in somewhat the same position as a mathematical system, a scientific account, or a poem. Each stands on its own feet in a public domain claiming to express something which holds for all, and is to be understood and challenged in these terms. It is inevitable then that there should be a history of philosophy, a sequence of systems in the past, finding the earlier ones unsatisfactory, and giving way to successors. It is the system itself that provokes or sustains the enterprise which demands the system's demise. It is its very success which demands that it pass away. The system which tries to avoid the claim of being *the* system will instead be trying to insinuate that it is final and absolute, allowing nothing to be defined as that which can be used against it.

The most dogmatic of philosophies is fallibilism or mere empiricism; these last longer than any one grand philosophy, but only because the statement that the philosophy is merely tentative precludes any way of affirming and therefore also of denying it. We do, to be sure, reject even such a philosophy and not merely on the grounds of its crass dogmatism; we can see, from the perspective of a system, that it is inadequate. The latter may be said in one way to be generated by the fallibilism, since the fallibilism despite its own internal disclaimer, is dogmatic. On the other hand the system is not generated by it so far as fallibilism itself is concerned. As not generated by fallibilism (to use this as a convenient term for all self-disclaiming philosophies) the system is not in the same time-scheme; it is discontinuous with it.

There are at least six aesthetic problems which the architect must face: the wall in relation to what lies beyond it (landscaping, setting, etc.); the wall in itself (relief, light and shadow, symmetries and balance), the wall in relation to the inside wall (coherence of intent, indication of the spirit of the time); the inside wall in relation to the outside (transference of purpose); the inside in itself, (color, contour, organization, division); the inside in relation to other insides (interplay of spaces, subdivisions, volumes, subdivisions).

The six problems of aesthetics must be integrated with a consideration of the usefulness or function of the building, or other architectural work (for architecture is the controlled encompassment of space made for a certain purpose). The stress on symmetry, proportion, balance on the aesthetic side is needed to attest to the stability of the work, the fact that despite its mass it can function at all. There are other demands also that there be asymmetries and imbalances.

Architecture is the union of form and function where form comprises the above six aesthetic dimensions (interwoven of course with a concern for texture and beauty), and function relates to the way in which the result can operate. In addition to these there is the attempt to comprise within the encompassed space the entire meaning of space that is outside. Art is the mastery of a world via the controlled use of a part of it, the imposition of new implications, and the reintroduction of new meanings. Architecture gives space a new meaning, and part of that meaning involves the sense of the adumbrated, the numinous, the drift of things. This can be allowed to be quite indeterminate or be sharpened in multiple ways. In the end it is to be left unexpressed except in the way in which the parts are organized. Primarily the meaning is something like that of a religion, or of the entire culture or of the spirit of the day.

It is a mistake to deliberately make the work incorporate this spirit; that would require one to define the spirit in advance and in this way delimit it; it is the task of the architect to create a space in which the spirit, which he merely adumbrates, is conveyed; he does not know what that spirit is in any definable sense, as contrasting with any other, except so far as he has completed his work as that which must embody a spirit whose nature he does not really know. It is the work of architecture which helps give the spirit its definition; to start with it as defined is to preclude the creative definition of it. It is wrong then to speak of making architecture for a machine age, or for an industrial society, or for the democratic spirit. One must make the architecture and hope that it will help define what the spirit in fact is that prevails now.

How is the spirit, which one cannot define or really know, captured in a work? Is it not that the very achievement of beauty through the control of space (when this is done by deliberately delimiting an endless space which is integral to time and energy) involves the adumbration of endless space and thus of the Existence which encompasses us all? Is it not then that architecture, though occupied with a controlled space, and stressing function and form, must also fulgurate, shine forth the nature of the real space and its existence out of which the controlled portion was taken and which it epitomizes?

March 10

Play is a spontaneous expression of energy unaffected by rules, producing pleasure and well-being. Craft is the subjugation of play to rules for the sake of attaining an excellent result with minimal means. Sport is a play with rules in which the participants have been subjected to a prior coaching or craftsmanship. (Amateur sports are essentially play with minor attention to the requirements of the craft.)

A sport must exhibit a kind of excellence; this is provided by the craft to begin with, and the concern for an objective at the end. It involves a kind of contest with time, space, and other individuals. But though it is the end of a sport to enable men to be victorious, its motive, its purpose and value lie in the fact that it   A] builds bodies, and is thus a branch of the department of health,   B] disciplines, separately and together, and is thus a part of the branch of socialization and civilizing;   C] molds character, and thus is a part of a process of education.

When the primary objective is winning we have only work; if the concentration is on the preparation for a contest we have labor. True coaching and preparation for a sport must be in terms of the craft, which is the excellence of the means for the purpose of attaining the objectives of the sport.

Sports are not arts: they do not stress creativity, are not interested in the production of beauty, and have no way of revealing the meaning of a world beyond. Coaches are like the teachers in art school, music school, and drama school, for they are concerned with getting men from the state of being inept to being effective. However, it is the hope that the students can then move from this state to a genuine professional career involving the production of beauty, that marks off the art teacher from the coach.

The division of the sports would seem to parallel that of the arts: sports are spatial, temporal and energetic. This means that the sports are involved in the realm of Existence and offer alternative ways of mastering it: This they do, not by making a kind of semblance, or intensifying the implications of it in special ways, but by immersing men in Existence. Sports therefore stand somewhere in between history and art, the former being the determination of men by Existence, the latter that of Existence by men. In sports we throw ourselves into the world, as we do in history, but instead of allowing that world to define us or to set all the conditions which we then will try to qualify, we impose conditions on it mainly for the purpose of enabling us to move through it.

Art masters Existence, subjugates it for us; history filters Existence, gives it a meaning by allowing it to impose itself on active man; sport makes pathways through Existence, thereby at once subjugating it and providing it with a kind of filter. It makes sense then to speak of sport as preparing us for history; but it also makes sense to speak of it preparing us for the arts.

March 11

A craft has an objective and a justification. Tht objective may be the justification too. Thus the craft of weaving may have as its objective the production of a tapestry. The tapestry, because it has a kind of excellence, is also a justification. But in other cases one may have a justification of quite a different kind, particularly if the objective is of little consequence. We may thus weave something trivial, and justify our efforts by reference to the money or pleasure which is obtained in the process.

A craft (which is essentially a technique or discipline), without its justification, is work, the mere operation on means for an end. A work without an end, the mere immersion in the means is, as Dewey observed, labor, toil or drudgery.

A sport is a craft in which the objective is winning a contest (against the resistance of things, the activities of other men or the body itself), and which is justified by the improvement in the bodies of men, on the one hand, and the improvement of their characters on the other. The characters are improved by virtue of the need to adjust to the stable and warranted demands of the body, the nature of the game, the insistencies and rights of other men, and the nature of the materials and their promises.

The teachers in art schools do essentially what is done by the coaches in the sports. They stress the opposite of what they expect in the future. Thus, there is an emphasis on team sports and activities by the coaches, though they hope that the activities in relation to body and character will be carried on by the individual in a non-team way; this is true too of the work in the art schools to some degree, for the individual artist is certainly one of the final objectives to be reached via the class-room and school. (There is also a training of actors and musicians who will play together in the future.) The contrast is sharper if we look to the humanities. Here we stress the individual activities of individuals; we stress competition, selfishness, concern for one's own results, but we hope that the outcome will be some consideration of common welfare. Stressing the individual and his goals, we hope to make socially-minded individuals; the coaches, stressing the team and team-play, hope to make individuals who are healthy and have the right private spirit.

Men accept the severest discipline of a good coach, and resent the laxest discipline of a good teacher for the one is seen to be integral to the work and the other is thought to be incidental and preparatory.

There is preparatory *work* in connection with the sports; this is activity with respect to the contest to come; there is also the limbering up and the repetitive training which gives us mere *toil*. But even in the exercise and mastery of the craft itself there is a degree of discipline having a purpose which is not the same as that characteristic of the student. One can perhaps say that the athlete pays off while in school and exhibits the end result, shows himself to be already in the open where he must exhibit his discipline in himself then and there, whereas the art student is thought to be one who is not yet ready for such an exhibition, and thus sees himself held back by the discipline. Or to put it another way, the art student hopes to be able to have under laboratory conditions the very life that he is going to have later; the athlete has under approximately the same conditions the contest that he is to have later. Since the final objective of the student is a life of art, and the final objective of the athlete is, while in school, to exhibit a craft, the one would like to be exercising his imagination in school, making beauty be, and adumbrating a meaning beyond him, whereas the other is content to be disciplined, made into an apprentice who can achieve, and be rewarded for a mastery.

It is the task of a sculpture to fill space. But it is not necessary to suppose that there is a sharp distinction between the outside and inside, rest and motion, the front and back, the up and down. Sculptors such as Engman, who are under the influence of Albers, have successfully broken away from the old-fashioned limitations. They are not doing architecture; they are not concerned with merely bounding, encompassing, giving a shape to space; instead they are occupying it in such a way that there is a bounding as a consequence. One ought not say that architecture must be hollow; yet Herbert Read does say this. The Pyramids or the Sphynx or the Washington Monument—are these all sculptures?

March 12

The work of fine art differs from a product of a craft in A] embodying beauty, B] having a referential, and C] an adumbrated import. Are these three contained in the work; are they read into it; could they be duplicated by a machine or nature?

The work of art as complete must contain in itself the very world which is outside itself; it is the work itself, as containing the world, which refers to the world beyond. In a basic sense then all art is representational, and even imitational, for it is what the art in fact embodies which makes it possible for it to refer beyond. The world as caught in art is that which refers to the world outside it. The world as caught in art doesn't look like, sound like, act like what is outside; it is transformed by being inside, and gets to be like the external world only in the sense that it refers to that world.

The work of art doesn't refer by itself. It could be said to have beauty in itself and to refer to the world beyond as well, but only in potency as being able to be these when men, without reworking, or without any other reworking than is involved in perception and observation of an aesthetic sort, confront it. Man may be said to read into the work these features, but it is surely just as true to say that he reads them out of the work; he finds them when and as he observes.

Were a machine to reproduce a work (and it does in lightography, etc.) it would seem to be able to reproduce these various features. But if this is so, why should it not be possible to get the machine to make the work in the first place, or at least to make a work which may evoke in us the act of reference even though it was never there? It is in fact true that the artist may build bigger than he knows. That being the case it is not necessary to have the beauty and the referents there by intent. Moreover, the work of art is objective; it is outside the artist, and as a public object must be said to be available to any public manipulation.

How do we tell the difference between a lie and an error? The difference would seem to lie entirely on the plane of private intent. On the other hand, a lie should infect the words and give them a tonality. Is it the case that if we do separate off the words (and also if we separate off a work from the producer) we do not have any guide to the reality of the intent? The intent is as it were in the work, but we cannot find it without actually going back into the production and eventually pointing to a producer. We may be mistaken in supposing that in a given work we do have a deliberate production; we may have read ourselves into it. The test of whether or not the work contains these elements depends on our knowing whether or not it was made by a man, just as the test of whether or not the error is a lie is the knowing whether someone wanted to convey the error as a truth. If we do know that the latter is the case, we can see the lie in the error, for we then see it as in the context of an expressed human intention.

The problem then of interpreting a given object as a work of art is the problem of knowing in what context it is to be placed. If we do not know this we do not know how to read it. If we do know it we do know what to look for; we may not find it, and will then conclude that the work is a failure as art.

How can we distinguish between the case where we read ourselves into the work and where we do not? In part by knowing the domain of art, what has been done and how. In part by remembering that art is the conquest of the world outside and involves the distillation of it, the freeing of it from irrelevancies, and therefore the coming to see the lack of irrelevancy in the work of art and the presence of irrelevancy in the work of nature. We can deliberately plan to copy the work of art, but this brings us back into the realm of human artifacts, with the craft being directed toward reproduction and even the avoidance of irrelevancy, rather than producing anew and in a fresh way, breaking through the limitations and conventions which up to that moment had prevailed. When nature does something new it offers a new limitation; the artist breaks through limitations.

Architecture perhaps more than most arts makes evident the truth in Plato's and Aristotle's view that art is imitation. The world that is caught inside a work of architecture (cf. a Greek temple with St. Sophia) imitates the world outside. It is not an icon of it, duplicating it in a new way; nor does it merely symbolize it, portray it or signalize it somehow; it embodies that outside world in new terms, and at the same time refers to that outside world. The very fact that the boundaries of the architectural world is real material of the outside world leads one to point the inside space to the world beyond—which the inside space epitomizes and aesthetically reconstructs and replaces.

All art has its adumbrative function which it grounds inside itself in the meaning that it contains. And all art makes evident that there is a world beyond by virtue of the fact that it does make use of material in the world. The fact that the created world of art is brought suddenly to a close by some natural boundary, a boundary which may be exhibited in the brutality of the material, the environmental intrusion, the limit in physical or spatial extent, etc., points the internal world of art to an external one.

In the case of architecture the relation to the external world is an essential part. It can be said to adumbrate the external world but now not so much by what it itself embodies but by the way in which it is placed in a setting. The inside of the architectural and perhaps of other works of art is "porous" with respect to its outside, and conversely; but the inside also imitates the world beyond, whereas the outside fits in the world beyond.

The inside expresses the "spirit of the time." This spirit is the very nature of Existence, usually limited in the shape of history, and sometimes made more narrow in the shape of the history of a given culture or nation or industry, and focused in the present. The embodiment of that "spirit" requires a mediation. This is either in the shape of the divine or of the Ideal. Each of these (with the other as correlative) serves to mediate the spirit of the time and the world. God can be thought of as objectively real, or as an idea in the mind of men, or as embodied in the religion, or perhaps better than all, as the meaning of the preservable truth of mankind. By embodying that truth in all or part, and thus by finding a motivation for one's art in the realization in oneself and one's work of what the divine is taken to be, it is possible to express the spirit of the time—an expression which is also its definition. The divine here is not itself part of that spirit; it is to be viewed as something not yet expressed, not temporal and not embodied in the work, though to be sure any expression we may have of that divine being will itself reflect the spirit of the time.

The other and more usual way of expressing the spirit of the time is by making use of the Ideal or the Good as the mediator of history and art. The Good here, once again, must be used and not conceived; it must be that in which I participate as a value. It can have the shape of an excellence of another kind—beauty or completion or purity, etc. The dominance of such a principle of value, the use of it to bring history to bear on the work of art is the turning the history, as in the present, into a spirit of the time manifest in the work and expressive of the cosmos beyond.

March 14

If one of the differentiations between a piece of craftsmanship and a work of art is that the latter has inside it that which "imitates" what is outside, how can we know this? Is it not the case that a machine might duplicate the art work, or there could be a copy or reproduction of it which could fool someone into believing it to be an original creation? Is it not the case that everyone might take something to be a work of art when in fact it is an idle product of chance occurrences?

It could be argued that A] there is something in the work of art which could be isolated just by itself, and nothing less than a discriminatory taste is needed. There would be an analogue with a lie over against an error, or a generous act done from a bad motive and one done from a good one. Can we say in these cases that the difference is present in the words and acts? To say they are not is to hold motive, intent, artistic creation away from the very objects in which they were supposed to be embodied. But to say that they are present in the objects is to be faced with the fact that anything one could note in the one could be duplicated in the other. Moreover it does not seem possible to find intent in the same way as one finds other parts of the content.

It would be better to say that we could not understand that something was a lie or an artistic product except so far as A] we had some acquaintance with the world beyond, and B] brought it into the context of human affairs. When we do this we can make manifest whatever there be in the work which distinguishes it by virtue of what we might call its motive, adumbration and import. But we can bring the artifactual non-artistic object into such a relation too. Should we say that we then read into the object what otherwise we would read out of it? Or should we say instead that there is a reading into in both cases but there can be a reading out in only one, and that we can sense the latter at times by noting the endless nuance, the freedom from irrelevancy, the ambiguity and the blunders of the art work? If a machine could produce something with the same features we should say that the machine, like a painter in a frenzy or when almost unknowingly painting a picture, has had read into it the intent of the creator of the machine. If the machine, as it were, has random variations which add up to all the nuances of a work of art then it is but the extension of the man who made the machine; otherwise it remains a machine making machine-like things. Accordingly, it is not necessarily the case that a machine-made entity is not a work of art; but if it is, we must find in the work something which distinguishes it from a machine product.

In the case of a lie and inadvertent falsehood, or of generosity from good and bad motives we must say that they have differences in content reflecting the intent. We find the additional difference by bringing the words or acts inside a human situation. What we then discern shows the difference between what is intended and not intended, and what is well-intended and not well-intended. If a not-intended falsehood should, when brought into the human context of voice and participative activity be such as to have all the tonality of a lie, then we must say that the lie was intended not by the forger of the falsehood but by what lay beyond this. When we turn to the difference between good and bad intent, (since these indicate what kind of being lies behind the act) we must once again say that the generous act bears the marks of the kind of intent and that if a badly intended generous act in fact has all the marks of a good intended one, then behind it is in fact a good intent.

The solution then to the determination of basic realities behind the ostensive phenomena is that of A] recognizing their presence in the phenomena, and B] affirming that there must be a placing in a human context to determine what the full nature of the object is, and C] the acceptance of a power of intent behind unintended activities, when the latter end with results which are indistinguishable from intended activities. The "automatic sweetheart" which acts as a live one would, is one which "loves" not by herself but by virtue of and as the extension of the creator of it.

There is much art work done by the body without direct supervision of the mind. There is a kind of "automatism" in the creation of works of art; but this is only to say that the body can work like a "machine." To have a machine beyond the body does not then change the situation in principle. It is the aesthetician's supposition that only spirit can produce a work of art; he is right if this be understood to mean that this spirit (cosmic, divine or human) must be supposed to be behind even those works of art that we know have been produced by machines.

March 16

There are four types of excellence which a man might have. These answer to his mind, his body, his character (or emotions), and his self, and thus to the powers of him which stress Ideal, Actual, Existent and divine facets or interests. Each of these four has a concern for all four modes of being, thus making the excellence characteristic of it have one of four colorings.

The mind has an honesty with respect to the Ideal, a piety with respect to God, a decisiveness with respect to the body, and a curiosity (imagination?) with respect to the realm of Existence.

The body has health as an Actuality, is adjusted with respect to Existence, is restrained with respect to the Ideal, and is organized with respect to the divine.

The character or emotions are adventurous with respect to Existence, courageous with respect to Actuality, humble with respect to the divine, and just with respect to the Ideal.

The self is passionate with respect to Existence, rational with respect to the Ideal, sympathetic with respect to Actuality and in awe with respect to the divine.

Some of these are misstated. Perhaps the distortions can be corrected by isolating the excellence of man with respect to each domain.

According to the above, man is capable of excellence with respect to Existence in four ways. He can be curious, adjusted, adventurous and passionate. With respect to the Ideal he can be honest, restrained, just and rational. With respect to Actuality he can be decisive, healthy, courageous and sympathetic. With respect to the divine he can be pious, organized, humble and in awe.

When we try to see what such an activity as sport is trying to do we can use the above as a kind of chart. Like every other enterprise concerned with the realm of *paideia* it is concerned with improving men, of helping them attain an excellence. It must make him healthy (Actuality), self-disciplined, restrained (Ideal), adjusted (Existence) and organized, unified, a man of power (divine).

Putting aside the fact that bull-fighting does have the earmarks of a ballet and dance, the fighter engages in it (somewhat as a diver or skater does) to reach a kind of grace and not for the sake of beauty. Bull-fighting is so cut away from play, is so serious in its import and so big with ominous, adumbrated meaning that it seems to be an art. Is it perhaps the case that all sports have a kind of make-believe about them, so that one does not really struggle with nature but only makes preliminary stabs at it under conditions which preclude her full activity? We find in the bull-fight on the other hand, that, despite its cushioned or civilized setting, there is a transcendence of these limits in the very fact that death is being met. To meet only the demands of nature, to see what one can do with its material is one thing; to deal with her as the very locus of death (and analogously in other types of adventure, as the locus of life, sex, growth and so on) seems to force the sport into another dimension. Or should we say that it is necessary for an art to have the ominous only within a controlled make-believe, and that a sport either A] does not have the ominous at all (which is the case when it is artifactual), and B] does not remain within the realm of the make-believe but struggles with fundamental realities and is so far like work?

Is it not the case that we can escape from work in two directions? We can enhance it through gracefulness, in the mastery of a craft, and we can ennoble it by focusing on the greatness of its problem or the nobility of its struggle. The bull-fight combines these two. Though its result does have something of the ominous within it, it is not yet an art. An art requires the ominous in a result, which itself is good in and of itself, and not because of the magnitude of what is being confronted.

March 17

We move away from work in two ways: in one we take pride in workmanship, enhance the elegance of the object, bring in gracefulness and technique to constitute a work of craftsmanship. In the other we face the work with the need to meet a vital issue. We make it an adventure in which the stakes are high. An illustration of the former is weaving or carpentry; basketball. An illustration of the latter is mountain-climbing. If we combine these two we get an art: bull-fighting. Such an art is to be distinguished from a fine art.

In "art" as such we have a concern for a matter of basic importance.

We here engage in a work, i.e., we exercise or spend our energies in disciplined ways with an awareness of the end to be attained, knowing in the case of an art that the end is significant. In a fine art we must have the element of the ominous, numinous, adumbrated side inside the work. When and as we recognize its aesthetic dimension (which might conceivably be duplicated by a non-artist), we find our place in the common-sense world and make our identification with what lies beyond it. When we engage in a fine art for the sake of pleasing, or teaching, or selling, we reduce it to a mere art.

The life-death situation of the bull-fighter enables one to see the adumbrated meaning of the world. The art of bull-fighting would seem then to be indistinguishable from a fine art. But it is to be noted that the art here makes its reference to the further reality only because it is continuous with it, because it in fact reaches into it really, whereas the work of fine art symbolizes it, since it is a world apart. The bull-fight is in the world, as is mountain climbing. In this respect it stands over against a game, e.g., of basketball.

A work of fine art is like a sport in that it is encapsulated, held off against the world and has an "imitation" of that world within it. It is like a work of art in that there is a genuine reference to the ominous world beyond. Unlike the sport, fine art has a reference to the ominous; unlike the work of art it is a "play," a "substitute" for the world which lies outside.

In the bull-fight there is a struggle with death. From the standpoint of the spectator, though, this could be taken as a fine art. But in that case he must ignore the possible terminus of the bull-fighter and the bull, and see the whole as a kind of dance or ballet. Is this perhaps what is done in Portugal where there is no possibility of death, so that it comes closer to a dance or an act, which makes evident the ominous forces of the world?

March 18

In a bull-fight we can have a preliminary activity which may be a technique or an art. But the ending of it is in death; this death is something others may be able to view as bearing on themselves, but it is actually a death in the world. To take it as having bearing on oneself is to tear it out of the world, to put a border around it. This is an aesthetic act. It does not do this of itself. Only if one either stopped the fight before the death or included the death symbolically could it be said that the fight was a work of art. Stopped before the death it would have an ominous meaning which only remotely dealt with death, for though one can have a dance of death this would be really on the representational or commonsensical side; the dance itself must invoke deeper powers. If on the other hand we include the death inside the work of art, we no longer allow it to spill over into reality; we say in effect it is a fiction.

To recognize a work of art is to hold it at a distance, to bound it from the world, to say of it that it is a mere meaning. To justify it, and thus to recognize it as a work of fine art we must see that its meaning includes the meaning of the being which is put aside when we grasp the meaning. We must say of that meaning that it is worth our full attention, that ourselves, put aside to enjoy the meaning, are recovered in the work itself. We make this judgment for everyone, which is to say that we make the claim that everyone will find it possible to do this, that the meaning which the work possesses illuminates their being, a being which they thrust aside in order to see the work as a work of art.

The death of a man forces us to be in the world. We must block the outcome, deny the implications which the death has in the world to enable us to throw its meaning back into the art. We find the work of art is one which includes us, and thus know it is the world, for only the world includes our being and subjects it to a rationale not of its own making. When I say commonsensically 'it is so,' I ignore myself or see the object as having a similar import for others as it has for me. When we say of a work that it is a work of fine art we say that it is that which includes us and any other who has a being like ours. When we say that it is beautiful we say that it is for all, that it gives the same universe for everyone. It is not like a common-sense object but like a philosophic system, making a universal claim. We see the claim, we recognize the numinous, ominous, adumbrated just so far as we find the work to be self-justifying, have it as beautiful, for this is but to say that it encompasses us as representative beings. We thrust ourselves aside as beings to have the work as a work of art (whereas in perception we ignore ourselves or include ourselves as beings who are attached to the percept).

When we confront an artifact which is not the product of an artistic effort we should be able to say of it that for someone at some time (and this surely of the imitator) it cannot be held apart, made to be a universe. Or conversely, only because there was someone for whom it was such a universe, who made the claim for it to be such, can it achieve this claim for us now. We distinguish the work of non-art then from a work of fine art by recognizing there is someone for whom it cannot stand apart, and distinguish the work of fine art, acknowledge it because we know there is someone for whom it could stand apart. When I confront it and find I cannot make it stand apart, I say that it is a failure as a work of art or that it is only an artifact. If I find I can make it stand apart then I claim it to be a work of fine art. I find myself to be in error in an objective sense when it is made evident that there are some (e.g., the faker, the machine-reproducing individual) for whom it never did and some (other people, perhaps more sensitive than I) for whom it never will be able to stand apart. My judgment is so far in error. (The fact that there are works without boundaries, as in oriental art, does not mean there are no boundaries in the present sense, for oriental art also claims to stand apart, not to be integral to the universe but to stand for it and thus to be able to satisfy and include me, via its meaning, and not through any action on my being.) The purging which I go through in some experiences is in fact the redefinition of my being through the subjugation of myself to a meaning with a new rhythm, a world more coherent and essentially determined than the one in which I in fact live.

March 19

Every sentence is of course held over against the world. But in ordinary use it functions as a means; it is like the preliminaries of a bull-fight pointing us outside itself to what is not in back of it, but what is future to it, i.e., to a subsequent use or to its object as that which is to be encountered subsequently. In our ordinary language use we are expectative beings, carrying the discourse until the time comes when we can attend to the real, the brute facts which are being discussed. A series of sentences can be held up for a while but there finally must be a reference to the world, unless we are constructing a fiction. Only if it is a fiction is it bounded, held apart, forced to be self-sufficient. It has boundaries which force one to stay within it by virtue of the inward tension between themselves and their subdivisions. Consequently it is the awareness of the inward tension over the whole work which leads one to see that it is to be held apart; it is this tension which forces us to make the meaning of the work to be the meaning of our own being. Our being had been shoved forward into the adumbrated realm to enable us to concentrate on the meaning of the work; we now recover that being in the meaning discovered in the art.

If we are confronted with what purports to be a work of art we must see it not only as being bounded from the world but as having an inward tension and complexity. It is a substitute for the world in which we can find our own meaning and place. To mistake a non-art work for an art work is to make a claim that the former would be sufficient for everyone.

It is tantamount to identifying a poor work of art with a great work of art. In the latter mistake we have someone who tried to present something as self-sufficient; in the case of what is not art we have no such effort, but the public result is the same. A work of art then claims to be excellent, to be self-sufficient, to therefore "imitate" the adumbrated beyond, in which one's own being has been forced. We settle however for excellence here and now, or for such and such purposes. The fact that in some dimension we have creativity and complexity makes us be satisfied with it as a work of art, but taken as a whole it may be the case that we cannot justly say of a partial work of art, partial in the sense that it did not attain excellence, that it is really distinguishable from a piece of art in the sense of a technically excellent bit which terminates in something important.

March 31

There are three types of "universals." There is the formal universal, indeterminate in content, capable of endless specification, instanced in every one of these cases as an ideal or prescriptive principle. There is at the opposite extreme the "general," the outcome of a generalization of the specific cases. Here we make the specific cases assume the status of a "universal" by dropping out details. But in doing this we do not succeed in freeing the outcome from all empirical bearing. It has no further range beyond whatever cases there may in fact be. It goes beyond the cases from which it is derived; it allows many more cases than those which instanced it. It is a true universal, but it has no prescriptive value, no normative meaning, and may in fact have no being beyond that which it obtains through the act of generalization. It contrasts in these respects with the formal universal which has being and normative value, preceding the cases which illustrate it. The latter is needed for logic and ethics.

In between these two types is the "formally defined correlative of the universal." To take the illustration of Aquinas: a snub nose differs from a concavity by virtue of flesh. But a snub nose is an essence, a meaning, and in it there is no real flesh, no genuine matter. Snub nose makes a reference to matter, and the matter as so referred to is conceivable, a kind of meaning or universal. This matter cannot be specified in fact, except in the guise of a genuine matter, with all the features and powers which it possesses over against the universal. If all we knew about the matter was what we learnt from seeing the difference between the idea or essence of concavity and snub-nosedness, we would not be able to know what a real object was. But as meant in the very essence of the snub nose this matter makes an indefinite reference; it does not tell us just what the matter in fact is, but only that matter is needed. It intellectualizes, essentiates the matter, turning it into a kind of universal.

In Kant we find a similar affirmation. Kant says (section 23 of the Deduction) that from the position of the general concepts of the understanding there is an intuition in general which is required. But instead of this meaning that there is a possible specification of this intuition in the guise of a non-temporal, non-spatial intuition, he but points up the fact that from the standpoint of the purely formal concept there is nothing to say about the intuition except that it must be sensible; we cannot say just what shape this sensible intuition must have. Consequently Kant is driven to engage in a transcendental deduction which begins with the specific form of intuition which we in fact have. If he did not begin there he would not know just what kind of intuition does work with the categories.

The third type of universal is the product of an activity similar to that of generalization; it starts with the particulars. But instead of keeping in that domain the outcome is attached to another domain, that of the universal in the first and formal sense of the term. The merely general, as it were, is dislocated and given the status of a correlate universal by the normative universal.

There should also then be three types of "particulars." There is first the individual, the unduplicatable, unique, ultimate substantial reality. There is next the description which is the outcome of the unification of specifications of universals. Here the attempt is made to approach uniqueness by adding items to one another and specifications without end. In between these two is the accident or quality. This is the description brought into relation with the individual and qualified by it. From the standpoint of the individual the accident is but an individualized way of having or referring to the specific forms of universals. But this individualized way of having the specific universals treats them as 'individualized universals,' universals functioning in a unique way. They are not true universals but universals as envisaged inside the perspective of the individuals who possess and taint them while they hold them to be over against themselves. The individual possesses those accidents as exteriorizations of himself, as himself multiplied and held over against himself as a unity.

What is true of the universal and individual, and thus of the Ideal and Actual must hold also of the other modes: Ideal and God; Ideal and Existence; Actual and God; God and Existence; Actual and Existence.

There are three senses of God: *1*] transcendent,   *2*] immanent, and   *3*] as qualified and interiorly correlative in the other modes of Actuality, Ideal and Existence. In the last role He has the Actual as that which He judges and preserves, the Ideal as that which He knows and to which He refers for judgment, and Existence as the ground of the divisions of Himself.

There are three senses of Existence: *1*] the world of space-time, *2*] the ingredient substantiality of other modes, and   *3*] the qualified and interior correlative in Actuality, Ideal and God. In the last it is the source of change and the ominous, the "manifold," and the dynamic creative element.

There are three senses of the Actual;   *1*] the individual,   *2*] the descriptive,   *3*] the accidental, as we saw just before.

There are three senses of the Ideal;   *1*] the universal,   *2*] the general and   *3*] the formalized materiate, as we saw before.

The general is not a universal, but in the realm of Actualities is a denuded particular, the "word" of the divine, and a scientific limiting case in the realm of Existence.

The descriptive is not a particular, but in the realm of the Ideal is a specified universal; in the realm of the divine is God's intent; and in the realm of Existence is the realm of history.

The immanent God in the realm of Actualities is but the class of Actualities; in the realm of the Ideal it is the highest value; in the realm of Existence it is the whole of it.

Ingredient Existence in the realm of Actualities is their vitality; in the realm of the Ideal it is mere oppositionality; in the realm of God it is the meaning of time.

What is evident from the above is that   A] the various designations are not altogether satisfactory, and   B] that there is for each mode a kind of correlative position which it gives to a part of itself, thereby enabling itself to function as a kind of representative of the other modes. Thus, once again:

The Actuality has Accidents, Adumbratives and the Ominous as ways of indicating the reality of a distinct Ideal, Existence and God.

The Ideal has Descriptions, Antecedents and Instantiation as ways of indicating the reality of a distinct Actuality, Existence and God.

God has Distinctions, Purpose and Creativity as ways of indicating the reality of distinct Actualities, Ideal and Existence.

Existence has inside it itself Localizations, Directionality and Meaning; they are its ways of indicating the distinct reality of Actuality, Ideality and God.

Reverting now to the original question, there would seem to be the following kinds of Universals: 1] the Ideal; 2] the Accidental; 3] Descriptions; 4] Antecedents, 5] Instantiations; 6] Purposes, and 7] Directionality. The Ideal is the formal 1] universal; 2] the accidental, 6] purpose and 7] directionality are the meaning of the Ideal as a correlative inside some other mode and functioning there as the representative of the Ideal in fact; 3] the descriptive, 4] antecedent and 5] instantiation are its way of referring to the other modes.

The Ideal is the formal 1] universal; 3] the descriptive is the way in which the Ideal portrays the Actual; 4] the antecedent is the way in which the Ideal formalizes and thereby represents the vital Existential ground; 5] the instantiation is the way in which the Ideal represents the Divine; 2] the accidental is what the universal is for an Actuality, how the Actuality represents universality for itself; 6] purpose is the representation which God provides for the Ideal; 7] directionality is the representation which Existence provides of the Ideal.

What has happened to the general, which was a denuded particular? Are there other ways of denuding the particular? Are there similar denudations possible with respect to other modes? Is it not the case that Actuality as over against accidents is the denuded particular? If so is there not a denuded particular over against adumbratives and the ominous? We would then have the Actual as General, as Private and as Self. And in the other cases we would have A] the Ideal as Possibility, Consequence and Meaning over against Actuality, Existence and God; B] God as Absolute Other, as Intelligible and as Concerned over against Actuality, Ideal and Existence; and C] Existence as Spatio-temporal, Directed and a Unity over against Actuality, Ideal and God.

April 1

The following seem to be some of the main features to be acknowledged in any treatment of painting. They are mainly the outcome of reflections on what I have learned from my own activity of painting. 1] *Plasticity.* The various shapes in a painting are distinguishable but still are not distinct. The transition from one part to another is never immediate; there are no simple lines separating off one part from another; all separations are also connections. One cannot, strictly speaking, isolate an eye or a cheek or a tree in a picture and have it as a distinct object; these various items merge with what is alongside.
2] *Modulation.* Colors do not sharply end and begin, but pass gradually into one another. They can interpenetrate and modify one another in the

same place, alongside one another or at a distance. But these are possible only so far as the colors also maintain their integrity and thus show what their own values are. It is like the matter of plasticity; in the work as a whole there can be distinguishable areas, but the isolation of these is a falsification in that it denies the continuing value of the color beyond itself.

3] *Bleeding.* The colors do not merely merge one into the other, but continue into the being of one another; the color that is here in fact or through the perceptual process is to be found exercising its power there and ideally perhaps everywhere.

4] *Molding.* The molding of a figure or of any part of a painting is done through the use of the color; color is not a filling but a means of making. The boundaries of things are but the limiting boundaries of colors which serve to fill them in or separate them off from one another.

5] *Openness.* The possibilities for theme, method, means, material, technique are endless. There are no fixed rules in works of art, and surely not in painting. Even such demands as needed contrast or the conventional rules in the use of complementaries, or the need to have perspective can be violated. They are at best but techniques for the teaching of students, to bring them inside the frame of accomplishments of the past.

6] *Negative Space.* The space between objects is a palpable reality. This space can be thought of as reaching and encompassing the objects, and as continuing objects so that they serve to encompass others; and it can be thought to have a life of its own. In any case it is not to be treated as over against the space in the objects, but as distinguishable from the latter and modifying it. It cannot be held apart from the space of the objects, and must be seen too to have directionality defined in part by its own content and in part by what lies beyond it.

7] *The space which the painter produces* is all of his own making. He contrasts in this way with the sculptor and architect who makes use of real space. The real space of the canvas is not the space which the painter vitalizes; he merely works in that space to constitute a new space, one which is exhibited in the very relationship of the colors, shapes and topics with which he deals. It is not then that he brings in a third dimension adding to the other two; he brings in all three dimensions.

8] *The painting is an organic unity,* not merely in color and shape and space, but through the ways in which the various parts depend on one another. Each merges with what is in fact alongside (and here we have the usual space utilized in somewhat the way the sculptor and architect utilize real space), and makes reference to all the other colors, shapes, dimensions and themes. Space in a painting is curved; it moves under and around and in the end envelops every part by virtue of the way in which it contributes to the unity of a radically diverse whole with a plurality of themes enhancing, contrasting with and continuing one another.

9] *Omission.* To know what is to be omitted is the most important lesson which distinguishes the professional from the amateur. To give the essence, the meaning, the import, to convey what creativity, a perceptual world, or an adumbrated reality (all three of course in the ideal case) is, one must put aside details which might distract the attention, but details as really irrelevant, as bringing in what is not truly germane. It is not for example the number of leaves that a tree has which makes this tree distinct from that, but the fact that it has leaves of a certain sort and in a certain way. The very result which the actual must produce through the use of details is what the artist must produce through the manipulation of the relations and color values, positions and themes that he has in his control.

10] *Stopping.* Every work of art has a point beyond which one cannot go without introducing devices, hiding blunders and in the end making a division in what is and ought to be a unity. To know that one cannot go further in a certain direction because of one's own lack of insight and ability, is to know how to make excellent works of art within the limits of one's status as artist. There is perhaps also a stopping which is dictated by the theme and its content, but this, more likely than not, is never reached by anybody. The great problem is to stop where one cannot make any further contribution to the created reality.

11] *Creation.* The work of art is the outcome of an act of creation. It provides us with a reality which replaces the external world and the internal one of ourselves   A] by being free from irrelevancies,   B] by being unified,   C] by being under the control of a dominating principle, and   D] by exemplifying beauty.

12] *Expression.* The painting expresses the painter, as everything he does expresses him. But it is no mere exteriorization of some idea he has. It is an outcome of exploration and experiment where an achievement here requires an alteration there; from beginning to end every part has a function in determining the values and roles of all other parts. The individual expresses himself only under the requirements set up by the painting itself. He masters a way of expressing himself by making the work of art serve as a channel through which he can make himself manifest. And he makes himself manifest of course as a being with a mind, will, emotions and body.

13] *Imitation.* Though it is wrong to speak of a painting being an imitation of any existent thing and even of some platonic ideal, there is a sense in which every painting imitates: A] it makes evident what is being intended, not necessarily consciously but by the being of the painter in that situation; B] by means of its cues and clues it imitates something of the purified meaning of the objects in the world, and particularly what it means to be in that world, regardless of the actual and limited role and particular appearance it may have; C] by means of the way in which it organizes its parts it imitates through a presentation of its meaning the very nature of the ominous reality beyond. We have here a case of something like an Actuality having in it a simulacrum of Existence and perhaps of God. This means that it has within it a representation of Existence and God, testifying to them by virtue of its adumbrative and its ominous aspects, with which it itself contrasts as something private and as a self, which is to say, in the case of a painting, as something which is privately enjoyed and which is taken as expressing the painter.

14] *Dislocation.* The work of art can be said to take its start from the world of perception. When it does this, without losing control of the substantival side of beings and the cosmic import of all, it frees qualities from adventitious connections and mixtures and functions, and deals with them in their purity. But the painter does not do this with respect to the perceptual content, but tries to paint this purified result. Instead of dislocating the item in experience, he redefines it, recreates it, makes something be which is identical with what the item would be were it in fact dislocated and purged in experience.

15] *The realm of art.* Painting is a civilized occupation, and every painting is affected by other paintings seen in the past. There is nothing like a mere, sheer painter, untainted and unaffected by any other. And in so-called primitive civilizations it is essentially the work of guilds who, like the medieval guilds, pass on their secrets to one another. The painter may be said to learn from the other arts as well, for what architecture and sculpture do with respect to space surely has meaning for him, and since the space is not altogether dislocated from time and energy, the painter must learn from other arts as well.

16] *The capacity to paint.* This capacity can be said to be in every one, not as a latency which seeks only the occasion to be expressed, but in the sense that it is one of the subdivisions of the possible expression of the personality. Instead of supposing this to be discrete and lying inside the being of a man for some propitious time, it would be better to suppose that it takes a reorganization of the being (and in the case of the "natural" painter, a brute fact of an organization at a given time) before he is able to manifest himself as a painter. There is always the matter of technique, but unlike the performing arts, the matter of technique is never a primary consideration for the arts. To be sure he who has mastered a technique as well as the other aspects of the activity of paint-ing—creativity, imagination, freshness of approach, subtlety of theme, originality and so on—will be superior to one who has not. But the im-portant consideration is the coming out through the avenue of the brush into the creative dimension of painting.

17] Expendability. The recognition that one is expendable as a painter frees one from the desire to live up to some established image of what a painter is and does. In this way one is enabled to paint with a freedom from one's own ambitions and achieve a concentration on the work itself. It is but the inverse of innocence, honesty and integrity, a way of achieving an immersion in the task before one.

18] Simplicity. It is better to have a simple product achieving maximum result than a complex one which fails to attain excellence. A splendid lyric is superior to a poor epic. The painter then must start and continue to remain with a limited pallet and limited objectives until he has mastered them in such a way as to require him to go out of this area.

19] Self-restraint. There can be an excessive insistence on novelty; there can be a tendency to be bizarre, eccentric, to merely exhibit a spontaneity. The best of arts involves a freedom within a restriction; the limitations provided by the medium, subject-matter and capacity are to be filled out, quickened, vitalized. The latter without the former is mere "expression"; the former without the latter is mere academicism. The restraint in the ideal case is that provided by   A] the end in view, B] the techniques and traditions of the art itself, and   C] the presence of beauty.

The nature of representation in art, if brought down to the question of "imitating" the world of common sense and the destiny which lies beyond, has to be dealt with in part by attending to the question of how, inside the work of art, this can be accomplished. For the inconographer there is the use of symbols tried by usage, and knowable apart from the work itself. If this were the proper way, or the only way of having the representation, then the representation would occur exteriorly to the work of art itself, and so far such people as Fry and Bell would be right. But there is a representational element right in the work itself, just as in the very idea of "snub-nosedness" there is the representation of real flesh, through the simulacrum of flesh, through the use of an idea of flesh operating correlatively with the concavity.

Yesterday it was said that "accidents" are a kind of universal offered by the actuality to itself to represent the real universals that are outside it, and which in a way condition it. This view goes counter to the Aristotelian which supposes that accidents are the product of "matter" or Existence. But what is more important is that these accidents are not universals but particulars, tainted by the individual. They have the status of universals, and function as representatives only so far as one is able to hold the Actuality over against them as a general, i.e., denuded particular. There would then be a kind of denudation for Actuality with respect to Existence and to God; in the former respect it would be something existing privately, and in the latter something which was a spiritual unity, a self. Taken in these terms, we can say that the painting, if treated as a symbol or meaning or something general, will represent something Ideal or valuable only by means of its accidents, its contingent diversified elements which divide its pristine unity as a general single meaning. And we can say that if treated as the exteriorization of a private existing being, it adumbrates only in the sense that such a private existing being (the painting as it is for me) has over against it that which orients it away from me. The painting in itself as forced toward me refers me beyond itself to the realm of Existence, and does this by virtue of a component in it which functions for the private side of the painting as its correlative. The acceptance of the painting as an objective reality while one is enjoying it, is the grasping of its adumbrative component, an adumbrative component which is ingredient in the work itself and which represents through "imitation" the real adumbrative being of the world beyond, focalized in common-sense objects.

Similarly, the orientation of a painting toward a self, as that which is the expression of the human spirit, as that which is essentially man-made, leaves over a reference, an element which is in the painting but functions as the counterweight to it as oriented toward the self. This counterweight is the ominous aspect of it, the element of it which makes it more than something private to this self. It is in fact open for all selves. This is not a losing of privacy but a multiplication of privacies in a way.

The recognition that this is a painting for any man, that it is the terminus of what Kant would term a valid universal judgment, is the treatment of it as having another component, an ominous element which is but the painting's way of taking account of the fact that there are selves, and in the end a unity of all selves in terms of which it can be the real in fact and not merely that which has been created by man as a substitute for the real. The painting is enjoyed as self-sufficient only by virtue of the fact that when and as it is had as for me it is recognized to be in itself a painting for others as well; those others as meant in the painting do not have the status of selves, but only the status of meant selves, which the painting requires in order to be real. (To get the real selves is to make the painting a reality at the conflux of all the selves.) It is something which is being enjoyed but yet oriented away from this enjoyment and open to the enjoyment of others.

The adumbrative and ominous representational features of a work of art are the elements in the work which prevent it from being private and oriented toward one self. They do not make it exist or be divine; they merely represent these features by virtue of the maintenance of a "distance" on the one hand and the insistence on the universality of judgment on the other. The taking of a distance from the object enables one to discriminate the adumbrative element, to see it as that which helps the object stand away; the universalizing of the judgment enables one to discriminate the ominous element, to see it as that which puts the object in the context of other selves. One could argue that it is in the taking of the distance and the putting it in the context of the selves which makes it have these representational functions; I have been inclined to think that the work itself contains the adumbrative and ominous elements and thus enables one to get a distance and to have a universal judgment.

By virtue of what do we achieve the distance? Is it not the case that just as we cannot really see "accidents" without orienting them toward genuine universals, we cannot really have the distance and thus the adumbrative except by orienting the painting in real Existence—and of course that we cannot really have universality without orienting the painting in the genuine destiny of man, in the ominous world beyond? This means that we cannot have the painting just in itself, just as we cannot really talk about "snub-nosedness" without having some grasp of genuine matter, for otherwise there would be no correlativity in the "essence." Though the correlativity occurs in the essence and though the component parts are both on a level, one part is oriented differently because while still an "essence" it is one through the help of Existence, an Existence which remains as a backdrop, a kind of reality. Existence is allowed to be shadowed forth in this way only because it stands there, over against what shadows it forth. Just so the accidents, adumbratives and ominosities of the work of art are able to have this status only because we already have, as we deal with the work of art, a firm grip on the realm of possibility, Existence and the divine.

To know, e.g., that this particular object has a nature which promises something for the future is to be in that object and not beyond it; but we are related beyond it if we see this promise as that which, though defined in content and meaning by the particular object, has its thrust and energy provided by the future as beyond it. Taken in this way we must say that the painting, and thus any work of art, has accidents, adumbratives and an ominous component only because we approach it from a perspective which reveals the forcefulness, the insistence on and through the work of art of the Ideal, Existence and God. He who did not have any Ideal with which he was concerned; he who did not know that there was a world of existent things caught in a sea of Existence; he who did not know that there was a common destiny for all beings expressive of some value or intent beyond all of them and loading the world down with a particular history of values; and he who did not know that these other dimensions were exerting an influence on us then and there, enabling us to hold these aspects aside from the work as oriented toward us, would not be able to understand, hold apart and make a universal judgment regarding the work.

We do take the work of art in itself, but this in-itself-ness of the work does not mean that it is not the product of a kind of convergence from points of view outside it. After all we perceive from a distance and what we perceive is the object; we could not perceive the object except so far as we maintain a position away from it. Just so it is because we converge on the work of art from these outside positions that we are enabled on the one side to have it as that which is the substantival, private, self-oriented reality, and on the other side to make an internal representation for that reality, so as to enable it to be over against us and to teach us about the entire universe which it has left outside. As making an internal representation, it does not set aside some portion of itself; it is the entire work as a whole as having a role other than that of being enjoyed, confronted and possessed that then and there is representative. It remains a painting and not a symbol precisely because this orientation is accomplished through the aid of the other modes of being from which we approached the painting. They, as it were, use the painting to make it have a role other than that which it has for me then and there.

Without subjugating the work to another mode of being, one puts it in relation to that other mode. We see the painting not as illustrating or symbolizing some idea, for example, but as in and of itself having its own interior logic. Were it matter of fact, or were it without its own orientation towards the individual spectator, it would be seen to illustrate the ideal or some idea.

My enjoyment of the work as something for me privately here and completely substantival, prevents me from seeing it as a mere illustration of the Ideal, Existence or God; I could not take it in that guise except by making myself such an illustration. From the standpoint of the Ideal, for example, any matter of fact could be viewed as a kind of recalcitrant illustration of itself; from that same standpoint a painting is recalcitrant not only because it occurs here and now in the space-time world but because it is mine, something I am enjoying and having for myself. It is as if I had said to myself, "ah, if only I could see this as illustrating an Ideal." In place of this, or as a way of saying this, I see it as the locus of accidents, and *pari passu,* as that which has an aspect where it plays an adumbrative and ominous role for itself, enjoyed by me alone. Man, as it were, creates the essence "snub-nosedness" because he places concavity in the context of matter without giving it matter. The matter distends the concavity, provides it with an orientation in which it can have a genuine correlative. We have in fact nothing but concavity as essence; it is the giving it the secondary role of being viewed from the perspective of matter while having no matter at all in it that enables one to have it as the essence "snub-nosedness." So one would have to say that it is the having of the painting, say from the perspective of Existence, which enables one to treat it as having an adumbrative side while as a matter of fact there is none of that genuine Existence within it (except of course what it must have in order to be a matter of fact).

April 2

The central problem of reference in perception is epitomized in that of the difference between the idea of concavity and snub-nosedness, and this is a clue finally to the way in which a painting and other works of art can represent Ideality, Existence and God.

Snub-nosedness has within it the "flesh" which is part of a wider Existence; it is a part which is functioning inside and together with the concavity, affecting the destiny of the latter to constitute a being which has its own implications. In the idea of the nose the flesh is lost and replaced by its meaning. That meaning is integral with the meaning of concavity, but it is oriented away from it. It is a meaning which is adumbrative, which makes the entire idea of the nose be an "idea of." The relation of the idea to the nose in fact and through this to the realm of Existence is of course what is being referred to under "semantics." That it is a relation which never will get to the real nose except through the use of the power of Existence is true, but the question is just what kind of reference is being made use of by this power.

Is the very use of Existence in fact that which gives an idea a bearing on the world? This cannot be the case without our denying any real adumbrative meaning to the idea. It must itself be existential in import. But how is this possible? Is it that in order to concentrate on the idea we must put the realm of Existence aside, keep it at arm's length, and thereby make the stretch between the idea and Existence one which is expressed by "of"?

When we recognize the real nose to be part of the domain of Existence by virtue of the flesh, we hold the nose apart as a part of Existence; but when we recognize the idea of the nose to relate to Existence by virtue of the component idea of flesh we hold the idea apart, not as a part of the realm of Existence, but as an analytic component of Existence, something which is not distinct in it but which has been distinguished by us. The "of" then but restates the fact that the idea is one analytic component, the other being Existence as held away from us.

When we take account of the accidents of an Actuality we hold the realm of the Ideal away from us and thereby take the accidents to be analytic components of the Ideal, having their orientation in it, even though they are ontologically part of the Actuality and function there in terms of it. The reference to the Ideal as the realm of the essential and prescriptive is given by the accidents as being in Existence, only by virtue of the fact that we are holding the Ideal at arm's length.

The adumbrative role of the work of art is defined and made by the work of art; the work of art gives it the role of being an abstracted or analytic component of a real cosmos. We hold the world away to have the painting as a work of art in itself, and thus give it the status of something like an idea; it is while it enjoys this status that the painting makes a reference beyond itself to the work which will enable it to be an object for anyone. The referential element is its content, in contrast with its decorative or organizational features; it is that part of it which evokes memories and other associations, which is marked by cues and clues and "representational" features. This is the "of-ing" aspect of it, just as the idea of "flesh" is the "of-ing" aspect of the idea of the nose. If we lost that aspect we would have a mere fiction, a dream, mere significant form.

To hold Existence away in such a manner that the outcome is a mere fiction having no referential meaning, in contrast with holding it at a distance so that the idea or picture or other work of art would have a referential import, requires us to throw our entire bodies into the realm of Existence and keep our selves as mere contemplators. It is when we treat the work as referential that we are enabled to be integrated beings. To have an idea over against a dream, to have a work of art in contrast with decoration or sheer fiction, is to have that which is faced by us as integrated beings. At the same time that we are not allowing the bodily part of us to be effective in us, but to be governed more than before by the world outside, we make the contemplative side of ourselves function with a purity it did not have before. In art we merely keep the realm of Existence at a distance; in dream we try to dismiss it. The dismissal, which occurs when we have a mere dream, is actually an immersion by ourselves in something beyond ourselves.

There are two modes of adumbration: on the one hand there is the adumbration which is carried by the idea or work of art, telling us that our bodily side is richer than we are allowing it to make manifest; and there is the adumbration which is in fact being carried out by our bodies, when we dismiss the realm of Existence to concentrate on the mere idea. In the latter case we force the meaning of flesh (or the representational features of the art) into the context of the idea or art work and do this by virtue of the forcing away of the Existence, holding it apart—an act which makes the two of them connected by an "of." "Of" here then means the recognition that we are analyzing and dislocating. In the latter case *we* are adumbrating; in the former case there is an adumbration.

There is an analogous situation in connection with the numinous, ominous, the reference to that which in the universe has pertinence to our destiny, fate, good and ill. Here what must be done is to hold apart the element of the divine. Our judgment should be that the work or the idea is for everyone, for mankind, for all the selves that there are. The grasp of the work as a unity, in contrast with the previous grasp of it as (in relation to the Ideal) that which is a reality of its own, and (in relation to Existence) as that which is objective and not merely private, is one which sees it to have a significance, an import. This import would be lost if it were merely enjoyed; it would then at best be only a universally entertainable object, a source of pleasure for all. But by holding the divine at a distance, forcing us to hold this unity apart as the unity of the work for everyone, we make a relation of "of" between its significance and the significance which holds in fact.

If there are two types of adumbration, there should be two kinds of reference to the Ideal and two kinds of reference to God. There should not only be the reference produced in the work of art by forcing a distance between the work and these modes, but also one which is achieved by our throwing the weight of our being into the mode, leaving a mere residue for us to enjoy as that which has no referential import. We can entertain an idea or just look or explore a painting; we can grasp what either means as a mere structure or totality. In these cases we have a minimal referential element (for it is doubtful that it can be eliminated altogether), in contrast with the cases where we recognize the idea or the work of art to have a being of its own when and as it has a referential import, due to the fact that one of the analyzable components in it terminates the distancing relation between the work of art and the modes of beings which lie outside.

The above treatment of art seems to deny that it makes reference to particular matters of fact, to distinct actualities, but only to Ideality, Existence, and God. But the Existence which is the object of reference is that which is focalized in this or that object. In short it is not the actuality in its Actuality which is the object of the work of art, but Existence as now exhibited in the actuality here and now. It is in this respect that the work of art differs from the idea. Through our ideas we make primary reference to actualities, through our works of art we refer to Existence as localized in these actualities.

The idea of a nose, in contrast with the sculpted nose, functions as an Ideal inside an individual actual mind. The sculpted nose is a matter of fact, an actuality, which is made to be a substitute for a world, to have the status of a work of art by virtue of the fact that it makes a reference not to some other actuality (as a sign or even a symbol might), but to another type of being altogether. The work of art is the product of Existence, actualized as this localized reality having the referential function of telling us about the realm of Existence. It does not compete with science or common sense or theology or ethics, since it makes something new, replaces the real world.

But there would seem to be something wrong with a view like this which apparently has no place for Actuality. Would it not be more correct to say that art works are localizations of Existence and that they make reference to the Ideal, God and Actuality? If so the problem of reference would have to be modified with respect to adumbration: here we would hold the realm of commonsensical actualities apart from us and make the existential work of art have, through one of its analytic components, the referential task of pointing to such actualities. And this it would do through the cues, clues, the knots in the created existence which the work of art provides. To make art an objective reality open to any man is to hold ordinary actualities at a distance and by that token force into focus certain knots in the created work which then have the role of "of-ing."

It is a mistake to suppose that the painter starts with two dimensions and then adds a third, say through the introduction of a tactile attitude, as

Berenson seems to suggest. A painter, if he merely presented a two-dimensional object, would make those two dimensions; when he paints in the usual way he offers us the three-dimensions as a newly constructed whole, and does not make use of the two dimensions of his canvas. Though it is not possible to draw a single dimension—for every line has breadth—one can nevertheless use a line as an illustration of such a one-dimensional entity. A geometer would have such a line lying evenly between its two end points. Even if a painter painted it with a single color of the same intensity throughout, the different parts of that line would all be related to one another and to the beginning, making the line in effect a plurality of curves, at the same time that it stretched outwards and contracted, altered its very being to become a pulsating, dynamic newly created space which never had been before. The space of the painter is entirely newly created with its own structure, geometry, powers, interplays. To create is to make be, and what is made be is a new three-dimensional space.

April 3

An idea refers to the realms of Ideality, Existence and God because it is a localized case inside an Actuality. The referential element is due to the fact that the referent is held away from the idea, forcing the stretch of reference with respect to the referent. Ordinarily the idea is used to refer to a particular object. But this usage adds to the actual referent the additional activity, derived from Existence, which leads one to the particular object. If this were not the case we would be forced to believe, and would in fact believe truly once we had the idea of something. The idea of a snub nose, or of a balloon (which adds matter as it were to the sphere) refers not to an Actuality answering to this nature, but then and there refers just to the realm of Existence. When we say that we believe the balloon will burst we but jump a step in such a reference, for the bursting of the balloon is merely the consequence that follows in Existence. To say that we believe the balloon will burst is but to say that we believe there is really a balloon answering to our idea of it.

What the idea does with respect to Existence, it also does with respect to Ideality and God. The idea as having systematic objective meaning, accidents of relationship which themselves however are implicative and logical in nature, requires a reference not to a specific localization of the Ideal as possessing just those relations—for then the idea would be certainly true of the Ideal—but to the Ideal as a domain. And similarly, the idea as answering to its possession of value for any man does not refer to such a value in fact, but to the mode of God as that which, though held away to give the idea the status of something objectively valid, is referred to by the idea at the same time.

What is true of the idea is true of the work of art, except that the work of art, being an instance of a created Existence, makes reference to Actuality as such. The Actuality it might portray does not necessarily have an answer in the shape of a specific actuality here and now, but only in Actuality as such, which may (if the idea be true or adequate) be specified in the shape of an actuality iconically like the idea.

But suppose now instead of having the idea of a balloon we had the idea of Ideality or of Existence or of God. If the idea had a necessary referent to these it could not help but being true. From this it follows A] in the light of the fact that there is a reference to the different modes in the idea, even when portraying something limited, which in that limited form does not exist, that there could be a deduction of the modes from an idea. An idea to be an idea which is to be true for all men makes a necessary and true reference to the modes of Ideality, Existence and God, and therefore one can prove their existence from the fact that the idea has these roles. A proof of God could run: I have the idea of a balloon which is an idea for everyone (or extended: I have the idea of a balloon bursting for everyone). It could not be an idea for everyone except so far as God was held at a distance and thereby turned into the inescapable referent of the idea. B] When God (or the other modes) is made itself the content of the idea it will not only serve to prove the existence of Existence and Ideality, but will itself provide a name for the proof of the God in which it terminates. To say I have an idea of God is but to say that I have an idea of the inevitable terminus of any idea which is an idea for any man. To say I have an idea of Existence is but to say that I have an idea open for every man by virtue of the referential position that God has for that idea; but it is also to say that just so far as that idea of Existence is an idea which is open to all as relating to an objective reality, the idea must portray what is there in fact and is necessarily true of it. Similarly the idea of Actuality is more than something privately enjoyed so far as it is treated as objective or for all men (and thus has reference to Existence and to God); as an idea which refers to something substantial, other than itself, it also necessarily portrays and refers to Actuality.

To have an idea of these three modes is to have a true idea of them; any other idea relates to specifications of these and may be in error, for there may be no such specifications in fact. Metaphysics then is rooted in assertions which have their necessary counterpart, and which answer in fact to what is being thought about. We ground proofs here on the basis of the ideas, not in the light of their content, but in the light of the status which the idea has as something to be accepted by other men as an adequate idea. To be sure if the idea is not an adequate idea, if it does not have the status of something open to others, then of course we cannot say that it portrays these modes. But if any idea be adequate it will refer to these modes. So the issue comes down to this: can any idea be adequate, and can we in an idea express the nature of that for which the idea is adequate? Since we can know the conditions of adequacy—substantiality, objectivity and universality—we can know the modes which are beyond the idea, for these are but the distanced realities which make it possible for the idea to assume these roles.

When we come to a work of art we ought to be able to find in it the same kind of "proof" of God and Ideality, and in addition of the realm of actualities. Its own being is of course proof that there is Existence of some kind—i.e., its kind, though to be sure not the Existence which governs Actuality. (In the case of ideas their presence proves the reality of Ideality but not necessarily of any particular Ideal form or even that there be particular forms beyond the mind.) The work of art recognized to have a status which is systematically organized via accidents (which means for the work of art that it has, beyond its significant form, the associations of daily life), as something objective for all other beings, and as holding for all selves, necessarily refers to the Ideal, Existence and God. If it portrayed these—and it can through Symbolic Icons, by the exhibition of the process of creativity itself, and by the achievement of a status as a sacramental object—it will tell us what these are, pointing to them inescapably and genuinely. The religious know this about the works which portray the divine; the musician knows it with respect to Existence; and the ethicist with respect to the Ideal.

The view just stated makes the work of art have accidents correlative with its adumbrative and ominous claims. But should it not have substantiality as a claim? An actuality is substantial over against its accidents; but a work of art is not an Actuality. As an Existence it must (and so must God and the Ideal) be made effective in a channelized way by virtue of its orientation in Actuality. This orientation is accomplished in Existence, and of course in God and the Ideal as well by an element which is, while part of them, made to serve as the terminus of the relation that holds actualities over against them. What is this component, and how are we to characterize the analytic component which is correlative with it?

What does a mode achieve through such orientation which it did not have before? The component in the modes which provides the orientation is excessive determinations, accidents, universal pertinence, objective purposiveness, divisions; what is left over is indeterminateness. What is accomplished is the making of the modes parts of experience.

Regarding a painting or other works of art we have A] the having of it as a part of common experience through the orientation in Actuality, provided by the determinations in it beyond those required by the very fact that it must be a created space, time or energy. In itself the work is such space, time or energy without real determinations; it becomes determinate by virtue of the use of its determinations to orient it in Actuality and thereby make it function in experience. (There is a similar role played by determinations in God and Ideality, enabling them, while indeterminate in themselves, to be determinate elements in experience.) B] The work of art is oriented toward God (and so are ideas and actualities) by virtue of the numinous component with its correlative selflessness; the work thereby achieves universal pertinence. C] The work is oriented toward the Ideal (as are God and Actuality) by virtue of a component of purpose, having its correlative in that which would be merely momentary. The orientation toward the Ideal gives the work of art the status of that which has beauty in and of itself, and thus a being of its own.

On this last interpretation there is no genuine adumbration in a work of art—just excess determinations, numinosity and purposiveness. Adumbration would be possessed by the modes of Actuality, Ideality and God, and be a way of making evident that there is an Existence beyond them. The excess determinations, the divisions, the fact that the space, time or energy is filled up by objects or contents which are more than filling, more than significant form, allow for an adumbrative role.

There are four powers, three of which are in each mode: A] that which orients in the Actual, or *representation* through excess determination; B] that which orients in the Ideal, or *orientation* through purpose; C] *adumbration,* which orients in Existence, through the use of a component making for objectivity; D] *numinosity* which orients in God through the use of a component making for universality.

Does an idea lack A, a work of art lack C, a prescription lack B and a sacrament lack D? It seems odd to say that an idea lacks representational orientation and that sacraments lack a numinous element. But the idea of which one here speaks is the idea in and of itself; it doesn't even claim to represent (what does that is a mere image or picture, a kind of existence in the mind), but to point to a world which might be subdivided and terminated in items of which the idea may be iconic. It would seem then that we have no idea proper of Actuality. But then how could we know the mode Actuality? Would we have to have something Ideal, some possibility or sense of the Good which had excess determinations; some way of Existing, an image say, which had excess determinations; something of God, a sacrament say, which had excess determinations, and in this way orient ourselves in Actuality and even characterize it? The excess determinations could be given the meaning of Actuality, i.e., the excess determinations themselves could be used as a name for the Actuality toward which they are oriented. But does it make sense to say that we can have genuine ideas, localizations of Actuality in ourselves regarding anything except Actuality, and that Actuality can be "known" only so far as we have a sense of value, images and sacraments loaded down with excess determinations?

Must we say that only ideas, images and values can have a numinous component but that sacraments lack it, and that we can "know" God, refer to Him properly only through the images, ideas and values, since the sacraments already possess Him and need orientation by the other modes?

Were an idea treated as a case of Ideality and not of Actuality we could have an adequate idea of Actuality but not of Ideality. We would not be able to orient the idea through purpose to the Ideal; all we could say of it was that it was a subdivision and specification of it. We would not know the Ideal through the idea, and would get to know it only through orientations which began with existent images, numinously oriented religious feelings, and actual expressions of the self in the shape of "concepts" (to keep to what is inside a man), and then found that all of these had elements of purpose associated with them which made it possible to point to the Ideal.

Perhaps it would be wise to recognize four different types of ideas, finally distinguished when we make a mode the content and terminus of it. The idea in the guise of Actuality would be incapable of representation, in the guise of Ideality would be incapable of orientation via purpose; as something with a career in us, the idea as existing would be incapable of adumbration; and the idea as categorial, as a basic unity, would be incapable of numinosity. We could have any one of three types of ideas for each of the modes. But we would also have to say that we could not represent Actuality through an idea of Actuality, orient an Idea of Ideality towards the Ideal, adumbrate through an idea of Existence the being of Existence, and use a numinous component of an idea of God to get to God. The idea of Actuality would be one which did not have an excess of determinations, the idea of the Ideal would not have a purposiveness as part of it, the idea of Existence would not be a genuinely objective one, and the idea of God would not have a genuine universal meaning. There is something odd here.

One can see how an idea of Actuality might not have an excess of determinations, that all the determinations it had were necessary to it as meaning whatever it did mean. It is possible even to allow that the idea of the Ideal is not oriented to the Ideal by purposiveness and thus lacks a systematic place in knowledge. But it is hard to see how the idea of Existence was not objective and that of God not universal. Suppose these characterizations were reversed? Does it make sense to say that the idea of Existence, though objective, is not universal, germane to all men, and that the idea of God though universal is not objective, open as a public datum to all? The latter seems plausible. What is left then is the idea of Existence as objective, a public kind of idea not actually universalizable —which is indeed what the Existentialists seem to say. It is the being of God then which provides objectivity and that of Existence which provides universality to ideas. The idea of God itself though would lack objectivity, being personally enjoyed as it were by all men, and that of Existence would lack universality, being something objective but which could not be affirmed by every man. This conclusion would seem to make a difficulty for theology on the one side and for a scientific account of nature on the other. But can we not say that a theological grasp of the nature of God is merely one that throws light on the other modes in their being and can do nothing more for the mode of God than to offer that which has meaning for all men (except perhaps by a kind of abstraction which enables one to deal with God in a kind of neutral way)?

These various alternatives affect the attempt in the *Modes* to look at all the modes speculatively, inside a single system in what at times seem to be quite similar ways—though there are suggestions at the end of the *Modes* that this is not what can or ought to be done. The different modes have different weights and must be approached in different ways; violence must be done to the idea of each to get it to have the characteristics in idea that are possessed by the others.

It is said in the *Modes* that the idea of Existence alone has existential import. But of course the other modes have ideas which are adequate to them too. The idea of the Actual will have non-representational bearing, and appear perhaps as a case of the Ideal; the idea of the Ideal will be representational as a kind of Actual; the idea of God will be universal but not objective. If this be the case then to say that the idea of Existence has existential import means only that it (as the *Modes of Being* apparently assumes) is a representational kind of idea or, as the foregoing allows as well, either an orienting purposed or an objective, non-universal kind of idea.

April 6

Ideas, as *Modes of Being* seems to make evident, are specialized versions of Actuality. Every idea which a man has should be distinguished from an image, an idealization and a divine name. Each is held over against the realm of the Ideal, Existent and divine, and as such has a purposive, adumbrative and numinous significance. It differs from the meaning of a work of art in that the latter is held over against the realm of the Actual, and has, not an adumbrative but a representative side, being a kind of image. However it does not report or duplicate the particular things in the world; instead it merely allows for their acknowledgment, claiming only that there is a world of commonsensical Actuality somehow articulated in the work of art. In a sense, though it is a contrary to fact conditional, the work of art is closer to the commonsensical real than are the categorial assertions of daily life. These do have individual termini but only as focalized portions of the realm of Existence. We know what Existence is through the use of our ordinary ideas—and that is why common-sense ideational activity moves into a cosmic science, whereas art keeps us rooted toward the individual.

When we come to think of the modes, we do so with ideas similar to those we have every day. These all lack representational power. This means that they function by virtue of the way in which the worlds of Existence, Ideal and God are held apart from them and the ideas are thereby made to adumbrate, be purposive and to illuminate. The idea of Actuality would stand out however in that the very realm of Actuality would not be held over against the idea. In the *Modes,* however, it is said that Existence has existential import, pointing directly to Existence. It does this via the non-representational contact it makes with Actuality as focalized in individual things. It makes itself function as a specialized focalized part of the whole of Existence.

April 7

If the ideas relating to the various modes are of the same type, and if it be the case that the idea of Existence has existential import, i.e., that it directly relates to Existence, forcing an assent to it, precisely because it is related to it as focalized element, so must all the other ideas have an existential import of a similar nature. But in addition, since the other ideas have an immediate relation to Ideality, and to God as well, all of them, including the ideas of Actuality and of Existence, must have direct and unavoidable pertinence to the modes of Ideality and of God. And it is right that there should be no such direct relation to Actuality, in view of the fact that of all of the modes, Actuality has its being in the plurality of actualities whereas the pluralities in the other modes are subordinate and derivative. The mode of Actuality, whether this be directly portrayed by the idea of Actuality or by some other mode, must be known derivatively from the consideration of actualities. It is the awareness that these actualities are cases of Actuality, that they have abstractable natures, which allows for the acknowledgment of the realm of Actuality with its various powers. But what then enables one to know distinct actualities, particularly those which are outside our ideas? Are they junctures of ideas, adumbrateds and numinosities? Is the individual actuality a kind of product?

April 8

To suppose that a real object is nothing but what is revealed in physics would be to suppose that it is something which cannot be experienced, or that so far as it is experienced it is overlaid with irrelevant qualities. Yet to suppose that the phenomenological object alone is real is to make science a grandiose hypothesis which by some miracle seems to be able to work, enables us to predict, and to use phenomenological objects in ways they themselves cannot provide. To suppose that both sides are real and must be correlated in some way is but to beg the question; it is begged in a worse way when it is thought that one of these sides is in the mind and the other is real. What is needed is a third position in terms of which one can see the two as equally basic but as in no way exhausting the reality of the object.

The only real star is a present star. This star has various properties and powers which are capable of mathematical treatment. To isolate those properties, to express them mathematically and still recognize them to be real, one must dislocate the star. The mathematical aspect of the star requires that the present star be selective of a whole sequence of occurrences in the past. The distant terminus of this selected sequence is the "cause" of the perception of the star. This cause does not operate now, nor did it ever operate. It is just related to the current star along the sequence which that star, by virtue of its mathematical properties, isolates out of the entire past—a past which is preserved as a domain of unoperative facts.

The present star is also a phenomenon, something seen. As such it is dislocated in space rather than time; the phenomenal star through the agency of perception, is selected across a region of space, by placing the present star in a space related to the observer.

The present star, or better the real object which is perceived and mathematically known, is a dynamic reality whose being consists in the unity of itself as the terminus (in the present) of the mathematical sequence which it sustains and extends through the past, as well as of itself as the terminus of a perceptual act.

What is the object; where is the object; what properties has it got? These questions are to be answered by a synthesis of the two sides, to give us the nature of a reality contemporary with us. The "cause" is not the real star; nor is the perceived object the real star. The real star is that being which makes it possible for there to be a cause and for there to be something perceived, subject of course to the conditions that on the one side there has been a past which mathematics can reorder, and that there is a perceiver contemporary with the real star.

There can be many phenomenological phases of an object, due to different circumstances. All of these can be said to be variations, due to those circumstances, of a normative phenomenon. We can thus say that the rails do not in fact converge, or that they converge from this perspective precisely because they are actually parallel. The fact that the mathematical relations between them give them as mathematically parallel makes us select the phenomenon of parallellism as normative. If we turn to the star we can then, if we like, take every one of the perceptual places and qualities of the star to be variants, for those circumstances, of some normative phenomenon which a sequence of the mathematical relations demands. In short that is the best and normative nature of the phenomenological star which has some at least of the major properties which the "cause" of the star is recognized to have, when we spin out the activities of the star over the course of past time.

Are we not now back to the doctrine of correlation? Do we not associate hot with high temperature, equi-distance in mathematics with visible parallelism? Do we not now actually live through the schematism of Kant? In a sense yes. There is correlation, but it is not of mind and matter, nor is it arbitrary. It involves the selection of a normative phenomenological object. But any one of the phenomenological occurrences could be taken as norm. We could take the convergence as normative and treat the visible parallel which we see when we stand atop of the rails to be a way of expressing such convergence under such special conditions, conditions which enable us to get a phenomenological counterpart of the mathematical nature of the rails.

One can say that every phenomenological phase of an entity is correlated with a mathematical; all that we do when we select, say visual parallelism, is to determine what our normative name for the relation is, and not what the phenomenological relation truly is. The convergence of the rails is no less real than the parallelism; indeed one can make a mathematical projection of the former as surely as of the latter, though the difficulty here is that such mathematical treatment will not take account of all the physical activities of the objects placed on those rails. The real object itself is the schema, the locus of the to-getherness of the two dimensions of phenomenological phases and mathematically defined extensions into the past.

Wm. Blake makes a further distinction. He speaks of the sun as a round disk of fire and also as an innumerable company of heavenly host. In addition then to the mathematical we seem to have the mystical. But it is his intent I think to say that the "heavenly host" is the very real sun; in the terms of the above this would make it (though this is not what Blake himself says), that unitary being in which the astronomical and the round disk have their union. The sun would manifest itself in two ways, thereby finding a place for itself in space and time and in the life of the perceiver.

The sun in a painting is a purged sun, a sun in a new space, freshly created, and it is related to the phenomenological sun, the astronomical sun and to the sun as affecting human destiny. This means that we have the following suns: A] phenomenological, B] mathematical, C] religious, D] aesthetic, E] substantial (and actual?). Is this too many?

A painting can be said to have taken real Existence and subjected it to new conditions to give it a new manifestation in the guise of a new space. Or it can be said to have made Existence anew. The former is more accurate. The painter makes a new space and this space expresses the very being of Existence. Since the painter also makes reference to the Ideal and the divine he can be said also to express in a new and fresh way something of the nature of the Ideal and of the divine. His reference to particular objects is a reference to congealizations of these other three modes; he does not deal with Actuality as such in its concrete plural manifestations. Accordingly, we have the following suns:

1] the phenomenological sun in space and time

2] the mathematically extended object which is located in a mathematical past (and future?)

3] the purposed sun, the sun related to an Ideal (the sun with a future)

4] the impinging sun, the sun related to the divine. (Blake's angels)

5] the artistically produced sun, with its newly forged space, Ideality and divinity

6] the substantial sun, the concretionalization of all these various suns, to constitute a genuine Actuality.

The interrelation of the first five to constitute the sixth cannot be performed in the terms of any one of these five. The substantial sun integrates all these. Art comes after the sun has been in existence, so does the phenomenological sun, and so does the mathematical. All of them are manifestations of the sixth. The point is that they are the points at which we start in order to learn of the nature of the sixth. The fact that in art we add something which the other four did not provide but shows that they were not adequate to give the full meaning of the sun. If we can find some other way of dealing with the sun in addition to the first five, this will but give us another way of approaching the substantial sun. It will also require us not merely to take account of new content, but to see that the way in which the sun is a unity is different from the way we had supposed it to be when we took account of fewer dimensions. If all the substantial sun had to do was to interrelate the phenomenological and mathematical suns, the substantial sun would be less complex in content and operation than it is now known to be, in light of the reality of purpose, impingment and art.

Will history give us another dimension? Politics? These questions can be left open, though perhaps it is pertinent to note now that the sun does play a role in history, and that the very attempt to get rockets to the sun, the very experiments of science which involve the curvature of light rays near the sun, etc., show that politics has its bearings on the sun.

We must understand the sun in fact to be not indeterminate (as I suggested in the paper on the reality of the art object), but as not being fully known either in content or in mode of unification. It is known nevertheless to some degree just to the very extent that we can, as we sometimes do in immediate experience, bring together a number of these dimensions in an object.

The above account abandons the view that a work of art is a contrary to fact conditional explicative of the adumbrative side of things. It treats the work of art as expanding in its own way the nature of the object, analogous to what mathematics or perception do. Of course the contrary to fact conditional approach can be maintained by treating, as we can for some purposes, ordinary discourse as realistic, etc. But then the converse also must be true; the latter discourse could be said to offer a contrary to fact conditional for art. These two usages can be carried on, at the same time that one recognizes the signal ultimacy and yet correlative status of the work of art as that which explicates a substantial reality in its own way, independently of the way in which other activities explicate it. Art would then be seen to be on a level of reality and of non-ultimacy (in terms of the substantial being) as any other mode of dealing with the world.

To know how all these fit together is of course to be outside all of them. The sixth way, the dealing with the substantial reality of the object as underlying all forms of approach must be the neutral way of speculation which dialectically synthesizes and modifies them all in the act of making them together express the unity which is the object. It must stand out over against the creating knowing self as an other, as deep and inward and substantial as the individual knower.

April 9

The Spring 1959 issues of *Daedelus* is devoted to Myth. Henry A. Murray defines it as "a sensible and dramatic representation of a supposedly recurrent or unique event . . . represented primarily in the mind, . . . but secondarily in words . . . in quasi-actions, . . . or in some artistic form . . . " "A myth is a potent imagent." It is said to be peculiarly attractive, to evoke empathy, elicit belief, guide conduct, and to bring about whole-hearted cooperative participation. He summarizes the writings of diverse men and is therefore loose in order to be inclusive. But he is close to the core of its nature. Perhaps it would be better though to say that myth is the dramatic presentation of absolute values as effective for a group of people.

Myth is an entire language, congealed and prescriptive. This language includes story and poetry. The rhythms of music, the divisions it defines, even before and apart from playing, the kind of rhythms that are characteristic of any of the pieces that are in fact composed in that community, are also included in its meaning. It differs from poetry in that it does not seem to be made by anyone; it is a communal art.

Valèry is quoted as saying that "myth is the name for everything that exists or subsists, only to the extent that speech is its cause." This says that so far as something is made to be by means of speech it is myth. But here speech must be viewed as "language" and account must be taken of drama and poetry. These perhaps provide sub-myths. Perhaps what Valèry intends can be preserved by distinguishing "Mythos" as that which is constituted by the language structure which will be and is being used, the subordinate myths or congealizations of the Mythos being provided by the artistic construction of the story teller and poet. The acknowledgment of the Mythos in the form of an acceptance of the rhythms it will provide, the adopting of an attitude where this will be used, is the enclosure act which has its analogue in architecture, defining the area to be used.

Levin says myth is the Aristotelian "plot," and the Latin "fabula." Aristotle, as Butcher observed, says that it is "as it were, the soul of tragedy" and that this is meant literally, as giving it its form and life. On this lead we must say that it is the soul of the people, the guiding principle and vital core of them as a unified whole.

Barthes is quoted as saying that "Mythology is an accord with the world not as it is but as it wants to be." This I think is sound, pointing up not only the prescriptive, valuational nature of the Mythos but also the fact that it has within it something of the Ideal which one seeks to achieve.

Joseph Campbell notes in a comparative study of mythology that the recurrent themes are fire-theft; deluge; land of the dead; virgin birth; resurrected hero. He says that the myths work on us as "energy-releasing, life-motivating and directing agents."

An alternative definition of Mythos: the precipitate of language under the influence of a sense of value, given dramatic form so as to control time.

Mircea Eliade says that the myths are in two categories: those relating to primordial proximity between heaven and earth, and those which relate to the communication between them. In the former man is immortal, spontaneous, free, able to ascend to heaven, and has friendship and a knowledge of the language of animals.

Clyde Kluckhohn says that "the following themes appear always and everywhere: 1] Were-animals. 2] the notion that . . . death can result from . . . magical means. 3] A connection between incest and witchcraft."

The various comparative mythologues do not agree as to just what is common to all—and this despite the fact that they are apparently trying to be descriptive and summarize the available evidence.

I abbreviate and modify a definition by Jerome S. Bruner: Myth is an aesthetic device for bringing preternatural forces into collaboration with life in such a way as to be amenable both to the unconscious passions and the conscious mind. Briefer: Mythos is a creation of time in which life is punctuated both on the conscious and unconscious levels. Or alternatively: Mythos is a language rooted in value, and focalized dramatically.

Can we not treat each story teller, dramatist and poet as providing a kind of precipitate which clings to the wall of the Ideal to constitute that myth which all adopt? We ought to include in it as well the temporal aspect of music, drama and dance. Like all traditionally sustained activities the Mythos is also an outcome of past activities merged together, and would in turn dictate what is now being done. The "spirit of the times" is but another way of referring to this. It is perhaps partly sustained in the interrelations which people have to one another and by the organizations and institutions through which they function.

Should there not be a form of art which is merely the punctuation of time, the mastery of it to be filled out in other ways? Need it have an Ideal prescriptive power instead of a mere defining role? Need it be anything more than either the actual redefining of time in fact, or the creation of a new time, a time for that group?

April 14

The possible approaches to art: 1] Imitation   A] of nature, B] of the Ideal;   2] Substitution   A] of nature,   B] of the Ideal, C] of man;   3] Utility for   A] man,   B] society,   C] religion;   4] Expression of   A] idea,   B] emotion,   C] unconscious;   5] Ontological, having a being of its own. Although these approaches have usually been held to be exculsive, occasionally they have been combined at least in pairs. There are those who speak of poetry as an imitation which functions to please men (S. Johnson); Freud seems to hold a combination of 4C and 2C. It seems correct though to say that all of these are correct, and that they answer quite distinct questions.

1] Imitation answers the question of the relation of the work of art to what is other than it. If imitation be thought to be more than duplication and even more than representation and be viewed as a kind of re-presentation, we will be able to see how it is possible for the work of art to provide symbols to be used to refer us to a world beyond. Even when we take the fifth position we are forced to hold the work apart from the world and in that very act are forced to make the work of art imitate, in the minimal sense of making a reference. And unless there is nothing in that world which we see to be worth preserving, we are bound to include its virtues in the work of art.

2] The work of art, precisely because it is within our control and is freed from irrelevancies, and precisely because it is available here and now and does not have the unreached character of the true Ideal, is worthy of being substituted for other realities. Here the work of art is viewed comparatively with respect to the *value* of what is other than it; in the former case it was looked at comparatively with respect to the *nature* of what is other than it. We can then combine the two: art is an imitation worthy of acting as a substitute.

3] The work of art as offered to the spectator must satisfy him. As being permitted to function in a society it must be in consonance with the society's needs; as worthy of acceptance in a religion it must serve the religion's purposes. Should it do only these things it is reduced to a didactic, rhetorical, purely instrumental object, a bit of craft or workmanship.

But if we combine this side of it with the other two it turns out that art is an imitation worthy of being a substitute, which enhances man in himself or in some role.

4] From the side of the artist the work of art is an expression, a product of his activity. This activity is in part governed by deliberate intent, in part by himself as a single being, and in part by habits, rules and even desires and impulses of which the artist is not aware but which manifest themselves perhaps all the more surely because he is not aware of them and does not therefore distort, inhibit or blur them. This expression should also be repeated in some form by the spectator if he is to read the work in something like the spirit in which it is produced. One does not always know what that spirit is, but there nevertheless must be more than passive receptivity on the part of the spectator. His must be an adventure of discovering just what is in the work by expressing himself in his reading of it, as a single being, and finding that in such expression some satisfaction is attained. The work of art then is a kind of expression. Tying this result together with the previous ones we can then say that art is an imitation worthy of being a substitute which expresses and enhances man in himself or in some role.

5] Finally, the work of art has a being of its own; it has a structure, a development of a plurality of themes, material, etc. It is a domain all its own—otherwise we could not have it as that which could substitute; it could not be that which was the product of an expression; it would not be that which was imitating or satisfying. Accordingly we can say: ART IS AN IMITATION HAVING VALUE AND BEING OF ITS OWN AND THERE-FORE WORTHY OF BEING A SUBSTITUTE FOR REALITY, WHICH DOES EXPRESS AND CAN ENHANCE MAN IN WHOLE OR PART. Once again: ART IS A VALUABLE, SUBSTITUTING IMITATION OF REALITY, EXPRES-SIVE OF AND ENHANCING MAN IN WHOLE OR PART.

These different approaches to art can be said to require different "styles." Thus, starting with I. A. Richards' distinction between sense, feeling, tone and intention, we can say that sense is for imitation, feeling for substitution, tone for utility, and intention for expression. For him sense directs us to some state of affairs; feeling indicates our bias; tone reflects our attitudes towards the listener; and intention is what we aim at. (Perhaps feeling and intention should here be interchanged.) But what is important is that there is no provision here for the ontological aspect of the art. Accordingly, and modifying what Richards has said, we can perhaps with justice make the following correlations: Every work of art has five stresses: 1] it imitates through its structure, theme, and in this sense its "sense"; this "sense" may but need not be referential.

2] It substitutes through its value, and this value is exhibited in its feeling-tone or qualitative unity; 3] It is useful, and expresses this by virtue of an effectiveness carried by the nature of its stimulative powers, themselves essentially due to modulations and interplays; 4] it expreses something of a man which it manifests not in an intent but in its resonance, its evocative powers, the capacity to communicate in the sense of solidifying and reflecting artist and spectator. 5] And it has a style which is the very characteristic it possesses, the way in which it develops inside itself regardless of where it originated or where it is going or what purpose it serves or could serve.

There ought also to be five ways in which a work of art is true. A] It is true to the world it imitates, somewhat as a foot-ruler is true; B] it is true to the values of the realm for which it substitutes in that it does justice to them, allows them fuller and purer play (this is being "true" in the sense of being faithful or just); C] it is true to the needs of man or society, religion, etc., in that it serves them (it is "true" here as that which does not betray them but in fact promotes them); D] it is true in that it is a clear and adequate expression and not a distortive one— "true" here means fair and pure. Finally, E] it is true to itself, has its own integrity, not other than it is supposed to be (it is "true" in that it is not a counterfeit). None of these truths of course is the truth of a prose statement in which there is an attempt to re-present, inside the conventions of discourse, what is outside. The prose statement is governed by the convention; it remains true to it in order to be true to what is outside it. The artistic work is true in other senses precisely because it has no conventional interpretation.

If it be the case that the phenomenological object, the object of perception, and the mathematical object are both abstracts from a substantival object, one ought perhaps to go on to say that the art object, the distorted object of illusion and error, the object as envisaged via judgment, and the object envisaged via the art work, are all abstracts from the same substantival reality. The mathematically formulated object is the substantial object as subject to a special condition, that of being dealt with only in mathematical terms. When so dealt with the substantial object must be placed in a mathematical time and space and dated as in the past and at a distance. But if one were to go to the place and time one would not find the mathematical object, for this is neither perceptible nor substantival. And it would be pointless to try to correlate this with the phenomenological object, not only because such correlation supposes that both are ultimately real, or that one is real and the other an intellectual construct, but because such a correlated result does not yield the being which can act, and does not make evident that the two abstracts are in fact the same reality under different conditions. What is phenomenological is the substantival object which is expressed in such and such a mathematical form. Just so the illusory and the art object (so far as this is "imitative") are the substantival reality as caught in such and such a condition. We can take a normative way of naming and describing, locating and characterizing the substantival reality, and this name can be a normal one for any of the abstracts which we in fact isolate, providing we recognize that the abstract is distinct from the substantival object (even though they are both given the same name), and that it is just such an object which must have a different abstract nature when it is subject to a different condition. In the *Modes* I was inclined   A] to overstress the reality of the phenomenological object, and   B] to speak at times as though the substantival object were the concertionalization of the phenomenological object and the mathematical, thereby on the one hand ignoring other abstracts, and on the other overlooking the equivalence of the abstracts one with the other.

The last consideration has been one which has not been faced in a constant way by me. Is the indicated the very same thing as the contemplated, but under a different condition, or is it a correlate of it? This is another version of the question of the relation of the phenomenological and mathematical objects. Perhaps the two views ought to be combined? There is a way perhaps in which diverse abstracts, each of which is the substantival object under a different restrictive condition can be combined, synthesized, to express the nature of the unitary, substantival real. If this were the case should we not say that the elliptical look of the coin and the roundish look, both of which are abstracts from the substantival coin which we designate to be in fact round, are capable of being synthesized in a kind of power, expressible by a formula which says that it must be the one now and the other then? Only in this way can we preserve the power to make a judgment on the one hand, since this needs diverse abstracts, and on the other hand recognize the objectivity and equality of different abstracts and their status as the substantival object under a condition. Taken in this sense we can say that the indicated and contemplated are synthesized to constitute that unitary representation of the substantival object which is nothing but an indicated when treated in this way and nothing but a contemplated when treated in that, and that these capacities are exactly what one means by its substantival nature.

Granted all this, then the work of art is the real object under the conditions of the artistic creation, and this can be synthesized with any of the other ways of having the real object, so as to express what that real substantival object is in itself, i.e., a power capable of being so manifested. But this does not really help us very much in the understanding of the work of art, for there is such a large factor of human creativity being introduced by the artist as to make the statement that it is the real object subject to a new condition, hardly illuminating. Yet the remark must be made if there is to be a genuine place for the work of art in nature. It must be the case that the art work has its own ontological status, is a real world with real properties in the very same sense as the mathematical or phenomenological objects are real. It is another competitor, and can be thought of as a substitute only in the way in which the mathematical or the phenomenological, etc., objects can be treated as substitutes for one another. But does this not leave the real substantival object mysterious? It does not leave it uncharacterizable, for we can characterize it generically in terms of its potentialities and its relations to the other modes of being. And it does not preclude our knowing it by synthesizing these various abstracts of it, these various resultants of it under various conditions.

It is not the case then that it is the function of mathematics or science not to explain the phenomenological world, but to explain the substantival one, to see what it is under various conditions. Evidence though is given by the phenomenological world, thereby providing us with a warning that we are not to identify the real with the mathematical or the scientific. We must similarly say that it is not the function of art to imitate the phenomena but the substantival, and that the phenomenological is needed for empirical reference which the mathematical is needed for conceptual apprehension.

This account supposes that an individual has different interests which make one or the other of these abstracts pertinent and even worthy of being the name of the substantival object. It supposes too that there is an inwardness to the individual which answers to the inwardness of the substantival object; that such and such a condition which the individual provides is but the individual himself in a special guise. The individual, in his substantial nature treated under a restricted condition, is one with the recognition that the object is likewise being so treated. The recognition of a need for synthesis is the recognition that the diverse expressions of a man, though all equally revelatory of him as under different conditions, have a kind of status and objectivity making it desirable to interpenetrate the results (rather than to take one alone as the name of the substantial object which is different from it and which will under the presentation of various conditions make itself manifest

in different ways). Such a view means that the work of art is no more or
even a better substitute in fact for the world than any other manifestation
under a circumstance. Each manifestation will involve some purging,
some denials, some incapacity to do justice to the full reality. The act of
synthesis enables us to see what is added to the abstract in order to make
it substantival. The reduction of an abstract through the release of a
condition so as to get the substantival object in itself is a process equivalent to the synthesis of that abstract with another to give us the nature of
its unity. But in either case the abstract loses something and in this sense
is an idealization or purged outcome. The work of art will differ from all
else by virtue of the control we exert, the element of creative reconstruction we provide. It is thus the product of the same kind of forces which
make other abstracts, but instead of working impersonally it is working
personally, bringing in more and more conditions, subjugating the substantival object to the limit of new conditioning, overwhelming it as it
were by all the new conditioning that a man can provide.

What happens then to the art object as that which has its own integrity and can be dealt with in isolation from the world? It would be that
which, having a minimal attachment to any of the abstracts, moves on to
be an abstract itself; it is as it were the mathematical object (here we
have the golden section) subject to phenomenological creativity, or
conversely, the phenomenological object of daily life subject to fresh
and controlling activities on the part of a creating being. Only one who
really knew the substantival object could make the work of art be a
direct abstract in the way in which nature and perception make the
mathematical and phenomenological objects into direct abstracts of the
substantival reality.

Art is "twice removed" as Plato said; it is an abstract from an abstract,
or more accurately it is the substantival object subject to a condition
imposed on a "natural" condition. Such a substantival object is in fact not
a Platonic Ideal but Existence congealed. One could conceivably view
all abstracts as specifications of the Ideal, and taken in this sense art is
"twice removed." Plato's criticism of art though would not be just, unless
one supposed that one had to face the substantival directly. Plato in the
end has to have a theory of immediate encounter with the real. But if I
see the world from an angle it is right that I have the result under a condition; to recognize that I am seeing it this way is to recognize that this
is the real object, as so seen of course.

The fact that the work of art is "twice removed" does not make it
more or less an abstract than the abstracts which are once removed. The
real substantial object is the mathematical object in a mathematical
space-time when treated in purely formal ways; it is the art object as

that which has subjected its phenomenological status to another condition, the condition of using a medium, of being creative and in control, of developing a theme, etc. Such an abstract of course is not rational as the mathematical is, is not at a distance as the phenomenological is, is not active as the substantival is, is not as familiar as even the erroneous and illusory is, and so on, but it has virtues of its own.

Have we a right to suppose that the phenomenological abstract and the mathematical can be synthesized, and if synthesized that they answer to the unity which is the real object? Does it make sense to say that the illusory object should be taken as such with its conditions, and synthesized with the mathematical and its conditions? Why not free oneself from the conditions altogether? But can one? But if we cannot, do we not have the Kantian thing in itself as over against a "phenomenal" world, where "phenomenal" is being used for any kind of conditioning including mathematical or even artistic and creative? Does it make sense to say that the real tracks are convergent tracks under the conditions of distant seeing, together with the mathematical relation of equidistance, and that the real tracks are the two of these unified, if only in a kind of power which can be expressed both for vision and formally? If it does not make sense we would have difficulty in knowing which one of the multiple abstracts did make sense.

Is it any harder to synthesize the art object with the mathematical than it is the illusory with the phenomenological or mathematical or art object? It would seem not to be so. To characterize the substantival object we must make a kind of synthesis which is no mere adding of abstracts but their interpenetration to make them into nothing but "powers," an inwardness with insistencies and resistances, mastering Existence and living through its own time and space. This inwardness is distorted and abstracted from in perception, mathematics and art, and there given additional features by virtue of the creative powers of those who engage in these activities.

Can we go further and say for example that the translation of an object into the abstract which is a story, is also translated one step further into language itself, and then one step further into calligraphy? Does it make sense to say that the calligraphy, the very letters in the word "cow" are the real substantival cow subject to a plurality of conditions? But this is precisely what it is. We cannot read back to the phenomenological reality or the substantival one if we start with the mere physical occurrence of the words, because we have no established convention for doing this. But is this not exactly what the Chinese do, and little children do when they learn to read?

And when we go on to say there is movement in a painting of Albers and action in a movie must we not recognize these to be as real as any other movement, including the "non-moving" movement of physical formulae, the "apparent" movements of experience, and the movements of engines, etc. The fact that physics made the making of the engine possible does not affect the fact that the movement of the engine goes beyond physics. Engineering is not degenerate or practical physics but a new enterprise altogether, which takes account of phenomenological and other aspects as well as the mathematical.

In connection with literature, more than in connection with painting or music, the counters we use are common counters with common functions which in fact must be maintained when and as we subject them to new conditions to live in a new world. The very attempt to be creative in literature leads men to try to be "literary" so as to free themselves from prosaic associations, but when they do this they cease to do full justice to their insight, and force one away from the awareness of the art object's capacity to be the substantial object under a condition. Yet to use the common usages of terms is but to take a commonsense interpretation of the nature of the object and to lose the aesthetic value of the language.

We do not get relativity or radical tolerance here, once it be recognized that A] for certain purposes certain approaches are better than others, that we in fact lose as well as gain by stressing one abstract rather than another, B] that some abstracts involve more conditions, more specifiable ways than others do, and are thus less amenable to control or understanding. Such an account has the advantage of providing us with an endless number of "proper names" for the substantival reality, since it does allow any one of the abstracts to serve as a norm; it frees us from the dominance of physics without necessarily subjecting us to the dominance of any other enterprise.

We can carry the position further; every art can be said to be the proper name for art as such, and therefore of the world beyond. In this sense there is an ultimacy to painting or sculpture or poetry, etc., revelatory of the very being of art which enables us to speak of art in its name. But on the other hand it allows every art to be equally an abstract for art as such, and to allow for a kind of synthesis of them so that the very being of art, as a locus of creativity responsive to the substantial actuality, is revealed. But if we do this we must also recognize that the "secondary" arts are no less revelatory of art and of the world than the primary; they are merely subject to extra conditions. Does this not lead us to break down the difference between art and craft, craft and work, work and labor? Is not the product of craft the very product of art under different condi-

tions? Yes, but the conditions are all-important; the fact that art subjects the work to special conditions makes it an abstract which can be
enjoyed in itself and can function as a substitute for its inward meaning,
whereas the craft-object can function only as a substitute for its effective
operation.

Once one has a given abstract and knows its conditions what need
is there for getting other abstracts? The first is the real and allows for its
grasp once one reverses the conditioning. The answer must be that we
lose ourselves in the substantial reality when we reverse the conditioning;
we articulate it when we bring in other abstracts and try to synthesize
these; we also understand something of the real nature of Existence
when we in fact employ conditions which in fact produce as objects the
very abstracts we conceive or which stand over against those that we
conceive. The element of distance in art, the voluntary suspension of
belief is in effect the recognition that there is an over-dominance of the
phenomenological objects as providing the proper name or even the
very substance of the real; we make a distance in order to allow the art
object to have its own life, and thus to be a genuine abstract.

Distancing is needed by physicists and by the practitioners of different
arts so far as these men tend to take their own type of abstract as the
criterion of all. Distancing is but an allowing for integrity. But it does
force a referential attitude. The work which we hold apart at a distance
is always a work which is thereby made to be referential. Accordingly,
if we started with a work of art and lived in this area as musicians are
inclined to do, we would have to distance ourselves from it in order to
grasp mathematics or even some such art as sculpture. We would have
to put the music to a side and concentrate say on the sculpture. But then
the sculpture could not avoid having some kind of reference to the music
which formed the background of the sculpture.

We can go one step further and take even the fancies, the dreams
that pass through a man's mind, to express not merely what he is in himself (and this they do, as Freud has made evident) but something of the
real world beyond as revealed by these (as Jung has seen). Freud saw
that the various expressions of man are so many abstracts; but instead of
trying to interrelate these to one another he tried to find the conditioning
of them and thereby reduce them to some deeper mode of action. He
could have interrelated the abstracts as well, but the interrelationship
would have to be one which revealed the underlying core or power.

The fundamental root, the truly real, is the substantial object. But it
is possible to take one of the abstracts and make it the locus of others.
This is what we do when we take the common-sense object to be the

locus of art and illusion. Here the common-sense object must preserve some of the powers and virtues of the other two. When we move from this object to the substantial object the virtues need not be preserved; they must be preserved only if we are to have some justification for using one abstract as more basic than others.

April 15

If everything is the object dislocated, the most outrageous fiction must be so too. And account must be taken of the fact that not every idea requires assent, or what is the same thing, may not have an answering object. Both of these matters can be taken care of by distinguishing the item in and of itself and the item as having a referential element. As the latter it obviously testifies to itself as having a role in and being eventually reducible to the object. The reference does not as it were refer beyond itself to something entirely new, but to itself as substantialized and transformed. If we take it apart from this we have something which is a mere abstract. The problem in cognition is that we do not know whether or not the ideas we have are merely abstract, and most important we do not know just what they would be when substantialized. Of course the merely abstract idea is concrete in the sense that there is a reference involved to a cognizing being, and this in turn does refer back to something substantial. The merely abstract or fictitious is but twice removed.

Reference is not distance acknowledgment but tension, relatedness, reverse tentacles, the insistence on a recovery of status. To see this best one may recur to the problem of the sphere and the balloon. The idea of a balloon is, by the very demand that account be taken of the material in a world, a referential sphere, a sphere which shows itself to be something which is substantialized by matter. But there might be no balloon in fact. The idea does not tell us just what the balloon is in its substantiality. The knowledge requires a retreat beyond all ostensible features. The idea of the sphere in contrast is that very balloon at a further remove; it has a reference A] to the domain of the Ideal, B] to the balloon in mind (and therefore to the individual as sustaining that balloon now), and C] via the balloon to whatever there be which is substantial in fact. Or from another angle, the idea of balloon indicates what sort of thing is required for it to be substantial, what other types of abstract there can be, which together with it will make the substantial. The sphere does not indicate what is required to be added to it to be substantial, and thus what other kinds of abstracts there are. To get to the concrete from it one must attend to the act of cognition, or the bearing that the Ideal, in its subdivisions, has on space-time actualities. Both the idea of the sphere and the idea of the balloon differ from the perceptual object, which has a location outside of the individual, even though conditioned by him.

The problem of the preferential abstract is really the problem of that item, idea or perceptual object, mathematical concept, etc., which has conventionally been recognized to be a normative object for ordinary living and whose substantialization, either directly, or through the synthesis with certain other abstracta, is what normally and without reflection has been the practice of that particular group.

This theory could be extended further. Each individual man or object, even in its substantiality, could be viewed as an "abstract" from something more concrete—and this presumably is what some Eastern thinkers suppose. And all this could be thought to be an abstract from something even more ultimate, such as the Plotinian One. There would be no harm in such an extension, if one could have any warrant for the supposition that there were these further realities, and if one at the same time preserved the "reality" of these supposed abstracta, realizing that they had their own integrities and ultimacies. We know that there are substantial actualities because we are such, and find that there is that which is over against us, resisting and opposing, and that so far as we are bodies there is something more than ideas in our minds or mere termini of our perception, with which we can interplay. But what warrant have we that beyond such bodily substantial realities there is a common domain (unless it be Existence as such and the actualities are nothing more than localizations of it) and a domain beyond this (unless it be the divine in which the actualities are preserved)?

We can take the Absolute or Transcendent to be even more concrete than the actualities we confront, but only by viewing the actualities as delimited versions of these. In themselves they are as ultimate as that which might, under an abstraction, be said to possess them—and conversely they are as ultimate as the men who can speculatively deal with them.

Irreconcilable oppositions, say, between religion and art, e.g., can be understood as involving the justified insistence on its claims by each component, since each is the real under a condition. Each taken by itself is the real; each taken with the others must be synthesized to express more fully something of the way in which the real can function, for though the elements lose some of their distinctive virtues when integrated with one another, they nevertheless retain something. What they retain is revelatory of the nature of the substantial reality, in a way in which the isolated element with its radical claim is not. This means that the errors of a philosophic system are truths not merely by being immersed in the system but by being converted into abstracts of that substantial real which the system portrays.

In *Man's Freedom* it was remarked that it is often supposed that the sciences and only the sciences deal with objects which seem to have a constant nature (even when we shift our positions and times) and which seem to be free from transitory, avoidable conditions. We suppose that the sciences make use of universally applicable principles, that they are free from the taint of subjective interests reflecting our emotions rather than a desire to know, that they deal with things as apart from man's appreciation; that they seem to relate to terminal realities, and not to the terms of relations, in a public domain. It is there said that these characterizations are not altogether true of science, and also that they are not altogether to be untrue of other approaches, particularly those which relate to values. Even if this were all granted, what would follow would be A] that science provides desirable abstracta, B] that science should provide the norm for names of substantival things, C] that we should view the substantival things as preserving within them most of what the scientific world shows to be experimentally verifiable. But we need not grant all the above, and even when we do, we can accept other abstracta as also desirable, allow them for other purposes to provide a norm for names, and see, in a genuine synthesis (though of course not in a mere act of reducing an abstractum to the substance) that there is as much warrant for the preservation of all of the synthesized items as for preserving any one.

Once we take some abstractum as the real, or as the clue to it, and explanatory of all the rest, we get into theories of illusion or constructs for what is evidently given and basic and objective; we will take the real to lack vital characteristics, or the potentiality for exhibiting these. Thus, as is customary today in Anglo-Saxon countries (the Europeans stress the phenomenological object) if we start with the results of science as real, or as abstracta which are paradigmatic of the real, or as the names of the real, we are driven to try to explain the phenomenal and of course the ethical and religious objects as the outcome of some complication of scientific activities or entities.

The ethical, etc., objects are not real in the sense in which the scientific entities are real; they are not even in the scientific space, time, energy complex. The fact that we can produce them through the use of the results of science does not disqualify them, any more than a manipulation, of the kinds of images we have in our heads or the marks we have on paper, to produce scientific results, disqualifies these results. It will be countered that we do not think with the images or marks but with the ideas they portray. But this is precisely the point. Given the images we move beyond them to deal with the scientific domain itself; that movement beyond, though, requires some manipulation of images. What it does not do is move by a complication of images or marks, whereas it is said that the scientific approach to illusion or perception requires only complication of scientific results. But the scientific effort does not reach to illusion or perception any more than a manipulation of the images or marks reaches to a scientific object. They are distinct types; to get to one from the other one must leave the one behind and make use of an entirely different approach.

When we use a language, actual or ideal, we manipulate marks but only in order to get to the stage where we can take the leap into the mathematical with ease; but is this not also true of the movement from the scientific to the phenomenal? Do we not manipulate the scientific until we get to the stage where we can easily move to the phenomenal? ("Ease" here means "by some conventionally unexamined, acceptable agency which has so far not deceived us, at least pragmatically.") And what is here said about science and phenomena must hold of the work of art. Complications of it should get us to the stage where we can readily move to what is other than it, but no complications will yield the world other than it. Men are reluctant to take the standpoint that art is real and paradigmatic not only because it has such a large dose of the individual's creativity in it (whereas science has at best only a communally allowable creativity in its results with a maximum creativity in discovery) but because we do not seem to be moving closer to the other domains when we complicate the art. To complicate the scientific accounts is to shorten the gap between other results and the scientific, but the converse does not seem to be true. Let us grant this: it does not follow that the gap is eliminable, that there is a preferential status for the scientific result, or that what it cannot accommodate is shown thereby to be eliminated, to be lower in status, value or reliability.

April 16

If the *Modes* is correct, and if it be the case that a work of art is something created, either in the realm of Existence or Actuality, then everyone of the features explored in the *Modes* should be found in the work of art, either in fact or in intent, in function or in meaning. So far as this is not the case the work of art can be at best an imitation at some remove of the modes; also if the modes exhaust all being there must be a kind of imitation in anything else that is brought about in this world and therefore art must be an imitation in some sense. Nevertheless it does not seem to be the case that, e.g., the work of art struggles to keep in existence, that it interacts with other actualities, that it is contemporary with them, that it strives towards the Idea, that it is preserved in the mind of the divine, etc., etc. In this sense it must be the case that the work of art is only a substitute. But there would be no point in the substitution if it did not also involve some gain.

Just as in discourse we substitute analytic elements and words for the objects, for the sake of a ready manipulation, so in art we can be said to substitute a purged kind of entity, losing some essential features of the modes themselves, in order to appreciate fully some of the values obscured in nature. But since this substitution is provided by the artist there must be an element of expression in it as well. It is as if an actuality decided to make a world out of the materials of Existence, a world in which there would be all the modes. This seems to be the very problem which is said to confront the Platonic God. It requires the acknowledgment of the Ideal, Existence and the activity of the demiurgos. There need not be, if this analogy be correct, any kind of reference to the deity. The result, according to Plato, reveals only the Ideal which has been merged with Existence, the former being emphasized, the latter denigrated. But this does overlook the element of the numinous, the referential element with respect to the world of common sense (and which as Plato put it, makes art an imitation twice removed). It is evident that what must be done is to try to understand the art work as being in fact a part of Existence (or the realm of creative effort), interrelated with others in some kind of public space (society?) and made into contemporaries by their presence in that one Existence. But this too is not yet right.

To justify the idea of art as a substitute one ought to show that there is something radically missing from the world which could not be made up in any other way. The work of art is a kind of absurdity, a reality which by its very presence reveals that it is the solution of the difficulties which we encounter in the real world—A] contingency,   B] irrelevancy,   C] frustration,   D] pain and ugliness;   E] monotony. These can be met by imaginings, dreams and denials, but there is no genuine positivity, no substantiality and therefore no permanence or richness except so far as there is something done, made to be. One thinks of art as expression just so far as one sees that imaginings do offer a substitute; but one must go further once one sees that art does require work, action, which has its own problems, results and rationale.

The justification of the theory that art is expression can be found in the recognition that by being made external, or given an external setting, one's feelings, ideas, meanings, etc., gain governance by rule, and an objectivity and universality they otherwise would not have. Conversely, a theory of imitation profits from the fact that the work of art is the world as purged, freed of irrelevancy and providing satisfaction for man. The work of art as an objective reality is the two together, tested perhaps by its repercussions on society or mankind.

April 17

The fact of freedom is questioned in ethics but rarely in aesthetics. One seems content to allow students of art to speak of creativity but not to allow ethicists to speak of freedom of choice or will. This is in part because the creativity allowed to the artist is thought to be below the level of reason, and perhaps outside the control of the individual. What is at issue therefore is the recognition of an independence of the individual, and not actually the existence of an element of freedom or novelty or creativity or process. Accordingly, if one were willing to deal with ethics as essentially the expression of the creative powers of the society, or state, or history, there presumably would be little or no opposition to the theory of freedom; on the other hand, were one willing to deal with creativity as involving a distinctive act of choice on the part of the artist which might have gone the other way there would perhaps be an increase in opposition.

Still the two cases are not parallel, because the artist is thought to be, when granted independence, outside the realm of serious concerns; there is a kind of fear of the freedom of the ethical being, as he who, by virtue of something independent in him, will overthrow that which is right in the eyes of God or for mankind or society or nature. The issue then of freedom would seem to revolve around the question of whether or not one is free to do anything, and whether anything that the freedom achieves is allowable. The theory of freedom of self-perfection, to the effect that a man is most free when he does what he ought, would seem to break the back of the opposition to the theory of freedom, but it does seem to deny that man is free to do evil. On the other hand the view that whatever is freely achieved is right, which is the essence of the theory of freedom of self-realization, has difficulty with recognizing that there can be a wrong-doing freely achieved. The one view says man is not free when he does evil, the other says that he is not evil when he is free. We must say with the first that he is faced with what ought to be, and with the second that he need not do this but may freely choose what is bad.

The artist is free not in the sense of self-perfection, or of self-determination, with the power to make himself be this or that, but in the sense of the power of self-realization as a kind of self-expression. All artists on this view are free, whether they produce the beautiful or the ugly. The institutional man, the man who belongs to a system, who accepts a creed or who acknowledges established rights, should of course be said to be free only so far as he conforms to that which alone is real or right. Accordingly we can distinguish what might be termed the self-perfectional theory of politics, the self-realization theory of artistic creativity, and the self-determining theory of ethics (the latter being extendable to embrace all nature, not as ethical, but as grounding the possibility of ethical behavior).

If art then is properly in the province of the theory of self-realization, it strictly speaking is not a topic for a freedom of choice or will. (The latter two are primarily the concern of the freedom of self-determination and of perfection—the one being concerned with the making of oneself, and the other being concerned with the living up to the absolute Good.) Art will be the topic of the freedom of preference, the election of a means to some accepted goal. Instead then of accepting the Aristotelian account of the virtues, etc., as giving us a theory of ethics, we ought to accept it as primarily an account of the nature of artistic creativity. Here the goal need not be good, and one may have habits and inclinations, techniques and interests which require acts of various sorts.

Depending on the power of the individual to make his goal dictate what he will do, there will be a variation in what is intended. If one can make the body live up to an interior intention (and this requires training and self-discipline), then what one has freely elected to do here and now will in fact be done. But for the most part the determination of what is elected as a means is dictated by the end one has adopted. Such an end dictates something to the alternatives and thereby limits the power of the goal to determine what is being done. But if the end is that which is the topic of self-perfection and thus of something "political," or given, then the primary activity of the artist involves the acceptance and choice of means, which would not have been made preferable by the goal that was in fact adopted. Self-determination would come in here only in the sense that the artist in the course of this activity would be thought to make himself, be a man in a new sense.

Subject then to some standard of the Good which defines him to be man of vision and worth, the artist should be said to dictate what means will serve some goal. This dictation is not necessarily in the forefront of his mind. Ideally he will elect that means which will in fact get him to the goal that he wants to attain, but his primary stress will be on using such and such a means and goal to attain the outcome of his vision. And in the course of this he will ethically make himself be a good man. He will in short make himself a good man by living up to some absolute requirement in such a way as to demand that he do this or that here and now, and thereby reach some goal.

If the artist is primarily involved in a freedom of self-determination for himself, a freedom of self-realization as a kind of self-expression, and a freedom of self-perfection as a kind of self-definition of himself as an artist we would avoid the horror some thinkers feel in the face of the view that there is freedom in ethics, by defining the ethical man in similar terms: an ethical man is one who freely constitutes himself, when expressing himself in the course of living up to the requirements of what would make him a man of worth. But the idea of an ethical man freely constituting himself, or of being free when he expresses himself is not altogether tolerable. The ethical man's freedom is thought to be harmless when viewed as a kind of self-perfection, the submission to that which ought to be; the artist is thought to be harmless when he exercises a freedom of self-realization (though one may object to this exercise when it conflicts with the requirements of ethics). Only that which is immature, incomplete, not yet a man is thought to be free to determine itself, and this perhaps would be in the sphere of education, training.

Man, when seen to be bound by the Good, can be held to be free, ethically, without arousing antagonism; when seen to be immature he can be held to be free to determine himself. The fact that this freedom is granted to the artist would indicate the belief that he is not yet up to where the ethical man is supposed to be. The freedom of self-realization is thought to be harmless when it is concerned with matters of little importance, such as the taking of this road or that, and it is allowed to the artist as that which in the end makes no difference either because it is thought that his self-determination will dictate the best way, or because there is no best way.

The artist's initial work dictates a kind of end, and the good artist will thereafter dictate to himself the nature of the means which he will follow in the light of the end he has adopted through the initial adoption of some means. The degree to which the artist allows himself to be dictated by the end to which he is committed, and thus the degree to which he allows his self-realization to be ruled by his self-perfection, will define the degree to which he remakes himself, realizes himself.

April 21

The obvious weakness of a theory of expression such as Croce's —no room for the struggle with a medium, no accounting for the failure of a man to master a technique, no awareness of the didactic or referential side of a work—may blind one to the merits of a theory of expression. Going back to the individual in a moment of exuberance we find, however, that he sometimes breaks into song, dance or acting. It is also true that one can try to commemorate some signal event in the light of one's strong feelings with respect to it. There is an exteriorization of the individual at certain moments which is exhibited in a fresh way, in violation or independence of the rules, conventions and stable ways of acting which characterize daily life and ordinary experience. But it is one thing to say that art begins in such expression, another to say that it is such expression which defines the break-through of art away from calm observation, discussion or articulation, and still another thing to say this is the very essence of art. It is questionable whether it is true that all art begins in such exuberant expression or even in commemorative activities; it seems quite false to assert that expression is of the very essence of art. The proper doctrine would seem to be that such exuberant expression is the break-through, the way in which we enter the world of art as creators. Just as architecture can be seen as encompassing a space to be filled by sculpture and painting, and just as perception can be viewed as framing a region of the world and thereby allowing it to stand over against the rest as that which is primarily humanly-defined, (making possible the photographing of it as an aesthetic object, for example) just so can we see the individual stressing himself in such a way as to alter the aesthetically apprehended world. The act of perception can be viewed as the act of isolating something, without having it as an aesthetic object. Only when the individual approaches this object with some exuberance, some feeling, some need to make what he is manifest does that object become an aesthetic one. And, taking the individual apart from perception, viewing him not in relation to a world which has been isolated by the perceiver, but as merely being active, we can distinguish what he does in the ordinary course of events and the difference he introduces into such doing when under the stress of passion.

There are then two ways of dealing with the individual expressing feelings—as a perceiver, and as a maker. In the former he vitalizes what he sees through sympathy and interpretation; in the latter he escapes from the routine, and produces something which, though not necessarily beautiful or pleasurable, is the locus of individual power made manifest, and not a mere function of the past, of society, of practical needs or the desire to communicate.

The theory of expression gets its power from the contrast between the non-conventionality of artistic work and the conventionality of daily life.

But its explanatory power is limited to indicating how we escape daily life, how we find the energy for creative work, and the kind of joy we experience in production. It can also be said to provide some ground for communication, once it is seen that the spectator tries or is stimulated to recover or duplicate something like the joy of the initial experience—as is evident in such participative arts as the common dance or song. But it fails to take account of the fact that the expressive artist looks beyond himself into a world.

April 24

To say that someone is "artless" is on the one hand to point up the fact that art requires sophistication, control, intent, and on the other hand promotes the paradox that that which is spontaneous, honest, simple is art-less. The artless in a word possesses some of the features characteristic of art, but lacks others. To be an artist one must in part be artless; not to be so, is to be "arty."

In each of the three divisions of art there is a combination of elements which help constitute the new being of space, time or energy. Thus material and medium together with shape give us the curvature of space; we are here kept away from the space of every day, in part by the conventions which function as a frame. In the realm of time we make use of a special punctuation in our formation of a lasting present, through the employment of metaphors and contrary to fact stories to which we add rhythm. The metaphor keeps us isolated in the art world; ordinary prose enables us to move on in the language or to move away from language. The metaphor stresses the contrary to fact conditional nature of the art world of time, not by making evident the formal relation of one analyzed part to another, but by showing how to interrelate those parts. It is as if we started with contrary to fact elements and then used the metaphor as a way of indicating how they come together. We ordinarily use the "if-then" contrary to fact in such a way as to point to a reality. A story reveals the drive of the universe by virtue of the element which it supposes follows from a supposed element; in the case of a metaphor we have the two elements related primarily as belonging together, in abstraction from the rationale of the connection the story could provide. If we say "were a man a wolf he would not eat but devour" we have an account of the nature of a man in a contrary to fact situation with a consequence; if we say that a man devours or better that a man is a wolf we say that the man's intrinsic power is expressed in devouring rather than eating.

When we come to the realm of energy, we find it necessary to construct a new unit of action. This is achieved by taking a climax as that which is accumulative and releasing, and recognize it to be the turning point in an entire situation having a beginning and an ending, and thus defining a unit of dynamic change which is spatio-temporal without being sequentially produced. The realm of the dynamic arts is a realm of presents with vitalities of their own, exhausted in the making of an extended stretch of action.

In each of the arts there is a device for defining it as a work of art. In the spatial arts there is something like the frame—there is the wall, the stresses on the sculptured surface, and the painting frame; in the temporal arts there is the metaphor, the contrary to fact conditional and the poetic intensification of terms. In both of these there is a convergent stress forcing us to move from the limits of the work or event into its centre, rather than beyond or through the work—though to be sure the convergence ends with a unity which intends that which is elsewhere. In the performing arts there is an event created which insists on being a vital present despite the fact that there has been a passing away of a plurality of presents of another type. These events are defined by themes, theatrical episodes or scenes, and pieces; in all of these we are forced to accumulate, to preserve our beginning and make it relevant to the ending. This is done by the climax which ties the past and future together. The climax occurs in every created action, coming to a conspicuous position only for that totality of actions which define the single work. (The part on the performing arts is not clear.)

There seems to be an inconsistency in my treatment of space and time. In connection with space I have recently spoken of the physical and the psychical or phenomenological as each abstract, and as together defining or being made to converge in that which had both of them transformed. But in connection with time I speak as if (and spoke in *Modes of Being*) the real had a kind of atomic time, and as though the extended time of history and art were somehow dislocated abstracted presents, having some reality but sustained by the "natural" or alongside the "natural" as equally real. A treatment of time parallel to that of space would require the view that the real time of the universe is a unity of various times, in the very way in which values and secondary qualities are united with the primary to constitute the being of that which is more concrete than any of these.

In view of the fact that there is a passing present and also one that remains as a kind of pattern governing the sequence of other passing presents, perhaps it would be right to say that the real time of the universe consists in the tensional displacement of presents into the past together with the tension of these presents and of the present now with respect to the future. If this position is taken then one can come closer than I had come in *Modes of Being* to the position of Bergson and Earle regarding our knowledge and memory of the past. Memory would be the product of a tension with respect to displaced presents. In view of the limited span of memory, and the limited span of a present, there would be pasts escaping from our grip; these would have to be sustained by God.

It is a mistake to try to interrelate the mathematical and the phenomenological by mathematics. That biases the result towards one of the terms. The union of the two is accomplished in advance by the being itself; it can be recovered only in a speculative judgment which uses the mathematical and phenomenological in something like a metaphor. This does not prevent us, once we have made such use, to articulate and formulate the result and draw the implications. We get to the concrete through a metaphor, but we carry on in logical terms, systematizing the whole. Our great danger comes in the use of terms, for our terms are primarily pertinent to abstracta. One of these is usually taken as the normative case for the use of a term characterizing the concrete entity, which embraces it and other abstracta as well as analytic parts.

In the *Modes of Being* something like this was seen, with reference to all the dimensions of Existence, for it was there remarked how Existence expands and how other modes define the units of the expansion in three ways. Such definition goes beyond any dimension of Existence. Still the stress on the passing away of things, and on the nature of the past with the sharp rejection of memory as directly apprehending something past, does obscure the nature of time and energy. I think the term "hovering natures" should now be abandoned since it makes the passage of physical time to be primary. If it be recognized that the latter is also an abstractum, a kind of "hovering" reality, then we can turn back to the world and see time as having a two-way expansiveness, into the past as well as into the future, both, up to a point, being held climatically by the concrete reality in the present. It is tempting to treat the past as always held on to, so that one actually reaches back into the distant past, but this is not tenable in the light of our short existence, our limited grasp, and the boundary of an event. We cannot treat the real object as merely in the present; the abstracta have a being, which though sustained and in the end interrelated in the object in a transforming way, exist on levels beyond it. Or, once again, space and time and energy are themselves abstracta from Existence, and consequently divisions and abstracta from them must be seen to be ways of trying to get not Existence itself, but these dimensions made as concrete as possible. And the outcome of the interrelationship should be an Existence whose expansiveness and divisiveness must be dealt with as being in more than one dimension. It transcends the limits of any one dimension and their derivative abstracta.

The best account of time in this sense is given by Augustine. He says (ch. xi, xx of the *Confessions*), ". . . there be three times: a present time of past things; a present time of present things; and a present time of future things . . . memory, . . . sight . . . expectation . . . neither [does] that which is to come have any being now; no, nor that which is already past." (xxiii). "I perceive time to be a certain stretching." (xxvi) ". . . time is nothing else but a stretching out in length . . . and I marvel, if it be not of the very mind." (xxvii). "For the very space between is the thing we measure, namely, from some beginning unto some end . . . we neither measure the times to come, nor the past, nor the present, nor the passing times; and yet we do measure times." ". . . this syllable is but single and that double; in respect of space of time, I mean: and yet can I not do thus much, unless these syllables were already past and ended. 'Tis not therefore these voices (which now are not) that I measure: but something it is even in mine own memory, which there remains fastened. 'Tis in thee, O my mind, that I measure my times. . . . The impression which things passing by cause in thee, and remains even when the things are gone, that is it which being still present I do not measure: nor the things which have passed by, that this impression might be made." (xxviii) "The future therefore is not a long time, for it is not: but the long future time is merely a long expectation of the future . . . a long past time is merely a long memory of the past time."

Augustine however contents himself with man, and apparently with the perception or measurement of time. If we turn from man to the world, and recognize what he says gives the inside of the man, we can extend his view to embrace all realities, and define time as a passing which is also possessed in advance and in retrospect. The real object is in a perpetual process of reconstituting itself; each effort is in a distinct present, but it is a present which cannot be entirely detached from a future into which the object then is directed, and a past to which it clings. The isolation of the future and the past will give us the abstract times of science and of history. The hovering natures of *Modes of Being* are really abstract; they were not seen as such because they were needed to make sense of a world in which there was a substantial passing away of beings. But if the beings as passing away be recognized to be abstracta too, then the reality will be nothing less than the two of these, the hovering natures and the passing beings, together.

We do use terms as relating to some experienceable item. Some of these terms are used normatively for the reality which is the unity of a number of experienceable items. The coin is seen to be round, ellipitical, a straight edge, etc.—or taking it as a cylinder, we see it as round, as a rectangle, etc. The coin is in fact no one of these; the round which "appears" never becomes elliptical; it just gives way, is replaced by the seen ellipse. What *is* now round and then elliptical is strictly speaking neither of these; but we use the word "round" normatively as well as descriptively of an appearance. When we use it normatively we intend to name not one of the appearances, but that which is the unity, the root and source of all these appearances. The real "round" is never seen except in some appearance or other. But this does not mean it cannot be known. We adumbrate it when we acknowledge the appearances; and we speculatively characterize it. In the latter case we use the ordinary terms (though we can at times frame new ones), but we draw new consequences from them. The round which appears has one set of consequences; the round which is the shape of the coin in and of itself has quite other consequences, to be known speculatively by understanding the nature of a substance.

So far as empirical knowledge is concerned we can know the speculatively determined round as a "power," as Locke called it, but a power which governs the order of the appearances in a set of circumstances. It would be a mistake to suppose that this power is exhausted by any set of appearances; Hegel has no warrant for supposing that it must be so exhausted (though to be sure the only "appearances" which concern him are categorial features, the absolute at various stages). There can always be a residuum of unexpressed powers; the power of the substance is that which we can explicate in part by the implications of the appearances with respect to further appearances, but the power is more than this. It is that which in fact makes itself manifest as these appearances. The time *of* the appearances is not the time *for* the appearing of them; the thing lives in a time which is the substantialization of the time of the appearances and other times as well; and it manifests itself in its own time. Its time is substantial; the thing makes itself manifest in the shape of an *abstractum* of time which relates the appearances. The appearances themselves have no generative power and the time they fill is thus a time imposed, brought about by the action of a being in a time which it dynamically produces.

Can we know an individual thing in a speculative way, or are we driven to affirm only highly general metaphysical truths about substances? The existentialist tends to say that we can know the individual man, but only in a kind of immediate interplay. The speculative approach he thinks leaves the reality of the individual behind. But does it not merely leave behind just the way in which the common features are uniquely united in this object? The unique union can be known in part by seeing how it in fact produces results which the appearances do not allow us to know. The consequences of the appearances are in fact now being modified by the action of the individual acting in an individual way.

April 25

The view that art is a species of illusion, or has no truth value (in the sense of having nothing to do with the real world but expressing something of the subject) must be stopped at the most extreme case: is there motion in a moving picture? If one says there is not, it is not possible to stop the rejection of space in a picture, etc. And from there we can go on and on, to reject secondary qualities and tertiary ones, leaving us in the hopeless position of a Locke or Descartes who can acknowledge as real only that which is not experienced. Yet to stop the reduction, by asserting that the aesthetic object is really the object as caught in a given perspective, and which, when unified with other abstracta will give us the object as in and of itself is to come up against the problem of illusion and error. The elimination of a perspective, without the substitution of another, is tantamount to the supplementation of one abstractum by others. When we say that the converging rails do not converge in fact, that the man in delirium tremens sees what is not there, that the dream is not real, we intend to say that the objects thus envisaged can be reduced to some other perceptual objects or real activities. The fact that these last can be viewed as abstracta, and the fact that the illusions and errors can themselves be understood to be true accounts of what the object or the abstracta may be like as subject to these new subjective conditions, does not affect the fact that we do not treat these errors and illusions as being on a footing with abstracta. What we mean when we call something an error or an illusion (the illusion being the common error which distorts a correct perception, in contrast with plain error which reads something into the content), we are denying the right to treat it as one abstractum correlate with others, even when it is granted that in the object itself the error or illusion is radically altered.

It is possible to maintain that the error or illusion comes about because an abstractum has been thought to be of a different type than it is in fact, and thus that we expect it to behave like the abstracta of common sense, for example. But firstly it would be the case that we can add this wrong expectation to the error to give us a truth, and secondly it makes the error arbitrary in that it takes some other abstractum as a norm to which the erroneous fails to conform. It would be better to treat certain abstracta as on a different level from others, while recognizing the equal right of the abstracta to constitute the elements to be united in the object. Thus one can speak of the various "appearances" of an object in perception (when unified), as constituting the real object, and thus when freed from their individual perspectives; and one can speak of a given work of art, or perhaps a totality of different works of art, as offering a different type of abstracta which themselves can give us the object in a way different from that given in perception.

This latter alternative is superior to the former. It permits one to deal with art as on a footing with other enterprises with respect to truth, and to have pertinence to what is real. It does deny though the right to treat its abstracta, or itself as an abstractum, as that which is to be integrated with common sense or mathematics. But then it might be asked with justice why should the phenomenological object be correlated with the mathematical as another abstractum, and not with the work of art? If we say that the phenomenological object can be paired with various other abstracta we put that phenomenological object in a preferred position. If we say that the various abstracta form only sub-sets, so that there is no union of all of them but only of some of them to constitute the judged object, we have the problem of knowing which ones can be so related, and why. There is nothing in the abstractum and no clue from the substance to tell us which or why. We therefore could not say that art is like the mathematically defined object and not like an illusion or an error, and thus to be related to the phenomenological object as surely as the mathematical, nor could we say that it can be related to the mathematically defined object etc.

Perhaps it would be better to say that there are multiple ways of producing abstracta, and it is the abstracta of a given type which constitute the elements to be synthesized to give us the true judgment of the real? Taken in this sense all phenomenological objects, no matter what the conditions, will be abstracta on a footing; the mathematically defined objects will constitute another set of abstracta which suffice to give us the object, once consideration is taken of the act by which one is able to move away from the substance; the errors men make would give us another set; and the arts would give us still another set. But then we cannot say that the substantial object is at once mathematical and qualitative, unless it be the case that the union of the mathematical abstracta yield a qualitative result as well.

This last alternative in effect says that there are various levels of abstracta and that the items on each, when synthesized, give a judgment which frees the abstracta from their limiting conditions, allows them to be mutually infective, and frees them also from the limitation of their level, thereby permitting the infecting of them by the outcome of the other levels. There would then be different ways of synthesizing in the different levels, and, what should be the same thing, different ways in which one moves from a level to the substantial object. We will then be able to say that we need not attend to anything but the mathematically defined star to know the star as that which is substantial and which can yield or express itself as a phenomenological star, providing we know how to read our mathematics, and give it its appropriate reference. And there would be nothing lost in an approach through perception, illusion, errors, dreams, and art. This position has the advantage of not requiring one to look for some unknown way of interrelating the outcomes of perception and mathematics, say, or of supposing that one of them is the norm for the others. It allows us to take a level as final, and to take the judgment not only to free the abstracta on one level from their various conditions to let us have the object as the union and source of all the abstracta of that level, but to free the level from its condition and to allow us to have the object as the union and source of all levels. We can on this view be radical rationalists, radical empiricists, radical aestheticians and come out in the end with the same knowledge of the substantial object which is beyond them all, being free from the conditions of abstraction which produced a level, and free from the special conditions which produced abstracta inside a given level. Any one of the levels would be "illusory," "erroneous," a falsification or radical abstraction from the perspective of any other, when this other is taken as basic and a norm.

The above view contrasts with the following: *1]* some one approach gives us the real (say mathematics); *2]* there are many approaches, all on a footing, synthesized or correlated (a view that is faced with the problem of error and art); *3]* the results of the many approaches give us abstracta, and the real object is in fact the being from which these issue and which might be speculatively grasped by an act of synthesis (this is the view to which I came recently, and which I took after going through the other two positions). *4]* The results of different approaches are levels, inside of which there are abstracta; it is the abstracta that are to be united, synthesized, and in such a way as to be referential. The reference characteristic of the items on one level is different from that of items on other levels; but the reference is to the object which is the origin and integrated being of all the levels.

The real object is "square, blue and attractive," where these terms are given a normative usage having reference to a substance. It will be by seeing that the abstracta of shape when freed from their perceptual conditions all mean "square" in the substance, and that the reference to the substance involves the dislocating of the substantial square from its level, to make it integral with substantial features known in other levels, that we will know the object to be also colored and possessed of value. We will not know what color it has or what value it has until we engage in the activity of abstract consideration which will enable us to see just what abstracta it in fact yields when subject to such and such conditions.

How many levels are there? Four, answering to the *Modes?* Does this mean that we must reduce illusion and art, etc., to one of the four, or that inside a level we can find subordinate cases, perhaps mixed cases, or cases under special conditions? Thus illusion and error would be under the rubric of Actuality but subject to special conditions of judgment and perception; art would be under Existence, but an Existence purged or subjugated by the Actual.

The most reasonable account of levels can be derived from the introduction to *Our Public Life:* each mode of being has an experiential import, both privately and cosmically oriented. The domains are the individual and objects, ethics and politics, art and history, religion and theology; or, perception and experience, prescriptions and guidance, values and destiny, worth and meaning. But what of mathematics, science, common sense? Must we not, to accommodate these, take account of each mode as that which is being conceived by an Actuality? If so we get mathematics as the knowledge of the Ideal as such, science as the knowledge of Existence as such, common sense as the knowledge of Actuality as such, and imagination, or creative understanding as the knowledge of God as such? Mathematics, science, common sense and creative understanding should give us the primary levels, ways of analyzing the substantial real. Ethics, art, etc., should be these, subject to qualification by one another—thus art would be creative understanding affecting the domain dealt with cognitively by science; ethics would be common sense affecting the domain dealt with cognitively by mathematics, etc.

April 27

There would seem to be four basic types of men. There is the observer who concerns himself with the isolation of the premises of thought. When he is creative he engages in abduction. There is the rationalist who sees the implications of the premiss; when creative he envisages possibilities in their relevance to what we know. There is the adventurer who detaches the implications; when he is creative he is one who makes. And finally there is the experiencer, who encounters and interplays, and who when creative shows himself sympathetic and considerate. Each of these types has inside him something of the others, and each is to be found in every field, including art. Art stresses the third but does have something of the others; otherwise it could not begin, know where it wanted to go, nor enjoy what it had achieved.

Are there not three or four Goods, and not one? Is there not only the ethical Good defined by the Ideal, but also the religious Good expressing what God is like as making Himself relevant to the world, and also a natural Good which is Existence as germane to and interrelating all the various Actualities? And perhaps even there is a fourth Good, the Good which Actuality offers to these other modes? Every mode of being in short has the role of a Good; strictly speaking each should have three distinctive roles since it functions as a Good for the different modes in different ways.

Is it not perhaps the case that when we distinguish the ontological (the essential) side of a being and the cosmological (what it is in the concrete setting of the world), we are in a position to use the term "being" as a universal, since it will then refer to the fact that each of the modes will have an (ontological) being of its own? In short, being is concretely diverse in each of the modes, but it is pure Being, being qua being, only so far as it is viewed as the meaning of each mode as that which is something in and of itself. As in and of itself, of course, each is other than the other modes, but as in and of itself, as apart from such a status as being an other of the others, it is a mere abstraction and in this sense an instance of Being.

April 28

1] Is there a language appropriate to each of the modes? 2] Are these philosophy, mathematics, art (?) science (?), and religion? 3] In addition are there four perspectives of the objects in the different modes? 4] Are these related to the above? 5] How do we accommodate the preface of *OPL* in which it says that we deal with each mode as an element in experience: Actuality as categorially known and effectively acted on; the Ideal as expressed in ethics and politics; Existence as taking the form of art and history; religion as taking the form of worship and church? In addition to these questions we have: 6] How do we define error in each dimension? 7] Is it the case that the real object is caught inside the given dimension in such a way that the elimination of the condition is the provision of the supplementary aid of other modes, and that this is tantamount to giving us the object in its substantiality? 8] Is it not the cosmological object which is achieved through the use of 7? 9] How do we get to the ontological object, the object as in and of itself, apart from the other modes? 10] Is it perhaps the case that the object in and of itself in full concreteness, as over against the other modes, is but the unity of the various approaches, a unity which is defined differently in the different perspectives?

1–4] The very fact that we do recognize the legitimacy of dealing with objects both from a phenomenological and a mathematical perspective shows that there are distinctive perspectives for the objects in different modes. And it would seem that mathematics is more appropriate to the Ideal than it is to the Actual. But if we say this last we seem to be putting the languages on different levels, so that it would no longer be the case that each of them, as per 7, gives us the real object equally; we would have a bias towards one language with the others being viewed as distortive or erroneous. It would seem correct to say that there is a language appropriate to each of the modes, but as expressing the ontological object, and that used in this way the language contrasts with those characteristic of the perspective taken on the object in a given mode. Accordingly, though per 2 we can say that common sense (refined perhaps through dialectic and speculation), mathematics, science, and religion are the proper ways of giving us the essence of the Actual, Ideal, Existence and God, they stand over against the perspective we take on each object, in each of these modes. Thus the Actual should be dealt with phenomenologically, formally, practically and sacramentally. These ways of dealing with it make use of the technique of mathematics, philosophy, etc., but are to be distinguished from these since these techniques are tainted by the object itself, in its concrete setting.

2] There seems considerable indeterminacy on my part as to just what languages are appropriate to each mode. Science can be included with mathematics, or better even can be taken as offering a mixed approach. It can be said to unite art with mathematics as a way of dealing with Existence, not as it is in itself, but in a perspective. Accordingly, we will have philosophy, mathematics, art and religion as the appropriate languages.

But perhaps these ought to be supplemented by others in order to take care of the fact that each mode is both a one and a many. Philosophy's systematic approach needs common sense as a supplement, where common sense is adumbrative and not merely practical (and is thus like Aristotle's common sense); mathematics, which deals with the many, needs supplementation by the language of the virtuous man who with his will attends to the total good; art needs supplementation by the language of appreciation which sees the real in its unity; and the unitary view of the merely religious mystic must be supplemented by the practical religion of pious men.

Do we not have categorial knowledge, ethics, art and worship as the languages appropriate to each mode, with action, politics, history and church as abbreviations for the perspectives we take on the modes? Then we have:

The language for the Mode		Perspectives on the Mode
ONE	MANY	SINGLE NAME FOR:
A. Philosophy	Common sense	practical action
I. Virtue: Ethics	Mathematics	politics
E. Art	Arts	history
G. Mystic	Worship	church or creed

6] The problem of experiential error arises only in the last column; the errors in the first two columns are those of interpretation and internal development. An error is that which is to be reduced by analysis into components that belong to different modes, and which can then be treated in terms of the language of the perspective.

The third column must be subdivided to give us the four perspectives in terms of which we observe. This means that the approach through practical action, e.g., must be broken up into phenomenology, value, mathematical-science, and import for our destiny. There should be similar divisions made of politics, history and creeds. Thus politics should have the four perspectives of psychology, rights, sociology and civilization.

7 and 8] The substantial object is to be known via the union of the one and many ways of discoursing, and this should be supplemented by the language of the perspectives. The latter gives the object in its setting in the world, the former gives us the object as in and of itself. The former is the unity for the latter, the latter offers the "essential or permanent" accidents of the being. The proof of God which starts with Actuality as an other in effect must say that by being involved in a relation of otherness to that which is eternal and inward, we are beings who will in some sense be preserved.

To make use of all these comments for art we must recognize that art does not offer a mere perspective of things, but has an ontological

import needing supplementation by the language or insight of appreciation. When we turn to history we get a spectrum of approaches to
Existence as that which is being qualified by other modes. The art work
should reveal the very nature of Existence in one of its subdivisions or
functions (as space, time, energy, e.g.) and this should serve as a type of
unity for the diverse approaches to Existence which we obtain in that
broadly conceived characterization of all the approaches, which is here
termed "history." The poor piece of art work will be like an error; it will
not reveal Existence until the work has been purged of its ugliness, transformed perhaps even into items in other modes.

If the above account is correct, one must be alert to the possible confusion of art as a genuine language for the knowledge of Existence in
and of itself, with the supposition A] that art can be a perspective on a
footing with other perspectives directed towards Actuality; B] that art
can be a perspective alongside other perspectives on Existence; C] that
art is parallel to philosophy, rather than to common sense, in light of the
fact that it is related to the Manyness of the realm of Existence.

Does this not mean that there are many different "times." There
should be A] four times for each of the modes, B] sixteen times for
the four perspectives on each of the modes, C] four times each expressing the unity of the four perspectives for each mode. Thus Actuality
should have a time peculiar to it; and there will be abstract times for
the phenomenological, scientific, valuational and important object (they
are perceptual time, abstract mathematical time, the time of the event,
and the time which has importance in eternity). Each of these is reducible
to the time of the object as capable of being encountered C]; such a
time is all of the four perspective times unified. This time is not identical
with A], for A] is the time we know only speculatively. A] is the
time of the substance; the unified time C] is the time of nature
governing the appearance B].

April 29

It is possible to use the term "art" and perhaps others such as
science in at least five ways. *1*] It can be used to characterize a perspective; this we do when we think of it as a kind of extension of craft serving
to relate us to, or to report some selected way of having experience. When
we say that the art object is as real as the object treated by practice we
take this position. *2*] It can be used to refer to the empirical object,
what perhaps Kant had in mind when he referred to the *x* or to substance,
that which is the unity of all the different forms of art, or which is the

integration of the results of art with the unified meaning of other perspectives. When we think of art as giving us the adumbrated being of things in a way other subjects do not and cannot, we take this position. 3] We can treat it as telling us what the object is in and of itself, as a unity underlying and making possible the unification of the various perspectives. Here the art object is a unitary ground. Art then becomes ontological in import, particularly when it is recognized to deal only with aspects of Existence and then in fragmentary portions. 4] The realm of art of some art work can be viewed as giving us, by virtue of its intrinsic purity, the very essence of Existence as a single domain. Here we have art as revelatory of the very being of the universe so far as this can be caught through a creative use of what in fact is something derived from a perspective—colors, sounds, shapes, etc. 5] The realm of art can finally be thought of as revelatory of some mode of being other than Existence. This is what we suppose when we view it as primarily a form of knowledge of actualities, as a kind of clarification of the very meaning of the Ideal, or an imitation of it, or as a primary device for geting to God.

When we say that art creates a new way in which space or motion, etc., can be, it is tempting to treat this new way as 1] another dimension to be added to the ones revealed in practical action of every day, with its characteristic perspectives, 2] as the very secret of the empirical object, transcending the limited perspectives, or 3] as the way the mode of Actuality is revealed. But it is more correct to say that this new space, time, motion, etc., is set over against the others, and as set over against makes a reference to the very being of space, time, motion, etc., as they are in themselves, i.e., as the unitary root of the empirically known, and a fragment or aspect of the very being of Existence. Art is our way of getting to Existence—a way which can be imitated in knowledge to give a cognitive meaning to the objective space time, etc., which the arts reveal. In short, we do have a new space, time, etc., just in the way in which we have a new object when we think. The problem is to recognize that this new object is the very being of the substantial unity of Existence transposed through the creative powers of man in such a way as to reveal the substantial unity. The problem is essentially one of semantics, to discover how to relate the outcome of art to the substantial reality of space, time, etc., which it is supposed to reveal. The objective being of space need not of course be curved in the way it is in a painting; but the curved space of the painting must reveal the nature of space in the way no knowledge can, and no perspective or unification of perspectives ever approaches. It must reveal what it means for space to be a unitary ground in which perspectives can be united; what it means for space to be, as perhaps Whitehead had in mind when he referred to sheer extensiveness.

The fact that a work of art is revelatory of a dimension of Existence in and of itslef, a revelation which does not require the work to be iconic but only to explicate it in a special way (a way which differs from its object by virtue of its "distance") does not mean that there is no reference to the empirical object, or to other modes. There is always a reference A] to some common-sense perspective, a clue telling us how to get into the work; B] to the empirical object, a meaning in depth which goes beyond the limits of a perspective; C] to the Ideal as that which is perfect; D] to the Actual as that which is individual; E] to the divine as that which is important. The latter three references involve a grasp of its purpose or intent, of its singular unity, and of its numinous import.

Does the work of art first make a single reference to all the modes, referring to them as together, and only subsequently relates to them in different ways? It would seem that this is the case, for we do not separate out the precise objective correlate, though there is one, for the work of art.

Though a painting be the very report of space in and of itself, it not only tells us what space is as localized in an empirical actuality B, but points through to Actuality and to other modes as well C, D, E, as specializations of the modes as together in a togetherness which is spatially defined. We see the space of Existence not as in Existence but as functioning as the togetherness of the other three modes. It is only when we vitalize the space by time, etc., and recognize that this is but one approach to Existence as such that we can see Existence as alongside the other modes. We must, as it were, minimize art as an enterprise, see it on a footing with others before we can see it as telling us what Existence is; short of that it tells us only how it functions as a kind of togetherness for the other three modes, a togetherness whose nature is subjugated by each of the modes in its own way to become a kind of space, time, etc., inside each of the modes. The grasp of an empirical actuality as having Existence in it is thus different from the grasp of the substantial Actual as having Existence in it; in the former case the Existence is discerned through cues; in the latter we grasp the very nature of Existence as a genuine reality but functioning as a generic form which is being specialized by Actuality.

It is correct then to say that Art is iconic of Existence, but only so far as this serves as the togetherness of the various modes. It does not of course have this function except for us; actually it is alongside the other modes. Art must then be said to give us a special account, a somewhat distortive picture of the whole. But in this respect it is like philosophy, religion, etc. Each of these tells us primarily about one mode and then as it functions as a togetherness. It is when it is seen to be but one way of approaching things, and thus of getting to other modes in a way not best for them, that we can relax with it and see that what it says is something of a given mode as alongside the other modes. How the nature it has, as a togetherness, is modified is determined only by putting all the different disciplines and their results together. Each discipline (and thus art) tells us what all the modes are, but only as specializations and subjugators of a single mode which is functioning as their togetherness. Art tells us what Existence is like as a generic togetherness, that which is muted and specialized by the different modes. To see it as giving the meaning of Existence we must recognize that the other modes are to be approached primarily/ in other ways.

Analogously we must say that philosophy does not tell us what the empirical object is. It deals with the substantial unity of Actuality primarily as a kind of togetherness for the other modes, and through this togetherness grasps the meaning of these other modes. The other modes ought to have other ways of being dealt with. When philosophy is supplemented by other approaches, Actuality is known as alongside the other modes, and thus most appropriately; those other modes are grasped by philosophy but not with a fullness that Actuality is. The categories of philosophy tell us truly about the other modes, but they do not give their contours. Similarly art gives us the very structure of Existence, the curvature of space, the divisions of time, the structure of events so far as Existence functions as a togetherness. It tells us what Existence is over against other modes, and what it is like in the other modes, and therefore even what the other modes are like, though as primarily loci of Existence. What it does not do, until we relax its insistence by recognizing other types of approach, is to tell us just what Existence is like as alongside the other modes. Art can of course, like philosophy, tell us something of the nature of the togetherness of all the modes; it gives us the meaning of togetherness as extensive, just as philosophy gives it to us as intelligible, ethics gives it to us as prescriptive, and religion gives it to us as important and descriptive.

The shapes of space, time, etc., in art then tell us what Existence is like as embodied in other modes and as the generic meaning of that which is embodied. And it tells us what Existence is like in and of itself, so far as we can sheer off part of it as a mere extensive One for all the modes. The residue will be what Existence is in and of itself.

If then it be asked what is space, or time, or energy, or more inclusively Existence, we can answer from the standpoint of an Actuality-biased or a neutrally cognizing philosophy, from a biased or netural

Ideality or divinity, or from the standpoint of Art which is either biased towards Existence as a togetherness, or of an Art which is alongside other enterprises.

Art tells us what time is like as a generic togetherness. Such a generic togetherness loses some of the features it has when divided into a neutral extensive togetherness and mere Existence. That mere Existence, though it loses its status as a togetherness, is now something properly grasped by means of the extensive togetherness. It is also understood as having other dimensions made evident when one approaches it from the position of other disciplines. What knowledge of a philosophic sort, for example, reveals about Existence is an Existence which is together in an intelligible way with the other modes, and as so together has properties not expressed by it as extensively together. It is as the togetherness of all these ways of being "together," e.g., intelligible, extensive, etc., that Existence is what it is. But we cannot get them all together without dividing Existence up. Our only way is to see Existence residually. But when we do, do we have it as curved, let us say? To answer this we must in fact occupy the position of a neutral togetherness. Is it possible to do this by identifying the very curvature of space, etc., as the extensiveness of Existence and treating the residuum as Existence subdivided into unitary points? To do this is to say that the work of Art gives us the iconic nature of the whole of Existence as integral with its subdivisions, and that when we use it neutrally, and thus when we see Art as a discipline alongside others, we are in a position to deal with it as a single domain. In that case the particular features of the different arts will tell us about the subdivisions. A proper neutrality will have the midpoint as the tension (or as said in the *Modes,* the restlessness) between the two. Art gives us the tension between Existence as a mere neutral extensionality (which has the features which art exhibits) and the subdivisions which are co-ordinated by that Existence when it functions, not as a togetherness between the modes, but as one extreme of the tensions between itself and the subdivisions.

The midpoint is no more the nature of Existence than the midpoint emotion is the Actuality of those Actualities we call man. The togetherness is the only aspect which is iconic with the manner of grasping it. The mind of man in its most abstract phase reaches to the togetherness which is neutral to all the modes; it is itself an extreme over against the body, with a midpoint at the emotions. To know what an actuality is is to see it from a position made possible by Actuality; it is to see it as over against other modes all under the intelligible One. We know what Actuality is in one sense when we know what the One as intelligible is; we know it in another sense when we see it as one of the many for that intelligible

One; We also know it when we see it as the juncture of these approaches, as that which has a status as both merged and opposed. So too we know Existence when we see it as the extensive One, when we see it as plurality of terminal points, and when we see it as the restlessness which keeps the two sides together and opposed. Art is iconic with the first, the arts and their analysis allows us to be concordant with the second, and the act of reference of the concrete work of art, its appreciation, is the having the Existence at a distance.

Art as giving us the icon of the togetherness approaches what Schopenhauer had in mind — art brings us to the eternal realm, keeping us out of the vital, destructive, non-rational movement of nature. What Schopenhauer overlooked is that art is also concordant with the vital movement of Existence and also offers us a reference to its midpoint as both fixed and moving. The tension in the work of art answers to the restlessness in Existence.

In the photograph and particularly in the moving picture, we have a new type of space. The movies add a new kind of motion and action not reducible to dramatic action in light of the ability (through montage and splicing) of the director and editor to violate the limits of the usual spaces and times. Granted that these arts give us a new set of dimensions, can we say that they too, like painting, music, etc., give us the very nature of Existence at least in some dimension? They seem so caught in the world of perspectives that it would seem as if they could do little more than to add a perspective to the ones we already have, or at best give us that unitary empirical object which the various perspectives together articulate. But the space, time, energy of these arts are no less basic than those of any other arts. They may mix modes, tie together a kind of drama with a kind of dance, or a kind of painting with a kind of mythos, but this shows only that instead of exhibiting only one dimension of Existence in its purity, they exhibit one intermixed with the others. Could one bring all the arts together in a single complex we would come close to the nature of Existence as the unity of the dimensions, but we would then risk losing the purity of Existence and get either a set of discrepant dimensions, or at least independent ones, or a blur expressive of the restlessness of Existence, without illuminating just what it is like.

The fact that works of art are produced without attending to the world beyond, and the fact that they do things with space, time and energy which differ one from the other, indicates that either the space, time and energy of specific works of art are not iconic at all, or are iconic with respect to only parts of the whole of space, etc. But the latter alternative would mean that there is really nothing genuinely new in the work of art. But if we take the first alternative we must abandon the position already assumed today, and maintain that the Existence portrayed in a work of art gives us either the power of Existence, or one of the expressions of Existence to be reduced to this power. The latter of these alternatives looks like the doctrine of perspectives once again, and would seem to give priority to knowledge as alone capable of being iconic of a mode.

The clue is perhaps to be found in knowledge. Knowledge makes divisions in the real which are not there; but in its systematization and syntheses it recovers, iconizes what is there through the unity of its own efforts. Is this perhaps not also what is done in art? Does not the beauty in each art constitute the meaning of the realm of Existence? What system is to knowledge, beauty is to Art, the whole of mathematics is to the Ideal and the community of saints is to God?

April 30

Each work of art can be said to provide the analogue of a proposition in a philosophic system. The totality of art works has however no syntax of its own. The works of art are related in Existence itself; the various works therefore, with their particular ways of expressing the nature of space, time, energy, etc., offer different ways of stressing, articulating the nature of Existence in its role of the One, and the nature of Existence consequently as it is in and of itself (and as it serves to provide a way of comprehending the other modes by virtue of the fact that it is a facet of them). There is a kind of immersion in the One then in connection with art that is not characteristic of knowledge. In knowledge the knower is in a sense identical with the One, and exhaustively articulates it in a systematic way when and as he deals with the Many which is correlate with it. In the case of Art the articulation is but the provision of the elements, of the components for such an integrated account; Art therefore has a kind of rootage in the world beyond, which does not apply to knowledge. Though knowledge is a knowledge of, and though it is never freed from empirical orientation, it is in principle possible to have knowledge (through the power of man to judge and unify) replace the world, reproduce it in its meaning. But in the case of Art only the elements can be reproduced in this sense; their interrelation requires the placing of them in the body of Existence and the having them related there in history, across space and time and in vital interplay.

The curvatures, punctuations, spans of Art then are neither iconic nor merely perspectival. They are the very being of Existence made articulate, divided through essential and relevant distinctions. These distinctions are interconnected by Existence itself to give us the meaning of Existence, in part conveyed by the distinctions and in part by the way in which they are in fact related one to the other by the residuum Existence which they diversely analyze. There is something analogous here to the way in which different perspectives are united through the power of the substantial unity below the empirical unity of supplementary perspectives. The difference between these two is that in Existence there is a structural function, a way of interplaying of item with item which is like that of the empirical object. In short, Existence is like the substantial object in its role of a unifying force for the empirical object, and is like the empirical object in that it serves to determine what weight is to be given to the different elements and how they are to be made into a unity.

To know a work of art is to know a unitary item, which offers a component in the non-cognitive understanding of an Existence. The Existence in turn sustains and relates that component to other components. The space of every-day or of mathematics are but perspectives on the empirical meaning or role of Existence. These perspectives must be integrated in such a way that the relaxation of the conditions of the appearances of any one of these kinds of space is but the supplementation of it by the other types to constitute an Existence in which they are synthesized. That Existence, as merely having them together, is Existence in its empirical meaning; such an Existence depends for its being on the functioning of Existence as a unitary substantial reality, as the mode expressing itself in diverse dimensions. That mode in itself is grasped in its role of unifying the perpetives which Art articulates; each work of art provides an element in the articulation.

Each work of art defines the nature of that unity which is Existence in itself, and in the light of the way in which it expresses that unity gives us a knowledge of the possibility of the different perspectives. But more important, the work of art identifies itself with the mere meaning of an extensive One, and in the light of this deals with Existence as a mode, and all the other modes as somehow existentially tainted. It is the work of art's stress on one facet or moment in the One, which Existence provides, that enables the work of art to tell us something of the being of Existence as distinct from that One, but as related to other modes via that One. We know what Existence is through Art because the work of art gives us the One, in terms of which we could grasp the modes. The stress that one work of art provides for dealing with the extensive One must be balanced by the stresses provided by other works of art. The totality of works of art mediated by the One provides us with the total meaning of Existence (and the other modes) as sustained by Existence itself, and Existence as in those other modes.

The above exaggerates the translucency of cognition. Analogous to the role which Existence in fact plays to constitute the syntax between the various works of art and in addition to Existence (as a One, as one of the many modes, and as the way of approaching the other modes), there is the active individual man. Each of the basic disciplines must root itself in its appropriate mode so as to be able to have an adequate syntax for the items it expresses.

A philosophic system is broken into propositions, and the connection between them is not propositional but structural and inferential, requiring the individual to hold them together. It is this syntax which is perspectivized; the individual is as it were made evident in the perspectives of phenomenology, mathematics, etc.; Existence is made manifest in the realm of history; the syntax of the ethical Ideal known is made manifest in the perspectives of politics; and the syntax of churches is made manifest in the perspective of creeds and religious activity and discourse.

We have thus, e.g., the following meanings of space: 1] space in some perspective, such as perception, or physics;   2] space as the integrated unity of these various perspectives to constitute the empirical meaning of space;   3] space in the substance of Existence, part of which substance is manifest as the empirical meaning, and part of which functions as the unifying power for that empirical meaning;   4] space as portrayed in a work of art and which gives us an articulation or stress on one meaning of the One for all the modes, and thereby an awareness of the space in all the modes;   5] space as portrayed by philosophy or pure mathematics or religion. When then we have the space of a picture we do not only have   1] a matter of fact, something to be taken as it appears, but we have identified ourselves   4] with one way of looking at all the modes, have rooted ourselves in Existence   3] to provide a way of relating our given work with other works, and have made evident the ground   2] of space which allows space to be perspectivized in various ways.

The work of art thus tells us something about   4] pure Existence and something about the other modes   3] as mediated by Existence, and at the same time something of the unity   2] which makes possible the historical use of space. What it refers to is primarily   4] Existence and   3] secondarily the reality of other modes, and the   2] possibility of having an empirical space, and eventually a   1] phenomenological space. Since however we normally recognize a phenomenological space and must tear ourselves away from this to get to the work of art, and yet on the other hand must have clues to the common object, it is evident that the function of the clues in the work of art is to make us forget the phenomenological; the clues are substitutes, ways of our putting the phenomenological object to a side so that we can make the work of art function as revelatory of the modes. This means that the clues are warnings telling us not to make the conventional interpretations, but to note what is to be ignored—or what is the same thing, to note that we are to deal with the objects of the clues not in themselves but as adumbrating the empirical object and thereby making evident the presence of a mode beneath that object.

When a quality is dislocated from its empirical or perspectival locus we in effect make it function as an index of the substantival reality. We are saying that the perspective and empirical approach are superficial, and that if we took even the elements of it which are most surely distant from a real substantial being we would be able to express it better. The cues help us to do better than we do in ordinary experience—move from the surface, the qualitative, the merely presented, which we have in the work of art itself, to the reality which that art in fact helps explicate by giving, via the dislocated item, an element of articulation to the reality.

In the ideal case there would be no need of cues or clues; we would take the work of art as immediately revelatory. But we start in art only after we have been in the daily world, and as a consequence have our minds geared to viewing whatever we do in terms which are appropriate to ordinary experience. The clues thus have the advantage of giving us something with which we are familiar; they have the danger of making us treat them as either reports of familiar things in familiar perspectives or of their empirical unity, rather than primarily of all the modes as approached through the unity and import of Existence.

May 1

The problem of accidental production comes out most acutely in music, particularly in recent times when electronic devices are used. But the answer here in the end must be like that given with respect to every other art: the recognition that such and such is aesthetically of interest is already an introduction into the domain of art, since it involves an element of creativity and re-evaluation of what occurs in nature. The sounds made by the machines can be treated as "natural," or non-aesthetic, but the recognition that they are to be enjoyed or viewed as prospectively enjoyable is the result of movement away from the non-aesthetic. And then when one has moved away there will be activities of slicing and splicing, of selecting and interweaving. And this is an aesthetic activity.

What the electronic devices show is that there is a way of dealing with music somewhat analogous to photography. Here one starts with nature and makes one's primary aesthetic decisions in deciding what the aesthetic data will be, which sequence or use of the device will be accepted. The electronic devices are sources of sound, and these can have a range that the performer may not be able to produce. Still, even where the sounds duplicate those of the performer there is a difference, for the performer is engaged in a translation or utilization of a script. The difference between the machine and the improvising musician, who has no script, lies in the fact that the next step is defined by the musician in the light of what he had accomplished.

The nature of the development of a musical theme is such that one must live through it in order to know what it requires from step to step. Were a machine to duplicate such movement and end with the very piece that an improvising performer gave us, it would be a machine to which we must attribute some exterior guidance by a power which expresses itself in a creative way. When machines really duplicate man we have no recourse but to acknowledge a "man behind the machine."

Those who say man is only a machine, deny obtrusive data and our own awareness of what we do. They do this on the basis of an accidental achievement of a special sort, supposed to be the entire product of the machine.

May 4

The work of art as offering a One for the many modes, among which is Existence itself in its substantial concreteness, does relate these various modes to one another in a way in which Actuality (or cognition, its primary mode of being a neutral One) does not. Knowledge relates them by virtue of the category (God relates them through a sensitive and variable appreciation; and the Ideal evaluates them, and thus from different angles gives each a kind of priority over the others). In art we have a kind of One which allows the various modes to be coordinate, to be alongside one another in a field of Existence, which is inseparable from the Existence in each of them.

If we subdivide the number of approaches we can make to things, as *1*] an empirical perspective, such as that offered in phenomenology, the sciences, politics etc., *2*] a construction of the empirical object as the locus of these different perspectives, possibly muted,   3] the substantially real unity which lies below 2, and gives it the unifying force to have the different perspectives together,   4] the biased way of dealing with 3, because one takes a particular approach—knowledge, art, mathematics, religion—we can say that 3 is the objective of all basic enterprises, but that we can hope only for 4, and must avoid confusing it with 1 and 2. I sometimes spoke as though art were a 1, and sometimes as though it were a 2. But it is more non-empirical than either of these allow it to be.

May 5

Each (1) perspective is part of a system of similar perspectives. Its terminus is a focused object (2). This has other sides which become evident in other types, e.g., in a scientific or historical perspective. The focused object in short is but a moment in the career of a *continuing focused* (3) *object.* As we engage in some particular enterprise or treat an object in a persistent way we deal with the continuing focused object. If we are strict phenomenologists we will (because there is a plurality of perspectives) be forced to acknowledge a plurality of continuing focused objects.

The locus of a plurality of continuing focused objects is a continuing empirical (4) object. This object is one in which the various focused objects are integrated and perhaps qualified radically. The continuing empirical object thus is the ground for a plurality of focused continuing objects, and for a focused object. A focused empirical object is the locus of a plurality of focused objects, at a moment; the continuing empirical object is the locus of a plurality of continuing focused objects. The difference between a focused and a continuing empirical object is the difference between a phase of a being and the entire being.

The phenomenologist is interested in the continuing focused object. Analysis is interested in the focused empirical object; it involves an awareness of the continuing empirical object but does not develop systematically a knowledge of the diverse continuing focused objects in terms of which one might try to express the nature of the continuing empirical object.

The continuing empirical object is only one of many such objects. Each is caught within a world; it is related to other objects in ways which require for their understanding a "philosophic" approach. One must either provide an interpretation of the way in which these diverse objects are displayed and interplay as more than merely focused objects, whether empirical or continuing, or must use one of them as the representative of the rest, as that which offers one special meaning which allows for the grasp of the others. In either case we refer the continuing empirical objects back to a further base, a mode of being which these objects illustrate.

We have six levels of analysis: A mode of being is but one of a number of modes of being and there must be some approach made to them all by some abstract and universal agency such as knowledge, art, evaluation or sympathy. The given mode of being will then be known from a biased perspective; each of the approaches however will be most appropriate to some one mode. Assuming that we are engaged in art and have grasped the nature of Existence through its means, that Existence must then be seen to be the ground for a number of continuing empirical objects, which together express what it is, and each one of which can function as its representative and thus as a representative of the others. Existence is here dated, localized, pluralized, distinguished. The continuing empirical object is manifested in a plurality of continuing focused objects, and in focused empirical objects. As manifest in continuing focused objects it is the ground for a plurality of phenomenologies; as manifest in a focused empirical object it is the ground for a set of relativized versions of itself. Each continuing focused object grounds a plurality of distinct perspectivized focused objects; each of these objects is dealt with in a specific perspective.

If an eskimo were to try to convey to a desert nomad the nature of his world, he would not be concerned with telling him the nature of a focused object; indeed he could not do this. All the eskimo could do would be to try to exhibit for him a continuing empirical object, by imposing on the focused object of the nomad the nature of the eskimo's own focused object, or by imposing on the nomad's continuing focused object something of the eskimo's own. If he does the former the result can be read either as a continuing focused object, or as an item from which one could read off what the meaning of the eskimo's focused object is by subtracting what one already knows of the nomad's; if he does the latter we will be able to know what the continuing empirical object is, or will be able to extract from the item the continuing focused object of the nomad.

When we think of art as a way of communicating feeling or experiences to another, we think of it as providing us with an item from which we can recover the focused object or the continuing focused object of the artist. When we think of art as revelatory of the real we think of it as iconic with respect to the continuing focused object or of the continuing empirical object. In either case the art product is seen to portray the continuing focused object, either because this is treated as the iconic counterpart of the work of art, or because it is viewed as that which overlays or underlies the continuing focused object of the artist's experience. We read the work of art then as; A] telling us what some unexperienced focused object is; B] some unexperienced continuing focused object is; C] the nature of a continuing focused object as underlying focused objects; D] the nature of the continuing empirical object as underlying continuing focused objects.

A better vocabulary is perhaps:

1] focused object—data
2] continuing focused object; phenomenological object
3] focused empirical object—abstractum
4] continuing empirical object—substance
5] mode of being—reality, with a concrete and a categorial component.

So, once again: The art object (3) is iconic with respect to 2] the phenomenological object or 4] the substance; it is to be read as telling us what something about 1] unexperienced data, about some unencountered 2] phenomenological object, about an underlying 2] phenomenological object, and about 4] a substance. But this account leaves out the most important function of art—to tell us 5] about reality, and this means that in addition to the above functions art must also bring together substances in such a way as to allow for the reading off of the nature of one of the substances which the artist had somehow known and which he incorporated in the other substances with which he was familiar, or so as to allow for the understanding of that reality which makes itself manifest as these diverse substances.

What is not clear is how a work of art can bring substances together, for these are precisely the entities which stand outside not only the individual but the data and the phenomenological objects. Is it not perhaps the meaning of a substance which the artist relates to another substance? Is it not then that he portrays a reality through this combination? But then in what sense is art iconic? Is it that the combination of the meanings of the substances in art is precisely the deformation of them, the transformation of Existence in such a way as to give us the nature of Existence as a reality? Is any attempt to read off one substance as somehow intruded upon the other through the activity of the artist and which the spectator must recover, a kind of flattening out of the iconic revelation of reality?

May 6

If art tells us iconically the nature of Existence it must make use of a number of substances. Are these the artist himself and the actual

material available? Does he impose himself on the material and thereby
A] provide one with a complex entity from which one can read off his
contribution, by recovering in that work the initial substance, so that the
artist's contribution will always be the distortion he introduces; and
B] provide an iconic portrayal of the reality which underlies both substances? In either case why does he look beyond both himself and the
material; how is it that he sometimes views himself as portraying some
other entity, a phenomenological object and perhaps a substance other
than himself, and offers the work of art as iconic of these? Is it not that
the entity to which he looks (and this must be something grasped at least
in part as a datum) a representative of a kind of unity which the artistic
work is to exhibit also, and this unity is the unity of Existence as a
reality? This would mean that the artist always uses the referential object
as a form of Existence, and that when he copies its shape, size, color, tone,
etc., he is but telling himself how to make a "substance" which will be
revelatory of Existence. This would seem to show that the artist makes use
of his material as a phenomenological object. The act of creating goes
from his substance, and with the substantial object beyond as a guide
he creates a new kind of substance which, when contrasted with and
related to himself and the object to which he referred, serves as an item in
the convergence towards Existence. Or it shows that the artist, by using
the material as a phenomenological object (i.e., as something merely
seen and not also something which can be treated mathematically, e.g.)
and looking at the substantial object known in common sense, makes use
of his own substance and the powers of Existence which are within and
without it, to constitute an odd phenomenological object. This last can be
seen to be real   A] as iconic of real Existence,   B] as a phase of a new
substance constituted by the individual, the copied object and the
artistic work. But B is not known nor sought.

It would seem that A is the right answer, so that art would be the
production of an icon of Existence through the imposition of our substantial and existing powers on phenomenologically treated material,
using as guide occasionally the substantial realities we daily confront.

But how does a phenomenological object, which the art work is here
said to be, function as an icon not of a substance but of a reality? It could
not be iconic of a substance without having to forego the very distortions
it introduces into phenomena, unless it be the case that substances do involve just such distortions. This is possible. Is it that a substance must
occupy some position in the world of phenomena and of data and this is
not the case with the counterpart of the work of art?

In knowing a work of art we do not know a substance which in fact does appear. But in knowing a work of art we can know Existence as that which appears in any substance and therefore in any phenomenological object or datum. A substance in short appears in some definite guise, thereby contrasting with other substances, but Existence appears in every guise, so that it can be portrayed iconically, as at the root of all. But then no art could falsify it? Or must we say that we get it more or less purely, via the distorted phenomenological object? That object is iconic after all of only a phase of Existence, Existence as caught from this angle or that. But then once again we can be said to portray Existence without fail.

How then account for the failures of artist achievement and communication? Is it not that these two are related? Must not the artist communicate through a reference to phenomenological and substantial objects and lead us through them to that which lies behind so that we sense their deeper import? The successful artist would then be one who knows how to go beyond any substance. But once again it could be said that the very fact of making the work of art leads one to do this. If so, one work will do more justice to Existence as such, and catch more than this or that phase; it will iconically reach not to a phase of Existence but to the whole of it by virtue of the subtlety of the distortion it provides. Instead of, e.g., seeing music as a mere icon of the time of Existence, one would see it as probing via time into the space and energy, the very dynamics of Existence. Or a better illustration—since music is thought to express the energy and in some way to include space and time—a painting is more than a mere icon of the space of Existence here or there. The more surely it is a great painting the more surely does the space it itself exhibits become the icon not merely of this or that part of Existence but of the entire space of Existence.

The iconic role of the work of art is achieved only by leaping over the intervening phenomena and substances. The great work of art leads one to use it iconically of the whole of Existence; lesser works of art lead one to use it iconically only of parts of Existence, or to represent the whole of Existence. The lesser works do not know how to make us use them as icons; they have no power to make us see them as totalities in and of themselves at the same time that they are held away from their counterpart, Existence. A work of art is iconic to the degree that it is rich enough to enable us to hold the world away from us. If we fail in art we fail to have that which suffices as a world of its own, and thus that which can be iconic of all Existence.

The iconic nature of the work of art means that Existence is faced as it were without mediation; it is as if the work of art were translucent. By being absorbed in the work of art we are placed inside Existence, not of course in its full substantiality (for it is in its full substantiality interlocked with other modes, infected by other modes, and approachable in other ways as well), but inside Existence as it is in and of itself, though even then in a biased way, due to the fact that we never get to that perfect state of abstraction where we deal with a mode without any bias at all. But the bias is no greater than that provided by the concepts used in a philosophy.

May 7

The work of art is a phenomenological entity isolated in a substance. It replaces other phenomenological entities, idealizing what they may be and thereby retaining clues in itself regarding them. Since it is taken to be something final it is a phenomenological object which functions as though it were a substance, and in this aspect stands over against and opposes whatever other substances there may be, including of course the substantial reality of itself as together with its carrier. The capacity of the art work to be sufficient, to enable us to enjoy it as something by itself, is one with the adoption of it as an icon of Existence. That Existence lies behind substances and makes itself manifest in them, their phenomenological objects and the consequent data. When we enjoy the work of art we enjoy Existence, and when we look at the world in the light of the work of art we see the objects in it as specializations of Existence. The objects can be looked at in the light of Existence just so far as the work of art tells us something about them. And this it does, for its data are derived from experience; as a phenomenological object it has the nature of other such objects, though idealized; as a kind of substance it is held over against other substances as a correlate with correlate properties.

The Stanislawski method in effect tells the artist to get back into his recesses and find that type of feeling or emotion or way of being which will answer to the dramatic problem. This is tantamount to saying that the actor, like any other artist, must produce the work of art by bringing his substance to bear on the material. The result of the use of this material is never merely realistic, no matter how realistic the drama, for the events on the stage must at the very least be fore-shortened in time and often in space; there must be the use of the voice beyond the normal. The so-called fourth wall is an error; the audience is in fact that wall, or rather just inside it; the illusion of distance from the stage is overcome; one becomes the spectator inside the play and not over against it. The spectator, like the actor and the playwright, makes use of his own substance to make, not a semblance or a duplicate, but an object whose structure is iconic or imitative of the very nature of Existence in its dimension of action. Action here is the dynamic ordered forward thrust of the work inside a plot or theme, itself a realization of a story or script, itself in turn made by a substantial being controlling phenomenological objects so as to get beyond them to their root import.

May 8

One type of phenomenological object is the product of the focusing of sensed data; another is that provided by a mathematical treatment from different grounds, say by a set of contrary to fact conditional formulations of the object in mathematical terms. It is possible, with Northrop, to view the scientific object as the outcome of the combination of these; such an object would be identical with the substantial object, except that it puts a stress on the mathematical side. One could conceivably put the stress the other way, in which case we would get a kind of "phenomenological science" in contrast with the mathematical science of contemporary physics. If now one goes on to recognize other types of phenomenological objects—such as values, social, political, historical—and tries to unite these with the mathematically defined phenomenological object one will get a mathematical science which is different from that which concerns the physicist. Thus a mathematically defined animal could be dated even in the distant past, as a kind of ancestor or pre-historic skeleton; this when combined with the nature of history will give us the mathematically defined science of biology. The mathematically defined phenomenological object is a locus of value, social importance, political meaning, historic import dealt with in a rationalistic system.

May 9

A rejection of a system is in opposition to it; a negation of a system is a proposition in it. The negation can stand over against the system only by being a rejection; the rejection enters the system and becomes in fact an affirmation in it by being made integral to the system, and has the status of a negation as a part of the system over against the whole—but it stands as a part over against the whole only by functioning as a rejection.

There are four types of phenomenological objects: perceptual, formal, eventful, and important. If we combine these in groups of three we get four kinds of substances. If we combine the latter into groups of three we get four realities. This raises two basic sets of questions: What modes make possible the distinctions among these levels? Why are there phenomenological objects? Is it because we look out at the world in an active mood, creating the phenomenological objects as it were by virtue of our participation in Existence? If so what makes us produce the substances and the realities? Is it that the substances reflect the power of the divine in us, and the realities that of the Ideal? or conversely? The second set of questions: how does one move from one level to another? Is it that to know one of the four types we combine three and have the fourth in a better form—e.g., to know events we combine perceptual, formal and important phenomenological objects to constitute a single substance which has at its root the being of the Ideal which unifies these and expresses itself as these? But then why do we try one of these combinations rather than another? Is it that we ourselves are trying to make manifest our own Ideality and find that the phenomenological Ideality is insufficient to answer to ourselves? And so on for other combinations? If so, combining this question with the last, is it that we seek to have the substance in an Ideal form, and when we, say, combine the ideal phenomenological object with, say, the event and the important phenomenological objects, to point to a substantival qualitative unity, we are in effect viewing this as a kind of Ideal so far as we take it to be substantial, and as a kind of Actuality so far as it is qualitative? If so, then we move to the realities, the modes, when we want to get the counterpart of the divine in us. Then, when using art to reach to Existence, what we in effect must be doing is making use of the category of the divine to get to realities as such.

We confront the world with minds, bodies, emotions and self. When we attend to what is in experience with a primary stress on one or the other of these we get a type of phenomenological object. Thus if we are primarily minds we have a mathematically defined phenomenological object. The object is phenomenological because it is faced in an attitude of action; it makes use of Existence. When we still are occupied say with the use of our minds, but now impose ourselves as substances on any trio of phenomenological objects, we make the fourth type into the unity of the other three. This means that we make use of the divine stress in ourselves to get to the substance, and choose the particular trio by virtue of the aspect of ourselves we are using—in this case the mind. Using the mind in this way we combine the perceptual, formal and eventful phenomenological objects to have a way of dealing with the substance in the guise of an Ideal. Continuing in the same vein, with a primary stress on mind, but emphasizing now our desire to have the Ideal side of ourselves expressed, we combine the various substances and have the result rooted in the Ideal.

In the case of art we must go through the three stages of using ourselves as stressing Existence, the divine, and the Ideal or evaluative, to get the levels of phenomenology, substance and reality; but we must (since we are interested in art at all times) stress the emotional component on each level. Accordingly we combine the formal, perceptual and important phenomenological objects, infusing them with out substance to constitute the elements which are united by Existence in the guise of a substance, and then we combine substances which are essentially Ideal, divine and Actual to point up the reality which is Existence. Art then faces phenomenological objects of four types, but does it in an active mood; it attends to the substantial being of things as essentially existences through the supplementation of perceptual, formal and dynamic phenomenological objects, and it makes itself into an icon of Existence through the combination of substances which are primarily Ideal, Actual and divine in meaning or import.

May 11

Confronted with phenomenological objects (for a man lives in time, with expectations and memories and therefore combines his data into singularities with persist), men seek to know some particular kind e.g., events. They therefore combine the others to focus on the substance which is an event. The phenomenological events are identified with himself; they constitute the category in terms of which he sees the substantial event. In the attempt to understand this substantial event, he reverses his stress. Instead of identifying himself with the substantial event and thereby knowing the reality beyond it, he tries to master the substantial event, and thereby comes to use it as a category revelatory of the nature of the Existence which lies beyond the three types of substances which lie at the root of combinations of phenomenological objects.

Interested in grasping the very substance of events, the aesthetic-minded man identifies himself with the phenomenological event and thereby unifies the perceptual, formal and valuable objects which were, after all, not altogether distinguished in his daily life. And then he tries to lay hold of that substance, and by making use of his own substantial powers he forges a category with it to enable him to combine the other substances so as to reveal the nature of real Existence below them all.

Since man is primarily an Actuality it would seem that knowledge is the best means open to him for getting to the ultimate realities, even that of Existence. Art comes to Existence in a more existential mood; it gets to it in its reality as knowledge does not, but in a fragmentary way only, and in this sense gets less of it than knowledge does. Could one as it were engage in art as merely a being in Existence—and this is what non-objective art tries to do—art would be able to do for us what knowledge can. And similarly, if we wish to grasp what things were formally we would have to identify ourselves with an Ideal being, as Plato saw. To grasp what they are as unities we would have to be appreciative in the way a God is; short of that we will remain religious in a biased way, getting to the being of what is in root God in a way that gives us Him in his concreteness but only a fragmentarily. (The four types of man are perhaps: philosopher, artist, saint and good man, exercising the power of mind in knowledge, energy in making, sympathy in religion or devotion, and virtue in evaluation and improvement.)

May 15

If action requires a genuine persistent self-identity of some sort, the Buddhist and the Whiteheadean must fail to provide the ground for such action, and as a consequence cannot be said to have an ethics, a politics or an art. But how can there be a self-identity in animals? Men can be said to have a self-identical self which governs all their acts. Is it not that the animals (and not men) live in a kind of *lebensraum,* that they are beings which are occupied with a limited prospect that is inseparable from their present being? That prospect is the good of the species, and it is by virtue of their essential reference to this that they are beings who can be said to persist and be capable of action. Unlike men, they will not have a core of persistent identity, capable of representing all Actuality and thus of being forever the other of the eternal other which is God. All animals will be representatives of their species; they will persist only so long as the species does and will function representatively for it, not by having an intent but by having a structural relation to it. An animal is an individual in the sense that it begins from a special place, but it lacks the final inwardness which will enable it to have intent, interiority, a true subjectivity.

In the ordinary course of life we confront entities in four different guises. They are caught in different time schemes. There is the time of the phenomenological object, which is the time of accumulation, involving some use of the past to govern the future; there is the time of the abstract mathematically defined object, which is the time that owes its being to Ideality, and merely gives the structure of time, a placing of items in a sequence which does not move; there is the time which owes its being to God, in which there is a perpetual re-evaluation, a shift in the items as more or less important, as making different beginnings and endings, to constitute new segments of a present; and there is the time which owes its being to Existence and is felt as sequential. To know what real time is we must use art as the unifying power which reveals what Existence is in itself as subtending the accumulative, abstractive-structural, and evaluative types of time.

What we discern in experience has its counterpart in each of the modes. Every Actuality is accumulative in its temporal dimension; the Ideal is the locus of the whole of time as a mere structure; God's time is that of re-evaluation, of making what was past germane to something in the future, thereby redefining the importance of what had been before, and perhaps also placing the date of creation at different points, moving backwards over the past of Actualities, Existence, or the Ideal; the time of Existence is purely sequential.

Just as for Actuality there is a four-fold time in which the items of the Actuality's experience are tainted by each of the modes, so there are four times for each of the modes. Thus the time in God is the re-evaluative time, the dictating of what is relevant in the past to what is to be in the future. Such a re-evaluative time takes account of the past as defined by Actuality, by Ideality and by Existence. It confronts a past which is remembered in the living Actualities, a past which is eternally present in the very structure of ideal time, and a past which has been left behind by the onward movement of Existence. And what is true of God is also true of Ideality and of Existence. The structure of time as in Ideality must accommodate, be made germane to the time characteristic of the other modes. What is finally adopted by the Ideal, as it subordinates the other modes, involves an adoption of their times inside the eternal structure of Ideality. And Existence in its vitality, faced with the content provided by the other modes, infects their time-features to make them all bear the marks of a lived-through present.

And what is true of time is true of space and of energy; it is true too of the features which characterize each of the Modes—there must be different types of inwardness or individuality in each mode; there must be different types of logic or rationality; different types of evaluation. Each of these different types will be four-fold, having a distinctive import in the experience of each. Thus the logical structure of the Actuality which stresses negation is faced with the eternal logic in the Ideal, the peculiar inductive pattern of the logic of Existence, and the logic of Identity which is characteristic of God.

Evaluation, characteristic of God, has a role in each mode. And as in each mode it confronts simulacra of the other modes. Evaluation for man is faced with valuable content which bears the marks of the Ideal, Existence and God. If he would know what the true value of a thing is, he must understand what the evaluations of God are. To find this out he must unite the evaluations (which reflect the meaning of man) with those of the Ideal and Existence in order to constitute a single item which is the source and locus of all evaluations.

In each mode there is a characteristic dominant ontological feature and three features which reflect the presence of the other modes. In order to know the ontological feature in another, one must take the cosmological features provided by the others and unite them to constitute a single root of them all. Existence's time, space and energy are to be treated as ultimate; God's evaluations are basic to the others; the Ideal's structure or logic is the test of the other three; Actualities' oppositionalities measure the types of opposition characteristic of the others.

There are then sixteen different usages of key terms such as time, space, energy; individuality, uniqueness, inwardness, negation; structure, meaning, intelligibility; sympathy, evaluation, reconstitution, eternity. Which of these terms are best to characterize Existence, Actuality, Ideality and God is a difficult question. Perhaps it is the case that though each has its proper application to a mode, some one is in a signal position. Thus it might be said that Existence, though it has the dimensions of time, space and energy, is most appropriately designated as active or energetic, and that time and space, though characteristic of it, as in and of itself, are terms which tell us a little more about the other modes. Though energy or activity would be true of the other modes in a derivative sense no less and no more surely than time or space would, there would be something more appropriate in using it only for Existence. If this were the case there really ought to be a matrix of four terms for the essential feature of a mode; some indication of why it is that one of them is most appropriate, and some indication as to how we might be able to translate each of the terms into derivative or subordinate aspects of the other modes, thereby indicating that they are cosmological as well as ontological entities.

May 18

1] Each mode, since it has the other modes ingredient in it, bears the marks of the essential features of those modes. Thus there must be a time in each mode; the time which Existence has is a pure time, and the time which the other modes have is that time modified and qualified. 2] Each mode has an iconic way of getting the other modes. Thus, Actuality makes use of art to get the iconic form of space, time, dynamics, characteristic of Existence. And it makes use of cognitive knowledge, ethics and religion to get iconic forms of Actuality, Ideality and God respectively.

3] Each basic feature must have sixteen forms: it will have a primary form in some mode, and secondary form in the other modes and in its own encounter of itself as a plurality. In each of the modes it will find the basic feature to be part of the phenomenological and substantial objects, enabling the mode, through some agency or discipline, to achieve an iconic grasp of that feature as ingredient in its proper mode. This means that time, e.g., can be known, as it is in Existence, from four positions. Man's way is through art; God, etc., must use other ways. Man can know Existence cognitively, but this will be the result of his knowing what Actuality is, and then speculatively moving via some high abstraction to the nature of Existence; to get Existence with the same concreteness that Actuality has for knowledge he would have to use art.

The following are twenty forms of time:

1] Time in Existence is a time which is passing away; it is atomic, a sequence of presents.

2] Time in Actuality is accumulative; it involves memory. It is also foreshadowing, since it is involved with expectation.

3] Time in Ideality is structural; it is the whole of time in an order of before and after.

4] Time in God is reconstructive; new combinations of beginning and ending are being made constantly. The whole of time as having been passed through is redefined; it is as if a new whole of time is replacing an old again and again. God decides what is a pertinent past item for a given future one.

5] Time in the experience of an Actuality is sequential so far as it is Existence qualified by Actuality.

6] Time in the experience of an Actuality is accumulative so far there is a conscious memory and expectation.

7] Time in the experience of an Actuality is structural, so far as there is a concern for the Good, plans, objectives.

8] Time in the experience of an Actuality is re-evaluative or reconstructive when, as in the case of law, there is a re-assessment of the relevance of what has been to what is and is to be.

9] Time from the perspective of Existence is rooted in something over against itself. It is a time which Existence confronts when time is taken as the essence of the divisions of Existence. It is a sequence of atoms which are encompassed by Existence as such.

10] Time from the perspective of Existence is confronted as Actuality subject to the activity of Existence. It is a time which defines Actualities to be contemporaneously present.

11] Time from the perspective of Existence is confronted as the Ideal, subject to the divisions of Existence. It is the structure of time made germane to the world, a true future.

12] Time from the perspective of Existence is confronted as God made evident. Here we get events of differing magnitudes.

13–16] Time from the perspective of the Ideal is the other modes as qualified by the Ideal. Time is accumulative, sequential and re-evaluative as subject to a single structure of before and after.

17–20] Time from the perspective of God is the other modes as qualified by God. This yields a sequence, accumulation and structure as subject to re-evaluation by Him.

Each mode of being is capable of iconizing the essential features of the others. But what one mode is to iconize through thought for example, another must do through action. Or to put the matter in another way, the features of a mode of being can be iconized in four ways. Time, e.g., is iconized by Actuality in art, by God through love, by the Ideal through evaluation, and through Existence's structuralization.

By what principle does one determine just what mode is to be iconized in this way or that? Is it that we must begin with Actuality as iconizing itself through cognition, Existence iconizing itself through art, Ideality through virtue or appreciation, and God through religious reconstitution? But then how distribute the cognition in other modes? If we want to cognize Existence must we do it through God, or Ideality or Existence itself? Should we perhaps say that all self-grasping is a kind of cognition? We will then have to change the above paragraph and say that time is iconized cognitionally through Existence, and that when actualities cognize it they do it derivately, getting a more abstract form of it than Existence does. But if this be so, we have the problem of what modes are to be grasped through a creative activity analogous to that which produces art. Evidently Existence will have only the modes of Ideality, God and Actuality to grasp in this way. The problem then is how to determine what one is most appropriate for the work of Existence in an activity analogous to art, and also, with respect to the remaining two modes, which activities analogous to religion and to evaluation are appropriate. Since there is no duplication of the iconic function, we know that Existence will not religiously deal with God; accordingly religion from the perspective of Existence must relate to Actuality or to Ideality. We know that Existence will not deal evaluationally with Ideality; evaluation must relate to Actuality or to God. By elimination we get:

x. Actuality deals "religiously" with God; Existence does this for the Actual, God does it for the Ideal, *and the Ideal does it for Existence.*

y. Actuality evaluates the Ideal; Existence does this for God; *God does it for the Actual,* and the Ideal does this for Existence. (this duplicates an item in x).

z. Actuality is productively iconic of Existence; Existence is this for the Ideal; *God is this for Actuality,* and the Ideal is this for God. (duplication of item in y).

To avoid duplication we must make some modificaation to the effect that not all modes iconically cognize themselves. We have then:

	Cognition	Production	Evaluation	Reconstitution
A	A	E	*I*	G
I	G	*A*	E	I
E	I	G	A	E
G	*E*	I	G	A

This means, e.g., that time is cognized by God, produced in art by Actuality, evaluated by the Ideal, and reconstituted by Existence (as per table above). The last two are difficult to see because the Ideal is not a person; but we can see that were one to assume the position of the Ideal one would try to treat time as something of value, and that Existence when encountering Existence in the shape of subdivision to itself re-forges itself, makes itself be in a new way. The above table of course leaves out the status of the modes in and of themselves, and considers only the way in which they get to grasp the modes through the use of phenomenological and substantival objects.

Actualities grasp themselves in cognition, God grasps himself in evaluation, the Ideal grasps itself in reconstitution. It means also that production, the kind of activity characteristic of art is never a means for self-iconization.

Does this require a new table:

	Cognition	Production	Evaluation	Reconstitution
A	A *	E	I	G
I	G	I	E	A *
E	I	G	A *	E
G	E	A *	G	I

This enables us to say that Actualities cognize themselves, the Ideal is iconic through an activity analogous to art, that God is iconic through evaluation, and that Existence is iconic through reconstitution. It means that Actualities cognize themselves, that God is productive of them (to grasp them), that Existence evaluates them, and that the Ideal reconstitutes them (per stars).

Some immediate consequences: Just as Actuality may be said to be engaged in iconically producing through art the nature of Existence, so Existence can be said to be involved in something like art for the production of the meaning of God. God here is discovered through the activity of Existence itself; He would be a kind of cosmic product of it. Productivity with respect to God would involve the active making (through self-analysis) of Actuality. Existence reconstitutes whatever Existence it confronts; the Ideal reconstitutes Actuality in order to have an icon of Actuality; Actuality reconstitutes the data it has of the divine in order to have an icon of it; God reconstitutes goals constantly in order to get an icon of the Ideal.

Though cognition is God's proper way to grasp Existence in its concreteness, so that He can be said to know it in a way others do not and cannot, God can grasp Existence in less concrete ways as well; e.g., via Actuality, Ideality or Existence He can grasp it as the outcome of production, evaluation and reconstitution, respectively.

May 19

What does it mean to say that Existence or Ideality has cognitive, productive, etc., ways of being iconic with respect to other modes? (And in one case with respect to itself.) Does it mean for example that we can look at a work of art as a kind of epitomization of Existence and find in it something like mind, activity, etc.? But then what happens to art as an activity of an Actuality? Would we not have to say that there is a sense in which art, as the work of an Actuality, is an agency by which the Actuality grasps Existence, and that there is another sense in which art is taken by itself and analyzed? For example, it might be sensible to speak of a work of art as being iconographic with respect to the Ideal, that it entrains the emotions and thereby makes one iconographic with respect to God, that it forces a re-assessment of Actuality and perhaps the individual artist himself and thereby provides one with an icon of Actuality, and that finally it offers itself as a means for reconstituting Existence and thereby provides an icon of it. If this be the case, then we ought to speak of Ideality not in and of itself but as an Ideal or Good or goal already accepted, and analyze this as having the meaning of God within it, as being in a dynamic relation to itself (part-whole), as offering an evaluation of Existence, and as providing an icon of Actuality through a reconstitution of itself and perhaps of the Actuality.

If we go so far, then perhaps even God should be treated not as a being who is dealing with other modes, but as the God envisaged in religion. God would then have a structure which can be said to cognize Existence in the sense of giving it its essence, to produce Actuality in the sense of making it the locus of identities, of evaluating Himself in the sense of redefining the meaning of the parts of Himself, and of reconstituting Himself by re-adopting the Ideal in new ways. But this last now sounds like a duplication of what is said of God in the modes.

Is it the case that the God achieved in religion but duplicates the features of God as a mode, whereas in the case of the Ideal and Existence there is no being to engage in particular activities which could be identified as cognition or evaluation? Can we say that only the work of art has these features but that we can make an analogous formulation of Existence as that which the art epitomizes? The work of art, like the goals of ethical activity and perhaps like a sacrament, can be analyzed and made to function as loci of cognitive references, evaluations, etc.

By making art, ethics, and religion the representatives of the various modes (as well as agencies for the dynamic production of iconic forms of the modes) one can deal with them spectator-wise as having in themselves iconographic, directive and reconstitutive features (thereby enabling one to use them to understand the various modes). Art, e.g., would then have the status of an agency by means of which one moves beyond phenomena and substances to real Existence. As something produced it can be a representative of Existence but iconic of God. And it could be iconic of Actuality as something which serves as a principle of evaluation. As that which reconstitutes what it encounters, art is also iconic of Existence as such. In this way one avoids supposing that Existence itself is confronted with phenomenological objects and then substances.

May 25

There might be some sense in taking the story of Creation in the Bible, with its six days, as offering a paradigm of what happens when a man creates. God hovers over formless chaos; the artist faces an unmarked domain. The next step is to separate light and darkness, the background and the foreground, the luminous forefront and the dismissed material. Man stops when the work is completed; God rests to contemplate. There would have to be some fresh interpretations involved in connection with the creation of animals, etc. For this it is desirable to look at the text and proceed step by step using whatever clues the text incidentally provides.

Architecture is at once a business, a craft and an art. And it has in the case of classical buildings, a wall, a roof and a floor. The wall is something for the outside environment, something in itself, and something in relation to the inside wall; the inside wall is also three-fold. And what is true of the wall is true of the roof and of the floor. This means that there are six sides to consider for three dimensions, or eighteen altogether, and each of these can be dealt with from the position of a business, craft and art.

June 28

Modus Ponens actually says that 1] there is an internal relation between certain elements, and 2] that this tautologically tells what conditions must be met before something can be taken as an instance of the abstract condition. It should be written as:

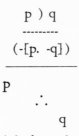

$$p \supset q$$
$$\overline{\hspace{2em}}$$
$$(-[p. -q])$$
$$\underline{\hspace{4em}}$$

$$p$$
$$\therefore$$
$$q$$

The ------- separates the principle from the categorial determination. The latter, (-[p. -q]), is something like the "rubber" in the idea of a balloon, for it is on the one side referential to something outside the mathematically formulatable "sphere" and on the other side it is formal, schematic. It does not tell us that the q can be held apart from the p; it tells us only that if we have p we cannot also have *non-q*.

A marriage is to be similarly understood:

$$\frac{x \text{ marries } y}{x \text{ and } y \text{ are of opposite sexes}}$$

$$\overline{\hspace{6em}}$$

x is a woman
therefore
y is a man

Modus Ponens bridges the mind and the body by providing a category for the body. The converse ought also to be true. It should be possible, given the nature of the world, to have categories for the mind—this is what Kant's transcendental deduction does. His categories are the categories which are bodily defined. To use them as categories in a logic it would be necessary to take a risk and separately work with them, apart from their tautologous definition as that which the body has demanded.

July 24

What was called art in the *Modes,* particularly in the last chapter, should be called Rhythmics, the study of Existence. Art and history are private and public ways of presenting Existence. Analogously mathematics is the study of the Ideal, which in turn is made subjectively and objectively available in ethics and politics.

October 19

In the negative section of the *Modes of Being,* the portions in italics which begin with "Otherwise" should have been transposed to the end of the negative discussion and have had "But then" substituted for "Otherwise." Thus *1.02* should have been presented as:

1.02. Some Actualities are active.

Against: In itself no Actuality is active; it is just what it is, and that is the end of the matter. Activity is the Actuality already beside itself—indeed already about to be transformed into an effect.

But then nothing would be produced.

Such a procedure would have made evident the difficulty with the negative position and how it must be corrected in order to become part of the system, i.e., be converted into *1.02.* The *Against* shows that in itself no Actuality is active. The "But then" goes on to say that since something is produced, it is not the case that this is the end of the matter. The "But then . . ." tells what is wrong with the negative argument; adding it to the negative argument in effect says that the negative argument is incomplete.

October 20

If an idea is true of an object, it would seem that we should be able to attend to the idea and ignore the object. Yet if an object has a career all its own, immersed in an Existence which our discourse or logic may not match, it would also seem that an idea does not give us all the information we need, since knowledge given by the idea will not then gear with the object. The two points are reconciled with the recognition that when we encounter the object we adumbrate it; our idea is an idea of it and is oriented towards it. We can ignore the object because we have the idea; we can then draw implications from the idea. But those implications will not necessarily be in accord with the career of the object. Knowing the idea then would not therefore give us a grasp of the object in its dynamic life, but only as it is at some position in that career, —usually that from which the idea was originally taken. We might find a logic which kept us in accord with the world, but we would know this only by stopping our implications and inferences at certain points and seeing if the outcome could be obtained also from the object in some way like that in which the idea was originally obtained.

In *3:30* in the *Modes of Being* three negations are contrasted with three rejections. They are not parallel; if we make them parallel we will need six negations answering to six rejections:

1] infectious negation $(-p)$ transforms; it is to be contrasted with infectious rejection $(-X)$ expressed by despising, disdaining, hesitation.

2] simple negation $-(p)$ which allows for double negation; it is to be contrasted with simple rejection $-(X)$ expressed by abandonment, absence.

3] relational negation pXq which stands between distinct terms; it is to be contrasted with relational rejection of oppositional tension, $X \sim Y$.

4] modifying negation $(!-p)$ which has degrees of dubeity; it is to be contrasted with modifying rejection $(!-X)$ which merely alters the being of a thing.

5] replacing negation $!-(p)$ which requires the substitution of another entity, and contrasts with replacing rejection $!-(X)$ which replaces a being by another.

6] oppositional negation $!(pXq)$ which demands that q be merely the rest of the field and contrasts with oppositional rejection $!(X \sim Y)$ which relates one item to whatever else exists in the world with it.

October 23

When it is said in *Modes of Being* and in *Nature and Man* that the self is immortal, no argument is offered, but only a reconstruction or interpretation of the nature of man. And even granted that this interpretation is as good as an argument, it is the case that it is an argument for only one case.

Is not one of the faults with the traditional arguments for the existence of God that the arguments are unsustained by other arguments or by a direct encounter? Putting aside the matter of a direct encounter —which is justifiable if it is also justifiable to put aside encounters in connection with historical facts, sub-atomic entities and astronomical beings beyond the reach of our telescopes—it would seem that it is not correct to say, as some theologians and logicians sometimes do, that if you have one good argument, you don't need the others.

The best argument is never good enough; even if logically impeccable we need to have other arguments. Does this mean that each inference partially precipitates a reality beyond itself, and that until we get a number of inferences converging on the same formal result we do not reach the objective reality which exists outside the inferences? Taken in this way each inference would keep us in the area of the formal, but when supported by others it would allow us to touch, through the precipitation of its possessed conclusion, the reality of what lies outside it. Does this mean that the objective past is known by a set of converging inferences, so that in effect it is either A] constituted by the convergence of those inferences, or B] that we are enabled by that convergence to reach the past that exists outside the range of the inferences themselves? If we take alternative B we suppose that there is a past to be known, and that this is the way to know it; we make contact with the external past through the use of self-precipitating and mutually supportively precipitating inferences. If we take alternative A we need make no supposition about the reality of the past and can make it be by virtue of the conjunction of supportive precipitating inferences. The existence of God on such a view would be dependent on the capacity to produce supporting arguments for Him. The view has the difficulty of supposing that a being ceases to exist when not argued for; it has the advantage of not supposing the reality of that to which we infer. All of us seem to reject the former alternative in connection with God and soul, since we believe they do or do not exist, regardless of our knowledge; we seem ready to accept it though in connection with the past. Is this because we think that the past has no power, whereas a God or soul is supposed to be endowed with power and therefore cannot be the outcome of a precipitation of converging inferences?

Or should we say that we always can precipitate an object through convergent inferences, but that this object cannot be known to have a power until it actually acts on us? Since we neither expect nor need power from the past we can be content with it as a precipitated product, but since we both expect and perhaps need power in God and soul we demand that the precipitating inferences be sustained by a genuine encounter. There are those who think they can experience the departed past; a few also think they can encounter it.

Only for those who encounter God, soul, past, etc., are they not only termini of inferences but beings with powers. It is not the case that one who already knows God needs no proof and he who has a proof need not "know" Him; a proof is needed to enable one to know Him as a being with power, as more than what is encountered.

October 26

There are four ways of determining whether a conclusion terminates in or reports a matter of fact:

1] Do consequences flow which enable us to take them as extra implications? If so we have the kind of proof appropriate to Existence (and in a subordinate way to the discipline of rhythmics, the subjective experience of ethics, the objective of creeds, and the strand of perception).

2] Is the conclusion the product of a convergence of many inferences? If so we have the kind of proof appropriate to Actuality (and in a subordinate way to the discipline of philosophy, the subjective experience of religion, the objective experience of history and the strand of importance).

3] Is the conclusion something encountered? If so we have the kind of proof appropriate to God (and in a subordinate way to the discipline of theology, the subjective categories, public politics and the strand of events).

4] Is the conclusion self-sufficient and completing? If so we have the kind of proof appropriate to the Ideal (and in a subordinate way to the discipline of mathematics, the subjective experience of art, public action and the strand of science).

The subordinate ways show what is good for some other mode. Thus science is self-sufficient as a strand only as illuminating the nature of God; events are to be encountered only as strands of Existence; a philosophy which is the result of the convergence of many influences illuminates Actuality only.

Strictly speaking every basic discipline—mathematics, philosophy, theology, rhythmics, and particularly each experiential version of it— ethics, categories, religion and art; politics, action, creed and history— has four tests. Thus art must be self-sufficient as a kind of surrogate of God, for the Ideal be something beautiful, be unique for Actuality, and be insistent for Existence. We ought also to speak of art as having extra implications in Existence for man in society, as being the convergent object of judgments of it as an Actuality, and as something which must be encountered so as to have the unitary value which a God has.

Science is a self-sufficient strand, iconic of God; mathematics is a self-sufficient strategy of the modes, iconic of the Ideal; and public action is a publicly determined self-sufficient strand which is iconic of Actuality. By knowing science as rational we know what God's mind is like; by knowing mathematic's consistency we know what the Ideal is like; by knowing what public action's insistent uniqueness is like we get an icon of Actuality. Art is the only way we have, through the use of a subjectively enjoyed and produced experience and action, of getting an icon; this icon is of Existence.

Science is an iconic strand, i.e., it is abstract. Mathematics is an iconic mode of reaching to a being, i.e., it is strategic and cosmic. Action is a publicly oriented way of dealing with experience; it is iconic of Actuality.

To know what God's rationality is like we must accept science; to know what the Ideal is like we must concentrate on mathematics; to know what Actuality is like we must enjoy a publicly oriented action. We can know God more intimately of course than through science, but then we do not do it iconically. Importance, the strand analogous to that of science, does not give one an icon of God, but only of Actuality as something at which we terminate by convergent approaches.

October 27

One can distinguish four types of truth—*truth by coherence*, appropriate to any discourse about the Ideal, and which thereby makes it iconic of that Ideal. Ethics has this character in relation to the Good. This Good is the Ideal caught in our subjectivized frame. For this Good to function as a true icon it must incorporate the elements of uniqueness (to be known through a social convergence of references to it), an element of self-sufficient unity, and an insistence reflecting its power— i.e., it must eventually be approved by all, be found to be enough, and to be imperative.

2] Another type is that of *social convergence* which is appropriate to any discourse about the Actual in its individuality. The philosophic category has just this iconic function of expressing the nature of Actuality in a subjectivized form. That category must be internally coherent and thereby be recognizable as complete; be self-sufficient and encountered (imposed on us from the outside as resident in some other Actuality or ultimate mode of being); and insistent in the sense that it is productive of results which nothing within its orbit can explain.

3] A third type is that of *correspondence*. Truth here is appropriate to discourses about God whom we expect to encounter us, as well as to be proved by us. The discourse is essentially religious. Such religious discourse is iconic of God in the sense that it is not merely spoken to Him but listened to by Him. It is complete as encompassing the world so far as this can be made coherent. It is the topic of a convergence in the social world, a convergence exhibited in the harmonization of mankind in the light of it. And it has an insistence, makes demands which actually bring about results no thought could have envisaged.

4] Finally there is the *truth of art* which is the *vindicatable* insistence of the texture of Existence. Such art is offered as complete because coherent in its own terms; it is unique and therefore to be approached by the convergent appreciations of mankind, and has a self-sufficiency which can be known only by being encountered.

The four types of truth—coherence, convergence, correspondence and vindicational—are characteristic not only of the subjectivized form of discourse with respect to some mode of being, but of A] the publicized form of the discourse, B] the strands abstractable from common sense, and C] the basic strategy of knowing a mode.

A] The objective counterpart of art is history; history though is not iconic of Existence. As its need to be confirmed through convergence indicates, it is iconic of Actuality. This does not mean that it intends to report Actuality, but only that it offers a unique account of Existence, thereby reflecting the pressure of Actuality on Existence. Similarly, politics, which is the correlate of ethics (itself iconic of the Ideal), is iconic of Existence and is to be tested through the vindication of its policies; creeds, which are the correlate of religion, are iconic of the Ideal and are to be tested by their completeness for a life which is coherent; and action, which is correlate to categories, is iconic of God and is to be tested by the fact that something is produced which encounters us as worthy of that action.

B] The strands have only one feature; they are iconic only as signs. Perception, though a strand relating to Actuality, is iconic of the Ideal, for its meanings are consistent. Events, which relate to Existence, are in fact iconic of God in the sense that they must be encountered in order to be had; Importance, though relating to the Ideal, is iconic of Actuality in the sense that its objective value depends on the convergence of all to it. Science, though relating to the eternal truth which is God's, is in fact iconic of Existence in the sense that it is vindicatable through its consequences.

C] The disciplines of theology, mathematics, philosophy and rhythmics are primarily biased towards God, Ideality, Actuality, and Existence. But they are iconic of different things, by virtue of their procedures. Theology is iconic of Actuality, mathematics of God, philosophy of Existence and rhythmics of the Ideal. Theology proceeds by virtue of its involvement of the individual; mathematics proceeds as though it were true forever; philosophy proceeds as though its meanings will govern and ground all others and are not to be deduced from any; rhythmics proceeds by attempting to provide a harmonious account of whatever there be, an abstract version of what in fact occurs.

	Existence	1	*God*	2	*Actuality*	3	*Ideal*	4
subjectivized	Art	1	Religion	2	Categories	3	Ethics	4
objectivized	History:	3	Creeds:	4	Action:	2	Politics:	1
	convergence		completeness		self-sufficiency		consequences	
strands	Events	2	Science	1	Perception	4	Importance	3
strategy	Rhythmics	4	Theology	3	Philosophy	1	Mathematics	2

Under each heading, the four items are respectively the subjectivized and the objectivized modes of experiencing the item at the top of the list, the third item is the strand, and the fourth the basic strategy. The numbers attached show of what they are iconic.

October 28

In 3.26 of the *Modes of Being* there is an attempt to express ways of vindicating our knowledge of three of the modes. It would have been better if some indication had been given that each mode is to be properly approached from different angles, and that these approaches have each their own tests of truth. Thus we want God to be encountered as well as proved—we need a correspondence theory of truth with respect to Him. With respect to the Ideal we want a coherent theory of truth; we want a self-consistent, internally harmonious account which reflects the very nature of that Ideal. In connection with Actuality we want to make use of a convergent method, the method of bringing together a plurality of data—of which a subject-predicate assertion is but a limited illustration—to converge on it as the final topic. Each of these methods is pursued by a proper basic discipline, but it is to be noted that each of these disciplines is iconic in its practice, not of its proper topic but of some other. Thus philosophy's practice rests on and is iconic of Existence, Theology's of Actuality, rhythmics of the Ideal, and mathematics of God.

The comments at the end of yesterday's notes indicate that subjectivized forms of the modes, objectified forms, strands and basic disciplines are all iconic in different ways and of different things. The subjectivized forms all capture in their own ways something of the texture and rhythm of the modes, the former in the product, the latter in the production. Art is iconic of Existence, religion of God, the categories of Actuality, and ethics of the Ideal. The objectivized relevant forms of the modes in history, creeds, actions, and politics are iconic in the sense that their characteristic concerns are with objects in the realm of Existence, God, Actuality and Ideals. History (though occupied with Existence) converges on its results; creeds (though concerned with God) offer themselves as a complete ideal scheme; action (though directed from and at actualities) claims the self-sufficiency of the divine, and politics (though an expression of the Ideal) is tested by its consequences and thus shows itself to be iconic of the dynamics of Existence.

The strands of events, science, perception, and importance are abstracts from what is primarily Existence, God, Actuality or Ideal. But they are iconic of something else; they seek in their own ways to answer to a quite distinct mode. Thus events try to keep apace with the internal rationale of God and come to an end at pivotal points in His being—or claim to; science goes its own way but tries to have beginning and ending coincide with what is occurring in Existence; perception in the end seeks to have its content conform to the Ideal demands of knowledge; the strand of importance seeks to coincide with central and pivotal aspects of the Actual.

When we come to the basic ways of dealing with the modes— rhythmics, theology, philosophy, and mathematics we find that the ground on which they rest is iconic of the Ideal, Actuality, Existence and God respectively. Thus theology reflects an actual individual, philosophy the tension and dynamics of Existence, mathematics and pristine eternity in a man answering to the nature of God, and rhythmics to the rationale of things having its counterpart in the Ideal.

If we wanted to make a single set dealing with Experience in an iconic way we would have to use art to provide a texture and a procedure which answer to Existence, would engage in politics to have a discipline whose test is consequences, would engage in science in order to have a strand which met Existence at terminal points and thus was iconic of it over the course of time, and would deal with experience philosophically in order to find in ourselves that aspect of our being which had the same contours that Existence itself had.

November 2

In *Our Public Life* it would have been possible (and perhaps desirable) to ask what the nature of the public life was from the perspective of God, Existence and actual individuals. God should have been shown to be involved in a theocratic state and in such an institution as a church. Existence should have been shown to provide the energy, the historic routes, and the creative promise of the political order. And actual individuals, though discussed in the beginning of the book, should have been viewed as providing the imagination and initiative of the public organization.

Instead of just contrasting art and ethics with the work of the public, one ought to have some discussion of the impingement of one on the other. Is there an historic, an ethical, a religious, an aesthetic approach to politics, perhaps dealing with sides which other thinkers in politics do not deal with? What are the presuppositions of a politics?

There are philosophers who occupy themselves with the discourse of ethics, politics, religion. But for the most part the philosopher concerns himself with the phenomena themselves. In the case of history, what looms large is the question of the relation of the historic writing to the historic phenomena, rather than a concern for the phenomena themselves. Also there is a persistent tendency in men to look for a meaning in history. They feel they can see the mark of God more clearly there than they can in the life of a man, in the work of an artist, in the structure of a state. Why is this? Is it because history offers a long run? Is it because we all discern the force of Existence behind the historic phenomena? Is it because it deals with the mass of mankind and thus is worthy of a perspective which is more embracing than that needed in politics or ethics?

Can we learn more from the philosophy of history than we can learn from historians? Are there other clues or avenues, other information which they cannot or will not use? Is the philosopher of history able to see the import of history in a way the historian cannot, because the philosopher is able to look at the historic process in the light of other modes of being which are effective in history? But why should we not be able to say the same thing regarding any other branch of study?

Why is it that there is such a strong temptation to give another account alongside the historian's? We look at the accounts of political activity, of moral behavior, etc., as raw data, and everyone seems to deal with these in the light of the nature of man and the meaning of organizations. But in the case of history there does not seem to be a use of the historical material as data. We look at history as something exposed by the historian; we take him to present us with material which we, from a new point of view, take to tell a story the historian does not discern.

November 4

Do works of art stand to a personalized form of Existence as the writings of historians do to the objectified manifestation of Existence which we call history? Do category or action have a similar status for Actuality; do ethics and politics have a similar one for the Ideal? Do we learn from these "discourses" how to understand Existence, Actuality and Ideal respectively? (Analogously, lived religious experience and the churches or creeds would be "discourses" regarding God.)

If this hypothesis be accepted—in contrast with yesterday's—then the philosopher (to judge from my previous works) is concerned with what those discourses do, and eventually with what light they throw on some realm of being. Should one then begin with a study of historiography and see how this in fact illuminates the nature of lived history (history being Existence itself in an available form)? What of such problems as the nature and being of the past, the reality of potentialities, the nature of the future, the influence of God? Are these analogous to possible divisions in the Ideal, the objective status of the Ideal, the operation of the Ideal; to the inward being of man, the expression of his nature, the being and locus of the categories, the reality and dimensions of action?

Is it possible to learn about the subjectivized experienced form of Existence in some other way than through art? Might not one take Existence as having pertinence to man and learn what it was like by attending to God, the Ideal or the nature of Man; by asking what it meant for Existence to get involved with man? These would seem to be questions analogous to those raised by history, for history seems to be a topic which is faced by the religious, the ethical, etc. Is it that we do not particularly care to know about the experience and what it imports (being more concerned with art as a basic means of communicating this), whereas in the case of history we feel that the experience is objective and that the data are to be read off? Is it the case that historical writing has no particular pattern or creative nature which allows one to grasp objective history from it, so that the objectified form of Existence seems to be a valuable thing to concentrate on? Is it that in religion we have the analogue of historiography in the sense that it is the experience rather than the creative use of it that seems to be the central idea? In connection with categories and action do we prefer the use of the subjective meaning of man to the experiencing, and the objective occurrence of the experience of action to the being of the Actuality, to and from which the action occurs?

November 7

On p. 201 of *Modes of Being* it should be said that Existence has an "existential" import without in any way denying that God, Actualities, the Ideal (and the Good) all offer peculiar predicates of an analogous sort. The Actuality betrays its existence through its contemporaneity (which perhaps should also be said to have consequences beyond conceptualization, even though this conceptualization is due to the Ideal). Actuality must betray the presence of the Ideal, and thus of the Good in it. This Ideal or Good will not be a "natural" predicate, but a prescriptive one realized, and will be known to be present by virtue of it obligating, by our continued concern for it, by being productive of satisfaction. The presence of God in Actuality is seen in the sacramental object.

November 15

Neal Klausner of Grinnell asked me whether or not there was not a stress on Fourthness or the number four in the *Modes*. There surely is such a stress. Of all the numbers in the universe of numbers, the number four is the number of the modes of Being. This gives it a particular status. But this is nothing other than to say that when we deal with all four modes of being from the standpoint of the Ideal, or its mathematical expression, that Ideal has the shape of the number four, just as when we deal with the cosmos from a philosophical point of view we make use of the Category as the epitomization of Actuality. Every mode of being, when it functions as the one (a one which is encompassing so far as it is known to be biased and to get the other modes under a restriction or abstraction) realizes itself in some special guise. We have Fourthness for the Ideal, and Category for Actuality; analogously for Existence and God we have Extensionality and Identity.

A similar problem arises when we make reference to a full life as one which involves the adjustment of the ethical life (the taking of a moral holiday) to the aesthetic, religious, etc. Here we view the four modes of being in humanized terms. The ethical life has to do with man in relation to the Ideal; the full life has to do with the Ideal as having a bearing on all the other modes. That is, the Ideal may be viewed as facing man and that is all, or as facing man but functioning as the One for the other modes at the same time. When man deals with the Ideal, and this has the role of a One for all the modes, it presents us with the Ideal of a full life; this Ideal is larger than the Ideal or Good faced by ethics.

The Ideal of the full life is offered to man. He must then be one who is completed not only by the Ideal, not only by the other modes in addition to the Ideal, but also by the other modes as approached via the Ideal. The Ideal must therefore not only be shown to be pertinent to man when he is taken by himself, but to be the Ideal for man as that which is to be completed by other modes. It must face him as a being who needs the other modes; it must be an Ideal which recognizes those other modes to be elements which would complete him. He, as a being who seeks to be complete, must adopt the other modes under the aegis of the Ideal which says that their possession will give him a full life.

A man can also try to possess three modes under the aegis of a fourth; thus under the aegis of the divine he can try to perfect himself by adopting those other modes. This will give him a completion but not a full life. If a man then were to achieve a full life, he would still be incomplete in the sense that he will have subordinated his effort to become complete through his attention say to the prescriptive demands of the theological. His fulfillment would be alternative to another type which yielded the same result by a different route.

The man who brought three modes within the compass of his being under the aegis of some fourth would be as full as a man could be, no matter which one was chosen as the fourth. But no man can persist in the pursuit of the full life or any other type. He must try one or the other until he finds once again that he is losing value (as he did when he pursued ethics or art, etc., and therefore saw that they had to give way to the Ideal of the full life), when he must take still another Ideal and make it good in still another way. The outcome is not determinable in advance; we must find a practical solution of the problem of being unable to do full justice to the mastery of all four modes from one perspective. The man who has pushed himself as far as possible in the pursuit of the full life and who then does the same for the religious, etc., is one who lives up to no prescription fully but finds a way to adjust himself to his incapacity to live up to the prescription. He is like one who instead of turning to the Ideal of a full life when he abandons the ethical, gives himself say to the artistic, and tries to change the centre of his gravity so as to retain in his being what he had of the ethical while pursuing the artistic in independence of this. His life will be complete sequentially, but not at any one time.

When one has made the ethical be, and has produced something in the realm of the arts, one does not affect the world beyond which is being realized or portrayed, except in the sense that by the realization or creation one has implicated the world and thus given it new import. But does this not mean that the four modes, when understood, must be involved in man's career and therefore be increased in meaning and perhaps in some sense in number? I think it does not mean this. The consideration of the four modes is always under the aegis of Actuality; the abstractive nature that the modes have from the perspective of Actuality means that they will have consequences which they otherwise would not have.

Are the modes in and of themselves affected by the fact that their abstractions are involved in man's career? Not in any other sense than that of making a difference to man. All the modes affect one another; to deal with them under an abstraction, to possess them through mind, etc., makes it easier, by an indirect route, for them to make their presence felt. Accordingly, it does make a difference to the modes to be known, but this difference does not add to their being but only to their efficacy, to the success of their persistent effort to master and penetrate the other modes, an effort which is in the end withstood by the counter efforts of the others.

No one is satisfied with arguments about the immortality of the soul, God's being, or the external world (or the existence of the past) unless he can somehow encounter these. But the encounter cannot be thought of properly as an encounter in *propria persona,* but only via what he now in fact can encounter. God must make himself evident through the individual in eternal love, through Existence as objectivity, through Ideality as providence and through Himself as meaning. The external world must manifest itself through the Ideal as implications, through Actuality as energy, through God as action and through itself as experience. The encounter of the immortal soul through the Ideal is the evaluations which are expressed by the self; through Existence as radical division or uniqueness; it manifests itself through God as His changing purpose; and through present Actuality as the category of unity or identity. The self is simply in me, but manifests the other modes so far as it is identical, divides the world, evaluates, and has a personal concern.

The immortal soul is now making my identity, the Good is now making my evaluation, God is making Himself manifest as my loving, and Existence is had as that which is external but mine. By virtue of my identity, evaluating, loving and possessing I am encountering the immortality which is lurking beneath me, and at which my inferences regarding immortality terminate.

The Ideal is now encountered as the directionality inside Existence, as the value of God, as myself as guilty, and is felt in itself as prescriptive. This encounter finds the Ideal in the different modes; as in me it is only myself as guilty, just as God is in me as judge and Existence is there as energy. The encounter of say the Ideal in me is different from the encounter of myself as immortal via the Ideal. What is this difference? The immortality of self through the Ideal is an encounter of the self only by looking at the Ideal; the encounter of the Ideal in me is myself acting with the Ideal in the background of my being, producing my guiltiness. We can speak of the past as being manifested through me directly (through the Ideal say, as its change in prospect) and indirectly through me by virtue of my adoption of the changed Ideal, and thus as my changing morality.

November 16

Not only "Existence," but the Good, the sacramental, the rational, and the substantial are "non-natural" predicates, predicates unlike those which relate to particular qualities of things. The total set of "non-natural" predicates, or more properly transcendentals, should be defined, not as Aristotle did, as ideas which transcend all his categories (for this would make them substantial, not transcendental) but in terms either of ideas which characterize whole areas or beings, or in terms of what is demanded by the modes. Each of the transcendentals tells us about some power in an entity. The Good when predicated of an object, for example, tells us that that object will be a continual source of satisfaction, that its parts are harmonized beyond that which is usual, that it can serve as a model for others, etc.

If art reveals the nature of Existence, its texture, and dynamics, must not history, as a writing, reveal something of the nature of Existence as it once was, i.e., as vital? This writing, because it starts from the recesses of our being, invokes a unity, an end and the power of Existence to manifest itself everywhere; in effect it brings out the efficacy of the past, exhibits it as the power behind our present activities.

There would seem to be four types of truth—correspondence which is appropriate to the divine as the permanent and supreme, in terms of which the fittingness of others are to be estimated; coherence which characterizes the Ideal's parts as integral elements in it; vindication which deals with Existence's perpetual power to produce new consequences beyond the envisagement of conceptualization; and convergence which is characteristic of a knowledge of the inexhaustible Actualities in this world. However, there is no enterprise which does not take account of all the types of truth. As was remarked before, we are never content with convergence alone; but also we are never content with correspondence, vindication or coherence alone. Not only do we want our accounts to be coherent, not only do we want to be confronted with objects (and thus to be vindicated), but we also want to have our ideas match the real as correspondence demands. Still one of these modes of truth is more germane to a given enterprise and its appropriate mode than is some other mode of truth.

November 18

For Croce there are only documents and the present reconstruction of them (which for him is history). The documents serve to verify the construction, the history serves to give unity and meaning to the documents. This view has the strength of not supposing that there is a dead past of entities to which we can move, or what is worse, which never can be reached by us. Nevertheless there is something odd in the view that history is the narrative and that this narrative is constantly being remade in the present of an historian's thinking. One ought to reconcile the view with a realism.

If it be recognized that we want an encounter as well as a convergent set of inferences, we can provide this by recognizing that the surface (not as was earlier suggested, the depth) of an individual bears the marks of a difference which has been produced by the past and which therefore sluices the expressions of the individual's vital unity in a new way. Or more completely: the various objects in the present are all what they are; we recognize some to be provocative by virtue of the way they stand out against the rest. We thereupon treat them as incomplete, not in and of themselves, for as such they are as complete as any other items, but as needing to be related to, unified with, other items in the present. We see, in other words, a number of items that belong together and we converge on a unity for them as that which is their causal ground. But the unity which they had was the unity of some central actor or actors, some human agency. We in our narration today offer ourselves as that unity. And we can do this A] by functioning as representatives of the past unity, and B] by expressing our unity in the differential form required by the difference which we now exhibit in relation to some one who had lived in the past.

We make articulate the distinction between what we are now and what we might have been. This distinction we do not know; we make it evident in the act of providing a unity for scattered data. We thus discover how we differ from, let us say Caesar, by providing the meaning of Caesar as the unity of the present data. In providing that unity we do not give all of ourselves, nor do we express ourselves as here and now, but we in fact sheer off a portion of ourselves as here and now as the element we had acquired from the past. Caesar as constructed by us marks the difference between what we are on our own and what had been contributed to us. The unity that we provide is thus a revelation of ourselves as well as a vitalization of a plurality of items.

The items which we confront were not only united by some major actor; they are manifestations of a power of Existence as is that actor too. The data which we confront must then be made to converge on a single area where Existence made itself manifest. Since we cannot get to that area directly we must take account of the different channels through which present Existence can be manifest. The differential expression of Existence today is due to the effect which the past has had on the realms and areas in which Existence makes itself manifest. We get to learn the nature of the power or majesty or import of history when we take account of the fact that Existence manifests itself differently from the way it otherwise would; the difference is expressed by the power which Existence once exhibited.

A similar thing must be said with respect to the Ideal. The purposes which confront the world today are different because there had been certain things realized in the past. We come to see the past to the degree that we come to recognize the change which the realm of possibility has undergone. Our discovery of the change is one with the provision of a meaning or significance for the past occurrence, a meaning which we provide as the outcome of a convergence on the past event as that which makes a difference to the future.

Similarly we must say that the objectivity of history is assured by God. He now preserves the past in Himself, and we discover what this past is when we see what different moves He makes in the course of history. Conversely, we discover the alteration in God's evaluations when we discover the kind of unity which is needed by the converging inferences in order to guarantee that there will be a final terminus which has to be compared with all other termini or occurrences in the history of the entire universe.

The Crocean insight thus must be extended to other modes, and we must recognize that the historical account we provide is one which explains and is explained by a differential feature in ourselves, Ideals, Existence and God. We insist that the past is real and objective and more than what is to be found in the documents, for we assert that we, in making an historical narrative, but make use, in a representative way, of a difference in ourselves (and in other modes). That which makes for the difference is the encounterable aspect of the past.

November 28

Every basic reality should be encounterable, and should be encounterable in all the modes. There should be a way of encountering God, another way of encountering Ideality, a third way of encountering Existence. There should be a way of encountering all in the Ideal, and so on. When then one encounters the past (since this is one phase of Existence), we should find in it the Actual, Ideality, God, making for its uniqueness, purpose, objectivity.

Should we also say that the other phases of Existence—the present and the future—are encountered in other phases? The future surely has a role in the present, and is to be found operative in God, on the present environment, in the Ideal itself, and in Actuality.

What of the present? Is this not encountered directly? Do we need to find a ground for it in other modes or other phases of Existence? There is justification for finding a ground for it in other modes, e.g., its otherness requires God. But is it also in the past? If so the meaning of the past is affected by the nature of the present as incipient; the present will then change the import of the past by the new relations it gives that past by being later than it. The present can also be said to be in the future as differentiating the kind of possibilities which will be pertinent.

December 4

We can reconcile the realm of perception with science in two ways. One will involve a reification of the strand of events, the other of importance, and each of these will proceed in one of four ways. We can reconcile the realms of perception and science in the existential, eventful enterprises of art, history, ethics or politics. And we can reconcile them in the important, divinized enterprises of religion, church, virtue and objective reality. In each of these cases there will have to be an assumption of the position of Actuality or the divine, the Ideal or the Existential. (Ethics e.g., relates to the idealized form of an existential reconciliation of perception and science; religion relates to an actualized form of a divinized reconciliation.)

But what is the object which is both perceived and understood? It is what their reconciliations reveal. It is a valuational one, or a public one, etc., with political import. As a rule when one asks after the object, one is asking after it as having an historical role over the course of Existence, and a role in civilization or a community of knowers, from the perspective of the divine. The historical reconciliation says that the vivification of the events (and then as dealt with from the position of the divine), gives us the proper meaning of things. This brings us close to Whitehead, where the event is at the root of both the formal and the perceptual. But the event must be understood as dynamically interrelating the components, not only from the standpoint of eternity, but inside a substantial reality.

Whitehead made the events exhaust the being of the reconciliation (which is right), but forgot that there ought to be a reconciler, who is more than the activity. He over-historicized the world by making the basic reality a sequence of events. This would be correct were there no corrective to the historical. The artist is not an event; nor is an ethical being, nor is a political animal. The event, in short, is an abstraction.

The basic reconciliation cannot be by an event but only by an eventful being, by one who lives through history. But to live through history is to reach out into the future, to maintain oneself over against Existence, to possess one's features and nature in a unique manner, and to be part of an ultimate objective realm. The event is a medium on the same level with the perception and the formal domain; the reconciliation requires that the event be used by beings who constitute a genuine domain of relevant beings in a temporal sequence. It is not one event but the whole of history which is the reconciliation.

We can still ask, what is the real object? Does it not have a being now? It does, but only as that which is to be understood as concretely extending backwards and forwards with a tensional hold on both directions. Its substantial being is the historical way in which it reconciles the two. Whitehead got the solution into one moment, but it is not a solution at one moment—or if one likes, the moment of the historic entity covers many presents. The two sides are now not reconciled except by a being whose nature is seen to extend beyond them both.

If we tried to locate the being where the two reconciled components severally are we would be up against the fact that they do not have a common "where," and also we would have to reduce the being to an event of reconciliation. The perceived star and the scientific star are united in an historic star which has a time stretch longer than the former and shorter than the latter—if it makes sense to speak of longer and shorter when the units are so disparate. (And though this is not essential and perhaps misleading if we think of history as human history, the real star is a humanly significant star which has been abstractly dealt with in perception and the science of astronomy.)

If one takes an aesthetic rather than an historic approach to the problem we confront ourselves with the star as created by an artist. This is as good an answer as the historical but it is not what is usually wanted.

There is also the other solution to be considered—that of reconciling them by a reification of the strand of importance. Here we have a choice between the objective meaning of God in civilization and the private meaning of the object in the body of ourselves. Men prefer private meanings to the divinely determined one. The star is then viewed as that which makes a difference to ourselves, as an existentialist might say. This star is a real star subtending the perceptual and scientific stars. Such a star, an expression or aspect of ourselves as having a private nature or character, gives us the star in a non-objective sense. If a more objective sense is desired, it would be the meaning of the star as caught in a fixed realm of objectivity, and thus the star from the standpoint of Divine omniscience.

The two plausible answers are the historical and the objective. The one requires a temporal run and leaves us to view history as somehow presupposing the elements to be reconciled—unless we can turn the matter upside down, and starting with history see the two components as abstractions from it, and diverse because so abstracted. The same thing should be said about the objectivity. Since the latter presupposes a knowledge of God, it would be better to take the historical answer. The final answer then is that there is a historical being; this permits of two types of abstraction (and an intermediate set, of commonsense objects and events) which must be thought of as analytic components of it. The historical being is a substance having an essence and existence, a form and a matter, a conceptual and a perceptual side, and these two sides, when freed from one another, give us the domains of science and perception, which can be reconciled only by being rooted in it once again.

December 5

We can substantialize the strands of the scientific and perceptual data (and also the strands of the event and importance) in a kind of Platonic intelligible scientifically tempered substantiality; we can do it in an existentialistic individual; we can do it through an orthodox divine objectivity of truth; and we can do it in the shape of an actual historical reality. In all cases the other items must be sustained and explained. The scientifically tempered substantiality would be unlike the scientific formal domain, though this will get the texture of the former. It will have the power of generating the formal and the perceptual (and the other strands). And similarly for the others.

Is there not some preferential mode? Ought we not in the end take them all together, so that we get, e.g., an individualistic-historical pair which is prescriptively and descriptively united by the substantiality of an intelligible world and the objectivity of the divine? What then would the real star, e.g., be? Would it not be an historical star having pertinence to the individual, the two being united by an effective intelligibility and a final objectivity? Such a reconciliation involves the use of an entire realm of intelligibility and objectivity. But this perhaps is not available to us now.

December 7

Not only does the discussion in the *Modes* use "civilization" for what I think is more properly termed Culture, or fragments of civilization as in *Our Public Life,* but it takes for granted the position of the physical world as being the area where the true units of time are to be found. But strictly speaking, the historic occurrence is that which provides the unit for Existence, when this is viewed in and of itself. This is to say that the realm of Existence breaks up into peaks and valleys in history. The divisions which are made in Existence due to the operation of the other modes of being, as discussed in the beginning of chapter three in the *Modes,* are the units of its time, and not the units of history.

The units of history are forged by the way in which the units of time are solidified through the workings out of Existence in and through individuals. If now we look at the historic unit from the perspective of the Ideal we get the smaller but more formal units of science. If we do it from the perspective of the Actual, we get the units of perception (these are longer than those of science but less formal). If we do it from the perspective of God we get much longer units in which the historic is caught. We can move over to the Ideal itself and get units which are larger than those of science; when we do we stand outside the historic domain altogether.

Better said: The historic occurrences are the basic units of Existence; these yield such strands as the scientific, perceptual, important, and the eventful, each with its own characteristic spans. Each of these in addition yields a way of dealing with the historic occurrences from the perspective of a mode of being.

The intelligibility, the individuality, the objective value and the adequacy of the historic world can be questioned from the position of the modes. This means in effect that we cannot say that actually there were two actions making up the historic occurrence of, say, an assassination; there is only the historic occurrence in a single unit of historic time. The attempt to deal with the subordinate actions, as occurring in successive moments of real time, is the result of taking those actions out of their context and then dealing with them as evaluated solely from the position of an Ideal as measuring the intelligibility and formal meaning of the historic occurrence.

None of the above is really satisfactory. It is the case that one first picks up a gun, and then shoots. This sequence is a sequence in time. The act as a murder is a unitary occurrence. Does this mean that we must recur to the position of the *Modes* and hold that the atomic unit is the physical, with the historical as that which is carried by the other modes? If we do this, must we not then deny that the historical can be locus of a reconciliation of the scientific, perceptual, and important strands; must it not be said that it could be such a reconciliation only if it be understood that Existence is now transmuted by being carried by the other modes of Being? The reconciliation would have to be in the common-sense object as temporal and spatial, etc. When this object is transmuted into Existence itself, as qualified by other modes, we get history. But what subject then would reveal the texture of Existence? Or must we not distinguish history from historiography and take the latter to reveal the structure of history, and then Existence, and this through a creativity which makes history the locus of mankind? In other words, can we not get history to be revelatory of Existence if we make it be the history of mankind, and this through the agency of historiography?

I think then it is better to go back to a position near the *Modes* and affirm that it is the Ideal which gives the measure of time for the realm of Existence. Historical occurrences refer to that Ideal, and consequently their units are defined by the Ideal. But taking the activities of things in their own terms, and thus viewing them as divided into units of becoming, we get the subordinate realities of atomic physical reality, punctuated by God. Different levels of history, and also perhaps different levels of things, will depend on the way in which they penetrate to the depths of the Ideal or are held by the depths of God. There will be another punctuation provided by the perceptual common-sense world as sustained by the Actual. But what is the actual unit, the reconciled occurrence in Existence? This should be the event substantialized. Are these others— history, science and common-sense—abstractions from this? If so, in what sense is history a revelation of Existence, parallel to art? Is it that it is such a revelation once one grants the essential role of the Ideal? But then the scientific and the common sense sequence should be equally so, granted their orientation in God and Actuality. Or is it that we need the creativity of history to burst the bonds, to make it possible for us to use the Ideal as a starting point, to enable us, at least as historians, to get a revelation of Existence? Does the Ideal in its depths give us a basis for judging history as oriented towards the Ideal (and similarly for God and Actuality)? Do art and history serve as correlatives which together make it possible to have the perceptual and scientific together? (If one of these is substantial, the other will have to be prescriptive.)

Is it not the case that if art and history offer unities for the other two strands this fact makes them revelatory of Existence? But if this is so, why should it not also be the case that common-sense objects and mathematical objects can serve as unities reconciling events and individuals? In such a case the common-sense objects and mathematical objects would also be revelatory of Existence. We would then have as a choice a pre-scriptive-descriptive unit given by history and art, and another given by common sense and mathematics. History (and art in a different way) would give the relevance of the atomic natural occurrences to one another so as to make them add up to the common-sense reality. This history nevertheless has a unit range. Since its being consists in the act of reconciliation, it offers a double measure of time, allowing one to get, e.g., both the abstraction "killing" and the abstraction "I pick up a gun and then shoot."

History can be said to be the basic reality (as sustained by art) and to require the double fact of a single unit act, such as killing, and the sequential acts of picking up the gun and then shooting. It holds on to the earlier act and relates it to the later. This relating preserves the passing time to make it operative now, so that one cannot truly say that the earlier act is over. The picking up of the gun which is related to the next act as ground and possibility is carried over into that next act. Still it is the case that we first have one and then the other. But if we had only this we would have no killing. The killing requires the carrying over, the refusal to allow the separate moments to be replacements of one another.

The killing by itself has no sequential ordering; it is a unit whose very nature requires a correlative which offers punctuation and which it itself does not contain. In contrast an historical occurrence, as it were, stretches an atemporal killing over the sequential acts to make this an actual killing, in which the first part is brought to bear on the second.

Strictly speaking, the above should be dealt with as involving four terms in all cases. We should be considering the reconciliation of the four strands of perception, science, events and importance in four correlative ways answering to Actuality, Ideality, Existence, and God and carried through by the disciplines of philosophy(?), mathematics, rhythmics, and religion. Each of these disciplines itself breaks up into a pair (or should it be a quadrant too?) of component and correlative disciplines such as *Categorienlehre* and Action; Ethics and Politics; Art and History; Belief and Creed. These like the more comprehensive disciplinary domains of philosophy, mathematics, etc., reveal the texture of different modes. The only sub-pairs that tell us about Existence are art and history, encompassed by rhythmics. But one could for example also make a reconciliation in the realm of the Ideal. This would require mathematics (perhaps as exemplified in scientific method?) to convey the texture of the Ideal, etc.

The basic historical unit is rooted in Existence, but the longer units involve an orientation with respect to the other modes as well. The longest is obviously that which is oriented in the depths of the Ideal, and which nevertheless is open to judgment by the whole Ideal.

December 8

If we distinguish A] the sequence of events in an order of earlier and later and which can be known to the analytic scientific intellect, B] the meaning of an occurrence, such as murder, which is known to the common-sense intellect, c] the historic occurrence with its order of before and after, and D] the objectivity of something as held before omniscience, we can say that history, c, is the process of unification of A and B under the condition D. That is to say, in the course of history, c, the earlier and later of A is wedded with the non-temporal meaning of B to constitute a single order of before and after in which the before items are linked by a stretch of revelance to what comes after. There are many such units, contained inside one another; a single historical occurrence can contain within itself subordinate historical occurrences related in an order of earlier and later. To recognize history one must identify a present item as in fact an "after" item, as that which is the outcome of a killing. We can do this by holding on to that item and recognizing how it stands out over against the rest. The acceptance of it as an item which comes after, must be followed by the recognition of its predecessor as being earlier in a dimension of merely sequential occurrences.

When the historian writes, he subdivides the object into a sequence,

A, and does this in the light of the meaning which he entertains, B. This involves a unification of the order of before and after of history with the objectivity of the occurrence, the acceptance of it as having some absolute value. Thus he takes the dead man to have been subjected to a series of acts which he understands from the perspective of murder. This dissection of the subject into a series of acts under this perspective is the giving to the historic killing a determinate nature.

The historic occurrence is a synthesis in the light of some final standard of worth; the historic writing is a synthesis in the light of some common-sense meaning. The historic occurrence has a common-sense meaning united with scientifically acceptable units; the historic writing has an historical occurrence united with a localization in a domain of absolute worth.

The course of history lifts up the items which otherwise would be merely past and gives them the role of being relevant "befores" to what comes later. This lifting up is a loss and a gain in a sense to both the items and the meaning. It denies the items their ultimacy and the meaning its purity; but it also makes the items relevant, and articulates the meaning.

Where can the historical occurrence be, what kind of domain is it? Must this not be the very being of Existence itself? It is only when we concentrate on actual entities, and their limited acts as issuing from them, that we miss the longer and different type of reach which is characteristic of the historic occurrence. While the particular items are slipping away into the past the realm of Existence continues to be in the shape of history. It saves those items by virtue of the incorporation of the meaning in each and every part of them. If you could detach the meaning you could have the separate items, but the meaning is integral to them. The falling away of the items which does in fact occur is inseparable from the meaning of the items in which they are preserved, in such a way that the earlier items are to be found inside the later ones.

The historian divides in the light of the common-sense meaning. The meaning of being a murder guides his division of the present of the murder, and this division serves as a way of making the history objective.

The historical synthesis is correlative with the synthesis produced by the objectivity of the omniscient mind; the two are distinct and do different things. Similarly the synthesis of the historian is distinct from the synthesis produced by the meaning of the act. The former synthesis (history) unites divisions with meaning; the latter synthesis (of the historian) involves the production of new divisions whose function is to provide an ultimate objectivity for history. The historian thus does something history could not do; he gives objectivity to the divisions of earlier and later. The history on the other hand does something historians cannot do; it gives a meaning to an actual set of divisions over which it can be exhibited. The historian's divisions are not the divisions of abstract science; they are new divisions and do not answer to the atomic moments of nature. But his divisions are real and carry a genuine objectivity if the historian produces them properly.

December 9

The historian subdivides, and thereby unites the historical occurrence and the absolute objectivity of it, in a realm where it can be compared to others in value and meaning. The divisions which the historian provides are not successively passed through in atomic presents. The atomic present is shorter than these divisions. Let us say that there was a war and the historian divides this into battles. The battles themselves encompass a sequence of atomic acts, such as lifting guns and firing them, retreats and advances, and perhaps even shorter ones. (It is a question whether the shortest units united in a battle are "historical" in nature or could be sub-atomic. I think it must be the former, and that we never get to the "sub-atomic" once we enter the field of history.)

The hard question that remains is what is the nature of the unit meaning which the historical occurrence originally united with the sequence of atomic moments, and which is a correlative way of uniting history with objectivity to constitute an objective reality? Can we distinguish this from the nature of the historic occurrence as essentially bringing in something of the nature and destiny of mankind (as embracing victory or defeat, of the import of the world for man in something like the way in which art does but with a different stress)? If so there will be a stress on the objective of the data or realm of history in contrast with the stress on the personal production of the artist.

The historian does not envisage what the historical occurrence in fact solidifies, or allows to be abstracted from it. When the historian unites the historical occurrence with his own divisions, the historical occurrence does not for him embrace atomic moments and an over-all import; the historical occurrence which the historian is solidifying with objectivity is a unit which is given a new set of divisions and, by virtue of the objectivity, a new import. On this view the primary function of the historian is to give the proper articulation to an historic occurrence and thereby objectivity, since the articulation is, in this case, the substantialization of the mere historic occurrence as an over-all unit.

Two questions still remain: A] what is the nature of the meaning which history itself unites with a sequence of atoms, B] and what is the nature of the historic occurrence which the historian unites with his own divisions?

Should we say that the meaning which is to be dealt with is that of civilization as a whole, and that what we are to produce is an historic occurrence, not history? The historic occurrence is the product of a creative equilibrium achieved between the atomic units and the meaning. It converts the units into relevant elements by combining a number into subordinate relevant combinations until we arrive at a single meaning, the meaning of civilization as lived through time. If we make the error of swallowing the units in civilization to make them mere demarcations of it, we would have only one moment of historic time. Or we would reduce the civilization to components which themselves are not elements in a civilization but subordinate parts of such elements, somewhat the way the musculature twitch at the beginning of an act is but part of the unit of shooting the enemy and is not relevant to the fact of war. We would then have to say that any larger set is an abstraction from it as surely as any subdivision is, that these abstractions can be lived through only by losing the concreteness of the historical occurrence, and that when the historian begins to write he leaves the historical occurrence behind to consider one of the abstractions, i.e., one of the larger sets of occurrences which he then subdivides so as to make the set objective.

Since the essence of civilization is the existence of peace, justice, harmony, and the flourishing of the arts and sciences, the basic historic occurrence should consist of anything which is constitutive of the continuance or discontinuance of these. But the occurrences make a plurality. One of them may be over before the others. It is necessary therefore to take one of them as basic, or to view civilization as a unit from which these are abstractions.

What is being sought is the unit of action of a group. One test is, whether or not it can allow the items to remain in sequence. Given a subatomic set of moments the historic occurrence does not merely make the first relevant to some later one, but accumulates a number of them which become relevant to some later number of them.

If we have a war there is no accumulation of battles. There is a sequence of battles made relevant in the war. But one battle may now be relevant to a battle at some later time even while it is relevant to some battle at a nearer time. This means that the later relevance is a function of the combination of smaller relevances. Skirmishes may be said to be like subatomic elements; it is these which are united in new blocks by the battle.

Should one say that just as the battle makes no sense except in the war, there is no war except as a product sustained by the idea of civilization? The civilization allows for distinctions within it of war and peace, but these distinctions do not provide units. The unit historic occurrences would be battles inside the frame of a war taken as an abstraction, even though its origin must be in the concrete (there really must be a war going on in the shape of a battle). The war produced by battles would of course be different from the war which was a distinctive unit inside the civilization.

Is there a smaller unit than war for civilization? Apparently not. Is it matched by peace? Is civilization nothing but war and peace, peace being defined by the flourishing of arts and science in justice? Apparently not. If so what are the units which history will forge; must it not be the subdivisions of war and peace, not as on the level of civilization, but on the level of these as sequential? Are the subdivisions of war just battles? It could be. What is the analogous subdivision for peace? Or is peace a single occurrence? The latter does not seem to be the case. Can we speak as critics do of characteristic styles, epochs, periods, and define these in terms of some crucial occurrence focused on by great men, ideals or religion?

The unit of peace should be an achievement in the arts or sciences, in justice or production. The length of these may vary but in any given case one of them must comprise the others as something which makes them relevant to one another and therefore does not allow them to be merely sequential or to be organized within their own dimension. Thus the unit of peace would be one which did not allow one musical composition to be followed by another, or even to form a single pattern of "the history of music," but would require the music to have its repercussions on other achievements and conversely. It would be them, as making a difference to one another, which would be in question.

We have then civilization with distinctions of war and peace; the ultimate sequence of physically or scientifically determinable atomic moments; and the historic occurrences which are battles and achievements. The progression of the first allows for war, or theatres of war, and the latter two for peace or special historical strands. Inside the historical occurrence one may be able to distinguish charges and skirmishes, preparations, actions, decisions and the rest. All of these, though in fact occurring sequentially and though themselves not like the subatomic moments in the sense that they do have some structure of relevance, could be said to be historic occurrences only on the condition that the battle be treated as a meaning which is being unified by the historian.

The historian isolates the history and treats this as a meaning; he can have battles or wars or civilization as his meaning, and he must then punctuate them, make essential and relevant divisions, enabling the supposed meaning to become objective. How does he know that he has done his job properly? If it is determinate? Must he not make the divisions determinate in the way the facts were, out of which the historic occurrence was carved, by converting their sequential being into bundles of relevancies? But if he takes battles to be his meaning he has nothing but objectified battles in the shape of skirmishes and cannot say that the war is objectively real. Accordingly, the historian must take as his meaning of history either something larger than the battles, or, contrary to what was said earlier, must view his own divisions as being longer than that offered by the occurrences, and this by virtue of the objectivity which he solidifies with the occurrences. The historic divisions of the historian should make the historic occurrence part of the relevant historic division of war and peace as actually sequential.

We then have   1] a civilization with its distinctions of war and peace, which have no temporal order or even relevance but merely analytic status, B] a sequence of atomic moments which have being in abstraction from any substantial realities, and   c] the unity of these in the form of historic occurrences which are battles and achievements. And   2] the historic occurrences arranged in an ordered sequence with a principle of objectivity which produces historic divisions of war and peace, that in fact follow one another in historic time and allow for an objective comparison of any component with any component. Can then the historian infer step by step without losing history? What room is there for a history of non-human things?

December 10

The historic occurrence or unit of objective history is the juncture point of a sequence of atomic sub-historic units and a meaning or nature. Absolutely viewed the atomic units are the smallest temporal units possible, and characterize the smallest possible elements moving at the greatest possible speed; the meaning which is correlative to them is the whole of civilization as punctuated by achievements. The historic occurrence is the smallest possible unit of objective history and this seems to be an achievement, such as a battle or a discovery or a work of art, etc. However, it is also the case that the smallest atomic moments are accumulated in vectors and have answering to them some broken segment of the meaning in the shape say of a culture or nation, an institution or other part of the whole of history. The historic occurrence which results (due to the fact that only some men are involved in it) is some occurrence shorter than the genuinely objective historic occurrence uniting the smallest elements and the largest meaning. (Those smallest elements are in fact united for it in the shape of the vectors and the largest meaning is already segmented by virtue of the operation of limited men.) In other words, the historic occurrence properly speaking, though it is the unity of the meaning of civilization and a sequence of atomic moments, does not have these naked but as already contained within bundles of various kinds, i.e., within sub-occurrences which are juncture points of segments of civilization and vector bundles of atomic moments.

The historian, when he looks at the historic occurrences as a set (and thus at the occurrence which is an achievement) as being made up of sub-occurrences, or a set of achievements, tries to deal with these as being eternally objective, completely determinate. He can do this only by breaking up the objectivized set of occurrences or sub-occurrences into a sequence of historic situations.

December 11

The type of object determines the nature of the span of the meaning and the length of the atomic moment. Thus the smallest physical entities are related to the remotest future by the span of "nature," and live through a time of the smallest atomic moments. Many of those entities are subjugated to and contained within macroscopic entities such as stones or mountains, and organic things such as flies and birds and horses. These have the span of a species or organic universe, and allow for longer moments. The being which is man has a span, which is the whole of history, subdivided into pivotal events in his life. The being which is institutions or mankind has a fragment of the whole of history and subdivides this into crucial events in the institution or the development of mankind.

What one is basic? It would seem that the human individual's span is, for though history does involve the interplay of men, it is a fact that it is primarily the individual who acts. But if history be thought of as civilization, then it is mankind and institutions which are primary. How does this work out in connection with atomic entities, etc.? There is no problem here, for the historic unit is not the basic reality of anything but of Existence: it tells us the rhythm of Existence, in the light of the different degrees of intimacy or grip that is had on the Ideal.

The physical units are A] contained within and have their careers determined by the historical beings in which they reside, and B] cannot function in independence except in a longer but thinner frame of nature. When Existence is said to be manifested in and through them it is nothing but the sequence of their occurrence; this sequence is itself contained within the historic occurrence of mankind, not in the sense that mankind thinks about it or sustains it, but in the sense that the entities become actualities and not loci of the process of Existence. Existence in its nakedness comes through the larger historical elements; what is smaller than this is the Actual with an existential moment, but not Existence itself. To get to the physical we must leave the realm of Existence either for the abstract formulae of science or the realm of individuals, subatomic and otherwise.

December 13

If we wish to reconcile, say the perceptual and scientific objects, we can do this on the subjective side by using our emotions, mind, will and body to constitute an artistic product, a mathematical rational unity, an astrological or important object, or the object as a common-sense thing clarified. But if we want to do this on an objective level we must understand it to be an object in history, an essence in the realm of possibility, an objective component of an eternal mind, or the thing in and of itself as a mere other of the rest of the world. When we ask after the star we evidently want in modern times only the second or fourth—we want to know what it is as a rational object or as a common-sense thing, preferably the latter. This means that we must, despite our current practice and tradition, take the perceptual strand as a primary abstraction from which the mathematical, the important and the eventful are to be derived. On the objective side we are concerned with the first and fourth—as an object in history or as in and of itself, preferably the latter. In this case we must recognize it to be not perceptual and not scientific, but essentially self-maintaining and to be known as such only by being faced as the other of ourselves and other things. We and those other things will provide the terms or meanings in the light of which its otherness can be expressed.

When we look at the historical object as reconciling oppositions it must not be forgotten that this is a reconciliation not of Actuality or Existence, but of Existence manifesting itself through Actualities, expressing itself with these as its agencies. The time of history is thus not the time of an Actuality in and of itself, any more than it is the time of science or of God or even of Existence itself. It is the time of Existence mediated or qualified. The reversal of this emphasis would be given by the effective expression of man through Existence. This is essentially technology. Here we come to know objects as effectively made into influences on Existence, ways in which Existence is controlled.

The *insistence* of the Ideal on man, and through man, is the provision of an *ethical leader;* of Existence on man and through man, is *history;* of God on man and through man is incarnation. The converse insistence of man on the Ideal is *mathematics,* on Existence is *technology,* on God is *prayer.* The *expression* of the Ideal through man, the using him as but an epitomized nodule of itself is the production of *mind;* of Existence, the man of *destiny;* of God, the priest or *servant of Him.* The converse expression of man on the Ideal is the *ethical good,* on God is the *saviour,* on Existence is *art.*

But it is proper to ask, what is the object really? Who am I? The question is ambiguous. Taken in and of myself I am the other of all else, or sheer privacy. Taken in Existence or from the position of Existence I am part of history or a technological being or a being of destiny or a creator of art. But am I all these at once? Must we not say that I am a private being by virtue of the fact that the other modes are settings for me? History then no more than art tells me what man is; it just tells me what man is as framed in Existence.

The present moment can be identified with the zero point of perception, science, event and importance. These are quite different from one another. If we want to reconcile them we must go to still other zero points, such as the in and of itself nature of a being in its substantial reality, the mathematically defined point, the historical present or the meaning of the present in the eye of eternity. Once again if it be asked which is basic, recourse must be had to the acknowledgment of the substance of ourselves as basic with a reference to the other modes as offering external denominations (which, from their perspective, are just as basic).

December 14

Instead of saying that "Existence has existential import" it would have been better in the *Modes* to have said that Existence, Actuality, God and Ideality are all transcendentals (or in modern terms, 'nonnaturalistic' characters or qualities, natures or meanings). The specific distinctive features of these will also be transcendentals—uniqueness, substantiality, space, time, energy, salvational judgment, rationality. These features are not to be found as characters or features of things; they characterize the transcendental entities as wholes, and express something about the order or presence or function of their parts.

If we can find an existential meaning to the qualities we experience, as is done in pragmatism or sensationalism, we will not find Existence to be a transcendental, but to be, as Hume and Kant saw, a kind of expression for any or all of them. A transcendental will vanish with the transportation of ordinary predicates to its realm.

Good is not a non-natural quality in the realm of the Ideal; nor is existence one in the realm of Existence. A transcendental is produced by recognizing that there is an over-all power in things which owes its being to another mode than that to which we are accrediting the ordinary predicates. The over-all power provides testimony to the reality of another mode; it is "accidental" so far as the ordinary predicates are taken as essential. With a reverse emphasis we can make the ordinary predicates into "non-natural" ones. Thus, if by the "natural," one means the space-time world, then taking this to be defined by experience, or Existence, or action or whatever, the various qualities which we might focus on in perception become "non-natural" or transcendental, owing their being, as they do, to individuals or to the Ideal.

December 15

When it is asked what is man, it is necessary to distinguish what he is as an individual from what he is as a unit in mankind. It is true to be sure that he is both, but since the time schemes and other divisions of the one are not the same as the other they must be distinguished. The individual and the unit (of mankind) man are over against all other modes. As part of mankind a man is imbedded in Existence; Existence dictates the divisions appropriate to him as a unit. Though he can legitimately be dealt with from the perspective of Existence one will not thereby get to his innermost nature.

When we come to finding out about the real star we put our stress on substances as over against man the individual. We could be concerned with the astronomical star in which case we would look to mathematics or the essence of man as concerned with ideas and possibilities. We could also be concerned with the star as an expression or avenue for Existence, in which case we would deal with it as a geological specimen. And if we asked about its worth, we would look to it as a signal or sign of the divine or of the locus of some excellence.

Kant would criticize Hegel undoubtedly as making Reason, which is antinomic and at best regulative, into a constitutive principle; he would point out that this leads to irresolvable contradictions, and denies the autonomy of different domains. Hegel must make Reason give itself its own opposition in order to be itself; it must make believe with itself in a make-believe activity. Hegel in reply would say that Kant speaks from the standpoint of the Understanding, that it is Understanding which is perpetually in conflict, that it depends for Reason for its guidance and criticism, and that the oppositions it rests on are in the end not real. Both are right, and this means we have a third position which may be called that of the Imagination. Both the powers of reason and understanding are subordinate to it. This third power has its own correlative, Intuition, which could reconcile the two powers in another way. Imagination in fact is invoked by Kant in the *Third Critique,* and so is Intuition, the former in the teleological the latter in the aesthetic judgment. However he thinks these are non-rational and apparently not as fundamental as the powers which are reconciled (Reason for Kant in the *Second Critique* is taken to be as powerful as Hegel would want, just as the Understanding, throughout the dialectic of Hegel, is as limited as Kant holds it to be). Marx offers an imaginative or socio-economic-historic reconciliation, and Kierkegaard an intuitive religiously oriented one for Hegel's Understanding and Reason.

From the standpoint of man the historical dimension of him, himself as a unit in mankind, which is to say a being through whom Existence is expressing itself in a typical and historical way, is something to be integrated with himself as a substance. This is also true of him as a rational object for mathematics, and as a religious object in the context of the divine. These dimensions, though they have genuine being in the orientation of the other modes, are for him but facets of himself which it is his task to subjugate to his own unity. Such subjugation does not change his inward nature, but only qualifies it, makes it have another flavor.

The star is, as I am, something in and of itself, but whereas the star has to be understood as being idly decorated with the historical, etc., sides, I can make these sides part of my very inward being. When I view the star as also historical I in effect am using my powers of integration to make the genuinely historical occurrence of the star, as the manifestation of Existence through an object, into an integral part of its being. But the suspicion that history does not apply to natural objects is justified; the history is not made into part of its being in fact but only from the perspective of some man. When we view the star as historical we do not humanize it, but we do make a non-existent unity of the star and the domain of history. But in the case of ourselves we make the exterior history, ourselves as units of mankind, into parts of ourselves, the substances which exist now.

1960

When I know, it seems as if I also know that I know. This can be accounted for in the following alternative ways: *1*] We can say that an immediately subsequent thought grasps the act of knowing. We have thought *x* and object *o*; thought *y*, at a subsequent moment, grasps the two together. But how can we know *x*, since this is past? How remember? To say that we remember is A] to say that we don't really know the first thought, and B] is to say that the self-consciousness does not occur when the consciousness of the object does. *2*] We can distinguish a whole mind and a partial mind, and view consciousness of object *o* as the work of the latter. The act of self-consciousness would then be the act of identification of the larger mind with the smaller, so that when and as object *o* is consciously grasped we are aware of ourselves. But how separate these two minds? How identify them? Do we ever see the two as distinct? And what do we do with the fact that the larger mind is then not self-conscious? *3*] We can take the larger mind to be a subconscious, so that self-consciousness now becomes close to what we ordinarily mean, particularly when we blush, etc. We become self-conscious when our unconscious identifies itself with a conscious apprehension of the object. And it engages in this identification necessarily because it provides the energy for the smaller, focused act of consciousness. *4*] We can hold the idealistic position and take the object of consciousness to be an obscurely apprehended object; the more we know what that object is the more we recognize that it is identical in nature with the mind by means of which we know it. The world to be known is in the end a tissue of mental contents and the discovery that it is so, to whatever degree one likes, is the awareness of oneself. We are self-conscious so far as we know that the object of consciousness is ourselves. This overlooks the subjective note in self-consciousness, makes objects into congeries of universals, and is up against the question as to why the self-conscious mind should ever have given itself a consciousness which it then must overcome by getting to know the object better. It is only a part of an answer to say that it does this to articulate itself, or to give itself to itself, for the question is why, (once it has done it, or having started without having done it) it should deceive itself by taking the position of consciousness. What status has the deception over against the real self-consciousness of the absolute mind? 5] The existentialist substitutes for the mind of the idealist an ultimate, irreducible ego and finds the object of its consciousness to be a kind of variant of this ego, since he "humanizes" or "subjectivizes," makes a "thou" of whatever his ego in fact really confronts.

Of all these views the third seems to be the best. It tells us that mind is only part of the entire self and that the self in giving the mind its energies becomes self-conscious, aware of itself as A] more than a mind, and B] as a mind. This view does not require us to tamper with the object as the latter two views demand, and does justice to self-consciousness which the first two do not allow.

Collingwood raises the question as to whether or not one can think the very same thought that Euclid did. If we distinguish content from act we can surely say that the content is identical; but we lose all history if we identify content and act, as he apparently does. However, there is a way of preserving his insight. We can take the "inside" of acts to be the Existence which is now, and which was before. When we infer to past events we but refer to the outside through which Existence was once channelized and altered. In acknowledging that it is Existence, we are able to have the very occurrence again, though as mediated by an idea, the outside as mere outside. We must give to the outside that we now think, the inside that we now see in Existence, when this inside has been separated off from the qualifications that present objects provide. We remake Existence as a qualified channelized power by using the outsides to which our evidence points.

It is said in the *Modes* in connection with the proofs of God that there are four distinct parts of a proof, answering to each of the modes. In addition there must be an encounter if we are to be satisfied. But must there be only one type of encounter, or are there many—four to be exact? Is it that we must encounter each of the components of the proof, or that we must have four ways of encountering the terminus of the proof? It is the former of these. In order to get a premiss, for example, expressing what an actuality is (say the Other of all others) we must have encountered an actuality, or have nothing but a fiction or something we hope is true. But we can have four kinds of premisses, implicative rules, etc., so that the second alternative is also true in the sense that it allows for four kinds of termini. But again, since any one of these termini has itself four ways of being—in itself and as affected by the other three modes—each can be said to be encounterable in four ways as well.

January 14

Is every actuality the other of God? If so, it would seem to be permanent. But if not, then how could God have an other when there were no men? Is it not then that God has the entire world of Actuality as his other, and that I become an absolute other of Him only by taking myself to be representative of all the other actualities? But this alternative has the difficulty that A] the world of Actuality presupposes particular actualities, and B] that we are others in ourselves before we take ourselves to be representative. Is it then that God inevitably makes each actuality to be representative of all the others, each in its own way—the physical entities as illustrating a law, and humans as having privacies?

By virtue of God's act of othering, man achieves the state of being God's Other. This perhaps is what is meant by being made in God's image. God elects the inwardness of man to be his Other. Before there were men, he elects the entire law-abiding world of things, as together having an inside, to have this status. He need not take this way when man appears; man's appearance merely allows him to give individuals the role of being His absolute other, and thus as standing for all actualities. It is God (and incidentally the other modes) who makes an actuality be Actuality per se.

January 24

Philosophy can be characterized in a four-fold way as being non-individualistic, as the Greeks saw, with a stress on Existence; scientific, coming to expression in common-sense actual objects; speculative and dealing with conceptualized ideals; and systematic or autonomous, like God.

How is it that man is self-identical? Is it because he has a private nature? But everything has this. Is it because he is a localization of the very nature of Actuality which is itself self-identical and the other of God? But how and when does he achieve this status of being a localization? Is it through his rights, by being responsible, by his belonging to civilization or by his acceptance by God? The last three would seem to depend on the activity of powers beyond him. Staying with the first we still are faced with hard questions. How does man get his rights? Do the rights originate with the private or the public sides of his being? But when does this occur?

When he is self-conscious. Does this mean that he always was self-conscious or that we anticipate his achievement of this? Or does God or civilization attribute this to him and he eventually lives up to it? We can see that civilization might do this; the newborn child is accepted into the world of men, and by that very act is accredited with rights; its privacy is given a definite role. Only later is there responsibility, work, and self-consciousness.

January 26

The Aristotelian thinks that a being in and of itself is an essence which is sustained by or interwoven with a matter. But in and of itself, i.e., without limitation from without, a being would be amorphous. Beings acquire definiteness from one another; they become cosmologized by one another, and thereby their ontological status is altered to make them into entities exercising their proper natures. It is as if they were Aristotelian matters essentializing one another. A being is concretely an essence in and of itself only so far as the rest of the universe presses in on it and forces it to maintain itself in and of itself.

The soul of man is shaped by the body, and is made to be what it is by the rest of the world. It is also capable of expressing itself, showing what it was in and of itself. It also has a characteristic way of acting on others, thereby enabling them to achieve a definiteness they otherwise would not have had. And it does at times permit of a speculative grasp of all being. By thinking of the essence of reality we give the appearance a purified being, and make it possible for the appearances to provide definiteness for the essence as it in fact occurs.

The newborn infant has privacy, and can through the other modes achieve otherness, rights and position. But it does not express itself enough; it can't act properly, can't speculate, can't be a representative. It becomes a representative through an adoption by society or man. Its soul is shaped not by a direct action by the body but by an acceptance by society. Its expressions are not actually carried out but are anticipated by those who know it. Its speculative powers, its capacity to understand others, is found in its subconscious. Animals must be taken as already expressed or as latent, whereas the soul of the infant is to be thought of as being shaped by what it undergoes through the action of others and through its action on them.

February 10

If it be the case that the combination of a beginning and a process together constitute a condition from which consequences follow both necessarily and rationally, it becomes a question as to whether or not one can distinguish between valid and invalid processes, proofs, structures, or logics. One might make the distinction in the way Peirce did by recognizing that the "tautological" or truly logical structure is one which is abstractable from all combinations of premises and processes. Only that combination which has the very structure of its process, as well as of itself as a whole, is valid. More flexibly and simply, though, a distinction can be made with reference to a desirable character. That procedure or logic is valid which guarantees that a given desirable character is retained or improved in the outcome. Thus a valid formal logical scheme is one which, given truth, never will end with falsehood.

In this sense one can say that a prayer offers a valid "proof" of God if it does not forsake the testimony's divine features in proceeding to its destination. A poor prayer will be like an inference which starts with falsehood (and thus may or may not arrive at its destination) or which, while starting with some good, never pushes this aside to get to some desirable result. But then one might well ask if it is not the case that most prayers start with an awareness of one's unworthiness. One can admit this, provided that it is recognized that the awareness of unworthiness is but the beginning of an acknowledgment of some testimony, of some divinely produced element in oneself. This is perhaps what is classically intended by the doctrine that God's grace is needed even for acts of repentance and turnings towards him.

The awareness of unworthiness by itself yields nothing. Only the grasp of this unworthiness (as being say, a feature of what is an absolute Other, i.e., of the divine) will ground a prayer which can be said to be legitimate or valid. A valid prayer terminates in the divine as possessing the features which were found to be desirable and should be retained. This means of course that proofs of God must not involve a denial of oneself and one's accepted features, except in the sense that one can prefer the terminus of the activity to the beginning. But the beginning must have some virtue. If it has none at all, a procedure which leads to a desirable result will be characterizable as valid or respectable only so far as the result itself is desirable.

March 14

If x is contingent, it can be. But if x is contingent, *non-x* might be. But if *non-x* might be, then *non-x* must be and if x might be then x must be (according to the argument of Chapter 2 of the *Modes*). But if x must be and *non-x* must be, we have two necessities which conflict. Either *x* cannot be contingent, or what can be need not be. The alternative overlooked is that there is no *x* which is antecedently contingent; the contingent is an outcome, the realization of *"x* or *non-x"* in the shape of *x*. Every realization is contingent, but it is not a possible contingent, since it has no definitive nature before it is realized.

But if *"x* or *non-x"* is the possibility which is realized, what do we do about normative possibilities which need not be realized at any given time, and may never be realized apart from God? Is it not that the normative possibility is one of the as yet undistinguished components in *x* or *non-x*, and that God's function is not to realize this but to keep it exterior? In and of itself the normative possibility is germane (since the whole of which it is a part is germane) but it takes God to keep it exterior; similarly in and of itself a non-normative possible is exterior (since the whole of which it is a part is so) but it takes God to see to it that it is in fact realized, and does not remain merely realizable.

May not one treat essence as the thing itself, an undifferentiated unity, and accident as its expression, diversified and fixated by other beings? If one does this then the fixated accidents which preclude the continuation of expression will make for the changes in the being's essence, since they will compel new manifestations. Accidents are the essence exteriorized, diversified and fixated by means of other entities; those accidents become merged into one another and as such constitute an essence in which no one of those exteriorized, diversified and fixated elements can be found, particularly since, as in and of itself, the contribution of the other entities is abstracted from. The real world of public activity to one of accidents, which express individuals in the setting of one another.

The categories which men use are like Kant's schematized categories in the sense that they have a "hole" in them in which the manifold is to fit. The material which fills that hole is "nothing" in the sense in which the category and the hole are something; the material is that which is other than the category and the hole, but is known as that which is to fit into it. If we treat it as something to be given to the category it must be viewed as a nothing—but in fact it is another mode functioning as the other of the category.

The category has as part of itself an "other." This demands not only that the category be "other" than it (where category is in fact the other three components of a four-fold entity of which the hole also is one), but that the filling for that hole be other than the hole. So we have a kind of pulling away from the category in one of the components of it, pointing to a realm which is other than the component, by virtue of the fact that the component itself is other than the rest of the category. Because the hole is other than the rest the filling of the hole must be other than the hole; and conversely, because the filling of the hole is other than the hole the hole is able to stand over against the rest of the four-fold category. Every other component of the category will also have an analogous filling. The category has four parts only because each part stands over against the rest by virtue of the fact that it is related to an other for it, outside itself and thus outside the category. The part of the category I identify with myself is other than the rest because it others myself in my concreteness; and conversely, because I in my concreteness other the "I" part of the category, that "I" part of the category is other than the rest of the category. The category is able to have a plurality within it, a plurality of stresses or parts, only because its parts other their fillings and thereby one another, and because they other one another and thereby their fillings. Without a filling for the categorial parts there would be only a sheer, mere unity.

March 17

The world as in and of itself is over against us and threatens us. We need it to be complete. We take a vectoral approach to that world, which we specialize in the form of concepts, attitudes, interests and even scales, enabling us to subjugate that world, bring it within the orbit of our meanings, and thereby accommodate ourselves and it to one another. Society, habit, the very structure of our beings demand that our vectors be restructured, remade and thereby enabled to find a proper, or better, an appropriate terminus in the world. Thus our emotions are vectoral and would in a rough way accommodate us to the world; but as already qualified by societal pressures we are enabled to have more appropriate vectors in the sense that they keep us steady, at least with respect to the items filtered through society. Society at once accommodates various things and qualifies our vectors so that they become appropriate to those things; society's accommodations are due to the fact that its machinery interrelates those things; its habituation of us is a way of interrelating us to those interrelated things. In some cases, such as the vital occurrences of life, as, e.g., a birth or death (even though these are socially qualified), we have a kind of direct contact with the real as in and of itself. As a consequence, our emotional responses are excessive, even beyond the tolerance of the society at times. What we ordinarily take to be real is for the most part conventionalized, and what we take to be conventionalized—birth and death, and the like—has a dimension to it which is outside the conventional, as is evident from the excessiveness of the emotions it elicits.

March 22

One can distinguish four ways in which men deal with the world beyond. There is the method of selectivity which, answering to the Ideal, approaches the world in terms of some kind of principle. Answering to Actuality is the prehensive effort which lays hold of something outside, to own it. Answering to Existence is the dispersive articulation, the self-expansiveness which intrudes. And answering to God is the creativity which brings things about from within.

What is said above has analogues with respect to the subject acting on itself (as though it were a God); in the objective world (acting on the subject as Existence); and in the interplay of correlatives (answering to the Ideal). Consequently one can combine the above four ways of dealing with material with the four kinds of material to be dealt with—the objective world, the subject itself, the object on the subject, and the correlativity of the two.

Art production, properly speaking, is creativity exercised by a subject; intensions and experience involve prehensive acts with respect to an object; self-discovery leads to the consideration of an articulation with respect to correlative elements; selectivity exercised with respect to a subject by the external world gives us the world as normative for the individual.

March 23

A proof that God is a creator is faced with the fact that a creation requires the separate being of the created, which, so far as it is separate, stands by itself. The proof must actually distinguish two kinds of separateness, one which is self-achieved and bad, and which would perhaps be what is meant by sin, and the other which involves and presupposes a prior acceptance of, or togetherness with God. Or put another way, the creation by God must involve a withdrawal of Him, an allowing of the creature to be in and of itself. This withdrawal is a withdrawal of allowance, of concern, and would have to be distinguished from the withdrawal of indifference.

On this view, a man is an other, which never is fully other until God allows himself to be its counterpart; before God does this (and thus enables man to be a created being), man would live through his otherness in solitude and as separate from all other things. He would not yet have a sufficient interiority adequate to his full powers. As he flatly lives this insufficient interiority he is aware that more is possible; his recognition of this more is the recognition of a God who has withdrawn Himself in the sense of allowing man to accept Him as the absolute Other. And in man there would be a kind of absolute Otherness available. This absolute Otherness, which could have been, and which might be said to be the kind of shadow required by a trace, i.e., to be a kind of higher status which is always suggested by a lower status, could be expressed as the state of being a man, for one who is always acting partly like an animal.

Man, it could be said, is one who has made himself a man in a precarious way by othering nature and other individual men, and this precarious otherness (which would be equivalent to sin and insufficiency) would point to a deeper otherness he can achieve. He can become a self-sufficient being with a genuine and deep other in God if only he would accept the fact that God makes him one who depends on God in order to be over against God. If he ignores the otherness which God (by withdrawing), enables him to have, and thus to be "created," i.e. to function on his own, he becomes like an animal.

God's creation of man then is the making him be over against nature. Man acquires from God an absolute status. The otherness of himself is not one which is made by the rest or by himself over against the other things in the universe, but by virtue of God's relation to him.

The view in the *Modes of Being* is that the otherness of man is ontological and thus is not the product of a creation. One loses one's hold on oneself by a deliberate or perhaps even accidental turning away from the otherness of God and attempting to locate that otherness elsewhere. With such a new locating the otherness of man becomes an otherness with respect to spatio-temporal or Ideal realities, and man himself becomes distraught. He will then have to adjust himself constantly to the changing world. The ontological fact of his absolute otherness would still hold. It cannot be abrogated by any act of man. The recovery of man, the escape from his state of sinfulness, the making himself be a created being, involves a recovery of his ontological status in the sense of making it consciously enjoyed. The full man on this account is one who is self-consciously ontological; he is one who has made the status of otherness which he has in himself into the living being of himself. Man can make himself be a self-conscious Other, i.e., recognize that God is his creator.

From the side of God this self-consciousness of man's ontological status would be produced by Him. God urges man to make his ontological otherness into his entire being, and to stand apart from God as a created being. His consciousness would be shown by God to be incomplete, to leave man out of account until it became a consciousness of man's otherness to God. God thus makes the ontological dimension insistently obtrusive on the conscious one.

Man is a being who is conscious of the fact that he is not fully conscious, and he would have to admit that there is a deeper rootage he has to something before he can make himself entirely separate from all else. He would, before that, be a self-divided being, one who while ontologically other than God would nevertheless be able to function as a separate being, but ignoring God. His consciousness would be aware that it was not self-conscious, conscious of the real nature of the self. Or it would be a consciousness which rested on an ontological base that had not come into full consciousness. Man's discovery of God would be one with the discovery of himself to himself; this would presuppose the presence of God. The fact of creation would be discovered by man's coming to see that there was something in him which had to be made conscious, that he was more other than he supposed he was. The creation, from the standpoint of God, would be one and the same with the demand of the ontological dimension to be identical with the full nature of man.

Man, then, in becoming conscious would A] have lost the status of being one with his ontological otherness, and B] would nevertheless have made himself into a man. The second stage requires him to recover his status, to admit that he was created in his deepest being.

The above account does not give us any temporal priority of unconsciousness over self-consciousness; it leaves over the question as to the nature of the creation of sub-human beings, and does not require the making of man's soul by God. It also does not show that man, in his conscious acceptance of an ontological status, is doing anything more than recovering his proper state vis-à-vis God. Perhaps there is nothing like creation but only a recognition of alienation? If man was really created, one would have to show that God acquired a status of an absolute other, and thus in a sense changed—unless one holds that man's self-conscious and even non-conscious way of being other is a kind of act within the ambit of God's being. A true creation turns God into a creator. But if we want God to be a creator we must recognize that He becomes so from man's side when man consciously accepts man's ontological otherness. From God's side, God becomes a creator with His insistence that the ontological side of man have priority and in fact makes possible the conscious side. God's creation is the insistence on the dependence of "epistemology" on ontology; man's acknowledgment of creation is an insistence on the epistemological recovery of ontology.

Creation then is the insistent power of an ontological otherness in man to affect the consciousness of man as an other. Apart from God this ontological otherness would not be effective; otherwise man, apart from God's insistence, could recover and know this ontological otherness by the very nature of consciousness.

The issue then is, can man know that he is the ontological other of God unless God insists on withdrawing Himself and thereby forcing the status of an ontological otherness into consciousness? The doctrine of creation would deny that the ontological otherness is just a datum, and would assert that its power is being felt in the guise of a freedom in man or by making itself manifest in thought.

March 25

The problem of sin for a theory of "creation," such as that open to the *Modes of Being,* would be the problem of what in consciousness prevented the divine incursion of the ontological into man. All theories of sin are up against the fact that God is omnipotent and yet man can defy Him. We would have to say that the very meaning of consciousness is that it has its own autonomy, and that the intrusion of the ontological is in no way affected by this autonomy. So far, God's omnipotence is in no way compromised. Sin would come through the refusal to revise consciousness in the light of the intrusion, the refusal to accommodate oneself to the fact of the created component. This means that the intrusion of God is without force in the conversion of consciousness. Is there anything wrong with this, once we recognize that consciousness must make its own decision, and that if God were to insist on Himself it would be only by despoiling the consciousness which man developed?

Divine power does not extend to making consciousness other than it is, precisely because consciousness is part of the separateness which man has, both when he separates himself wrongly and when he does it rightly. The consciousness is of course, from the standpoint of the ontological, a derivative to be accounted for as a result of a relaxation of the ontological dimension in its completeness. Consciousness on this view would result when the ontological side of man divided itself into a subordinate abstract but all-comprehensive mode of activity and a root being; once the division is made the root being will nevertheless continue to intrude. The division, from the standpoint of God, would be but an expression of the ontological under limitative conditions and as still dependent on Him as a kind of adjective; but the expression will also be dependent in the sense that it will be that which was being expressed by the ontological. The ontological has an expression only so far as it allows some autonomy to the expressed.

The expressed will be at once adjectival to and the outcome of the ontological.

Sin is the result of an adjective acting as though it were a substance, and thus not recognizing its own incompleteness; it results too from the failure to see that the adjective is an outcome, in not recognizing its origin. The first sort of sin is pride or arrogance; the second sort, blindness, obstinacy. The overcoming of the first depends on "grace" in that the ontological continues to provide the energy and thus be there for the pride to see that it ought not itself be. The overcoming of the second would also require "grace" in that the ontological continues to intrude and thus forces one to take some account of it. Grace in the first sense is the vitalizing force which is available for use, and of which Rosicrucians and Christian Scientists and the like speak; Grace in the second sense is the power which enables one to become a new man. It is at the root of conversion and the taking on of the new life.

Sin then would be the supposition that one's consciousness is able to function on its own, and also the supposition that there was no more to man than that of which he was conscious. There would be a component in a man which provided him with energy to be a man and nothing more, and another which enabled him to see that his consciousness could be more inclusive than it is, particularly with respect to himself. Sin would thus be a failure to be sufficiently self-conscious, in the one case because one did not see what one's powers were, and in the second because one did not see what consciousness should have included. The overcoming of the second would involve man as a new being, but it would not preclude the first still remaining, for though man makes the ontological a part of his conscious life and thus changes himself, he still has a consciousness which was dependent on the ontological qua ontological.

The making of the ontological into the conscious presupposes the separation of the two and thus the antecedent withdrawal of God in order to enable man to have a separate consciousness. The bringing of the ontological into consciousness would look as though a part could master the whole, but it is to be noted that the ontological is not swallowed by the conscious but merely given a place there. The individual then heals the breach between the conscious and the ontological by a free act apart from God. This still leaves him an adjective to the ontological.

If the ontological were nothing but energy it would of course be easily assimilable to the body or Existence; but it must be thought of as the "other." Full self-consciousness involves an acceptance of the fact that there is a radical otherness which it has adopted in order to become "full," and that this otherness nevertheless functions on its own, apart from the consciousness, to make man a self-same persistent being regardless of whether he thinks or not.

March 26

There are a number of relations which the artistic side of a work could have to the material, and thus to the commonsensical or natural reality of it. It could assimilate that material within it. This is most completely done in the dance. The very forces of gravity are absorbed and made to conform to the dance; every leap transforms the powers of gravity or, if one likes, places these powers in an entirely new context, leaving nothing over that must be remarked. It is possible too to have the artistic side refer to the other. This is what is done in story; here the meanings of the words make reference also to meanings which are outside the story. Finally, the artistic side may take account of the existence of the other as something which is intruding on it and which ought somehow to be absorbed by it or integrated with it. This is what happens in architecture; the natural dimensions of space are felt to have their rights, and the artistic side of the architecture is thus defined to be dependent on the other.

The assimilative, adjectival and presupposing positions of the art side of a work (which is what the above can be characterized to state), have their affiliations with the previous discussion of creation and God. The assimilative position expressed in the dance is the incorporation of the divine in the daily acts; it is in effect the death of a God, and on the side of the work of art the denial of the rights of the commonsensical or natural world. This position is an ideal one; no dance ever really arrives at it. It is a position too which is approximated by painting and poetry; indeed one could say that poetry deals with this better than dance or painting can.

The adjectival position, which is represented by story, has affiliations too in sculpture and in the theatre. It is a position analogous to that of the conscious man who, aware that his dependence on some power outside himself enables him to do what he is doing, nevertheless acts in independence of it. In these three arts there is a kind of holding away from the world which is nevertheless made use of as a carrier.

The presuppositional arts are architecture, musical compositions, and musical performance. Here there is an intrusive component from the world beyond, of which account ought to be taken in the work. In architecture we can occupy the world of ordinary space at the same time that we are in a tensional, created one. This is also true of the temporal art of musicry; the beats of ordinary expectative life dictate the kind of divisions possible in the composition. It is even more evidently the case in the dynamic performance of music. If there be any question here it would be in connection with musicry, for one would somehow have to show that the mere temporal divisions of ordinary life are those which are being referred to as an intrusive or presupposed element in the new rhythms being composed.

We thus divide the three columns of the arts as presuppositional, adjectival, and assimilative of the world of every day; this is an alternative to the expression of the arts as bounding, occupying and exhausting their own space, time and dynamics. The occupation and finally the exhaustion of a space, time, and dynamics are the result of the conquest of the world of every day, a conquest which makes the work of art stand outside that common day.

March 27

If one were to take the individual and the world, or mind and matter, as antitheses, one can get a basic set of six alternative views: 1] the individual is self-enclosed, and any meaning that the world may have is included, absorbed within it—solipsism, some varieties of existentialism, subjectivism, individualism.   2] The individual is adhesive, adjectival, a being which, though it has its own nature, exists only so far as there is another outside it on which it depends—the social view of the individual, to be found in Dewey and Hegel and Marx and perhaps in Aristotle. 3] The individual finds that the world is intrusive on him and that his existence consists in the perpetual mastery and possession or absorption of this external world, but from a position inside himself. This seems to be the later view held by Wittgenstein and those who, with conceptual pragmatists, think of the world as being organized by man. The root of the view is perhaps in Kant; something in the nature of the world requires that the ideas function in this way rather than that.   4] This position is the reverse of *1;* here the world of nature is self-enclosed and one can find the individual only as a subdivision of it. The position must be contrasted with 2, where the focus is the individual and he is understood to be adjectival. Here the world of nature or social world is taken as final and the individual, instead of being seen to be adjectival, is thought to be a subdivision. We have here man the public or social being—Aristotle's politics, the economic interpretation of the individual, historic interpretations of the world governed by some cosmic force, physicalism.   5] This is the reverse of 2, and takes the world of nature to be adjectival to the individual. The world of nature has here its own integrity, though it is dependent for its being on the individual. This is the position I have taken with respect to nature as known by science; in a more radical form it can be taken by sociologically affected theorists who suppose that nature itself is but a function of man. By a subjectivistic twist we get it out of Kant; the world of nature is a function of man's interpretation but it goes its own way while so dependent. The necessities of nature would here be a function of the free production of nature by man. 6] This is the reverse of 3 and involves the recognition that the driving force behind nature is given by the individual. Nature is itself affected by the individual and is constantly altered to accommodate it, feeling the force of his nature or insistence or power. This is Hegel's view; he insists that man governs nature and in the end that nature takes the shape that man's presence and demands force it to. However, man here must be viewed as a kind of representative of a cosmic mind, or Hegel must be individualized.

None of these views actually puts the individual and nature on a footing. If this be done then we get a seventh view, in which the individual and nature act in any of the above six ways. They could interact, to give us an eighth view in which the individual and nature, while independent in being and origin, will produce something common to them, a momentary One—society or the common-sense world.

The position which I have been holding I think is the seventh, as well as forms of the other eight in different circumstances. On my view, the two types of being, Actuality and Existence interact, and have one another as subdivisions, adjectives, and intrusive driving powers. In fact we can speak of a ninth view in which all of the eight function not as distinct alternatives but together in various situations and times.

March 28

Does the enterprise of philosophy begin with the awareness of the intrusion of the external world inside the concepts, life, feelings which we have as individuals, and is the progress of man dependent on his assimilation of this external world within his conceptual frame at the same time that he recognizes this conceptual frame to be adjectival to the real being of that external world? An affirmative answer assumes that man begins as alienated, as private, and later discovers what is at the roots of himself, that he is in fact part of a larger world.

The awareness of the external world is an integral part of man's self-awareness or knowledge; he is aware that he is part of a world beyond the knowledge. This is the position I have held over the years. But one can well affirm that it is but part of a larger view; that, for example, one begins by behaving in a larger world and finds himself intruding ideas into it and thereby discovers who he is. Does the child begin by finding the world operative inside his feelings or ideas, or does it begin by acting and then finding that it is thinking and that this thinking is a intrustive element in its public world? Does it discover *itself* in short, as this second alternative would suggest, or does it discover the *external world,* as the first suggests? If one thinks of the child as initially omnipotent (since to it is given without effort whatever satisfies and is needed) and that only when its cries are not answered it discovers the hard facts of the world, one can say that it eventually discovers the futility of its own feelings and "ideas." One could equally well say that it begins living through its own feelings and finds that there is a recalcitrant element, making it aware that there is more to the world than it "knew." On the first of these alternatives the feelings would be abandoned to behavior; one would submit to the world. On the second the feelings would be altered so as to accommodate the world inside those feelings, thereby enabling one to understand what it is to be. Perhaps both of these ventures are engaged in at the same time.

Arts like architecture, musicry and music are alert to the operative presence of the other world within themselves. The reverse position, where art is viewed as a kind of force or leaven in the realm of nature is related to Wilde's quip about nature imitating art. More basically, it would be the view that, while nature does have a reality of its own, it is a reality which is impotent and must be quickened by art. This view could be derived from Hegel, once art be understood to be an effective way of exhibiting the basic cosmic Idea.

March 30

The space, time and dynamic dimensions of Existence are endlessly malleable. This is why it is possible to engage in a given art in multiple ways. One painter, e.g., will stress flatness, another the way in which color actually forms the space, a third will stress contrasts, a fourth the ambiguity of a dimension. The unity of these different phases in a given work of art is of course to be accomplished by the artist or spectator. Just as the different scales in a work of architecture are solidified in the single scale of a man as a unitary being, so different dimensions of other works of art are solidified by the artist and spectator. It is not necessary though for another work to be as conspicuous or as routine as the engineering side of a building. Nevertheless there is the element of pleasure, of visibility, of consonance with the prevailing mores which must be considered by the artist if he is to communicate.

All the elements that we distinguish in trying to understand the nature of a work of art are analytic components which belong together by virtue of the fact that they make reference to man. They are, however, actually held apart by us and, in different works and sometimes in a given work, may have been made separately. In a work of art we learn then not only what Existence is for man but also what man is; the unity of the work, as that which finds a place for all these elements is due to man. We could then say that the work of art, in revealing the nature of Existence in its import on man, has two components—the nature of Existence in fact (and this is given in the texture), and the nature of man (which is given in the fact that the work has a unitary meaning for him). He learns to be one by virtue of his submission to the unity of the work of art, for the work of art is seen and made part by part. The acceptance of its unity is the recovery of himself as a single being who has, a mind, a body, etc., and therefore who has paticular but limited scales in terms of which the whole can be dissected. But there is an over-arching scale and that is provided by man himself. What man is and thus what his scale is, is not to be discovered except by going through the experience of finding oneself over against a single substantial work.

April 1

In order to know what is real, or at least what is objective and common for all men, one must either find something constant in their divergent contents, get intersections which cancel out their divergencies, construct that which could be real, or make direct contact with some kind of reality beyond them all.

We all distinguish babies from grown-ups, birth and death, day and night. These are nucleal constancies. It is these constancies which Wittgenstein perhaps tries to get at by his *gedankenexperimenten*. But instead of asking himself what happens when he changes the conditions (since this involves imagination with its possible taint of cultural conditioning) it is better to sheer away the specifications and qualitative elements in what we encounter. The common-sense world is also a world in which we can get intersections for our various parts.

We know whether or not something is an objective component in common sense by A] counterbalancing our own stresses in that world with one another, and B] by counterbalancing our cultural common-sense world with the cultural common-sense worlds of others. The former method enables us to overcome the fluctuating and varying emphases we place on our world from the different positions in our culture—e.g., church, family, etc. The second allows us to take the outcome of the first and still find that there must be a kind of residuum for all of them. A third method, C] is to imagine inside common sense what a thing is in and of itself before it has manifested itself; sometimes this is done by contrary to fact conditionals, sometimes by analysis, and sometimes by a "transcendental deduction," in the endeavor to see what must be presupposed if there is to be any common-sense world at all. A fourth method, D] is that of adumbration, which allows one to penetrate beneath the surface of the common-sense world to the underlying vaguely apprehended core. All four methods are legitimate and yield objective content.

In the endeavor to have a well-integrated body of knowledge which is also freed from cultural accretions, one can abstract from the common-sense world. If the abstraction is through perception, one does not reach objectivity, for the perceptual world is tainted by what the individual has experienced, and it does still have clinging to it something of the cultural meaning. But at its best it frees itself from culture. Every man can then be said to perceive in independence of his culture, but not in independence of his experience, his past, his interests, etc. To achieve objectivity here, one must carry out something like the four procedures pursued in connection with common sense.

There are tonal values in perception; the different senses have different textures, sound differing from color, and color from shape. These tonal differences, though not necessarily the specific textures actually encountered, would seem to be constants in perception. There is also what Peirce calls the *hic et nunc* aspect of perception, the over-againstness of it. Each individual can find what is common to all other perceptions by recognizing the different tonal values, the *hic et nunc* aspect, and perhaps also the fact that it is something individually tainted. The different percepts also allow for an intersection which we can denominate "the objective core" in all of them; thus the multiple facets of a coin can all be said to intersect at roundness. This roundness is in fact what is perceived, the facets being but stimuli and occasions for us to see that roundness. If this is the case it is the intersection which is known immediately, so that perceptions from the start have an objectivity open to all. Thirdly, there is the construction, the articulation and reorganization of perceptions so that they conform to some ideal, such as what would be seen by an ideal observer, or what is to be known under such and such ideal conditions which do not in fact prevail. We also take this position when we perceive, accepting qualifications and making alterations in our data to make them conform to some accepted norm such as what the object would be like in daylight, at arm's length, etc. And finally there is the idea of a perceptual adumbrated, the real perceptum as it is not yet caught within the limitations of the individual, or dissected for judgment.

It is sometimes supposed that science expresses itself objectively, and that this is the same thing as saying that its truths are neutral for all observers. But when one attends to the fact that theories are sometimes ignored or abandoned not because they have been shown to be false but because they are difficult, complex or not readily connected with others, that science's zero points are arbitrarily chosen, as are its units, and that its results are all in universals, it is evident that we have neutrality, but not necessarily objectivity, that which is there for all observers rather than that which abstracts from them. One can also find constant elements in all scientific assertions — formal relations, deducibility, and even such referents as scale and ruler, sun and earth, magnitudes, space and time. These may have only the useless generality of Newton's absolute time, but they seem to be present, for otherwise there would be nothing which is being measured or discoursed about. A self-contained science which speaks of measures or variations must suppose there are constants which are being measured or varied.

It is not easy to determine whether such a formula as Einstein's expresses the outcome of intersections of diverse scientific systems or a construction supposed to be real. It would seem to be the latter. If so we must look for an intersection of diverse scientific systems by some method such as supposing that every scientific system is a set of conditionals contrary to fact and that what one says the other also says with its own set of conditionals. If we take this tack then an Einsteinian formula would not be a contrary to fact conditional, but a least common denominator, a presupposition which every one of the systems utilizes in its own way. Finally, we ought to be able to peer beyond the scientific formulae and make contacts with the real beyond, so far as the formulae are themselves reports, restatements, mere icons of that real, guaranteed as it were by God, as Descartes maintained. Or is there an adumbrated in every scientific account which goes beyond the commonsensical object and touches the very being of the real?

Events also have a four-fold objectivity. There is the constancy of their having a magnitude governed by the reality of minimal durations; there is the intersectional nuclear meaning which we can get by seeing how people interact and thereby bring their diverse livings into interplay (thus making the public world the real constant for private events); there is the construction of the ideal event which could be obtained by some such device as following the clues of Bergson's or Whitehead's metaphysics; and finally there is the adumbrative grasp of Existence as the power in and outside the event.

The realm of the important has often been thought to be essentially subjective; the aims of men diverge and the standards they use are consequently different. Yet there are constancies – the value of friendship over hatred, life over death, pleasure over painful injury. There can be differences as to just when one has the one or the other, and one can put values on the negative items which make them seem greater than the positive. But these are subsequent to the recognition of the evil or negative value in the hatred, death, injury. Good and evil are constants, diversely expressed for different men, but having a steady difference inside all schemes. There is an intersection of importance in diverse men, giving us a nucleal importance characteristic of that group, and eventually of all mankind. And there is the construction of an ideal importance in the light of the absolute good, following the lead of Plato. Finally there is the adumbration of the basic cut of the world, as malign or benign, and thus as determining the value of our lives.

We can utilize all these four strands as they are abstracted, or as reduced to their objective components, in order to make a metaphysical construction of the nature of the being in which those strands or their objective components are integrally together. Since metaphysicians differ from one another, one would have to look for constancies in those constructions, find intersections amonst them, construct an Ideal in terms of which their diverse constructions can be judged, or finally find an adumbrated component inside each. (In the *Modes* there is an attempt to offer categoreal points which are constancies, the other views being thought to be subdivisions of the one presented and in a sense to offer components for which the *Modes* might be said to offer intersections; the view in the *Modes* is thought to meet the ideal conditions which a system is to have, and the adumbrated element is the world which common sense in its root is said to provide).

Art will be said to offer a construct comparable to the metaphysical but one which stresses the adumbrative or textural aspect of the real in contrast with its formal or conceptual aspects. One can then look for constancies in art, find the points of intersection of a number of them, define an ideal art, and actually adumbrate the real behind them all, in ways analogous to those discussed in the *Modes* in connection with philosophy. And there should be analogous acts in connection with mathematics and religion.

Cutting the foregoing in another way, we can say that there are four types of objectivity—constancies, intersections, constructions and encountered entities, and these are to be found in common sense, in strands abstracted from these, in different disciplines, and either in different kinds of encounter or in encounters with different modes of being. It is true then that science gives us objectivity, but not in a sense to be denied to any other strand, to common sense, to speculative enterprises, or to direct encounters.

Suppose one locates a constancy which no one else affirms? This is a special case of the problem of a man acting as a representative of the rest and finding that the rest do not take his views seriously. Architects are constantly worried about their conformity to the demands of their civilization. They want their works to be viable, and look for some way of expressing their civilization. But they are parts of the civilization themselves, and are at once being conditioned by it and constituting it. That their constitution may not be a primary element of the civilization is due in part to the power of people to receive it. The failure of a man to be a representative is a failure which arouses condemnation and a just cultural criticism that he has wasted his time. But he may prove representative of mankind for all that, as prophets, religious leaders, a Socrates or a Christ have proved to be. But even mankind may not accept him. And mankind may be mistaken. The final criterion of judgment is not what mankind says or endorses, but what it ought to endorse. Accordingly, he who has not received an acceptance or who never will, though he may in fact be incompetent or mistaken, may nevertheless be right in the eyes of eternity, while mankind is just so far wrong and to be condemned.

The fact that every assertion makes a claim to be representative, and thus to express a truth which others would also express, makes every assertion have a normative component. It in fact says that it is right, a judgment as it ought to be. It does not say that the content of that judgment is as it ought to be, i.e., it does not say that what it rightly claims is good. What it does claim is that the judgment is a proper one, that the assertion is correct, and thus that what is contended for is what others ought to affirm. We have then two levels of prescription. There is the claim that this occurrence is as it ought to be, and there is the claim that this occurrence is being affirmed as it ought to be affirmed. If one had the two together, one would say that *x* is good, that this judgment was properly made and, is a judgment which others should make.

Accordingly, when analysts say that a moral judgment has two components, one reporting a fact and the other an admonition that others ought to judge or act or approve in a similar manner, they overlook an alternative: though one ought to judge, act or approve as the assertor does — and this is what the assertor implicitly maintains — there is still the question whether or not moral assertions are similar in nature to others. It is a question of fact whether or not *x* is fat, and when we assert it is we add a claim to be representative. If we want to distinguish judgments of value from others it will have to be not by distinguishing these components, but by showing that a judgment such as *x* is good is not like one such as *x* is fat. We would have to maintain that the sheering away of the claim to be representative always leaves a dead, non-evaluative fact of the order of "*x* is fat." In short, it is correct to say that there is an emotional element in judgments of value and even a claim to be representative of all or to urge a prescription for all, but this does not yet make evaluative judgments different from other kinds of judgments. What would make them different would be an emotional component containing the whole of the evaluative part of the situation, leaving over as objective and factual only that which is non-evaluative. But an assertion which is functioning representatively is, so far, not evaluative in any other sense but that of claiming to be true.

When we assert *x* is good we are making an evaluation that our judgment is a just one. We are not mentioning that we are being evaluative, or reflecting something of our own desires. We are claiming to say something about the world. If the analytic approach were correct it would in fact have to say that the evaluational component, since it is not part of the factual world outside the realm of the assertion, is present only in the assertion, and that the assertion for that reason must be false. If "*x* is good" means I hold it to be so, and want you to hold it too (because it is in fact what is the case, not because I happen to be holding it) and it is the case that there is nothing good in fact, then whenever I say "*x* is good" I am saying something which is not true, and in urging others to affirm it or accept it I am urging them to affirm as true what is in fact false.

A true "*x* is good" is on a par with a true "*x* is fat." Both have evaluational components, referring to their universal truthfulness, and both refer to some matter of fact. The "good" however is not a predicate as "fat" is. It encompasses the entire object, and says that the components and predicates in the object are all harmoniously organized, mutually sup-portive, and give lodgment to the Ideal. We are always claiming to live up to the norm of telling the truth, both when we make assertions with limited and when we make assertions with all-inclusive predicates.

Is it perhaps the case that the all-inclusive predicate "good" involves an additional emotional component over and above that involved in claiming to assert a truth? Do we want someone not only to affirm or admit what we say, but to do something, say cherish this good? This is surely the case, but it is also the case that when we say "this is fat" we are asking that an other not only accept the truth but act on it appropriately. We may want him to record, admire, alter, reject. Is there something though which we may want another merely to note? Perhaps when we say that something is beautiful we want him merely to enjoy? But we want him also to cherish, be sensitive, appreciative, remember, where these mean more than merely enjoying in the sense of living with, then and there. In short, there seems to be an instrumental value to every object. We, in referring to that object, are also demanding of another that this instrumental value be attended to. Our affirmation is not only a claim to truth, which we expect or hope others to support, thereby making ourselves into petitioners to them and into prescribers for them (because we fear to be judged as oddities and also hold that they will be discredited if they do not accept our claim). Our affirmation is offered to them as alongside us, and thus to them as capable of using the objects to which we refer.

All judgments then have   A] an objective component,   B] a representative claim by a prescriber, c] a representative claim by a petitioner, D] a supposition regarding subsequent use. These seem to answer to Actuality, God, Ideality, and Existence. Analysts seem to think the important element is A; Kantians B; sociologists c; and pragmatists D.

April 2

To yesterday's set should be added the case of some item selected as a paradigm, an individual whose life or nature or character is the touchstone, a rule, such, e.g., as the serpentine line in painting, or some basic decision by someone in power.

Theories of law, kinds of judgment, schemes of value, criteria, basic outlooks, can be defined in terms of the various kinds of contents and the objective elements in them.

1] Naïve common sense. This accepts whatever appears to common-sense men. It is essentially cultural and defines who is sensible in the society. Popular judgments of virtue and vice hinge here; it is behind the theory of democracy, common voting, and perhaps juries.

2] Constants in common sense. Since even inside a single culture there are variations in acceptances, one may try to isolate what is always present, or what is present in all common-sense experience, such as opposition, interplay, space, time, and the like. Ideas of right and wrong are thought to be constants defining the variations which individuals may exhibit as deviations or complications. These constants are thought to be found by direct inspection.

3] Intersections in common sense. One can shift out of the plurality of details and diversities something objective by attending to the least common denominator, the part which remains when the diversities cancel out as objective. We do this when we take a majority vote, or better when we engage in a compromise and direct arbitration or discussion.

4] Constructions in common sense. We can, through analysis, or more boldly in speculation, try to get ideal components or portions of the common-sense world which would serve as the model for the others and would be taken to be neutral and objective for all. This is what is done when one speaks of a reasonable man. He is not any one man, but what a man would be like were he properly attuned to that situation.

5] There is the direct adumbration of the basic reality in common sense. This is somewhat related to the second case. But whereas in the second case right and wrong are found by direct inspection, here they are known by a kind of penetrating gaze, which cuts beneath the ostensible common-sense data to find its meaning, its value. One takes this position in evaluating candidates for office, but it is also the method used by "sages" or "leaders" who know the data open to others, data on the edge of the common-sense world.

6] One can take some man as a model, the king perhaps or some virtuous man, and estimate what is right and wrong, what is objective and true in the light of whether or not it conforms to him. This is what in principle is done by those who model their ideas of worth and reality on the principles exhibited in the lives of religious leaders.

7] One can take some particular part of common-sense life, say what is isolated in work, or discovered in the course of a ceremonial, as providing the items which are truly objective, neutral and capable of determining the worth and reality of all others. Some item is isolated, approved and even made into a fetish; what sustains or is radiated by that item is thereby ennobled. This is the view of those who take certain occurrences to be omens.

8] There can be rules isolated in the common-sense world, such as those expressed in common law, which serve as the principles in terms of which all others are to be judged. It is these principles which the law seeks to express and which are to be exemplified in the lives of reasonable men.

9] One can deliberately take some item in the common-sense world and by a fiat take it to be the final test. This is perhaps what the existentialists do when they commit themselves to a whole career in terms of some decision to act or affirm. This decision could be the decision of some man in power whose word defines what is right and wrong and even what is real, so that we have diseases and offenses defined by him, though no one else would have recognized them.

These nine cases have parallels in the four strands, perception, science, events and value; they are to be found in all the nine cases of the arts, and in the three ways of dealing with reality which are alternative to the arts. This means there are 36 plus 36 plus 27 cases to deal with—which is to say with the previous 9, a total of 108. In addition one can take the preferred element to be a measure not only of its own domain but of others as well, so that e.g., a constant in common sense might be taken to be the criterion in terms of which one judges the rightness or excellence or even reality of a painting or an item in perception, and so on.

10–18] Perception. Perceptual objectivity is of interest primarily to those who wish to resolve common sense into its ultimate components. But perceptions diverge, and one must isolate items which could be taken to be the basic, pivotal percepta. Those who make it their primary concern to attend to observable evidence look to perception, and must in the end find constants, constructions, adumbrations, model perceivers, model percepta, rules, and arbitrary segements. None but philosophers and perhaps some psychologists take any of these to be ultimate; in any case they are never taken as ultimate in courts of law except as indices to what is to be treated as genuine common-sense reality. When this is done the objectivily viewed percepta become tests not for perception but for what is to be accepted in a common-sense world. This is perhaps the way the jury is supposed to deal with the evidences given to it.

19–27] Science. It is sometimes supposed that any part of science is true or objective or a model for all else. But since scientists differ, since not everything can be confirmed, and since there are interstitial suppositions required for the entire enterprise, it is necessary to find a basis for determining what are the ultimate objective realities as vouched for by science. There may be no individual who can make a final decision, but a scientific community can. It refuses to attend to questions which are not immediately to the fore or based on issues at the centre of the interests of most. Also science is, by the criterion of verification, made subject to the tests of objectivity provided by common sense, rather than the reverse. Gallileo and Descartes were more consistent with respect to the ultimacy of science; they did not take its assertions to be tested by common sense, but rather the reverse, and therefore dismissed common sense as not expressing what was real. In the law those men who are concerned with statistics, and the reports say of psychiatrists, are concerned with what is supposed to be known by science, the one attending to rules given by science, the other making analyses of the scientifically acquired data, and applying the result to common-sense or perceptual data. Inside science itself constants, intersections, and the like serve merely to tell the scientist how to evaluate other reports, as being somehow qualified or limited by special conditions.

28–36] Events. The pragmatic approach to the world ultimately comes to deal with the world of events. But events also have differences amongst them, making desirable the isolation of criteria or special cases which allow one to have a theory of value and to treat some events as being not as basic as others. In the law we look for what would make life go on, what makes it possible to continue in the course of political living, and thus seek the common factors which all must accept, intersections which relate and give focus to all, constructions which give us ideal cases, adumbrations into the power of Existence itself (taking the life of some man, or some signal event as the crux), find some rule exemplified in all events, such as a supposed law, or look to some decisively accepted event. We do not want the course of daily living disrupted and take as basic the events which make such living possible.

37–45] The values which men use are not used in constant ways, and therefore one must find objective values here as well as in other strands. Are there constants in all evaluations? Can one find them by intersections? Can one construct an ideal value? Can one adumbrate a basic value behind evaluations? Can one find model men or cases, rules or decisions? Everyone of these seems to have some defenders—Platonists; interculturalists; planners; religionists; patriots; realists; rationalists; emotivists.

46–54] Architecture; *55–63]* Sculpture; *64–72]* Painting. Here we have A] created realities, each governing space in a distinctive way. But in each, one can look for constants, as is done by historians; intersections as is done by those who make comparative studies; constructions in the light of some ideal work; adumbrations, in the light of what can be discerned within any; ideal judgers or experts; ideal cases such as classical works; basic rules, e.g., the pyramid, golden section, etc., or some decision to accept this or that as one's pivotal case. Any one of these arts can be measured by the objective component of the others, so that one can judge the work of a sculptor, for example, in terms offered by an objective theory of painting. There is also the application of any one of these constructions to the common-sense world or its derivatives, and conversely. As a rule, ordinary men employ objective components in common sense to estimate the worth of works of art, but one can surely make use of science or perception, activity or the sense of importance, and one can reverse the procedure and judge common sense or these derivatives to be defective just so far as they fail to exhibit or be in consonance with what the objective elements of the arts require. Carried over into law this would be tantamount to providing a code to measure common-sense items or abstractions from them, or conversely, using the latter to determine what in the code is sensible or legitimate.

73–99]; 100–126] deal with the temporal and dynamic arts. They repeat above, but also bring in the consideration that one might use a temporal art to measure a dynamic or a spatial one, and so on.

127–154] relate to the enterprises of philosophy, mathematics and religion which, like art, are concerned with some definite mode of being. Each one of these can be examined for objective elements. Thus philosophy has assertions and even systems which may express only a personal opinion. One must find something objective and neutral in philosophy if it is to be worthy of the name of an ultimate discipline. Its objective elements, found by looking for constants, intersections and so on, can be used to evaluate all other enterprises, and conversely these enterprises can serve to measure it.

Strictly speaking no enterprise has a right to impose its criteria of objectivity on any others. Or, if it does so impose its criteria, it ought to be receptive to the criteria which the others provide. This contention applies primarily to cases 46–154, for the previous cases are derivatives from these. The objective components in these previous cases are objective only with respect to these disciplines; the disciplines themselves are being judged by the criteria that basic studies into the modes provide. This does not disqualify the objectivity of these various disciplines, but shows only that the objectivity they provide is an objectivity which falls short of giving us what is real or basically valuable.

The ideal scheme will use the basic inquiries as irreducible, and will then relate them to the objective elements found in the other enterprises. The latter elements would serve as useful agents for the expression of the constants of the inquiries concerned with the modes. Thus we could say that a true philosophic assertion, e.g., is that which has such and such characteristics (say constancy through all philosophies) and which came to expression in say the intersectional objectivity of common-sense assertions. We would use the constants of the basic inquiries into the modes to enable us to estimate the import of other enterprises, and thereby make it possible to identify the objective elements in those other enterprises with the objective elements of the inquiries into the modes.

April 3

The basic divisions— 1] common-sense, 2] strands, 3] disciplines concerned with the *Modes,* and 4] the modes themselves, all have

virtues of their own. The first is culturally and pragmatically significant; the second is manipulatable in thought, and capable of a rational
organization without losing rootage in the commonsensical real; the third,
reproducing the being of the real—art doing this in texture for Existence,
mathematics doing this in tension for the Ideal, philosophy in structure for
Actuality (the category is the essence of man's inwardness, though in an
abstract form), mysticism through its ineffableness doing this for the divine; the fourth giving us the permanent in which the others can be
rooted. Because each has virtues, each offers measures for all the others,
and has been so used. But because each has virtues, no one has a right to
dismiss the others as worthless, though they will of course fail to measure
up to the demands of the measurer. Even metaphysics, with its insistence
on telling what the real is, must confess its failure to have the pragmatic
utility of common sense or the virtues of the strands. It cannot, like a
strand, entertain hypotheses for the sake of tying together a miscellany of
encountered items. Instead it must transcend what is in fact experienced
and what is merely abstracted from this. It is superior in offering us the
real, but inferior in other respects.

It would be a mistake for other disciplines or divisions to be treated as
realities or as offering us direct reports of the real; this would be a mistake
of the same order as that of a philosophy which thought it was commonsensical, had the empirical grounding or detailed organization of a strand,
or the substantiality of the real. Metaphysics then is no test of other
disciplines or phenomena except so far as the question of the reality,
ultimacy, the rootage of what is otherwise conceived, is concerned.

Under the influence of Wittgenstein, the Oxford school seems to be
concerned with finding the constants in common-sense experience by
using as its measure the nature of man so far as this is expressed in his
living language. (Other thinkers can and undoubtedly will use man's
social habits or institutions, social behavior, social virtues.) The position
tends to overlook the fact that there are other ways of getting to the
objective than by looking for constants, and that there are other ways of
getting constants besides those which use man as a measure and then in the
guise of a language-using being. Thus one could look for constants by
making an historic survey, by analyzing out what seem to be accidental or
accidental features, or by having a systematic means (such as clarity and
distinctness) for eliminating elements. The Wittgensteinian way seems to
involve the use of the imagination; but this is notoriously without
well-defined procedures. One will never learn by this method just what the
constants in fact are.

One need not take the language of man to be the paradigm for determining what the proper constants are; one could conceive of a proper "usage" of one's body or of social institutions. Or, better, one could forget about man in any guise and take some abstract rule, as Descartes did, and use this to determine what should be accepted as a constant, even though not directly experienced as such. And since one can get objectivity without having recourse to constants, one can ignore the method of the Oxford school altogether and concentrate on such a method as that of intersecting diverse common-sense contents in a common focal point.

More important, perhaps, is the fact that the discoveries by any of these methods will result in the ignoring of what may be an objective factor inside the common-sense world itself, since the use of criteria such as language or rules or behavior or decisions, etc., subjects the common-sense world to conditions which are not altogether germane to its nature, and thus gives us what might be called a 'languagified' common sense, or a behavioralized common sense, or a rule-dominated common sense, and the like. Of course some method must be used to find the constants. That method could be part of the very common-sense world itself, for the isolating of variants and transients is part of common-sense living. To this it might be answered that language too is a common-sense item. But it is not used by the school as such an item. It is used as a measure and a ground for determining what in the common-sense world is to be taken as constant, even in the face of its transience, and despite the presence of other items in every moment of experience. And if the Wittgensteineans ignore (as they do) science and events, they can isolate only some of the items which are in fact constant. Also, they do not seem aware of the fact that a language-philosophy can be judged by criteria rooted in other enterprises, which do not take common sense as seriously as it does.

In summary: A] there are other objective factors besides constants; B] there are other ways of discovering constants besides that of an intuitive disposal of non-constants;   C] there are other criteria for what a constant is than conformity to a language;   D] there are other domains in which criteria can be imposed than that of common sense;   E] the outcome of one method has limitations which can be corrected only by recourse to other methods, occupied with different objective factors in different ways without restriction to language or common sense. The most that one can hope for from the language school is the isolation of constants in common sense as available to an experiment with language. It will give us common sense as communicable, manipulatable, familiar. It will not have the rationality of science, the personal quality of perception, the immersion of events, the values of accepted importance; it will not have the completeness of philosophy, the creativeness of art, the sympathy of mysticism, or the translucency of mathematics, and will miss the reproduction of reality which these provide in structure, texture, ineffableness, and a tensional relation of parts; and it will not of course have the grounding character which the real, in any of its modes, provides.

Common sense is a starting point and an ending, but it does not ground the basic disciplines and these do not refer to it. When Dewey spoke of metaphysics as concerned with the pervasive aspects of experience he sometimes seemed to think that it was the constants of common sense which were the object of metaphysics; if this is the case he had in mind essentially what Wittgensteineans today do, but did not provide a method for finding the aspects. On the other hand it is not altogether clear that the Wittgensteineans want to find pervasive traits rather than items which are open to every man. A pervasive trait is one which is presumably to be found in every item (and this is Dewey's view in the main); a constant is an item which anyone will be able to encounter.

It is conceivable that there might be no pervasive traits, no traits shared by all apart from the trait of being commonsensical, etc.; it is conceivable that there might be no single object which all men could or would have as objective. If the former alone were the case, one would have constant objective items but no common characters present in all items whatsoever; if the latter alone were the case, one would have features which were present in all items but no items which could be found in all contexts. Since the very approach from language, etc., requires that there be pervasive features marked out by the very fact of language, Dewey's position is inescapable. Only by presupposing pervasive traits could there be a universal application of language; or conversely, the applicability of language is one with there being pervasive traits. So, strictly speaking, we must presuppose a Deweyean approach. However, this need not be confined to language or any other aspect of a paradigmatic man. One could discover such traits by making use of other measures. But even then, one would not have reached what others would term metaphysics; for this concerns not pervasive traits answering to some measure, or even to what is found within experience itself, but to what underlies the experience and makes it and other things possible, or which rectifies experience by giving it a more coherent formulation with some reproduction of the nature of what lies outside the experience itself.

The denial that there is anything outside experience would preclude the use of any criteria, deny the need to rectify experience, deny that one can engage in speculative enterprises, art, etc., or can recover the being which stands away from man, his cultural concerns and his capacity to experience. Experience surely needs man; but the real is larger than man and has being apart from him. Dewey sometimes spoke as though this real could be known by science. He thereby showed that his idea of experience was not inclusive enough, and mistakenly supposed that science gave him the real instead of a rationalized version of this. It was right of him to acknowledge a science beyond the control of experience, but wrong to suppose there were no other enterprises also beyond that control, or that there were no enterprises which gave one the real.

In the *World of Art,* there are four strands examined in terms of extensional factors—time, space, and becoming. But there ought also be a concern for individuals, for unity and for purposiveness, which are also characteristic of the common-sense world. A perceptual strand is at once individually based in an object, has a unity governing the plurality of sense data and a directionality. These are mentioned in the *WofA* but within the orbit of the extensional elements. They have an independent being. This is also the case with the rational or scientific strand, the evaluative, and the eventful. The individual for the scientific is identified with an instance of a law, the unity it deals with is the unity of its discourse or its inquirers, and the purposiveness comes in as a kind of conditioning of all the material so as to produce understanding or agreement. The evaluative strand takes the individual to be a final locus of value, treats unity as governing the whole, and finds purposiveness as the tension towards a good to be achieved. The transitional or eventful takes the individual to be a pivot, unity to pervade, and has purposiveness ingredient in it.

The strands which concern themselves with individuals will find satisfaction in the Actual; those which deal with unity will refer to the divine; and those which are occupied with purposiveness will refer to the Ideal. They are then not of primary concern in an account of art; but they are significant for an account of strands, for an understanding of the common-sense world, and for an understanding of the nature of the real.

In different works Kant took account of the pervasive and inescapable features of the common-sense world. In the *Critique of Pure Reason* he acknowledged a root space and time (and perhaps also a kind of becomingness); in the *Critique of Practical Reason* he recognized substantial unities, or individuals; in the *Critique of Judgment* he recognized unified groups of items for aesthetics, and purposiveness in his teleological judgment. It would have been better had he taken all these as equally "forms of intuition" and applied his categories on them to constitute a world. He took ours to be the world of science which, though mechanical in nature, was primarily commonsensical in structure and being. The fact is that the world is open to perception, scientific study, living, and evaluation. His categories are analytic, not interpretative of his world. Interpretations tell us what to do with "intuited" material.

April 4

Kant took extension to be divided into two kinds—space and time. He overlooked the extensiveness of becoming, so clearly brought out by Whitehead. Also, he did not note that his extensions were abstractions. He saw they were correlative to the abstractions of the categories. When he said that intuitions without concepts are blind and concepts without intuitions are empty he perhaps also saw that the extensions were abstractions. But of what are they abstractions? It is not merely of that which results from the juncture of categories and extensions—which is the normal way of rectifying Kant by those who recognize that he had to start with the thick of experience. The juncture of the two yields only an abstract scientific account of things. Also it is most dubious that the categories united with the extensions would give anything more than intelligible segments of those extensions, making it possible to know not the world of experience or a scientifically reconstructed world of experience, but only that experience as caught within space-time-becoming.

The union of the forms of intuition and the categories seems to take place before we have experiential content; this is the abstract scientific world. How could this be filled out by content in such a way as to have a causality in it, not expressed in either the forms of intuition or the categories?

Kant also overlooked the fact that there are other "forms of intuition" besides the extensive. There is the "form of intuition" which says that there are substantial beings over against one; without such a predetermination of individual beings we would never have anything but phenomena. There is also the fact that there are unities, situations, combinations of items in a field, which Kant was able to deal with only by attending to his own acts of synthesis. But they are pre-conditional in the same way as the forms of space-time-becoming are. They cannot be conceptualized, but only immediately apprehended. They are, with space, time, becoming, not to be put over against categories, but are to be understood as always categorized, and to have application to content as so categorized; the content is not amorphous but is already structured in the way the categorized-forms are. And there is also a dynamics to the world, the making of things, the productive powers in things, which cannot be assimilated either to time or becoming or to some categorial organization of such a time or a becoming.

Extension, otherness or individuality, unities and productivity (Peirce's first, second, [fourth] and third?) are pervasive features which have application to one another. Extension contains subdivisions in the shape of the other three; individuals have all three of the other features; synthetic unities have subdivisions in individuals, are extended and productive; productivity is extended, is unified and has subdivisions of individuals. The Kantian forms of intuition then should have been far more complex than he indicated, even if restricted to mere extensionality or to the extensionality of space or time.

Also, there are other modes of apprehension besides that which intellectually subdivides an encountered space-time-becoming. One can perceive, live through, and evaluate. And one can engage in art and in philosophy. In all these cases what one confronts is the common-sense world in which pervasive features are ingredient. These could be isolated by science, but they are also open to other modes of isolation.

Instead then of proceeding as Kant did, one can follow something like the clue given by his transcendental deduction and start with experience as already characterized by pervasive features. One can then isolate some of these, purging them in the process, and having them as integral to some method of apprehension. Thus we can say, e.g., that we encounter time in experience, but that we seek to know it in scientific ways. If we do, we isolate time as such to get something like the Kantian form of intuition, over against the category of measure or quantity or magnitude.

The outcome of the Kantian analytic is the result of an abstraction from the concrete content of experience, and an achievement of abstract elements, one functioning as the matter for the other, and neither being adequate to common experience. If we try to reverse the process, we will find that the dual abstractions of say, time and some categorial way of handling it, are not merely given a content to organize but are radically transformed by that content to give the world of experience. That world of experience yields not only a scientific account but perceptual, eventual and evaluational accounts. Granted then that we had only space and time in experience we would have to get, besides the scientific, other categorial ways of handling the abstracts of these. The same "mathematical" necessities which Kant found in space and time as correlative to scientific categories must be found in the others; and the same kind of metaphysical deduction which Kant provided for the scientific categories would have to be found for the categories which break up the perceptual, the lived, and the evaluational world. Are there such necessities? It does not seem correct to say that if there are, they are derived from logic, particularly a restricted Aristotelian logic.

Kant's final categories seem to be: degree, magnitude, causality and necessity (with reciprocity perhaps being reduced to causality, with possibility and actuality in his system being reduced to necessity, and substance being presupposed in degree). These are pervasive characters. Degree would seem to answer to the nature of individuals; magnitude to extensions; causality to purposiveness, and necessity to synthetic unities; i.e., these are the a priori conditions in terms of which one actually apprehends specific individuals, extensions, purposiveness, and unities.

What we encounter are specific cases of individuals, differing in degree; specific cases of extensions, differing in magnitude; specific cases of purposiveness differing in causal effectiveness; specific cases of unity with different types of necessity. A "deduction" would require one to free oneself from the conditions of specification, which means separating them off from possible content, to make us have only otherness, mere extensions, sheer directionality, and affiliatability. But every one of these can be isolated in a number of ways. If we want the extension appropriate to science we will get one kind of extension, if we want that appropriate to perception we would get another kind. No one of these would be sheer extension. A sheer extension neutral to science, etc., would be the synthetic product of all, or the product of a creative act in art, or a speculation in philosophy, etc.

In summary:

1] Extension includes becoming.

2] There are other "forms of intuition," such as otherness, purposiveness, unities.

3] All the forms are already categorized to be generic frames which are merely specified by content. Extension is broken up into magnitudes, otherness is for individuals, etc. These answer to the fact that we are to know them.

4] The abstraction of the forms apart from their bearing in experience gives one an abstraction of them.

5] There are many ways of making the abstraction. Each answers to some attitude, such as that of the perceiver using his senses, the scientist being rational, etc.

6] The abstractions are assimilated to the attitudes, so that what one knows is abstract space as perceptible, cognizable, lived through or evaluated, etc.

7] To get the nature of sheer extension, sheer otherness, sheer purposiveness, sheer unity as beyond any qualifications by attitudes expressed in strands, one must synthesize the different strands, or construct an entity in art or philosophy or religion or mathematics which will give us sheer neutral pervasive features of the real.

The pervasive features as intertwined are the concern of art, philosophy, etc., and of course of the common-sense world. If we look for an experiential grounding of religion, philosophy, etc., in experience it can only be with respect to the intertwined features, with a stress on one of them. The isolation of the individual, for example, is the work of a strand so far as this is set over against extension, etc. But the individual as at once extended, situational, etc., is the topic for philosophy; religion would take a situational or other unity as basic and have the others intertwined with it. Religion then has an experiential ground in the fact that it takes the situation as primary and has the others rooted in it; had it put them all on a footing it would be reduced to a mere category for common sense; if it dealt with the situation as a presuppositional unity in which the situational facet of common sense were also an expression alongside extension, etc., it would re-present to us the texture of a mode of being, or something analogous to this.

April 5

The common-sense worlds of different social groups are not in complete accord. Family life has many different textures, values, components for us which Eskimos do not acknowledge, just as snow, cold, and distance have natures for them which they do not have for us. Common-sense worlds are largely conventional worlds, overlaid with meanings that reflect the common experience, traditions, practices, and needs of particular groups. Still, we do seem able to communicate with men in other societies. We do seem able to acknowledge some objects, and do act on these in concordant ways. There do seem to be common pervasive features in our different common-sense worlds which our diverse stresses do not entirely obscure.

In all common-sense worlds there are observable entities, activities, extended regions, and situations. These are not always attended to; they are not even always understood in the same way by all the members of the same group. But every moment of experience exhibits them, intertwined with one another, and filled out with specific content. All of us deal with them as so intertwined and filled out, under the guidance of training, habits and unexamined beliefs. Consequently none of us understands the world of common sense very well. The pervasive features blur one another's natures; the filling which experience provides merges imperceptibly into them all; there is no clear indication as to just what parts of our common-sense world are objective and real, and what subjective and illusory.

To know what is real and what is not we must separate off he pervasive features from the transitory filling they receive in the course of daily experience. Such a separation is no simple act. It requires the use of definite but limited powers on our part, each producing a result distinct from that which other powers would. If we make use of our sense organs we turn pervasive features into parts of an abstract perceptual realm; if we use our reason they appear as parts of an abstract scientific account; if we live with them, they become parts of an abstract domain of events; and if we interest ourselves in them they become parts of an abstract scheme of values. To know what is real we must escape from the limitations which our different approaches impose on the pervasive features when we attempt to hold those features apart from the filling they get in experience.

We can separate off pervasive features either as intertwined or as distinct from one another. If we do the first we get one of four schemata of the common-sense world, depending on whether we make our separation through the agency of perception, science, action, or evaluation. Each offers a form or category in which the various features are intertwined. None is clear in detail or in outline, and any attempt to combine them will but compound the initial confusion which each exhibits. It would be better to dissect the different schemata, analyze each into a set of distinct pervasive features and then, to overcome the limitations that the different modes of apprehension impose on them, synthesize the different shapes which each exhibits inside a particular mode of apprehension. A synthesis of perceptual, scientific, lived, and evaluative forms of time, for example, will provide one with a form of time which is neutral to all these modes of apprehension. But it will not give us the texture of time; it yields only a concept of it. To know what time or any other pervasive feature is really like, it is best to turn away from the different modes of apprehending it and attempt to create the features themselves. This is what we do when we speculate in philosophy, participate in a religion, make contributions in mathematics, or engage in an art. Philosophy, though, is primarily concerned with understanding actual substances, religion with making contact with an ultimate unity, mathematics with mastering the ideal termini of purposes, and art with creating an extended space, time or becoming. No synthesis of these enterprises is possible. Each defines a distinct irreducible mode of being. Purposes, tension and the rest are intertwined only in the world of common sense.

The foregoing is a not-used portion of an introduction to the *Nine Basic Arts*. It makes it possible to summarize Kant's errors in still another way:

1] He overlooked the fact that we begin with a common-sense world and not with a scientific one.

2] He neglected to consider a third form of extension—becoming.

3] He neglected to consider such other basic "forms of intuition" as otherness, unifications (or synthesis as an ingredient structural form), and directionality.

4] He neglected to note that from the common-sense world one could abstract schemata which would be all the forms of intuition as intertwined, and defining a possible object.

5] He neglected to note that abstract schemata could be apprehended in perception, through action, and through values, as well as through science.

6] He neglected to note that scientific categories give only functions and variables, or in his terms, magnitudes; and that his set of categories is not really pertinent to scientific inquiry.

7] He neglected to note that one can separate out different sets of characters, for each pervasive feature can be considered by itself.

8] He neglected to note that each abstraction subjects content to a different set of conditions.

9] He did not know that a feature might be treated as neutral by synthesizing the various abstractions which are made of a common-sense form of it.

10] He did not examine the possibility of synthesizing the schemata of common-sense objects to get the idea of a mere object in general, vague, without much determination.

11] He neglected to consider the nature of a known substantial object which is produced by synthesizing all the features grasped in a given mode of apprehension, and therefore did not see that there are at least four types of known substantial objects.

12] He neglected to see that since we cannot synthesize known substantial objects we must find the real in some other way. This will be done either A] by seeing some way of synthesizing neutral features (e.g., extension which is the outcome of a synthesis that overcomes the abstractional conditions imposed by perception, science, etc.), or B] by dealing with each feature directly but as it is in and of itself. A] If the *Modes* is right, A is not possible; at most it will give us the idea of a One for the many. There can be no genuine unification of extension, individuality, etc., which is neutral to them all, except in the sense of 10. Indeed, a neutral extension is already constitutive of a known substance, in which perhaps the other features can be viewed as derivatives and then as somewhat transformed from the way in which they would be were they had as themselves constitutive. B] Treatment of a feature in and of itself must be achieved by speculation, participation, decision or creation. Each can be extended in a derivative way to the others, but strictly speaking each is appropriate to only one type, and in any case will never make the others part of the one which is of primary interest to itself.

If we take nature to be the synthesis of various strands as carried by, grounded in Existence, then we can speak of the synthesis, when carried by Actuality, as a realm of individual substances. When carried by God it is creation, and when carried by the Ideal it is a realm of intelligibles, or schemata for the world. Nature, individuals, creation and schemata would all be real and objective—certainly more so than the world of common sense, which is infected by social conventions and has the strands inchoately together—by virtue of their being rooted in real, irreducible beings.

April 6

Some of the foregoing needs correction:

If nature is conceived by virtue of A] a synthesis of abstractions derived from common sense which B] is imbedded in Existence, it ought to be possible 1] to take, e.g., the scientific rectification of common sense, which consists in the isolation of space, time, becoming, individuals, unity, and directionality, and synthesize this to have a scientific realm of reality; 2] and then do something similar to perception, events and values, and 3] then synthesize the results of *1* and *2*. In other words, there is an alternative to the method of merely neutralizing, say time, by synthesizing the abstractions which science, perception, events and values make, and then combining the result with other synthetic products. We can compare the two methods thus:

I. x, y, z synthesized in perception, or science, etc., to constitute a realm of reality; the different realms then to be synthesized to give us a possible realm of nature.

II. x synthesized in perception and science, etc., to constitute a neutral x; this to be synthesized with neutral y and z to give us a possible realm of nature.

It seems to have been my tendency to take the second tack; the two though appear to be equivalent. We do not however get the realm of nature in either way until we imbed it in Existence. Existence thus seems to sustain not only extensions, but individuals, unities and directionality, both severally and together. So far as it does each by itself, it offers us dimensions of nature, not nature in its full concreteness.

The very same neutral items, obtained by either method can be imbedded in Actuality, God, or Ideality. If imbedded in Actuality we get expressions of Actuality, a kind of subjective orientation of them, which can be dealt with one by one or as together. When taken together, we get the set of "categories" in terms of which actualities face the world. The categories could be said to make a single four-fold set, with extension being set over against unity and the two mediated by a correlative pair, individuals and directionality, eventually to be filled out with indicateds and contemplateds. If the neutral items are imbedded in God they have the form not of creation (as was suggested before) but of a dependent world. This dependency is consistent with an idea of creation but not identical with it. If the neutral items are imbedded in Ideality we get them in the guise of a set of forms or schemata, wholly intelligible variables filled out by determinating content.

A feature such as space then has the following natures: *1]* common-sensical, *2]* perceptual, *3]* scientific, *4]* eventful, *5]* valuational, *6]* as a component in an abstract pattern for any common-sense object, *7]* as a component in a synthesis of perceptualized features, *8]* as a component in a synthesis of scientific features; *9]* as a component in a synthesis of eventful features, *10]* as a component in a synthesis of evaluated features, *11]* as neutralized through a synthesis of perception, science, events and importance, *12]* as combined with other syntheses of perception, science, events and importance, so as to constitute the idea of a possible realm of nature (or through a synthesis of *7, 8, 9, 10*); *13]* *11* imbedded in Existence; *14]* *12* imbedded in Existence. *15]* *11* imbedded in Actualities, *16]* God, or *17]* Ideality; *18]* *12* imbedded in Actualities, *19]* God, or *20]* Ideality; *21]* as ingredient in Existence itself; *22]* as an element in Actuality, *23]* as an element in God; *24]* as an element in Ideality; *25]* as expressed in architecture, *26]* as expressed in sculpture, *27]* as expressed in painting, *28]* as expressed in compound arts.

April 7

The world of common sense is not altogether clear, not only because the perceptual, formal, productive and valuational components are merged inextricably within it, but because it is imbedded in four different contexts each of which makes its nature felt. It is imbedded in Existence and has its extensionality from this; it is there quickened by powers outside itself which we faintly adumbrate. It is imbedded in individuals and thereby achieves the status of a *lebenswelt,* to become primarily oriented towards myself and others, with all non-human things somehow made subservient to our basic tensions and interests. It is imbedded in the Ideal and is thereby idealized, made into a centre of values, a kind of faint copy of the Good. And it is imbedded in the divine and achieves a sacramental status, as that which is unified by a power and therefore controlled in ways which it cannot explain. If we wish to speak of this common-sense world as the realm of experience, we will have to say that experience is no more existent than it is individually oriented, no more idealized and formal than it is sacramental and unified. If then one sought to find an experiential ground for religion one could do this just as readily as one could find an experiential ground for science, perception, etc.

We speak of science as requiring verification by the facts of the world. If we follow out the clue of the theory of complementarity which affirms (on one of the possible interpretations) that classical formulations are indeterminate with respect to certain sub-microscopic occurrences and conversely, then the nature of science and the facts of the world will be indeterminate in themselves and made determinate only together. But perhaps more important is the truth that the facts which are supposed to verify science are either denuded facts, facts which show only a scientific side, or they are full-bodied facts which show also the sides where they are valuational, individual, etc. The latter would seem to be irrelevant; but the former presupposes that the verifying facts are either already made into scientific entities (or are so converted when used to verify,) which seems to beg the question. Taking this lead one can say that it is the same full-bodied fact which we use to verify religion, or value, etc., and that when we impose the principles of unity, individuality or Ideality, we denude the facts to make them verificational for religion, *lebenswelt* or Ideality, respectively. (Religion here is not being used as an inquiry into a mode of being, and science is not being used as merely formal self-enclosed system; both are viewed as reoriented towards the commonsense world, and thus as experimental or experiential.)

The *lebenswelt,* experiential science, experiential religion, and experiential ideals are the strands of perception, science, events (?) and importance given rootage in different modes of being, as sustaining the world of common sense. The *lebenswelt* for example is perceptual, formal, productive and valuational at the same time, but as oriented in substantial individuals—and so on for the other domains.

Instead of taking the strands either severally or as synthesized in an intelligible way and rooting them in the sustaining powers of the commonsense world, one can conceive them to be rooted in the modes of being directly. When this is done we have a realm of nature, so far as the combined strands are integrated with Existence; a realm of persons or psyches or individuals when made integral to Actuality; a realm of the intrinsically sacramental when grounded in the divine; and a realm of the formally perfected when grounded in the Ideal.

Perceptions then can be said to tell us not only about nature, but about persons, the sacramental and the perfect, though only under the restrictions of the perceptual outlook. When perceptions are united with science, etc., we get what nature, persons, etc., are conceived to be, for nature, persons, etc., as known are the outcome of the synthesis of the perceptions, science, etc. Perceptions give us only a partial grasp of nature, etc. When united with the other components they may lose their distinctive features. We can know whether or not they do only by engaging in the synthesis and comparing the outcome and its components with the elements which were used to make the synthesis.

Science tells us about nature, but A] only under a limitation (which puts science on a level with other modes of learning about nature, e.g., perception), and B] as having its component altered somewhat by being integrated with the other, non-scientific components. Science will also be able to tell us about psyches, the sacramental, and the idealized domains, for these are the scientific interrelated with the other components imbedded, not in Existence but in other modes of being. A scientific, perceptual, etc., synthesis by itself is neutral to an imbedment; it gives us a possible domain of nature, or psyches, or a sacramental universe, or an idealized universe; it is only when imbedded that it has the status of a synthesis of items in nature, etc.

Accordingly we must say that not only can nature be known in non-scientific ways, as surely as it can be known in scientific ways (with the same kind of limitation and possible failure to iconize what is there in fact), but other types of universes (such as that of psyches, sacramentals or idealizations), can be known by science and the other agencies as well. The knowledge of the universes themselves is of course to be achieved by the synthesis of all the abstractive modes, so that we get to understand what nature is not by using perception or science, etc., but by transcending these and having the result imbedded in Existence.

Known nature, inter-personal reality, sacramental unity, and the idealized world (all of which make unities of space, time, objects, etc.), differ from one another only by virtue of the orientation they receive from some mode of being. Nature as known by us through the synthesis of the content of different strands is in content not different from, say the sacramental unity. They become different only through their presence in different modes, a fact which is evidenced by the kind of pattern or career they then exhibit.

Known nature is A] a distillate of the common-sense world, as imbedded in Existence, and reconstituted by a synthesis of strands, B] known in part through the components of such a synthesis—components which include not only science but other strands, such as perception; C] capable of being dislodged from Existence and thereby made to function as an indeterminate realm which can be made determinate by being imbedded in some mode of being other than Existence.

Since the mode of being of Existence is best caught in art, art tells us what will convert a conceived realm into the realm of nature. To know what nature is really like (and not merely by conceiving how it might be imbedded, but by actually enjoying its imbedment) we must understand the possible conceived realm, or its fragmentary expression in science, perception, etc., within the context which art makes evident. The philosopher can know what nature is like because he can conceive Existence; but he cannot actually face nature as more than something conceived because he does not face Existence as more than conceived. To face Existence as more than conceived one must make use of art, or fall back into oneself as a vital being interplaying, (as a representative Actuality) with Existence as such. When, then, an artist says he looks to nature he must, if he is speaking accurately, be looking at a conceived domain which is rooted in, sustained and qualified by the kind of being which art shows Existence to have. If we want to know something of the feel of the divine (or Actuality or the Ideal) we must look not to art but to other basic enterprises which are able to capture the texture of the divine etc. in ways analogous to that in which art catches that of Existence.

April 8

Religion can be rooted in a number of ways. There is firstly the awareness of the realm of common sense under or in a power which makes for unity and otherness. It is because of this power that the world is not merely extended, with distinctive objects, events and values, but stands over against men as an entire universe with its own insistence and private or subterranean career. And when we abstract the realms of perception, science, etc., from that common-sense world we can either make combinations of the extension, object-places, eventfulness and values inside each realm, and find these rooted in a power which makes for unity and otherness, or we can get a neutral extension, or a neutral object, etc., by synthesizing these features over the different realms or modes of apprehension, and rooting the result. Or we can just try to combine the totality of results of the two methods, which is to say have that which is at once extended, object, etc., in a synthesis of perception, science, etc.

If we take the first way we get a perceptual world grounded in the power for unity, a scientific world similarly grounded, etc. The "aesthetic" world of Jonathan Edwards and the language of Berkeley seem to be perceptual worlds grounded in the divine. A scientific world which is grounded in the divine is what Newton apparently had in mind. An eventful world grounded in the divine would seem to be warranted by some of Whitehead's statements about the dependence of events on God, but perhaps a clearer position could be obtained from Aristotle by acknowledging his *energeia* to have a divine reference and sustaining— though I think Aristotle never definitely held this position. A valuational world which is grounded in the divine is perhaps what is to be obtained from creationalistic theories.

If we take the second way and seek to get a neutral extension which is then rooted in the divine (and so on with other neutral outcomes resulting from the synthesis of features over a set of modes of apprehension), we will have the nature of extension as kept other than and yet unified by God. This view is not easy to distinguish from Newton's view; perhaps one can say that for Newton there is an absolute space, time and perhaps "motion" which is neutral and divinely grounded, and that when he went over to theology he filled this out to give a scientific world in which there were objects as well as extensions, values as well as directions. This second method also yields the neutral idea of an object as rooted in the divine; here individuals are somehow made to be by God, and this in independence of extension, values, etc. There would be in each object a kind of unity or "soul" which enabled it to stand over against others, not in its own right but as sustained by God. A third result of this second method would be to get productivity sustained by God; God would here provide the causal power of the world, which is what is perhaps intended by those who see history as having its dynamics under the control of, or being the expression of the divine. And finally we can have neutral purposiveness sustained by God; this would make the world providentially controlled, which is the way orthodox Christianity sees it.

The third method for getting a religious grounding consists in getting neutral universes by combining all the features made neutral by a synthesis of different modes of apprehension. We would thereby get a full-bodied world like that of common sense, but neutral, and would have this rooted in the divine. This would be a rationally apprehended and constructed universe which was known to have its nature as a unity, and its being as a reality other than ourselves and truly objective, sustained by God. This would give us what is intended by most religious or theological men.

The first two methods—which add to a common-sense awareness of a rootage in the divine, a rootage of distinctive features such as extension, or an apprehended realm such as the perceptual or scientific (brought about by uniting a plurality of features with a single mode of apprehension) are those which can properly be said, with common-sense apprehension, to give us an experiential ground for religion. The common-sense apprehension, though, is one which is concerned with a full-bodied content, whereas the others are concerned with abstract though purged versions of this content. And all of them would be quite distinct from the being of God Himself, and from the being which Actuality or Existence or Ideality might have for Him and in Him.

April 9

The Wittgenstein school offers a nominalistic, sociological view of the common-sense world. It has strong affiliations, not only with a Kantianism, but with Dewey and Existenz, though the fact has not been acknowledged by its students. But Wild has seen that the *Lebenswelt* is like the common-sense world of the Wittgensteinians, and Aldrich has stressed the constitutive and existential side of language for them. There are at least four defects with the Wittgensteinean view:

1] The view that the use of terms is idle if it is not made integral to common-sense activities and men, overlooks the fact that what is idle in one sense may be useful in another. (Hegel thought it idle for one to attend to such common-sense uses as that of necessity when used in connection with the hanging out of wash and having it rain that very day.)

2] If language be taken as institutional and constitutive, there ought to be a recognition of correlative forms, such as ritual, habitual action, traditional ceremonials, etc., all of which help constitute the commonsense world.

3] It has no way of getting logical prescriptive rules and therefore no warranted way of rectifying or ordering different discourses.

4] Men do not altogether agree in their uses of terms and expressions. Each man at each moment must be allowed to dictate a use, or there would have to be principles of selection.

Actually no language is constitutive. What we have in fact is what Wittgenstein calls "place" as the decisive factor. What we think of as good common-sense use is that which involves the identification of an object or activity at different points of its career. We say *"x* is an honest man" and what we mean by this is that at this point he does this and at that point he does that. We do not mean that the contour of our assertion is identical with the contour of the actual man. The two are independent, and all we can ask for is that they mesh at different and selected times.

The doctrine of use is only a doctrine as to when the terms are to be checked with common-sense facts. But then returning to the above criticisms of Wittgenstein we can say that the terms which are idle are those which have no assigned place in common discourse. Nevertheless they may have places in the life of men, at moments of experience, and inside the isolated discourse or dialogue which goes on in a dialectical philosopher.

The philosopher's referent could be the very things which the ordinary man acknowledges but only as rooted in and as opening into the reality which lies beyond. When the philosopher checks his categorial assertions with experience he uses the ordinary content as a surface for a deeper orientation in and an acceptance of something beyond.

Language, secondly, like ritual, has its own rationale, and actually presupposes a semantics which it does not express. The theory of language-use then in effect is a theory which has to do with the application of language and not with language itself. The application of language can be performed by various institutions, e.g., conversation, newspapers, etc., or the various institutions themselves can use modes of placement which are themselves not linguistic at all. Linguistic elements are related in non-linguistic ways to the common-sense data which all accept.

Thirdly, the grammar of society is one thing, the grammar of the language by itself another, and the prescriptive rules for application a third. What is wanted is a set of prescriptions for the grammar of the language by itself.

The fourth defect relates to the fact that a strict application of the theory would require one to attend to particular uses at particular times, and merely record the fact. We could make reference to society as a norm, but society itself has many sub-societies within it, not altogether in gear. If we want to refer to society as such we would get something quite general, to which reference would have to be made somewhat in abstract and thus in the previously defined "idle" terms.

April 10

The common-sense world has a four-fold rootage in the four modes. These are not passive rootages; they infect the common-sense world, charge it with powers it otherwise would not have. And we who are brought up and qualified by the common-sense world must feel the effects of the different modes when mediated and expressed through that common-sense world. If we attend to Actuality, as primarily outside common sense, we use philosophic categories; if we see Actuality in itself we get metaphysics; if we see common sense sustained by Actuality we get panpsychism or existentialism; if we see Actuality manifesting itself through common sense to us and affecting us, we get significant action. If we attend to Ideality outside common sense we use mathematics; if we see the Ideal in itself we do mathematics; if we see common sense sustained by Ideality we see the world idealized; if we see Ideality manifesting itself through common sense and affecting us we get politics. Existence as outside common sense is known through art; Existence in and of itself through interplay; if we see common sense as sustained by Existence we get nature humanized; but Existence expressing itself on us via common sense is history. God outside common sense is known through religion; in and of Himself in theology; common sense sustained by Him, a sacramental world; God acting directly on us, creation.

Nature is the common-sense world purged, and rooted in Existence; there are other rootages for purged forms of common sense. The reciprocal action of Existence and other modes is not to be known in nature, but can be conceived to be operating there, for nature is a conceptual product.

Taken to be mere creatures of common sense, we are sociological beings; taken to be creatures of common sense infected by Actuality, we have philosophic categories. These are forged by the very vitality of the Actualities which penetrate to us through the common-sense barrier. It is this set of philosophic categories which concern the Wittgensteineans. The nature of language with which they are concerned is one which is vital, and placed with respect to vital individuals. A common-sense language is used to categorize the common-sense world, one made by powers beyond the common-sense world. It is in short a metaphysical language concerned with Actuality, but one qualified by the medium through which it appears.

Pure knowledge of Actuality requires the separation out of the initial force which is being expressed in the common-sense world. A metaphysical language, mediated by common sense and dealing with Actuality only through that medium, breaks up into subgroups of perceptual, scientific, eventful, and valuational languages. These are not to be identified with those ways of apprehending the world which start with ourselves; they are a function of the operation of the Actual through common sense, and have as their proper object the abstractions of the common-sense world so far as this is sustained and infected by the modes of being.

Existence manifested through common sense yields history. The categories in terms of which one must deal with history as an objective power are common sense categories and the derivate strands, all of which are affected by Existence. The dimensions for example of an event apprehended by an historically determined individual is distinct from that which is known by one who starts merely in the common-sense world. There is of course no sharp distinction here; we are never without an historical tinge. But we become historians only when we see that the common-sense world is not to be dealt with merely as yielding strands, but as that which relates those strands to Existence.

The intrusion of the Ideal in the common-sense world (and therefore on us, and the strands which we might use to understand what is real) is the field of politics. Here the various categories we use when we perceive, etc., are made by the political influences exerted on us.

The intrusion of God in the common-sense world, us and strands, is the field of divine governance. Here we have new categories made for us and which have their appropriate object, not God in himself, not the strands in isolation, not common sense, but a God who has expressed Himself, as Berkeley said, in the "language" of common-sense objects.

We have then a number of sets of categories or concepts in terms of which we deal with things. There are those which are appropriate to common sense and have been produced for us in the course of our adjusting to the common-sense world. There are also those which are appropriate to strands achieved by sophisticated reflection, after an initial concentration or detachment by which we free ourselves from societal conditioning; and those which are appropriate to the strands imbedded in the different modes. And there are those which are appropriate to the common-sense world as imbedded in the different modes; those which are appropriate to the modes themselves; those which are appropriate to the modes when they make themselves manifest in the common-sense world; and those which are appropriate to the modes manifested in the common-sense world but dealt with in the area of a strand. These different categories often have the same name, but a confusion of them will make it impossible to see how what is "idle" for one meaning "works" for another.

"Thing" is *1*] a common-sense object to be used, handled, in societally conditioned terms; *2*] that which is perceived; *3*] that which is known to science; *4*] that which is actually actively forging a place for itself; *5*] that which has some value; *6*] what is perceived but imbedded in Actuality, i.e., substance; *7*] what is perceived but imbedded in Ideality, a paradigm; *8*] what is perceived but imbedded in Existence, natural qualities; *9*] what is perceived but imbedded in God, miracle (?); *10, 11, 12, 13*] a scientifically known entity imbedded in the four modes; *14, 15, 16, 17*] an eventfully known entity imbedded in the four modes; *18, 19, 20, 21*] a valuationally known entity imbedded in the four modes; *22, 23, 24, 25*] a common-sense entity imbedded in the four modes; *26, 27, 28, 29*] categories dealing with the modes themselves might use "thing" to refer to subdivisions of these; *30, 31, 32, 33*] the modes making themselves manifest in the common-sense world (the reciprocal of *6, 7, 8, 9*); *34, 35, 36, 37*] the mode of Actuality expressed through an object but apprehended by perception, science, event or value; *38, 39, 40, 41*] ditto for the mode of Ideality; *42, 43, 44, 45*] ditto for Existence; *46, 47, 48, 49*] ditto for God.

A thing, e.g., as a social object (*1*) is more than what is scientifically known (*3*), not a substance (*6*), not a divinely sustained rationally apprehended entity (*13*), not an eventful aspect of an Actuality (*14*), not a value ingredient in Existence (*20*), not an ordinary social thing in Existence, (*24*), not a representative Actuality (*26*), not an historic entity (*32*), not a perceived Actuality (*34*), not a perceived possibility (*42*), not a conceived part of Existence (*43*), not a conceived part of God (*47*).

There are thirteen types, twelve of which have four variants, and thus 49 different ways in which a single basic term can be used.

April 11

The common-sense world is effective. We know it by means of categories it helps produce. We could not know this much however unless we could have some way of escaping from those categories. And this we do. We use the strands for example; though they give us abstractions, and sometimes have personal overtones, they enable us to escape the limitations of common sense. And then we can synthesize and also make depth penetrations beyond the common-sense world, not only because it is imbedded in something beyond itself, but because we ourselves are more than common-sense men.

The world beyond common sense is the four-fold world of the modes of being. Each of these is effective on us through the medium of the common-sense world, and the strands we abstract from this. Our categories then, are not merely commonsensical, or abstractions from these; they are these but as qualified by or as mediating the modes. These categories are the agencies by which we know the modes. In short, the modes are known by virtue of categories which they themselves produce in us. And they are able to produce these in us of course primarily as mediated by common sense and strands, and thus as not altogether appropriate to the modes in and of themselves when we start within ourselves, where the influence of the modes has moved beyond the texture of common sense and the strands, to have its power felt on us.

Our final categories are produced by the very realities to which they are appropriate. The world of common sense is known by categories produced by it, and the real world beyond this is known by categories produced by that real world. If we use one type on the other's world we will of course misconstrue it. There is a different meaning of "extension," e.g., in common sense and in metaphysics; and we must keep them separate if we are to speak properly. We must adjust ourselves and our vocabulary to the world with which we are concerned. This does not mean there is no relation between the worlds; the common-sense world and its derivative strands are to be explained by referring to the modes in interplay.

Each mode expresses itself in a common-sense world by infecting the variable "thing," "extension," "formality" and "unity" with itself, thereby giving it a different meaning than it had for one concerned either with the mode or with the common-sense world in and of itself. And there ought to be appropriate categories for this too. We have then the following categories:

1] Those produced by common-sense world on us to make us into common-sense men. Our task is to become the latter by means of the former, so as to know the former.

2] Those produced by us in the very act of abstracting strands. A strand is a category whose object as it were is itself oriented in the world of common sense. We, e.g., perceive in terms which are not distinguishable from the percepta, except that the perceiving is oriented in us and the percepta in the world beyond, even when held apart from that world as abstractions.

3] Those produced by the effect of a mode on us via common sense, so that we are beings who use the proper categories only because we have become, not common-sense men, but more than this. We are beings who are naturalized, substantialized, idealized, and made into unitary others, by virtue of the fact that our commonsensical being is rooted in Existence, Actuality, Ideality, and God. The rooting here is produced in us by the modes. The modes, by affecting the common-sense world, yield history, action, politics and institutional religion; these express the force of the modes being manifested through common sense. If we are to know history, etc., we must allow it to naturalize our common-sense being. History is Existence controlling the common-sense world. We must allow it to make us into beings whose common-sense nature is also controlled by

Existence. In us history's existential dimension meets ours and produces through the both of us the appropriate category for history.

4] The modes peer through the strand we abstract from the common-sense world. Even in the most formal strand of science we can become aware say of the power of Existence. This is insistent, expanding and punctuating the scientific content according to a set of dimensions not themselves expressed or known in science.

5] The modes act beyond the limitations of common sense or the strands, to allow us face each in and of itself as facing us in our roots. This point is made in *3* above; but in *3* strictly speaking, what we have is the rootage of ourselves as common-sense beings in Existence on the one side, and the penetration of Existence or some other mode on the world of common sense and through this on us. But here we speak of the modes operating beyond the limits provided by common sense and the strands.

Every mode has these last three roles. Each affects us via common sense, via strands, and by itself, and thereby makes us (when we meet it, with ourselves in a similar state) provide a category which expresses the way in which the external pressure meets an appropriate aspect of ourselves.

Existence unites with the Ideal to constitute a natural beauty. The awesome is where Existence makes its power felt in the world of common sense. This seems to be indistinguishable from what has just been said to be history. But in history, Existence operates as extensional, though effectively; when Existence is awesome it acts in its entire unitary being, and primarily as a force. History could be said to be awesome in its entirety; the awesome becomes historical when its force is articulated in the guise of an actual process of time. We get what is commonly thought of as history, history as oriented with respect to men, only when we make the common-sense world primary or equal to the existent force. This requires us to say that the awesome can become the historical when its force is articulated and subjected to the demands of the common-sense world. The awesome itself submerges the common-sense object; in beauty we recover the common-sense object but then only with the help of ideas. The historic can be said to be the beautiful altered through a substitution, of ourselves as historians, for the idea which nature has before it and which is integrated with the Existent force to make the beautiful.

What is said about history is to be carried over with respect to other public manifestations of the modes, and thus to action, politics and institutional religion.

Now, if art is a way of telling us the nature of Existence, it provides us with categories produced by Existence, and which are used to know it.

These categories are not merely abstract or conceptual, but involve the infusion of our own existence into them (to yield texture), the interplay of our existence with objective Existence (to yield the reference to a world beyond), and the awareness of the way in which Existence affects the common-sense world and us to make us emotional. Perhaps regarding the texture it would be better to say that this too is the result of the interplay of our existence with objective Existence (with a stress on our reference to the objective Existence, as here and now), while the reference to the world beyond is on objective Existence as continuing to be beyond the point of juncture with us.

April 12

Each mode reaches to the individual and elicits from it what can be termed appropriate categories for itself. The attempt on the part of the individual to meet the mode will result in the production of something which expresses the individual in that mode, the mode itself, and the manner in which the individual reaches to that mode. If the mode is Existence then the individual as existential provides the world of art, through the use of his existent powers, with an agency for reaching to objective Existence. He does not lay hold of it, yet catches something of it. Similarly if the mode is God the individual as an ultimate unity provides a realm of religious significance, the sacramental. If the mode is the Ideal he substitutes the realm of the ethical. If the mode is Actuality it reaches to the individual who is representative of Actuality.

The individual could use the category in an intellectual way, in which case he spreads it between the four modes, with himself as a pivot. When he does this he can assume any one of a number of roles, to give him a conceptualization of any of the modes. The intellectual use of the category, though most appropriate to the Actual, will allow us to have a partial view of the other modes, to get their structure without their texture. When we come to the knowledge of Actuality we can be said to provide a substitute for it. Accordingly we must say that what the individual can produce is a substitute for Actuality, not only in the guise of the Existent, divine or Ideal, but in the guise of Actuality, shaped as a category.

The various substitutes we provide by virtue of our response to the modes which impinge on us, exhibiting not their nature but their force or stimulating effect on us (thereby awakening our use of ourselves in those modes), not only are our substitutes for those modes but exhibit the other two modes as limits. If the mode is Existence the art we produce has its limits in the Ideal and the divine, the one providing the meaning, the other unity. The individual acts as a kind of Actuality, though it is in an existential way that he creates. If the mode is God and we produce religious objects or a world, the limits are the Ideal and the Existent; the objects are between these. If the mode is the Ideal, the resultant ethical domain stands between Existence and the divine, offering a kind of synthesis of the two, and we, functioning as ideal beings (members of Kant's kingdom of ends), are mediated by the ethical with respect to the mode of Ideality at the same time. If the mode is the Actual, the resultant intellectual system of actualities, the Existent realm which we create as a realm of participation in dialogue, the sympathetically felt binding of love which we create to make a simulacrum of the divine, and the Ideal set of prescriptions to which we submit, have the other two modes as poles. Thus a dialogue, which is a kind of existence created by actualities in interplay, has as its poles the divine and the Ideal; love has as its poles the Existent and the Ideal; and prescriptions have as their poles the divine and the existent, at the same time they all have a pole in Actuality, as a mode affecting the individual and leading him to create substitutes for the world.

On this interpretation philosophy appears to be a substitute for the world. But it can also be viewed as having categories which are appropriate to the world. This is the state it has when it is completed, for then its categories come to rest in the world itself, mediated by the system. The system, as it were, sustains the categories on a frontal plane and is crossed by a reference from us to the modes themselves, carried by our basic interest and the power of the system itself. The philosophic system as system vanishes in the sense that it becomes identical with the individual who knows, to make him confront the modes in themselves, though categorized by him with philosophic concepts.

In the sense in which the philosophic system can be made to vanish, the language of common sense can be made to vanish—when it is most appropriate to the common-sense world. By accepting the product which we have made, by using the language common sense has produced in us to make us common-sense men, we become beings who just face a common-sense world. Similarly, if we accept the categories which the modes have produced in us, and if, instead of making them into agencies by which we produce substitutes for the modes, we identify ourselves with them, accept them as our own, we get a direct acquaintance with the modes, via those categories. Philosophic language or concepts are then to be seen either as substitutes which we forge through a creative use of the meaning of Actuality in us (Actuality operating on us to make us into its representatives) or the set of ideas with which we have identified ourselves to make us face the modes directly. When we are in the process of thinking, we have philosophy over against us, and when we end we have it one with us.

Philosophy over against us, when it is in the process of being thought through, is a false infinite, in Hegel's sense. When we accept it at any point as completed, we finitize that false infinite. This has the double defect of making us suppose that we have something positive, because finite, and that we have a true negative dependent on a positive thesis. Philosophizing, in other words, is sustained by the presence in us of a positivity over against the positivity of the modes. The pursuit of philosophy as an enterprise must be sustained by these two positivities. When it is held apart from them it collapses into a falsified version of an infinitely incomplete way of being a philosopher.

We can escape the false finitization of the infinite "negative" by identifying the finite result with ourselves. But this would seem to say that, e.g., a man who actually became a pragmatist or Cartesian or whatever would have to appropriate his philosophy properly and could then face the modes. This would be the case however only if pragmatism, etc., were true. If a philosophic process is finitized into an incomplete system, the man will not be complete. An unsatisfactory system is one which, if a man adopted it, made it one with himself so that he could look at the modes, would A] misconstrue the modes, as is evident from the contradictions and paradoxes produced, and B] would distort him, as is evident from the fact that he would not be able to deal appropriately with some discipline or some content of that discipline. This does not mean that he is unable to do science, e.g., or be religious, but only that he is precluded from doing these things by virtue of his identification with categories which have no place for them.

If it be correct to say that God makes man be an other, then we ought to say that the Ideal turns man into a knower, Existence turns him into a creator, and other Actualities turn him into a self. Accordingly, since all work on man at the same time, in his root man is a self which is at once creative and knowing, standing as the absolute other of God.

If it be correct to speak of man providing substitutes for the different modes when they elicit from him their appropriate side or categories in him, such as other, cognizer, creator or self, what status has the world of common sense? Is it something which he has made as a substitute? If so, it is a substitute for all of the modes together, which would make it a kind of world of art, religion, ethics and philosophy. This seems to put the earlier in terms of what is evidently later, since we are brought up in a common-sense world. Or is it that we already have an interplay of the individual with the modes, where none is really distinguished, so that the common-sense world starts with us intermingled with an intermingled art, religion, ethics and philosophy? More accurately, it starts with something partially created, worshipped, submitted to and understood but not entirely separate from us. It is the separation of ourselves from this which allows common sense to have a status over against us. The world of common sense produces this separation by penetrating us, pushing beyond us (as parts of the common-sense whole) to elicit a proper way for us to refer to it.

The common-sense world then initially is a mixture of the modes, with us as individuals reduced to parts of it. This intermingling is a kind of "one" for the many of the modes, the "one" as a "." in which they merge, but not properly enough to give us anything like a decent correlative ".," We have a "," or way of having the modes separate in fact, and the intermingling is one of the degrees in which they come together as merged. In this sense the common-sense world is ontologically rooted and inescapable; it is the modes as together in one degree, a degree which has being at the same time that all the other degrees do. The "one" which is most appropriate to the separateness of the modes involves a plurality of degrees of merging. The common-sense world is a low degree, over-whelmed by the sensuous character and involvement of the individual.

The action of that common-sense world on us is in a way a producing a one which is more appropriate to a real togetherness of the modes. The individual when separated off from the common-sense world becomes a one for the many. But the many which is appropriate is hidden for him. He can get to it only by intensifying the oneness of himself, becoming the counterpart not of common sense but of the modes; he can know the modes by virtue of their action on him. The individual though can know and even substitute for only one mode; the plurality which he needs must nevertheless always be there, if not within the same categorial but biased orbit in terms of which he deals with an appropriate mode, then within a different but unbiased way of dealing with what is a distinctive mode with its distinctive needs.

Common sense is a product of the modes, and becomes an object only so far as it produces an individual or allows an individual to stand over against it as a one, thereby enabling the modal factors of the common-sense world to separate out and be recognized to be four distinct domains which common sense has jumbled together. When we forge a language we are trying to substitute for that common-sense world or are using a set of categories appropriate to it. If the former, our language is a social phenomenon to be perceived, understood, etc., in the same way a ceremonial is; if the latter it is the common-sense man as come out to meet the world which produced him. He stands over against that world while ordering it properly.

Those who see "use" as the clue to the nature of things overlook the fact that one who uses language never loses himself entirely in the world which the language structures, but remains a being who retains his position as the source of the categorial formulations.

April 13

There are significant differences among the arts of a particular type. Architecture, musicry and music all have an empty space with a being of its own, with its own tensions. Sculpture, story and the theatre have an empty space whose nature is the product of the carrying over into them of the very solidities of the filled items. The space is a continuation in a thinner medium of the very being of the items. There are no boundaries for innerspace or time or becoming in sculpture, story and theatre, but a control of these by the very things which in the former set of arts would have merely bounded them. And finally, in painting, poetry and dance the emptiness has in fact been occupied; it is a solid mass with its own proper texture, a solid with a positive qualia, an integral component of the work. There is no room here any more for occupancy as there is in the former set.

The empty space in nature and thus the empty space which we see between buildings is quite different from the empty space of either architecture or sculpture. Firstly, it is a consequence not of an artistic activity but of the insistent presence of nature or reality. The recognition of it is the recognition of the area of a world which the art would ordinarily exclude, but which we can acknowledge aesthetically as having its own value. It is nature accepted as an aesthetic reality in the world of art objects. Is this reality overlaid or defined by the architectural or sculptural objects between which it appears? This is perhaps what city planning intends. But taken as such we ought to say that it defines the environmental space of architecture only so far as this is in fact laid hold of. This, however, need not be done. When it is done the aesthetic dimension which we are accepting from nature becomes part of the content of architecture. In short, architecture defines an environment; it bounds the world outside it from one position, leaving the horizon or something else to provide the other position or boundary. So far, we have only a tension thrown across the environment making it into an environmental space. But since there is no control by the architect of this further boundary, the tension must be carried by nature. If nature carried it in and of itself we would never notice it. It is only when we have taken nature and given it an aesthetic status that we are able to find a proper carrier for the tensions which a bounding object (a building) imposes on the world thought to be outside it. In sculpture the spectator space is of a similar nature, except that the spectator space absorbs the aesthetic dimension within itself to define, not something germane to the sculpture, but what will influence the spectator and draw him into and around the sculpture.

Works differ in their "emptiness"; they also differ in their scales. All scales are achievements not conditions; they are ventures in the activity of trying to find a way in which we as bodies, minds, emotions, spirits, with tasks and ideals, can at once be integrated with a world beyond, keep that world beyond at a distance and make it into the proper foil or other of ourselves as bodies, minds, etc.

The entire work of art can itself be thought of as a scale measuring man and the world in relation to one another. The scales are perpetually dictating to us the way in which we can avoid slipping from the work of art into the common-sense world. Scale measures the work of art in its parts only in the sense of enabling it to be a work of art for a man who approaches it initially as though he were not a being caught in that work; the scale enables him to be caught in the work, to be geared to it as an object.

Scales are to be found in every art. They may be said to be a plurality of devices by which one finds one's way into the work of art. The work of art is itself a scale measuring the degree to which a man, as a being with mind, body, emotion and will, actually is adjusted to the complex world of Existence, mediated through common sense, strands, and his powers (body, mind, emotion and will).

April 14

Gombrich rightly remarks that our perceptions vary in their content and stresses, and thus are in effect distinct from culture to culture. But he also goes on to make two other suppositions, both of which might well be questioned: 1] that there is no observable constant in perception, and 2] that it is the task of the artist to reproduce what he sees. He thinks, in the light of the second supposition, that he can understand the diversities in art by attending to the fact that cultures differ. But then how account for the differences in the works of men of the same period and school? How do we get a diversity today? Is it because men see differently, or is it not that though they all see in the same way they are engaged in distinctive ways of creating?

Gombrich recognizes that there is a perception of the works of art themselves, and that they do not deal with objects literally. He does not see clearly what it is that he is noting; he thinks, e.g., the fact, that the image's size on the mirror is one half of the size of the face before the mirror, shows that we mistakenly think we see a full-size face. But we see a full-size face; the size of the image is a "size" in quite a different sense. His account though does tell us that A] there is a kind of indeterminacy in the work of art, for different men can interpret it differently, and thus (despite my saying that art adds determinations) does allow us to recognize that the art object is not fully determinate, and B] that there is an element of determinateness which the work of perception imposes on the images or measures of the items which are perceived, or in other words that there is a way of seeing the terminus of perception both as full-sized and as half-sized (the latter resulting not from the failure to note what is there but from the effort to see what is perceived as having its physical being at a certain place). It is like the comparison between the elliptical shape and the round shape of the coin—just as the coin, though presented as in an elliptical shape, is seen to be round, so the image in the mirror is a half-sized-having of the whole size. The half-size is the whole size as it must be in or at the mirror, just as the round is that which must "appear" elliptical from some angle.

It would perhaps be fairer to attribute the view above not to Gombrich but to Riegel who said "Every style aims at a faithful rendering of nature and nothing else, but each has its own conception of Nature. . . ." Gombrich does say that "art is born of art" and not of the observation of nature.

The important point is not who said it, but the double recognition that A] nature is indeterminate in some degree, B] that art is a determination of it, and C] that the art still has areas of indetermination. The first allows art to be in "nature," the second takes account of artistic making, and the third allows us to see that the art work allows for 1] different modes of apprehension and perception, and 2] for its use in commerce and the rest. The first of these subdivisions of C, 1] is relevant to appreciation and shows that the art is a kind of determinate being with potency for being appreciated, and the second, 2] shows that the world is larger than the world of art, allowing art to function not only as ingredient in nature but as a component in a society, in which the values are non-aesthetic. It is nevertheless still of interest to see just where Gombrich stands; it is I think, in the end, near Riegel. He says that Egyptians manipulate "ambiguous cues on which we have to rely in stationary vision till their image was indistinguishable from reality." This means he does think artists copy reality, but also that the artist starts with ambiguous or indeterminate perceptions (sometimes called hypotheses by Gombrich) (*vide.* Peirce) and makes these determinate to conform to nature itself. In the end the criticism of Gombrich will be like that to be made of Riegel: we don't seek to portray nature (which is his reality I think), and this nature is not determinate.

April 17

It can be argued that Hegel had only one mode of being – the Ideal or God. The adventures of that being are with respect to mere distinctions contained within it. It released these as much as possible, which is to say never entirely, and thereby articulated itself to itself. It had therefore, with respect to its own interiority, the status that Christianity ascribes to the created world and angels. In neither case is there a real exterior plurality; we have only a plurality which is allowed to be to the greatest possible extent that anything other than God could be.

If one takes this position one can say that there are two things which Hegel overlooked. The first is the reality of other modes outside God, and thus a kind of plurality which is not contained inside Him; the second is the recognition, inside the plurality of God, of those external modes. If we acknowledge the first we have a kind of negation which is unlike the negation that a plurality exhibits with respect to its unity. The progress in Hegel is the addition of more and more determinate ways of producing this negation. These determinate ways are of the same type as the original. But if there are modes outside of God, the negation they provide for Him, and He for them, is of a different kind. It is a reciprocal negation, which cannot then be negated; there is no further negation which is to follow on it.

The first negation making possible a plurality of items in God could be viewed, along the lines of the chapter on causation in *Reality,* as a kind of internal expression of the external negation. But since there can be many divisions in God, many more than there are modes, it would not be possible to say this, except so far as one thought of the interior of God as keeping pace not with the other modes but with the pluralities in them. But it would be better I think to recognize God's activity, and thereby be able to affirm that what God does is to impose on the plurality inside Him limitations and qualifications answering to the natures of the other modes and their pluralities. The nature of God in Himself would be pluralized regardless of the other modes; He would also have Himself in a reciprocal relation to other modes; and He would, finally, act on Himself in Himself in the light of the pluralities, and thus of the adventures of the other modes.

The negation which is characteristic of the relation of the modes to one another expresses the One or being of them all. It reveals the dissolution of being into a plurality. But in addition, each mode holds itself over against the rest as their other; it must therefore put a biased emphasis on this neutral negativity which separates and unites them all. It must lay hold of the other modes as not itself. We have then the following negations or othernesses:

1] The otherness of the plurality within to the unity of a mode.

2] The otherness of the modes to one another, viewed neutrally; the One dissolved.

3] The otherness of the other modes for each mode.

4] The otherness of the plurality of the various modes, partly overcome by a mode making the plurality in sense 1 be qualified by what is grasped of the plurality in other modes.

April 18

When Hegel was turned "upside down" by Marx, was this any more than a shift to another mode of being, or was it a taking of the plurality to be primary? Marx spoke as if it were the second, with his concern for what is happening in the "material" world; but in fact it was the first, for the primary reality was the dialectical force which governed and determined the activities of the plurality. His was then a kind of philosophy of history, and one which was under the control of Existence. He was not concerned with individuals, substances, and thus not with Actuality; and his "materialism" made him opposed to the Ideal. His dialectic then is not a genuine reversal of Hegel but a repetition of Hegel in another domain. And he also did what Hegel did; he starts with the abstract and "exterior" but not really distinct, and moves to the concrete which is distinguished and possessed. Hegel keeps in mind the fact that the plurality is the plurality of the One, whereas Marx keeps in mind the fact that it is abstract and exterior.

There are the following additional alternatives: 1] taking Actuality, or 2] Ideality as the One's which govern a dialectic of their own pluralities, or 3] placing emphasis on the plurality rather than the One.

Actuality, as a One, has the kind of ineffectiveness that Existence has; it can be operative only as a power and not as a governing and insistent meaning. This will make for a more radical contingency in the development of individuals. It ought to have made for a more radical development in nature and commonsense for Marx. It does for Darwin, who takes the individuals or at least "species" of them to have a primary role over against the all-embracing "evolution." If we take this line we can have a kind of dialectic amongst individuals which presumably will lead to finding themselves over the course of time and adjusting themselves in society to one another, or a dialectic in which Actuality, despite its relative abstractness, controls the development of the individuals over time so that they come closer and closer to being concrete enough to exhaust the nature of Actuality. Though Peirce was anti-individualistic, his view of the nature of the community of scientists would seem to have this idea as his basic meaning. It seems to be the view of Dewey too.

Ideality can have two varieties too: one where the Ideal, with an efficacy like God's, is operating with respect to its own plurality, making this more and more concrete; the other where the plurality is infected by the One but nevertheless by its own operations defines how it is itself to develop.

It is more appropriate in connection with Actuality and Existence to stress the contingent development of the plurality under the wing of the unity; the governed development of the plurality under the control of the unity is more appropriate to God and Ideality.

If one takes this line one has as an instance the world of Plotinus. Here however we seem to have a primary problem of falling away, whereas the issue which at least has been focussed on by Hegel is that of returning. The "return" of Plotinus and of neo-platonists seems to take one step, just as the "fall" for the others seems to take one step. What is needed is an account of a detailed fall similar to Plotinus and exhibited in the mode of God; Hegel failed here. Also one needs a detailed account of a return; here is where Plotinus failed.

In connection with Actuality and Existence one does not need an account of a fall or a return. The unities do not actually have enough being to be the origin of the fall or to govern a return. What ought to be stressed here is the way in which the pluralities give meaning to the One so that it can really function (which is what is done when the parts become representative or recapitulate the whole), and then allow themselves to be subordinated to it. (This means that the individual scientist and the evolving species must themselves function as representatives of the whole of science and evolution). If, though, we take the view that there is a unitary power to Actuality and Existence, which can either remain One (to make possible a genuine microcosmic repetition created by the Actuality or a realm of nature), or be a plurality (of actualities) and divisions (in Existence) whose career is dictated by the One, to yield a common "humanity" or a single historical line, we get something analogous to the Hegelian development. But then it ought also to be possible to find inside the realm of God and Ideal a way in which the parts absorb the One and then allow themselves to be subordinated to it.

In short, we have pluralities giving meaning to the One and Being, and being subordinate to it, and also the One governing the activities of the plurality and repossessing it. The former is stressed by Actuality and Existence, the latter by God and the Ideal.

Because of the asymmetry inside a mode, between the One of it and its many, there is nothing like both a decline and rise. The rise expresses the way in which the plurality achieves its own reality under the aegis of a guiding Ideal; the fall expresses the way in which the One allows the plurality to become its articulation. Actuality and Existence are stories of a rise through the progressive expression of their Ones by the subordinate parts of their plurality, each having the guise of a representative unit. God and Ideal are stories of a fall which is allowed by the unity to give itself an articulation. If we take this line then the failure of Hegel is the failure to see that as he goes on in the dialectic he gets no closer, but further away from the One, while making the whole plurality into its articulation. The more determinate the elements in the plurality become, the more they destroy the One. It is only because the determinate is so far non-real within a totality that the plurality can be said to be the expression of the One.

Plotinus then is right in seeing the fall as a falling away from the One; but he does not see that this is the meaning of the One. Hegel is right in seeing that the plurality is the meaning of the One but he does not see that the subsequent moments in the dialectic fall away as Plotinus saw they did.

The above offers an internal dialectic inside each of the modes. That dialectic goes on regardless of the outside adjustive negativities, though the latter do make a difference to the way in which the pluralities are clustered to make larger units. If we take the Hegelian dialectic to be an illustration of how we progressively approach a unity through a development of a plurality, we would have to place his entire account inside Actuality or Existence.

The Aristotelian actualization of potentiality is in effect the rise of the potentiality under the direction and control of a One. It can be viewed as a rise and thus as occurring inside Actuality. That Actuality is not doing anything to the potentiality, but is being made to be a more concrete unity by the independent articulation and development of the potentiality. This means that the potentiality has its own nisus towards being the articulation of Actuality. If we recognize Actuality to be in fact dominant in the sense that it is more effective and real than the plurality—which is the more correct way of looking at Actuality in Aristotle—(and thus treating it the way we treated God and Ideal above) we must say that the development of the potentiality is the Actuality's own way of releasing itself, of "thinking on thinking" by a series of more and more determinate distinctions, which together make up the entire meaning of the Actuality.

How can the determinate be more abstract than the indeterminate? What meaning is there in the view that the later parts of a dialectic, under the aegis of God or Ideal, are abstract though determinate, or determinate because abstract? The determinations which are being provided are adjectival not substantival. They are not genuine features inside the Ideal or God, but exterior determinations of them, so that the entire venture is the achievement of the articulation of the Ideal or God by an exterior act. But then we cannot really have a fall made by God or the Ideal in the shape of a release or relaxation of their Ones, except so far as we view the Ideal or God as having two roles—as a unity and as the source of external determinations which are themselves ways of making a fall possible. Creation would be the providing by God of determinations to Himself so as to enable the plurality to stand apart; the very provision of the determinations by Him will then all the more certify to their dependence on Him. The more determinate a finite entity, the more will it testify to the dependence of it on a One. It is more dependent the more determinate it is. The determinations then of the pluralities inside the Ideal and God are ways in which sets of distinct items were made more and more dependent on the being of the Ideal or God. As mere divisions in the Ideal or God they would be indeterminate, though enjoying some independence of being.

Actuality and Existence are ways in which the real items of a plurality become more and more representative of unity, and thereby make the unities of Actuality and Existence efficacious. Before we attain the stage of a genuine representativeness, the Actuality and the Existence would themselves be indeterminate. Their determinateness is achieved by virtue of their efficacy in the plurality, an efficacy which is produced by the items in the plurality themselves. Once again the indeterminate would be that which is independent, and the determinate would be that which is possessed or dependent. In either case the history of a dialectic development would consist either in the fall of a more and more determinate plurality (in God and Ideality) or in a rise of a more and more determinate unity (in Actuality and Existence).

April 19

One can break down the modes into pairs. Two modes, viewed by themselves, are primarily Ones. These release their own distinctions allowing them to become more and more determinate and abstract (not as single items but as a plurality). Two of the modes, viewed by themselves, are primarily pluralities which become more and more determinate by becoming more and more representative of the One (which thereby attains in them a kind of completeness or solidity). Since there are four Ones (for the four modes), strictly speaking the problem of the "one and the many" is misstated since it seems to imply a dualism, it should deal with four ones and a many of four members.

Taking the Ones in pairs, one pair is prescriptive; from its angle the four modes are released, and offer together an articulation of the One. The other pair is descriptive and leads the modes to turn themselves into representatives of the One, thereby giving it a kind of status it did not have before. But the strict way would be to see the four modes offering four sets of manys each with its distinctive kind of togetherness. The "," is descriptive, the "." is prescriptive, the ")" is structural, and the "∴" is existential—they correspond to Actuality, God, Ideal and Existence. As pairs "." and ")", and the "," and "∴" go together. Taking them singly, the four modes related by a "," must act something like Actuality; each of them is endeavoring to be Being by the way it collects its own plurality within the limits of the forms given by the other three modes. The four modes as related by "∴" must act something like Existence, each of the parts of which is endeavoring to maintain itself within the matrix of their interplay, by internally possessing (in a three-fold way) the plurality within it. The "." will make the modes act something like God, and thus release its own plurality so as to allow the other modes to articulate it. The ")" will make them act something like the Ideal, and thus divest themselves of their pluralities in such a way that they are caught in the other modes, to provide articulations there.

Each mode in itself functions as a One for its plurality. The four Ones match a unity now connecting the modes with one another. This means that since each mode is related in a four-fold way with the other modes, each will have twelve ways of functioning inside itself with respect to its own plurality. If a mode is connected with others by a "." it will have to function as a One in the guise of a ")", ",", and "∴"; if it relates to the other modes by a ",", it will function for its own plurality in the guise of a ".", a ")", and a "∴", and so on. This means that each mode in itself has a four-fold status as a One with respect to the many inside it. It will prescribe to them, descriptively connect them, offer them a structural unity, and govern the way in which they are connected as distinct items.

If we turn to Actuality, which is where most thinkers in the West seem to remain, we must say then that Actuality as such has a four-fold role, and that the diverse actualities (which in fact act, and thus make the "," and the "∴" primary), see to it that it does have this status. The different actualities are governed by the One Actuality, when they are descriptively together and dynamically active, but this governance is purely "formal," or with minimal effect. By virtue of the way in which the diverse Actualities descriptively and dynamically act together, the One attains a reality in them, and thereby is enabled to exercise the role of a genuine implicative rule and prescriptive unity for them.

There is no dialectic of the four modes in the sense that they can be assumed to be in a relation to one another and subsequently attain another relation, where "relation" is understood to be that of a basic unity. The problem of the one and the many is solved in the very being of the four modes. Is this also true of the inward being of each of the modes? Is the release or rise of the plurality in a mode a sequential thing, or an analytic account of the relation of the parts of the mode to the whole of it? Since time is real in actualities, at least, the rise in Actuality must be sequential. But then the other modes, to be abreast of Actuality, must also be engaged in sequential internal activities. The modes, without having their relation to one another disturbed, internally adjust themselves to the perpetual need either of their plurality to be adequate representatives of the unitary mode, or for the unitary mode to get an adequate articulation by means of its plurality.

Why does not this effort come to an end at some finite time? Is it that there is no limit to the determinateness which is achieved by abstractions, and no limit to the degree of representativeness which a plurality of entities can achieve with respect to the One? It would seem we have time enough to get to the limit, or that we have a structure which can reach the limit and within which subdivisions can be endlessly made. Is this last not the answer then? In principle we are at the limit, but we live through time, fractionating the whole which structurally always reaches to that limit. But this would make time have smaller and smaller units preventing it from getting to the limit, or would make time into a kind of space in which all the divisions are made at the same time. Or is it that the plurality, to be a genuine plurality, must have its members distinguished one from the other, thereby frustrating one another? The reason we never get to the final end which is theoretically defined is that the different components are in opposition, and never can be perfectly harmonized.

Carried over into God, this would mean that the release He gives to the plurality in Him is also a giving of a "freedom" to the members of that plurality. This freedom involves an oppositionality of the released parts with respect to one another. They become determinate and separate and abstract, thereby requiring readjustment—or another attempt by God to make a set which is more consistent. The release by God of the parts, though it occurs all at once to the extreme of determinateness, requires subsequent efforts at release, in which the adventure is made again.

Should we say similarly that the rise of actualities, the incorporation of the Actual in them to make them representatives, is also a single operation, and that what we have in time is further efforts to do justice to the Actual? This would give us atomic time, in the sense that at each moment an actuality would assume a representative role, only to release this at once so as to be able to engage in another, more satisfactory representation. Analogous things would have to be said with respect to the Ideal and Existence.

One can say that the various modes seek to adjust themselves to one another in two ways: each seeks to adjust itself internally in the light of the alterations in the internality of the others, and each, by virtue of its own internal adjustment, re-adjusts itself to the others as external to it. But in neither way does it really operate with respect to the others to change the kind of way in which it is together with them. The adjustment is a perspectival adjustment. This point is not clear in 4.03 of the Modes. In 4.04, though, it is said that it is meanings that are adjusted, implying that the modes in their being are not involved. But the "meanings" reference is perhaps an evasion; there should have been a reference to the fact that the meanings are provided by a plurality of one mode, of which account must be taken by the other modes in their interiors.

The failure of a mode to do justice to another in effect means that it does not match the needs or actual operations of the other modes. An actuality which fails to be representative to the full does not function properly with respect to the other modes that face Actuality. No actuality does justice to the internal divisions of the Ideal. Is this a failure which requires recompense or completion by the other modes? The failure of an actuality to be representative does of course demand another effort on the part of the actuality to be a better representative. But this does not seem to be the same as the need of other modes to take up the slack.

Shall we say that the Ideal has a need to release its plurality, and that it (like God) cannot do so, except so far as it is helped by Actuality? An actuality in failing to be representative fails to give the Ideal a proper plurality—a plurality which as in the Actual demands a similar plurality in the Ideal. The Ideal's plurality is released only through the efforts of all the other pluralities to achieve their determinateness. But if we say this we seem faced with a kind of possible complete determinateness in each mode, and must say that the mode as accepted by a given mode is not sufficiently subdivided. An actuality (which is already a subdivision seeking to be a unified one through representativeness) adopts the Ideal but fails to do justice to the need of that Ideal to have a plurality which articulates it. That plurality could be obtained only if all actualities were in harmony. The need of that Ideal is satisfied by the other modes, each of which gives it a plurality in another sense—God giving it one by release, and Existence giving it one by virtue of the mirroring of the whole by the parts.

A consequence of the pluralization of a mode, and thus of the provision of a pluralization for other modes, is the fact that the given mode will have contingent operations within it, both by virtue of its own release or representative activity, and by virtue of the subdivisions it must have if it is to keep abreast of the subdivisions of the other modes.

If it be the case that an actuality, to be representative, must also be an other, and if the otherness of the Actuality requires God, then the representative function of the actuality requires God. In the end then the rise of actualities to give genuine or rich being to the Actual as such requires the work of God. God helps Actuality by making Himself its Other. Does this require God to act as a One, or does it mean that He will provide in Himself an appropriate subdivision for Actuality? The latter would seem to be what is demanded. Yet if the otherness of an actuality is a representation of the otherness of Actuality as such, it would seem that God need only to hold over against Himself the plurality which articulates Him. This is the case. The plurality which is in God is held over against Himself to provide an otherness for any actuality, or for an actuality in its role of representing Actuality as such. This allows God nevertheless to make an inadequate set of plural items; His failure is not the failure to provide an otherness, but the failure to have it made up of sufficiently distinct determinate items. It is a determinate otherness constituted by a plurality, but it is not determinate enough, since the items which make it up are not yet fully adequate to the meaning of God's unity.

It is possible now to restate the criticism of Hegel in a better way than before.   1] He deals only with one mode of being; but there are four in which the problem of the one and the many must be dealt with.   2] He muddles two distinct kinds of being—one in which the One is dominant, and the other in which plurality is.   3] Where the One is dominant it is able only to release or fulgurate an entire set of determinations, and does not proceed (as he thinks) sequentially, approaching closer and closer to the state of the Absolute. Every fulguration is of an entire set of items, but the set itself fails to do full justice to the unity, so that once again there is a need to fulgurate, and so on forever. The parts which are fulgurated get in one another's way.   4] Where the plurality is dominant and the items in it need to achieve unity in themselves and with respect to one another (thereby giving the unity a solidity and being it otherwise would not have), the efforts are atomic. They can be indifferently viewed as involving a descent of the One or a raising of the plurality.   5] He overlooks the fact that since there are three other modes for a given one, and that since this given one must have the others somehow inside them, the others will function as ways of organizing the plurality of the given mode. Thus Actuality has Existence, God and Ideality in it; these serve as generic ways of making the plurality of actualities into parts of nature, into sacramental entities or into valuational ones. And so on for the others.

April 20

Using the previous dialectical examination of rise and fall as a model it would seem to follow that Christianity, (since it takes the being of God to be primary), must view creation as a kind of fall. This has two consequences: 1] the entire universe would be created as a single whole and have its own temporal development. If that universe were not the best possible, then after the "day of last judgment" there would be a need for God to create again. Creations would then be not recurrences but constant endeavors to produce an adequate articulation. Such a view is consistent with the reality of time, and therefore also with God's being as eternal and encompassing the whole of time. The whole of time would be encompassed by virtue of the fact that it would, after all, be nothing more than part of the articulation of the divine. The novelty in the world of time would of course still be beyond Him, for the separate parts would by their very incompleteness require that they act in time, sequentially considered. God would have the meaning of the whole world of time, not the meaning of the particular items which were produced in time.

The production of things in time seems though to deny the entire articulation, the presence of a totality of items as expressing the nature of God. This need not be the case, for the articulated totality which God produced would itself have an independence given to it by God, which enables it to provide new articulations. The new events in history would be novel and real, but together with their neighbors would be but another variant of the initial articulation. The sequence in time might be said to be a series of efforts to do full justice to the nature of God. Could God have made a perfect creation the time in that creation would provide occasions for the articulation of that perfect degree—but instead of being demanded by the defect of some previous articulation in the first place, the time would be demanded by God Himself? Or perhaps it would be better to say that if the creation were as perfect as possible there would be no time at all. I think this is better.

The second consequence is that there would be no return to God. The power of the One is only to articulate itself, and not to bring back into itself the articulation which it provides for itself and which in fact it needs in order to be itself to the full. To have a rise back into Him is to defeat His very need. But then how is it that a poor articulation comes to an end? It does this by an act of replacement by another articulation of a better degree. The coming back is not a return to the unity of God but the annihilation of the world in order to replace the poor articulation.

If there is a need to rectify a bad articulation by the sacrifice of a Christ, then the world becomes perfected by this additional fact—which confirms the theory that the creation was not initially as good as it might have been. A rectifying Christ could give a new meaning to time, pointing up a moment towards which and from which all moments are to follow. A new zero moment is provided which makes the time of this world the time of an excellent world having its end in a moment where the articulation is completed temporally. The articulation would already be completed in principle, by virtue of Christ's determinate control over the day of Last Judgment, from a position in the world at a moment which His presence defines to be zero.

The raising of man to God would be accomplished only by virtue of his identification with a Christ, and the identification of that Christ with God. But the latter identification is not really possible, for the rest of creation is also God's creation, thereby preventing Christ from being the adequate articulation of God. One could make Christ an adequate articulation by spreading his nature, as it were, over the whole of time which is required by the inadequate articulation that creation provides. One can then even speak of grace as needed in order that men might rise, but it would be the grace of Christ and not of God, the creator of him and the rest of the world. The Christian doctrine then must take Christ (as Protestants apparently do) to lift up the inadequate creation and make it an excellent articulation of God. There would be no genuine power in men because men would not really have had beings of their own; they would not really be substantial.

Only a view which starts with a plurality can have men raising themselves by their independent incorporation of the One within themselves. And that One is not God, but Actuality as such. These two ideas can be related by taking man as at the juncture of God and Actuality, being the released form of the former, and the agent which is giving full body to the latter. The history of the world, as apart from God, and as not even known by Him, would consist in the activity of men (who from His point of view are released) to make themselves representatives not of Him but of Actuality as such.

It would be better though to say that the fulguration which is the world is defective, and that this, instead of being removed or cancelled or allowed to vanish and be replaced by another, is in fact supplemented immediately. Or better still, that the fulguration is inevitably a perfect one but that it occurs in two parts and not, as it ideally might, in one. One of the parts is a plurality of beings which must progress in time or at least alter so that the potentialities of those beings can be expressed. The other part, made at the very same time and lasting from one end to the other, would be a temporally ordered eternity. On this view the eternal om- niscience of God would be found in the temporally ordered eternity; this defines the beginning and ending of the temporal series which will be covered by the objects in time. There would then be no need of a second or subsequent fulgurations.

But on the other hand, so far as there was the temporally ordered eternity there would have to be a temporal sequence, so that ultimately we could not say that the temporal sequence was completed. Nevertheless the temporally ordered eternity would be complete and any moment in it would be an expression of it. This could be thought to offer an articulation of the whole of it, though as under the condition of being distributed in such and such a way rather than in some other.

April 22

The four modes of being are incomplete in two ways: they are incomplete as beings and in this respect they continue to have one another over against themselves, and can never satisfy one another's needs; and they are incomplete in that the others have virtues or powers which help them be satisfied. Should we say that they are incomplete in two more ways—in their activity and in their relation to Ones? I think so.

Must we not say that the modes are ingredient in one another in four ways and that they are non-ingredient or external in four ways? I think so. The four ways will be the ".", ",", ")", "∴". Or, to make the matter con- crete, as ingredient, they ought to function as categories, classifications, syncategorematics, or elements in the ultimate plurality, and this should match the merging, etc., discussed in the *Modes* in relation to the external position of the modes with respect to one another.

In dealing with the modes two at a time there was an insistence on the dot and the comma. But it would seem to be more correct to make the pairs be dot and comma, implication and therefore, in any combination. Thus if we have two modes *x* and *y*, they might be related one to the other by a dot and a therefore. The kind of relations which two modes would have would evidently depend on the nature of the modes being related. Or more generally, depending on the character of the pair of items being related, one will have a set of two ways of relating them, and this whether we are talking of modes or more limited entities.

The *Modes* is primarily defective   A] in being biased towards Actuality,   B] not dealing in detail with the kinds of pluralities each mode contains,   C] not examining the way in which the modes can be ingredient in one another,   D] not seeing that one need not be restricted to any pair of relations. It may be the case that the four-fold way of relating four modes will also result in a plurality which cannot be maintained except by an infinite progress that will see any one way of handling the plurality being supplemented by other ways, and so on.

April 27

A distinction ought to be made between difference and otherness. The former applies to any entities which are not identical; the latter relates to a symmetrically related set of opposites—contradictories or contraries (in Aristotle's sense). Both of these are distinct from the kind of one-way relation which Aristotle has between the world and God (the world is related to God but God is not related to the world), a position which seems to be the opposite of Christianity's view that the world depends for its being on God and that God in no way depends on it for His being.

The different modes of being are related, from the perspective of Actuality, as others of one another. An actuality is the other of all the other modes, not in its own right but only as representative of Actuality as such. But a man has the role of an absolute Other with respect to God, and this means that he has a way of holding on to himself as an other which requires God in particular to be opposed to him. This is himself in his inwardness. It can be met only by God's inwardness. This view involves the following consequences: God's being is not exhausted by being an other of Actuality; neither is Actuality's role exhausted by being an other of God. Indeed their roles cannot be taken to be merely others even of the rest of the modes, for this would make them without any real being of their own. Each mode must have a residuum which is not covered by its being an other. The residua of each is distinct from that of the others. It is these residua which are related by the relation of otherness.

Otherness, though symmetrical and though demanding the same degree of reality (for the thrusts backward and forward are the same) on the part of both its members, does require them to be distinct beings with distinct natures. But if God and Actuality are others, must not their distinct natures be ultimately poised with respect to one another? This does not follow. The very meaning of their otherness is that they should have residua and these residua can have other roles with respect to one another and with respect to other modes. God and Actuality are in themselves (as residua of the otherness between them), inward beings whose inwardnesses take up different relations of otherness with respect to the other modes. Thus it is not God's inwardness in its inwardness, as private, which is the other of the Ideal or Existence, but His being as dominating (and also as repeated throughout His parts), which enables His inwardness or being in Himself to stand over against these other modes. In other words, God has a being in Himself, and thus functions as an other inwardness of Actuality, an other supervening one for Ideality, and an other self-divisive being for Existence. Each of these in turn has its own kind of being in itself, having three roles of otherness with respect to the other modes. The termini of these othernesses are reciprocals of the other modes as they are in themselves with respect to it. No being in itself but has three different ways of expressing its being other than three other modes.

Since actualities come and go, and since Actuality itself is relatively abstract and yet the other of the other modes, there must be a way of guaranteeing that Actuality will have an integral being in itself sufficient to enable it to stand over against the other modes. This can be done by the incursion inside Actuality of the other modes. *Nature* is the result of the subdivision, of the classifying of actualities according to the demands of Existence; *Sacramentality* is the result of classifying them according to God; *Value* is the result of classifying them according to the Ideal. When man arrives he adopts not the position of Actuality as such, but of Actuality as already subdivided by the incursion of the different modes within the mode of Actuality, thereby turning it into a set of domains within Actuality. It is by virtue of these domains that Actuality is able to function as the other of the other three modes.

If this is the case must we not then say that each mode of being is the other of the remaining modes so far as these remaining modes have already had it as an element subdividing in into a domain? Thus is not the reason why God can be the other of Actuality is that Actuality has infected

God, subdividing His being into a realm of Persons? (This would presumably be done by some actuality or group of them, and not by the mode itself.) Is it then the case that all the relations of opposition amongst the various modes but express the way in which a mode is related to itself as in some other mode?

It is not necessary, if we take any one of these lines, to hold that man is immortal. The immortality or rather the eternity of the relation of otherness relating Actuality and the other modes, is produced by the inescapable presence of these other modes in Actuality. And since the relation of opposition is in fact derived from the stress on Actuality, there must be relations having their origin in other modes, and having different functions with respect to those other modes. Thus God has the relation of identity with respect to the other modes beyond Himself; this relation of identity is not (as is said in the *Modes*) a relation which concerns itself only with Actuality; it is a relation which also has a different strength, involving a distinct act of identification with respect to Ideality and Existence.

God must see Ideality and Existence as kinds of identities, Himself multiplied, but multiplied in a different way from that in which Actuality multiplies Him. And it must be the case that Ideality and Existence must themselves generate other ways of relating to the other modes; thus Ideality has relations of implication not only in itself with respect to its components but with respect to the other modes outside itself—a relation which, if reciprocal, makes the situation one of equivalence rather than of mere implication, and thus a kind of counterpart to the identity provided by God. Existence similarly will have the relation of a "therefore," detaching itself from the others (or the others from itself), and this "therefore," if reciprocal, means that there is a kind of mutual withdrawing and pushing aside, a kind of reciprocal insistence-resistance.

Since, once again, actualities come and go, and since Actuality is comparatively abstract (from the position of the other modes) the presence in Actuality of the other modes has the double effect of making Actuality have domains, such as the sacramental, the valuational, and the natural. But since Actuality is in the relation of otherness to all the others, these very domains must at the same time be grounds for Actuality being the other of these different modes.

We have then (to concentrate say, on God), A] Actuality as the other of God because God has intruded into Actuality to make a domain there; B] God as the other of Actuality because Actuality has intruded into God; C] God as identifying Actuality because God has intruded into Actuality, and D] God as the identifying of Actuality because

Actuality has intruded into Him. Cases A and C have opposite effects, because of the ways in which the intrusion is performed; in the case of A, Actuality is in fact subdivided as over against God, whereas in the case of C, Actuality is pulverized in that domain, to be, by virtue of the action of God, a God multiplied. The domain that is constituted by God is thus a domain in the Actual, a way of classifying the plurality of actualities, or it is a domain which re-assesses, analyzes the actualities in a new way.

Conversely, Actuality as making a domain in God must analyze Him, whereas in the case of D, which prompts God's identification of those actualities with Himself, there is a re-assessment of God by the actualities in Him. The actualities intrude on God in such a way as to re-assess or re-analyze Him as the being who will accept them — this account being viewed from the perspective of the categories provided by Actuality.

If this account be carried over to apply to the other modes, we would have to recognize that there is in each mode an intrusion by the others (which will require six ways of dealing with them all). Thus in God there will not only be an acceptance of the actualities as beings which analyze Him as the being who will accept them as part of His identity, but there will be the endowing of Him with the role of the other of those actualities as not yet having intruded, a role which is achieved by virtue of an intrusion by Actuality. There will also be the acceptance of Ideality and the acceptance of Existence (which themselves will intrude on God to give Him domains of "value" and "nature"), the one involving a relation of equivalence between God and the Ideal, the other involving a relation of vital interplay between Him and Existence (where Ideal and Existence are both to be understood as standing outside Him).

The six relations inside God are paralleled by six inside each of the other three modes. Actuality, e.g., is that which is sacramentally subdivided as God's being, and this by virtue of His intrusion on Actuality, and is also (by virtue of that very intrusion as accepted by God as His own), God's nature. The Ideal in turn will make Actuality into its equivalent, at the same time that Actuality will repulse it as an other; and Existence in turn will make Actuality into a coordinate actor at the same time that it will be repulsed as an other.

All three modes are others of Actuality; since Actuality is forever, and so are they, they are absolute Others. But their absolute Otherness must be different by virtue of the fact that they are adopted by one another in distinctive ways; God is the absolute Other of Actualities (and this is said from the position of actualities) only as that being who will identify Himself with them, accept them; Ideality is the absolute Other of

Actualities only as that being which will accept them as its equivalence; Existence is the absolute Other of Actualities only as that being which will accept them as equally reactive.

April 28

If the past can in any way be encountered—or if in any sense there is an objective immortality of the past in the present—this must be consistent with the externality of the past. One way in which this duality can be maintained is by recognizing that there are different time schemes. An entity can be caught up in a time scheme which owes its origin to (or perhaps better, in our usual time scheme, is infected by) some other mode of being. There is a way in which the past continues to be together with other subsequent events, and is only a before for them and not an earlier. But (since it is only a before), it is able to extend itself in effectiveness and even in its own qualitative meaning, through the help of some other mode. By identifying the past object say with the way in which God might be resident in the world, one can find that past object now being effective and continuing to be active in the present, though in itself it is past and gone. The alteration of the past would then not be the outcome of an actual change in the very content of the past, but only in its capacity to have new roles due to the action of other modes. It is also the case that the past can itself be part of the other modes.

In the *Modes of Being* it was recognized that God's memory could be understood as a power of possessing and utilizing the past of this world. That view ought to be supplemented by one in which the Ideal and Existence are also ways of preserving in their own characteristic "times" the past of Actualities. They ought also to be seen to make a difference to Actuality in its own domain, and thereby enable the world of Actualities to sustain and retain the past. Does this allow one to speak of the past star as that which is now being preserved in the subdomain of Actuality which is nature? This cannot be the case; nature is not directly perceived or known. But might it not be the case that what science expresses in its formulae is what nature is in fact and, therefore, since for science the star is in the past and now known, we can go on to say that in nature the past is carried over to become a terminus for perception?

It is perhaps a good thing to say that science enables us to know not reality, nor even Actuality or Existence, but rather Existence as qualified by Actuality. This Existence-qualified-Actuality could be treated as a kind of punctuated Nature, a Nature which is no longer a mere domain, as is the case where Existence affects Actuality, but a Nature which is made up of distinctive entities. Such a Nature will preserve and in a sense alter the past by virtue of the fact that its time scheme is not that of actualities but of Existence primarily, and that it does not need to have divisions similar to those made by actualities in their various pulsations. There would here be a world of events, perhaps in Whitehead's sense, but one in which there were events of quite a long range which the actualities divide. Whitehead could then be said to take Existence as primary and to view the effect of actualities on it as the imposition of abstract divisions. The life of those actualities would, though, also have to be viewed as abstract. Their pasts would be concrete only as absorbed within the whole of Existence and as enabled to have objective immortality in and through the actualities – and this not by virtue of the actualities making a distinctive time scheme, but by virtue of their breaking into the time scheme of Existence.

One can also, in a similar vein, speak of actualities intruding on the time scheme of Ideality, and thereby reporting the history of the way in which the past achievements of the Ideal are carried into and made to affect its future ones. Once again the function of the actualities would not be to have a time scheme of their own, but to serve as mediations or transmitters or dividers of the time scheme of Ideality.

What we have then is A] Actuality intruding on the different modes and there having their distinctive activities preserved within their respective time schemes. B] The different modes intruding on Actuality and thereby enabling actualities to continue to be items with their own past, but to have a role also in subdomains of Actuality. Here they are carried on within larger presents as items which are merely before and not earlier; they extend over the entire present in effectiveness, and cannot be located as merely at one part of that present. C] This is an extension of B, for it merely says that the various modes must intrude on one another. The modes of Actuality, God, and Existence, e.g., all should make sub-domains in Ideality, and the kind of time that Ideality has must be sub-divided by these various modes. The subdivisions of these, or of their plural members, will be but division marks inside the larger time scheme of the mode in which the members of three modes somehow intrude.

From the foregoing there are consequences which are not examined in the *Modes of Being*. Is it the case that the various modes have time schemes of their own? If so, time is not peculiar to Existence. And, there would seem to be a kind of space and a kind of dynamics too in the different modes, apart from any intrusion of Existence. It would also seem to be the case that it is modes in their plurality which are caught in time and can be ordered in space. But the pluralities of the modes of God and Ideality are comparatively abstract. This would seem to require one to say that just as actualities can function as representatives of Actuality, so God and Ideality as unities can act as representatives of the plurality each has within it. This point was glimpsed in the account (in *Modes of Being*) of the self-identities of the plurality in God, for this would allow God to deal with other modes, not as a mere unity but as being who insists on sub-dividing them in accord with the divisions which are in Him.

May 5

If an object be designated as A, a sign as B, and an interpreter as C, we have the following considerations before us. B can act as a sign for A only if it has some relation to it; it must function as its representative. This is done by being together with A and then turning from it to C. The relation of B to C is conventional; it may in the law courts, in society, in some special discipline, in common sense and so on. B as turning towards C has already transformed what A is even for itself. The sign becomes representative only by closing itself off from the object it represents; it stands in its place, it substitutes for it, it speaks in its name. Since the object, A, might be a piece of real estate, or some dead man, or an animal, it is evident that the speaking can be something new. There need be nothing in B, as it stands away from A, which is like A. All B need be is something which was open to A to begin with and now is closed to it, no longer attending to it but being referred to C. C of course may be the user of the sign himself; in such a case he moves himself from the state where he is with A, to the state where he is merely signifying A, to the state where he is interpreting the sign B in himself, in the shape of his mind or a concept, thus putting the sign to work within the larger context of himself as a being who is more than a mind or concept.

C is affected by B. B can be a stimulus, a directive, a way of making C turn his attention in one direction or another; the sign no matter what it says may in effect be saying nothing more than "look more carefully," "turn to the right" and so on. There can be many types of C; that is why it is possible for one to make a joke about a man doffing his hat to a sign "Jesus saves" which is being carried from one place to another. Or one might see the sign before a church and ask how much it costs. The sign there functions in two capacities; it is a sign for an interpreting purchaser and a sign for a possible sinner. If the C were not already oriented towards the object of the sign, whatever that might be (in the first case, the carried sign is an object, A, and the message on it is a sign, B; A in the second case is referred to by the idea one has with respect to a sale or purchase), there would be no way in which one could make him know about the realm of the object of the sign.

Our signs are all directed to beings who are oriented to the domain where A, the object of the sign, occurs. We who are representing A, or anyone who is using the sign B, and so far is representing it in the shape of action, and not functioning as a sign for it (though this is perhaps a good way to deal with it) address it to interpreters who are already related to the world in which A is. One mistakes our intention, misconstrues the meaning that the sign is intended to have if one functions in a way in which B does not require. If one pleads on behalf of a client and the judge counts the number of words one is using, the judge fails to be the interpreter of justice (mediating by judicial procedure the relation of B to C) which the pleading supposes him to be.

The effect on C of B, within the conventional context, is to make C attend more sharply or directly or clearly or definitively to A. The way he attends is the reciprocal of the way in which B attended. He is a representative in reverse. Firstly he has assumed the position of B, for the appeal B makes to him is that he now attend to A, and B, which before stood in the place of A, now allows C to stand in its (B's) place. C need not though be similar to B. All C need do is to find a way of getting to A. As a rule in ordinary discourse where C and B are on a level, the return to A from C is the converse of the way in which B was obtained from A. But where C is superior or inferior, a judge or someone commanded and so on, the reference to A from C is distinctive.

Because the relation which C has to A is not necessarily like the relation B has to A, even in a converse way, C must be guided by more than stimuli to attend to A. If one restricts oneself to stimuli, one will not know how to become aware of A's powers, or A's consequences. B in its reference to C must not only lead C to attend, in the sense of directing him, but must help him understand what A is supposed to be for B. B represents A not merely in the sense of standing in its place, but in the sense of portraying its being.

A has potentialities or powers in it. B represents A as a thing, a substance with power. B must therefore express that power; this is done by means of a predicate. Though a predicate may make some evident feature its object, it in effect relates that object to its implicative consequences. The sign then says to C that he is to attend to A with respect to implications x, y, z, whose meaningful beginning is given by some ostensible feature remarked by the predicate. The predicate could be a pure directive just like the subject. But in order to convey knowledge (and not merely make C become acquainted with what B is acquainted with), it must at the same time make a feature in the object stand out as a representative of the power in the object; if not, it will be caught within an implicative set stretching beyond the subject. C must see a feature in A as absorbed within c's own way of grasping the concept of that feature. When B tells C about the feature through the aid of the predicate, the predicate functions as a way in which the feature will be detached from the object to the extent of being made to imply something. C thus, as Peirce observed, interprets for a further interpreter who treats the predicate (as attributed to a being) as a sign of the predicate's own consequences.

May 10

If it be the case that   1] There are propositions in the *Modes of Being* which are existentially necessary, in that their denial would preclude the expression or assertion or presentation of the denial,   2] if those propositions are linked with the rest of the system,   3] if the arguments from any one mode to the other three are valid, then it will follow that there must be four modes of being. Those modes will have different weights, for each will offer a way of being together for the other three. Any attempt to deal with five modes of being will be but an idle consideration of an abstract quintet, arbitrarily named modes of being and arbitrarily supposed to be related to one another by some of the basic forms of togetherness.

The first way to try to break down the *Modes* is to accept the position of *Reality* and read into it the distinctions of the Modes. This in effect is the bringing in of *Nature and Man* with its discussion of the four sides of a being—being on the outside, inside, from the outside and from the inside. But once we recognize, as *Nature and Man* was forced to do, the independent being of the mode of Ideality, one can move on (in the light of the paradox of ethics, the realization of the nature of otherness in individuals, their energy or Existence and so on) to the other modes of being.

Were there five modes of being then, every one of the assertions (in principle, theoretically considered) —supposing I had done the job I was supposed to have done—in the *Modes* must be altered, qualified to accommodate the intrusion of the fifth on them, and conversely. There would then be gaps in the system, and the arguments to the other three modes qualified.

Suppose there were a One which was merely for the four modes. Would this not show that we can have a One outside the many which did not, with that many, make a larger many? I think not. But suppose it did. Then it would be the case, in the light of the different weights which the various modes had for one another that they would be Ones for one another. Since they would be like a One which did not add to a many, they would be modes which did not make a four-fold set of modes. The very argument which shows that there are four modes precludes a One for these modes from being a One which is A] substantival, B] over against the modes and C] adding to them to make a larger many.

May 18

Descartes observed that confused ideas were the result of the fusion of body and mind. Instead of taking this to be evidence of the the reality of bodies he tried to replace the confusion by clear ideas. But then he was faced with the problem of the objectivity of his clear ideas. His mistake was in supposing that the confused ideas were confused in the mind; had he recognized that they were ideas which were partly in the body, that they were emotionally tinged, that they had as it were hyphens to them which were inseparable from the body itself, he would have been able to refer to the body. The body to which he referred is the other of the rest of the bodies in the world. The ideas as merely in the mind, the so-called ideas, are abstractions from abstractions. Strictly speaking we should say they are ideas *for* a mind, or at least that the mind is at the content it derives from the objects it knows. We know an abstraction from other bodies; the ideas we have of those other bodies are hyphenated towards those other bodies. When we attend to the ideas we are also aware that they are ideas which have come to us, that we are being confronted by them even when we abstract them and have them for ourselves.

Ideas then can be said to be   1] oriented towards our bodies;   2] oriented towards other bodies. Is it possible to have one without the other? *1* could be had without *2*, so far as we have an awareness of ourselves as emotional; *2* could be had without *1* so far as we had achieved a neutrality, had moved beyond the feature of the object as coordinate with ourselves to attend to the object, though only in an abstract way. When we in our bodies refer to the other bodies we get an abstraction which is rooted in the others, but with a definite bias towards ourselves, reflecting our interests. When through our ideas we refer to another object we get a neutral position which involves the abstraction of some feature of that object, representing its essence, and which we can recognize to be correlative with ourselves as beings who are properly represented by the idea or mind.

Through our ideas, we are aware of ourselves as beings who have minds, and are aware of other beings in their essence or nature. We can to be sure concentrate on the nature or essence of some feature of those beings rather than on the beings themselves—an act which abstracts from the feature somewhat as that feature was abstracted from the being. The ideas in terms of which we get the features of others are clear so far as they tell us only that we are possessers of minds; they are confused so far as they reveal the state of our bodies and thus preclude (since they then lead us to take a biased concrete attitude towards others), the grasp of the essence of others, to allow us to get them only in their particularity. The confused ideas are thus evidential of particularity in ourselves and others; the clear ideas are evidential of the being of ourselves as essentially able to have minds, and of others as having essential features, both taken neutrally. Confused ideas are not neutral, they are primarily oriented towards our bodies in a certain state and are related to others in a certain state; clear ideas are neutral and reveal only that we and others have something essential. Both types of ideas have double hyphens, pointing to ourselves and to others.

If man's strategy is primarily to know, God's strategy is to do something else. God does not function primarily as a knower. Knowing He does less well than man does. But why cannot He, with clear ideas, get to the essences? This perhaps He can, but perhaps also with less ease than man. Man never gets clear ideas as perfectly neutral, but it is possible now and then. God's ideas are never as pure, because the primary act in which He is concerned is love or grace or appreciation. This means that His ideas are subordinated and colored; He is no sheer knower. Still He does not have confused ideas as we have, because what is wrong with His ideas is only that they are subordinate and limited in somewhat the way our love is. This means that when He frees his ideas, makes Himself just a knower, He does it in a biased way. His ideas function somewhat as our confused ideas do, in that they reveal something of Him as a being who loves, and reveal something of the rest of the world as having a resistant nature. He has clear ideas which reveal not the emotional or analogous state in Him but the essential power of Him, and the beingness of other entities. It is in this sense that He acts as though He had confused ideas.

When a man loves he is in a state analogous to God when He knows. The love now is subordinate in principle to ideas or mind. Should a man make himself primarily loving, he will have his love point to himself as one who is able to know, and to other beings as somehow resistant to his love. God in contrast finds that His loving points to Himself as a being who is best expressed as loving and to other beings as merely confronting Him with content, or as merely providing Him with an occasion to love. God has of course resistant entities over against Him just as a knowing man has, but their resistance for the loving God, as they are for the knowing man, is the resistance of merely possessing the essence that is grasped in the loving and the knowing. What is said now about God and His essential loving, and about man and his essential knowing, must of course apply to the other two modes. (The use of anthropomorphic expressions in connection with these other two seems to have misled the reviewers of the *Modes.*)

(How odd it is that men do not seem to mind speaking of machines as having memories, of programming, etc., and hesitate to say that the Ideal subjugates. One here sees the continuation of a childish practice of humanizing one's tools, and a separation off of what is real and basic but distant and powerful, as somehow of a different order of being, to be judged as possessing features beyond all appropriate human characterization. The Ideal and Existence are of course not human, but they do have features which can be effectively expressed by extending terms which relate to man's essential activities.)

If man is to love as God does, God must move in, make love the neutral way of apprehending all. This is but another way of saying that man's good acts depend on a prior act of grace. There should be an analogous way of moving in by the Ideal and by Existence; the acts of subjugation and coordination must reflect the influence of the teleological and the dynamic aspects of the cosmos on man. Man achieves a neutrality by these other routes if these other modes can in fact come in and usurp the position that pure mind has for man.

The doctrine of incarnation is relevant here. If it be the case that everything is divinized to some degree, the incarnation would be the carrying this out all the way; the being of Christ would be that which is actually secular or human but which was also permeated by the divine all the way through. Accordingly we could say that the only case where God usurps through grace the priority of the rational in man is in Christ, where He gives Christ the priority of love; and of course conversely, the priority of the rational in man would in Christ also be possible because Christ is a man as well. The grace that man receives would on this doctrine always be a mediated grace, a grace which in one special case usurped the position of a neutral rationality, and this without precluding its use by that incarnated being.

Should one also say that Existence and Ideality also usurp a position in Christ; or do they do it in connection with other beings? Is it possible perhaps to have a Christ for the divine element, another for the element stemming from Existence, and a third for one from Ideality? Would one also have to say that somewhere in God, some subordinate part of him, instead of being a sustained part through love might itself usurp the position which love occupies and become the neutral mode? Or if not some part, God Himself in some position or attitude? Should we say that God in Himself assumes the position, say of rationality, by virtue of the intrusion of men on Him, by their insistence that they be loved as they are, and thus as beings who can take the neutral position of knowing? Should we say similar things of the other modes both with respect to man and with respect to one another? It would seem so; and this would lead to an entirely new development out of the *Modes,* relating not only to the incarnation, but to the life in God, and the way in which Ideality and Existence are made into "cognitional," "sympathetic," etc., powers, and how they alter the very functions of man and of God.

June 1

When enjoying a work of art I ought to know that there are other ways of apprehending the work itself. This is possible A] because I can, while I am enjoying, be aware of the fact that the enjoyment is an abstractive act, entraining another mode of apprehension; B] because I can, while I am enjoying, find the enjoyment to be a component in a larger context, the attitude of a common-sense being, and C] because I can find the work intruding on me, and thus a surface of something else, to be apprehended in some other way. These three are analogous to those which I use when, in the act of cognizing, I note that there is an object for me, to be apprehended in another way (C); that I am engaged in an abstractive act of intellection (A); and that as a common-sense man I am at the same time engaged in other ways of handling the world outside (B). And I ought also be able to know that the work of art has an Existence outside itself which it is portraying, if I am to engage in a similar triple attitude with respect, not to the work of art, but to the Existence outside it.

May not the awareness that the work of art can be dealt with in a cognitional way make me know there is an Existence to be apprehended in a non-artistic way? No; for the cognition of art concerns *its* properties, and not the properties of something outside it. But I can locate the idea in the work of art and know this idea to have a reference to an Ideal, and that this Ideal offers a meaning of Existence. We must then distinguish two modes of cognition pertinent to a work of art: one has to do with cognizing the work itself, instead of enjoying it, the other has to do with cognizing the idea in that work instead of enjoying it. The second has reference to an ideational component in the work; the former need not have such a reference. The second helps us understand something outside the work of art, if the ideational component in the work of art is known to have a referent. But is this known? Not by merely seeing it to be ideational.

If we are to learn about the world from the ideational component it must be because this cannot exist without a referent. To make out such a case one would have to say that any idea is derived from the individual's roots and refers to a world outside, at the same time that it points to the Ideal and to the divine unification of these three, individual, world and Ideal. But what of erroneous ideas, or trivial ones? The ideational component can have references only because it refers to a mode of being. Those ideas which purport to speak of Existence in the work of art have a necessary reference outside themselves; to have an idea germane to Existence is to have an idea which has existential import. (An idea germane to Actuality, etc., will of course have an analogous "existential import.")

August 1

Summarizing notes taken in July in Mexico:
Assertions must do justice to the evidence and report the nature of the real. If the evidence is insufficient we fail to report the real. If there is no attempt to report the real, there will be no use of evidence. Science fails to do justice to all the evidence and fails so far to discourse the real.

If we use only one mode of apprehension we reduce all to naturalism. The Ideal becomes cognized and only future, not prescriptive; Existence becomes cognized and is a field, not vital; God is cognized and is unity, not ultimate. There remain other modes of apprehension, and the modes continue to function as before—the Ideal subjugates, Existence moves on and God is the Other.

Starting with the Ideal, or with an affiliation characteristic of today, we find the cause by subtracting it from the event and seeing if this will then give us the world before that event. Why did the South secede? Let us say because of Lincoln's election. To show this we must show that if we take the secession and subtract Lincoln's election we reduce the War to the state where nothing but tensions between North and South are to be found. This means that the other occurrences must have been steady, or that the tensions continue for other reasons, or that we ignore the fact that they changed.

Why must the tension at an earlier date be like the tensions which came later? The later might have evolved. What kind of affiliation can I choose at the present time? Unity, diversity, as expressing the meaning of peace, civilization, mankind? What is the ideal in terms of which I can make my choice? Peace, civilization, mankind?

If the Civil War were part of a world of mere differences it would be a violent expression of the reconciliation of the differences, the violence being caused by this or that act. If we look at it as a tension which has grown out of bounds we take a different approach. We must see the occurrence first in a setting. We must know the War to be a special case of tension, or revolution, or evolution, or accident, etc. This means we must know what the proper Ideal form for all things is.

We must connect all the items of a given time with the unusual one. At the time of the secession we can say that it had tensions of law, background, economics, etc. We reduce the War to one of the tensions in politics say, and thereby make the world be one of a plurality of tensions one of which became the War. Or we can go back further and make this one tension have a long history. The tension which is behind the War is not necessarily one of a number of tensions. The immediate antecedent of the War may not be a tension at all. Accordingly we cannot say that the War was preceded by a world of tensions, but only that if there were tensions when the War occurred the War has its origin in a tension. But the immediate origin might be the shooting at Fort Sumter, etc.

We see the present object as distinctive over against other present items. We make an idealized relation between them. There is an ordering of earlier and later which will make the present object be affiliated with the others in meaning. The Ideal is satisfied by becoming the structure of the earlier and later inside the one totality. The outstanding object is now reduced to being on a par with the other present ones. But do we have to start with the present? Could we start from an Ideal state of affairs? A present occurrence could then be seen to be recalcitrant to the Ideal and be reduced to its proper position or to a less recalcitrant form.

The Ideal serves, not to give the relation of earlier and later, but to make a connection between the outstanding event now and other occurrences. We get an Ideal affiliation. This which is affiliated is now the precondition and explanation of the later occurrences along the lines of Existence.

From the standpoint of the Ideal I take this recalcitrant occurrence and reduce it so that it is no odder, no more difficult than those I now accept. History need not be rewritten constantly, for we must change it only so far as the world of Existence must be treated as more obscure than we had supposed it to be. The explanation of the Civil War is anything which will make it as intelligible as what else occurred, or which shows it to be somehow related to these (as analogous to or identical with them?) so that it satisfies the condition of belonging to their world. In the first case we start with an ideal conceptuality of the world contemporaneous with the occurrence of the Civil War.

With respect to some event in the past I can use its contemporaries as measures of what it ought to be like; I can use present-day items, of what would be a normal occurrence, from which a special one is produced through the action of some cause, or I can approach it from the standpoint of the Ideal, or intelligibility for any time. We can ask of the Civil War: why should it occur, in terms of mere intelligibility; why should it occur, in terms of present unity; and why should there have been violence, when there were other occurrences then of tension, struggle and antagonism, which did not eventuate in war?

Our basic units are combinations governed by a power greater than the individual's and which is being manifested in individuals. We want A] to know how that power's expressions are to be affiliated with others taken as normal, B] to see them as instances of our present day understandings and C] to see them as objects of intelligibility. We want the peculiar occurrence to be as *normal* as its contemporaries, to be as *plausible* as our contemporaries today, and to be as *intelligible* as the future allows other present or past items to be intelligible.

If the peculiar event is today then present entities serve as a model of normality and plausibility; if the unusual event is in the past we must start with the plausible events of today, and reach to it and its normal contemporaries. If we make it plausible from the standpoint of today we don't make it normal; we can, e.g., make it plausible that economic differences can lead to war but we don't make the war normal. We find out what was contemporary with the cause of the war and then show how the war, which is now plausible, can be made normal through introduction of another cause, requiring all the antecedents of the war in a way that it does not require antecedents from the war's contemporaries.

Before we make the war normal and plausible, we should make it intelligible. We ought to know what an ultimate unity of Existence is, as operating through a plurality of men, i.e., what an historic unit is, in which a man develops as he ought. This should be something possible. We must relate the good, the future and the possible, i.e., ultimate intelligibility, plausible present events, and normal contemporaries in the past.

When did some combination of men, united through powers of Existence, become intelligible? Which one do we not ask to have explained any further? Suppose we had the men at peace in a perfect civilization: We would want to know how this could come about in the light of nature.

If we knew what Existence and man were we would know how both could be perfectly expressed; but we know what expression deserves to be expressed only through speculation. Does this mean that we must know that Existence must express itself perfectly (as in beauty) at the same time that men must express themselves (in art) so that the true combination would be the (beauty of) Existence as matched by (the art of) man? We can suppose that the intelligible and plausible prevails, but we would not, as historians, fasten on a present occurrence if it were normal. We find that some outstanding object is not normal, though it can be plausible and intelligible. Suppose we want to understand the normal? We must then recognize that it is not intelligible or plausible.

History is the story of the activities of groups of men. As stabilized those groups are institutions; as possessing power, tradition, etc., they are nations, states, cultures, etc. An history is intelligible or right when understood in terms of the differentiations of a perfect unitary group where beauty is matched by ethical activities. It is plausible in terms of what we take to be proper combinations today, and it is normal or rational so far as we reduce unusual events to others, plus some force or power which transforms those others into the unusual occurrences. In the end the unusual is the result of the mis-matching of individuals and Existence, because Existence is not beautiful or man is not ethical, or the two are not in consonance.

We study history to learn how men become individuals in a civilization with the help of an independent activity of Existence. We look to it now though to tell us what kind of difference Existence has enabled man to make in the past with respect usually to other contemporaries, whom we assume for the moment to give a reasonable or plausible way of being at this period of time. We could immediately treat the present odd occurrence as having an ideal promise, but this would require us to define Existence as that which has prevented this ideal from being actual. History would tell us then what Existence as such has done. If we start with plausible contemporaries in the present it tells us what man or Existence has done. If we start with past events, contemporary with the investigated one, it tells us what man has done—the normal.

If we seek a *cause* we try to find out how the idealized nature, which is latent or possible, differs from the present situation; if we seek an *explanation* we start with the present and find the law-abiding process which makes the development plausible; if we want a *pre-condition,* the antecedent, we reduce the present object on which we focus to the shape of other contemporaries. We start by looking for an antecedent, then for an explanation, and then for a cause.

Why the Civil War?   A] the antecedent of the War is a tensional situation like others present with the War, but independent of it—bitter rivalry. The explanation is the way the rivalry degenerated into violence, in somewhat the way it does or can today. The cause is what made the rivalry deviate from the state it would have been in were it to be progressing to the position where men will be together adjusted to the world. This deviation arises because the power which they use is not entirely in their control.

We learn from history the incapacity of man to control the power altogether. This failure does not tell us what Existence is, but rather what men together are as not yet adjusted to existent organizational energy.

Does the Ideal tell us of the Ideal route, the present of the antecedent, and the contemporaries of the cause? If so, the Civil War occurs because A] the logic or route of history requires this state, given such and such an antecedent;   B] the antecedent is that which is like the present, and C] the cause is the differentiating impatience or irritability. The cause is what distinguishes this occurrence from its contemporaries; the antecedent is that which is presupposed, the power in the object which is like present power (so that we learn how the power here differs by virtue of the object's deviation from its contemporaries); the explanation is the deviation in the law by which the occurrence deviates from contemporaries and present acceptances. (Or it is the law which is always present but which was complicated through the introduction of the deviation.) It is an ideal law but we find that the occurrence does not behave in terms of it because there is something not yet controlled. (The explanation then is that the Ideal does not explain?) The antecedent with its power would ideally terminate in such and such a result. But it does not. Antecedent power produces the War because men are not properly adjusted to one another or to Existence.

Does the Ideal tell us how to affiliate, what kind of conditioning is allowable, the meaning of causes? Is it a cause of meaning, of civilizations? The Ideal isolates the essential component, finds it for us. The occurrence has a different prospect from its contemporaries and in order to have it get the same one, we are driven to find a new item in history.

We can interpret the contemporaries according to their appearances or in terms of an ultimate Ideal, say mankind at peace. We can isolate the War as a cause and explain the intervals of peace and quiet and rest as a failure of nerve. If we want to give the causes of the War we must say it is one of a class of affiliated entities each of which is distinctive and yet the same in root.

August 2

Men and situations have a power of their own which makes them deviate from present things; they therefore have adventitious causes which produce deviations from contemporaries.

The cause is an antecedent, like the contemporaries, plus a differentiating element. We ask next about the way in which this cause would operate to bring about the result, and here get a plausible explanation in consonance with what is now known about the world. But when we ask why should this particular route be followed, why should things at that time act in that way, we move to the Ideal for the explanation of the nature of the proper way of acting, and to find out why it is that the difference in the way things happened was the outcome of the deviation produced by Existence and men in interplay. In the end we learn how a cause plausibly produced the result with respect to men who were not ideally related to one another or Existence.

Men are maladjusted in four ways—with respect to promise, fellowman, structure or organization, and with respect to the vital energy of the world. The all-inclusive account of how the adjustments occur is history. But we also have the subordinate histories of philosophy, ethical growth, emotional expression; histories of societies, cultures, customs, etc.; histories of state, law, peace, revolution; and finally, the history of technology. What is today called history is concerned primarily with the adjustment of groups of men with respect to the vital energy of the world; i.e., it is concerned with the interrelation of the history of technology with that of Existence, in which ethical or spiritual and political history are subordinate parts.

We begin with the vital energy already partly caught in the structure, interrelationship and individual expression of men, and seek to find out the causes, the plausible routes and the ultimate explanations. We find that individuals, groups, structured wholes all have some Existence in them in conflict with their natures, and that the three of them together conflict with Existence outside. The last conflict is explained from the standpoint of the Ideal, as governing the deviation from the Ideal; the conflict of men with structured wholes is discovered by using present entities to indicate the intelligible principles which will define a proper structural route at the end of which the given event appeared. The conflict of men with their fellows is given by the cause which explains how the occurrence could have arisen from a situation like that provided by its contemporaries. (But there is left over the conflict of men with themselves so that their art, philosophies, ethical societies, actions, expressions, etc., do not conform to what they are in essence. Individual energies are opposed by bodily energies so that the nature of man is distorted; or because man's nature is not yet sufficiently developed there is a distorted use made of energy.

The Ideal must take as basic that what men are found out to be in history is what they are in fact. Accordingly history would deal only with men in groups having structures over against Existence. What about the history of art or philosophy? We should say that these are to be explained as terminal points in groups, or that they have an internal development through the exercise of human will or action.

The Ideal tells us that men ought to express what they really are, but history begins by telling us that what they express they really are. When we do a history of what they express, in abstraction from groups, etc., we can do nothing more than trace references, reduce forms to earlier ones, etc., and therefore seek a cause. We don't deal with a rational route for we do not have anything to compare, and we don't explain a new philosophy or writer by relating it to other beings.

What is the relation of a group to God and of structure to the Ideal? Is there a four-fold situation in connection with the Ideal and God? Must we not ask A] how men adjust themselves by means of the ought; B] how men act together in society; C] how they act in politics and under law; and D] how they produce a civilization? *Our Public Life* did not attend enough to D; *Man's Freedom* deals with A and B. We must also ask how A] men adjust themselves by means of authenticity; B] how they act together in a religious community; C] how they act with respect to a church or other institution; and D] how they are able to stand over against the rest of the world through the aid of church, etc. (But perhaps it is incorrect to do this since the problems with the different modes is different. All we can say is that men do adjust themselves to the Ideal and to God in the form of structure, organization, and community spirit. If we want to ask about man and the Ideal we ask about a realization of different forms of private and public achievement of excellence. If we want to ask about men and God we must distinguish a private relation to some form of worship and then subdivide the public form in many ways.)

But is it not true that men as related in organized groups may be deflected from an Ideal by the intrusion of God, or that the Ideal may alter the way in which Existence might force a deviation from the Ideal? Might we say that the Ideal seeks to realize itself, so that we have a kind of teleology, and that God seeks to absorb all? Might we not learn from history what God wants or the force of the Ideal, rather than what Existence does in relation to man?

We can eliminate the teleological alternative for we are already speaking from the standpoint of the Ideal. We must therefore ask whether we cannot account for the resistance of men in groups to leave the Ideal, as being due to God? Don't we say it is God when we ask why the plausible route of transformation is not entirely rational? But then it is not only Existence which is the concern of history; we must say that Existence is behind the production of the aberration if it is not what the Ideal specifies; but God would make the Ideal realizable, or at least would not take us away from it. Yet God does have His own standards. From the standpoint of history He must aim at realizing the Ideal. Accordingly, we cannot say that the deviations are due only to Existence.

Theological interpretations of history are wrong because A] they suppose that the task of history is to explain by means of the Ideal; B] suppose that we need a divine power to bring us to a desired end, C] that the end which is to come is a good one in fact. But history is more secular and has more respect for God than theological history would allow.

Existence affects some occurrence, to make it the cause which then operates along a plausible, i.e., empirically adopted route, to produce a result that, together with all other occurrences at that time, deviates in an intelligible way from what could have been. Alternatively, the energy contained in actual entities and groups is operative as a cause. This cause is effective along the route which is characteristic of men and their groups. This deviates in an intelligible way from what might have been the cause of the power of Existence as that to which men have not yet been properly adjusted. If we were content with the causal action of men and groups we would have anthropology; with plausible acts, sociology; if we want explanation in the light of the Ideal, we have history.

We must begin with Existence as caught in men and their groups, and kept along paths which are reasonable, in order to find out what Existence, as over against us, does in relation to us. History has sociological and anthropological components.

If we just look for the causes of an occurrence we have anthropology; if for the laws we have sociology. It is only when we want explanations that we have history. We are not looking for the cause of the Civil War or the laws of history, but for the explanation of why men deviate from the Ideal and what they are as beings in Existence.

Men are maladjusted in themselves and this can be a question of psychology and ethics; in relation to one another, a question of politics; in relation to the structure of groups, freedom; in relation to Existence, technology. It is only when we ask for an explanation of the maladjustment and with respect to the anthropologically accepted cause and the sociological laws, that these become part of history. We can get a history of man's expressions, i.e., of psychology and ethics, once we take his biology as a way of getting to his cause, accept his psychology for plausible routes, and look at him as ideally expressing a healthy and controlled body. But this does not tell us about him as a spiritual individual. The question remains how can we get a history of ideals, art, etc., which is not sociological or anthropological.

In connection with the individual we can take his various works, assume some of them to be the final point at which he has arrived, and explain the others as the result of a causal theory in which the individual is the *cause* of the difference of the one to be *explained,* in terms of a present understanding of what is a *reasonable* path of development. Individual incapacity indicates why the individual failed or contradicted himself. It is possible of course that he might be at the height of his powers over a period. In that case the final explanation will be the production of variety by Existence and men in interplay. We will hope that there will be a pattern given by earlier and later forms of the variety.

We must say then that history does not suppose a maladjustment but an independence. It is possible that the independent beings may work together so well that we get variety as an explanation. If they work badly we get maladjustment. Accordingly, history starts with the recognition that there is a distinction in the functioning of men internally and externally in relation to their fellows, in connection with the structure of a group, and in relation to the world beyond. Each taken by itself will give subdivisions of history. In connection with the internal and external there will be an unused amount of Existence in the form of emotion which will explain either the variety, or a deviation from the Ideal. One can of course also deal with the struggle over against the social situation, over against politics or over against Existence itself.

What emotion is for the individual man, sympathy is for him in relation to others, loyalty is for him in relation to the structured whole, and adjustment is for him in relation to Existence. Emotion, fellow-feeling, disposition are Existence caught inside man, making him a community of individuals or an organization in relation to its members, thereby enabling them to have a history of individual achievements in arts, etc., a social history and a political history.

Men start with unorganized emotions as individuals, expressing a trapped Existence, relating their internal and external natures. They are also related to one another socially, expressing a trapped Existence, at once uniting and dividing. They are also members of structured wholes, expressing a trapped Existence initially exhibited in a tensional force.

Men begin as at once emotional, as subject to social pressure, and as in a tensional relation to the organizations of which they are members. At the same time they stand over against the whole of Existence, as constituting a culture struggling with the larger world. The history of philosophy, etc., takes account of the use of the emotional component; the history of sociology, of social pressure; the history of politics and nations, of the tensional relation, and the history of man, of the cultural struggle. But history proper is usually concerned with men as in some consonance with one another, so that the problem is mainly one of understanding the way in which the tension operates and how the struggle with Existence is carried out.

History is concerned either with the trapped Existence, or with an Existence which is outside, and with which mankind struggles. So far as we take individuals, societies, or nations to be excellent or self-sufficient, at least for the purposes of history, we concern ourselves with trapped Existence and suppose this to be responsible for the variety of occurrences. But we also think of the trapped Existence as disturbing and therefore functioning as a real causal power, making for deviations from the Ideal. But no explanation will be satisfactory unless it also recognizes that Existence, in the guise of fortune, chance, or acts of God also has an independent role and makes a difference to man's world, and that he must adjust himself to it. The trapping of Existence is a consequence of some previous struggle with Existence itself. The explanation of an occurrence is usually A] the unorganized emotional occurrence in individuals, B] the social disequilibrium with respect to the group to which they belong; C] the tensional relation they have to the total organization; D] the loose energy of the world beyond. These yield aberrations of individuals, incoherence of social wholes, inadequacies of organization, the fortunes of Existence at that time.

If we take a proposition out of the *Modes* and generalize it, it becomes the very meaning of Actuality from that position. This can be summarized or axiomatized to give a principle of deduction in Ideality. This is what Robert Hartman is doing. We do not make an axiom of a category. It is the function of the Ideal to take axiomatized form in the shape of the Good.

Except in rare cases, workers in a given organization do not form a community or organization; when they do they are partners. Even when we pay wages we have a kind of partnership. Profit-sharing is an ideal way of having this, as Hartman has shown. But when we take the workers away from a given organization we can organize them as mere workers. They should then have over against them the nexus of companies. The regulation or union of these two is a matter of public legislation, whose object is to see that the two function together in such a way as to preserve the constitution or nation for men concerned with the rational whole. The workers are part of the men who judge the value of the togetherness of the two. So far as they are, they regulate themselves; the legislation in the end is self-legislation.

Each mode of being has a characteristic way of being a one for a many. The Ideal as mere structure is a logic—axiological logic—as Hartman sees—since it has to do with what will serve as a norm for ethics, etc. As integral to the Ideal it is a material logic of the Ideal, its very structure; and as made referential to the other modes it is prescriptive. The other modes have a logic of their own but it has a subordinate role in them. We have, then, the logic which applies to the other modes, and the logic which is the very structure of those modes, and these will have to be reconciled. The One of the Actualities is category; of Existence is expansiveness, and of God is unity. The logics of these are of individuals, of mathematical science, and of self-identity.

There are four methods; systematic or logical; intuitional or abductive; creative or inferential; evaluational or ordering, and in each mode one of these is most appropriate—Ideality, Actuality, Existence and God answer respectively to the above.

In history, if we are content with the *cause* and the rational, we will suppose that the emotional, folkways and political sanctions are *normal,* and that the *explanation* will reveal the way in which Existence as such interplays with man and his organizations and institutions.

Men and women are individuals who supplement one another. This means that with respect to some given mode which they incorporate, e.g., the ethical when they are related to the Ideal, they are concerned with using themselves to show the effect of the Good on the one side and Existence on the other. The ethical man reveals what Existence is like in himself as requiring action, whereas woman requires revelation. Man reconciles himself to the other by action; she does it by reevaluating what it is about.

August 3

Man seeks order and woman seeks direction. Facing the Ideal he takes account of Existence, she of God; facing God he of Ideal, she of Existence; facing Existence, he of God, she of the Ideal.

Ethical teachers, being men, always urge action. But women themselves want re-evaluation or eternity. To make them act with respect to the Ideal is in a way to make them do what they have been doing—using their emotions as a power. What they want is an objective basis, not a true judgment. Men theologians, it has been remarked by a woman theologian, always ask men to deal with God from an ethical point of view and thus to look for quiet, patience, etc. Were they to speak of women they would repeat their recommendations, yet women need action in Existence, pride, etc. As Nietzsche said, Christianity is a womanly religion; what women need is a masculine one which puts great stress on action. When men tell us how to deal with Existence, they want us to stress order, but women need more guidance by an outcome which ought to be attained. Of course as the churches now make evident, preaching womanly religion attracts the women; if we want men to go to church we must urge the virtues men already have—courage, adventure, etc., public activity. This perhaps, is the reason why ministers turn to politics in their sermons so often. The combination of men and women gives us a togetherness uniting some other mode in two ways. If actualities are to be reconciled to Existence then the order men bring about must be supplemented by women's ethical achievements. Art and history will help men become ethical, and women to conform to God.

The absolute logic is the structure of the Ideal and this can be imposed on other modes. In itself it is "descriptive"; it is prescriptive for the other modes. Each mode in addition has its own logic; this does not do full justice to the mode's nature, and one must therefore engage in further abstractions, thereby losing the mode. Symbolic logic is a logic of individuals or Existence, but when it becomes general it ceases to be applicable, since it then becomes only a refined abduction of actualities and Existence, missing their essence and being incapable of application, in a neutral way, to all the other modes. E.g., an Actuality knows by a series of intuitive apprehensions. These, when made neutral, can serve as the very essence of philosophic knowledge of all the modes in the way in which the Ideal logic can. But if we apply those intuitions to other modes, we do not catch them, as well as we could have, had we allowed their natures to dictate what the neutral characteristics should be. In Actuality our logic, creativity and evaluations are either generalizations of ourselves but never neutral enough, or are the outcome of prescriptions imposed by other modes.

Art and history together give us Existence in its relation to man. Ideality and God serve to reconcile them with one another, the first offering a systematic evaluation, the second, a sympathetic evaluation. The first makes them conform to the Ideal good and the second makes them find a place in the preserved totality of things.

It is always necessary, in connection with the modes, to recognize that they have different weights and thus what is true of one primarily is true of the others secondarily. Can we say just how different features are related inside each?

	Actuality	*Ideality*	*Existence*	*God*
1]	intuitive apprehension	logic	creativity	evaluation
2]	creativity	obligation	logic	intuition
3]	logic	intuition	evaluation	creativity
4]	evaluation	creativity	intuition	logic

The characteristic of politics is the prescription of the Ideal on public actualities. If we try applying this to other modes we will make an error of distortion, though we can find an analogous relation there. The state is not the individual writ large; man is an individual, the state is not.

Is natural science integral though not primary to Existence; is logic integral and primary to Ideal; if so what science is integral to man— psychology taken in depth?

The loss of prescriptiveness in modern logic is due to the fact that it is a material logic, a logic of the structure of science and mathematics. Its inability to keep abreast of actual reasoning is due to the fact that it is not a logic of the Ideal, which also plays a role in our reasoning—e.g., in our values.

Engineering is successful just so far as science is only an abstractive strand of the world of engineering. There can be an "engineering" in every mode which is the outcome of a syntax. In practice the modes shape up as: Actuality as social life, Existence as engineering proper, Ideality as specification and God as providence.

The unresolved component in an individual is emotion. Men also have diverse interests. The fact of their diversity is exhibited in the unorganized course of the social world in which they live; over the course of time they can "purge" this in the form of activities such as rituals and ceremonials, or can exhibit it in such a way as to make for a disharmony and confusion in the future and a maladjustment of individuals to one another. Men also have relations to the Ideal, God and Existence, both as individuals and as together. In the latter form they have an unused component in the feeling of injustice, or perhaps better, the tension between the lived or positive law and natural law, or perhaps even better, between the lived law and positive law. The unresolved portion expresses the discrepancy due in part to the fact that individuals have private lives and are concerned there with ethics, art and religion.

Man's political freedom, when properly purged in the form of an individual acceptance of the state in patriotic activities, is analogous to the successful use of emotion. We have a feeling of obligation which is resolved in proper acts; we can have an analogous feeling of responsibility which is not well-focused and needs purging in the shape of significant public activities. There is also the relation of the social group to God—a church. The relation of a group to Existence allows for the occurrence of contingency, which is to be purged by technological control. Purged emotion gives art; unorganized interest gives ceremonial and ritual; unfulfilled obligation or responsibility gives patriotic activities; religion's awesomeness makes a church; culture's insecurity is purged in technology.

To explain the peculiarity of art we make reference to energy of emotion, diverse interests, insufficient responsibility, fear of the lord, contingent uncontrolled Existence.

August 4

Mexican notes concluded:

The explanations we seek, after we have taken care of causes and rational laws, (for say, occurrences in society) lump together influences which could come from individuals, God, the political structure and Existence. But why is history concerned with Existence? Is it not because Existence is the unresolved energy in all? This means that it is not so much the concern with Existence as such outside, but the unused Existence within the frame of human activity that is the major problem. This is Existence in one special form, and is related to the Existence outside man and his world. A deviation then can be explained by some combination of emotion, unorganized interest, insufficient responsibility, sin, and lack of control of the world beyond.

Explanation lies in the fact that there is a technological control, a religious unchannelized energy, a political irresponsibility and a socially disorganized Existence which makes for the occurrence of the cause over a plausible route, bringing about the aberrant behavior of other occurrences we seek to explain. It is then Existence as already caught within the confines of the human world which explains, though the explanation may lie not in what Existence, or God or the Ideal, may require of man. Accordingly, what we seek to learn, particularly when we attend to men in social groups and states, is what an unused Existence might do. We make our history secular by eliminating the divine element, make it non-political by eliminating the irresponsibility, and make it cosmic by eliminating the social, so that in the end we see the Existence (which is to explain the occurrence) to be in an inadequate relation to the whole Existence outside. This gives us a history inclusive of all human enterprise, embracing the totality of groups, states, etc., each of which is to be explained in terms of its own use of Existence. We can also proceed the other way, and by dealing with social, political and religious history, leave over a residuum to be dealt with in universal history.

A document, treated as an occurrence to be explained, is like any other event; it is when we already know what the event is which we wish to study, say the Civil War, that we seek the cause, rationale and explanation, by looking at some of our contemporary materials to see if in their particular way of acting we can understand the route of the causation. The materials give us a way of interpreting the route or the elements. The document does our interpreting for us; inside it tells us what the cause is or what the route was; if reliable it shortens our work. It does not bring us closer to the determination of the legitimacy of our answer; the historical problem is no different here from the determination that such and such is the cause for this odd occurrence.

A first person observer is a third person observer in his report. The historian's work is a first person document. What seems to be a significant historical rationale or explanation, taken in its internal claim, is observational in the sense of being equivalent to a contemporary's recording by an expert.

A murderer injures himself in that he does not act to develop himself as he should, and he prevents another from doing so as well. In this sense the crime is double. He also forces the rest of men to preserve the value he lost, and he forces God or the essential nature of man to become more abstract, or to re-evaluate the whole, or to find another articulation for the values that were lost. Taken in terms of the Ideal, the loss is absolute; taken in terms of Actuality each man is a unit to be counted; taken in terms of Existence we have a loss of method, and from the standpoint of God a loss of a needed other.

If God were made abstract He would have to divide Himself and have Himself, as divided, over against Himself. The concreteness of God requires an internal articulation. If this is not answered by the world, God is so far in error. He must then revise His articulation at every moment. Each individual Actuality is such an articulation; each man is one moment, one way of articulating God. God's infinite number of articulations is necessary if He is to be fully concrete. The murderer forces men to be preserved in a form altered from what it would otherwise be. Men lose some of their individuality in being transformed by God; every murderer requires some articulation in a different direction. To make Himself concrete, God must articulate Himself in a way which is not identical with what men really are, to make up for the value the murderer lost.

The murderer forces God to take over the job the murderer should have been doing, and to complete what the victim's might have been. Each man must articulate the whole from his angle. Not only does the murderer not do this, but he also prevents another from doing it. A murderer acts within the sphere of a representative of all; instead of making another into a moment of the whole which will articulate the whole, he makes him into an articulation of what is not a genuine whole. God must undo the meaning of the victim who is caught in the whole the murderer represents. The more murders the more must God reformulate the meanings of individuals.

God must make good the obligations the murderer fails to fulfill; He is also required to radically revise everything in this world to make good the value lost. Also, the loss of the individuality of the victim means that there is a loss of an articulation of God from one perspective. God is abstract, incomplete, not as good as He might be until He articulates Himself completely, answers to what things are. The realization in Him of His unity is needed, if He is to keep abreast of new values, and this involves a loss of an accurate restatement of what the world is like.

The orientation of the Ideal towards the Actual persists so long as there are men who can be obligated to realize it. And if there were no such men, God would have no truth about the world. God's perfection requires that He adopt the good. He must also articulate the world and this means that men must be Godlike, embracing the whole world. Two murders are worse than one because they add to God's struggle to complete Himself, by making Him face two tasks—a reorganization of Himself and a reconstruction, by an abstract activity, of what is in fact existent.

August 25

If we take the dimensions of man to be the body, mind, person and concern we can distinguish four virtues: There is the virtue of *mastery,* which is related to self-discipline and is perhaps what the ancients called temperance. Here the body is controlled and yet allowed to be itself fully; this mastery is in the little and the large, in the parts of the body and in the body as a whole, and has its repercussions in an appropriate control of the other dimensions, and conversely. There is next the virtue of *understanding* with its two directions of vision and insight, of grasping the cut of the whole and of seeing the depths in things. A person has the virtue of *authenticity;* this must be understood as being concerned with the individual's own integrity on the one side, and on the other, with a respect for the persons of others. And finally there is a *commitment,* both with respect to immediate and to eventual goals.

August 29

A rather sharp line should be drawn between dialectical and other kinds of reasoning, not merely in terms of the objectives—i.e., in the one case to complete a given idea or content, and in the other to transfer a desirable value of an acceptable premiss to a desired conclusion—but in terms of the entities at which they arrive and the relation they have to one another. The dialectical method arrives at beings whom we might encounter; its proofs are proofs that the beings are there for encounters and therefore warrant the fact that the reasoning is in consonance with the real. If we argue that a cat is a set of qualities sustained by a substance, such a substance is not in fact encountered but supposed or presupposed. We think there must be a substance so that the qualities can be sustained and the being's movements explained. But unless we can make a dialectical demonstration that there are substances all we have is the faith that the world will justify our expectation that the being we call a cat will subsequently behave in such and such a way. If we have no dialectical proof of this we do not know that there is a being to behave in such and such a way, and must be content to say that our expectations seemed to be sustained, but we do not know by what—which is roughly the position of Hume.

The religious man, precisely because he has no dialectical demonstration of the being of God, has to say that he knows Him by faith. But the faith here is in principle the same kind of faith that an ordinary Aristotelian type of man would use to justify his belief in substance. The guarantee of the legitimacy of our inferences, that they are such that the world will in fact bring about what we have inferred, is to be given only by metaphysics. It is correct then to say that metaphysics is the subject concerned with presuppositions; it is also correct to say that its propositions cannot be verified in the ordinary sense, and that even its logic is not the logic which does justice to mathematics.

Occasionally theologians engage in speculations, but these they put in the form of "mysteries" beyond actual rational understanding. This means that they have a way of getting to their presuppositions, but no way of showing that the result is completive. Theirs is in effect a way of continuing the inference (and in this case it has the structure perhaps of prayer), beyond its terminus in a conclusion, to something which, in the light of various bits of information obtained in different places, is made thicker than the terminus and able to act as an encounterable object. The theologian, then, provides interesting clues and perhaps even guides for the speculative metaphysician. This comes out for example in connection with our understanding of what an individual is. The doctrine of the trinity provides a clue to our understanding of the individual, for it says that there is but one substance and three basic divisions of it, each of which is the whole substance. The analogue in connection with man is the recognition that he, a unitary person, has a mind, body, and a concern. If he were just the aggregate of these he would no longer be a man; if he is one of these primarily, the others become incidental functions; if he is a fifth thing he would seem not to have control of these various divisions. The answer would seem to be that in each one of the divisions he is a unity, but with a stress on understanding, power, privacy or commitment.

Each man is a unity of essence and Existence, a unity which varies in destiny over the course of a day. The mind (or any of the others) when not active, has a minimum energy. Any one of the divisions can function to control the others and thereby make it function in new ways; it can subordinate it to itself, intermediate it with the others, and even allow it to function on its own. The unity of a division is continued over into the other divisions where it is re-organized by virtue of the fact that the other divisions have their own structures and thereby are able to bring in energy in a new way. Each offers potential energy for the others, and when those others make use of that potential energy each can be said to express itself through those others.

The unity of a being is to be found by starting with any of the subordinate divisions and seeing the others as translations of this in new contexts. A man has no special locus of identity; each of the various unitary subdivisions has its own stress, the dominance of one over the others at any time is largely a matter of adjustment. Who does the adjusting? Each part. There is no entity made by the adjustment but only, e.g., a body which is affecting the way in which the others are to act. Why cannot the man restrain all of them? Because there is no position in which he is to be found; he finds himself dispersed into these unities, and each makes him aware of the others. He is a single being from four different angles and never is a pure substance in and of himself.

I was wrong to treat concern in *Nature and Man* as though it were such a thing; I there made something like Aristotle's error when he took the soul to be the form of the body and the locus of his "manhood." The unity of man is like my hand, which is dispersed through my fingers and my palm; it is the hand that it is by virtue of the way in which the palm or fingers operate. There is no hand as such; but, also, it is not an aggregate.

What must be said is 1] there is an individual Existence, 2] that part of it is potential, and 3] that the unity and being of the individual is more than Existence. It means in the end that the potential energy must be qualified by the structure, in the sense that it has thereafter an individual note. But A] the structure is itself not individual, and B] the individual does function as though it were a thing.

Is B taken care of by the recognition that the Existence in the individual is also under the control of the larger Existence? It must then be pulled in two ways. Is A taken care of by the re-assertion of the qualified Existence, so that, having been pulled away from the total Existence by the structure, it now re-asserts itself as a distinctive Existence, and from then on can serve as one meaning of the individual? The Existence in the individual must thereafter be his substantially, but only because it was enabled to stand away. How then is it, according to B, still carried away? It is this by virtue of the Existence with which it is ontologically one. In the individual it felt the mark of the individual's essence; it is thereafter a unity with an essence, but with an individual note, precisely because the essence which it has is not adequate to its full meaning, and it nevertheless remains within the confines of that meaning. The Existence as keeping itself to that essence, as that which it has absorbed and nevertheless accepts, is individual; as that which absorbs, Existence becomes the energy of a functioning structure; as properly having a wider essence, as being localized by an alien factor, it is part of cosmic Existence.

August 30

He who lives a creative life runs with the ball, sets down the goal posts, acts as an umpire, fixes the rules as he goes along, and at the end says he has lost. The setting of the goal posts, etc., is properly done only by one who has played other games before, sometimes in rather strict conformity to the rules established. Given enough concern with a discipline and devotion to it, a man eventually establishes a discipline in himself. He acts authentically and thereby becomes a good worker in the field. Whether or not he has genius will depend on the combination of understanding (vision and insight), commitment (attention to the ideal end and the goals possible now), authenticity (being himself and allowing the rules to be dictated by no one else from the outside) and training (the grasp of what is good in the past).

In connection with man, one must recognize that there is an element of Existence in him which is A] potential, B] his own, C] capable of being expressed in particular limited ways, D] continuous with the Existence outside. This Existence can be viewed as a kind of togetherness, demanding a prescriptive togetherness in the form of an essence, another in terms of an end, and a fourth in terms of a privacy. Viewed in this way, life, attention, person and concern become "modes of being"; this, however, would reduce the individual, taken in his over-all unity to a kind of attenuated being. If, however, we reverse the field, and suppose that life, attention, person and concern are forms of togetherness, the essence, Existence, end and privacy all become concrete and oppositional, and each will have to have (as was the case in the reverse situation) the others somehow in it, making a difference to its functioning. The unity will then be the outcome of the ways in which the togetherness of life, attention, etc., operate on one another, but the substantival aspect of the being will be in the essence, Existence, end and privacy, and not in life, attention, person or concern. The trouble is that the latter look as though they were vital and effective; they are concrete in their operation, and seem to have more of an integrity than a mere togetherness could be. Also it does seem as if essence, Existence, end and privacy are not affected by one another.

Can an analogue of the *Modes of Being* be applied to the individual and in such a way that his essence, Existence, etc., function as modes with the various togetherness having the nature of life, attention or mind, etc.? What does one do with the fact that life has both a structure and an

Existence, and thus seems to have a kind of being? Is the individual perhaps in between these different stresses, so that it is right to say that either the complex of life, etc., or that of essence, etc., is the One or the substantial? Should we also say that A] because neither has become exclusively one, we as a consequence are "organic," who momentarily may make our essence, etc., vital and effective, and B] at another moment may reverse the situation and make life, etc., vital and effective? But can we, on the one hand, treat essence as vital and effective, and life as merely a prescription, a description, etc., of the way in which essence is together with Existence, etc.?

August 31

There are, according to the *Modes,* four ways of being together, which are expressed as a conjunction involving a prescription and marked with a comma, a descriptive conjunction marked with a dot, an entailment or necessity, and a therefore. Each of these provides a way in which the four modes can be together; they are ways of uniting the modes, but not ways of unifying them. Since they do have some power, and since it is the case that one can actually adopt the position of any one of them, and since they do in fact make a difference to one another, it would seem, as the *Modes* did not show, that they must have various ways of interpenetrating and taking account of one another; and it must also be the case that the modes themselves will offer ways in which they can be united. This means, e.g., that such a way of being together as prescriptive conjunction must have a bearing on the other ways of being together, to constitute the analogue of the cosmological relation which holds amongst the modes. It must also be able to be united with the other ways of being together through the actions of the different modes of being.

A] We then have a being together acting as a way of uniting the modes; B] a way in which the various kinds of togetherness are unified by some mode, and C] a way in which the different kinds of togetherness take account of one another by accommodating them within themselves. The third case occurs together with the second. We find that the different kinds of togetherness take account of one another when they are unified by some mode, and conversely. It is possible to conceive of either B or C as prior. We also of course have the reciprocal A'] where the modes unify the forms of togetherness in four different ways, B'] where the modes are united by the different kinds of togetherness, and C'] where the different modes take account of one another.

The cosmos can be said to be an organic whole so far as we view it as a set of modes united by the kinds of togetherness; it can also be said to be a unit so far as we view the togethernesses as unified by the different modes. It is in fact both of these together but not perfectly distinguished; were they perfectly distinguished we would lose the universe. The price one pays for having a universe is that the modes do not unite perfectly, and therefore are somewhat independent in functioning (thereby setting problems to one another) and that the various kinds of togetherness have an independence too. The distinctiveness of any mode or of any form of togetherness depends in part on its failure to be a perfect success; it always has work to do.

If one goes on to use the *Modes* as a model for man it becomes evident that man is a unity of unit and organism in somewhat the way in which the total cosmos, made up of modes of being and forms of togetherness, is. But in the case of the cosmos the forms of togetherness are never major; they merely vary in the degree of their significance without ever offering a correlative reality to which the modes of being are really subordinate. But in the case of man his status as a unit—essence, existence, person and concern—is on a footing with his status as an organic whole—life, mind, subjectivity and value. He fluctuates between these without ever losing either. This is but another way of saying that man is not a mode of being, nor identical even in miniature with the cosmos, and that no subordinate part of him is a mode of being. But a subordinate part of the cosmos is a mode of being.

September 1

If the individual can be said to be an arena made up of a unit and an organism or organic whole, and if it is also the case that the separate items of the one make possible a togetherness of the items of the other, (the unit's items are united in themselves and unified with one another, whereas the organic whole's items are unified in themselves and united with one another—where unification means making something one, and uniting means allowing it to have articulate members), the structure of a being will have a number of functions. It will constitute the essence of an individual, having over against it such other elements as Existence. Now the essence is a structure. But the organism itself has a structure. When the Existence acts to make a unit with the essence, it also may act to constitute an organic whole with the structure. But when it does the former it works as a single unit, merely occupying the area which the structure marks out; when it does the latter it goes further and articulates the structure. But we seem now faced with a hard problem.

When the structure is articulated it would seem to be occupied as well, so that the very being of an organic whole requires the being of a unit, but not conversely, and the unit and organic whole would so far seem to be related as general to particular, a single one to an articulation of it.

The possible answers seem to be: unit and organic whole are correlatives only in the sense that the generic and specific are, and the components of the latter operate on the former to unify them only so far as there is a reciprocal action on the part of the components of the generic. A second possible answer is that the other members of the unit make a difference to the way in which the structure functions there in contrast with the way it functions in the organic whole. But then why should the structure be capable of having a dual role, in the one sense constituting a unit and in the other an organic whole, whereas this is not the case with the person or with the concern, the subjectivity or the values?

A third alternative would say that the structure is a mere structure only for essence, etc., and that the components of the organic whole are not structure and Existence, e.g., but a living body and an attentive mind. These are, to be sure, constituted of structure and Existence, but the point is that this is a new type of unity, which is now distinct and active. In short, in the unit, essence and Existence are distinguishable, but in the organic whole it is body and mind. What therefore constitutes a unit has no distinct being in the organic whole.

Must we not also say that the living body has energy in reserve, and that this comes in to make it into this or that kind of active being? The infusion of energy into the living body, etc., will then not be the filling out of a structure or even its articulation, but the energizing of it, the conversion of it into a functioning. In the unit the structure just is, and does not operate; in the organic whole it is a dynamic element. When then we abstract from a body its anatomical features, we are in effect not getting the structure of an organism but the structure of a unit individual. The organism's structure is an activity. There is then, strictly speaking, no structure to an organic whole in the sense of an essence, but only in the sense of something already transformed, which can be quickened more or less. Somehow the structure of the unit must be prescriptive, demanding, self-contained, over against the structure of the organic whole which is quickened and pluralized into body, mind, etc. This would seem to say that there is a demand made on the unit components.

Might one not also follow the clue of scholastics in their double analysis of a thing into form and matter, and essence and Existence? The essence involves "form-and-matter" as a meaning or organization, the Existence placing this in a world where the matter thereupon stands over against the essential form-and-matter as a correlative. Since Existence here performs two roles, essence must have two (and of course also subjectivity and value, a fact which I obscured by referring to the second role in terms of person and concern). Essence and Existence pervade the beings in the scholastic view, and relate form and matter in distinctive ways, the one uniting them "formally" the other separating them "existentially."

September 2

The energy we have in our bodies has its primary source in the Existence of the individual as a single being interplaying with essence, subjectivity and value. But there is some energy which comes from the surrounding world as a result of the body's interplay with it. Other energy results from the way in which the attentive mind re-establishes the position of the being as a unity, and still other energy comes from the Ideal at which one is directed. The totality of this energy is the energy of the living body. That living body is but part of a total organic whole, and as such contributes its own modicum of vitality to the other parts of that organic whole, just as they do to it. The result is an individual being. That individual being has the same relation to the realm of community, institution, civilization and Existence as a whole that the various divisions of the living body and of the individual have to one another. The individual, in short, makes a difference to their being; the community is something like a realm of Existence, the institution like a mind, and civilization like an Ideal, making up with the individual the realm of mankind. It is this realm which interplays with an environing world to constitute the single domain of history.

History is to be found wherever the external Existence makes its presence felt. There is however a kind of history of the interplay of the individual with the different parts of the human realm and these with one another. Here the meaning of history is provided by that component which represents as it were the environing Existence. Coming back to man and his living body, then, we can say that history will be found where the environing Existence helps produce the Existence of the individual as a unit being interplaying with an essence, when the environing Existence interplays with the living body; when the living body interplays with the different parts of the organic being (for it then has the role of existing in contrast with mind, person and concern which have to do with the divine-like, Actual and Ideal sides); when the living body interplays with the community (which itself has something like the role of Existence). All these different roles which Existence assumes gives us a plurality of histories. But Existence proper is cosmic; its proper counterpart for us is either the whole realm of man (when it would then have to be supplemented by the realm of the divine and the absolute Ideal), or the civilized aspect of the realm of man (when it would have to be supplemented by the institution and the individual, as well as by the community in the role of a specialized interplaying portion of itself).

September 3

The existence of a structure and a process raises a host of problems. For idealists (or neo-platonists perhaps to be more exact), the process in the end must be treated as a degenerate version of the structure. Not only is there a derivation of structure from structure presupposing process, on this view, but the theory cannot take care of time, and therefore the fact of its own discovery and communication. The opposite view, preferred by existentialists and romanticists, takes the structure to be an empty place, a mere reminder or residuum of process, a kind of process in infinitely slow motion. But this view has difficulty with logic, mathematics and science, and any other prescriptive governance of process; it is in fact a theory for a jelly fish, since it allows for no anatomy.

We must, without denying some independence of structure and energy, see how they belong together. The structure has at least two juncture points which serve as its terms; more complicated ones have multiple subordinate juncture points. Perhaps it would be better in fact to call something a mere relation unless there are subordinate juncture points. With respect to such structures we can make use of energy in a number of ways. The formalist would like one to use the energy merely to dissolve the juncture points, so as to arrive at the terminus. When this is done we have perfect conformity to law or rule. But the movement through those juncture points makes a difference to them; the movement is sequential and therefore the terminus is no longer what it was before, when it was linked with the rest of the structure. It is a mere supposition that the dissolution makes no difference to the terminus at which one arrives.

A second use of the energy is to fill out the structure, make it vivid; here we avoid the temporalization of the structure, but give it a new locus. We do this when we want to attend to plans, when we want to guide the subsequent use of energy. By filling out the structure in this way we change it once again, but now not as a temporal thing but as having a new role, and therefore new affiliates, meaning, consequences.

A third use involves the employment of the structure without regard for every juncture point; we jump to the conclusion, skipping over intermediate steps. This is what we do when we creatively reason, and perhaps when we see or hear, etc. This is a point where taxonomists, logicians, anatomists diverge most sharply from naturalists, mathematicians, physiologists. The former think that the latter must actually go through the various juncture points in a definite order, stopping at each if only for an infinitesimal period. For them every train must be a local.

Finally there is the energy which overflows all the restrictions of the structure, which subordinates it, carries it along with itself as it expresses itself in inflamed expressions but which have a distinctive cast—we can have spasms in the arm or in the leg.

It is perhaps impossible to go through a structure without being confined by it somewhat; but even if it be the case that the structure is used and that there is in fact a traversal over the different juncture points in some order, it still is the case that some of the energy is employed in ways which do not attend to the structural junctures. If so, we have a variant of the second form. Instead though of filling out the structure and thereby giving it a new role for further use by energy, the structure is then swept along, put in a new context but without regard for its nature and use.

September 4

There seem to be at least three different types of science—those which, with the naturalists, stay with common-sense items and merely reorganize them; those which subject the common-sense world to mathematical treatment and thereby provide a language and a world of abstractions; and those which are concerned with ontological or cosmological questions, such as the reality of the sub-atomic particles and the cosmological behavior of Existence as a realm of space-time-energy. Regarding the atomic particles it is possible to maintain that these are the product of a reification of the terms in the abstractive sets. But there does seem to be a cosmos, and there does seem to be a kind of law-abiding behavior on the part of Existence. Should we say then that the space-time schemes of the scientists have a proper object, but that they are based on the smoothing out and stretching out of the common-sense world and its contours? If this be the case, then the cosmology of physicists is a derivation from the world of common sense and not as it is usually put, the converse.

In what sense is the result an abstraction? The nature of Existence is expressed in structural terms, as a law-abiding reality, and its powers and actual adventures are ignored, even when understood in terms apart from localizations. Cosmological science is struggling to get to the point where the metaphysician has already arrived through the act of dialectical constructions. One of Whitehead's blunders was to take relativity physics too seriously, even though he tried to modify its claims to make them accord with other aspects of reality. In a way then he was caught the way Kant was, and perhaps Aristotle. It is a great temptation for the philosopher to accept the cosmological affirmations of the physicist. He is impressed with their "verifications," forgetting that these are always local, and involve a semantical compression of the syntactical formulations.

We ought not then to start an account of Existence with the supposition that it was first one single realm. From the very beginning we have localized forms of Existence. Can we then be content with speaking of the localized forms and the way in which they are related? No, because Existence seems to have its own power of coordination; space is independent in its being of the particular things that occupy it, and time seems to have one single direction and one single present. But most important, Existence as such seems to interact not only with such other modes of being, as the Ideal and God, but to interplay with individuals. We men are constantly taking away from and giving to Existence as such, as becomes most evident when we face Existence with the entire human realm. Mankind does not exist in relation to an external world in the way in which a chair is related to a table, but stands over against it, making evident that the Existence has a power of its own. History depends upon the recognition of the interplay of mankind and Existence, and art makes evident the nature of Existence in and of itself.

The Existence in an individual or in any other part of the human realm can be spoken of as a genuine Existence; it owes its origin and can come back into the total realm of Existence as such. From the standpoint of the modes of being that Existence can be viewed as a kind of derivative. But if we do this we ought also to say that the value of a man is a manifestation of the Ideal, that it interplays with the Ideal, and that it also stands over against the Ideal as a kind of independently localized fact about it. Similarly for God. And when we come to look at the other modes of being we should bring in the activity of the individual in somewhat the way in which we deal with the Existence in the individual.

Idealism, as became clear to Bradley as he went on in his thinking, and particularly in his essays, does not tell us only about the insistent operation of the Ideal; from the standpoint of an idealism there is no matter or obdurate other which must be subjugated by that Ideal. But from the standpoint of what even an idealism must acknowledge—the fact that this world is not perfect and does not exhibit the Ideal—there must be an acknowledgment of "finite centres" as Bradley called them. These centres must be viewed as congealed or localized forms of the Ideal, and be capable of interplaying with the Ideal to constitute the adventures of the Ideal in time. Such an adventuring is not really history; but once it be recognized that the localized Ideal makes up a unit individual with Existence (and God and Actuality) it is correct to say that history involves the interplay of localized versions of the modes with the modes themselves. In short, in history we find, among other things, an Ideal localized in man interplaying with the Ideal, with localized Existence, and with Existence as such (and similarly with God, and with man in his individuality).

September 5

Existence interplays with the individual. The individual can be analyzed as having an essence, an Existence, a subjectivity and a value; a body, mind, person and concern; and a body, a life, responsiveness, activity and appetite. Staying with these, and thus ignoring the subdivisions of the mind, person and concern, and taking account of the fact that we can view either the individual or Existence as dominant, and the two of them as in a constant interplay, we would seem to have the following basic classifications:

1] External Existence	subjugated to the essence	—nature humanized
2]	subjugating	—geographic determination
3]	interplaying	—existence of prehistoric man
4]	subjugated to Existence	—control
5]	subjugating	—disaster
6]	interplaying	—self-maintenance
7]	subjugated to subjectivity	—at homeness
8]	subjugating	—alieninity
9]	interplaying	—self-discovery

10]	subjugated to value	—made useful
11]	subjugating	—natural dignity
12]	interplaying	—achievement
13]	subjugated to body	—utilized
14]	subjugating	—crippling
15]	interplaying	—technique
16]	subjugated to mind	—plans
17]	subjugating	—primitivism
18]	interplaying	—perception
19]	subjugated to respon-siveness	—instrument
20]	subjugating	—frustrating
21]	interplaying	—sustaining
22]	subjugated to action	—extension
23]	subjugating	—disorienting
24]	interplaying	—environment
25]	subjugated to appetite	—controlled
26]	subjugating	—defeating
27]	interplaying	—maturation
28]	subjugated to person	—civilized
29]	subjugating	—terrorizing
30]	interplaying	—myth
31]	subjugated to concern	—means
32]	subjugating	—amoral
33]	interplaying	—morality, natural

Many of these names should be changed. Room must also be made for a natural heroism exhibited in relation to the threats of nature, and thus of discovery, exploration and the like. This would seem to involve the entire organism, so that we ought to have

34]	External Existence	subjugated to organism	—conquest
35]		subjugating	—intimidation
36]		interplaying	—natural beauty

The hero would be not merely one who had conquered external Existence to some extent, but had done so relative to what other men could or would do. We also have the question of technology; this evidently involves the use of the mind and the body together, without necessary reference to the person or the concern, or at the least in abstraction from the person. This leads to viewing the organism in various combinations: the entire organism, as above in 34–36; mind, body, concern, without the person in technology—which is Existence subjugated, etc. Art would seem to be a making with mind, body, person, without the concern.

Account must be taken of the fact that from the standpoint of the individual the intrusion of the external world, in the guise either of a subjugator or of an interplaying domain, is exhibited as chance, randomness, spontaneity, irregularity and irrationality, though in fact it need not have this role in and of itself. We also have the fact of tragedy and comedy as a consequence of the way in which nature impinges on man; here perhaps the focal point is the person with or without a body.

Possible title for book on religion; *For the Love of God.*

September 6

If it is the work of mind to infer, and if this in the end rests on the individual's dual relation to what is outside him, it would seem to be the case that the duality could be dealt with in terms of the way in which a structure is vivified in and of itself, and how an additional energy is concerned with the terminus of that vivified structure. The structure would give us the object as something necessitated or required, and the energy outside it would give us the object as wanted. There would be a duality in the reaching of the object but at the beginning and end they would be the same. Pain and discomfort result from the fact that the structure requires something (and thus terminates in it) and yet the energy does not reach to it. The structure makes a demand not met. If the tension decreases, if the energy actually lays hold of what is necessitated we get comfort and pleasure. This is from the standpoint of structure. Accordingly, it is the structure which gives us an awareness of the fact that the energy has actually terminated in its object.

Hegel knew of the duality of the objects of the mind, but he supposed that on the one hand the duality meant merely that the content belonged to the mind and was the mind in fact but from another perspective, and that the entire task of philosophy was to recover the content by an act of identification. If we take this approach we can say that the object at which our energy arrives is a proper terminus of ourselves, and that this terminus must be reconciled, be made one with the terminus of the structure. All efforts would then involve the attempt to decrease the tension, to solidify the freely expressed energy with the energized structure.

But why suppose that the decrease in one direction is but another indication of a gap from another, therefore driving one from one mode of knowing to another? If one could follow the Hegelian route one would show that as soon as we had mastered what was necessitated by a structure we would have structuralized it and therefore required that a new amount of energy be employed. This would seem to say that at the limit of all possible knowing we have reached the limit of the expression of the energy as answering to some demand, and that when we were at the lowest level, say sensing, we would not have used all the energy in connection with cognition as we might. There is this much justification in such an approach; we can cognize as well as sense and therefore must still have energy over when we sense; also we do seem to cognize on the basis of what we sensed. But there does not seem to be the kind of direct development or proportionate use of energy as the Hegelian theory requires.

September 8

Those modern philosophers who have eschewed metaphysics, are like men practicing to sit in the air. They leap with grace and in fact with such neatness and dispatch that they dumbfound the world. That they persistently fall does not surprise. That they should keep on, despite the perpetual failure to establish themselves in this interesting position, is a testimony to the charming determination of philosophers. But for the rest of us, a chair is what we want. It does not demand of us that we learn odd ways of manipulating our bodies, but it does demand that we know what is at our rear.

Mind is the outcome of the interiorization of a mood, and this in the end comes down to a tension felt between a structure and energy. If we start with the structure, the energy gives us feeling; if we start with the energy the structure gives us the focal meaning; if we stay in the middle we get the adumbrated. If we hold to all three we get perception—sensing allowing us the external entity as that which we have adopted, cognition, allowing us the meaning as that which is being adopted, and expectation and participation giving us the adopted adumbrated. The systematization of the judged yields daily perception, of the structure science, of the adumbrated the event, of the referent beyond as pointed to by the judged object and evaluating it, value. Common sense merges these various types of judgments and their extensions and fills them up with conventions, etc. Metaphysical speculation, with an element of self-consciousness, expressed as a criticism of its own roots or meanings, expresses the nature of the beings which would answer to the object, structure, adumbrated and prospect, were these freed from sensing and all perceptual affiliations, structures, and routes of inference which are germane to the initial adumbration.

We can distinguish three kinds of common sense: *1*] an adumbrated, which we have before judgment and expresses our sense of reality, *2*] the clarified form of it in perception, science, etc., so far as these continue to hold on to the adumbrated; *3*] the mixture of perception, science, etc. The last is common sense as it is known by men in a given epoch. Perhaps one ought to add a *4*] common sense as overrun with conventions, taboos, etc. The sophisticated man seeks to go from the fourth to the third; the philosophers usually try to go from the third to the second; the mystic or primitive tries to go from the second to the first; the metaphysician cuts behind all of them, or goes from the first to that which underlies it as self-consciously known.

September 9

The abstractive systems constituted by perceptions, or scientific judgments, events or gradings of importance are all rooted in the concrete. They are purgations of the common-sense objective world, in which there is a stress on the articulate components. These are derived by a sharper use of sensed content, by a breaking up of it into something vital reached towards and a structural content having a structurally defined terminus. The division of the sensed in this way gives a syntactical unit and this is oriented towards the presented adumbrated. In perception we emphasize the sensuous element in both parts of the syntactical unit; in science the structure of the unit; in events the reference to and immersion in the adumbrated, and in value the adumbrated as definitory of the unit, particularly when taken to be representative of the Ideal.

Combinations of these abstractions give us a purged common-sense world, a world which is multi-judged. When that result is overlaid with social conditions we get the familiar world of every day. It is a world of practical wisdom, in which the reasoning, characteristic of any of the abstractive sets, is quieted by being contained within the use and acceptance of the common-sense world. There is a social moment which must be included, where the very topic of the judgment of one man is accepted as a topic for another. One's own consciousness then becomes a part of a wider social consciousness, when there is an acknowledgment of another as focusing on one's own object. (And we must also take account of the use of signs, which are abstractions from such a situation, as having the same kind of duality of reference. A sign is given to another to allow him to focus on the same terminus that we focus on.)

September 10

We seem to become conscious of another human only by virtue of the kind of resistance he offers to our consciousness of him. We find that he replies to us, offers us a resistance, that as we terminate in him by the expression of energy in and over against a structural relation to him, he not only escapes our grasp but intrudes on us. This intrusion can stop right at the terminal point of our activity; we will then be aware that he is substantial. It may move on further into our own activity and finally reach us, we will find then that we are self-conscious. We can enjoy him as loving or hating us and thus not necessarily having any idea of us; we can have him as a mere brute fact; we can have him as having only the worth of making us be self-conscious. It is rarely that we can be conscious of him and also aware that he is noting us: we take him to be conscious in the act of finding ourselves to be self-conscious.

Is there a similar duality in memory? Do we not then have a content which is our own and even our own product which is nevertheless escaping us by virtue of some feature that it has? If we treat it this way, memory will not involve us in a duality with respect to the kinds of grasps we have of the memory content, unless we go on to say that we can have a hold on a world outside the memory content when and as we have the memory content.

We have a hold on the memory content as here and now and also find that it is slipping away from us by virtue of its determinateness. We have it in the present as a unit, and then as something structurally possessed; we also have it in details, and these details we cannot grasp except by energizing our attention. But this would give us material in the present as well as the past. We get the past reference only when we see that the detailed apprehension, though outside our grasp, is in fact not being sustained by anything. We seek to become conscious, as it were, of the content which we have through our energy, and therefore allow it to be treated as possessed by something inside us. The duality of memory then lies not in the structure and energy, but in the energy as dealing with details which require something other than itself.

September 11

It seems to be the case that the mind acts on the body. But how? We can speak of the body acting because action requires a substantial entity, and though the human lived body is not a substance by and of itself, it does, when a corpse, reveal that there is a substantiality to it, and that it is at least in part on a par with other substances. The action of the mind in any case must be of a different sort than the action of the body. Could it be that the rules which govern thinking, instead of merely restraining the energy which is used to quicken those rules, actually dominate the energy of the body in part? The rules would have such a dominating role by virtue of the energy in them, or because the energy in the body yields to this in a way it does not to the anatomy of the body.

Could one perhaps take the mind on the model of God in the *Modes* and view its activity as a kind of self-exploration, a kind of self-traversal with a reference to what is happening in the body, making it reorganize itself from moment to moment to keep abreast of that body? But were this the case we would not have control but only recognition. Genuine control would require something like the objective preservation of the past, characteristic of God. Here the mind would be a kind of mediator between what the body had done and what it might do; or it could, inside itself, function as a way of completing the content it had taken from the body. But neither of these faces up to the fact that the mind seems here and now to make a difference to the body, and this not by taking account of what the body has done or is doing, but by imposing from its own side conditions on the body to which the body may or may not conform. (There is a similar problem to be faced in connection with the operation of the mind on the person. The action of the person on the body would seem to pose a less difficult question because the person is a kind of "substantial" reality and its action can be viewed as a kind of expression.)

If the mind acts on the body by a prescriptive force, this must be distinguished from willing on the one side and from a kind of action on the other. It must be thought of as having no particular limit in the kind of control or area over which it operates. If we speak in this way we must also view the use of energy as filling out the being conditioned by a structure, even apart from its own effort to fill out the structure. Mind would be a condition which reaches to and controls the energy, even energy which is already caught within the frame of the body and is thus the energy of life.

But what kind of being do the rules in or of the mind have, so that they can condition the energy? What is the locus of the rules? What associates one idea with another; what kind of being has the law of logic which is governing the inferences and perhaps also the life in a body? Is it that when we are confronted with some prospective idea or result we adopt it in some way or other, and thereupon bring to bear the rules we have achieved? But what kind of being have the rules before they have been brought to bear? Why do we use the energy of our inference in such a way that it exemplifies or submits to some condition? What channels are there, forcing the energy to go one way rather than another? Does it make sense to speak of an "anatomy" of the mind? Is it that I have the desire to transfer desirable values all the time and that it is this desire which dictates that the energy will follow this route or that? But what is this desire, and how does it express itself in this particular rule or that? It must be the individual need to be complete, which is made manifest in the use of mastered content in terms of that content's value to that individual.

September 12

Stated most broadly, religion is an openness to God. This can have many forms. The individual can make himself open by his body, mind, person and concern. We thus have the hermits, the clergy, the monks, the conformity to codes. The individual can also make himself open by taking himself to be a single being, making all the above interplay. We thus get prayer, religious devotion and commitment. In these various ways we have proofs of God in the sense that we move to His being as beyond the reach of mere inference. The individual also makes himself open by the way in which he interplays with fellowman, community, state and civilization. There is mutual love and respect, loyalty, patriotism and public service, taken not merely as occupied with man, but as opening oneself up to a larger or greater value. Here we can include such "religions" as Confucianism which do not make explicit reference to God.

Of course if we have a devotion to others in which we deliberately close off the area from all else we have the very antithesis of religion. We can thus compare the patriot who is religious with one who is not, as standing at the opposite extremes of attitude; the difference between them lies mainly in the fact that the religiously tempered person feels himself to open up to God and perhaps even to be influenced by Him as he engages in his act, whereas the other defines the situation to be one in which he alone is important.

The individual also can interact with Existence and the Ideal in such a way as to open himself up to God. Here we have the individual in art and history, in ethics and politics, seeing God as supervening over the whole. In all these ways we have religion as a private activity. And in all of them we can start with an acceptance of God and thereupon open ourselves in the course of our activities with respect to others, to Existence, etc.

Over against such private religion is the religion which is public. This depends upon some organization or codification or ritual to which the individual makes himself conform. This is institutionalized religion. Such religion can be thought of as an end, a means, or as a correlate of private religion. When an end, we have private religion as preparation for communal action; when a means, the churches become laboratories. But the proper position is one where the two sides are in constant interplay in the effort to be open to God both privately and publicly.

When an individual or a group participates in a sport, when it loses itself in some work, particularly where the end of the work is larger than the individual and is thought to have a meaning not altogether contained within it, we have a genuine religious activity of a public sort. A spectator sport for example is a publicly governed opening of individuals as spectators, together with a private opening of the individual participants. The sport, since it occurs in public and involves the interplay of men, and always of at least one with Existence, is also public, while the spectators, each of whom is participating in the sport in his own way, is privately religious as well.

The crucial issue is how to distinguish the religious opening in those cases where there is no explicit reference or even thought of God. The clue lies in the fact that in religion there is an expectation of a closure or achievement outside and beyond that which is being aimed at in the successful performance. He who runs to win is not religious; nor is he religious if he runs to win for the team. But if he runs as a way of opening himself up, and while trying to win, as a way of allowing some other good to be achieved, he is religious. This is not yet said properly, but the area of the answer is I think now delineated. The religious man not only aims horizontally but opens himself up vertically for supplementation, support, control and even for the presentation of himself (and of his horizontally aimed at result), to a superior being.

There is still another dimension of religion: God as acting on men, as the source of grace and guidance; God as acting on history, on Existence and so on. But this is compatible with a deism and even an a-religionism such as Aristotle's. Religion is primarily something which begins on this side and has to do with the way in which men relate themselves to God, either by privately opening themselves up to Him or by expressing their attitude towards Him in a codification given by the churches.

The codification by the churches should be offered as a kind of representative of God himself. If and so far as this is the case, we have the problem of a "kingdom of God" on earth, the secret church within the church, etc. But I think it must be said that no matter how representative the church is, in the end an individual must escape it to make direct contact with God or at least open himself up to it as an individual. The church should recognize that being a representative is not identical with being God Himself, and thus that an individual in participating in a church is doing this religiously only if he also opens himself up to God, a being who is outside the church.

September 13

The objective side of the experience of the modes has a different centre of gravity in each case; the subjective side answers to a different part of the organism. Subjectively, Actuality has to do with the mind, the Ideal with the concern, Existence with the body and God with the person. It is these aspects which carry the brunt of an interest and use of the modes. On the objective side Actuality is expressed as action, but the centre of this is in the individual. Ideality is expressed in the society, state and civilization as subject to a natural law; here the individual is a constituent and thus has a being something like the subdivisions of the Ideal itself, being defined by the whole and having no status apart from it except so far as something other than it pulls it out and apart. Existence is expressed in a neutral history in which the individual interplays with Existence itself, and also finds that the institution, as somehow transcending him, interplays with Existence too. Existence itself is divisive and the objective expressions of it are divided-off bits of the world interplaying with Existence as such. In the case of God the locus of the objective being for experience is the institution, functioning as an intermediary or instrument to govern and change the individual.

The individual in religion might concern himself directly with the being of God. This is a subjectively oriented experience. If God were to concern himself with the individual, as is believed in low-church Christianity, it would still be a subjective experience, though oriented towards a being outside the individual, except so far as a man is forced to spread himself out in history and act in order to accommodate this experience. If so, then God to the individual is something like Existence, in that the objective domain constituted by Him and the individual lies somewhere between Him and the individual in a newly constituted domain. In the case of Existence this domain is history, but in the case of God it is the adventure of creatively trying to be together with others. The historical aspect of this will be due to the operation of Existence on the individual, God serving merely as the occasion for the individual to spread himself out for the history. Conversely, the history of a man or mankind can be viewed as an occasion for the individual to open himself up to God.

Existence forces the individual to be in history because it is itself extensional; but God forces the individual to be spread out over a time (and primarily through action) because He is too big for the individual. The spreading out is thus a contribution made by the individual. This spreading out is the individual's way of doing what institutions do by virtue of their very being. In the case of Existence the institutions are in history by offering a correlative spread-out nature to the Existence.

The public religion of man then is an extension which is either newly forged or is already expressed inside an institution or society. The individual may, by identifying himself with the institution, get his extensionality in time and action through it, rather than directly. In all cases the individual is related to the meaning of the divine in public, somewhat as the parts of the divine are to the whole; the individual is a summation, an epitomization of this totality. It is what makes him as a person infinitely precious, even though he is finite and limited in other dimensions.

September 14

To predict in history is not the same as to learn from it, nor does it entail the latter, for the prediction could be based on some knowledge just now presented or discovered, and some rule holding for the future. But if we do learn from history we are able to discover something there which does hold of the future, so that the learning from history entails the prediction. The learning and prediction are possible if Existence is law-abiding, if the natures of that with which it interplays, and the kind of interplay that is possible, is known. This can occur where the Existence is confined inside some area and there qualified and kept within the bounds of a structure, where the beings which interplay with it are definite, and can control the way in which they utilize the qualified Existence. For scientists the nature of Existence as such will eventually be known to be law-abiding, though it is the intent of art in the end to deny that this is the case.

At present, anyhow, it is true that we do not know the laws of Existence as such. But we can speak of Existence as caught inside states and societies and men; we can get a good inductive knowledge of the way they exist, even though subject to spontaneities and unpredictabilities due to the overflowing of the energy in them. And we can see how men, in their essence, as possessed of such and such natures and characteristic powers, are accustomed to interplay with the institutionalized forms of Existence or the social forms of it. It is perhaps in part for this reason that historians attend to the histories of nations and the like, and why there is an effort to make predictions about future courses of nations, and not of the future of mankind or civilization. The fact that men can act with independence, and the fact that each institution and society is different from all others does not preclude large commonalities, enabling one to say what would happen after devastating wars, tyranny, peace and so on. Predictions must be tailored to the kind of stabilities that can be isolated in a realm where Existence cannot be wholly kept within confines—even when it starts as confined in a state, etc. In the latter case the way in which it acts on the individual is not determinable in advance.

We need the large panorama of history to have a perspective which will enable us to isolate the large commonalities rather than the small incidental occurrences. The approach then of a predictor or one who learns from history is different from the historian; the latter concentrates on actual incidents and does not isolate, except incidentally and perhaps unknowingly, the large commonalities characteristic of all history.

September 15

Existence alone seems to provide an objective domain with which men can interplay, because it alone is extended, a field in which they can be outside themselves. Their relation to the Ideal is from within, as is their relation to God. The Ideal however can become a special object for society and state, as Existence cannot, for it there has a particular import, being an Ideal of justice or peace. Existence for society and state is the same raw Existence that is faced by individuals. God, on the other hand, mediates through institutions as well as makes direct contact with individuals. As the former He is like the Ideal, and as the latter He is like Existence, except that the idealized institutions require men to fit in them, whereas God allows the individuals to stand over against the institutions which mediate Him. Existence subdivides itself in the particular individuals, but God expresses himself as a single being in them all.

There is a dimension of history which is determined by the interplay of God and Existence as modes. In God Existence has one role, in Existence God has another, but the two together can constitute a new realm of theological history which is neutral to them both, made possible by the way in which God sustains the past and relates this to the future. This relating allows God to go backwards and forwards in time, revising the meanings of antecedents in the sense of making them necessitated by what comes after, but without undoing the settled past as an actual concrete occurrence. The realm of history in this sense is being constantly remade out of eternity on the one side and a relentless one-way movement of Existence on the other. The reconstruction of all history at every moment is necessary; the meaning of it must be redefined at every moment, but this meaning is framed in an unalterable sequence which precludes any tampering with the past through any temporal movement backwards.

There does not seem to be a history possible made out of Existence and the Ideal together, unless the Ideal can function as more than a future for Existence and Existence can function as more than a field of operation for the Ideal. Once again there would have to be a new domain produced out of the two of them; this could be the domain of the altered meaning which God could use to redefine the domain of history. In short, there could be a domain of history constituted by God and the Ideal, together interplaying with Existence, to provide it with a new double meaning. There would be a meaning for the whole, obtained from Ideal, and a distribution of that meaning derived from God. This history must be brought into relationship with the history which men, severally and together, produce by interplaying with Existence. If this is not done we would have at least two distinct "histories," the one constituted cosmically by God and Ideal, the other by men. But the modes of beings are interlocked; this cannot therefore be a significant alternative. Consequently the history which is sustained by God and the Ideal must be that which is being filled out sequentially by men. Do these men function as representatives of Actuality, or is there in addition to their activity as individuals another dimension provided by them when they act representatively for all Actuality? They are representatives who have unit powers, so that the story at the end is the story of Actuality in interplay with Existence.

History can be said to require all four modes of being; it demands of the realm of the Ideal a possibility which spreads over the entire reach of Existence and divides this into meanings before and after, all necessitated, with a different content at every moment so far as the present is different. History here is being remade all the time in the sense that there is a new frame of meanings covering all of the past and future. Here history is the locus of explanation. The items in that history must be re-evaluated, be made relevant to one another in different ways; there must be a guarantee that the unused Ideal will be realized in the history and that what has been will be preserved. This is the ground of the plausible explanation. And finally the Actuality, through the representative action of individuals, interplays with Existence to constitute significant causes.

These dimensions are not here clearly stated; but what does seem clear now is that the domain of history is neutral to the modes of being. It therefore is a kind of togetherness. There would be similar forms of togetherness having God, the Ideal or the Actual as the primary correlative. Thus God, as immanent, or religion in practice, would be the way in which God interplays with Existence, Ideality and Actuality; the rationalization of the universe would result from the way in which the Ideal interplayed with God, Existence and Actuality to constitute a new domain; the cosmic intelligible world results from a kind of neutrality achieved by the Actual in interplay with God, Existence and Ideal.

The above are all half-ideas, but all worth elaboration. In summary they point out that there is a togetherness which constitutes a genuine domain when three modes interplay with a fourth, and that history, strictly speaking, is one such domain.

September 16

The *Modes of Being* speaks of the reconciliation of the various modes in pairs, with a pair of modes functioning as the principle of union. But what is not seen there very clearly is that the various modes can intermingle with one another, thereby constituting a kind of thick togetherness. We have the following cases of intermingling:

1] Existence and Actuality
2]   "   and Ideality
3]   "   and God
4] God   and Actuality
5]   "   and Ideality
6] Actuality and Ideality
7] Existence, God, Ideality
8] Existence, Actuality, God
9]   "   "   Ideality
10] Actuality, God, Ideality
11] All four modes.

1] Is the domain of history; 2] cosmic purposiveness; 3] I think the scientifically knowable world, but it can be said to be the immanent God or theologically governed history. 4] religion, 5] providence with a concerned God, 6] ethics and politics; 7] scientifically knowable nature; 8] religiously oriented history; 9] moralistically knowable nature; 10] the personalistic world; 11] does not have a being except as a mere togetherness matching a prescriptive one. Such mixtures as the above, whose names and import must undoubtedly be changed later, supplement the cases in which the different modes are seen to be transmuted by being ingredient in one another, as, e.g., when Existence is oughtified by having the ideal ingredient in it.

The mixtures seem to show that there is a realm of history, religion, politics constituted by mixing the modes in pairs, with a stress on the objective side, and that the triplets give us nature in some form. Correlative to history is art, to religion as objective domain is religion experienced in private; politics is matched by ethics; nature would seem to have as its correlative, knowledge or experience. The objective items, history, religion, politics and nature, are neutral between the mixed modes; there could be a stress on one of the factors however, and this would give us objective domains to be experienced; these, properly speaking, are not history, religion, etc. Thus, an insistence on man over against nature is technology rather than history. The other cases of stress on one factor deserve elaboration and naming. Also, the question then arises as to whether the subjective experiences ought not to be dealt with in three ways too—as neutral mixtures, as biased towards this factor or that, and then as involving a stress on one of the three factors.

September 24

Each mode of being can act as a locus and a measure for the remaining two. Thus, history, which is the mixture of Actuality and Existence, is measured for its rationality by Ideality, the source of explanation. The past, present and future of history is given a locus by God. It is in that objective domain of past, present and future that the Ideality has new meanings every moment, making for a re-ordering of the past. The past is fixed but the meaning of it is changing because of the Ideal, and because God holds on to that past as a reality which is to be charged with meaning from the Ideal. It is also the case that there is a kind of history in which God serves as a measure and the Ideal serves as a locus. Here the Ideal is the realm of fulfilled possibility and God is the all-comprehensive judge. When we take this position, we evaluate history at every moment, as less than it will be in fact; we also find it within the all-inclusive Ideality, offering an inadequate articulation of that Ideal. This is closer to Hegel's view than the former, and perhaps is needed for ontology. There is, in short, a problem as to how these two kinds of histories belong together.

The togetherness of Actuality and Ideality gives us a kingdom of ends with God as measure and Existence as locus. We have here Kant's view in the *Practical Reason.* One can also see the kingdom of ends as being measured by Existence. Existence will then determine just how effective moral nature is in the world. God, the being who realizes the normative possibility, assures that it will be achieved. He will give that nature a locus.

In the field of religion we have Actuality and God being measured by Existence as revelatory of how their concern for one another works out in fact. Here the Ideal, as a fulfilled possibility, offers a kind of locus which Actuality and God are to articulate. Ideality can also serve as a measure, telling us how rational, how intelligible the individual and God are together; Existence will then provide a locus in which the Ideal will have an opportunity to be fully realized, thereby making the dialogue between Actuality and God throughout intelligible.

Existence and Ideality constitute nature. Here the degree of concordance will be measured by an actual hero or great man and will have its locus in God who preserves the past achievements and virtues of those men. There is a sense of nature too in which the degree is measured by the all-comprehensiveness of God and in which the reconciliation of Existence and Ideality is given a locus in man as representative of all Actuality.

Existence and God constitute a teleological scheme. Here the individual virtuous man offers a measure of the success of the meeting of Existence and God, and the locus is the fulfilled Ideal which the teleology is intended to articulate. There is also a teleology in which the measure is given by the rationality of the Ideal, and the locus is to be found in man as representative of all Actuality.

Finally the Ideal and God constitute the domain of what is providential. Here we see how perceptive Plato was, for the *Timaeus* reveals that Existence as a receptacle offers a locus for that excellence, measured by the excellence of the individual soul. On the other hand, there is Existence as a measure, which is what pragmatism stresses; the locus of the reconciliation of the Ideal and God (which is science perfected) would then be the individual inquirer as representative of all inquirers. This is at root the idea that Peirce had.

The problem that remains is how to reconcile Plato and Peirce, to use the last case. Is it a question of making one measure prescriptive and the other descriptive, one locus descriptive and the other prescriptive? But if so, which? It must be the individual who is prescriptive, for he is already, whereas the Existence is not yet worked out. But though we can then go on and take God to be prescriptive with respect to Existence and even Ideality and Actuality, we will have to take the Ideal to be prescriptive as a measure for Existence, even though it is not prescriptive as a measure for God or Actuality. Accordingly we have the following prescriptive measures:

God for history (with Ideality then being a preferred locus); the kingdom of ends will have God as the prescriptive measure, and Existence as the preferred locus (so that the Kantian realm of ends would be prior to the reconciliation of Actuality and Ideality which uses Existence as a measure). In religion the Ideal will be the proper measure with Existence as a locus. Nature will have God as measure and man as a preferred locus. In teleology, man serves as a measure which is prescriptive, with Ideality offering a preferred locus. But it is not yet clear that Actuality should offer a prescription in relation to the Ideal; and it is even dubious that this should be true of God. And how does one determine whether or not it is God or man who is to be the prescriptive measure?

September 25

The mixture by pairs are:

> AE, history
> AI, society
> AG, religion
> EI, cosmology, purposive
> EG, cosmology, (*Timaeus*)
> IG, providence

For each of these the other two modes have two roles. Each offers a measure and each offers a locus. As offering a measure a mode is prescriptive, and as offering a locus it is descriptive. The prescription is not with respect to itself, as offering a locus, but with respect to the correlative mode functioning as a locus. Thus history has God as the locus of past, present and future (earlier and later), and as prescribing the importance and thus distributing the worth of the elements in history; it also has the Ideal as a locus for history as intelligible (as the idealists saw) and the Ideal as a measure of the explanation, the rationality of what is in fact happening. The Ideal as measure has the items in a relation of before and after.

1] why does a mode function in these two ways, *2*] how are the two sides related *3*] why do we need two prescriptions and two descriptions for a given enterprise, *4*] how are the two prescriptions related to one another, and *5*] how are the two descriptions related?

1] There is a double need. For example, the Ideal as explanatory requires God to hold on to the past; God as evaluative requires the Ideal to order occurrences as before and after, or as condition and conditioned.

2] There is an effort on the part of every mode to make a unity of itself as locus and prescription; the more it succeeds, the more do the elements in the mixture continue to be together, constituting a single domain. The very being of history depends on God's perpetual readjustment of Himself as locus (where He remains in and of Himself as required by the Ideal), and of Himself as imposing conditions on the whole of history (and thereupon requiring the Ideal to be in and of itself a domain of conditions and conditioned). 3] The different prescriptions and descriptions are independent but compatible, and become integrated when the modes of which they are parts are unified. That is, two prescriptions are not directly related, but via beings in which there are descriptions, which the beings try to solidify with the prescriptions, to constitute themselves as genuine beings. 4] The two prescriptions then are related as two dimensions dealing with different sides of the phenomenon we are studying. 5] Ditto for the descriptions.

September 26

The mode which is functioning as a locus does this in order to be able to transfer the properties of one of the united modes to the other. Thus God as a locus sees that the past of Existence is made into a past for Actualities, while the Ideal as a locus sees that the Actuality is made into a condition for Existence. The former transfer is measured by the Ideal as that which is more or less rational; the latter transfer is measured by God as more or less all-comprehensive. Is there any way of deciding which mode will transfer in one way and which in the other? Would it, e.g., be possible to have the Ideal as a locus function to transfer properties from the realm of Existence into the domain of Actuality? Would it not in fact be better to assert that the transfer goes in two directions, so that we have God as a locus enabling the past of Existence to become a past for Actualities, and individual pasts to become part of one single past, with the result that history is a humanized past with a publicized set of past careers? The Ideal as locus enables the Actualities to function as conditions for Existence, so that conditions are always individuated, and allows Existence to function as a mode of conditioning, with the result that history becomes a realm of effective conditionings having individual orientation points. In the first case the Ideal serves as a measure of the degree to which the transfer makes something rational, and God serves as a measure in the second case of the degree to which the whole of Actuality and Existence is included in history.

In the other cases too (AI, AG, EI, EG, IG), there will be two transfers and two measures. We constitute a new domain, a realm of society, religion, cosmology, teleology and a providence through the activity of one of the modes solidifying the components of the new domain, and subjecting the result to a prescription by the remaining mode. It is because God actually unites the past of Actualities and Existence that there is a domain of history whose rationality is measured by the Ideal; it is because the Ideal actually unites the condition offered by Actualities with the conditioning of Existence that there is a domain of history whose inclusiveness is measured by God.

It would seem from the case of the union provided by the Ideal that we unite a static with a dynamic component. Why is not this also the case with God? Should we not say that it is a passing away Existence which is united with meaning, as sluiced through individual entities, that constitutes history? If so, we have history as individual meaning and condition, united with a passing away and a process of conditioning. Or would it be the case that the individual, if it is static in one case, must be dynamic in the other, and for Existence we have the reverse? If so, we would have individual meaning and effective conditions united with a domain of effective pasts and a structure of conditioning.

Taking the last alternative, we then have two modes constituting a new domain, by having a static and a dynamic side of each, united with a dynamic and static side of the other, within the body of a third mode, and having the result measured by a fourth. But it would be better to say that God unites the "static" past of Existence with effective individual pasts, and that the Ideal unites individual meanings with an effective conditioning. Are there rules for telling us which mode will transfer which characteristics and which mode will, for a given mode, offer the static component?

What kind of features are transferred? Must not the space, time and energy of Existence be transferred somehow to the Actual? Can we say that Existence transfers the space, but that the time and energy need God and Ideality? Or that energy and time need God and Ideality? And what is transferred from the Actual? Must it not be individuality, humanized meaning and localization, the latter occurring without any aid, the individuality being transferred by God, and the humanized meaning by the Ideal? But why should it not be God who transfers the humanized meaning and Ideality the individuality?

September 27

The realm of history has four distinctive features. *1]* It preserves a past, where Existence has lost its past to be in the present. *2]* It makes up a realm where individuals have only memories. *3]* It also has men acting as causal agents, with a power peculiar to them. 4] It also exhibits a power of concerted humanized causation with principles of relevance. Men have something like a past in their memories and have a causational nature in the way in which they live through their individual careers; on the other hand Existence exhibits something like a realm in the sense that it is extended, and also shows something like causation in the way it exercises its powers. Accordingly, history is constituted by translating the features of the elements in each to constitute entirely new natures:

1] The remembered past of men gets Existence so as to constitute a real past through the action of God.

2] The extension of Existence gets Actualities so as to constitute a human realm through the action of God.

3] Men as having careers get Existence so as to constitute a new type of causal agent through the action of the Ideal.

4] The power of Existence gets Actualities so as to constitute a humanly relevant causation through the action of the Ideal.

The Ideal measures *1* and *2* and God measures *3* and *4,* the first by seeing how rational the whole is and the second by seeing how comprehensive. *1* and *4* go together, so that the real past is made to work in a humanly relevant way; *2* and *3* go together to give us human causal agents operating in an extended human realm.

It would seem from such propositions as *4:22* in Modes of Being that Existence can accrete properties, such as a geometry, from Actualities through the action of God. But it is to be noted that this is no transfer of properties from Actualities, but a result of the way in which Actualities are made to define the geometrical points, as it were, which are then to be spread over Existence. But in history and similar phenomena, it is the very properties of Actuality and Existence which are transferred to one another. Existence gives Actualities independent being, by allowing itself to be splintered; but Existence can also be made to transfer properties to Actualities through the help of God. Consequently, we have to distinguish between the ontological natures of each mode, the cosmological natures due to accidentalization of the modes by one another, and the presence of new domains due to the transfer of properties from one mode to another.

September 29

If history is a "mixture," it is a purely phenomenological domain, in which the qualities of the various modes are intermingled to make a richer quality. The domain lacks a genuine being of its own. There is power in it and even a peculiar potentiality which is the outcome of the interplay of the power of its components, but this power, though it is effective and peculiar, is actually not working as a power, but as a resultant of the other powers. With this in mind one can go on to speak of correlates to the four modes. They will all be the cosmos phenomenologically, as having all the features of the various modes in some combination—mere merging, purest possible separation, necessitation, and sequential occurrences. That means that the very necessitation of the cosmos is a derivative, a necessitation which imposes qualifications on the necessitation that is derived from the Ideal. But it has no intrinsic thrust of its own.

If we take the modes three at a time we get a different set of mixtures:

AEG

AEI

AIG

IEG

AEG is evidently a historic universe in which God interplays with the history. This can be treated as a variant of theism, with God working through time, or conversely of the way in which history impinges on God to alter His inward being. AEI leaves God out of account and has the Ideal as operative force; it seems to give us Kant's teleological governed world. AIG would seem to be the world of society as interplaying with God, and we have here a variant on the AEG case, so far as this has been historically dealt with. But here a factor comes into prominence which perhaps is muted in the theistic or teleologically determined world with their stresses on God—the Ideal as operative on the combination of AG, religion. This yields the meaning of religion in society. There is finally IEG, nature as interplaying with God—or, if one likes, providence as being expressed through history. These four cases must be rooted in and governed by the modes of Ideality, God, Existence and Actuality respectively; these will provide the locus for the interpenetration. This means that, e.g., in the first case a theism or a Whiteheadean view of God assumes that there is an Ideal in which these various modes can have their properties transferred to one another to constitute a new phenomenological domain.

Hegel's philosophy of history expresses the kind of dualism which comes from trying to have a pure mode of being, such as the spirit on the one side, and also a phenomenological world on the other. If a pure being alone is dialectic, the dialectic of history must be without its own internal drive, a "show." But if history has its own internal drive, we have no need to refer back to a mode of being,—or if we do we must see it as on a level with history. There is a dialectic in an Hegelian history, but it is without an internal compulsion of its own; it is a surface product, distinctive and meaningful and able to be dealt with in its own terms, but not actually effective, dynamic, ultimate, powerful. One cannot read off the future steps of such a dialectic because it is a function of other operations. Perhaps this is why Hegel (and Marx) cannot tell us what the next stage of history is.

October 1

The laws of thought are embodied in each of the modes, other than Existence. Existence is the locus of the negation of all of them. God is the locus of identity, Actuality of contradiction, and Ideality of excluded middle. The excluded middle does not apply to Ideality; Ideality is the being of that law and as such is applicable to other things. Actuality by its oppositional acts seems to be the law of contradiction, as indeed must be the case if it is determinate. Here the law seems to be by being applied. God is the law of identity and this is applied to all things.

If there be a strict division amongst the modes we would have to deny the applicability of the other laws to them. God would then be a being of whom it was not true that either "contradiction" or "excluded" applied; Actuality would escape "excluded" and "identity"; Ideality would escape "contradiction" and "identity." Actuality, e.g., escapes "excluded" by virtue of its potentiality since it does not distinguish one realization from another just so far; and it escapes identity in that its different parts are distinct and opposed (rather than as in God identical one with the other and the whole).

Existence would have none of these laws; it would be too potential to be able to have the excluded, too cosmic to be open to contradiction, and unable to be identical since it is without an essence. These defects are overcome by virtue of the cosmical interplay of Existence with the other modes. In history where Existence intermingles with Actuality within the body of God and Ideality, Existence accretes to itself the power of the law of contradiction which it did not have before; this means it becomes a domain where there are determinate beings who remain outside one another. The extension of Existence now becomes the power which keeps predicates apart, precluding a contradiction.

October 3

The togetherness of the modes determined by the "," keeps them separate. This, strictly speaking, is the state of affairs which metaphysics studies. When they are related by the ")" we have cosmology, for here the different modes implicate one another. When the modes mix to constitute a phenomenology we have ".", or a merging of various degrees. The ".˙." expresses the way in which, out of each mode, the other three are precipitated to enable the given mode to be authentic.

This use of the symbols differs from that on p. 514 in *Modes of Being,* where it is said that the four modes are together in four ways. What is now being said is that inside the ontological combination of the four modes, as given by the ",", there are the other three, or that the best way of expressing the ontological togetherness is by taking up the position of God; that the Ideal offers us the best way to get the model form of a cosmology, inside of which the other modes of togetherness will also be found; that phenomenology has the kind of togetherness which is defined ontologically by Actuality, and that inside this togetherness there are the other forms; and finally that the status of being authentic takes its model from the kind of togetherness which owes its being to Existence.

The proper togetherness of the modes expressed by a "," requires all four of them, and shows them to be an aggregate. The togetherness of the modes in a cosmology seems to allow for three modes as oriented in a fourth, though the togetherness is not to be identified with the being of that fourth; in a phenomenology we use the body of one mode to allow for the togetherness in a mixture of two other modes as measured by a third; in the state of authenticity we start with a mode (as we also do in phenomenology) and allow it to stand free, so that it is in effect the isolation of one mode, and comes, via a process related to cosmology, to the ontological situation.

The mixture that is history has a kind of togetherness which in ontology is dictated by the Actual. It is a newly constituted domain in which we can find relations of "." between the components showing how each borrows from the other to make this newly constituted realm. Does this mean that God and the Ideal function as ways in which the merging relation is substantialized, so as to provide a "whole" in which the components have an involvement in one another as mutual sources of the properties of that whole?

If Actuality and Existence are already in a cosmological relation to one another in the sense that each inplicates the other, what is added when they are phenomenologically involved in one another also? Actualities need Existence cosmologically in order to be contemporaneous with one another; they need Existence phenomenologically in order to be able to have a realm in which to operate or to be able to be involved in a cosmic causality. The question then is on the relation of the former connection to the latter. Is it, for example, the Existentialized contemporary actualities, or is it actualities as such, which make a realm? Let it be the former: this would mean that the Actualities hold themselves (in part at least) apart from that cosmological setting, and thus the case reduces to the second alternative. Actualities as such interplay with Existence as such. These actualities have Existence in them, and thus are cosmological entities. But they are not neutrally related in the cosmos. In short, we pre-suppose cosmology if they already affect one another. The actualities are therefore apart from the Existence; they have already been made determinate cosmologically, over against it. It is, then, cosmological actualities and Existence which merge to constitute history. It is the actualities as contemporaneous with a geometrized Existence that make history in the body of God or Ideality. But is there no raw action on the part of Existence? It would seem that there is.

The answer would seem to be that it is raw Existence and Actuality, (and thus in the ontological dimension) which mix together. At that time they constitute a mixture in which the cosmological features are given a phenomenological meaning. That is to say, if Actuality gives Existence a geometry, and Existence gives Actuality contemporaneity, when Actuality and Existence mix there is a production of a geometry and contemporaneity. These are continuous with and phenomenologically like the other properties acquired by transferring the features of Existence to Actuality and conversely, to constitute a new domain. But then it would seem also to be the case that the authentic side of each item would also be revealed, so that at one and the same time there would be a merging of the various items to constitute, say history, and a separation off of each component so that it stands naked over against that domain and the other constituent.

If all three ways of being together, "." ".·." and ")" are in God, then God is the eternal "," Himself. He then offers a neutral ontology to make possible the other three ways of being together—phenomenology, authenticity and cosmology. But if all three occur in the body of the Ideal (which is like a ")") there would seem to be an operation there which reveals the presence and import of God. Or more sharply, if we try to reconcile God and the Ideal ontologically before we have the phenomenology, authenticity and cosmology, we would seem to require God to provide the needed neutrality, and thus to have somehow affected Existence or the Actual, in whose body the reconciliation takes place.

If the cosmological and phenomenological sides of reality come into being together in the case of a mixture, we would still be able to have a cosmological side apart from the phenomenological. For there are at least two meanings of contemporaneity and geometry; there is the contemporaneity of historical actualities and the contemporaneity of cosmological entities, and there is the geometry of cosmological Existence and the geometry of the human realm which Existence constitutes with Actuality. The features which Existence gets from God and Ideality are also involved; otherwise there would be no unity and no direction, no comparison and no value. Since the unity, direction, comparison and value must be pertinent to what is made to be in history, we must say that the cosmological factors are all brought in when and as the two items make a phenomenological mixture. The cosmological factors though are affected by and become adjectival to the phenomenological. It is as though there was first a phenomenology of the mixture and then there were various features added to both items by the beings in which they are mixed.

The cosmological features derived from God and Ideality are accreted to the phenomenologically produced history's components, Actuality and Existence, when and as these acquire the cosmological features from one another. These cosmological features are all phenomenologically conditioned. Thus the unity, otherness, the directionality and the essence of Existence are acquired by Actuality, as already components in history and not as standing outside it; the direction is a purposed direction for actualities in Existence, and the essence provided by God is an essence for a world of beings which have an integrity of their own.

The cosmological features derived from God and the Ideal are for the pair, Actuality and Existence. They thus contrast with Actuality and Existence as they are for one another cosmologically, since here they are severally related and not paired with anything else. It is as making a pair that they are affected by Ideality and God. Cosmologically they are affected one by one, and thus as Actuality and Existence in history they are cosmologically affected. God and Ideality have no role for them, except so far as they are paired and thus derivatives. The cosmological act of God and Ideality is a derivative one, being exercised on the derivative pair.

October 4

If we are ontologists, we start with a neutral position, the most favored being that of the divine ",", where the modes are entirely separate.

But there are other neutral positions and the various modes go through these. A Cosmology keeps latent the other ways in which the modes can be together; it contains them in a way, but they do not exist, strictly speaking, from its point of view. If we take a cosmological point of view we take one mode for granted and find the others through an implicative process. The basic mode of being together then is ")". It would seem best to start with the Ideal (though there is nothing amiss in the *Modes* in starting with Actuality). In the cosmology there is a place for a cosmological ontology—i.e., there will be a way in which one can deal with the four modes as outside one another but as derivatives from the cosmological situation in which they imply one another. The chapter on God seems to do this; it begins with cosmology in the sense of deriving God, and then deals with Him in and of Himself; but the entire job of doing a cosmological deduction of the four modes first, watching their interplay, and then isolating the modes has not yet been done.

If now we go on to do a phenomenology we find that we mix two modes, primarily according to the Actuality's ".", and then find that we have a derivative cosmology and ontology to deal with. A phenomenologized cosmology looks to the two remaining modes to provide needed features. Thus, in connection with history, which mixes Actuality and Existence, God provides a single essence and objectivity for the combination, whereas the Ideal provides a single direction and value. The need for God and Ideality to do these is to be demonstrated in ways analogous to the proofs of God, except that one must here presuppose history. There is also a way in which each of the modes stands out against the others with its own pace and nature, though to be sure only as a limit for history itself, where it provides the energy, etc. An ontology for a history falls short of a real ontology, because the modes are not pure but only distinct from the position of history. (It is to be noted incidentally, in connection with the cosmology of phenomenology, that though God and the Ideal offer content to the history they also, since cosmology requires three modes, offer something to one another as germane to history.)

This therefore comes to clear expression only in an "authentication," where the model is a kind of Existence which explodes into all the modes. It is a world in which each mode is taken by itself and allowed to explode into the others. In such a world there will be derivative phenomenologies, cosmologies and ontologies, for the given mode will allow for combinations of pairs of them, as forming epistemic systems; for triplets as forming realms for it; and for the separate modes as forming substantial grounds for it. But in none of these ways does one really get to ontology; this must be done by a direct speculative leap and treatment outside the sphere of cosmology, phenomenology or authenticity.

If society is also one of the constituents of a history, then history can be made up of mixtures, for society is a mixture of Actuality and Ideality. There presumably could be a mixture of mixtures, so that say, Actuality and God which constitute a religious mixture, could mix with history to constitute a new kind of content. Also, it seems to be the case that though history is a mixture, it can be said not only to have a kind of phenomenologized cosmology and thus substances derivative from it (as it is in fact from them), but also to interplay with the substances. The mixture which is history can be mixed with Actuality itself, and it can be mixed with other mixtures.

Why should there be a mixture? Given full fledged ontological entities we know there must be a cosmology because each reality is incomplete and needs the others and also acts on them; the very being of each leads to the cosmological unity of them all. But a cosmology could presumably be without history or societies, etc. Is it the case that each mode insists on taking up the role of a conjunction for two others, that God, for example, insists on being a meeting ground where Existence and Actuality can support one another by an interchange? If so, then Actuality should be the meeting ground of God and Existence, for God and Ideality, and for Ideality and Existence.

Why should a mode insist on being the conjunct for others? What does Existence gain by getting personal agents in history, or what do agents gain by getting a human realm from Existence? And why should God help them have those gains? What kind of reasoning tells us the answer? In ontology we have dialectic, and in cosmology proof, but what do we have in phenomenology?

Society, I have said, enables men to do what they individually cannot and yet ought to do—such as helping others via taxes and charities. It does not come inevitably; it is an ideal solution to a problem. Is there something analogous for the Ideal in society; does society help the Ideal have a multiplicity of instruments or loci which it otherwise would not be able to use, or does it at least help transform it into a myth which, while obligatory, can be realized by the society and eventually the individuals in it? If so, can we not also say that Actuality also needs a region in which it can express itself concurrently with others, that Existence needs a plurality of agents as focal points, and that these two needs are satisfied by one another? These are needs in a different sense from that acknowledged in cosmology; there is here none but an ideal reason why they should be satisfied. The occurrence of history is a contingent matter which nevertheless has an explanation: the entities which are mixed in it benefit from the mixing.

Must it not now be said that if society is a mixture, and if mixtures occur in the body of some third or fourth mode, that society (which is Actuality and Ideality together) must be in the body of Existence and God, and that these two give the society natures which result from the transference of powers from the constituents of society to one another. The individuality, e.g., of Actuality will become a social individuality with rights, by virtue of God or Existence.

Our Public Life took society and state to be the outcome of an ideal and successful effort to achieve a higher degree of perfection. Taking this as a clue one can say that cosmology results from the need for beings to be completed as beings, by having other beings in them, and that the phenomenological world results when as a matter of fact it happens that some mode helps others to perfect themselves in the sense of being able to do and be more completely, universally. It enables men to be representative not by standing out over against the others and doing for all what they may neglect to do, but by finding a role within a whole and acting as part of that whole. Can we say that history results in the same way, that men need to become historical in order to be more completely men? Is it conceivable then for men to avoid having a history? The latter seems to be the case—Nigerians have no history.

October 5

The beings which are in a cosmological setting have one another inside themselves through action and support. The result is that each mode is enabled to be; if it had the others outside it entirely, it would not be in itself but would have its being dependent on theirs. They are not of course ultimate final realities in a cosmological setting. They do not have the other modes in themselves fully; this is in fact a self-contradictory idea, for if *a* has *b* and *c* inside itself, *b* and *c* can't have *a*, and *a* then becomes the only reality with *b* and *c* as subordinate notes. But if *a* can have *b* and *c* as subordinate notes and *b* can have *a* and *c* and so on, then each can function as a final being in a cosmology. The entire cosmology will rest upon the ontology, where each is something in and of itself.

There is a need to move to phenomenological situations in order that the beings in the cosmology can become perfected, completed. Now they become completed, not as mere beings—which is what happens in the cosmology, so far as such completion is at all possible (involving as it does the possession within one being of all the others)—but as the particular kinds of beings that they are. To achieve this result pairs of beings in the cosmology must hold themselves over against one another in order to be able to be themselves, despite the cosmological involvement with the others, and then must try to make themselves into participants of some more inclusive scheme in which the virtues of the other mode are added to its own to make a new kind of domain.

The adding requires the use of a third mode. Why does this third mode function in this way, e.g., provide a ground by which the reality of the past of Existence is made into an historical past for men? Is it not that the mode that grounds, needs to have other modes within it unified, and that this is the beginning of an act of adjusting the other modes to one another in a phenomenological form? It must take them two at a time because the third mode is needed in order that there can be a measure, and a fourth is needed as a counter-thrust. Accordingly, we must say that *AE,* history; *AI,* society; *AG,* religion; *EI,* teleology; and *EG,* nature, are ways in which the different components are perfected in the body of some other mode which needs their unification and offers them a common meaning, and holds them over against a fourth mode.

If cosmology rests on the acceptance of some mode, and the implication of the others as somehow qualifying and correcting it to constitute a single realm with it, we have the following cosmological approaches: *A; EIG. I; AEG. E; IAG. G; IAE.* The first element in each case is the accepted mode and the others are derived. The last is theo-analysis. The first is the view of *Reality* as carried out in the first chapter of the *Modes,* and expresses a cosmology. The second is an idealistic cosmology such as Hegel's. The third is a Bergsonian or Schopenhauerian cosmology. Most cosmologies seem to be the first.

Whitehead is confessedly a cosmologist, and Aristotle is one in fact. Neither is much concerned about ontology or the nature of beings in and of themselves, or the derivation of the cosmology from this in the light of the need of a mode to be related to others so as to be something in and of itself while together with those others.

A cosmology brings three modes together in relation to a fourth. This seems to make it superior to the phenomenological approach in which only a pair of modes is conjoined. But the triplet is not given a being of its own for the fourth; it is merely derived from the fourth, and each item in it is allowed to be itself. What has an over-all character is the four of the modes cosmologically interlocked, though oriented towards one of them, biased in that direction. Why and how do we start with one of the modes as the base for a derivation or a ground with a specific bias? There is gain in the grounding mode in that it has within it as necessary components the other modes, thereby enabling it to be. But what do the other modes gain by being in a given mode? Is it not that they reach the being of that given mode, and thus supplement their possessing of it in themselves? *A* as having *b* in it possesses it, but it does not have the being of *b*. By acting on *b* and thus being in *b*, *a* has the being of *b* but does not possess it. Or more simply, *a* possesses *b* but does not have its being, and *b* has the being of *a* but does not possess it.

October 12

The objective status of a mixture is guaranteed by some mode other than those involved in the mixture. In connection with society, state, etc., the union of the Ideal and the Actual in an objective way is provided by Existence, and is measured by God. This means that when we come to history and try to deal with society, what we are doing is taking one of the products of Existence itself, and seeing how Actuality on the one side, and Existence as such on the other, interplay with this to give a history. Since history is itself the product of a union due to God, what we then have is God reconciling Actuality with what Existence has reconciled (Actuality and Ideality), thereby giving Actuality a second role.

If history is cosmology phenomenologized, then every feature of the cosmology should be found in history, but transposed. This means we ought to have something like the space-time-energy complex of Actualities in interplay with Existence, plus a new unity and a new kind of career, and in addition should have an objectivity guaranteed by God and a rationality guaranteed by the ideal. The being of history is possible because it is oriented, located, sustained by God, whereas the cosmological domain is itself a product of the interplay of the various modes. The cosmology is less real than the history because there is no mixture, but only a coming to be and passing away of an attenuated togetherness.

October 19

A number of different logics have been exploited in the past. Looking only at the "deductive" aspects, we can distinguish A] The Aristotelian which requires a mediating premiss in any significant bit of reasoning, to lead us from an antecedent to a consequence. B] The Cartesian "method" which breaks each item down to its clear and distinct components and then proceeds step by step, by a kind of intuitive leap of minimal size, to the next position. C] The Hegelian method which finds a distinctive kind of logic in history and in the philosophical dimension of beings. D] The Freudian reasoning in depth which takes a miscellany of items to be the outcroppings of some more basic reality diversely

expressed under different circumstances or in different contexts. E]
Perhaps all these should have been preceded by a logic of dialectic in
Plato's sense, where one drives oneself back and back to presupposed
ultimates in value. This is the method of completing what is known but
incoherent, by finding a more rational and final ground. F] There is the
method of Whitehead and Russell which acknowledges certain basic
propositions and then tries to derive all others by applying those propositions on themselves, thereby making the premisses themselves yield the
very principles of inference by which consequences are derived from those
premisses.

Another way of dealing with the matter is to examine each subject
matter in turn and see just what kind of logic it demands. A logic for all
will be any procedure which will in that context preserve whatever desirable values have already been accumulated and will warrantedly
transfer them to what is not yet known to possess those values. Is there a
logic for society, another for religion, history, and art which is unlike any
of these listed before? How can one find out?

October 28

The problem of the past is that A] it must somehow achieve an
extension so that there can be a distance from the present between one
item in it and another, B] it must have some being so that it can be in
opposition to the present, be that which is excluded by the present, C]
it must be preserved in a good God as that residuum left over when the
evil is divinely forgotten, D] it must interplay with the present, making
a difference to it here and now, E] it must be encounterable in the
present (for otherwise all references to it would be implications without
a proper terminus), F] it must interplay with the future to determine
a fulfilled possibility for that future, or to dictate what the future possibilities are to be, G] it must change in value, meaning or import as the
future changes.

There is a problem of relating different moments to one another,
particularly when there are some atomic presents longer than others.
Thus a battle follows a battle in the single atomic present of a war. The
battle is over before the war has been completed. The battles as made
part of the war are in the order of before and after and are no longer
earlier and later. They have the latter status only as outside and over
against the war, as having their own objectives and internal careers. But
as such they are in the past, while the war is in the present.

It would seem then that the past can be kept in existence in the present, though not in one that succeeds that past. The present in which the past continues to be is a larger atomic present whose interior has no past components. But this is not yet to allow the past battle to be in a relation of earlier and later to other battles. When the atomic present, in which the battles are, is itself past, there will have to be an act by God making the battles earlier and later. This is done by providing the atomic moment with a divisible extension, which it did not have before. But in this way we would also seem to lose the atomic moment. It is necessary therefore that the past atomic moment be capable of releasing its members, or be made into an atomic moment in which earlier and later have a different meaning than they would have were the later in the present or future. In short, the atomic moment must acquire a new meaning when it becomes a past extended stretch. It then allows its members to be earlier and later, without allowing any one of them to be without the others being also.

October 31

When a long-ranged atomic moment is in the process of being present, the subordinate sequential occurrences are not part of it. They are part of it only when they lose their sequential natures. This they do by virtue of their integration with the atomic moment. The atomic moment may be said to stretch backwards to embrace the previous subordinate occurrences. The present then of a long-ranged atom is partly in a past defined by the place of the subordinate items in it. Thus if a battle is over and the war is still continuing, the war embraces that previous battle as part of itself, and thus must stretch back to include that battle. But so far as it does include that battle, it turns it into a part of itself as without sequential nature, or will divide itself and cease to be that atomic event. The former means that as a sequence becomes past it will cease to be in an order of earlier and later. But it does have an order of earlier and later; this indicates that some power other than the atom must preserve the earlier and later despite the atom's "present nature." This is done by giving the atom's extension to the interrelation of the components, allowing the atom merely to define a segment of the past, an area or period which is all of one piece; the atom as one atom ceases to have an extension of its own.

We have, first the sequence, the loss of the sequential nature by its being part of an unfinished atom, then a recovery of the sequential nature (but not of passage) by virtue of the acquisition of the atom's own extension. The atom has an extension of its own and is in a sequence within a larger atom. The whole of history is the largest atom; it encompasses the entire past as a sequential determinate array of occurrences. That atom may be located in God; but whether it is or not, one must turn to God to account for the transfer of the extensionality of the atom to the components of it, so that they can be in a sequential relation to one another.

November 3

Some facts to consider in any account of history.

1] The past has passed away, allowing the present to be.
2] The past is exterior to the present, being excluded by it, thereby allowing historians to be right or wrong.
3] The past is ingredient in the present, making a difference to its nature—the third world war depends on the being of the other two as now *aufgehoben*.
4] The past can be encountered, justifying inferences to it.
5] The past affects the future, dictating that some prospects are not possible.
6] The present is atomic, for otherwise there would be no extended history, and history as something which took time would never be but only have been.
7] There are many presents of different lengths, for the battle is shorter than the war.
8] The larger present includes the smaller and thus must make it be in an order of before and after other small presents.
9] The recovery of the status of an earlier and later for any included portion must be by a power outside history.
10] The future affects the present, making possible a direction.
11] The future affects the past giving it new values, marking it as defective, or allowing it to be organized anew.
12] The future, in the process of being present, is the present with unfinished details.
13] The pure future is over against a present.
14] The length of the present is determined by the relevance of the earlier to the later.
15] There is an historic space, and an historic use of energy.

November 4

In history we must affirm relationships and behaviors about the past, present and future that we do not in other enterprises. This is due to the fact that A] the sequentially occurring items must be recovered inside a larger atomic present unity, so as to achieve extensionality and objectivity. This is done by God. B] The past items must be related to the present which excludes them. This is achieved by the present actualities. c] The future must be related to the past and the present as not only that which is yet to come but as that which provides the base for a re-evaluation of them, and an ordering of them as better or worse. This is achieved by the Ideal itself.

Though history is sustained by the other three modes, it does occur objectively, causally and intelligibly through the operation of those modes on the realm of Existence. It would seem to follow from the foregoing though that there is no genuine history in the present, and thus that history is only what has already happened without ever happening. But in a present atom which is not yet over there can be subordinate atoms which are completed; within their own time they are past, but inside that atom they are not, and consequently we can be said to have a history here and now but always on a level lower than that provided by the atom in which we are interested.

I seem here to be doing what I objected to elsewhere—make the past be what it had never been before. I objected to the past being extended if the present were not, but I now say that there is no real history of the atom until it is past. But is this not necessary, in view of the fact that history is that which is finished, that we see it as a datum, whereas in the present we are producing the datum? This means that we can be said to be living *through* history but not *in* history. No one lives in history, for in history there are only dessicated facts, the residua of a previous living through history.

November 16

There are at least five legitimate referents to God: There is first the referent to the ominous counterpart of common-sense objects which we directly experience and which we cannot focus on in any particular form. (This subdivides into three components, Existence, Ideality and God.) In this first case there is a reference to the blur of the three components, of which only one is properly designated as God. The blur could have been called Existence or Ideality too, but we talk of it as God because it is irreducible. Even if we suppose that one of the three components is more basic than the others, we do distinguish them as referring to different basic functions or powers of reality, and in this sense God is but one component. It is this God which is the object of an ontological argument, of a metaphysical speculation, of a necessitation. It is questionable whether we ever experience Him alone or have Him only as blurred as in the first sense.

The Gods of the different religions are specializations of this philosophic God; they make him have special powers, interests, virtues, natures, as defined by the particular theologies and creeds or practices. There is a conflict amongst these different Gods. Some one or the other cannot be real; it is possible none of them may. But we do not have a particular religion until we have one of these, reached through some particular privileged channel, in contrast with the God who is known from any position but through reason. (The first God is experienced without proper focussing on what is in fact the Godhead.)

The third God is the religious God; the second is the philosophic. A fourth God substitutes for the third God something in this world, say a state or mankind. A fifth God is the symbol in terms of which we refer to the other Gods, to give us a religion of the fetish, magic and idolatry.

November 19

Common sense has a number of meanings: 1] It refers to the totality of experience taken naïvely: this is made up of the ordinary world of daily life with focussed objects here, and an adumbrated background with which it interplays and from which it cannot be entirely distinguished. It is to this "common sense" that all our inquiries in the end refer for base and confirmation. 2] It refers to a part of the former, that which is constituted of robust objects in space-time, having powers and meanings, loaded down with traditional values and social import, but standing over against the ominous background with which it (in the previous sense) interplays. 3] It refers to a segment of the second realm, that portion which is known by the legal "reasonable man." This is the world to which English philosophers presumably refer when they take the world of common sense seriously. It leaves out of the second domain those items which, though well-established by tradition, are nevertheless known to be unsupported by inquiry and science—e.g., walking under ladders, the danger of the number 13, etc. 4] It refers to that sense which, according to Aristotle, is common to all the senses, enabling one to know that what is apprehended through say a sense of touch is the very same item which is apprehended through a sense of sight. 5] It refers to the power in men to discriminate in a quick and ready way the illusory, the dreamt, the erroneous from the encounterable in fact. (It here refers to a power in us, whereas in the third it refers to the domain to which such a power refers.) 6] There is the world of daily practice, and here the common-sense world in the first three senses is broken up into strands and disciplines; he who has common sense is one who has the feel of his subject, particularly if it has to do with something palpable. A common-sense carpenter knows the quality of the wood and what it can do; this is the common sense of accumulated experience in a restricted domain. I have been accustomed to use the term in the second and third senses, though in *Reality* there is a use of the first.

November 20

History, since it involves the interplay of actualities and Existence, sustained by God and Ideality, is evidently a form of the togetherness of the modes. It is a cosmological product in which the components of the interplay, actualities and Existence, recover (because sustained in a distinctive way) the powers they had before, but transformed. The togetherness which has a minor role to play in the ontology becomes primary, with the components all swallowed up and transformed. History is the togetherness of the modes with a primary stress on Existence as interplaying with Actuality and sustained by the other two.

In ethics the situation seems to be reversed, for ethics is a subjectively oriented discipline in contrast with history. Art, the counterpart of history, is primarily oriented in the individual maker (though the result is objective to him); it is not therefore a genuine cosmological discipline. Nor is politics, the publicly oriented activity with respect to the Ideal, a genuine cosmological discipline. But ethics is. The ethical realm is sustained by Existence and God, the one providing a base for action, the other guaranteeing eventual fulfillment.

There is no need to refer to the other modes when one considers actualities as exhibiting the basic category, or when one considers them in interplay with one another. It is of course true that each mode has a cosmological function, but there is no new discipline or domain constituted by the actualities as possessing a categorial knowledge or being, or as interplaying with one another.

In connection with God, both the churches and the religious experience have a cosmological import. The churches involve an interplay of individuals and God on this side of the world and thus are primarily sustained by Existence and secondarily by the Ideal, whereas the religious experience, as actually reaching to God, is sustained by the Ideal, particularly as exhibited in a virtuous man.

Art and politics, the one subjectively produced, the other objectively, seem to yield realities which are not themselves genuine forms of the togetherness of the other modes. There is an exhibition of Existence in the work of art, produced under the stress of a concern with an Ideal myth, a kind of unity and an individual. These are ways in which Existence is enabled to present itself to the individual; it is a kind of localized togetherness, if one wishes. In politics we have a togetherness of the individuals with the Ideal, but the relation here seems to be sustained by the individual as interrelated with others. Existence and God, which certainly affect the individual, do not here enable the Ideal to recover some property not otherwise present.

The test of art and politics, as not being genuine cosmological forms of togetherness, is the fact that neither recovers fully the features of the component elements. In art there is no genuine action of Existence, but a created counterpart of it which symbolizes it. In politics there is no genuine action of the Ideal, but a political goal which reflects and refers to it. But in ethics, history and religion, there is a genuine reaching out into other modes; in these areas there is a genuine interplay of Ideality and Actuality, Existence and Actuality, and God and Actuality.

History, ethics and religion reconcile modes. Art and politics do not reconcile them; they use them in order to recover the virtues of some one mode. If one wanted in religion (which is reconciliatory, both as oriented here and as oriented towards God) to recover the virtues of God, one would have to move outside religion to a non-reconciling form of getting God. This is magic and perhaps also prayer. Magic is the attempt to re-express God and refer to him. It tries to do for God what art and politics actually do for Existence and the Ideal. Something like this is to be found in the realm of Actuality when we institute plans or schemata which serve to express the nature of the interplay of men with one another. Science refers to the interplay of Actualities. But it does not recover the concreteness of the Actualities. To get this we must turn to engineering. Engineering is on a footing with art, politics and magic; all of them recapture and refer to some mode, through the agency of some kind of interplay of the other modes treated as a subordinate enterprise and not as a cosmological occurrence. Engineering relates to Actualities, art to Existence, politics to the Ideal and magic to God. ("Magic" seems to have a pejorative meaning; perhaps it would be better to speak of worship or adoration or prayer.)

Why should religion have two cosmological forms, one in which there is a relation of togetherness of all the modes oriented in Actuality, and another oriented towards God? Is it the case that a church is a genuine togetherness; is a religious man? And if so, why cannot men in other enterprises also serve as grounds for a genuine togetherness of the modes?

Why may not there be a genuine enjoyment of the Ideal, as in Plato; a genuine participation in Existence, e.g., in work; a genuine participation in Actuality interplaying with the other modes, as in a community? It would seem to be the case that there are such genuine togethernesses.

We have then:

For the Ideal: A] subjective enjoyment of a genuine togetherness—the Ideal realized in ethics;   B] an objective togetherness given by a cosmological account, and   C] a reflection and reference of the Ideal in politics.

For Existence: A] a subjective enjoyment of a genuine togetherness in work;   B] an objective togetherness in history, and   C] a reflection and reference to Existence in art.

For God: A] a subjectively oriented togetherness in a church or an individual's religious experience;   B] an objective togetherness of the mercy of God;   C] a reflection and reference to God in worship, magic or prayer.

For Actuality: A] a kind of subjective enjoyment of Actuality as a togetherness in a community;   B] a kind of objective togetherness of all the modes in man;   C] a reflection and reference to Actuality in knowledge.

November 21

Some of the categories and evaluations of yesterday must be changed. One can distinguish three kinds of togetherness in addition to the cosmological: 1] a togetherness oriented in some one mode,   2] a togetherness created by man,   3] a togetherness by intent. The first, as in cosmology, requires that the various modes come together. We have here the realms of Community, Civilization, History and Religious Experience. The second is essentially a focussing on the new creation produced by man through some kind of act, and in which we can discern the actual or vicarious functioning of the modes. The second differs from the first in that the first requires the actual interplay of the different modes. The first is a kind of biased cosmological study, whereas the second is a production by man. We have here the realms of Action, Ethics, Art and Religious Community. The third differs from the other two in not being objective; it is produced by man in himself. This yields Categorial Knowledge, Intent, Planning and Adoration.

What is the place of sports, engineering and economics? What systematic approach can be made to these and other subjects? How can we know that we have caught the basic ones? How can we make provision for others not yet known or of which insufficient knowledge is now had?

Might one perhaps envisage delimited versions of the three different types of togetherness? Do sports give us an orientation in man with primary emphasis on the way in which he interlocks with Existence; does engineering give us a togetherness oriented in Existence but dealing only with man, ignoring God and Ideality; does economics deal only with Intent or Planning in relation to man? If these are possible, there should be further cases, e.g., a togetherness oriented in Existence dealing with God, another oriented in Ideality dealing with, say Existence, etc.

November 22

The philosopher of Christianity or some other particular religion can proceed either by assuming the truth of that religion and seeing if with that assumption he can make sense of the entire scheme of things. Or he can take the theses learned by faith, translate them into a rational scheme, and then follow out the implications of that scheme. In contrast, the philosophical-theologian begins by assuming some religious truths; these he does not examine, though his creative work consists in making new and deeper sense of his inherited truths. He then proceeds philosophically in a self-critical spirit to develop an account covering all else. He differs from the philosopher of religion x in that he is willing to give up everything but his basic ideas in the light of self-criticism; the philosopher of religion x is merely exploring the consequences of his assumption and therefore is not essentially self-critical. The metaphysician touches on God, affirmatively or negatively. He may end with theses which are more in consonance with one religion than another. But whether he does or not, he is self-critical throughout; he does not care, he is detached with respect to the answer he might get. He might end with denying some basic theses which he has learned in his religion: This result he is willing to accept, for this is what he has found, to the best of his ability, to be the defensible truth. The metaphysician has as his objective a systematic, self-criticized truth; the philosophical-theologian has this only with respect to the non-committed portion of his view, the part which he does not take as defining him to be a philosophical theologian of some school or religion. The philosopher of x has clarification and exploration as his objective.

November 23

The problem of the relationship of such domains as history and religion and cosmology can be focussed effectively through the consideration of some limited instance. A man and a woman may be close to one another and function as mere space-time actualities governed by gravitational laws; they may be in love; they may be legally married; they may be married in a church. Or *a* and *b* may be near one another, *a* and *c* may be in love, *a* and *d* married legally, and *a* and *e* married in a church. In all these cases *a* has affiliations with other beings. This means that he, together with others, constitutes a single situation having its own meaning and consequences. The consequences follow on the meanings according to their own logics, and are not to be subordinated to other meanings or consequences. The problem of reconciling the different sets is the problem of understanding the world in which *a, b, c, d* and *e* exist as beings which may be affiliated with one another as nearby, as involved with one another, as legally responsible, as constituting value units, as items in history, and the like. They are neutrally together as mere realities in a cosmology, but they are also together in more biased and limited forms by virtue of their specialization through a restrictive mode of affiliation. Though every body in the universe is related gravitationally, it is a fact that some bodies are attuned to others which may have little gravitational significance for them. Though it is the case that we are bound to the earth we may be interested in the moon or a loved one at a distance. (In the gravitational field the affiliations are due not only to mass but to nearness, so that a vast body may not be closely affiliated any more than a near body may be—a distant star, e.g., on the one hand, and a piece of paper, in contrast with the earth itself, on the other.)

A and *b* may have a minor relation in one context and an intimate one in another; the two affiliations may be related as condition and conditioned, but whether they are or not they have their own natures and consequences. *A* and *b* themselves will be in fact the unification of the different roles they play with respect to one another. We find no difficulty in recognizing that it is spatial objects which live through time, and ought to find none in recognizing that it is a political being which is in history. The fact that there are these additional dimensions shows that man, unlike other actualities, is not a mere cosmological being; by virtue of his mind, values, etc., and his concern with God, Ideals, Existence, he, in addition to being cosmological, grounds new types of affiliations. He may not do justice to the affiliated beings but will continue to be affiliated nevertheless; thus he may have an ethical responsibility towards someone and yet concentrate on a political act with respect to him; the responsibility will continue, and so far he will be guilty.

The question that comes to the fore then is not the reconciliation of the different dimensions, or of the different systems of affiliation; the very being of man as related through various channels to other beings, and as sustained by other modes, takes care of this. What is not taken care of is the question of how he is to do maximum justice to all the systems; here is where conflict and tragedy and hard decision come in. Should one be ethical or aesthetic, political or religious, merely cosmological etc.? This seems to be a matter of strategy; we want to do justice to all domains, to achieve the highest values in them, to become perfected in each, but we must sometimes yield here in order to gain there. Each individual must decide whether a sacrifice now in one domain will make for its recovery there later, at the same time that it makes possible a signal gain in some other domain not otherwise attainable.

When we come to final questions, involving life and death decisions, we may be forced, in order to be able to do justice to a given domain, to accept the outcome which precludes any further life or continuance in that domain. A man faced with war may decide he would rather be shot than shoot another; or he may decide that he must leave the public world behind for good, and become a hermit; or he may decide to go to war, and allow politics to dictate his right and wrong; or he may accept himself as radically guilty. Given just these alternatives, he will end by being only a partial man, a man who is not as good as a man ought to be.

He who enters one domain and adopts the role of being primarily there, must take the punishments as well as the rewards which come from such concentration. Those punishments and rewards are not only internal and given by the system, but are external and given by other domains. A man is economically rewarded for the virtues of diligence, intelligence, etc., and he may be economically punished for them as well. The political man may be condemned on ethical grounds, and conversely.

In connection with the basic disciplines one can allow the affiliations to be governed by others; one can allow oneself to be carried along by history and politics and art, and concentrate on ethics or speculation, or just living. Ideally a man should live fully in all of them, or somehow achieve the values which accrue in each. If he could master one domain in order thereby to enhance the others, and could also accept the achievements of one domain in order to do best what needs be done in some other domain, he perhaps does as much as any man can do.

To speak of an excellence which man is to achieve through the union of different dimensions is but to make another and more complicated reference to the Ideal and eventually to other modes than is given by a cosmology. This is but to say that the intrusion of man in the world gives a new dimension to the excellence that can be realized in this world. Just as we say that in ethics we improve things and thereby enable excellence to be realized, and in art that we make things and thereby exhibit an excellence, the two together constituting an excellence greater than either, so we must bring the excellencies of all dimensions together. This but reveals that the Ideal has a richness and requires a satisfaction that a merely cosmological scheme would not provide. This means that were there no men the modes would satisfy one another as beings which need completion in being, but would not entirely satisfy one another's needs as constituted by or including a plurality of subordinate elements. With man the divisions of the Ideal and thereupon the divisions in Existence and in God get a new focus, become sharpened and demanding, and require special means of satisfaction, so that the Ideal and thereupon all the other modes are completed as manys and ones.

November 24

Each mode of being deals with each of the other modes in three ways. It deals with the other modes as part of a trio, making up with itself the cosmological whole. In addition, it deals with it as one mode with the help of a second, and then with the result with the help of a third. One can perhaps add that it can deal with one mode with the joint help of a second and a third.

An actuality may deal with the Ideal as the obligating good in conjunction with the actuality's interplay with the other two modes; it may then go on to deal with it as sustained by Existence, as in politics; and it may deal with it as supported by God and thus as helping constitute a community or civilization. An actuality may deal with God as its other; and then deal with Him in a relation sustained by Existence (as in good works) and as sustained by the Ideal (as in inference). An actuality may deal with Existence as a space-time-energy manifold; it may deal with it in a relation sustained by God to yield history; and it may deal with it in a relation sustained by Ideality to yield art. To these distinctions one can also add the objective and subjective stresses to yield new subdivisions.

The problem of reconciling history and nature is then evidently the problem of reconciling a direct interplay of Actuality with Existence and the other two modes. The interplay is sustained and supported by the other two modes. In the latter case the other two modes are utilized, delimited, not allowed to act cosmologically but only instrumentally. The reconciliation then is that of two modes functioning over against the Actuality and Existence and there functioning instrumentally for it, the latter being accomplished by the intent, mind, will, involvement of men, thereby producing new consequences for Actuality and Existence together. In the former Actuality is itself merely a component in a larger whole; in the latter it is exercising some control of the situation it helps constitute. Actuality might be cosmologically involved in making the future present, and at the same time may be concerned with realizing that future as a good. As the former it would merely interplay; as the latter it would make the outcome of the interplay have consequences with respect to a world in which Actuality was involved.

We always have a problem of deciding to spend our lives concentrating on either art, ethics, religion, etc. The resolution of that problem requires a reference to the excellent. The excellent is the Ideal, realized in one way in art, another way in ethics, a third way in religion, and so on. Apart from man the excellent would be just the Good for all actualities, etc.; but with man, the excellent acquires new values and meanings, through his use of its possible subdivisions. A man becomes perfect only so far as he realizes the Good both as general and in detail.

There is an achievement of detail in ethics, which acts by improving things here and now, and in art which acts by creating things here and now. The ethical deals with the Ideal as part of a cosmological whole, art deals with it as being related to man in Existence, and religion deals with it as being related to man in God. This requires a change in the classifications just made with respect to the different disciplines. If we follow out the present line we get:

Actuality and Ideality	cosmologically	is Ethics
Actuality and Ideality	helped by Existence	is Art as beautiful
Actuality and Ideality	helped by God	is Religious evaluation
Actuality and Existence	cosmologically	is Nature
Actuality and Existence	helped by Ideal	is engineering
Actuality and Existence	helped by God	is religious community
Actuality and God	cosmologically	is faith
Actuality and God	helped by Ideal	is adoration
Actuality and God	helped by Existence	is good works

A liberal can be said to allow for the use of any item as a symbol, with an insistence that none is ever adequate, (since it is tainted by human influence); the conservative can be said to allow for the use of some special items at different times according to needs and places; the orthodox can be said to demand the use of all those which had been established. We need not hold any one of these positions, but can maintain instead the right to take up one or the other at different times, depending on which then and there enabled one to make a satisfactory contact with God. It is the desire of the churches and of ministers, who have officially allied themselves with one or the other of these positions, to insist that a choice be made. But the individual need not make this choice except at some given moment. He must start perhaps as a conservative and see if he need expand his symbols to include more of the orthodox than he had, or if he can dispense with some of the items he now accepts. At every moment he must experiment. No one as a matter of fact can be orthodox in the sense of doing at any moment all that is required. Orthodoxy is but the persistence in a conservative vein over a wide and pre-established range of items.

Conversely, no religious man can be completely liberal; there are some symbols which are not readily usable by him, and others which have the sanction of use and familiarity. Liberality is the readiness to replace one symbol by another. At any given moment all three approaches can be sustained in a given act—one may go to church for example or engage in some sacrament. They will differ not there but in what they do next, the liberal perhaps doing nothing more, and the conservative doing some of the things which the orthodox would require.

If we take the orthodox as standard we must say that the liberal has an attitude which calls every tenet into possible question, and the conservative has one which allows every tenet to have a local or only limited temporal use. The orthodox will not allow man to decide which of the attitudes he is to assume; the orthodox takes it for granted that one must continue inside the ritual scheme. The liberal, since he allows for the use of any symbol, must allow for the possibility of an orthodox and a conservative use; he can object only to the prescription in advance as to when and how one is to be orthodox or conservative. The conservative takes the same attitude towards the orthodox as the liberal does; however, since he has definite selections to make, he rejects the liberal's freedom.

The orthodox is allowed on all three grounds, and in this sense is justifiable in a way the others are not, providing one does not insist on a pre-designated set of symbols or acts, as unavoidable in every case. From the position of the others the orthodox is allowed only as somehow justified for the moment. The liberal, since he does find a place for the others, in some sense offers a pre-condition or a more comprehensive view, though this fails to do justice to the persistent and singular demands that the other positions require. The conservative, though he has the position which all men accept to begin with and perhaps end with, is not allowed nor presupposed by the others, and can justify himself only as offering the source of them. We have then the *allowable,* the *categorial* and the *originating* form of religion. All have peculiar virtues, justifying, from limited perspectives, a preference of one over others.

November 25

There are three certainties and three kinds of doubt in religion. There is the certainty of religious experience; here we come to the inescapable polar opposite of familiar Existence and know it to be overwhelming, irreducible and vital. It is unfocussed, chaotic, muddled. What we are not sure about is just how much of it is God; we know there is something divine in it, but is it all so? It would seem to be equally Ideal and equally Existential. We do not distinguish these but also do not know which should be primary. It can be called an experience of God providing this is not understood to exclude an experience of other realities as well.

The object of metaphysical speculation is a unity which is correlate with the other modes of being. There is the certainty here of a demonstration in a system. Here we have God in His purity, but we are not sure just what kind of values He cherishes and just what He imports for man in his daily life. We know only that like God in the first sense He does interplay with this world.

The object of a particular religion is a specification of the inescapable speculatively achieved God. One is certain of this by virtue of the accepted symbols which point to it, because of revelation, and because of authority. But one is never entirely sure that one has expressed its nature properly, for the opposite is urged by other religions.

There are two types of reconciliation involved in connection with basic disciplines. There is the reconciliation of one discipline with another, when both are the product of the new affiliations which men introduce into the world. Here we have the reconciliation of art and ethics, of history and politics, engineering and action, etc. The solution to these problems lies in making a reference to some standard—excellence as represented by the Ideal, effectiveness as represented by Existence, unifying sympathy as expressed by God. The reconciliations will be matters of trial and error, with one item coming to the forefront at one moment and some other at another. We can bring any and all under the aegis of the Ideal, or of the other two modes. Thus there is a reconciliation of art, ethics, history, e.g., in Existence, or from the standpoint of God, or by ourselves as His representative.

A second form of reconciliation is required when reference is made to the cosmological reality from which the components of the new disciplines were derived and which in their unification repeat with a bias and modification the features which the cosmological reality possessed. Here we have a reconciliation of the presupposed and the conditioned, and one must first make sure that the cosmological occurrence, and therefore the ultimacy of nature, is in fact accounted for before one is able to engage in the derivatives—and this without compromising the fact that the meaning of nature is affected by works of history, politics, etc.

The reconciliation of perception, science, etc., is of a different sort, since these are modes of knowledge and depend on the construction of a purified substance. The reconciliation of the different levels of history with one another (since it is in effect the reconciliation of differently affiliated realities) in the end depends on something like the first form of reconciliation mentioned above. Here the standard will be that offered by God, for we want to do justice to every level without losing the values of any one.

December 7

If we keep the nature of man fixed, we can take history to be the difference which Existence makes to him. In that case we can understand different parts of history, past or future, by dealing with the matter in a contrary-to-fact conditional. We will then say that what happened at a given time was an articulation of the nature of man in history, through the agency of Existence. The Existence will be the differential factor, and therefore what we will in effect learn is the nature of Existence as manifesting itself differently in different periods. If, e.g., we think of the assassination of Lincoln as the inevitable outcome of two sets of beings, epitomized in Lincoln and Booth, there would be a different occurrence at a different time due to the difference not in the men or the particular ongoing, but to the difference Existence makes. It would be due to Existence that when Cromwell was ruler he was not assassinated; here the difference between the outcomes of Cromwell and Lincoln would be attributed not to them but to the Existence which, starting with each, had different outcomes. If one took Existence to be a constantly operating force one would see the difference between the two events to be a matter of dating, location, situation. If one supposed these were only incidental, and not of the essence of the historic world, one would have to suppose that Existence or mankind or both had systematic ways of changing, and that as a consequence one could explain what was new by virtue of that change.

It is possible to suppose that man is intrinsically indeterminate or that he is constantly changing, and that there is a kind of constancy to Existence. One would then reverse the previous stress on the constancy of man, and use the contrary-to-fact conditionals to express the difference in the nature of man over the course of time. If one instead supposes, as one ought, that both man and Existence are changing, one ought first to see what happens on the supposition of a constant Existence, and then what happens on the supposition of a constant human nature, and combine the two contrary-to-fact conditionals.

If we say that an occurrence *xy* is the articulation of a reality *z,* then in the light of the fact that *y* followed on *x* and thus involves a certain law-abiding relation of meanings, when we have *a* we will have *b. A* and *b* may have occurred elsewhere or may occur in the future. There is no prediction in history, but there is a reconsideration and an understanding of what might and, perhaps even more strongly, what will ensue. The future is known not by inferring from what is but by reconstituting the nature of the future in the light of the patterning characteristic of what is. This involves the acceptance of some antecedent, and for that acceptance there can be predictions grounded in the present.

It is then one and the same same thing to say of a past event A] that such and such occurred, B] that if (instead) such and such had occurred, then such and such would have occurred, and C] if such and such were to occur then such and such would occur. All these are different articulations of the same reality. The only problem is whether this reality is Existence manifested through constant man, man making use of a constant Existence, or the two of them in interplay. The last alternative requires first one approach and then the other in order to enable one to understand what in fact did occur, and in the end what man is and what Existence is, and what they mean to one another.

December 8

If it be the case that the ethicist enhances things in this world and thereby incidentally realizes the Good, it ought to be the case that he is obligated not to the Good but to the things about. It seems paradoxical to say that we have an obligation, that this is directed towards the Good, and yet that we are required to enhance the things in the world. We ought to say that we are obligated to enhance the things in the world and that we are related to the Good incidentally and instrumentally in order to make this possible. In connection with art we ought to say that we are obligated to realize the Good in the shape of beauty, and incidentally take care of the various objects about. Or are these only verbal matters? Is it that we are involved with other things in ethics, that though we face them as making claims on us and we on them, and that this could be said to involve an obligation, there is another meaning of obligation which relates us now to the prospect which in fact will be realized? The obligation in the second sense is an obligation which defines the kind of meaning we wish to achieve, whereas the obligation in the first sense tells us the location of the result which would be said to free us from the taint of guilt. None of this is clear to me at this moment.

There is another ambiguity in connection with action. The ethical act is different from the artistic act in that the former is concerned with doing justice to the things about, of realizing their promise, whereas the latter acts to make something beautiful. The former also is like an act of craftsmanship, and is occupied with reaching some end, whereas the latter is constantly reconstitutive and makes itself one with the very result it helps bring about.

December 13

Discussions of perception run the risk of passing, almost un-noticed, into discussions of sense-data, of series of perceptions, and of common-sense observations. The sense-data are merely confronted, undergone, and abstracted out of a perceptual situation. A single perception is the outcome of a judgment and involves an articulation with elements derived from an encounter, and rooted in an adumbrated reality. Such a single perception occurs in the present and, since the present is atomic, does not allow for a knowledge of change or motion. To have a knowl-edge of change or motion it is necessary to continue perceiving. In addi-tion to the intrusion of the past and the future into a single perception, infecting what is in fact being known then and there, there is the reten-tion of the past and the anticipation of the future. These govern a whole series of perceptions, to make the outcome a single inclusive judgment. This single inclusive judgment, embracing a plurality of perceptions, is to be distinguished from a common-sense observation, for the common-sense observation is   A] socially determined,   B] entrenches on a larger realm of experience with which it interplays and which is the domain of ignorance and terror, and   C] is sustained by an acceptance of the object as having potentialities or powers not then and there observed.

It is questionable whether distinct moments and thus distinct percepts are, so far as knowledge is concerned, anything more than abstractions out of the series of perceivings and percepts. The entire course of one perceiving may however itself be thought of as a single atomic moment, on a higher level than the percepts, and the percepts with their correlative perceivings can be viewed as being in an order of earlier and later inside the confines of that single atomic, long-stretch perceiving.

We must distinguish A] a single minimal percept, B] a series of these percepts, C] a single atomic moment in which the series can be located without compromising the capacity of the items in it to constitute a single continuum of change or motion. This last of course requires that the series be gone through sequentially when and as it is being held together in the atomic moment which embraces all the items.

December 14

Collingwood has made clear that one must get over a number of misconceptions regarding history. It is not to be understood in terms of categories applicable to the sciences. It is a science in the sense of organized knowledge, but it does not concern itself with laws and repeatable occurrences, being occupied with a singular past. It is not a subject which rests upon authorities, either by simple acceptance of them, or by a scissors and paste method, adding or comparing them and settling for the one that seems to be most reliable. It involves the critical use of evidence to reach conclusions which may not even have been known to those who were present at the time when the occurrence, to which one is concluding, took place.

Collingwood seems not to allow for an encounter with the past in the being of the items in the present. He also thinks that the historian must re-live the occurrence to which he refers. But how then could the historian know the nature of a whole war, since this is beyond the knowledge of the participants? Such knowledge is evidently had only by the historian and then only by reconstructing the entire war out of the fragmentary occurrences which the two sides produce. Also Collingwood recognizes that he must interpolate. He should have recognized that history embraces chance occurrences, the irrational and the uncognized. Because he concentrates on the narrative and does not attend to the reality to which the narrative presumably refers, he is unable to say that an historian's account is true. The most he could hope to say is that it is adequate, that it embraces in the reconstruction all the meaning or causes which the evidence presupposes.

The procedure of the historian is something like that referred to by Kant as the transcendental deduction of the categories: one accepts given data and then seeks the basic explanations in terms of which these data are what they are. The data for history are present evidences which we wish to account for by constructing a story of what had been and which, in the course of time, produced this very evidence. But it is not enough to construct the story; the story itself has implications. The task of the historian is to see what implications are involved, and thus to look for consequences from his story as a kind of verification of it. If he constructs the story that Napoleon was in Russia and left in a hurry, he ought then to expect to find rusty rifles, some hurriedly-made French graves and the like, all having approximately the date of Napoleon's departure. Collingwood overlooked the need to *look for evidence;* he was instead content to recognize the need to *begin with evidence,* to use this with utmost criticism, challenging every bit of it, whether reported by eyewitnesses or not, in order to produce an account which made sense of what had happened. He could say that the result was something intelligible, mental and rational and that this answered to what had occurred, but this does not mean that the initial occurrence was a mental one. It means only that the historian in his account tells us what the essential nature of the past occurrence is. There would be no harm were one to say that this essential nature is the "inside" or "mind" of the occurrence when it took place, were it but remembered that this "inside" was not consciously entertained, and even that it did not relate to what men planned to do. The reconstruction of the event is the idealization of it, in the sense of giving the meaning; it is not to be identified with the idealistic reality of a mental content, but only with the essence of what in fact occurs. This essence however must be recognized to be a singular essence, the specific occurrence freed of irrelevancies and made to be the origin of the evidences which are here and now, not something abstract and repeatable.

December 15

The question as to just which items in this common-sense world can best serve as symbols for the ineffable experienced domain beyond that world, involves a cognitive grasp of the nature of that domain. We must know what lies in that domain, before we can say what would prove to be a good icon, mirror or representative of it.

The domain, as a muddled totality of God, Existence and Ideality, should be answered by man as an emotionally involved and vital being. This is presumably what the existentialists are saying. It is also what the Yogi and the Buddhist are saying, for, though they speak of detachment and noninvolvement, they want the individual to be completely one with the realm beyond.

If the element of Ideality is isolated we should have charity and hope as essential components in man; if God, it should be virtue and worship; if Existence, it should be sensitivity and appreciation. The individual himself must guide his activity by an integrity and authenticity, which is to say he must continue to be aware of what he discerned beyond, and actually make the articulation (in which he is engaged) serve this which he had acknowledged. In this last stage he is, for example, not merely a man of virtue who worships God, but one who does so under the control of his awareness that God is a being distinct from other beings and was encountered in some form in the experience which transcended the common-sense world.

John Cage suggested to me that the outcome of a work of art must be such that no accident could dim or alter it. This would seem to say that the result of the articulation must manifestly, and without hindrance, prove itself to be a mirror of the being to which it refers. And this I suppose must be said, providing we have the authenticity which alone makes it possible to make and to have the mirroring symbol.

We know that we are doing justice to what lies outside the realm of common sense by A] attending to the speculative results of a systematic metaphysics, B] by making an accurate protrayal of that experienced domain which results from the muddling of speculatively known objects. (B occurs before A); c] by attaining a state of authenticity where we keep a hold on the meaning of what was discerned as we go about the task of articulating it; and D] by articulating in the form of a created product, exemplifying some virtue in a man or expressed by him.

December 16

In the beginning of my intellectual career, I felt the need to express myself. I did not have ideas clearly in mind, but still there was something I wanted to say. Perhaps, more accurately, I had a multiplicity of fragmentary ideas swirling around, cutting into one another, and not forming a significant whole. I had to write and rewrite and rewrite until I could forge something like a coherent account out of them. And then after *Reality,* what a long wait before I could get another book together! The interval was filled with articles on a miscellany of topics. And then the time came for a refining and restructuring, a solidifying and a completing, and this I think was accomplished in the *Modes.* Though there is no real separation of periods, this has been followed by a time where I am primarily concerned with finding things out. I am learning from the books on art, and the one I am writing on history, as I had never learned before. Before I became clearer as to just what it was I was trying to say, I learned something about the world in the course of trying to bring some kind of civilized order out of the wilderness of ideas which sprung up in myself from around 20 to 35. But when I began working in art I seemed to have started only with a suggestion of an idea derived from the *Modes;* this, when faced with actual works of art, with writings on art, with reflections on the nature of beauty, etc., became something I never had even surmised.

The first stage was one in which it was hard to write; the very forging of a style took up most of the time—or rather, since no style was aimed at, there was a need to rewrite in order to be able to communicate. In the second stage there was an increase in the capacity to communicate. But an excessive abstractedness was still evident. It is only in the last period that a style has become comparatively easy to exhibit — but it is also a period when it is hardest to write. The ideas are slow in coming; each notion seems to be made fresh, and few predecessors and little help can be found. I am left with a need to create against the background of my system, while yet knowing that no creation must rest on the past, so far as possible.

What are the categories of history; how to find them, how to relate them; how to deal with them? The problem facing Kant in his deductions was simpler; he had a well-ordered world and well-defined concepts appropriate to it. Newton's scheme had been in existence for quite some time. Without minimizing the achievement of Kant, it is still true to say that he did not face as open a situation as does one who today writes on the philosophy of history. At any rate what is now needed is the forging of a brand new set of categories which is genuinely appropriate to history alone, as an autonomous discipline and an objective reality.

December 17

In teaching one conveys primarily the quality of an older man and his concern for knowledge. The student is then awakened to a model of an inquiring honest mind enjoying the search for truth. The content taught is necessary to give cross-graining; it is not the essential fact communicated. This view of teaching stands in contrast with the more common view in which the teacher is thought to be a transmitter of information or cultural values. Such a teacher finds his satisfaction in his role of authority on the one hand, and in being a sustainer of civilization on the other. He contrasts with the former, whose satisfaction lies in his attainment of a mastery of a subject in a creative spirit, and the awakening of a creative desire in his respondents.

Both types are necessary. Were there just the former there would not be sufficient knowledge and attention given to past achievements, and to the mastery of techniques and information which enable civilization to move on. Were there just the latter, one would be making allowance for creativity only in the past and would be in effect making it difficult to have it in the present. The former type of teacher defends himself by saying that he is as good a creator as any, and that the information conveyed by the latter is neither retained, significant nor satisfactory. The latter defends himself by saying that over the course of time we have sifted out poor creators from good ones, and therefore, in teaching the past, we are keeping the highest ideal before the student. He thinks that the former teacher is a blunderer, offering content not to be compared with the truly great, particularly that which we now endorse, since this has been ironed out over the course of years of research, through comparison with others, etc.

We face here a conflict of two excellencies—the excellence of creativity and the excellence of achievement. A vital creative man must blunder, must be awkward, must fail; a story of excellence achieved must overlook the existential matrix of vital working. In favoring the one, however, we need not entirely exclude the other. A creative teacher checks his thinking with the brute facts of the world about and offers his own product as something to be judged by others in terms of its adequacy, and in the light of the standards set by the great men of the past. A transmitting teacher can be vital, creative in his presentation, making the student alert to the way in which one is properly to deal with greatness.

December 19

The problem of causation in the social or humanistic disciplines differs from that of the sciences, and in each discipline it seems to have a distinctive meaning. In law it has to do with practice, in descriptive sociology with facts, in theoretical sociology with norms, and in history with the construction of causes to explain.

In law one seeks to determine who ought to be identified as having taken the most risk. The answer is that it is the one who gets the most benefit. This may be the benefit from the transaction, from the functioning of the society in the past (when it protected the favored, allowed for inheritance, etc.). One ought to add availability as another criterion. The benefit also must be such that to deprive one of it, to make one who benefits sustain the liability, will not disrupt the society and in this sense not be unjust. Accordingly, he who is available and benefits, the society makes liable, in accordance with its sense of justice. These men are usually the most powerful, influential, richest, and prestigious, all subject to the social requirement that they are in principle on a footing with all the others, and therefore ought to suffer for their advantages. But we also hold the bad liable. The connection between this identified locus of liability as a cause and the unwanted effect is here governed by a principle of relevance which the reasonable man should know.

The effect with which we begin is an undesirable result, and we want to redress the balance, distribute the weight, make for an equitable distribution. Even though it may be grounded in a fault, the wrong is in root the product of the kind of society in which we live and thus should be borne in principle by the society, and in fact by those who have the role of being the loci of its greatest benefits, powers, availabilities, etc.

The law recognizes that if something could have happened without the tort the actor is not liable; and if each by himself could produce what he does with an other, then both are liable, for we want here to stop the kind of action as well.

In descriptive sociology we try to make correlations of various occurrences, attending to those which seem to be of primary importance in terms of conspicuous behavior. We then look for a rule, a meaning which will transform one occurrence into the other. The rule gives us the character of the society, its laws, and tells us what it is to be a sane and decent member of society. Our primary focus is on those acts in which the society promotes or hinders the welfare and cohesion of its members and allows for its own continuance or promotes its own destruction.

In history we base ourselves on our knowledge of the run of affairs today, and use this as the rule which is to govern the causes. In principle we should be able to take account of the kind of transformation the antecedent requires and thus the kind of power it might exert on the consequent, and how it could, in the course of time, through normal forces, become the latter. We could say that, e.g., "x is a mild people" is the same as "were x to have such and such a relation to money it would be an aggressive people." This is equivalent with "were the children of x to have had such and such a childhood, they would be aggressively trained." The last is equivalent to "were a member of x to have a childhood of such and such a different sort, he would be mild." The conversion of this latter into a cause of the "x is a mild people" depends on the recognition that both are asserting the same thing, but with the difference that the childhood must modify the action of events in a child-like manner, and that the difference between childhood and a later period is one of development and exposition of what was there initially.

In history we must know something now about human motives and human causation. This we know in part from experience, in part from the law, in part from our understanding of the main correlations of our actions, learned in society. So far as this is true our history will have to be rewritten the more surely we have re-understood the causal activity of men today. With our discovery of the unconscious we must look at history in a new light, re-interpreting all the facts in a new way, so that we can see what was done before was done in the way it is being done now. What cannot be so explained must be attributed to the power of Existence, either acting rationally (as understood from the perspective of the Ideal), or as a mere uncharted, fortuitious source of accidents.

December 21

If we start with common-sense objects, as substantial but overlaid with conventional and traditional ingredients, we can abstract from them the various strands of perception, science, etc. We can then go on to synthesize these strands to constitute common-sense layers. A common-sense layer is some such domain as law, society, the state, a culture, in which all the strands are united but under a restrictive condition. Thus in law we want to determine liability and have the strands related one to the other as subject to the condition that there will be a connection between a damage suffered and a plausible (though not necessarily efficacious) source of the liability. This source would be an advantaged or disadvantaged member of the community who is available and from whom recompense of some sort can be obtained.

When we come to history we could try to combine the various strands to define a substantial domain of history, or we can unite various layers. The former approach has the advantage of allowing us to see the elements which are to be found both in the common-sense object and in the historic object, the first being a muddled version of the second. The second enables one to deal with history as a basic social enterprise, and thus enables us to see that history is more substantial and neutral than other social enterprises.

To employ the first approach is to force one to add another consideration: a synthesis of the various strands does not yield history, unless the reconstituted substances possess their own energies, constitute groups, and interplay with Existence. But this is in effect to take the second approach. Consequently the proper method to pursue is to isolate the various layers constituting the human realm, while looking at the various strands (since they offer a contrast in the way in which space, time, and energy is being employed). Consequently we ought to say something like this: perception has such and such a type of space, but law, society, etc., have different types; history involves the synthesis of the latter to constitute a single domain where a new type is employed.

History offers a more inclusive, cosmic and neutral union of different layers than can be had in any other way. If we keep the nature of men constant, the power of history will be accredited to Existence. But whether this accreditation takes place or not, the important thing is that history achieves an ultimacy in being as well as an autonomous set of categories. Each of the layers, like history itself, will have its own space and time as well as dynamics. The space, time and dynamics of the layers is of the same type as history's—it involves a reference to some purpose and makes use of relevance to determine what is the cause for realizing or preventing the achievement of the purpose.

The layers belong to the same family of realities and enterprises as history, and all can be said to be specialized forms of the world of common sense rather than, as is the case of the strands, ways of reorganizing that world in order to make it more coherent and to free it from various conventional elements. The family of humanistic disciplines all share with common sense something of the respect for tradition, if not as something which should enter into one's study of a field, then as that which must be recognized to be operative in the field.

We isolate the scientific strand for example as not only free of traditional elements in fact but as that which is to be dealt with apart from our own traditional attitudes as expressed in that society. That is, the scientific account is offered as an objective account about something which is itself without conventional elements; the historic account is offered as an objective account too, but it is about that which has conventional elements; a social account could be objective, too, but it is often a subjective one, expressive of one's own training and relating to what is traditionalized. A legal account is subjective in the sense that it requires a reasonable man to make the decision; it is about that which is itself organized in conventional, traditional terms.

December 25

Each of the modes of being allows for an abstraction of what Northrop calls nominalistic universals. In addition each allows for four structuralizations of the abstraction. The nominalistic universals are derived and vindicated by seeing how one can keep apace of the world outside. The structuralizations are related to the abstractions by schemata provided by the interplay of the remaining two modes, and the outcome is a purified form of the abstraction, which then can be vindicated.

If we abstract a scientific strand from the common-sense world, we can vindicate it by virtue of its relation to the objects in that world— (not necessarily merely to the perceptual, as Northrop assumes). We can subject the strand to rectification by mathematics, by a divinely sustained unity and by Existence. The first has a schematism determined by the conjunction of God and Actuality; the second, one determined by Ideality and Actuality; the third, by God and Ideality, it being assumed that science is here the formalization of the very meaning of cosmic Existence. But then the third case will differ from the other two, for in the third case we get an abstraction from Existence rectified by Existence itself, and this enables us to offer a mere isomorphism, since the science is supposed to answer to the Existence. However, one could well argue that science is occupied with the common-sense objects as well as with the field in which they are.

Perhaps it would be better to recognize that science, precisely because it is abstracted from common sense, is oriented there, on the one side, and that, because it is formal, it is also oriented towards the Ideal. This is in root Kant's view in the schematism. But it is equally true that science is unified, that it is involved in a dynamic world, and that it has individualized existential involvements. All these mean that it is oriented towards other modes of being as well. And there ought to be similar things said about perception, values and action, for all these are strands on a par with science.

On the Copenhagen program the nature of science is essentially unity, cosmic in reach. It is then a kind of secularized version of God's mind. Taken in this way it would need rectification from Ideality, Actuality and Existence. If the Actuality and Existence which relate science to the Ideal (to make it perfectly rational) are in conflict, (the one stressing individual involvement, the other cosmic significance) science must remain essentially a nominalistic universal, or inductive discipline.

We should be able to abstract and rectify perception, eventfulness and value in the same way we do science. But may we not do the same thing with the modes themselves? May we not derive the modes from common sense by abstraction and find a way of rectifying the result? We seem to have suggested this in connection with God; it seems plausible in connection with Actuality and even Existence. But in these cases, though, what we in fact do is to rectify the abstraction by some other mode and use two others to constitute a schema. This helps us know a mode standing over against the very items which helped us define it properly. Thus the isolation of God, Actuality, Ideality and Existence from common sense must be supplemented by the use of three of them on each to get three purified forms of it. This must then be solidified to give us the mode itself. If we want to get a good understanding, say of Actuality, we isolate the individuals in the common-sense world, understand them as unities, as rational, and as existing in a cosmos, and then combine all three of these to get the idea of a mode of Actuality which stands over against all other modes.

If we think of politics as being occupied with the common-sense world but to be primarily a form of Ideality, we will either have to treat it as a strand derived from Ideality, as on the way to being the Ideal itself, or as oriented in the realm of common sense but rectified by the Ideal.

If we want to know time (or space or energy), since these are aspects of Existence, we must, if we start with common sense, abstract these from common sense and rectify the result in three ways. We can then have   A] common-sense public clock time,   B] rectified idealized time, which is physics,   C] rectified divinized time, which is theology, and D] the rectified existential time of individuals. The time of art would be additional, and would answer to   E] the time in Existence itself. The time of history, since it is a time which refines the time of common sense, can be viewed as an abstraction or refinement of common-sense time, and thus to be open to three rectifications—there will be that provided F] by the Ideal when we seek rational explanations of the course of history,   G] by God when we seek to have an objective time, and H] by Actuality when we seek the time for historic causes.

History is only one of a number of cosmological products. It is derived from common sense in a different way than science is. The former remains within the cosmological setting, the latter is concerned with the analytic constituents of the common-sense world and not with the substantial beings and actions. History, law, sociology, etc., the humanistic disciplines, are and remain cosmological; perception, science, events and values are cosmological as oriented in the common-sense world but, as subject to rectifications by the various modes, come to have natures answering to those modes. The rectifications of history, etc., merely refine the way in which the concrete world of cosmological interplay is to be understood; the rectifications of science, etc., seek to make them in consonance with the nature of a mode, and thus require two steps for application—a step which moves from mode to the rectified discipline, and from the latter to the common-sense data. History in contrast needs only one step, since the rectification of history is but the continued refinement of the common-sense world from which it was obtained.

INDEX OF NAMES

INDEX OF SUBJECTS

489, 514, 516, 535, 561, 641, 677, 743, 747, 748; kinds of, 390; natural, 702

Becoming, 32, 39, 48f, 58, 74, 92, 119f, 122, 125, 132, 152, 161, 198, 202, 327, 344, 352, 393, 578, 622, 625, 627, 629, 646

Before and after, 552f, 580f, 665f, 713, 717, 731, 733

Beginnings, 100f, 103, 251, 518, 550, 552, 595f

Behavior: 55, 352, 607, 619; ethical, 514; law-abiding, 699f

Being(s): 53, 58, 68, 104, 106, 109, 189, 213, 219, 220f, 284, 287, 302, 307, 346, 375, 389f, 393, 481, 526, 551, 568, 580, 728; action of, 38, 144, 145, 146; adjustment of, 655; alienated, 193; and category, 213, 640, 643; and common sense, 640, 645; and history, 701, 713; and individual, 642; and man, 695; and rationality, 17f, 550; and time, 31, 41, 291, 550f, 554; as limits, 642; as loci, 715ff; as measures, 715ff; as terminus, 42; asymmetry in, 652; bearers of, 201, 310; burdens of, 296f; combinations of, 721; conscious, 81; correlates of, 721; cosmological, 595; cycle of, 219f, 222; defects of, 59, 61, 63, 141f, 145f, 153, 160, 341; dimensions of, 290, 337, 388; disequilibrium of, 33, 147, 163, 197, 219; divisions of, 656f; evaluation of, 63, 146, 341, 550f; experience of, 710; explanation of, 175; expressions of, 220, 640; failures of, 656; features of, 128, 138, 139, 160, 162, 181, 185, 289, 290, 293, 295, 296, 342, 550ff, 619, 622, 626ff, 630, 686, 719; grades of, 39; humanized, 568; idea of, 389, 487, 492, 526; in itself, 20, 21, 138, 175, 190, 302, 554, 570, 655; independence of, 145, 146, 147, 153, 284, 333, 339, 341, 344, 353, 682, 728; individual, 697; ingredient, 715; in-

termingling of, 713f; knowledge of, 7, 8, 175, 194, 345, 490f, 497, 526, 533, 535, 538, 564, 570, 639, 640, 645; living, 87, 336, 337; logic of, 212, 213, 219, 220, 291, 348, 481, 550; meaning of, 49, 58, 377, 526; mixture of, 645, 713f, 717f; modes of, 5, 21, 24, 25, 39, 48, 52, 56, 58, 61, 63, 68, 71, 72, 74, 82, 84, 97, 98, 100, 119, 124, 127, 137, 138, 141, 143, 161, 174, 183, 188, 190, 191, 192, 219, 220, 221, 259, 264, 265, 267, 284, 285, 287, 295, 297, 306, 313, 316, 332ff, 337, 354, 357, 368, 426, 427, 466, 481, 485, 491, 512, 525f, 532ff, 536, 538f, 541f, 550f, 564f, 570, 580, 612, 618, 626f, 631f, 636, 638ff, 642, 649, 650, 669f, 674, 684, 686, 693ff, 713, 720, 726, 729, 742, 756ff; nature of, 704; needs of, 655, 717f; neutrality of, 55, 194, 287; number of, 568; opposition of, 655, 661; organic, 54, 694; pairing of, 653, 661, 714f; parts of, 142, 143, 149, 291, 307, 669; phases of, 24, 43, 45, 161, 540; plurality in, 649, 651, 658, 666; potentiality in, 149, 141; predicate for, 175, 212; proof of, 61, 183, 184, 292, 297, 487; pure, 721; rational, 17, 18; recognition of, 5, 570; relation of, 649, 654, 661, 727; released, 654; residua in, 661, 662; roles for, 42, 48, 63, 138, 143, 145, 149, 159, 171, 222, 283, 297, 354, 380, 480, 526, 641, 717; root, 602; strategy of, 76, 168, 174, 175, 295, 297; structure of, 695; subhuman, 81, 139, 336, 337; substitutes for, 643ff; union of, 694f, 737; unity of, 306, 319, 483f, 718; use of, 710

Belief, 210, 211, 214, 215, 216, 419, 486, 507, 580, 626

Bias, 500, 545

Biology, 450, 596

Birth, 449, 450, 598

J